The Chinese Communist Party in Power

P'eng Shu-tse

Ch'en Pi-lan

The Chinese Communist Party in Power

P'eng Shu-tse

MONAD PRESS, NEW YORK

Edited by Leslie Evans
Copyright © 1980 by the Anchor Foundation, Inc.
All rights reserved

Library of Congress Catalog Card Number 79-92214
ISBN 0-913460-75-3 cloth; ISBN 0-913460-76-1 paper
Manufactured in the United States of America

Published by Monad Press for the Anchor Foundation

Distributed by:
Pathfinder Press
410 West Street
New York, NY 10014

First Edition 1980

Contents

Publisher's Preface   7

Introduction: Looking Back Over My Years
With P'eng Shu-tse—by Ch'en Pi-lan   13

The Theory of Permanent Revolution and the
Underdeveloped Countries   49

The Causes of the Victory of the Chinese Communist
Party Over Chiang Kai-shek, and the CCP's
Perspectives *(1951-52)*   71

Some Comments on the Draft Resolution on the Third
Chinese Revolution *(1952)*   138

The Case of the Chinese Trotskyists: Open Letter
to the Central Executive Committee of the CCP
(April 15, 1953)   145

The Third Chinese Revolution and Its Perspectives
(December 1, 1954)   153

A Criticism of the Various Views Supporting the
Rural People's Communes *(August 19, 1959)*   171

On the Nature of the CCP and Its Regime—Political
Revolution or Democratic Reform *(April 1960)*   224

Two Interviews on the "Cultural Revolution"
(Published August 1966 and February 1967)   268

Open Letter to Members of the Chinese Communist Party
(February 15, 1967)   294

The Relationship and Differences Between Mao Tse-tung
and Liu Shao-ch'i *(July 6, 1967)*   306

The May Fourth Movement and the Great Cultural
Revolution *(April 9, 1969)*   326

The Fall of Lin Piao *(January 1972)*   335

The "Criticize Lin, Criticize Confucius" Campaign
(Published January 1976)   340

The Meaning of the Tien An Men Demonstration
  (July 10, 1976)   361
Behind the Fall of Mao's Faction *(December 7, 1976)*   369
An Appraisal of the Political Life of Mao Tse-tung
  (March 14, 1977)   380
APPENDIX: An Interview with Ch'en Pi-lan on the
  Cultural Revolution *(Published July 14, 1967)*   417
Notes   435
Acknowledgements   459
Glossary   461
Index   499

PUBLISHER'S PREFACE

China in the twentieth century has been a focal point in the struggle between two world orders—the declining system of capitalist private property and the emerging socialist revolution, whose standard-bearer is the industrial working class. In no other country with the exception of the Soviet Union has this clash of social forces led to such immense and complex battles, and to such upsurges and reversals.

China has experienced three great revolutions in this century. In 1911 a bourgeois revolution toppled the last of the Chinese emperors and established the Republic. But because of the weak and vacillating character of the Chinese capitalist class this revolution failed to achieve its principal objectives: the genuine national independence of the country from foreign imperialist domination and the ending of semifeudal relations in the rural countryside. Instead the Republic collapsed into regional military governments under the sway of the imperialist powers of the West and Japan.

In 1925-27, the relatively small urban working class succeeded in sparking a great uprising of the urban and rural poor. This revolutionary upheaval promised to unite the dismembered country in a socialist revolution as the workers of Russia had done a decade before. But this priceless opportunity for an advance toward national independence and on toward socialism was betrayed and defeated when the young Communist Party of China was compelled by the increasingly Stalinized leadership of the Communist International to adopt a class-collaborationist policy, subordinating its forces to the leadership of the national bourgeoisie under the Kuomintang (Nationalist Party).

Finally, under the pressure of foreign invasion and peasant rebellion during and after the Sino-Japanese War, the Stalinized Communist Party of Mao Tse-tung found it increasingly difficult to move toward implementing its perspective of establishing a stable coalition with Chiang Kai-shek. Chiang would settle for nothing less than the annihilation of the Communist Party, no matter how opportunist its program or how willing its leadership might be to seek compromises. With their backs to the wall, the peasant Red Armies fought for and won political power, opening the door to a revolutionary social transformation in the largest country in the world.

Yet even this great revolution, despite its indisputable conquests in freeing China from imperialist exploitation and in breaking the power of the capitalists and landlords, did not lead to placing the working people of China in command of their own society. As the revelations following the death of Mao Tse-tung in 1976 have confirmed—revelations of years of repressive police rule and of serious economic failures and setbacks—the socialist revolution remains unfinished and undemocratized in China today.

P'eng Shu-tse lived through these tumultuous events, and, during a great part of them, not as a spectator but as a political leader and strategist of the working-class movement. His life is intimately tied to that of the Chinese working class, whose unyielding spokesman he has been for almost sixty years. His personal and political story is graphically told by Ch'en Pi-lan, his lifelong companion and herself an outstanding communist revolutionist, in the biographical essay that opens this volume.

P'eng was among the first to join the Communist movement in China and soon became one of its central leaders. Born into a peasant family in Hunan province in 1895, he enrolled in the Socialist Youth League formed by Comintern representative Gregory Voitinsky in August 1920, before the founding of the Chinese Communist Party. He studied in Moscow in 1921-24 at the Communist University of the Toilers of the East and was a delegate for the Chinese Communist Party to the Fifth World Congress of the Comintern.

P'eng was elected to the CCP's Central Committee and to the five-member Central Standing Committee of the Politburo by the party's Fourth Congress, held in January 1925. He was the chief editor of the party's official newspaper *Hsiang-tao chou-pao* (Guide Weekly) and of its theoretical magazine *Hsin Ch'ing-nien* (New Youth).

Within the top leadership of the CCP, P'eng became the most outspoken opponent of the disastrous course charted by Stalin and his agents in China. This was in sharp contrast to Mao Tse-Tung, who supported to the end the fatal entry of the CCP into

Chiang Kai-shek's Kuomintang, which led to the bloodbath against the CCP and the trade unions in the spring and summer of 1927.

As early as 1924, P'eng insisted that the Chinese bourgeoisie was incapable of pursuing a consistent anti-imperialist course and that the working class would have to assume the leadership of the revolution. He also insisted that despite the proven capacities of the peasantry to participate in explosive struggles against oppression, the peasantry alone was too dispersed as a class to give overall social cohesion and direction to a struggle against capitalism. A socialist revolution would require winning the peasants to follow the leadership of an independent revolutionary workers' party firmly rooted in the urban proletariat. On the basis of these positions, which coincided in their essentials with those of Trotsky and the Soviet Left Opposition—which were then unknown in China—P'eng argued against the subordination of the CCP to the KMT and fought consistently for the reestablishment of an independent Communist Party free of the control of the Chinese bourgeoisie.

P'eng's political battle was unsuccessful. The overwhelming weight of the apparatus of the Comintern was brought to bear on the CCP. All of the weak or opportunist party leaders fell into line. The results are well known: The brutal massacre of the workers of Shanghai in April 1927 at the hands of their supposed ally, Chiang Kai-shek. This was followed by a similar slaughter in Wuhan in July under the auspices of the so-called Left Kuomintang of Wang Ching-wei, who was supported by Stalin after Chiang broke with the CCP.

In the course of these events, P'eng won over Ch'en Tu-hsiu, the CCP's general secretary and the best known of its founding leaders. P'eng and Ch'en and their followers were expelled from the party in 1929 for adhering to the revolutionary criticism of Stalin's policy put forward by Trotsky. This marked the beginning of the independent Trotskyist movement in China. Ch'en Pi-lan in her biographical account provides the only reliable account available in English of the difficult years of the revolutionary struggle that followed for Chinese Trotskyism, beset by political and physical repression from both the KMT and the Stalinists. P'eng himself spent five years in prison from 1932 to 1937 along with Ch'en Tu-hsiu and a number of other leading Trotskyists after a spectacular trial in the courts of the Kuomintang.

P'eng Shu-tse today is one of the very few living links to the leadership of the Communist International in its revolutionary period in the time of Lenin and Trotsky. Forced into exile by Stalinist persecution in 1948, he and Ch'en Pi-lan have devoted their energies to the building of the Fourth International, the world party of socialist revolution founded by Leon Trotsky in 1938. Today they are among its most respected leaders. Their comrades who remained in China suffered the fate that every Stalinist regime reserves for loyal defenders of the interests of the working class: They were arrested in a nationwide police sweep, in December 1952 and January 1953, and disappeared into the CCP's prisons. They were held for twenty-seven years—the few dozen who remained alive were released in the summer of 1979.

The essays, interviews, and political documents in this collection are the writings of an active revolutionist. Some of the most important, analyzing in detail the social character of the Stalinist regime that came to power in 1949, were written not for the general public but to help orient the cadres of the Fourth International. These take the form of polemics with individuals or groupings within the Trotskyist movement that tended to one degree or another to identify the immense achievements made possible by the overthrow of the capitalist regime in China, and later of capitalist property forms, with the leadership of the Mao regime.

The disputes over China within the Fourth International hinged on the question of whether the CCP's immersion in such a deepgoing revolutionary process had transformed it from a defender of the privileges of a bureaucratic caste into a party that now reflected the real ongoing class interests of the oppressed. Viewing the Chinese revolution from afar, it seemed to some Trotskyists that Mao could only have come to power by definitively breaking with Stalinism. Such an evaluation led them to regard the Mao regime as moving in the direction of revolutionary Marxism, and, consequently, to hold out positive expectations that in the future the CCP would act to help promote the program of socialist revolution on the world arena.

As P'eng shows in his report to the 1951 world congress of the Fourth International, "The Causes of the Victory of the Chinese Communist Party Over Chiang Kai-shek, and the CCP's Perspectives," the premise on which this whole line of reasoning originated was erroneous. Mao Tse-tung had not aimed from the first at the seizure of power. Finding himself propelled by circumstances onto this road, he and his party then sought for a prolonged period to wield their power to preserve capitalist private property, not to abolish it. (In 1951 when this report was given Mao had still not broken with support to capitalist property forms—that decisive step took place two years later, under the pressure of procapitalist sabotage of the economy in the later stages of the Korean War.)

In the end, Mao carried out measures far more sweeping than he had intended or advocated. The sum of these changes amounted to the creation of a workers' state in China. But it was not a workers' state under the control of institutions of workers' democracy such as the soviets that had played such a decisive role in the early years of the Russian revolution. The Chinese workers' state suffered from the outset from the uncontrolled bureaucratic domination of the CCP high command. The CCP used its control of the state apparatus to consolidate a parasitic privileged bureaucratic stratum of the type that had come to exist in the Soviet Union. P'eng was sharply aware of this profound contradiction in the third Chinese revolution. In contrast to those Marxists who saw an identification between the Maoist leadership and the gains of the revolution, and who were led by this misperception to bend to or apologize for the Maoist regime, P'eng consistently differentiated his unswerving support for the revolutionary advances made possible by the nationalized planned economy from the totalitarian dictatorship that monopolized political power.

The failure to make this distinction could lead only to political disorientation and an abandonment of revolutionary perspectives. This was the sorry fate of Arne Swabeck, who entered into a sharp controversy with P'eng in the late 1950s over the character of the rural "People's Communes" instituted by the Peking government during the Great Leap Forward. Swabeck had behind him a long and honorable career as a class-struggle fighter in the American Communist and Trotskyist movements. Swabeck failed to grasp the reasons for Chinese Stalinism's rise to power. He persuaded himself that the organization of the "People's Communes" in 1958 represented an upsurge of popular democracy. This brought him by 1967 to desert Trotskyism altogether, although he had been a founding leader of the American Trotskyists in 1928 and a long-time leader of the Socialist Workers Party.

Some of the most fascinating sections of this volume are the numerous interview-articles through which P'eng commented on

Mao's last decade. These follow in rich detail the rise and fall of the "Cultural Revolution"; the successive waves of purges within the CCP leadership as the Mao cult became more and more entrenched—Liu Shao-ch'i, Lin Piao, Ch'en Po-ta; and, finally, the overturn of Mao's own coterie after his death. Here P'eng brings to bear an exceptional insight, founded on his more than fifty years of life in China, his long study of Marxism and of Chinese society, and his extensive personal knowledge of many of the central individuals involved.

*   *   *

The documents that comprise the first part of this book were written in Chinese and translated at the time for the press or for the internal discussion bulletins of the Trotskyist movement. The editing of them for publication here has retained the original translations but made minor stylistic changes. An exception is the 1951 report on "The Causes of the Victory of the Chinese Communist Party," where the translation as a whole was corrected for this volume. The interviews were originally given in English. In most cases P'eng quotes from Chinese-language editions of the many documents cited in the text. For the convenience of the English reader the editor has provided identifying English-language sources of these documents where they exist. The back-of-the-book notes as well as the biographical glossary have been supplied by the editor. Bottom-of-the-page footnotes are part of the original text. An effort has been made to conform Chinese spelling to the Wade-Giles system. The editor assumes the responsibility for any inconsistencies in the English transliteration of Chinese words and names.

In addition to the introduction by Ch'en Pi-lan this volume also contains as an appendix an interview with her obtained in mid-1967 on the effects of Mao's "Cultural Revolution" on writers, artists, and educators. This is an area that Ch'en Pi-lan follows with particular attention and her interview adds an important dimension in understanding the widespread popular hostility to Mao's faction in the last years of his rule.

INTRODUCTION

Looking Back Over My Years with P'eng Shu-tse

By Ch'en Pi-lan

I

It is not my intention in this brief account to write a biography of P'eng Shu-tse, but I shall attempt to sketch his thinking, his political positions, and his activities in the Chinese Communist Party from the time I first met him forty years ago. I shall also try to indicate his arduous struggle over the past thirty-six years for the Trotskyist movement.

I first met P'eng Shu-tse in the autumn of 1925, but I had already become familiar with his outlook by the end of 1924. At that time I was attending the Communist University of Toilers of the East in Moscow. I read articles by him that appeared in *Hsiang-tao chou-pao* [Guide Weekly], the official organ of the

---

This biographical sketch of P'eng Shu-tse was written by Ch'en Pi-lan, P'eng's companion since 1925. It was completed in November 1965 on the occasion of P'eng's seventieth birthday. It was first published in Intercontinental Press *(New York) between November 2 and November 23, 1970. Ch'en Pi-lan was born in the village of Huang-pei, Hupeh province, in 1902. She joined the Young Socialist League and the Chinese Communist Party as a student in Wuhan in 1922. In 1924 she was chosen by the CCP Central Committee to attend the University of the Toilers of the East in Moscow, returning in August 1925. She took part in the revolutionary upheaval of 1925-27, first in Honan, then, toward the end of 1925, in Shanghai. From October 1925 to April 1927 she was a member of the Standing Committee of the CCP's Shanghai Regional Committee, secretary of the regional committee's women's bureau, and editor of Chung-kuo fu-nü (Chinese Women). Ch'en Pi-lan helped to organize the Shanghai Women's Association's participation in the successful workers' insurrec-*

CCP, and in the theoretical magazine *Hsin ch'ing-nien* [New Youth].

In his first article, "Imperialism and the Boxer Movement" (published in *Hsiang-tao,* September 3, 1924), he analyzed the decline of China to semicolonial status, a process that began with the Opium War (1840-42), citing facts on the military, political, economic, and cultural penetration of China by the imperialist powers. He characterized the Boxer Movement of 1900 as an "anti-imperialistic movement of national revolution, undertaken by the peasant masses under the excessive pressure of the imperialists." [1] He thus took exception to the invidious terms used by many historians in referring to the "Boxer Rebellion," which they generally characterized as "barbarous" and "anti-foreign." P'eng correctly defined the Boxer Movement, not only for the CCP but also for the Chinese intellectuals who were arguing the question. The bourgeois historians, of whom Professor Hu Shih of Peking University was typical, maintained that his view flew in the face of the traditional interpretation of Chinese history.

P'eng's next article, which impressed me deeply, was entitled "Who Is the Leader of the National Revolution?" (published in *Hsin ch'ing-nien,* December 1924).

Early in 1923 the Communist International, claiming that the Chinese revolution was a national democratic revolution involving all the classes, had ordered members of the CCP to join the Kuomintang and to follow a policy of collaborating with it. The question arose—what class is the leader of the revolution? The Comintern's order implied that the CCP, representing the proletariat, could not carry full responsibility for leading the national revolution alone, since it had to join the Kuomintang and collaborate with it.

---

tion in Shanghai in March 1927. (She left Shanghai to attend a party conference in Wuhan a few hours before Chiang Kai-shek's anticommunist massacre on April 12.) Ch'en Pi-lan was a founding member of the Chinese Trotskyist movement in 1929. She carried out clandestine work in Shanghai under the Japanese occupation during the Sino-Japanese War (1937-45). In 1946 she was elected to the Political Bureau of the Communist League of China, the Chinese section of the Fourth International. She was editor of the League's magazine, New Voice, *from May 1945 until she and P'eng were forced to go into exile in December 1948. Since then she has been a leader of the Chinese Trotskyists in exile and of the Fourth International.*

Having accepted the order, the leaders of the party changed their previous views and shifted toward the right. Mao Tse-tung, for instance, in an article "Peking Coup d'Etat and the Merchants" (published in *Hsiang-tao,* July 11, 1923), openly urged that the merchants, i.e., the bourgeoisie of Tientsin and Peking, "rise and collaborate with those of Shanghai to advance the revolution. The greater the unity of the merchants, *the more powerful their leadership of the masses throughout the country, and the shorter the time necessary to bring the revolution to success"* (emphasis in original).

Obviously the author here recognized the bourgeoisie as the leader of the national revolution.

Later on, Ch'en Tu-hsiu wrote an article entitled "The National Revolution and All Classes" (published in the monthly *Ch'ien feng* [The Vanguard], vol. 2, December 1923). In this article, after analyzing all the social classes in China and their relationship of forces, he came to the conclusion: Only the bourgeoisie can lead the national revolution, since on the one hand the character of the revolution is inherently bourgeois, and on the other the proletariat is insufficient in numbers and lacks the knowledge needed to lead a revolution. Such concepts caused considerable confusion and bewilderment among the rank and file of the party. Although P'eng did not mention Ch'en by name, his article was in fact a criticism of Ch'en's view.

In his 1924 article, after analyzing in detail the economic basis and interests of all the social classes, from the bourgeoisie (i.e., the bank capitalists, merchants, and industrial capitalists) through the petty bourgeoisie, the artisans, the peasantry, and the proletariat, P'eng pointed out that the Chinese bourgeoisie, including the industrial capitalists, depended either directly or indirectly on the imperialists and Chinese warlords and therefore could not mount the determined struggle against them that was necessary for success in the national revolution. Furthermore, owing to its fear of the proletariat, the bourgeoisie would inevitably prove reactionary. P'eng drew the following conclusion:

"After analyzing all the classes . . . we may now affirm that from the standpoint of their material basis, revolutionary consciousness, and the conditions of the international revolution . . . only the working class can become the leader of the national revolution."

*   *   *

P'eng joined the CCP in the autumn of 1920. The following year he attended the Communist University of the Toilers of the East in Moscow. He was elected to serve as secretary of the Moscow branch of the CCP, holding this post until 1924 when he returned to China after attending the Fifth Congress of the Communist International.

In the Moscow branch, I was told, he gave many reports on Marxism and discussed all kinds of problems with the comrades. Small wonder that they regarded him highly.

When I was there, his successor as secretary of the branch was Lo I-nung. (Lo returned to China in the spring of 1925, soon being assigned to serve as secretary of the Shanghai Regional Committee. After the failure of the revolution of 1927, he was executed by Chiang Kai-shek.) At that time there were about 100 comrades in Moscow. Some of them had come from France and Germany, but most of them were sent from China. In addition to our regular classes, we often held discussions in the evening. When we took up P'eng's long articles ("Imperialism and the Boxer Movement" and "Who Is the Leader of the National Revolution?"), everyone agreed with the viewpoint expressed.

At that time, Li Ta-chao was in Moscow. He was one of the founders of the CCP. Following the Fifth Congress of the Comintern, he stayed in Moscow to do research work. After he returned to China, he was hanged in April 1927 by Chang Tso-lin, the warlord of Northern China.

Among the students was Liu Pai-chien, who later became head of Feng Yü-hsiang's Political Commission. He was shot by Chiang Kai-shek.

I recall that at the farewell party for Li Ta-chao when he returned to China, the chairman was Liu Pai-chien. In his remarks, the smiling Liu said proudly: "One pen has already gone home. That pen is our comrade P'eng Shu-tse. Now Comrade Li Ta-chao is going home, too. We believe that he will certainly make a great contribution to our party."

The word "pen" struck a chord because that was where my interests lay. That is why I began by saying that I already knew P'eng's outlook before I came to know him personally.

*   *   *

After returning home in the summer of 1924, P'eng, besides writing articles for *Hsiang-tao* and *Hsin ch'ing-nien,* participated in the daily work of the Shanghai Regional Committee. In

January 1925, when the Fourth Congress of the CCP was held, he was elected to the Central Committee and the Central Standing Committee (Political Bureau), and was assigned to be chief editor of both *Hsiang-tao* and *Hsin ch'ing-nien.* In the autumn of 1925 I came back to Shanghai to participate in a meeting for all women comrades in Shanghai. The man who gave the political report at the meeting, I learned from the brief introduction by Hsiang Ching-yü, who was in charge of the Central Board for Women, was none other than the author of the many articles I had read in Moscow. My first impression of him was his quiet and dignified manner and the warmth he displayed toward comrades.

*　　　　*　　　　*

The Central Standing Committee was composed of five members: Ch'en Tu-hsiu, P'eng Shu-tse, Ch'ü Ch'iu-pai, Ts'ai Ho-sen, and Chang Kuo-t'ao. But in fact there were only three, because Ts'ai went to Moscow and Chang was often absent from Shanghai.

Ch'en always stayed in the central office to meet comrades coming in from all over the country. P'eng also often assisted Ch'en in this. Ch'ü, owing to his better facility with the Russian language, was in charge of contacts with representatives from the Comintern. He did not like to participate in the Shanghai Regional Committee, which included three provinces (Chekiang, Kiangsu, Anhwei), nor did he like to meet comrades. Consequently, P'eng was the only member of the Central Standing Committee to attend the Shanghai Regional Committee meetings. He also regularly attended the meetings of the Central Standing Committee of the Chinese Communist Youth Corps.

Since P'eng often participated in the meetings of the Shanghai Regional Committee (of which I was a member) as well as in other meetings of cadres, I had occasion to see him frequently. When literary work was involved, I used to go where he was staying, as he was the director of the Central Department of Propaganda and I was the editor-in-chief of the monthly magazine *Chung-kuo fu-nü* [Chinese Women]. Some of the important articles involving politics and theory had to be taken up with him for approval or correction. Thus I saw him often, and after a certain time, understanding each other perfectly, we decided to live together.

*   *   *

In 1925 the May Thirtieth Movement stirred up resistance against imperialism and the warlords.[2] Throughout the whole country in 1925 and 1926, workers, peasants, students, women, and various elements of the petty bourgeoisie all took part in the revolutionary upsurge. For instance, whenever they were aroused by events, such as the struggle against the Fengtien warlord clique, the invasion of Manchuria by the Japanese, the March 18, 1926, slaughter in Peking, hundreds of thousands of persons demonstrated in the streets of Shanghai.[3]

Immediately after the emotionally charged demonstration protesting the March 18 slaughter, the news reached Shanghai of the March 20 coup d'etat in Canton.[4] Chiang Kai-shek, the representative of the bourgeoisie with whom the CCP had collaborated in the Kuomintang, had signaled his intentions. The event, which came like a bolt from the blue, paralyzed the whole party. Caught by surprise, every member of the CCP in the Shanghai region was anguished and bewildered.

On the following day, after the Shanghai Regional Committee had weighed the meaning of the coup, the activists were called together in a meeting. More than 100, sitting on the floor, listened to P'eng's report on the Canton coup and the opinion of the Central Committee of the CCP. By the end of the meeting they were seething with indignation over the coup. They were in complete agreement that it was a clear indication of the reactionary nature of the bourgeoisie, and that we Communists, standing firmly with the proletariat, had to reconsider the question of the CCP's collaborating with the Kuomintang, and take up the problem of what policy the party should adopt toward that formation. Everyone wanted the Central Committee to speedily work out ways and means of coping with Chiang Kai-shek.

After critical consideration, the Central Committee decided on a counterattack. This included an alliance with the armed forces of the left-wing Kuomintang, expansion of the army under the command of the Communist Yeh T'ing, and the arming of detachments of the proletariat and the peasantry.

At the end of April 1926, the Central Committee sent P'eng to Canton delegated to set up a special committee to discuss with Borodin, the representative of the Comintern, what should be done concretely with relation to Chiang and to express the views of the Central Committee.

The Third Congress of the National General Labor Union was

being held at the same time in Canton. The Shanghai Regional Committee designated me to help the delegation of the Shanghai General Labor Union in its participation, and so I went with P'eng on this trip.

* * *

P'eng, as the representative of the Central Committee, proposed taking a stand against Chiang. He also proposed, on his own, that the CCP withdraw its members from the Kuomintang, end the tactic of working from within, and conduct subsequent collaboration party-to-party.

Borodin, as the representative of the Comintern, continued to support Chiang and collaboration between the CCP and the Kuomintang. He was therefore opposed to these proposals.

Thus P'eng and Borodin were in sharp conflict. The outcome of this was that P'eng became isolated.

Borodin was a sophisticated bureaucrat, skilled at maneuvering. He was armed with the prestige of the Soviet Union and the Comintern, and had abundant material resources at his command (arms and money), which added to his authority and power.

The members of the provincial committee in Kwangtung (Chou En-lai was one of them), and the other member of the Central Committee such as T'an P'ing-shan, Chang Kuo-t'ao, etc., thus adjusted their views to fit those of Borodin.

Borodin turned the Central Committee's anti-Chiang policy around into a policy of supporting Chiang. P'eng's proposal to withdraw from the Kuomintang was converted into acceptance of Chiang's "Resolution Adjusting Party Affairs." As a result, the CCP became an appendage of the Kuomintang.

The "Resolution Adjusting Party Affairs" specified that criticism by Communists of Sun Yat-sen's San-min chu-i [the Three People's Principles] be prohibited; that no member of the CCP could hold the post of chief of the Central Headquarters of the Kuomintang; that not more than one-third of those sitting on the regional committees of the Kuomintang could be members of the CCP; and that the CCP must turn over to the Central Committee of the Kuomintang a complete list of CCP members in the Kuomintang.

Borodin agreed to this "Resolution Adjusting Party Affairs." Of course, Borodin's policy of surrendering to Chiang was put into effect under orders from the Comintern.

In order to successfully carry out the Comintern's, or, better put, Stalin's policy, Borodin told Ch'en Yen-nien, the secretary of the provincial committee in Kwangtung: "Unless P'eng Shu-tse leaves Canton, I can't start doing anything."

It was on Borodin's suggestion that Ch'en Yen-nien immediately wrote to his father, Ch'en Tu-hsiu, asking him to transfer P'eng Shu-tse back to Shanghai. This was the first harsh experience suffered by P'eng at the hands of the representative of the Comintern.

*   *   *

After P'eng left Canton and returned to Shanghai in early June 1926, the Central Committee of the CCP was forced to accept the Comintern's policy of surrendering to Chiang Kai-shek. With the support of Borodin, Chiang consolidated his military dictatorship without hindrance, manipulating the apparatus of the Kuomintang, the administration, and the army to his own ends, and assigning himself the post of commander in chief to undertake the Northern Expedition.[5]

In face of the mounting threat, the Central Committee of the CCP felt it necessary to correct the policy of surrender.

In July 1926 a plenary meeting of the Central Committee took place. Ch'en Tu-hsiu and P'eng Shu-tse submitted a proposal to end collaboration with the Kuomintang from within, substituting collaboration party-to-party, and thus freeing the CCP from the yoke of the Kuomintang. They also proposed putting into practice the CCP's stated policy of leading the workers and peasants in the revolution. Although the suggested course was not adopted, most of the members agreed to submit it to the Comintern for consideration.

The Comintern criticized it severely and turned it down. The CCP had no alternative but to obey the orders of the Comintern and continue the opportunist policy. This meant that the CCP had to mobilize the workers and peasants as a whole in support of the Northern Expedition headed by Chiang Kai-shek. From then on the workers had to restrain themselves from violating bourgeois property rights; the peasants were denied early possession of land held by the landlords; the CCP could not carry on propaganda work among the Kuomintang troops or organize anything within their ranks. In particular, the CCP was not to set up its own regime based on soviets of the workers, peasants, and soldiers, since this would be likely to injure collaboration between the Kuomintang and the CCP, and would constitute a "rash adventure" overstepping "the stage of the national revolution." The Chinese revolution was thus taken, step by step, down a blind alley ending in destruction.

Nevertheless, P'eng Shu-tse felt, as he still does, that limiting the Chinese revolution to "the stage of the national revolution" and confining it within "the bondage of Kuomintang-CCP collaboration," did not conform to the historical experience of the October revolution in Russia.

Early in 1927 he wrote an article entitled "Is Leninism Applicable to the National Peculiarities of China?" (published in *Hsiang-tao*, January 21, 1927). In this article he criticized the fallacious reasoning according to which the national peculiarities of China differ so much from those of Russia as to make Leninism inapplicable to China. After analyzing in detail the social and economic conditions in China, the relationship of forces among the classes, and the international position of China, he pointed out that these, in general, resembled those of Russia before the October revolution. Consequently, he concluded, the Chinese revolution could be expected to follow the Russian pattern, and Leninism was entirely applicable to the situation in China.

He acknowledged that "the Chinese revolution is a national democratic revolution at present, *but this revolution is absolutely not limited to the ideas of nationality and democracy; it will certainly turn gradually in the direction of socialist revolution*" (my emphasis).

Accordingly, he suggested the label "permanent revolution" and the following:

It should be finally understood that the national revolution is not the last stage of the revolution; *it is only a road leading to the socialist revolution.* The final and genuine emancipation of humanity depends solely on the socialist revolution being carried out by the proletariat as a foundation for the building of communist society. The ultimate objective of Leninism is to lead humanity as a whole from the oppression of various societies to the freedom of communism. *Thus "permanent revolution" should be understood to mean the process leading directly from the national revolution into the proletarian revolution.* [Emphasis in the original]

In the early part of 1927, when the revolution had reached a very critical stage, P'eng Shu-tse wrote another article, entitled "The Present Revolutionary Crisis of the Rightward Tendency" (published in *Hsiang-tao*, March 6, 1927).

> *The whole situation of the Chinese revolution is already clearly apparent. On the one hand, the power of the revolution, especially the power of the National Revolutionary Army, the workers, and the peasants, is developing with exceptional rapidity. The tide of revolution is still swelling and deepening. . . . On the other hand . . . a compromising and reactionary tendency among the leaders of the National Revolutionary Army has become apparent. . . . They have attempted, publicly, or secretly, to make a compromise with the enemy against the masses they confront. This is the most dangerous phenomenon in the revolution at present, and it may well destroy the whole revolution.* [Emphasis in the original]

This compromising and reactionary tendency to which P'eng drew attention was the bourgeois counterrevolutionary tendency represented by Chiang Kai-shek. P'eng continued:

> The so-called moderate group in the Kuomintang has fully disclosed its bourgeois tendency; *they . . . have seen the workers and peasants rising to fight not only for general revolutionary interests but in the interest of the workers and peasants themselves. They have also noted the concessions granted by the imperialists and the warlords. Hence this group aims at stopping the revolutionary process . . . in order to unify all the compradors, bureaucrats, and landlords, the rotten gentry and those enemies of the revolution, the imperialists and the warlords, for the purpose of striking back at the worker and peasant masses.* [Emphasis in original]

In view of this, P'eng drew the emphatic conclusion:

> *The Chinese revolution should create a regime of revolutionary democracy, and, above all, should not create a personal military dictatorship* (Chiang Kai-shek). . . . The present revolution is urgently in need of a revolutionary regime of democratic dictatorship. That means a regime for the masses in their majority, composed of workers, peasants, and petty bourgeois, in which they participate directly, thus controlling the government in order to carry out their interest in *striking down all the elements of the counterrevolution and in enforcing a revolutionary dictatorship over them.* [Emphasis in original]

P'eng's conclusions were advanced two weeks before the workers in Shanghai were victorious in their armed insurrection of March 21, 1927. His views were thus put forward five weeks before Chiang Kai-shek's next coup, on April 12, when he butchered the revolutionary masses in the same city.

Although P'eng's formula of a "revolutionary regime of democratic dictatorship" cannot be equated with a dictatorship of the proletariat in alliance with the poor peasants, it obviously excludes the bourgeoisie from the revolutionary regime, and can therefore be considered to be a formula calling for a workers' and peasants' government.

It is completely different from the policy of a "bloc of four classes"—the workers, the peasants, the petty bourgeoisie, and the bourgeoisie—insisted upon by the Comintern in preparing for the establishment of a coalition government composed of representatives of the workers, peasants, petty bourgeoisie, and bourgeoisie.

Furthermore, in an article entitled "After Reading Chiang Kai-shek's Speech of February 21" (published in *Hsiang-tao*, March 18, 1927), P'eng with the greatest precision exposed Chiang's calculations and his antilabor, antipeasant, anticommunist, and anti-Soviet course. P'eng uttered a grave warning: *"The coming struggle in China is a life and death struggle between the forces of the revolution and the antirevolutionary forces represented by Chiang Kai-shek"* (emphasis in original).

But the Comintern took a different attitude toward Chiang Kai-shek, since it still urged the CCP to continue its policy of collaborating with him.

Special attention should be paid to an article written by P'eng two years earlier entitled "The Banning of the Confederation of Trade Unions in Shanghai and the Ensuing Responsibilities of the Workers in the City" (published in *Hsiang-tao*, October 5, 1925). In this article, P'eng observed: "The success of the Chinese national revolution is possible only on condition that the Chinese workers arise and fight. Shanghai . . . is the equivalent of Russia's Petrograd—the February revolution and the October revolution in Russia were under the leadership of the workers in Petrograd."

He ended his article by forecasting:

> The hundreds of thousands of workers in Shanghai have gained much experience in the May Thirtieth Movement under the leadership of the General Labor Union, and have become familiar with a number of the elementary methods of carrying out a revolution. *In the future they will advance further along the road of armed insurrection . . . following the examples set by the workers of Petrograd from the February revolution to the October revolution.* [Emphasis in the original]

P'eng's prediction had proved to be accurate. The workers in Shanghai organized an armed insurrection on March 21, 1927, in response to the advance of the Northern Expedition. The following day, they occupied the entire city except for the foreign concessions. More than 2,000 armed pickets were organized to maintain peace and order. Workers flooded into the trade unions and the CCP, opening up the possibility of establishing a proletarian regime.

If, at that time, the CCP had not been controlled by the Comintern; if it had been permitted to follow its own assessments (such as those expressed by P'eng) based on the lessons drawn from the October revolution in Russia and its own experiences; if it had led the Shanghai workers in a determined way and drawn in those soldiers in sympathy with the workers;* if it had organized councils (soviets) of delegates representing the workers, soldiers, and peasants; if it had aimed a decisive strike against Chiang Kai-shek and had set up a proletarian dictatorship against the bourgeoisie; then the workers of Shanghai could have fulfilled their historical mission, as did the Petrograd workers before them.

Unfortunately the CCP had to obey the Comintern and, in accordance with its opportunistic policy, collaborate with Chiang Kai-shek. After having led the workers to victory in an armed insurrection in Shanghai, the CCP was soon disarmed politically. The CCP had to do what the Comintern wanted it to do—organize a "provisional government" in Shanghai in collaboration with the bourgeoisie.

The bourgeois elements participating in the provisional government did everything possible to paralyze it through sabotage and boycotts while waiting for Chiang's next move. The Comintern's policy tied the hands of the Communists and workers. Under these circumstances, the CCP was useless to the workers.

Early in the morning of April 12, 1927, Chiang, having been granted the time needed to work out another plot, gave the signal to start the slaughter of his second coup. Many Communists and workers in Shanghai fell at the hands of the executioners, and Chiang took over the gains made by the revolution. This was the inevitable outcome of Stalin's insistence on the CCP following a policy of collaborating with the Kuomintang and helping Chiang's Northern Expedition.

---

* The great majority of the Shanghai contingent of soldiers in the Northern Expedition were, at that juncture, sympathetically disposed toward the workers.

II

Stalin did not have the least inkling of the meaning of the Canton coup carried out by Chiang Kai-shek on March 20, 1926. That was why he continued the policy of having the CCP collaborate with the Kuomintang and of giving assistance to Chiang. This paved the way for the butchery committed in the Shanghai coup of April 12. Even this massacre did not open Stalin's eyes to the facts; the tragedy taught him nothing.

Now he shifted to Wang Ching-wei, placing confidence in him instead of Chiang Kai-shek. "Collaboration with the left-wing Kuomintang" replaced "Kuomintang-CCP collaboration."[6]

The Fifth Congress of the CCP was held when this shift occurred, from the end of April to the beginning of May, 1927. The basic policies adopted by the congress remained as before, inasmuch as Stalin's policy remained unchanged. The peasants were still restrained from demanding the land; the need to seek improvements in the workers' standard of living was ignored; above all, out of fear of damaging collaboration with the "left" Kuomintang, arming of the workers and peasants was rejected.

Stalin held that "Wuhan is the revolutionary center," and that naturally Wang's regime would solve the agrarian problem and improve the standard of living of the workers. Stalin's policy, however, paved the way for Wang Ching-wei, as the representative of the "left" Kuomintang, to purge the CCP.

At the time of the Fifth Congress, Trotsky proposed that the CCP, in order to establish its independence, leave the Kuomintang, and that soviets of the workers, peasants, and soldiers be organized in preparation to displace Wang's regime. Trotsky's proposals, which would have led to a showdown, were blocked by Stalin.

Stalin even withheld knowledge of them from the CCP out of fear that if the Chinese Communists became aware of the documents submitted by Trotsky, they would compare and weigh the two policies, with the chances being, in view of their recent experiences, that they would favor what Trotsky proposed. This in turn would possibly bring victory to the Chinese revolution, destroying Stalin's preeminence in the Communist Party of the Soviet Union, an outcome intolerable to the reactionary, privileged Russian bureaucracy. Thus the second Chinese revolution was sacrificed for the sake of preserving the privileged position of the bureaucrats in Russia.

A fact worth noting in this respect is that Ch'ü Ch'iu-pai came to Wuhan on a secret visit on the eve of the Fifth Congress. Without consulting the Central Standing Committee, he published a pamphlet entitled *The Problem of the Chinese Revolution*. It was directed mainly against P'eng Shu-tse's basic position in favor of "permanent revolution," but he also dealt with the schedule of the armed insurrection in Shanghai and the argument over the selection of members of the Shanghai provisional government after the victory.

Ch'ü had already learned from certain representatives of the Comintern that Stalin had opened a furious attack against all of Trotsky's views, particularly his theory of "permanent revolution." Citing P'eng's use of the words "permanent revolution," he said that this signified "copying Trotskyism and introducing it into China."

In point of fact, P'eng did not know what was going on in Moscow but had come to his views on the Chinese revolution as a result of the lessons of the Russian revolution from February to October 1917 and as a result of his own experience in the Chinese revolution. He was aware, of course, that the theory went back to Marx.

Ch'ü sought to pin the label of "Trotskyism" on P'eng so as to destroy him and earn Stalin's appreciation. Although it appeared on the surface to be directed only against P'eng Shu-tse, it was also aimed against Ch'en Tu-hsiu. Ch'ü was seeking to kill two birds with one stone—have P'eng excluded from leadership and Ch'en Tu-hsiu removed as general secretary of the CCP, thus opening up a vacancy into which he could step.

To promote this factional aim, he organized a small group and sought the patronage of certain Comintern representatives. The majority of the cadres, especially Roy, the representative of the Comintern, were very much against Ch'ü's intrigue and intervened in the affair. Ch'en Tu-hsiu was reelected as general secretary, but P'eng was excluded from the incoming Central Standing Committee.

In the period following the Fifth Congress, from about May to June, 1927, P'eng stayed in Wuhan where he wrote a pamphlet, *The Basic Problems of the Chinese Revolution*, in which he set out to explain and justify the "excessive actions," as they were called, of the workers and peasants. During these days P'eng met frequently with Ch'en Tu-hsiu to discuss the deteriorating situation.

I was sometimes there and can bear witness to the great

perplexity they felt over the dilemma that faced them. They suffered deeply from the painful experience of discovering that the Comintern's policy of supporting Chiang Kai-shek had already proved bankrupt. As for the Comintern's current policy of supporting Wang Ching-wei, evidence was mounting that this, too, was taking the party into a blind alley.

Ch'en, as general secretary, had no choice but to carry out the policy decided on in Moscow. At the same time he was well aware that Wang's "left" Kuomintang was giving more and more support to the counterrevolutionary army generals against the CCP, and turning toward an attack against the mass movement of workers and peasants.

Once more, Ch'en proposed to withdraw from Wang's Kuomintang so that the CCP could lead the movement independently. Again the Comintern rejected the proposal. In his disappointment over the leadership of the Comintern, Ch'en resigned shortly thereafter. (Ch'ü Ch'iu-pai was put in as acting general secretary.) Almost immediately, Wang Ching-wei cracked down, July 14, 1927, with his "Communist purge."

From now on, the second Chinese revolution met with failure and tragedy!

*   *   *

On the eve of the "Communist purge," P'eng was sent to the North to serve as secretary of the Northern Regional Committee. To renew contact with the workers and peasants, he set about working out a defensive policy and reorganizing the party in Peking, Tientsin, and other areas. This was the moment chosen by the Central Political Bureau, headed by Ch'ü Ch'iu-pai, to order an armed insurrection in Peking and Tientsin.

What had happened? Following Wang's coup, the Comintern switched its policy on the Chinese revolution from extreme right opportunism to extreme left adventurism. The Central Committee of the CCP met August 7, 1927 (hence the so-called "August 7 Conference"), for the principal purpose of absolving the Comintern of its responsibility for the defeat of the Chinese revolution and laying the blame on Ch'en Tu-hsiu as the scapegoat. Ch'ü Ch'iu-pai, who tended to follow blindly the adventurist policy of the Comintern, was chosen formally as the general secretary.

Disregarding the objective situation, Ch'ü had already ordered the troops under Ho Lung and Yeh T'ing to engage in an armed rebellion. This started August 1, 1927, in Nanchang. Then came the so-called Autumn Harvest Rebellions in Hunan and Hupeh.

P'eng held that the Comintern's policy of jumping from the extreme right to the extreme left was not only out of keeping with Marxism, but also lacked common sense. Although he could do nothing to change things, he discussed the situation with members of the Northern Regional Committee and a "delaying policy" was agreed on.

They clearly saw that Peking and Tientsin were completely under control of the reactionary warlords. Since neither a mass movement nor a mass organization existed, if they ordered party members and workers to engage in an artificial armed insurrection, the sole outcome would be the useless sacrifice of the lives of the cadres and militants. As a pretext for delaying, they argued that an armed insurrection takes time to prepare. However, Ch'ü Ch'iu-pai and the Political Bureau believed that P'eng was purposefully refusing to carry out the decision and dismissed him as secretary.

Ts'ai Ho-sen was sent to replace him and to organize the Northern Bureau. He moved toward an armed insurrection in the most energetic way, but this had not even begun when more than sixty cadres were arrested in Peking and shot. This was the outcome of only attempting to carry out the Comintern's policy of armed insurrection in North China.

After being dismissed, P'eng went back to Shanghai. This was in the days immediately following the failure of the Canton insurrection (staged December 11, 1927), when Stalin's adventurist policy was clearly an utter failure.[7] In Shanghai and throughout the rest of the country, terror reigned. Virtually not a day passed without comrades being arrested and shot.

The CCP became increasingly dependent on the Comintern as the sole source of funds, and there was no alternative to this owing to the defeat of the revolution. Under Stalin's control, the Comintern was increasingly being used as a device to housebreak the CCP by backing the more pliable leaders and cadres.

Thus the bureaucrats, especially Ch'ü Ch'iu-pai, utilized material means to advance their control. Those who demonstrated their tractability were assured of material help, which, to a certain extent, gained protection for them against danger. Those who dared to express doubts as to the effectiveness of the adventurist course, or to evidence dissatisfaction with Ch'ü Ch'iu-pai's bureaucratic measures, faced great difficulties. They would inevitably find themselves out of a job and denied living expenses.

This was a deadly threat to cadres who had become professional revolutionists. Working wholeheartedly for the party, making this their way of life, they had severed ordinary social relations, often even with friends and relatives. They could expect help from nowhere. Under the white terror those known as Communists could in no circumstances so much as apply for a job. Even in journalistic or translating work they were compelled to use pseudonyms. The bureaucrats exploited this situation to tighten their control over the cadres.

P'eng Shu-tse, our six-month-old daughter, and I underwent great dangers and suffered many hardships. Under the control of Ch'ü Ch'iu-pai, the Central Committee would give P'eng no work, although he was still a member of that body, even refusing to admit him to meetings. Out of fear that his opposition to adventurism and bureaucratism would affect other cadres, they wanted to isolate him.

They soon stopped his frugal living allowance, and Shu-tse was left with no other alternative but to make a living by translating books.

When we returned to Shanghai from Tientsin, P'eng Shu-tse could once again meet with Ch'en Tu-hsiu. Ch'en was P'eng's source of information on what had been going on in the CCP since Wang Ching-wei had launched his purge against the Communists. In August and September of 1927, Ch'en had written two letters to the Central Committee criticizing the adventurist course. Consequently, P'eng and Ch'en found themselves in common agreement on their political positions.

Their criticisms of the Central Committee of the CCP and of the Comintern were, of course, reported back to Moscow by Ch'ü Ch'iu-pai. As a result, just before the Sixth Congress of the Comintern, which was held in Moscow in 1928, Stalin and Bukharin sent a telegram to Ch'en Tu-hsiu and P'eng Shu-tse (the telegram was delivered personally by Chou En-lai to Ch'en's home), inviting them to attend the congress.

Ch'en Tu-hsiu and P'eng Shu-tse had already lost hope and confidence in the Comintern, and, clearly understanding that the real aim was to "persuade" or "detain" them and thus eliminate their influence in the CCP, they politely but firmly declined the invitation.

*   *   *

In the spring of 1929, P'eng Shu-tse had a long talk with several students who had just returned from Moscow. From them he learned of the struggle of the Left Opposition, led by Trotsky, against the Stalinists. They told him about Trotsky's view on the problems of the Chinese revolution. These students also gave him two important documents written by Trotsky on the Chinese question: "Summary and Perspectives of the Chinese Revolution" and "The Chinese Question After the Sixth Congress."[8]

After studying these documents, P'eng Shu-tse decided what political line he would take inside the Chinese Communist Party; he would fight in support of the line adopted by the Trotskyist Left Opposition. That P'eng so swiftly accepted Trotsky's program was by no means accidental. On the one hand he was grounded in Marxism and Leninism, and had a thought-out concept of the Chinese revolution. On the other hand he knew from personal experience why the revolution had failed and had seen with his own eyes the tragic results of Stalin's adventurist policy.

He was powerfully impressed upon reading how acutely Trotsky had criticized first the opportunist policies of Stalin and Bukharin during the rise of the Chinese revolution and then their adventurist course during its decline, and how Trotsky had advocated a defensive policy, calling for a national assembly as a general slogan, to replace the hopeless adventurism. The accuracy of Trotsky's forecasts had been registered in blood.

P'eng gave the two documents to Ch'en Tu-hsiu to read and study. The next day Ch'en came to our home to tell us that in his opinion Trotsky's criticisms of the policies of Stalin and Bukharin were completely justified. It was most urgent, he thought, in view of the current objective situation, to adopt a defensive policy centered around the slogan of calling for a national assembly, replacing Stalin's adventurist policy.

The outcome of this common understanding and agreement was that Ch'en Tu-hsiu and P'eng Shu-tse worked out a plan to bring together all the cadres in disagreement with the party's adventurist policy in order to discuss Trotsky's two documents and to organize a Left Opposition within the Chinese Communist Party.

Ch'en Tu-hsiu and P'eng Shu-tse each wrote a letter to the party's Central Committee, requesting that a discussion be opened to draw the necessary lessons from the defeat of the revolution and the results of the current policy. They asked that the party publish Trotsky's documents on the Chinese revolution so that they could be referred to in the discussion.

Our left oppositional work inside the party was very successful. Within two months we had assembled about fifty cadres and held a meeting that adopted the stand taken by Trotsky. A provisional central committee composed of three members (Ch'en, P'eng and I K'uan) was elected. The cadres, divided into cells, met constantly to discuss problems and activities inside the party. We also published a periodical, *The Proletariat*, and a book consisting of Trotsky's main documents on the Chinese revolution.

In consequence of our activities both inside and outside the party, and the dissemination of the ideas expressed in the letters addressed by Ch'en and P'eng to the center, the party was greatly shaken. The leadership of the party, under directives from the International, was compelled to expel us, one by one. The first to be singled out for expulsion were Ch'en Tu-hsiu and P'eng Shu-tse. It was then the turn of I K'uan, Cheng Ch'ao-lin, myself, and other cadres. News of the expulsions was published in the party organ *Red Flag*.

However, the expulsions, because of their nature, did not resolve the crisis in the party, but instead aggravated the shaky situation, causing a number of cadres to join us. On December 15, 1929, eighty-one outstanding cadres signed their names to the "Declaration of the Left Opposition." In the history of the Chinese Communist Party, this marked the most intense struggle and division between Stalinism and Trotskyism. Not only did it shake the Chinese Communist Party; it drew the attention of Chinese society as a whole and had repercussions in the Communist parties throughout the world.

A number of seasoned cadres, who had experienced the consequences of the defeat of the revolution and the bankruptcy of the policy of adventurism and who had suffered from the arbitrariness of the bureaucracy, yet had remained in the party, now indicated their sympathy for the Left Opposition as they observed their co-fighters in the revolution waging a brave and resolute struggle against the party leadership under the guidance of Ch'en and P'eng on the basis of the program of Trotsky.

These comrades were called "conciliators" in the party since they sought to bring about a conciliation between those following the party line and the group led by Ch'en Tu-hsiu. (Liu Shao-ch'i, now the chairman of the People's Republic of China,[9] also belonged to the "conciliators," and was sent to Moscow because of this.) According to Ch'en Shao-yü, who was one hundred percent for the line of the International (he later changed his name to Wang Ming), "the conciliators suggested that the Party welcome back Ch'en Tu-hsiu and P'eng Shu-tse, who had been expelled because of their opposition to the line adopted at the Sixth Congress of the Party."* These few words indicate the impact of the Left Opposition on the party.

*   *   *

While Ch'en and P'eng were forming the Left Opposition in China, some students who had recently returned from Moscow were also organizing Trotskyist groups and publishing their own periodicals. In these publications they not only quarreled among themselves, they also attacked Ch'en and P'eng, whom they considered to be responsible for the past opportunistic policy. In their eyes, only the younger comrades, who had not participated in the revolution, and who, therefore, had not caused it to fail, were worthy of being called Trotskyists.

This sectarian attitude was exploited by the Stalinist leadership of the party in attacks against Ch'en Tu-hsiu and P'eng Shu-tse. The "conciliators," noting the confusion and divergent views in the Left Opposition, gradually lost their sympathy for Trotskyism.

This was a heavy blow to the newly born Trotskyist movement in China. Later, when Trotsky heard about the confusion, he suggested that the various Trotskyist groupings unite. The unification took place at a conference held in May 1931. The united Trotskyist movement was called the Communist League of China.

Right after the unification, a number of leading comrades were arrested—a traitor had passed information to the military authorities in Shanghai. Shu-tse, I, and our daughter, then four years old, escaped only several hours before the police raided our home and confiscated all our belongings—books, documents, and clothes. This loss intensified our sufferings and difficulties in the years ahead.

Ch'en Tu-hsiu was not arrested on this occasion, since his address was not known to the turncoat.

It was a terrible situation, since the traitors to the party worked hand in hand with Chiang Kai-shek's agents. The agents waited at entrances to parks, theatres, department stores, major street

---

* See Ch'en Shao-yü, "For More Bolshevization of the Party."

crossings. If a comrade met one of the traitors, he would be followed and arrested by the plainclothesmen. His fate was then sealed.

*　　　*　　　*

Although our Left Opposition suffered heavy losses— demoralized comrades even left the movement—the objective situation changed as a result of the Japanese imperialist invasion of Manchuria on September 18, 1931, and of Shanghai on January 28, 1932, giving us new impetus. The invasions gave rise to a big anti-Japanese-imperialist movement which, in turn, scored the nonresistance of the Kuomintang government. During the mass anti-Japanese and anti-Kuomintang movement, the Communist League of China published, for the first time since its formation, an open weekly periodical, *Warm Tide*. It called for arming the masses against Japanese imperialism.

Our agitation and propaganda work had great influence among the students and working masses, and we met with an especially broad response among the lower levels of the party cadres.

Wang Ming, with Moscow's support, now ousted Li Li-san and Ch'ü Ch'iu-pai from leadership of the Chinese Communist Party, assuming leadership himself. During his tenure, he went to a bizarre extreme in his sectarian attitude toward the anti-Japanese movement and later toward the Nineteenth Route Army, then under the leadership of the left wing of the Kuomintang. In *Red Flag*, the official party organ, he advocated supporting the Red Army in its fight against the Japanese in the countryside, but he opposed arming the masses and backing the Nineteenth Route Army in its struggle against the Japanese.[10] That was on the political side. Organizationally he was just as bad. He expelled a great number of activists—the "conciliators" led by Ho Meng-hsiung—causing them to lose their lives. In one instance, cut off from financial support from the party and unable to rent a safer place to meet, some twenty cadres gathered in a small room in a poor hotel. They were arrested and shot. Many cadres left the party, and the disintegrating organization became a big field of recruitment for the Trotskyist movement.

Many rank-and-file cadres who read the documents of Trotsky and the anti-Japanese articles and criticisms of Stalin's policies published in *Warm Tide* got in touch with us. After discussing with P'eng Shu-tse, they joined the Trotskyist movement. Several dozen important industrial party cells came over to us, including the postal, power-plant, and textile workers. These cells totaled half the membership of the Chinese Communist Party in Shanghai. The Left Opposition was thus able to lead the workers' movement in Shanghai in several important strikes that met with relative success. The Trotskyist movement simultaneously made fresh headway in Peking, Wuhan, Nanking, Kwangtung, and Hong Kong.

The Trotskyist movement likewise registered progress in expanding the publication of socialist literature. First of all, we put out a magazine called *The Moving Force*. This was printed by a left-wing publishing house. P'eng edited it and contributed articles on the nature of Chinese society and on philosophical and political problems which he dealt with from the Trotskyist standpoint.

The magazine had considerable influence among intellectuals and students. Later it was taken over by another editor and renamed *Reader's Magazine*. However, P'eng Shu-tse encouraged continued contributions by Trotskyists to the magazine and they went on taking up the question of the nature of Chinese society.

The Stalinists maintained that China was predominantly feudal. This touched off a big controversy between the Trotskyists and Stalinists on the subject and related theoretical questions having to do with the nature of the Chinese revolution.

The Trotskyist viewpoint, which was based on the theory of permanent revolution, gained the upper hand in this controversy. As a result our influence increased on the Left. In addition we translated into Chinese various works by Marx and Lenin dealing with social science and philosophy and the first part of Trotsky's autobiography. These books were brought out by some left-wing publishers who were generally accessible to us.

As for us personally, P'eng devoted all his time and energy to the movement, neglecting our sole means of gaining a livelihood—translating books—and since I could not find a job owing to the witch-hunt kept up by the Chiang Kai-shek government, our resources touched bottom. I frequently visited the pawnbroker, and sometimes P'eng had nothing but a bun for sustenance throughout a whole day of meetings or discussions with comrades. He was often obliged to walk long distances because he had no money with which to buy a tram ticket. Several years passed, working in the movement in this fashion.

It was then that misfortune befell the harvest our movement was beginning to reap. On October 15, 1932, Ch'en Tu-hsiu, P'eng

Shu-tse, and eight other comrades were arrested!

The blow to our movement was extremely heavy, and this disaster was shortly to be followed by another. All the important cadres who had joined us from the Chinese Communist Party were arrested. As a result, nearly all of the workers' groups were broken up. Our contacts with the workers thus came to an end.

Those intellectuals that escaped arrest became very demoralized, many resigning and leaving the movement. Our forces were reduced to a few cadres faced with stagnation and isolation, a situation that was to endure for several years.

III

The big press reported the arrest of Ch'en Tu-hsiu and P'eng Shu-tse, especially the fact that they had been transferred from Shanghai to Nanking where they were to be tried by a military court. Fearing that the two revolutionary leaders would be condemned to death, many eminent figures sent telegrams to Chiang Kai-shek and his government, calling for their case to be transferred to a civil court. These included Ts'ai Yuan-p'ei, the former chancellor of Peking National University, Soong Ch'ing-ling, the widow of Dr. Sun Yat-sen, who is a vice-president of the People's Republic of China today, and a number of well-known professors. Because of these appeals, the two were finally transferred to a civil court in Nanking. The proceedings, which were made public, lasted two years, and were closely followed by the press throughout the country.

The Kuomintang government charged Ch'en Tu-hsiu and P'eng Shu-tse with violating the "Emergency Law Governing Treason." Both of them wrote statements defending themselves and chose several lawyers to represent them in court. P'eng, in addition to answering the charges in his statement, denounced as treason the Kuomintang's policy of offering no resistance to Japanese imperialism, abolishing civil liberties and democratic rights, and stated that in his opinion only communism could save China from disaster.

On the day of their open trial (the one and only time in the history of the Kuomintang government that communists were granted an open trial), the courtroom was crowded. Ch'en Li-fu and his entourage, the bosses of the Kuomintang, even followed the trial, although hidden from view behind screens.

In his speech of defense, P'eng boldly attacked the foreign and domestic policies of the Kuomintang, and affirmed his belief in the goals of communism. Ch'en Li-fu and his companions were particularly outraged at this.

Ch'en and P'eng were each sentenced to thirteen years and the other comrades to five years. The thirteen-year sentences, upon being appealed to a higher court, were later reduced to eight years.

Actually, P'eng spent five years in the Nanking Model Prison, not being released until the prison was destroyed by Japanese bombers at the opening of the Sino-Japanese War in 1937.

During the years in prison, P'eng converted his cell into a "study." His reading ranged from the works of Marx, Engels, Lenin, and Trotsky to the history of China and the Western world, philosophy, the natural sciences, and literature. He read every good book he could lay his hands on, broadening his knowledge as much as possible, including even the origins and social content of the Christian and Buddhist religions.

Unfortunately, during their second year in prison, differences arose between P'eng Shu-tse and Ch'en Tu-hsiu over problems involving the Soviet Union, proletarian dictatorship, and democracy. These were the outcome of a few articles P'eng wrote on these subjects. They found it impossible to reconcile their differing points of view and their friendship finally came to an end. During the same year, P'eng's younger brother, P'eng Tao-tse, one of the best cadres, who was also being held in the same prison, died of an illness left untreated for want of money. These two misfortunes greatly affected P'eng, as I could tell from his letters. Yet his fortitude, his patience, and his inner balance enabled him to take these blows and recover.

Over the long five years Shu-tse was in prison, I suffered greatly, personally, from the disruption of our family life, meeting with much hardship. I had to support our two children, yet be wary of the offers of help that came from many sides. Most painful of all, I had to face political isolation.

Whenever I participated in meetings of Left groups or engaged in political discussions, almost inevitably I encountered Stalinists and their sympathizers, very seldom Trotskyists. At first the Stalinists displayed sympathy and friendliness. They even went so far as to find work for me, thus hoping to win me to their ranks. However, once I had openly rejected their advances, making clear my political views, they cut me off from all their various activities.

On August 13, 1937, a few days after the Nanking Model Prison was bombed, P'eng, Ch'en, and the other comrades were released. P'eng was the last to be freed. Had it not been for the strong objections of the chief jailer, the Kuomintang hierarchy might still have kept P'eng locked up because of his strong attack against their regime at the time of his trial.

When P'eng Shu-tse returned to Shanghai, the nationwide anti-Japanese campaign was at its height. However, there were only a dozen or so Trotskyists left in Shanghai. On top of this, although a nominal central organization existed, contacts with other local groups had not been reestablished.

To begin swimming in the current of the anti-imperialist struggle, P'eng called a provisional conference of all the remaining comrades, including those newly released from prison. A resolution was passed at the conference supporting the armed struggle being waged by the Kuomintang government against Japanese imperialism. Accompanying this was a criticism from the political point of view of the government's reactionary policies.

A provisional central committee was elected and authorization given to publish a clandestine party journal, *The Struggle*. Shortly after this meeting, a number of small regional groups were again established. Owing to the favorable objective situation, the Trotskyist organization was soon expanding in areas such as Shanghai, Peking, Canton, Hong Kong, and the provinces of Kwangsi and Chekiang.

No sooner had our movement found its feet than two important events occurred.

The first was a rumor cooked up by the Stalinists and published in their press alleging that Ch'en Tu-hsiu and P'eng Shu-tse had accepted funds from the Japanese imperialists and had pledged to enter into their service. The tag they used for this was "Trotskyite traitors." The Stalinist newspapers in Shanghai followed this up with the slander that Li Kuo-chieh, a traitor who had just been assassinated by Kuomintang agents, and P'eng Shu-tse were good friends. The purpose of this was to provoke an agent of the Kuomintang into assassinating P'eng, or to provide a cover for one of their own agents to kill P'eng. They retracted the slander only after P'eng filed a lawsuit.

The second event involved Ch'en Tu-hsiu. He proposed to offer all-out support to the War of Resistance as led by Chiang Kai-shek. He objected to the political criticism of the Kuomintang published in our journal. His attitude gave rise to a severe dispute within our organization. P'eng Shu-tse, trying to overcome the confusion that had been created, had no choice but to criticize Ch'en Tu-hsiu's viewpoint. This ruined their relationship conclusively. For the Chinese Trotskyist movement, the loss was a great one.

Yet, as P'eng Shu-tse, Liu Chia-liang, Wang Fan-hsi, and other cadres released from prison collaborated with the few comrades who had remained firm in Shanghai, the movement progressed steadily despite the rumors circulated by the Stalinists and despite the difficulties caused by Ch'en Tu-hsiu's erroneous position. In fact, after the publication in August 1939 of an open periodical, *Moving Onward*, its influence was quite considerable. The periodical carried criticisms of the Kuomintang's passivity in the War of Resistance and of Stalin's signing the infamous German-Soviet pact.[11]

In this same period, various sympathizers gave P'eng substantial financial aid, enabling us to publish two books and a pamphlet by Trotsky: *The History of the Russian Revolution, The Revolution Betrayed,* and *The Moscow Trials.* We also published three pamphlets by P'eng: *The War Against the Japanese Imperialists, The Lesson of the Defeat of the Spanish Revolution,* and *The Defeat of the Austrian Revolution.* These received quite a wide response from workers and intellectuals. Once again our movement was moving forward.

At the outbreak of World War II, just prior to the attack on Pearl Harbor, a very serious internal struggle took place within the Chinese Trotskyist movement.

One tendency, headed by Ch'en Tu-hsiu, viewed the war as a struggle between democratic countries and the fascist Axis. He therefore argued for abandoning the policy of "defeatism" in democratic countries like England and France. In addition, in view of the tragedy of the Moscow trials and the Hitler-Stalin pact, he reached the conclusion that the Soviet Union was no longer a workers' state and consequently should not be supported.

Another tendency, headed by Wang Fan-hsi, held that if war broke out between Japan and the United States, China would become involved in an imperialist war. A consequence of this would be the conversion of the national war of resistance into an imperialist war. Thus he held that we should adopt a policy of "defeatism" toward the War of Resistance led by the Kuomintang.

These two tendencies, especially the ultraleft one, caused great confusion among the rank and file.

To combat this, P'eng Shu-tse wrote a long article, "On the

Struggle Against Two Deviationist Lines," explaining the dangers inherent in Ch'en's opportunism and Wang's ultraleft sectarianism. P'eng defended Trotsky's fundamental position on the Second World War and the Sino-Japanese War, including the possibility of war breaking out between Japan and the U.S.

The discussion in the membership ended at the National Convention of the Communist League of China in August 1941. P'eng's resolution was adopted by an overwhelming majority. No one supported Ch'en's position, and Wang's position was backed by only a few members.

After the convention, Ch'en Tu-hsiu broke with Trotskyism. He died in 1942, in Szechwan province.

The minority group led by Wang continued to maintain its position but then violated the principles of democratic centralism by publishing an open periodical of its own. Not long after the outbreak of the war between the United States and Japan, Wang and his small group of followers left the Communist League of China.

*   *   *

After the attack on Pearl Harbor, December 7, 1941, Japanese troops occupied the foreign settlement in Shanghai. This dealt a heavy blow to our movement. Communications between our central headquarters and the local organizations were disrupted. More important, a number of cadres were arrested. P'eng Shu-tse barely escaped.

The repression caused a number of activists to leave Shanghai. Once again our link with the masses was severed. A period of extreme terror opened under the Japanese imperialist occupation.

Despite the perilous situation, P'eng managed to bring together a group of young comrades. Using a pseudonym, he gained an appointment as a professor of Chinese history, Western history, and philosophy in two universities. In his classes, of course, he could not use Marxist terminology. Nevertheless, he oriented his lectures along Marxist lines and influenced a number of leftist students. Some of them wanted to meet him after his lectures and thus we welcomed a group of young people to our home, regardless of their political backgrounds.

We discussed various problems with these students, later converting even those who had come under Stalinist influence to our positions. These youths were to become the foundation of our movement in the postwar period.

We also became acquainted with several businessmen of leftist inclinations. They later became good friends of ours. After the war they helped the movement financially in an energetic way, especially in the publication of periodicals.

With the surrender of Japan, Chiang Kai-shek's government came under mounting pressure from the people to grant democratic concessions. This eased the political situation somewhat. Taking advantage of the opening, our organization once more moved actively forward. Our first task was to publish an open journal to stir up the masses.

On May 1, 1946, two open monthly magazines came off the press. *Seeking the Truth* was a theoretical and political magazine edited by P'eng Shu-tse. It was the most attractive magazine of the postwar period, openly propagating Trotskyist ideas. The second magazine, *Young and Women*, which I edited, was later renamed *New Voice*. It became the organ of the Trotskyist movement.

The two periodicals had a nationwide circulation, reaching all the important cities until they ceased publication at the end of 1948 upon our leaving Shanghai. Their influence was considerable among the intellectuals, students, and young workers. In addition they made it possible for branches of our movement, disrupted by the war, to renew contacts and to reach out to individuals who had become isolated.

The Communist League of China not only recovered its lost forces, it began to grow at a rapid rate. It reconstituted a number of cells among industrial workers and university students in Shanghai, Canton, Hong Kong, and other cities.

We devoted our most intensive efforts to educating young cadres. In addition to regular cadre schools, we held a seminar each week that was regularly attended by more than one hundred comrades and sympathizers. This weekly gathering continued for two and a half years, becoming a pole of attraction that recruited many youths and intellectuals into our movement.

P'eng Shu-tse was one of the principal speakers and organizers of these meetings as well as of the cadre schools. Despite sleepless nights, which he spent in writing articles for our publications, he participated in all these meetings with rare and unflagging energy.

In August 1948, when the Third National Convention of the Communist League of China opened, our membership stood at 350. This was a good gauge of our fast rate of growth. A new political platform was adopted at the convention, and it was decided to change the name of the organization to the Chinese Revolutionary Communist Party.

As our movement made these strides forward, a decisive change took place in the objective situation. The military counteroffensive opened by the Chinese Communist Party against Chiang Kai-shek gained victory after victory. The People's Liberation Army stood at the north bank of the Yangtze and was poised to take Nanking and Shanghai.

Under these circumstances, the Chinese Revolutionary Communist Party held an emergency conference at which measures were adopted in the light of the experiences and lessons learned from the treatment of Trotskyists by the Stalin regime in the Soviet Union.

All the members of the Executive Committee were present. They voted for a resolution recommending that the Political Bureau be transferred to Hong Kong and that a Provisional Committee be set up in Shanghai, charged with the responsibility of keeping in touch with the regional groups and giving directives as necessary.

It was also decided that all our party members and the members of the youth movement should do everything possible to integrate themselves into the Chinese Communist Party, the Communist Youth League, and the mass organizations of workers and peasants of various kinds in order to better support all progressive measures undertaken by the CCP.

The cadres who were too well known to the Stalinists were instructed to leave Shanghai for other provinces. Exchanges of cadres between different areas were also decided upon. Of the five comrades on the Political Bureau, Chin was already in Hong Kong; I K'uan, who was not willing to leave Shanghai, was soon arrested by the CCP regime along with many other comrades none of whom have been heard from since; P'eng Shu-tse, Liu Chia-Liang, and I set out for Hong Kong, where we arrived at the end of 1948.

IV

As soon as we had become settled in Hong Kong, we set up a printshop again and resumed publishing our party's journal. We also helped the Hong Kong branch in its activities and in improving its educational work. We projected the publication in Chinese of Trotsky's *Stalin* and Harold R. Isaacs's *The Tragedy of the Chinese Revolution,* succeeding in getting out the latter book.

The British authorities in Hong Kong, however, had already put Trotskyist activities on the island under close surveillance because of the strikes they had led, much to the distaste of the rulers of the Crown Colony. Our comrades had suffered frequent arrests and deportations. Since the leading journal of the Chinese Revolutionary Communist Party had now opened up offices on the island, the authorities tightened their surveillance of all our movements.

The Hong Kong police discovered our printshop, arrested two of the comrades in charge, and deported them at once. Two persons who received correspondence from the international movement and Western Trotskyist publications were jailed. They were not members but only sympathizers. However, by tailing them and following all the leads, the police also managed to arrest more than ten of our comrades. Most of them were soon sentenced and deported. Then the police discovered where we lived and raided our flat. Fortunately, we had left the night before. Two days after this narrow escape, the police found our temporary refuge at a friend's flat and we had to move again. No sooner had we moved into another friend's home than the police appeared once more.

It was evident that under these circumstances we could no longer continue to live in Hong Kong. Since Shu-tse had become the main quarry in the hunt pursued by the Hong Kong authorities, the comrades were of the opinion that the Political Bureau should move elsewhere. Thus it was that Liu Chia-liang, Shu-tse, I, and our children left Hong Kong for Vietnam. The move was made possible thanks to considerable help from our friends and comrades.

We reached Vietnam at the end of January 1950. Save for Liu, we found jobs to keep us going. Hardly a few months had passed, however, before misfortune struck again.

Two leading Vietnamese Trotskyists (René and Liu) were invited to participate in a conference in the zone controlled by the Vietminh. We had been assured that the conference was being organized by Trotskyist elements inside the Vietminh, among them being the chief of staff of the army in control of this zone. The conference was scheduled to discuss the military situation and organizational problems of the Vietnamese Trotskyist movement. Unfortunately, the Stalinists had prepared a trap.

When the conference came to an end, all the Vietnamese Trotskyists, and our Comrade Liu Chia-liang, who had been

invited to attend, were arrested. Shortly afterwards, Liu Chia-
liang died in prison. As for the Vietnamese comrades, the report
was that they were still alive at the time we left Vietnam, but we
have never heard what their final fate was.

The Trotskyist movement in Vietnam had suffered a serious
blow. Comrade Liu Chia-liang was now gone. Even Shu-tse's life
was in immediate danger because the Stalinists knew where he
was and could eliminate him whenever they pleased.

Upon learning of Liu's death, all our comrades and friends in
Hong Kong and elsewhere urged us to leave Vietnam without
further delay. They collected sufficient funds to assure our getting
to Europe. Thus we started out on our long exile to the West.

*　　　*　　　*

Despite hardships, poverty, and illness, the years of exile in
Western Europe have been instructive. Upon arriving in Europe,
Shu-tse was able to participate more directly in the international
activities of the world Trotskyist movement. This enabled him to
gain a better appreciation of world developments and, above all,
to gain a better grasp of where our movement as a whole stands
in seeking to achieve its tasks.

His contributions in the past fifteen years to the Trotskyist
movement have been primarily literary. First of all, he made a
detailed analysis of the victory of the third Chinese revolution, its
causes, its impact on the international situation, and its consequences in China in the initial and subsequent stages.

In his opinion the third Chinese revolution ought properly to be
characterized as a "deformed" revolution. The overthrow of
Chiang Kai-shek's bourgeois regime, the realization of such
revolutionary measures as national independence, land reform,
etc., showed incontestably that a deepgoing revolution had
occurred. But the regime established in China following the
revolution had to be characterized as a type of dictatorial
bureaucratic rule. Therefore the prospects in China were much like
those in the East European countries, that is, the formation of a
"deformed workers' state."

When the fanatical campaign to establish "People's Communes" was launched by the Chinese Communist Party, this led
to considerable confusion and the creation of illusions among
radical and progressive elements all over the world. P'eng
followed the events very closely and wrote about them in the light
of the fundamental principles laid down by Engels, Lenin, and

Trotsky on collectivization of the land, the experiences of the Soviet Union and the East European countries in this field, and in particular the existing conditions in China. To force the peasants to enter the People's Communes by ukase, he held, could only lead to resentment on their part and as a result an inevitable decline in agricultural production (see "A Criticism of the Various Views Supporting the Chinese Rural People's Communes").

When a few Trotskyists began to idealize the CCP and its regime, seeking to establish that Mao's party and regime are analogous to the Bolshevik Party and the revolutionary regime that existed in the Soviet Union during Lenin's lifetime, P'eng Shu-tse sought to refute their assertions by facts and theoretical arguments. The CCP, he maintained, still continued to be a Stalinist party and its regime a bureaucratic dictatorship. For this reason, he held, a political revolution would inevitably occur in China as had been forecast for the Soviet Union and the East European countries (see "On the Nature of the Chinese Communist Party and Its Regime," written in April 1960).

Within the Fourth International, he opposed the tendency represented by Pablo that inclined to take a conciliatory attitude toward the Soviet bureaucracy, and he also opposed the ultraleft sectarian tendency represented by Healy that appeared later (see "Pabloism Reviewed" and "Where Is Healy Taking the Socialist Labour League?").[12]

In the years following the split in the world Trotskyist movement that occurred in 1953-54, as soon as it became clear that a new basis for a principled unification existed, he became an advocate of reunification. In the International Committee he conducted a solitary battle for several years against Healy's stubborn hostility to reunification. At the Reunification Congress in June 1963, when he saw the actual reunification of the world Trotskyist movement with his own eyes, he said, "For me, during my stay in Europe this is the happiest event of the past ten years."

*   *   *

P'eng Shu-tse is now seventy years old. He feels extremely lucky to be alive. Most of the militants of his generation, with whom he fought side by side during the days of the second Chinese revolution and following its defeat, are dead. The majority lost their lives under the knife of the butcher Chiang Kai-shek.

For the past thirty-eight years, the years following that defeated revolution, P'eng Shu-tse has passed most of the time in privation, danger, terror, and exile. He has lived through the witch-hunt conducted by Chiang Kai-shek; arrest and imprisonment under the rule of the Kuomintang; the lies and slanders splashed on his name by the Stalinists, their attempts on his life; through the persecution inflicted by Japanese imperialism. To survive all this sounds like the role cast for the hero in popular fiction. Yet that is the way it turned out, and Shu-tse is a most fortunate man.

As early as 1920 when he joined the newly founded Communist Party as a youth of twenty-five, he made up his mind to dedicate his life and energies to the revolution. That is why, after so many years of hardships and setbacks, endured during his youth and manhood, he has never regretted his decision or felt disheartened. He knows to the bottom the contradiction that can occur between truth and reality, that all those who fight for a noble ideal have to suffer a hard fate as long as the truth is not definitively triumphant. So it has been that each time he has suffered a blow or setback, he has adopted a sort of "fatalistic" attitude, confronting life with the utmost patience and an iron will. "For gnarling sorrow hath less power to bite the man that mocks it and sets it light," Shakespeare said.[13] A real revolutionist has no choice but to forge his morality and his will through suffering. Out of this comes an even state of mind that makes it possible to avoid being overwhelmed by suffering; suffering can instead be reduced.

Of course, even revolutionists of excellent morality and firm resolution cannot defy the test of events and resist the incessant pressure of suffering and setbacks without being armed with Marxism. To mention only China, many revolutionists who are staunch and resolute to begin with, gradually lost heart and faith under the constant terror and persecution, under the rain of blows and unending hardship. They lacked a deep Marxist appreciation of the world. Shu-tse often tells comrades, "We must raise our own level by studying Marxism. This is not only an absolute necessity in leading the revolution, but is the most effective weapon in resisting the setbacks that come in a period of counterrevolution."

Through consistent study of Marx, Engels, Lenin, and Trotsky's works, and their way of thinking; through the experiences and lessons to be learned from the world revolutionary movement; by seeking to make these intellectual gains his own, P'eng Shu-tse has remained a revolutionary optimist. He firmly believes that Trotskyism, in which the heritage of Marxism and Leninism is to be found, is certain to carry out the tasks of the world revolution and lead humanity to freedom from capitalist exploitation and oppression, to deliverance from the threat of extermination in a nuclear war.

In the struggle against Stalinism, which still functions as a brake on the world revolution, P'eng Shu-tse is convinced that Trotskyism will emerge triumphant.

Stalin's successor, Khrushchev, in his report to the Twentieth Congress of the CPSU, revealed a portion of the crimes committed by Stalin, a portion of the crimes that were repeatedly exposed and denounced by Trotsky and his followers. At the Twenty-second Congress of the CPSU, further revelations were made. Since then the most revolting expressions of Stalin's self-adulation, such as statues and monuments, have been toppled, and Stalin's corpse has been removed from Lenin's tomb. Enough has been done to show that even Stalin's own heirs have been compelled to at least partially confirm the truth of the denunciations leveled by Trotsky and his followers.

After the exposure at the Twentieth Congress of the cult of Stalin and some of his crimes, the working class in Poland and Hungary rose up against the Stalinist bureaucracy. Then came the breakup of the Stalinist monolith on a world scale as a result of the rupture between Peking and Moscow. This was followed by splits among the Stalinist parties throughout the world.

All of this confirmed the correctness of the Trotskyist analyses and forecasts concerning the inevitable crisis and decline faced by Stalinism, thus reinforcing the convictions held by P'eng Shu-tse and all the Trotskyists internationally.

When Stalin's heirs, under the pressure of the Soviet masses, felt compelled to repudiate Stalin's crimes, this, I firmly believe, represented the opening of a new era for humanity in which the truths espoused by Trotskyism will gain ascendancy. These truths have been sown all over the globe and will be harvested in revolutions everywhere.

For forty years I have shared P'eng Shu-tse's fate. I believe that I understand better than anyone else his way of thinking, his enthusiasm in seeking the truth, his conviction in the truth of Marxism-Leninism and Trotskyism, his role in the Chinese Communist Party, and the extremely difficult conditions he had to face in struggling for the Trotskyist movement in the past thirty-six years. I have written this article as my present to him at his seventieth birthday celebration and to express my congratulations.

November 1965

THE THEORY OF PERMANENT REVOLUTION AND THE UNDERDEVELOPED COUNTRIES

We are witnessing a continuing upsurge of the colonial and semicolonial national and democratic revolution in Asia, Africa, and Latin America, shaking world imperialist rule. At the same time, however, we see the absence of revolutionary proletarian leaderships or of a correct revolutionary line in these movements. As a consequence, the leadership has fallen into the hands of opportunistic petty-bourgeois and even bourgeois parties. The result has been that, among those countries where revolutions have succeeded or are in process, not one has been able to thoroughly solve the national and democratic tasks: the securing of genuine national independence by breaking the imperialist yoke and eliminating feudal remnants through a revolutionary agrarian reform.

The revolutions either stop half way or end in a stalemate. In order to break the deadlock and open the path to victory, it is necessary to pose a correct strategy based on Marxism and in this way build a revolutionary proletarian leadership. There is no other road.

It was Trotsky above all others who put forward a correct strategy for the colonial and semicolonial revolution. He developed the conception of permanent revolution first enunciated by Marx and Engels in 1850 and perfected it in his own "theory of permanent revolution." This theory was first confirmed in the Russian October revolution, and was later confirmed negatively in the tragic defeat of the second Chinese revolution of 1925-27. It is now twenty years since Trotsky, the coleader with Lenin of the victorious October revolution, was murdered by Stalin. It seems appropriate to take this anniversary occasion to restate for today's revolutionists the theory of permanent revolution, which so decisively affects the fate of the colonial and semicolonial revolution. This brief exposition is based particularly on the historical experience of the Russian and Chinese revolutions.

Three theories of the Russian revolution

In analyzing the economic structure and social relations of classes in capitalist society, Marx came to the conclusion that capitalism must give way to socialism just as feudalism gave way to capitalism. This historic task of transformation will fall solely to the proletariat. This is because, as Marx and Engels wrote in the *Communist Manifesto*, "Of all the classes that stand face to face with the bourgeoisie today, the proletariat alone is a really revolutionary class. The other classes decay and finally disappear in the face of modern industry; the proletariat is its special and essential product."

Flowing from this analysis, Marx proposed the following strategy for proletarian revolution: that the working class under the leadership of its vanguard, the party, prepare an uprising to destroy the bourgeois apparatus, to fight for state power, and to establish its own dictatorship for entering onto the road to socialist construction.

Marx's program, of course, was based on the level of industrial capitalist development of his time, in particular on conditions in the advanced capitalist countries. But when capitalism has reached its highest stage, imperialism, when all the backward countries have been turned into colonies or semicolonies exploited and ruled by imperialism, these underdeveloped countries are compelled to engage in a revolutionary struggle for national and democratic liberation. Is the Marxist program for proletarian revolution applicable to the revolutionary movements in these countries? This question produced a serious ideological struggle among Marx's disciples and finally ended in an irreconcilable dispute between two opposing lines.

This struggle first broke out among the Russian Marxists (the Russian Social Democratic Labor Party). Though it became an imperialist country at the beginning of this century, Russia— because of the belated development of capitalism there— remained far behind the advanced nations of the West. (Its relations with French and Belgian finance capital still had a semicolonial character.) Above all, the land question remained unsolved and the state power remained in the hands of tsarism, which represented the landed aristocracy. As a result, the Russian revolution had an uneven and combined character, telescoping together the bourgeois-democratic revolution and the proletarian socialist revolution.

The immediate task facing the Russian revolutionists at that time involved achieving democracy. But which class could solve this problem and lead the revolution to victory? Three different answers to this question were put forward.

1. Assuming that the immediate tasks of the Russian revolution were bourgeois, Plekhanov considered that the proletariat should ally itself with the liberal bourgeoisie to overthrow the tsarist regime and establish a bourgeois-democratic government, thus clearing the road for capitalist development. Plekhanov's position mechanically followed the development of the Western advanced countries by dividing the Russian revolution into two entirely different stages: First a revolution led by the bourgeoisie to solve democratic tasks and develop capitalism; then, after several decades, when a high level of capitalist development had been achieved, the proletariat would proceed with the socialist revolution against the bourgeoisie. This was the "revolution by stages" line that was to be followed by the Mensheviks.

2. Lenin also began from the postulate that the immediate task of the revolution would be the establishment of bourgeois democracy. But in his view, the central question in this revolution would be the agrarian problem, a problem that could be solved only through an alliance of the proletariat and the peasantry. Lenin pointed out that the liberal bourgeoisie was tied in a thousand ways to the system of landed property that exploited the peasantry. This bourgeoisie not only could not solve the land question in the interests of the peasantry but would inevitably compromise with the landed gentry and tsarism against the revolutionary movement when the worker-peasant masses arose in struggle.

The land question can only be solved through an alliance between the proletariat and the peasantry that would resolutely oppose the liberal bourgeoisie's compromises and betrayal. Such an alliance would overthrow tsarism and set up a "democratic dictatorship of the workers and the peasantry." Lenin fully developed this thought in his *Two Tactics of Social-Democracy in the Democratic Revolution.* Here he emphasized:

> The democratic revolution is bourgeois in nature. The slogan of a general redistribution, or "land and freedom" . . . is a bourgeois slogan. . . . We must not forget that there is not, nor can there be at the present time, any other means of bringing socialism nearer, than complete political liberty, than a democratic republic, than the revolutionary-democratic dictatorship of the proletariat and the peasantry.[1]

Lenin's conception of substituting an alliance between the proletariat and the peasantry for Plekhanov's proposed alliance of the proletariat with the liberal bourgeoisie was undoubtedly a great step forward. But how this democratic dictatorship would be realized and what the specific weight of the proletariat would be in it Lenin did not clearly formulate until his April Theses of 1917. As a result, before 1917 the Bolsheviks' theory was confined within the straitjacket of the conception of a bourgeois-democratic revolution. In this period they viewed the socialist revolution in Russia as an event of the far future and believed the working class could only undertake such a thing after the completion of the bourgeois-democratic phase. Thus, the Bolsheviks before April 1917 also adhered to the line of a "revolution by stages."

3. Trotsky was in full agreement with Lenin in opposing Plekhanov's formula of an alliance between the proletariat and the liberal bourgeoisie to overthrow tsarism and secure bourgeois democracy. He also accepted Lenin's view that the central task of the democratic revolution would be land reform. But Trotsky strongly disagreed with the formula of a "democratic dictatorship of the proletariat and the peasantry," which Lenin had deduced from the workers' need for an alliance with the peasants. Trotsky argued that while the peasantry is a key force in the bourgeois-democratic revolution, it cannot play an independent revolutionary role because of the class differentiations within the peasantry and the dispersed character inherent in peasant life. Only by supporting the proletarian dictatorship and under the workers' leadership could the peasantry solve the land problem. But the proletariat, after taking power, cannot limit itself to the solution of democratic tasks. Socialist measures would also have to be placed on the agenda. Thus there would be no lag in time between the stage of bourgeois democracy and the proletarian socialist revolution. The idea of a separate phase of proletarian-peasant dictatorship was an illusion. This is the core of the theory of permanent revolution.

Trotsky made a systematic elucidation of the theory of permanent revolution in his *Results and Prospects*. In analyzing the social and economic relations of classes in Russia, and drawing on the experiences of the French revolution of 1792 and the German revolution of 1848, as well as conditions in the rest of the capitalist world at the beginning of the twentieth century, Trotsky developed the following conception of the Russian revolution:

The Russian revolution does not, and for a long time will not, permit the establishment of any kind of bourgeois-constitutional order that might solve the most elementary problems of democracy. . . . Consequently, the fate of the most elementary revolutionary interests of the peasantry—even the peasantry *as a whole*, as an *estate*, is bound up with the fate of [the] entire revolution, i.e., with the fate of the proletariat.

The proletariat in power will stand before the peasants as the class which has emancipated it.[2]

And further:

The very fact of the proletariat's representatives entering the government, not as powerless hostages, but as the leading force, destroys the border-line between maximum and minimum programme; that is to say, it *places collectivism* [i.e., socialism—P'eng] *on the order of the day*. . . .

For this reason there can be no talk of any sort of *special* form of proletarian dictatorship in the bourgeois revolution, of *democratic* proletarian dictatorship (or dictatorship of the proletariat and the peasantry). The working class cannot preserve the democratic character of its dictatorship without refraining from overstepping the limits of its democratic programme. Any illusions on this point would be fatal.[3]

The basic thesis outlined here was counterposed not only to the Menshevik theory of revolution by stages, but also to the Bolshevik conception of the "democratic dictatorship of the proletariat and the peasantry." If we compare *Results and Prospects* with Lenin's *Two Tactics*, we see that the actual events came much closer to Trotsky's prognostication than to Lenin's.

The three positions I have outlined had taken definite shape in the 1905 revolution and constituted the frame of the ideological dispute for a prolonged period afterward. It was only after the February revolution in 1917 that they were finally tested in practice on a large scale. In 1917, the Mensheviks, acting on their conception of the "alliance of the proletariat with the liberal bourgeoisie to establish bourgeois democracy," yielded the power seized by the proletariat in the February revolution to the bourgeoisie. The Mensheviks aided the bourgeois forces in the creation of the Provisional Government. They turned the soviets, which were spontaneously set up by the working masses during the revolution, into an appendage of the Provisional Government. The Mensheviks used the soviets to dampen the revolutionary struggle of the worker-peasant masses.

This Provisional Government not only put aside the land issue, but also postponed indefinitely the calling of a constituent assembly. It even devoted its energies to Russia's continued participation in the imperialist war. Consequently, as is well known, the Mensheviks became the last bulwark of the bourgeoisie's efforts to stem the revolution.

The Bolsheviks, represented immediately after February in Russia by Stalin and Kamenev, sought to apply the old formula of the "democratic dictatorship." As a result, they adopted a half-Menshevik position, seeking democratic reform through pressure on the Provisional Government, acting as a loyal opposition to the bourgeois regime. The Bolsheviks, then, were in a confused and helpless ideological state.

Lenin, in exile, witnessed the decisive role played by the working masses in overthrowing tsarism during the February revolution, their spontaneous creation of the soviets, the reactionary attitude of the bourgeois Provisional Government, and the betrayal by the Social Revolutionary Party, the organized representative of the peasantry. After returning to Petrograd, Lenin decided to junk the formula of the "democratic dictatorship of the workers and the peasantry." He now considered it a necessity that the democratic tasks of the revolution be accomplished through the seizure of power by the proletariat. Therefore, he immediately put the slogan of the proletarian dictatorship on the agenda—this is the essential content of his famous April Theses. With this declaration, Lenin's concept of the revolution conformed fully with that of Trotsky.

It was this uniting of Lenin and Trotsky around a common revolutionary strategy that made it possible for the Bolsheviks to take power in the October revolution. Leading the workers and armed peasantry, they established a workers' state based on the soviets and carried out the democratic tasks of the revolution (distribution of land to the peasantry and the proclamation of the right of self-determination for Russia's oppressed nationalities). The implementation of socialist tasks followed immediately—the expropriation of bourgeois property. Thus Russia entered the road of socialist construction.

In this way the theory of permanent revolution, propounded by Trotsky in 1905, was fully confirmed in historical fact. The bourgeois-democratic revolution developed uninterruptedly into the socialist revolution. The schema outlined in *Results and Prospects* was realized with striking accuracy in the October revolution. At the same time, the Menshevik theory of revolution by stages was shown to be completely bankrupt; it served only the antirevolutionary aims of the bourgeoisie. Lastly, the October revolution showed that the Marxist program of **proletarian** revolution, ending in the dictatorship of the proletariat, is applicable not only to the advanced countries but to the backward nations as well. The only qualification needed is that in the latter the path to socialist revolution takes a more complex form, combining two stages of historical development.

The theory of permanent revolution tested in the second Chinese revolution

The historical experience of the Russian revolution provides an exceptionally valuable model for revolutions in all the underdeveloped countries, whether colonial or semicolonial. In Russia itself, however, because of the country's backwardness and the failure of proletarian revolutions in the advanced Western countries, which could have provided aid to the new Soviet state, the leadership of the Communist Party of the Soviet Union fell into the hands of the bureaucracy, represented by Stalin. This process was speeded by Lenin's death.

Soon after Lenin died, Stalin put forward the theory of "socialism in one country." This nationalist and conservative line was counterposed to, and displaced, the objective of world revolution. Almost at the same time, Stalin used the leading bodies of the Communist International to impose the Menshevik theory of revolution by stages on all the backward countries. This was first put into practice on an extensive scale in the second Chinese revolution of 1925-27.

China was a typical semicolonial country. It was certainly more economically backward than Russia. At the same time, the relationship of class forces in China was more advantageous for a proletarian victory in the course of the democratic revolution. But the policy practiced by Stalin in China had gone much further and was more shameful than that of the Mensheviks in Russia. The latter at least supported the independent organization of the proletarian party, whereas Stalin ordered the Chinese Communist Party to join the bourgeois Kuomintang and lauded "the cooperation of the Kuomintang and the CCP." In fact, this policy turned the revolutionary proletarian party—which had the leadership of the impoverished masses (the peasantry and the urban poor)—into an instrument for the bourgeoisie to deceive the masses. This led to the tragic defeat of the second Chinese revolution.

After the outbreak of the revolution in May 1925, Stalin used the prestige of the October revolution and the Soviet Union's material resources to aid Chiang Kai-shek and Wang Ching-wei, the representatives respectively of the bourgeoisie and the petty bourgeoisie. Stalin promoted their influence and standing among the masses and proclaimed the Kuomintang Canton bourgeois government (set up in the autumn of 1925) to be a "revolutionary government" supported by all classes, or at any rate, a coalition government representing four classes.[4]

On the other hand, Stalin did his best to restrict the political activities of the CCP, submitting it to the discipline of the Kuomintang and limiting it to carrying out the KMT's bourgeois policy. He also ordered the CCP and the masses it led to give unconditional and uncritical support to the KMT government for the sake of maintaining the "cooperation" between the KMT and the CCP.

The aim of Stalin's policy was apparently to have the CCP help the KMT to carry out the "national revolution" against the warlords and imperialists, i.e., to assist the bourgeoisie in completing the democratic revolution, while relegating the anti-bourgeois, socialist revolution to an indefinite future.

But Chiang Kai-shek and the bourgeoisie he represented were not satisfied with the aid provided by Stalin's policy. Chiang saw the unchecked spread of militancy among the worker-peasant masses. This was especially marked in the resolute struggle of the workers under the leadership of the Canton–Hong Kong Strike Committee,[5] and in the rapid growth of the Communist Party and the extension of its influence in the mass movement. He instinctively recognized these developments as a mortal threat to the bourgeoisie which had to be deflected. This was the motive behind Chiang's coup of March 20, 1926.

In this coup, Chiang Kai-shek disbanded the armed pickets of the Canton–Hong Kong Strike Committee, arrested the CCP cadres who were carrying on political work (directly under Chiang's control) in the army, drove his political competitor Wang Ching-wei out of the government, and established his personal military dictatorship. This was followed by the KMT's adoption of the "Resolution Adjusting Party Affairs," which severely restricted CCP activities inside the KMT and prohibited criticism of the reactionary petty-bourgeois ideology of Sun Yat-sen.

What was Stalin's attitude toward this antirevolutionary policy of Chiang? He not only mounted no resistance to Chiang (to say nothing about a counterattack), but on the contrary forced the CCP to fully accept the status quo arising from Chiang's coup and endorse the military dictatorship. Stalin hoped that in offering no resistance, Chiang would proceed as planned with his Northern Expedition to overthrow the North China warlords and imperialists, achieve independence and unity, and set up a "bloc of four classes" government.

But as soon as Chiang's "Northern Expedition Army" arrived at the Yangtze River, he opened secret negotiations with the northern warlords. And when Chiang arrived in Shanghai, he repaid Stalin's aid by organizing a further coup in which he massacred the workers. Six days before the Shanghai massacre Stalin (in a speech to members of the British Communist Party) was still proclaiming Chiang Kai-shek to be a dependable ally in the struggle against the warlords and imperialism!

After the counterrevolutionary massacre of the Shanghai workers, Stalin transferred his hopes from Chiang to Wang Ching-wei, and announced that Wang's "left" Kuomintang embodied the alliance of the workers, peasants, and the petty bourgeoisie and could substitute for the creation of soviets. Stalin further proclaimed the Wuhan government led by Wang to be the "center of revolution" and instructed two members of the CCP to enter this government as the ministers of Labor and Agriculture. Their duties were supposedly the protection of the workers' interests and the implementation of land reform. In fact, however, they carried out Stalin's policy of suppressing the "overzealous" actions of the workers and the agrarian revolution of the peasantry. Hence, in this period, Stalin rejected all of Trotsky's proposals, including the demand that the CCP resign from the "left" KMT and organize soviets to rally the workers and peasants in order to save the perilous situation. (I will return to these points.)

But Wang proved to be no different from Chiang. He saw his opportunity and staged a coup on July 14, 1927, in which he arrested and massacred the leaders and members of the CCP and of the mass movement and disbanded their revolutionary organizations. The second Chinese revolution was thus tragically and shamefully defeated!

After this terrible defeat, Stalin sought to evade responsibility for the course he had charted, and to shield himself from Trotsky's criticism. He now jumped from ultraright opportunism to ultraleft adventurism, ordering the CCP to launch insurrections against the KMT. The remnants of the revolutionary forces were expended in the abortive effort to establish the Canton Soviet government.

Trotsky by this time had been expelled from the leadership of the Russian CP and from the leadership of the Communist International, but he continued to criticize the Menshevik policy carried out by Stalin and Bukharin and to offer proposals to the Chinese revolution. Already in 1923 he had objected to the CCP joining the Kuomintang. On March 4, 1927, he again formally proposed that the CCP immediately resign from the KMT. "If there is to be a leadership for the Chinese proletariat, a systematic struggle to gain influence in the trade unions, and finally, a leadership in the struggle of the proletariat to influence the peasant masses, there must be a totally independent, i.e., truly Communist (Bolshevik) Party."[6]

Trotsky later criticized the Comintern policy and theory regarding China in his article "Class Relations in the Chinese Revolution." He emphasized: "Despite the backwardness of the Chinese economy, and in part precisely due to this backwardness, the Chinese revolution is wholly capable of bringing to political power an alliance of workers and peasants, under the leadership of the proletariat."[7]

Trotsky further warned:

Having captured Hankow and Shanghai, the revolution has thereby drawn into itself the most developed class contradictions in China. . . . It is necessary to orient either on the proletariat or the bourgeoisie.

The proletariat must orient itself on the many-millioned rank and file in the struggle against the bourgeoisie. We have this on the one hand. And on the other—the imperialists show by their Nanking butchery [Trotsky is referring to the naval bombardment of Nanking by imperialist warships—P'eng] that they are in no jesting mood. . . . They desire above all to compel the bourgeois tops of the nationalist movement to understand that the time has come for them to break with the rank and file if they do not wish to have the guns of world imperialism trained upon them.[8]

Trotsky's article was written on April 3, 1927. Only nine days later Chiang acted on the imperialists' directive to "break with the rank and file" through his bloody coup of April 12. Chiang's break with the masses and his now direct dependence on the imperialists, however, did not teach Stalin any lessons. On the contrary, in his theses entitled *Questions of the Chinese Revolution* he defended his bankrupt policy toward Chiang, while at the same time proposing support to the "left" KMT of Wang Ching-wei. Thus Stalin laid a trap in the immediate path of the revolution.

At this time (May 7, 1927), Trotsky wrote an article, "The Chinese Revolution and the Theses of Comrade Stalin," which has a decisive signifiance for the second Chinese revolution. Here Trotsky made an accurate and profound criticism of Stalin's opportunistic theory and policy, and presented proposals for action. The gist of Trotsky's position was as follows:

It is a gross mistake to think that imperialism mechanically welds together all the classes of China from without. . . .

But everything that brings the oppressed and exploited masses of the toilers to their feet inevitably pushes the national bourgeoisie into an open bloc with the imperialists. The class struggle between the bourgeoisie and the masses of workers and peasants is not weakened, but on the contrary, it is sharpened by imperialist oppression, to the point of bloody civil war at every serious conflict.[9]

That Chiang Kai-shek played the role of a republican-liberal Cavaignac has already become a commonplace. The theses of Stalin, following the Opposition, recognize this analogy. But the analogy must be supplemented. Cavaignac would have been impossible without the Ledru-Rollins, the Louis Blancs, and the other phrasemongers of the all-inclusive national front. And who played these roles in China? Not only Wang Ching-wei, but also the leaders of the Chinese Communist Party, above all their inspirers of the ECCI. Unless this is stated openly, explained, and deeply impressed, the philosophy of the two paths of development will only serve to screen opportunism à la Louis Blanc and Martynov, that is, to prepare a repetition of the April tragedy at a new stage of the Chinese revolution.[10]

In order to have the right to speak about the struggle for the Bolshevik path of the democratic revolution, one must possess the principal instrument of proletarian policy: *an independent proletarian party* which fights under its own banner and never permits its policy and organization to be dissolved in the policy and organization of other classes.[11]

. . . they [Stalin and Company—P'eng] want to retain the ideological, political, and organizational dependence of the proletarian party upon a petty-bourgeois party, which is inevitably converted into an instrument of the big bourgeoisie.[12]

To declare that the time for the soviets has not yet arrived and at the same time to launch the slogan for arming the workers and peasants is to sow confusion. Only the soviets, at a further development of the revolution, can become the organs capable of really conducting the arming of the workers and of directing these armed masses.[13]

To strengthen this wave and to deepen it, we need peasants' soviets with the unfurled banner of the agrarian revolution, not after the victory but immediately, in order to guarantee the victory.

If we do not want to permit the peasant wave to come to naught and be splattered into froth, the peasants' soviets must be united with workers' soviets in the cities and the industrial centers, and to the workers' soviets must be added the soviets of the poor population from the urban and handwork districts.

If we do not want to permit the bourgeoisie to drive a wedge between the revolutionary masses and the army, then soldiers' soviets must be fitted into the revolutionary chain.

As quickly as possible, as boldly as possible, as energetically as possible, the revolution must be deepened, not after the victory but immediately, or else there will be no victory.

The deepening of the agrarian revolution, the immediate seizure of the land by the peasants, will weaken Chiang Kai-shek on the spot, bring confusion into the ranks of his soldiers, and set the peasant hinterland in motion. There is no other road to victory and there can be none.[14]

If this revolutionary policy proposed by Trotsky in his criticism of the opportunism of Stalin's theses had been adopted by the Communist International and applied in China, it would have turned the crisis into a victory. This would have been the case because, although the revolution had suffered a serious defeat in Shanghai and Canton, it still maintained tremendous force in the provinces of Hupeh, Hunan, etc. Had the CCP called for the formation of workers', peasants', and soldiers' soviets, and for land reform, the worker-peasant masses could have been rallied and in the process could have won the soldiers to them. This revolutionary tide would have submerged Wang Ching-wei's counterrevolutionary treachery, secured the reentry into the revolution of the worker-peasant masses of Shanghai and Canton, weakened Chiang Kai-shek "on the spot," bringing "confusion into the ranks of his soldiers." Instead, Trotsky's proposal—the only one that could have turned a very dangerous situation into victory—was suppressed by Stalin. The Chinese revolution continued along a Menshevik course and fell into the trap.

Watching Stalin push forward a policy that would strangle the Chinese revolution, Trotsky issued a sharp denunciation in a speech to the Eighth Plenum of the ECCI at the end of May 1927:

We have nothing in common with this policy. We do not want to assume even a shadow of responsibility for the policy of the Wuhan government and the leadership of the Kuomintang, and we urgently advise the Comintern to reject this responsibility. We say directly to the Chinese peasants: The leaders of the left Kuomintang of the type of Wang Ching-wei and Company will inevitably betray you if you follow the Wuhan heads instead of forming your own independent soviets. The agrarian revolution is a serious thing. Politicians of the Wang Ching-wei type, under different conditions, will unite ten times with Chiang Kai-shek against the workers and peasants. Under such conditions, two communists in a bourgeois government become impotent hostages, if not a direct mask for the preparation of a new blow against the working masses. We say to the workers of China: The peasants will not carry out the agrarian revolution to the end if they let themselves be led by petty-bourgeois radicals instead of by you, the revolutionary proletarians. Therefore, build up your workers' soviets, ally them with the peasant soviets, arm yourselves through the soviets, draw soldiers' representatives into the soviets, shoot the generals who do not recognize the soviets, shoot the bureaucrats and bourgeois liberals who will organize uprisings against the soviets. Only through peasants' and soldiers' soviets will you win over the majority of Chiang Kai-shek's soldiers to your side.

You, the advanced Chinese proletarians, would be traitors to your class and to your historic mission, were you to believe that an organization of leaders, petty bourgeois and compromising in spirit, which has no more than 250,000 members [Trotsky is referring to the "left" KMT—P'eng] . . . is capable of substituting for workers', peasants', and soldiers' soviets embracing millions upon millions. *The Chinese bourgeois-democratic revolution will go forward and be victorious either in the soviet form or not at all.*[15]

But this urgent call was censored by Stalin and could not reach the ears of the Chinese workers and peasants. Trotsky's prediction that the revolution would triumph "in the soviet form or not at all" proved to be tragically acute.

To the adventuristic policy adopted by Stalin after the defeat, Trotsky counterposed a strategy of defense against the victorious counterrevolution. (See "The Chinese Question After the Sixth Congress" [in *Leon Trotsky on China*].)

Finally, from the experience of the abortive Canton Soviet government, he pointed out the character of the coming third Chinese revolution, the future of proletarian socialism.

From the above highly condensed account we can see how Stalin's Menshevik line of the revolution by stages converted a revolution with every hope of success into a tragic defeat. At the same time, it shows the striking correctness of Trotsky's line based on the theory of permanent revolution.

After this terrible defeat, Stalin and Bukharin sought to blame the leaders of the CCP, especially Ch'en Tu-hsiu, to cover up their own crimes. But at the same time they continued to defend and to systematize the Menshevik line of the revolution by stages and incorporated it into the *Draft Program of the Communist Interna-*

tional as a rope to strangle future revolutions in the colonial and semicolonial countries.

Therefore, Trotsky in his "The Draft Program of the Communist International—A Criticism of Fundamentals," in addition to challenging Stalin's reactionary theory of "socialism in one country" and other incorrect conceptions, devoted an entire chapter, "Summary and Perspectives of the Chinese Revolution," to exposing Stalin's line for derailing the revolution in the colonial and semicolonial countries.[16]

At the end of 1928 in his classic, *Permanent Revolution,* Trotsky summarized his view of revolution in the underdeveloped countries as a whole, on the basis of the experience of the Russian revolutions of 1905 and February and October 1917, and of the second Chinese revolution. These were his main conclusions:

With regard to countries with a belated bourgeois development, especially the colonial and semi-colonial countries, the theory of the permanent revolution signifies that the complete and genuine solution of their tasks of achieving *democracy and national emancipation* is conceivable only through the dictatorship of the proletariat as the leader of the subjugated nation, above all of its peasant masses.

Not only the agrarian, but also the national question assigns to the peasantry—the overwhelming majority of the population in backward countries—an exceptional place in the democratic revolution. Without an alliance of the proletariat with the peasantry the tasks of the democratic revolution cannot be solved, nor even seriously posed. But the alliance of these two classes can be realized in no other way than through an irreconcilable struggle against the influence of the national-liberal bourgeoisie.

No matter what the first episodic stages of the revolution may be in the individual countries, the realization of the revolutionary alliance between the proletariat and the peasantry is conceivable only under the political leadership of the proletarian vanguard, organized in the Communist Party. This in turn means that the victory of the democratic revolution is conceivable only through the dictatorship of the proletariat which bases itself upon the alliance with the peasantry and solves first of all the tasks of the democratic revolution. . . .

The dictatorship of the proletariat which has risen to power as the leader of the democratic revolution is inevitably and very quickly confronted with tasks, the fulfillment of which is bound up with deep inroads into the rights of bourgeois property. The democratic revolution grows over directly into the socialist revolution and thereby becomes a *permanent* revolution. . . .

The completion of the socialist revolution within national limits is unthinkable. One of the basic reasons for the crisis in bourgeois society is the fact that the productive forces created by it can no longer be reconciled with the framework of the national state. From this follow, on the one hand, imperialist wars, on the other, the utopia of a bourgeois United States of Europe. The socialist revolution begins on the national arena, it unfolds on the international arena, and is completed on the world arena. Thus, the socialist revolution becomes a permanent revolution in a newer and broader sense of the word; it attains completion only in the final victory of the new society on our entire planet.[17]

The permanent revolution as reflected in the third Chinese revolution

The Chinese Communist Party, after the defeat of the second Chinese revolution, remained under Stalin's tight control. After going through a series of adventuristic uprisings, it established "Soviet" areas and its own "Red Army." This opened a long period of civil war. But even in the course of the fighting it clung to the Menshevik theory of the revolution by stages, developed by Mao under the slogan "New Democracy." According to Mao's theory, China would first have to go through a New Democratic revolution that would secure a bourgeois-democratic (i.e., non-socialist) political, economic, and cultural structure. Only after a historical period of New Democracy would the revolution proceed to its socialist phase.

The Second World War created an exceptionally favorable situation for the Maoists. The Chiang government virtually collapsed because of its own internal contradictions. At the same time, American imperialism found itself unable to intervene directly in support of Chiang. Under these conditions the CCP came to power. Significantly, Mao's first government was a coalition that included bourgeois and petty-bourgeois elements as well as workers and peasants. It represented a continued alliance with the national or democratic bourgeoisie. It proclaimed in its program equal status for both state and private industry, and equal benefits for both labor and the bourgeoisie. It even postponed land reform and protected imperialist property holdings in China.

The Mao regime announced a perspective of several decades—or as Chou En-lai said, within twenty years—to complete the New Democratic stage of the revolution. But the logic of class contradictions forced Mao to abandon his New Democratic front and step by step to concede to the objective law of the permanent revolution.

First, under the impact of the Korean War, in opposition to the direct threat of American imperialist invasion, the CCP carried out the seizure of imperialist property in China. At the same time, the bourgeois forces took advantage of the American imperialist presence in Korea to mount a campaign of outrageous antirevolutionary activities. This prompted the CCP to carry out a land reform in contradiction to its New Democratic pronouncements, in order to win the peasantry against the landlords. It also initiated the "Five Anti Movement" to strike at the bourgeoisie.[18]

Later, at the beginning of 1953, the CCP proclaimed its "general line of the transitional period," including its First Five-Year Plan for economic construction and industrialization. Faced with bourgeois sabotage of the economic plan, the CCP ultimately abandoned entirely its New Democracy line, substituting the policy of "state and private cooperation," which aimed at the gradual abolition of bourgeois property and the beginning of socialist construction.

It was only at its Eighth Party Congress in September 1956 that the CCP declared the Chinese People's Republic to be a proletarian dictatorship. (The report on this question was given by Liu Shao-ch'i.)

These shifts in CCP policy clearly show that the Maoists, under the pressure of objective events, were forced to give up the theory of a revolution by stages and to submit to the course of permanent revolution. In other words, the actual unfolding of the third Chinese revolution confirmed once more the theory of permanent revolution, though in a distorted fashion. But precisely because this process occurred in a distorted way, further advance of the revolution ran into a great obstacle.

The obstacle is this: the CCP lacked any conscious understanding of the theory of permanent revolution or of the meaning of the experiences of the October revolution and the second Chinese revolution. It did not seize power through a proletarian uprising with the workers in the leadership of the peasantry. It did not aim at the formation of a proletarian dictatorship, a soviet government, or the immediate resolution of the land question, the expropriation of the bourgeoisie, and the institution of socialist construction. Instead it depended on peasant armed forces to overthrow Chiang, surrounding and besieging the cities rather than involving the urban proletariat.

In the name of the "bloc of four classes" it established a coalition government that amounted to a Bonapartist military regime, a bureaucratic dictatorship that denied democratic rights to the worker-peasant masses. It also limited the revolution to its own soil, attempting to build socialism and even communism in one country. The result was a leap from the earlier opportunism to adventurism. This was strikingly revealed in Mao's forced collectivization of the countryside. Without providing any avenue for the peasants to express their own desires, they were compelled over a very brief span to join collective farms and even communes. This was accompanied by an unprecedented intensification of the volume and pace of their labor.

In industry, the workers are hard pressed by the administrative apparatus to step up production to fulfill the economic plan (including such goals as completing the Second Five-Year Plan in two years). The compensation for this extreme intensification of labor is meager indeed, especially among the peasantry, whose standard of living is the barest even in regard to food.[19] In contrast to this, the bureaucrats enjoy all kinds of special privileges and live far better than the masses. Thus, an irreconcilable contradiction is created between the disfranchised and abused worker-peasant masses and the privileged bureaucracy. Just as in the Soviet Union and the countries of Eastern Europe, the conditions are ripening for a political revolution.

Therefore, we can say that though the third Chinese revolution objectively confirmed the theory of permanent revolution, reflected in a distorted way in the course followed by the CCP, the completion of the permanent revolution in China will see one further step in this process; that is, a political revolution in which the Stalinist bureaucratic regime will be replaced by one of proletarian socialist democracy. Only with the extension of the revolution, especially to the advanced capitalist countries, will the inherent dynamic of the permanent revolution have worked itself out.

Experiences of the revolutionary movements in the underdeveloped countries since the end of World War II

Based on his reactionary theory of "socialism in one country," Stalin defined his line toward the Communist parties of other countries in the *Program of the Communist International* passed by the Sixth World Congress of the Comintern in 1928. This amounted to converting the Communist Party in every country into a simple apparatus for carrying out the Kremlin's foreign policy, particularly in the colonial and semicolonial nations. In the name of a People's Front or a National Front, Stalin transformed the CPs in these countries into appendages of the liberal bourgeoisie for deceiving the masses. We have seen the full application of this line in almost every country since the end of World War II. The most striking example is India.

India was a typical big colonial country, just as China was a typical big semicolonial country. Its objective conditions have long been ripe for permanent revolution. But the CP there, after applying an opportunist policy for a long period before the war, acted during the war as a plaything of the bourgeoisie. In accord with the Soviet Union's alliance with Britain against Hitler, the Indian CP openly repudiated the struggle against Britain for national independence and fell into a most infamous position.

Faced with mounting difficulties following the war, Britain reluctantly granted India "independence," turning power over to the indigenous bourgeoisie represented by Nehru. This regime has guaranteed Britain's economic privileges in India. The response of the Indian CP was to give servile support to the Nehru government, relying on it to secure national independence (the cancellation of Britain's special privileges) and to carry out land reform.

As early as 1930 Trotsky pointed out: "The Indian peasant wants a 'just' distribution of the land. That is the basis of democracy. And that is at the same time the social basis of the democratic revolution as a whole."[20]

In the same article Trotsky had this to say about the "passive resistance" movement led by Gandhi: "The passive resistance of the peasants as well as their bloody uprisings can be turned into a revolution only under the leadership of an *urban class,* which then becomes the leader of the revolutionary nation and, after victory, the bearer of the revolutionary power. In the present epoch only the proletariat is such a class, even in the East. . . . There is 'only' one condition missing: a *Bolshevik party.*"[21]

Trotsky's basic concept of the pattern of the Indian revolution is still valid and effective today. At present the Indian bourgeoisie holds the power yielded to it by Britain. But India is still a semicolonial country and its land problem has yet to be solved. This is the case because "there is 'only' one condition missing: a *Bolshevik party.*" The central task facing the Indian masses today is the formation of a revolutionary party based on the theory of permanent revolution.

Indonesia is another big colonial country, second only to India as regards population. The CP there has been playing the same shameful role as the one in India. Before and during the Second World War it acted as an instrument of the bourgeoisie. It thus paved the way for the bourgeoisie's rise to power as the "leader of the national movement." But just as the capitalist class was establishing its government, the Indonesian CP organized an adventuristic uprising that ended in a tragic defeat.[22]

After this it returned to a policy of faithful support to Sukarno's bourgeois government, relying on the bourgeois state to promote a land reform.

But the Sukarno regime is incapable of solving the agrarian question. On the contrary, it is intensifying its exploitation of the peasantry and using repression against the working class. In the past year, Sukarno has transformed his government into a military dictatorship and is preparing a counterrevolutionary coup against the worker-peasant masses at the first opportunity, just as Chiang did in China.[23]

A similar experience to that in Indonesia occurred in the Middle East, in Iraq. After the overthrow of the thoroughly corrupt monarchy in an army coup led by Kassem [in 1958], a revolutionary mass mobilization erupted. But the CP did its best to contain this tide within the framework of support to the landlord-bourgeois government, relying on Kassem for the completion of the democratic revolution. But Kassem, just like Sukarno, grows more and more hostile to the masses. The regime is striving to weaken the CP (for example, by granting legal recognition to only one section of the party after a split in the CP). The road ahead is one of military dictatorship.

Following the line of the alliance between the proletariat and the liberal bourgeoisie, the CP in Guatemala helped bring the bourgeoisie to power rather than arming the masses for a socialist revolution.[24] As a result, the military, representing the bourgeoisie and the landlords, carried out a brutal counterrevolutionary coup at the instigation of American imperialism, which crushed the workers' and peasants' organizations. This was the first tragedy in Latin America resulting from the Stalinist-Menshevik policy and should serve as a warning to the masses of that continent.

Cuba is presently in the midst of a revolutionary situation. Castro at the head of a peasant guerrilla force has overthrown Batista's reactionary dictatorship and established his own revolutionary power. Faced with the threat of American imperialism, the new regime has pushed through a series of revolutionary measures, including the taking over of American, British, and Dutch oil refineries and part of the land owned by American imperialists. All this shows that the new government is on the road of the permanent revolution, yet it is still a petty-bourgeois regime that can only be a transitional form. The completion of the permanent revolution will require establishment of a proletarian dictatorship which would expropriate all the lands held by American imperialism as well as by domestic landowners, and nationalize alike all capitalist property, whether domestically or foreign owned.[25] In addition to beginning socialist construction, such a state would seek to extend the revolution to the rest of Latin America and seek to inspire and stimulate the workers' movement throughout the Americas.

Taken as a whole, the fresh experiences since the end of World War II show without qualification that none of the bourgeois regimes that came to power in the backward countries has been able to win genuine national independence or to carry through a thoroughgoing agrarian reform. It has made little difference whether they came to power through a concession by the imperialists, at the head of a mass mobilization, or through a military coup. (Such varied roads to power as we have seen in India, Ceylon, Burma, Indonesia, Iraq, and Egypt have produced regimes that do not differ greatly in their social content.)

In addition we have seen that consistent application of the Stalinist theory of revolution by stages does not "neutralize" the national bourgeoisie in the backward countries but converts the Communist parties of those countries into props for continued bourgeois rule and a roadblock in the way of the revolutionary movement of the masses.

If we were to distill the revolutionary experience of the underdeveloped countries in this century down to a single summary conclusion it could perhaps be best expressed in these passages from the Transitional Program of the Fourth International:

Colonial and semicolonial countries are backward countries by their very essence. But backward countries are part of a world dominated by imperialism. Their development, therefore, has a *combined* character: the most primitive economic forms are combined with the last word in capitalist technique and culture. In like manner are defined the political strivings of the proletariat of backward countries: the struggle for the most elementary achievements of national independence and bourgeois democracy is combined with the socialist struggle against world imperialism. Democratic slogans, transitional demands, and the problems of the socialist revolution are not divided into separate historical epochs in this struggle, but stem directly from one another. The Chinese proletariat had barely begun to organize trade unions before it had to provide for soviets.

In this sense, the present program is completely applicable to colonial and semicolonial countries, at least to those where the proletariat has become capable of carrying on independent politics.

The central tasks of the colonial and semicolonial countries are the *agrarian revolution*, i.e., liquidation of feudal heritages, and *national independence,* i.e., the overthrow of the imperialist yoke. The two tasks are closely linked with each other.

It is impossible merely to reject the democratic program; it is imperative that in the struggle the masses outgrow it. The slogan for a national (or constituent) assembly preserves its full force for such countries as China or India. This slogan must be indissolubly tied up with the problem of national liberation and agrarian reform. As a primary step, the workers must be armed with this democratic program. Only they will be able to summon and unite the farmers. On the basis of the revolutionary democratic program, it is necessary to oppose the workers to the "national" bourgeoisie.

Then, at a certain stage in the mobilization of the masses under the slogans of revolutionary democracy, soviets can and should arise. . . . Sooner or later, the soviets should overthrow bourgeois democracy. Only they are capable of bringing the democratic revolution to a conclusion and likewise opening an era of socialist revolution.[26]

July 15, 1960

THE CAUSES OF THE VICTORY OF THE CHINESE COMMUNIST PARTY OVER CHIANG KAI-SHEK, AND THE CCP'S PERSPECTIVES

Report on the Chinese Situation to the Third Congress of the Fourth International

The victory of the Chinese Communist Party over the reactionary power of Chiang Kai-shek, its occupation of the entire Chinese mainland, and the establishment of the "People's Republic" (or the "People's Democratic Dictatorship") has marked a great and even a monumental change in modern Chinese history, and has also caused profound changes in the Far East and in international relations.

These events were unexpected both among bourgeois ruling circles and the petty-bourgeois politicians, the former being stunned and panic-stricken; the latter, perplexed or dazzled. But these events were likewise far from being anticipated by us Trotskyists (including Trotsky himself), owing to the fact that the CCP came to its current victory through its extremely reactionary Menshevik program of "revolution by stages," coupled with the fact that the peasant armed forces were completely isolated from the urban working class.

As a result, a considerable amount of confusion has been raised in our ranks regarding Mao's victory, and serious differences of

This is the edited text of the report given by P'eng Shu-tse to the Third World Congress of the Fourth International, held in Switzerland in August-September 1951. The edited text was completed in November 1951 and published in the internal bulletin of the Fourth International. The translation used in the internal bulletin has been revised for this volume.

opinion have occurred over its causes and significance, the nature of the new power and its perspectives. A few comrades have even begun to doubt the correctness of the theory of permanent revolution. If these differences are not clarified and resolved in time, the most serious consequences would ensue, especially in our Chinese section. Some of the comrades would proceed from doubting the permanent revolution to capitulating to Stalinism (some comrades in Shanghai have already shown signs of this tendency). Others would arrive at ultrasectarianism and complete demoralization in their revulsion against Mao Tse-tung's opportunist victory, which is the result of a complete violation of the permanent revolution. (The Chinese minority has already clearly demonstrated this tendency.) We must, therefore, very prudently and seriously examine Mao's victory and the extraordinary situation emerging from it.

First of all, we should not overlook the reactionary role of Stalinism independently of the CCP victory, and not reconcile ourselves or, even worse, surrender to it. We must still insist on the basic position of the permanent revolution, which is the only compass to guide China and all backward countries to genuine liberation; we must judge any further events from this position. But, in proceeding with the discussion, it is necessary not only to discard all subjective prejudices, desires, or mechanical analogies, but to free ourselves from traditional formulas (not, of course, principles). We must face the concrete living facts, whether desirable or undesirable, particularly the decisive influence of the situation created after the Second World War on the Chinese events. We must also take note of the specific function Stalinism played in these events, the distortion or deformation imposed by its rule on the events and their consequences. In a word, we should seriously and flexibly apply the dialectic method of Marxism to observe the facts, analyze the facts, and by analysis of the causes and effects of the realities, obtain a correct understanding, and thus form a correct appraisal of possible developments.

In other words, on the Chinese problem we must adopt the same spirit and method as our International has done in the study of the Yugoslav events and the question of Eastern Europe. Only in this way can we extricate ourselves from perplexity and extremely dangerous deviations to reach a decision on what the fundamental attitude and orientation of our party should be in respect to the CCP leadership. Thus this report is not aimed at supplying a great deal of data; it intends to provide necessary and essential facts in the course of the logical development of the events, and to explain certain opinions which have already caused serious disputes, as references for the International so that it can achieve a correct solution of the Chinese question.

The diverse causes of the CCP victory over the Kuomintang

One of the traditional concepts that Trotsky repeatedly put forward, and that the Chinese Trotskyists upheld for the past twenty years, was a strategy that ran counter to the Stalinist strategy of conquering the cities through the peasant armed forces alone. The Trotskyists maintained that the overthrow of the bourgeois Kuomintang regime was possible only if the urban working class stood up and led all the oppressed and exploited in the country, especially the peasant masses, carried forward a persistent struggle, and eventually brought about an armed insurrection. It was not possible to overthrow the bourgeois regime by relying exclusively on the peasant armed forces because, under the present conditions of society, the countryside is subordinated to the cities and the peasants can play a decisive role only under the leadership of the working class. But the fact now confronting us is exactly the contrary: it was a Stalinist party relying exclusively on the peasant armed forces that destroyed the old regime and seized power.

This extreme contradiction between the "facts" and the "traditional conception" first of all led to confusion and disputes among the Chinese comrades. Meanwhile, some comrades in the International, because of their inadequate understanding of Trotsky's traditional conception of the Chinese question and the specific causes of Mao's victory, emphasize the factor of "mass pressure" to account for this victory. So I think that an accurate and detailed explanation of the causes of this victory is necessary, not only in order to overcome the differences of opinion among the Chinese comrades, but also in order to correct the deviations of some comrades in the International. Moreover, the most important thing is this: Only from a correct answer to this question will we be able to go one step further and comprehend the objective significance of Mao's victory, as well as the twists and turns of all the measures taken by his regime, and the regime's possible perspectives. In order to best answer this question, I shall start from several aspects of the facts.

A. The complete rottenness and collapse of Chiang's regime

It is known to everyone that Chiang Kai-shek's regime was born amid the bloodshed of the defeat of the second Chinese revolution. Naturally it was extremely afraid of and hostile to the people. It oppressed the people and sustained itself on the exploitation of the masses (especially the peasant masses) by the most barbaric Asiatic methods. At the same time, since by its very nature this regime represented the bourgeoisie of the Orient (characterized in the saying that "the farther East the bourgeoisie goes, the more cowardly and the more incompetent it becomes"), Chiang's regime could only support itself on the imperialist powers (one of them, at least).

It united all reactionary influences, including the feudal survivals, to resist the masses and to suppress them. It was consequently unable to fulfill any of the bourgeois-democratic tasks, not even such a slight reform as a 25 percent reduction in rents. It was mainly characterized by consummate Asiatic despotism, corruption, and inefficiency. These characteristics were completely disclosed during the Resistance War. On one hand, after its policy of "nondefensism" failed and the long period of concessions to the Japanese imperialists ended with the Chiang government forced to fight, it revealed its complete incompetence by losing one city after another. On the other hand, it clamped an iron grip over any spontaneous activity by the masses, while its bureaucrats and warlords, profiting from this rare opportunity, exploited and plundered the blood and flesh of the people by hoarding and smuggling goods and other extortions, and thus enriched themselves through the national disaster. These deeds stirred up great dissatisfaction and bitterness among the common people—which was reflected in the student demonstrations and the peasant unrest in certain regions during the closing period of the war.

After the surrender of Japanese imperialism, Chiang Kai-shek's tyranny, corruption, and inefficiency reached a climax. First, in the name of taking over the "properties of the enemy and the traitors," the militarists and bureaucrats stole almost all the public property to fill their own purses, and indulged themselves in extravagant luxury and dissipation. At the same time, using the pretext of proceeding with the civil war, they extracted food from the peasants and imposed conscription upon them, did their best to squeeze and to oppress. (As some enlisted peasants could be exempted from duty by subscribing a sum of money, this became another of the sources of extortion on the part of the bureaucrats.) This further inflamed the fury of the masses, and provoked the eruption of several large-scale protest demonstrations (in which the students played a central part). But the only answer from Chiang Kai-shek to these bitter feelings, protests, and demonstrations was suppression, massacres, and even assassinations and kidnappings by gendarmes, police, and secret agents.

The financial base of Chiang's government had already been exhausted in the course of the war. Besides compulsory extortions, it could only resort to issuing paper currency to maintain itself. Consequently the rate of inflation climbed in geometric progression. After peace was announced, the pace of inflation advanced from geometric progression to lightning speed, terminating in the collapse of the "gold yuan" and the unprecedented economic chaos at the end of 1948.[1]

All commerce and industry halted and disintegrated, and the living conditions of the various layers among the middle and lower classes (including all the middle and lower functionaries in the government institutions) cast them into the pit of despair. Driven by starvation, the workers rose up in a universal strike wave (there were 200,000 workers on strike in Shanghai alone). Plundering of rice took place everywhere. At that time, the United Press gave a brief description of the situation as follows: "The people below the middle class are not able to go on living; discontent and resentment against the status quo prevail. Everyone wants a change." Chiang Kai-shek's regime was tottering. If the CCP had called upon the workers and the masses in the big cities to rise in rebellion and overthrow the regime, it would have been as easy as knocking down rotten wood. But Mao's party merely gave orders to the people to quietly wait for their "liberation" by the "People's Liberation Army."

Chiang's sole prop was his military force and so he continued the fight to the end and would never compromise with Mao Tse-tung. He hoped to exterminate the CCP's peasant armed forces through his superior military equipment and prevent his doomed regime from being swept away. In fact, Chiang Kai-shek's army far surpassed the CCP's, not only in numbers but also in equipment. A considerable part of his army (about six to seven hundred thousand soldiers) was armed with the most modern American weapons. But this army had two fatal defects: First, most of the soldiers were recruited from the countryside by compulsory conscription, some of them even by kidnapping, so they naturally more or less reflected the dissatisfaction and hatred of the peasants. Second, all the generals and officers of high rank were rotten to the core; they mistreated the soldiers and steadily reduced rations. This oppression inflicted much suffering upon the soldiers and deepened their discontent and hatred. Once this hatred found a suitable outlet, it would be transformed into a deluge of flight and surrender. Mao Tse-tung's "general counteroffensive" furnished this outlet.

All the above-stated facts demonstrate that Chiang's government was not only isolated from the people, who were hostile to it, but was also deserted by the majority of the bourgeoisie. Even those who formerly supported it turned bitter against it and were ready to sacrifice it in exchange for their own lives. This situation resulted in the appearance of various kinds of anti-Chiang factions and cliques within the Kuomintang itself, which was thus involved in complete decomposition. One of these factions crystallized into the so-called Kuomintang Revolutionary Committee (led by Li Chi-shen). In view of the inevitability of Chiang Kai-shek's fall, it anxiously sought an "understanding and reconciliation" with Mao Tse-tung.

Another group prepared to respond to the CCP's offensive by rebelling against Chiang (such as Ch'eng Ch'ien, the governor of Hunan province, and Lu Han, the governor of Yunnan), while still others were ready to capitulate, as in the case of Fu Tso-yi in Peiping and Liu Hsiang in Szechuan.[2]

The third group—the Kwangsi clique, represented by Li Tsung-jen and Pai Ch'ung-hsi—attempted to replace Chiang Kai-shek.[3] The bourgeois elements outside the Kuomintang gathered more and more around the "Democratic League," trying to find their way out through this organization. In a word, the structures of the Kuomintang regime were corroded from top to bottom and it could no longer stand up. The only remaining hope for Chiang Kai-shek was imperative aid from Washington. (He had sent Soong Ch'ing-ling on this special mission to bid for a last favor.)

B. Chiang finally deserted by American imperialism

Prior to the Second World War, the most powerful and decisive influences in Chinese economy and politics were the Japanese, British, and American imperialists. With the end of the war, the influence of Japanese imperialism vanished. British imperialism, because of its extreme decline, although still maintaining its rule in Hong Kong, has since completely left the political stage in China. The last one to attempt to control the country was American imperialism. It intended at the beginning to uphold Chiang's government with all its might in order to monopolize the Chinese market and use this country as a bastion against the Soviet Union. Acting from this motive, it had dispatched a tremendous amount of materiel and military equipment to Chiang's government at the close of the war. But it soon opened its eyes to the extreme corruption of this government's administrative and military apparatus and the crisis that created. (For example, most of the materiel given by the U.S. was swallowed by the bureaucrats, and American-made arms often found their way into the CCP's hands through the lack of combativeness of the Kuomintang officers.)

On the one hand, Washington still tried to "prevail upon" Chiang Kai-shek to make some "reforms," such as eliminating a few of the most corrupt and incompetent officials and generals, inviting some more able "democratic" figures into the administration, and curtailing some of the more excessive forms of despotic oppression and exploitation. On the other hand, the U.S. maneuvered for a temporary compromise between Chiang and Mao, in order to gain time to destroy Mao. This was the purpose of Gen. Marshall's special mission in China.

But Chiang not only refused to make any "reforms"; he also obstinately balked at any compromise with Mao's party. Ultimately, the Marshall mission was a complete failure. The only alternative left for American imperialism was to engage in a direct military offensive against the CCP in Chiang's place (as one group of Republicans demanded at that time), and to extend its direct control over the administrative and military power of the government. It was very clear, however, that the situation emerging from the Second World War would never permit this headstrong action. Had American imperialism pursued such a course, not only would all of its resources and energy have been drawn into the vast China quagmire, but a new world war would have been precipitated. American imperialism was completely unprepared for such a course of action, and, in face of the expected vehement opposition from its own allies, was not bold enough to run the risk.

The result was that the U.S. was finally compelled to abandon its aid to Chiang's government and adopt a wait-and-see attitude toward the CCP, pending a more favorable opportunity. This final decision by American imperialism came as a death blow to Chiang Kai-shek's regime, which was fully expressed in the atmosphere of dejection and despair hovering around Chiang's group when the news reached China of Truman's victory in the 1948 election and his refusal of aid to Chiang.

C. The CCP's subjective strength

The CCP's basic strength lies in its peasant armed forces. These originated in the successive peasant revolts that exploded in China's southern provinces after the defeat of the second revolution. While these revolts had no real hope of victory, the armed forces they assembled were able to maintain their existence, develop, and carry on a durable peasant war. This was possible because of the CCP's deep involvement in organizing and training the peasants, as well as the economic backwardness and other specific geographic conditions (the vastness of the country and the extreme lack of means of communication). Other factors included the utter despair of the peasants and the incompetence of the bourgeois government.

Later, when Chiang Kai-shek obtained enormous quantities of military aid from imperialism, the CCP's peasant army was forced to flee from South to North China, and even capitulated to Chiang's government by canceling its agrarian policy and dissolving the "Red Army" and the soviets.

However, as a result of the outbreak of the war against Japanese imperialism this armed force secured the opportunity for an unusual development. In particular, at the end of the war and right after it, the army made great progress in both numbers and in quality, becoming far stronger than in the Kiangsi period. This army thus grew into a strong military force.

Politically, the CCP always oscillated between adventurism and opportunism: it canceled its agrarian revolution and dissolved the "Red Army" and the soviets on the eve of the Resistance War; it collaborated servilely with the Kuomintang and supported Chiang Kai-shek's leadership during the war. But despite all these things, it also carried on a long period of resistance against Chiang's government. It made certain criticisms of the political, economic, and military measures of the latter during the war, and had put forward a number of demands for democratic reform. It carried out agrarian reform, particularly in some regions of North China. Furthermore it was backed by the prestige of the tradition of the October revolution in the USSR, as well as by the amazing record of the Soviet Union in the recent world war and the powerful position it has held since the war's end.

On the other hand, the common people had become desperate and deeply resentful under the intolerable oppression and exploitation of Chiang's utterly despotic, rotten, and inefficient regime. The petty-bourgeois intellectuals and peasant masses in particular, in the absence of a powerful and really revolutionary party to lead them, lodged all their hopes in the CCP. This was the source of the CCP's political capital. This political capital, plus the peasant armed forces, constituted the party's subjective strength. But without aid from the Soviet Union, this victory would still not have been assured.

D. *The aid from the Soviet Union*

Despite the Soviet bureaucracy's fear of the victory of a genuine revolution of the working class at the head of the peasant masses in China, and despite its foreign policy of seeking a compromise with American imperialism, in order to preserve its own privileges and resist the threat of American imperialism it would not refuse to give the CCP a certain amount of help, within the confines of its attempt to preserve control over the CCP. Therefore, in addition to its support in political agitation, the Soviet Union actually gave the CCP decisive material aid. The Soviet occupation of Manchuria (one of the greatest centers of heavy industry in China, built up during the several decades of Japanese occupation, and the area of the highest rural production), with its population of thirty million, objectively dealt a mortal blow to Chiang's government.

Despite the fact that the Soviet Union had recognized Chiang's regime as the official government, and had handed over to it the majority of the cities and mines in Manchuria, the Soviet bureaucracy had destroyed almost all the most important factories and mining machinery. (It also took away a part of them.) Thus industry was brought almost to a complete halt. Meanwhile, through its control over the two ports—Dairen and Port Arthur—it blocked the Chiang government's main lines of sea communication with Manchuria and barred its trade and commerce, especially its transportation of supplies to the army stationed in Manchuria.

On the other hand, it armed the CCP's troops with huge amounts of light and heavy weapons taken from the Japanese soldiers. (It is estimated that these weapons could be used to rearm a million soldiers.) This enabled the CCP to occupy the villages, smaller cities, and towns, and to besiege the great cities and mining districts where Chiang's army was stationed. Thus the cities and mines restored to Chiang Kai-shek did not benefit him, but on the contrary, became an insupportable burden, and finally turned into a trap. To begin with, Chiang had to send a huge army (around a half-million soldiers) with the best equipment, i.e., armed with American weapons, to stand guard. At the same time, the KMT had to provide for the enormous expenditures in the big cities and in the mines. Consequently, this greatly limited and scattered Chiang Kai-shek's military force and accelerated the financial bankruptcy of his regime.

The weapons taken from the Japanese captives by the Soviet Union served to build up the CCP's army and produced a decisive effect upon Mao Tse-tung's military apparatus and strategy.* We must understand that the CCP's original peasant army, despite its preponderant size, was not only very backward but also had extremely scanty equipment, especially in heavy weapons. Having obtained this gigantic quantity of light and heavy weapons through the medium of the Soviet Union (in addition to numerous Soviet and Japanese military technicians), part of the originally very backward peasant troops were modernized overnight.

The bravery of the peasants and the military adroitness of the Communist generals, together with these modern weapons, then enabled the Communist army to transform guerrilla warfare into positional warfare. This was fully manifested in the battles where the Communist troops gained complete victory in conquering the great cities and mines in Manchuria during the changing season between autumn and winter of 1948. (These included Changchun, Mukden, Chinchou, and the big mining districts, Tiehling, Fushun, Benchi, and Anshan.) This victory won for the Communist army an ample economic base. Moreover, in the military field, since the best-equipped of Chiang's troops (about 80 percent of those with American equipment) were destroyed, that meant that the greatest part of this American equipment was no longer effective.

Since the Communist army had taken possession of modern weapons and technicians, together with the Japanese arms handed over by the Soviet Union, that made it possible for the CCP to transform the former unfavorable relationship of forces toward Chiang's troops in the sphere of military equipment and technique into an overwhelming superiority. Henceforth the strategic attitude of the Communist army fundamentally changed, shifting over from guerrilla warfare to positional warfare and an offensive toward the big cities. This change was undoubtedly a decisive factor in the victory of the CCP inasmuch

---

* For example, Lin Piao's well-known and powerful Fourth Division was armed entirely with these weapons.

as it depended on the peasant army alone to conquer the cities.

From the above facts we can draw a clear picture as follows: Chiang Kai-shek's bourgeois-landlord regime collapsed in toto, both on the economic and political planes and in its military organization. Its only supporter, American imperialism, deserted it in the end. The CCP's peasant army, having won the support of the peasants and the petty bourgeoisie in general, and especially having obtained military aid from the Soviet Union, had become a colossal and more or less modernized army. The combination of all these objective and subjective factors paved the way for this extraordinary victory.

If we give a brief description of the development of this military victory, the truth of these factors as stated above can be made more explicit. Beginning with the "all-out counteroffensive" launched by the Communist army in the autumn of 1948, in the successive battles occurring in the Northeast, except for a violent fight in Chinchou, the other big cities, such as Changchun, Mukden, etc., were occupied without a fight as a result of the capitulation or disintegration of Chiang's army in their defensive positions. As for the great cities and important military bases north of the Yangtze River, except for an encounter in Chuchao and Paotow, the others, such as Tsinan, Tientsin, Peiping, Kaifeng, Chengshou, Sian, etc., were handed over either because of the rebellion of the army stationed there (Tsinan), or surrender (Peiping), or desertion as in Tientsin, Kaifeng, Chengchou, and Sian. In the Northwest, in the provinces of Kansu and Sinkiang, there was only surrender. In the city of Taiyuan, there was a comparatively longer struggle, but this had no weight at all in the situation as a whole. As for the great cities south of the river, except for token resistance in Shanghai, the others were either given up in advance (Nanking, Hangchow, Hangkow, Nanchang, Fuchow, Kweilin, and Canton), or surrendered upon the arrival of the Communist army (as in the provinces of Hunan, Szechuan, and Yunnan).

Thereupon, after crossing the Yangtze River, Mao Tse-tung's army marched headlong down to Canton as though through "no man's land," while the remnants of Chiang's troops either surrendered or withdrew and fled. Hence the peculiar situation whereby the "Liberation Army" did not conquer but rather took over the cities. From this concrete military process, one can get a clearer view of the amazing extent of the Chiang Kai-shek regime's disintegration and the exceptional conditions under which the victory of the CCP's peasant army unfolded.

Now we can comprehend that it was under the specific conditions of a definite historical stage that the CCP, relying on a peasant army isolated from the urban working class, could win power from the bourgeois-landlord rule of Chiang Kai-shek. This was a combination of various intricate and exceptional conditions emerging from the Second World War. The essential features of this set of circumstances are as follows:

The whole capitalist world—of which China is the weakest link—tended to an unparalleled decline and decay. The internal disintegration of the bourgeois Chiang Kai-shek regime was only the most consummate manifestation of the deterioration of the whole capitalist system. On the other hand, the Soviet bureaucracy, resting on the socialized property relations of the October revolution and exploiting the contradictions among the imperialist powers, was able to achieve an unprecedented expansion of its influence during the Second World War. This expansion greatly attracted the masses, especially of the backward Asian countries, who were deprived of hope under the extreme decline and decomposition of the capitalist system. This facilitated the explosive growth of the Stalinist parties in these countries. The CCP is precisely a perfected model of these Stalinist parties.

Meanwhile, placed in an unfavorable position in the international situation created by the Second World War, American imperialism was obliged to abandon its aid to Chiang and its interference with Mao. At the same time, the Soviet Union, which had secured a superior position in Manchuria at the end of the war, inflicted serious damage to Chiang's government and offered direct aid to the CCP. This enabled the latter to modernize its backward peasant army. Without this combination of circumstances, the victory of a party like the CCP, which relied purely on peasant forces, would be inconceivable.

For example, if Manchuria had not been occupied by the Soviet Union but had fallen entirely under Chiang's control, Chiang Kai-shek would have utilized the economic resources and the Japanese arms in Manchuria to cut off direct connection between the CCP and the Soviet Union. This would have blocked the USSR's armed support to the CCP. Similarly, the situation would have been quite different if direct intervention against the CCP by American imperialism had been possible. Under either of these two circumstances the victory of Mao Tse-tung would have been very doubtful.

To approach this from another direction, we could recall the defeat of the CCP's peasant army in the Kiangsi period, 1930-35, when the bourgeois KMT's power was considerably stabilized as a result of continual aid from imperialism, while the CCP was isolated from the Soviet Union. From this we can also derive sufficient reason to justify the conclusion that today's victory of the CCP is entirely the result of the specific conditions created by the Second World War.

Trotsky and the Chinese Trotskyists insisted that the overturn of the Kuomintang regime could not be achieved by relying solely on the peasant armed forces, but could only be accomplished by the urban working class leading the peasant masses in a series of revolts. Even today, this conception is still entirely valid. It is derived from the fundamental Marxist theory that under the modern capitalist system—including that in the backward countries—it is the urban class that leads the rural masses. This is also the conclusion drawn from numerous experiences, especially that of the October revolution. This is precisely one of the fundamental conceptions of the permanent revolution, which we must firmly hold onto despite the present CCP victory.

Let us take India, for example. There we should insist on the perspective that the Indian working class lead the peasant masses in the overthrow of the bourgeois power dominated by the Congress Party. Only this process can guarantee that this backward country will take the direction of genuine emancipation and development, i.e., the *permanent* transformation from the democratic revolution to the socialist revolution.

We were unable to foresee the current victory of the CCP for the same reason that Trotsky and we Trotskyists were unable to predict in advance the unusual expansion that Stalinism underwent after the Second World War. In both cases our mistake was not one of principle. Rather, because we concentrated so much on principle, we more or less ignored the specific conditions involved in the unfolding of events and were unable to modify our tactics in time. Of course there is a lesson in this, a lesson we should assimilate and apply to the analysis of future developments in those Asian countries where the Stalinist parties maintain strong influence (such as Vietnam, Burma, etc.). That should help us to formulate a correct strategy in advance.

At the same time, we must understand that the victory gained by a party such as the CCP, which detached itself from the working class and relied entirely on the peasant armed forces, is not only abnormal in itself. It has also laid down many obstacles in the path of the future development of the Chinese revolutionary movement. To understand this is, in my opinion, of great importance in our judgment and estimation of the whole movement led by the CCP as well as in determining our strategy and tactics.

Is the CCP's seizure of power the result of "mass pressure," and in opposition to the Kremlin's objectives?

Some comrades of the International, not being very familiar with the concrete process and specific conditions of the events in China, have particularly stressed the factor of "mass pressure," or interpreted the victory of the CCP by making an analogy with the Yugoslav events. For example, Comrade Germain says:

> Our movement has traditionally conceived the outstripping of Stalinism by the masses as involving profound splits inside the Communist parties. The Yugoslav and Chinese examples have demonstrated that, placed in certain exceptional conditions, entire Communist parties can modify their political line and lead the struggle of the masses up to the conquest of power, while passing beyond the objectives of the Kremlin. Under such conditions, these parties cease being Stalinist parties in the classical sense of the word.[4]

The ideas contained in this passage are obviously as follows: The CCP succeeded in conquering power, like the Yugoslav CP, under pressure from the masses, and in conflict with the objectives of the Kremlin. Unfortunately, this "traditionally conceived" analogy can hardly be justified by the facts of the Chinese events. Let us first of all begin with these facts.

Regarding the relationship between the CCP and the masses—including its relationship to "mass pressure"—I am not going to trace the facts prior to and during the war against Japan. To do so would, however, also fully demonstrate how often the CCP violated the aspirations of the masses and ignored "mass pressure." I shall start with the period at the end of the war.

The first period immediately after the war, from September 1945 to the end of 1946, marked a considerable revival and growth of the mass movement in China. In this period the working masses in all the great cities, with Shanghai in the forefront, first brought forward their demands for a sliding-scale increase in wages, for the right to organize trade unions, against freezing of wages, etc. They universally and continuously engaged in strikes and demonstrations. This struggle in the main did not pass beyond the economic framework, or reach a nation-wide level. But it did at least prove that after the war the workers had raised their heads and were waging a resolute fight to improve their living conditions and general position against the bourgeoisie and its reactionary government. This movement actually won considerable successes. Undoubtedly this was the expression of a new awakening of the Chinese workers' movement.

Meanwhile, among the peasant masses, under the unbearable weight of compulsory contributions, taxes in kind, conscription, and the threat of starvation, the ferment of resentment was boiling. Some disturbances had already occurred in the regions controlled by Chiang's government.

The students played a notable role, representing the petty bourgeoisie in general, in large-scale protests, strikes, and demonstrations in the big cities. These took place in Chungking, Kunming, Nanking, Shanghai, Canton, Peiping, etc., under banners and slogans demanding democracy and peace, against the Kuomintang dictatorship, against mobilization for the civil war, and against the persecutions conducted by the KMT agents.

On the other hand, when Chiang's government returned to the "recovered areas," it revealed its own extreme corruption and inefficiency in administration and stirred up strong resentment among the people. It already appeared to be tottering. Its power did not extend into North China for a certain period of time, especially Manchuria. (It was not until the beginning of March 1946 that the Soviet Union began gradually to transfer such great cities as Mukden and Changchun and the important mines to Chiang's government.)

During this same period the CCP's military strength and its political influence among the masses were growing rapidly. The workers' struggles, the ferment of resentment and rebellion among the peasants, and widespread demonstrations by the students, accompanied by the corruption and insecurity of Chiang's regime and the strengthening of the CCP, plainly created a prerevolutionary situation.

If the CCP had then been able to stay in step with the situation, that is, to accept the "pressure of the masses," it would have raised slogans for the overthrow of the Chiang Kai-shek government (i.e., the slogan for the seizure of power). It would have joined this slogan to other demands for democratic reforms, especially the demand for agrarian revolution. And it would have been able to swiftly transform this prerevolutionary situation, to carry through the insurrection, and thereby arrive at the conquest of power in the most propitious way.

Unfortunately, however, the fundamental political line adopted by the CCP in this period was quite different. Contrary to what it should have done—mobilize the masses in the struggle for power under the slogans of overthrowing Chiang's government and agrarian reform—it kowtowed to Chiang Kai-shek and pleaded for the establishment of a "coalition government." (For this purpose Mao flew to Chungking to negotiate directly with Chiang, and even openly expressed his support to the latter in mass meetings.) The CCP tried its best to pull together the politicians of the upper layers of the bourgeoisie and petty bourgeoisie in order to proceed with peace talks under the sponsorship of American imperialism.

As for the workers' economic struggles, not only did the CCP not offer any positive lead to transform them into political struggles, which was quite possible at that time, but on the contrary, in order to effect a "united front" with the "national bourgeoisie," it persuaded the working masses not to go to "extremes" in their conflicts. Moreover, it dealt obsequiously with the leaders of the "yellow trade unions" in order to check the "excessive" demands of the workers.[5]

The CCP's activities in the countryside were limited solely to organizing the guerrillas, while it avoided by all means broad mass movements which would have encouraged and unified the peasant masses. The great student movement in the cities was handled as a simple instrument for exerting pressure on the Kuomintang government to accept peace talks. It was never linked with the workers' strikes in a common struggle against Chiang Kai-shek's rule.

However, in May 1946, in response to the KMT's continuing military offensive, the CCP announced that it had begun agrarian reform in certain areas under its control. This served to strengthen the CCP's military position. Even then, this land reform was by no means thoroughgoing. It consisted largely of a compromise with the landlords and rich peasants, preserving all of their "industrial and commercial properties" and allowing them to get the best and most of the land. It was also quite limited in its scope. No land reform was allowed, for example, in the CCP-controlled areas of the provinces of Shantung, Kiangsu, Hopeh, and Honan.

Moreover, in its anxiety to accomplish its reconciliation with Chiang Kai-shek, the CCP dissolved the peasant army in Kwangtung and Shekiang, and removed only a part of it to North China. This caused great dissatisfaction among rank-and-file members within the party itself.

These facts should show that the CCP's policy not only did not bow to "mass pressure," but proceeded arbitrarily in direct opposition to the will and demands of the masses.

Chiang Kai-shek, for his part, made full use of the time during the peace conference to transport his army, with the aid of American planes and warships, from the interior to the great cities and the strategic bases in the "recovered areas." He solidified his position and prepared for armed attack on the CCP. In the meantime, he suppressed all the newly arising mass movements, especially the student movement. At the end of 1946, when all preparations were completed, Chiang's government openly barred all doors to compromise and peace talks by holding its own "national assembly" and organizing its own "constituent government," which showed its determination to reject the establishment of any coalition government with the CCP.

Following these steps, the KMT mobilized a great military offensive—such as the seizure of Chang-chia-k'ou [in Hopeh] and some small cities and towns in north Kiangsu. Yet up to this moment the CCP had not given up its efforts at conciliation. Its delegates to the peace conference still lingered in Shanghai and Nanking, trying to reopen peace talks with the KMT through the mediation of the so-called third force—the Democratic League.

Not until later, when Chiang Kai-shek drove away the CCP's peace delegation (March 1947) and succeeded in occupying Yenan, its capital and stronghold (April 1947), did the CCP begin to realize the hopelessness of this attempt and only then did it muster its forces to engage in a military defense. But even at that time, it still did not dare to raise the slogan of the overthrow of the Koumintang government. Nor did it offer a program of agrarian reform to mobilize the masses.

Even when Chiang's government published its "warrant" for Mao Tse-tung's arrest (June 25, 1947) and promulgated its "mobilization decree for suppressing revolts" (July 4), the CCP responded with several months of hesitation (during which it seemed to be waiting for instructions from Moscow). Finally on October 10, it published its manifesto in the name of the "People's Liberation Army" that openly called for Chiang Kai-shek's overthrow and the building of a "New China." It was also at this time that it once again revived its "agrarian law," ordering the expropriation of the land of landlords and rich peasants and its redistribution to peasants with no land or whose land was inadequate. ("Industrial and commercial enterprises," however, remained untouched.)

This was a remarkable change in the CCP's policy from the whole period since it declared its support to Chiang's regime and abandoned land reform in 1937. This policy shift marked a fundamental change in the CCP's relations with Chiang's government.

Was this change, then, the result of mass pressure? No, obviously not. The mass movement had already been brutally trampled by Chiang's regime and was actually at a very low ebb. With KMT agents active everywhere, thousands of young students were arrested, tortured, and even assassinated, and worker militants were constantly being arrested or hunted. The indisputable facts indicate that the CCP was compelled to make this change solely because Chiang had burned all bridges leading toward compromise and because it was confronted with the mortal threat of a violent attack designed to annihilate its influence once and for all. So we might rather say that this shift was the result of Chiang's pressure than of mass pressure.

In order to arm itself for a counteroffensive, the CCP began to make a "left turn" on the political plane. Only then did it begin to make concessions to the demands of the masses, or to bend before "mass pressure." In particular it gave in to the demands of the peasant masses in areas it controlled, with the aim of regaining and strengthening its military power.

Hence, from November 1947 to the next spring, it initiated a universal struggle to "correct the Right deviation" in areas where land reform was set into motion. In the course of this struggle, the CCP liquidated all the privileges previously granted to the landlords and kulaks, and reexpropriated and distributed the land among the poor peasants. It also deprived the landlords and kulaks of the posts they held in the local administration, the party, and the army. (As a result of the previous compromising policy, a great number of landlords and kulaks had joined the party and its army, and even occupied certain important positions.)

"Poor Peasants' Committees" were created and given a few democratic rights, to allow them to directly fight the landlords and kulaks. They were even permitted to criticize lower-ranking party cadres, some of whom were removed from their posts and punished. These actions as a whole were quite successful in winning considerable support from the peasant masses and greatly strengthened the CCP's anti-Chiang military forces. But we should not forget that all these "leftward" policies were taken in reaction to pressure from Chiang.

As regards the CCP's relations with the Kremlin, I can only offer as illustrations some important historical turns. After the disastrous defeat of the second Chinese revolution, when the Kremlin switched its policy from ultraright opportunism to ultraleft adventurism (the so-called third period in its general international line),[6] the CCP leadership followed at the Kremlin's heels without hesitation. Closing their eyes to the most grave injuries the party suffered because of this turn, and deaf to the unremitting and sharp criticisms from Trotsky and the Chinese Left Opposition, the leading bodies carried out these adventurist policies and engaged in a desperate struggle to "build up soviets and the Red Army" in the desolate and isolated villages. This was done without any connection with the urban workers' movement, and in the general counterrevolutionary climate of bourgeois victory and relative stability.

At the time the "Red Army" in China was driven out of the South and fled to Yenan in the North, the Kremlin, threatened by Hitler's triumph, turned away from the "third period" and back toward ultraright opportunism. This opened the period of building up the so-called Democratic Front and the Peace Front. Just as before, adjusting itself to this turn of the Kremlin, the CCP likewise unreservedly advocated the People's Front or the Front of National Defense, and renewed its appeal to the Kuomintang for collaboration.

A case in point was the CCP's reaction when Chang Hsueh-liang, commander in chief of the Kuomintang expedition at the time, detained Chiang Kai-shek in Sian under "pressure of the masses," particularly pressure from his own soldiers and lower officers, all of whom were Manchurians who nourished a bitter hatred against Chiang because his "nondefensism" during the Japanese attack on Manchuria had rendered them homeless.[7] This incident aroused delight and hope in the whole country, especially among the members of the CCP. As the news spread the whole nation was at a peak of excitement and passion, thinking that this counterrevolutionary butcher was doomed at last and that a new era was dawning.

But to everyone's astonishment, without resistance the CCP complied with the Kremlin's directives, calling on and compelling Chang Hsueh-liang to release Chiang Kai-shek, the chief butcher of the second revolution and Mao's mortal enemy during eight years of civil war.* This was the price paid to get from Chiang his agreement for a new collaboration in order to "fight together against Japan"! (And this was on the condition that the CCP cancel the agrarian reform and dissolve the "soviets" and the "Red Army.")

This amazing servile obedience of the Communist leadership toward the Kremlin not only stirred up discontent among the people in general, but also caused great disappointment and disturbances among its own members and followers. After the war, the CCP's desperate efforts to submissively follow the policy of compromise and peace with Chiang, in complete disregard of the aspirations of the masses, was the latest fact to show that it was entirely under the direction of the Kremlin. Its policy was completely subordinated to Moscow's foreign policy, which was aimed at seeking compromise with American imperialism.

Later, the "big turn" in the CCP's policy, from compromise with Chiang to urging his overthrow, was also in line with the turn in the Kremlin's foreign policy. Having failed in its attempt to achieve a compromise with American imperialism, Moscow turned to a defensive strategy as a result of the cold war. The timing of the CCP's "big turn" in October 1947 followed immediately the formation of the Cominform at the Kremlin's orders in September of that year. This was not merely a coincidence and should suffice to prove that the CCP's turn, far from violating the Kremlin's objectives, was completed precisely under Moscow's direction.

Some comrades of the International have cited certain facts regarding the isolation of the CCP from Moscow during the Resistance War, in order to justify the theory that the latest turn in CCP policy was a result of violating the Kremlin's objectives. But these "facts" are just the opposite of the real facts. Before the war, the Kremlin's agents stayed permanently at Yenan (not openly), and there was regular radio communication between Yenan and Moscow. After the war, the Soviet Union sent its ambassador to Chungking, accompanied by its secret agents, so that it could openly and legally establish regular contact with the Chinese Communist delegation and its special agents in Chung-

---

* Chou En-lai was the fully empowered representative sent to Sian by the CCP to confer with Chang Shueh-liang about freeing Chiang Kai-shek, and to negotiate directly with Chiang on the terms for "collaboration between the Kuomintang and the CCP."

king, to dispatch news and instructions. Therefore we have sufficient reason to say that during the war the relations between the CCP and the Kremlin not only were not cut off, but on the contrary became closer than ever. This fact is clearly revealed in all CCP newspapers and documents of that period, which quickly echoed all of Moscow's propaganda and strategic positions. As for the postwar period, since the Soviet occupation of Manchuria, and with so many Soviet representatives working in the CCP and the army, the intimacy between Moscow and the CCP has been too evident to need further clarification.

In view of the above-mentioned facts, it is perfectly clear that to place the Chinese and Yugoslav parties on the same plane and to consider the former's conquest of power as the result of similar "mass pressure" and as overstepping the Kremlin's objectives is both mechanical and misleading. If we make a comparison of the policies and measures adopted by the YCP and those of the CCP in the course of the events, the distance between them would be even more apparent.

In the course of the anti-imperialist national liberation movement during 1941-45, the YCP already destroyed the bourgeois-landlord regime, step by step, and consummated its proletarian dictatorship in the first period after the war (October 1945), despite its somewhat abnormal character. Simultaneous with or a little later than the creation of the proletarian dictatorship (1945-46), it succeeded in carrying out agrarian reform and the statization of industry and banking, and expropriated private property by law. Meanwhile, on many important problems, the YCP had already formulated its own views, which were different from and independent of the Kremlin. It pursued its course according to its own experiences, that is, it submitted empirically to mass pressure against the Kremlin's objectives.*

But the CCP not only closely followed the Kremlin's foreign policy during the national liberation movement against Japanese imperialism, and devoted itself to seeking a compromise with the bourgeois-landlord regime regardless of mass pressure; but even after it conquered full power, it persisted in forming a "coalition government" with the national bourgeoisie and guaranteed them protection of their properties. It even tried to postpone carrying out the land reform to the latest possible date. Here we must

* See the "Resolution on the Yugoslav Revolution" adopted by the Ninth Plenum of the IEC, and "On the Class Nature of Yugoslavia" by Comrade Pablo.

note that the differences in attitude expressed by the YCP and the CCP in the course of the events are not quantitative, but qualitative. To assume therefore that the CCP has completed the same process of development as the YCP and ceased to be a Stalinist party in the classical sense of the word is to go entirely beyond the facts.*

But what explanation should be given for these differences? First, since the CCP withdrew from the cities to the countryside in 1928, it established a quite solid apparatus and army (the peasant army). For these twenty years it used this army and power to rule over the peasant masses—as we know, the backward and scattered peasants are the easiest to control—and hence a stubborn and self-willed bureaucracy took shape, especially in its manner of treating the masses. Even toward the workers and students in the KMT areas, it employed either ultimatistic or deceitful methods instead of persuasion.

Second, in ideology the CCP has further fortified and deepened the theory of Stalinism through its treatment of a series of important events: the defeat of the second revolution, the peasant wars, and the Resistance War against Japan, etc. This was especially true in its rejection of the criticism of its concepts and policies by Trotsky and the Chinese Trotskyists. (I should call the comrades' attention to the fact that Trotsky's critique of Stalinism was more extensive on the Chinese question than for any other country except the Soviet Union.)

Mao Tse-tung's "systematic" and dogmatic "New Democracy" is nothing but an ideologically and politically deepened and crystallized expression of Stalinism; i.e., it is the expression of obstinately holding onto the "revolution by stages" in direct challenge to the permanent revolution.

---

* [In preparing the manuscript of this article for composition, the publishers received from P'eng Shu-tse a comment on the views he expressed in 1951 on Yugoslavia. He writes: "During the Third Congress of the Fourth International, in my report I shared the position adopted by the leadership on the nature of the YCP. At that time, having just arrived in France, I did not have any recent information on the YCP and, having no time to study the question, I based my position on the information given at the congress. After the Korean War, where the YCP participated on the side of imperialism, I immediately started a serious study of the development of the YCP. My conclusion was that the YCP remained a Stalinist party and that the conflict between Tito and Stalin in 1949, a fight among bureaucrats, did not change the nature of that party" (March 18, 1975, letter from P'eng Shu-tse to the editors).—Ed.]

Third, over these two decades the CCP has received special attention from the Kremlin, and it follows that its relations with the latter are particularly intimate. After the Soviet Union occupied Manchuria and rearmed the CCP with weapons taken from the Japanese captives, the Kremlin's control over the CCP became more rigorous than ever.*

Because of these three characteristics, the CCP has neither been able to yield to mass pressure and modify its own political line, nor has it been easy for this party to overstep the Kremlin's objectives and go its own way. The YCP on the other hand has traversed an entirely different course. This party was almost created out of the national anti-imperialist mass movement, and in a comparatively short span of time. It was not able to form a bureaucracy and Stalinist ideology as tenacious as that of the CCP. Since it was actually quite isolated from the Kremlin during its resistance war, it was more disposed to empirically bend to mass pressure. It gradually modified its own political line in accord with the development of events until it finally went against the Kremlin's objectives. Therefore, we must say that the conquest of power in these two cases has only an apparent resemblance. In respect to the motivating causes (in terms of "pressure"), the manner adopted in taking power, and in the content of the power, the differences are quite great.

* In fact, this control was effected through internal strife. When the Soviet Union started to arm the troops of Lin Piao and other generals, it expressed skepticism regarding Mao Tse-tung and backed Li Li-san, Mao's old adversary, to be the political leader of the Communist army in Manchuria and the spokesman of the party. Moscow thus calculated to take Mao Tse-tung in tow and tame him. However, this immediately aroused resistance on Mao's part. On one hand, he ordered Liu Shao-ch'i to make a public statement declaring that Li Li-san was not authorized to speak on behalf of the CCP Central Committee (about the end of 1945). At the same time, he mobilized a big "ideological campaign" within the party against "Li Li-sanism" (or "sectarianism").

In view of this situation, and apprehensive of untoward consequences, the Kremlin sent a special mission to negotiate with Mao Tse-tung, which consented to place its "full confidence in him" and "help," provided he would be "loyal in executing the international line." Of course, Mao agreed to these terms, and in turn won the Kremlin's trust. Then Li Li-san was deprived of his post and replaced by someone else sent by Mao. Only after the feud between Mao and Li was finally settled did Mao become more cautious and assiduous in showing his obedience and support to the Soviet Union and in carrying out its directives.

From this judgment and explanation, should we deduce a further inference, that the CCP will at all times and under any conditions resist mass pressure and never come into conflict with the Kremlin? No. What we have demonstrated above is that the most important turns the CCP underwent in the past were entirely the result of pressure from the Kremlin, and in violation of the will of the masses. Even the present "turn" toward the seizure of power was not a product of its yielding to mass pressure and going against the Kremlin's objectives, but, on the contrary, resulted from the mortal pressure of Chiang Kai-shek, and was taken in complete agreement with the Kremlin. However, .in ordinary circumstances, in order to maintain its own existence and continue its development, the CCP is obliged to seek support from certain layers of the masses and to establish a base among them. Accordingly, it would more or less concede to demands of the masses within certain limits and within the possibilities permitted by its own control; i.e., bend to mass pressure.

In the past, the CCP's policy passed through not a few "leftward" oscillations, such as the limited agrarian reform policy offered in May 1947, the "liquidation of the Right deviation in the land reform" in the period from the end of 1947 to the spring of 1948, and some comparatively leftward measures taken after its conquest of power. These are the solid facts of its yielding to mass pressure. It is possible that this kind of leftward turn will appear more often and to a greater extent in the future. Also, for the same reasons we can believe that in the past certain differences or conflicts must have occurred between the CCP and the Kremlin. But these conflicts have not yet burst to the surface. For example, the dispute between Mao and Li discussed above may be a significant reflection of this existing conflict, which is not only unavoidable in the period ahead but will be further intensified. So I must say that the error made by Comrade Germain, taken up earlier, is not one of principle, but of fact.

Yet I must also point out that the mistake made on such an important question may not only give rise to a series of other mistakes—such as underestimation of the bureaucratism of the CCP, its Stalinist ideology and methods, and overoptimism on perspectives concerning the CCP, etc.—but may also lead to errors in principle. For example, some comrades in our International have already asserted that the CCP regime is a "proletarian dictatorship," because they consider that events in China are in the same category as the Yugoslav events, and because the

YCP regime has already become a proletarian dictatorship. Proceeding by abstract deduction according to formal logic, the CCP regime is doubtlessly also a "proletarian dictatorship." (There will be further discussion of this question later in this report.)

Because this way of transposing facts to suit certain formulas carries with it the danger of committing mistakes in principle, we should be very cautious in applying "principles," and especially formulas deduced from principles. We cannot group events which are similar only in appearance under the same principle or the same formula, or force events into accommodation with a given principle or formula.

First of all, we must examine and analyze the concrete facts of the events themselves, particularly taking account of whatever exceptional circumstances have played a decisive role in the events, and judge whether this event conforms to a certain principle or formula, whether it actually is the true expression of this principle or formula. As Lenin said, the facts are forever alive, while formulas often tend to become rigid.

Our movement has assumed and stressed that it is possible for the masses to pass beyond the boundaries of Stalinism, and that hidden, profound contradictions exist between various Communist parties and the Kremlin. Under certain specific conditions an entire Communist party may modify its political line, go beyond the Kremlin's objectives, and lead the masses to the seizure of power. This principle and this formula is correct in its basic theoretical premise, and has already been justified by the Yugoslav events (or to be more exact, it is rather derived from them). But here we must particularly note one thing, and that is precisely the "certain specific conditions." Although under certain specific conditions a Communist party could be pushed by mass pressure to seize power in violation of the Kremlin's aims (as in the case of the YCP), under certain other specific conditions a Communist party could come to power not necessarily through mass pressure, meanwhile receiving instructions from the Kremlin (or at least not violating its objectives). This is exactly what has happened in China.

We believe that similar events may possibly be repeated in other Asian countries (Vietnam, Burma, etc.). What the Kremlin fears is the victory of a genuine revolutionary movement of the workers, especially in the advanced countries, simply because it will not be able to control this victorious revolution, which will in turn threaten its very existence. If it does not face this kind of

threat, and if its action will not involve immediate direct intervention by imperialism, the Kremlin would not give up an
opportunity to extend its sphere of influence and would naturally
permit a Communist party under its control to take power. This is
the lesson that can be drawn from the Chinese events and that
we must accept. While this still falls under the heading of the
conquest of power by a Communist party, we should at least see
it as something supplementary to the lesson of the Yugoslav
events. Only in this manner can we avoid falling into the mistake
of transforming a principle into a rigid formula, of imposing this
formula on every apparently similar event, and thereby producing a series of erroneous conclusions.

We Marxists react toward events by analyzing the concrete
facts of their development with our methods and principles,
testing and enriching our principles through this analysis, or if
necessary, modifying our principles and formulas, for the truth is
always concrete.

Is the CCP's victory the beginning
of the third Chinese revolution?

The resolution on the Chinese question of the Seventh Plenum
of the International Executive Committee stated, "The victory of
Mao Tse-tung over Chiang Kai-shek is the beginning of the third
Chinese revolution." When this resolution first arrived in China
(autumn 1949), the leading body of our party—the Political
Bureau—agreed with it in general. But because of the Political
Bureau's urgent need to move, it was not able to discuss the
resolution in detail and express its opinions in written form. Then
doubts arose among some comrades regarding the International's
resolution, and the most acute controversy of recent years began.*

Some of the responsible comrades are in complete agreement
with the views of the International (comrades Chiao and Ma, who
formerly expressed their disagreement are now becoming the
major supporters of the International's position), while other
responsible comrades are in strong opposition. We have selected
four of the most representative articles in this controversy and

* The first disagreement to appear in writing was "The Significance
and the Nature of the Victory of the Chinese Stalinist Movement," an
article written by Comrades Chiao and Ma, published in the Chinese
edition of *Fourth International*, vol. 1, no. 2, April 1950.

translated them into English for reference.[8] So in this report it is not necessary to recount in detail the points of divergence in their discussion. I am simply going to give my personal criticism and explanation of the essential arguments, particularly those of the comrades with oppositional views.

On the question of the revolutionary situation

The major argument of the comrades in opposition is that the CCP's ascent to power is not based on the revolutionary actions of the masses, especially the workers (i.e., from general strikes to armed insurrection), but has relied entirely on the peasant armed forces and purely military actions. On the basis of our traditional conception of revolution and the experiences of revolutions in modern times—especially the Russian October revolution—they conceive of the revolution only in the sense that huge masses, especially the working class, are mobilized from bottom to top, go beyond the domain of the general democratic struggle to armed rebellion, directly destroy the state apparatus of the ruling class, and proceed to build up a new regime. That we can call the beginning of the victory of a real revolution.

Now, this movement under the CCP's leadership not only did not at all mobilize the working masses, but even refrained from appealing to the peasant masses to organize, to rise for action, and engage in a revolutionary struggle (ousting the landlords, distributing the land, etc.). As the facts stand, the CCP relied solely on the military action of the peasant army instead of the revolutionary action of the worker and peasant masses. From this, these comrades asserted that this victory is only the victory of a peasant war, and not the beginning of the third Chinese revolution.

We must admit that the traditional conception of revolution held by these comrades is completely correct, and the facts they enumerate are irrefutable. But they have forgotten a small matter. That is, that the epoch in which we live is not that of the victory of the October revolution, the time of Lenin and Trotsky. It is the epoch in which the heritage of the October revolution— the Soviet socialist workers' state—has been usurped by the bureaucracy of Stalin and has reached the point of extreme degeneration. These are the main features of this epoch:

On the one hand, the capitalist world, having experienced two world wars, is in utter decay, while the objective revolutionary conditions have gone from ripe to overripe. On the other hand, the Stalin bureaucracy, by dint of the prestige inherited from the October revolution and the material resources of the Soviet Union, has done everything it can to retain its grip on the Communist parties of the world, and through them it attempts to subordinate the revolutionary movements of different countries to its own diplomatic interests. These exceptional circumstances have not led universally to the frustration and defeat of revolutionary movements in various countries; in some countries the revolutionary movements have only been deformed. The victory of the movement led by the CCP is a prominent example of this deformation of its revolution.

As we have said, viewed from the aspect of the CCP's attempt to avoid the mobilization of the masses, particularly the worker masses, and its conquering of power on the basis of peasant armed forces, this event is indeed far from conforming to a classic or normal revolution. But considered from the standpoint of its overthrow of the bourgeois-landlord regime of Chiang Kai-shek, its widespread practice of land reform, and its political resistance against imperialism and its struggle for national independence, it is undeniably not only "progressive," but revolutionary. Further, it marks a great dividing line in modern Chinese history. The destruction of the bloody twenty-year rule of Chiang Kai-shek and the blow dealt to the imperialist powers who have trodden on the Chinese people for centuries are quite sufficient to prove that this event can stack up with the first Chinese revolution (1911). Inasmuch as a sizable general land reform has been carried out (no matter how incomplete), the feudal remnants that have persisted for thousands of years are for the first time being shoveled away on a wide scale. And since this work is still being carried on, should we still insist that it is not an epoch-making revolutionary movement?

The comrades in opposition contend that they have completely acknowledged the progressive aspects of this movement, but nevertheless, they are by no means identical with the initial triumph of a real revolution, or the beginning of the third revolution, since they have been achieved by military and bureaucratic means.

Though we admit this fact, our conclusion cannot simply be a condemnation of the process and its outcome as "not revolutionary." The only correct view is to say that this is not a typical or normal revolution, but a distorted, damaged, and hence a deformed revolutionary movement. In order to obtain a more precise understanding of this question of deformed revolution, let us recall the discussions on the nature of the states in the buffer countries of Eastern Europe.

In these buffer countries, with the exception of Yugoslavia, the dispossession of the bourgeoisie from power, the land reform procedures, and the nationalizations of industry, banks, and means of transport and exchange were either not at all or only to a small degree carried out through the revolutionary action of the worker and peasant masses. The statized properties and enterprises of the new regime have never been placed under the supervision and control of the masses, but are, under occupation by the Soviet army, operated and monopolized by the Communist bureaucrats of the Kremlin order. Concentrating on this fact, various minorities among the sections of the International—which are in fact elements already outside of or on the way to quitting our movement if they insist on their views—dogmatize about the nature of these states as "state capitalist" or "bureaucratic collectivist."

However, the International Secretariat of our International, using the traditional method employed by Trotsky in studying and characterizing the nature of the Soviet state under the rule of the Stalin bureaucracy as a degenerated workers' state, has held that these buffer states have already become deformed workers' states assimilated into the Soviet Union. As the property relations in these countries have been fundamentally changed, i.e., statized, and since this statization is an indispensable material premise for the transformation from capitalism to socialism, on the basis of this fundamental change in property relations we can then assert the change in the nature of the state.

But while maintaining this assertion, the International has not overlooked the detestable way the bureaucrats of the Soviet Union and the Communist parties of these countries are monopolizing all economic and administrative power and the way the police and the GPU are strangling the freedom and initiative of the masses. It is precisely in view of these *facts* that our International calls these states *deformed* or *abnormal* workers' states. This is the only correct way to dialectically comprehend the events, the only way to "call things by their right names."

If our oppositional Chinese comrades would adopt the method used by the International in deciding the character of the state in the buffer countries—the traditional method of Trotskyism—to evaluate the victory of the CCP, it would be very plain that no matter how the CCP succeeded in seizing power, even though it was by purely military or bureaucratic means, the things it has accomplished are revolutionary. The overthrow of Chiang's regime, the land reform, and the relative political independence now won are goals that have to be achieved in the *permanent* process going from the democratic revolution to the socialist revolution.

But the CCP has not mobilized the worker masses. It has not pushed the revolution forward through the agency of the working class leading the peasant masses. In other words, because it substituted the military-bureaucratic methods of Stalinism for the Bolshevik revolutionary methods of mobilizing the masses, this revolution has been gravely distorted and injured, and its features are misshapen to such an extent that they are hardly recognizable. However, we Marxists judge all things and events not by their appearance, but by the essence concealed under the appearance. Therefore, no matter how ugly and abhorrent the appearance of the Soviet Union is under the rule of Stalin's bureaucracy, since it preserves the nationalized property created by the October revolution we still recognize it as a workers' state—a *degenerated* workers' state. And although from their very birth the buffer states in Eastern Europe were already seriously disfigured by Stalin's bureaucratism, and have revealed such monstrous deformity, we must nevertheless call them workers' states, although *deformed* workers' states.

In the same way, no matter how the movement led by the CCP is distorted and damaged by its bureaucratic methods, because it has overthrown Chiang's regime, has secured considerable independence, and carried out a certain degree of land reform, we must recognize it as a revolution, although an abnormal revolution.

We must understand that our epoch is a transitional one, lying between capitalism and socialism, the most consequential and complex epoch in the history of humanity. Hence, many of the events and movements, under the influence of diverse factors, develop out of accord with the normal procedures of our logical thinking that are derived from historical experience or principles. Moreover, the extraordinary expansion and interference of Stalinism following the degeneration of the first workers' state—which in the last analysis is also one of the products of this complex and convulsive epoch—has further pulled these events and movements out of their normal orbit and served to distort them. In this epoch, anyone who demands that all events and movements conform to one's own ideal or norm, and who would only recognize and participate in those that are considered normal and that conform to one's ideals, is a perfect utopian, who either hurls meaningless curses—or "criticisms"—at events and movements, or wages a desperate fight against history. These people have nothing in common with Marxists.

We Trotskyists must bear the responsibility for the coming revolution. We should not only maintain "our own ideal" and understand the "normal development of the movement," but should particularly understand the abnormal events and imperfect movements produced under exceptional conditions. In other words, we must recognize the situation already coming into existence, acknowledge its reality even though it may be inconsistent with our "norm" or unpleasant. And we must carry on an untiring fight in face of this situation to alter it in the course of the struggle and turn it toward our goal.

The entire Chinese mainland has now fallen into the CCP's hands. The whole movement has been placed under its control or leadership. This is an absolute reality, although distorted and contrary to our ideals. But unless we accept the reality of this movement, penetrate it, and actively join in all mass struggles, all our criticisms will be futile as well as harmful. We must seek to influence the masses with our Trotskyist revolutionary program, try patiently to convince and to win the confidence of the masses in the course of the struggle, help them step by step to disentangle themselves, through their own experiences, from the illusions and control of Mao Tse-tung's opportunism and bureaucratism, and eventually change the orientation of this movement. This task is, of course, extremely difficult and it will not necessarily proceed in tune with our efforts. But at least by participating in this movement we can lay down a basis for future work. Then, when we are faced with a more favorable situation, we shall be able to intervene and even to lead the movement.

If we refuse to recognize the CCP's victory as the beginning of a deformed revolution, if we do not participate in the movement positively in order to rescue it from deformation, or if we only express some passive criticisms of the CCP, we shall surely fall into the bog of sectarianism—as our Chinese minority has done. We would then quit the movement and the masses and finally, inevitably withdraw from all practical political struggles and be swept away by the historical current.

I must also point out that our oppositional comrades have committed another mechanical error by maintaining that the CCP-led movement was purely a peasant war and for that reason denying the significance of its mass character. The CCP's peasant army is itself a mass movement—the peasant in uniform—embracing the most active sectors of the rural toilers. But even more, behind it stands the great mass of the peasantry.

Historical experience has shown us that once the peasant movement erupts, it is often involved in armed struggle. In the second Chinese revolution, when the peasant masses in Kwangtung and Hunan were organized into peasants' associations, their armed forces appeared almost immediately, since it was quite impossible for them to fight the landlords and the country gentry without a substantial force. This has become almost a law of the peasant movement. We must also note that the present army differs greatly from any former peasant army. It has been systematically organized and trained by the Stalinist party, which is more or less equipped with modern knowledge and techniques. It has been endowed with a nationwide and up-to-date program of democratic reform as the general direction of the struggle, no matter how opportunist this program has been. It is for this reason that we cannot call this movement simply a peasant war but an abnormal revolutionary movement, and only this designation is true to the facts and to dialectic logic.

On the other hand, the Chinese comrades who support the International's resolution have gone to the opposite extreme in their attempt to demonstrate that the CCP's victory is the beginning of the third Chinese revolution, that the movement led by the CCP is a mass movement, and that the change in its policy is the result of mass pressure. They exaggerate or even misinterpret the facts. This is just as harmful. For example, Comrade Chiao and Comrade Ma arrive at the conclusion that the CCP's change in policy was the result of mass pressure and represented a mass movement by means of misdating the "beginning of the third Chinese revolution" from October 1947, when the CCP formally called for the overthrow of Chiang's regime. This is not only mechanical, but is entirely contradictory to the actual facts, as I have indicated above. Moreover, Comrade Ma says:

From the point of view of the number of masses mobilized, the present revolution is even more normal than the second revolution, because the masses organized in the latter numbered only about ten millions, while even before the "Liberation Army" crossed the Yangtze River, there were already more than one hundred million farmers rising to distribute the land.*

This kind of exposition is exaggerated and also fundamentally wrong in its conception of the mass movement. Comrade Chung Yuan has refuted and criticized it fully in his article "The Problem of the So-called 'Revolutionary Situation.'" I think that his refutation is correct and consistent with the historical facts. Here I would like to emphasize one point. In the second Chinese revolution, the majority of the working class was organized in such groups as the Canton-Hong Kong Strike Committee and the Shanghai General Labor Union (which were then functioning practically as soviets). The workers were mobilized, and occupied the leading position in the nationwide movement, launching a number of general strikes and giant demonstrations. In addition, the working class engaged in several victorious armed revolts, such as the case of the worker masses in Hangkow and Chiuchiang, who seized the British settlements, and in Shanghai where they occupied the entire city with the exception of the foreign concessions.

But in this movement of the CCP, from its beginning to the conquest of power, there has neither been the rising of the working masses in any city to the point of general strikes or insurrections, nor even a small-scale strike or demonstration. Most of the workers were passive and inert, or at most showed a certain hopeful attitude toward this movement. This is an indisputable fact. How can we compare this present movement with the revolutionary movement of the second Chinese revolution? The International's resolution has clearly asserted: "The victory of Mao Tse-tung over Chiang Kai-shek is the military victory of a peasant revolt over a thoroughly collapsed regime." That is to say, this victory of the CCP is not the political victory of a real revolutionary movement of the worker and peasant masses over the bourgeois power. So this only helps to prove that Comrade Ma, who ardently supports the International's resolution, has gone too far, has idealized the Communist-led movement. This idealization of events will not only foster illusions but will objectively lead to wrong judgments. Both will be dangerous, because illusions are always the origin of disappointment or

* See "Why Is This Civil War.Called a Revolution and the Importance of This Recognition."

discouragement, while wrong judgments will inevitably become the root of erroneous policies.

We should never overlook the extremely serious dangers implicit in the deformation of the third Chinese revolution fostered by the CCP: the tenacious opportunism, the imperious bureaucracy, the severe control over the masses, the hostility toward revolutionary ideas, and the brutal persecution of the revolutionary elements, especially the Trotskyists. (Our organization has been disrupted in many places on the mainland; many comrades have been arrested, imprisoned, forced to "repent," and a few of our most responsible comrades have already been executed.)

All these dangerous factors combined preclude any overoptimism in regard to the development and perspective of the third Chinese revolution that is now underway. They will make it extremely difficult for Trotskyists to work in this movement.

Despite all these circumstances we should never adopt a sectarian or pessimistic attitude, nor give up our efforts and our revolutionary responsibility to try to push this movement forward or transform it.

At the same time we must also reject all naive ultraoptimism, which always tends to disregard the difficulties in the movement and the hardships in our work. At the beginning, ultraoptimists might throw themselves into the movement with great zeal. But when they encounter the severe difficulties in the course of their work, they will become disheartened and shrink back. However, with the entire perspective of our movement in sight, we Trotskyists always hold firm to our unbending faith and revolutionary optimism. In other words, we profoundly believe that the victory of the proletarian revolution in the whole world and the reconstruction of human society can be accomplished only under the banner and the program of Trotskyism, the most enriched and deepened Marxism-Leninism of modern times. Yet we should not overlook the formidable roadblocks on the way from the present period to the eventual victory, particularly the obstacles laid down by Stalinism.

We must first of all bring to light these obstacles, then overcome them with the most precise program, correct methods, and utmost patience and perseverance.

The sectarians find their excuses in the fact that the movement does not conform to their preconceived norms and they attempt to flee from it in advance. The naive optimists idealize the movement. But as soon as they discover that the movement does not follow the track of their idealization, they leave it. Revolutionary optimists have nothing in common with these two sorts of people. Since we have the strongest faith in the victory of the revolution, since we understand the enormous difficulties lying on the road to this victory, we cut our path through the thorniest thickets only with revolutionary methods and absolute persistence to reach the ultimate goal.

Confronted with Mao's victory, serious controversies have been raised in the Chinese organization through the discussion of the party's past policy. These controversies have produced certain unhealthy effects on the party. Though it is not possible for me to dwell in detail on a description and criticism of these controversial opinions, I should express my fundamental attitude toward this discussion (especially since many Chinese comrades have asked me to do so).

It is altogether reasonable that a political organization, on the morrow of a great event, should examine and discuss its past policy carefully in order to readjust its political line. Therefore I do not agree with some comrades who object to this discussion. But I should also insist that we must proceed with the discussion in a fully responsible way, both for the revolutionary tasks and for our party, and in a circumspect, exact, and precise manner. It is absolutely wrong to criticize at will the party's past policy with giddy and bombastic gestures which create confusion and centrifugal tendencies in the party. The experience of history has already taught us that a political party is most susceptible to centrifugal tendencies under the pressure of a great event, especially in face of growing difficulties in its conditions of work.

If at this moment criticism of the party's past policy assumes an indiscreet, exaggerated, or unjust attitude, it will be most apt to cause the rank and file of the party to falter in their convictions, encourage the development of centrifugal tendencies, and finally lead to a terrible split.

Unfortunately, some of our comrades are not prudent enough in their criticisms of the policy we adopted in the past period. The article written by Comrade Chiao, "Thesis on the Ideological Rearmament," is a notable example. Though this article is aimed at correcting the "sectarian tendency," its criticism of the party's past policy is not only exaggerated but misleading. In his view, or at least according to his way of writing, it seems that the party's whole past political line was fundamentally wrong and therefore, following the example of Lenin in posing the April Theses, "the party must be ideologically rearmed."

However, as a result, this attitude only stimulated strong

protests and criticisms from another group of comrades. These criticisms found their first expression in "Rearmament or Revisionism?" written by Comrade Ming.

In reality, our party has maintained and struggled over long years for the traditional line of Trotskyism, the line of the permanent revolution. The great events—the Sino-Japanese War and China's involvement in the Second World War, as well as the party's internal struggles during the critical periods of these two events, first the struggle against Ch'en Tu-hsiu's right opportunism and then the fight against the ultraleft sectarianism of the minority group led by Cheng Chao-lin—have justified the political line we upheld in the past.

During the civil war between the Kuomintang and the CCP, our basic line and our position toward the CCP have also been correct and coincide with the fundamental attitude of the International's resolution on the Chinese civil war.*

After the CCP set out toward the seizure of power, the program put forward by our party—contained in "An Open Letter to the Members of the CCP" adopted by the plenum of the Central Executive Committee of our party—corresponded almost entirely to the program adopted by the Seventh Plenum of the International. Comrade Chiao's appeal for an "ideological rearmament of our party" is tantamount to saying that the party in the past, or at least in the course of the CCP's conquest of power, "deserted Trotskyist ideology" and needs to be "rearmed" by returning to Trotskyist ideas. This presentation is not only exaggerated and a distortion of the facts, but it is actually an insult to the party. Therefore it naturally has stirred up vehement indignation, outrage, and protests, and even, to a certain extent, confusion and vacillations among the comrades. It was with the premonition of such consequences that I forewarned our comrades not to be too hasty in making a 180-degree turn.

Nevertheless, I do not mean to say that our party has never made any mistakes in the past, especially in the recent events of

* See the "Resolution on the Chinese Civil War" adopted by our party in January 1947 and the International's resolution "Struggles of the Colonial Peoples and the World Revolution," adopted by the Second World Congress. [The first of these documents has not been published in English; the Second World Congress of the Fourth International was held in Paris in April 1948, and the resolution referred to here was published in *Fourth International* magazine (New York), vol. 9, no. 5, July 1948, p. 144.—Ed.]

the CCP's conquest of power. I have already pointed out that our party did not envisage the victorious conquest of power by the CCP. From this major error in estimating the whole event flows a series of mistakes on the evaluation of events in the course of their development, and certain tactical errors in our propaganda to the outside world. These errors in estimation have affected our attitude to the entire event, which more or less tended to passive criticism and an underestimation of its objective revolutionary significance. This is what we seriously admit and must correct. But, as I have said above, these are mistakes in estimating the events rather than mistakes of principles, and therefore can be easily redressed.

As we know, the best Marxists—Marx, Engels, Lenin, Trotsky, etc.—were able to maintain correctness in principle and in method, but could not guarantee accuracy in every estimate of the development of events. Marxism is the most effective scientific method of predicting social phenomena. But it has not yet reached such exactness as meteorology in foretelling the weather or astronomy in astral phenomena, since social phenomena are far more complicated than those of nature. So Marx, Engels, Lenin, and Trotsky also made mistakes in their evaluation of events. Examples of this sort include the estimation made by Marx and Engels on the development of the situation after the failure of the 1848 revolution; Lenin and Trotsky's optimistic anticipation of revolutionary possibilities in Europe after the October revolution; and Trotsky's appraisal of the prospects for Stalinism during the Second World War. What distinguished them was not infallibility in estimating any and all events, but their constant, cautious, and exact observation of the objective process of events. And once they realized that the development of events did not conform to their original estimates or that their estimates were wrong, they immediately readjusted or reestimated them. This is the attitude of a real Marxist, and is the example we should try to follow.

The class nature of the CCP and the new regime

Though there has not been much discussion among the Chinese comrades on this question, some opinions exist among the comrades of the International that tend to deviate from the Marxist line. I therefore consider it necessary to raise this question for serious discussion and to make a definite appraisal that can serve as the premise in determining our position in relation to the CCP and its new regime.

About the nature of the CCP, virtually all the Chinese comrades have declared it to be a petty-bourgeois party based on the peasantry. This has been a traditional conception of the Chinese Trotskyists for the past twenty years, and is one defined by Trotsky himself.

Beginning with 1930, Trotsky repeatedly pointed out that the CCP had gradually degenerated from a workers' party into a peasant party. Once in a letter to the Chinese comrades he even said that the CCP was following the same path as the Social Revolutionary Party in Russia. The main reason for this judgment was as follows: After the defeat of the second revolution, the CCP gave up the urban workers' movement, left the urban proletariat, and turned entirely toward the countryside. It threw its whole strength into village guerrilla fighting and therefore absorbed into the party a great number of peasants. As a result, the party's composition became purely peasant. Despite the participation of some worker elements who retreated from the cities, the tiny number of these workers was not enough to determine the party's composition. Furthermore during the prolonged period of living in the countryside they also assimilated the peasant outlook into their ideology, little by little.*

As we know, Trotsky's assessment of the nature of the CCP was never revised up to his death. The composition of the CCP and its nature as described in the last part of Isaacs's *The Tragedy of the Chinese Revolution* clearly reflected this conception because his book was read and corrected by Trotsky himself before publication.[9]

Has there been any alteration in the CCP's composition in the direction of the working class since Trotsky's death? Not only has there been no fundamental change, but the petty-bourgeois composition represented by peasants and intellectuals has, on the contrary, been strengthened. The unprecedented growth of the CCP during and after the Resistance War was almost completely due to an influx of peasants and petty-bourgeois intellectuals.

---

* All these ideas can be found in several articles written by Trotsky on the Chinese question and in his letters to the Chinese comrades. [These materials have since been published in English in the collection *Leon Trotsky on China* (New York: Monad Press, 1976).—Ed.]

Before its conquest of power, the party claimed about 3.5 million members. Of this total number, the worker element was very weak and at most was not more than 5 percent (including manual laborers). We can therefore confirm that up to the time it came to power the CCP still remained petty bourgeois in composition.

Despite all this, some of our International comrades consider that the CCP has already become a workers' party. Comrade Germain, for example, is of this opinion. When we referred to Trotsky's characterization of the CCP as a petty-bourgeois peasant party, he replied: "I know, I admit that was true before. But since the CCP seized power and came into the cities, it has become transformed into a workers' party."

This assertion is based on the argument that the nature of a party is not determined simply by the criterion of composition, but also by the role it plays. From the fact that the CCP has overthrown the Kuomintang bourgeois system and set up its own power, it is quite evident that the nature of the party has changed. Unfortunately, this kind of reasoning leads to only a superficial resemblance to the truth, because the CCP overthrew the Chiang Kai-shek regime not through the revolutionary action of the working class leading the peasant masses, but by relying exclusively on the peasant armed forces. Therefore the newly established regime still remains bourgeois. (We will return to the characterization of this regime.) So how can this fact be used as a criterion to judge the change in the nature of the party? On the contrary, we could say that the very fact that the CCP did not mobilize the working masses and depended solely on the peasant armed forces to conquer power reveals the petty-bourgeois nature of this party.

Has the nature of the party changed, then, after it came into the cities? The answer must again be in the negative. A political party can never change its composition in twenty-four hours, especially in the case of the CCP, which has an unusually large peasant base. We can be assured that up to now the CCP is still a party in which peasant members are predominant, and hence is still largely petty bourgeois in nature. But this does not mean that the peasant character of the party is now fixed and invariable. In fact, since this party has seized power and occupied the great cities, in its eagerness to seek support among the working class it has empirically stressed recruiting its members from the workers. At the same time, it has temporarily ceased to recruit peasants into the party. Following this bent, it is possible in the future for the CCP to gradually change its composition from a petty-bourgeois peasant party into a more or less workers' party. However, this is a future possibility and cannot replace the reality for today.

The resolution of the Seventh Plenum of the IS has pointed out: "*Socially*, the Chinese Communist Party is . . . a bi-partite party which even to this day has only an insignificant base in the urban proletariat."[10]

This is really a very cautious characterization of the nature of the party. If this appraisal is considered as a summary formula for this transitional period in which the CCP is attempting to transform itself from a peasant party into a workers' party (purely from the viewpoint of social composition), it is quite acceptable. But we must not forget the serious lesson disclosed in Trotsky's criticism of the "worker-peasant party": Any attempt to organize a worker-peasant party under the conditions of present-day society (including in the backward countries) is reactionary, petty-bourgeois, and extremely dangerous to the proletarian revolution. Because in a "worker-peasant party" it is not the proletarian elements who assimilate the peasant but quite the reverse, the peasant members overwhelm the former. Therefore, from the revolutionary point of view, it is never possible for two classes to establish an equal weight in a common party. Accordingly, a so-called two-class "worker-peasant party" is always a reactionary tool of petty-bourgeois politicians to deceive the working class.[11]

In the documents on China, the International has not yet specifically clarified the class nature of the new regime (the so-called People's Democratic Dictatorship). Despite some differences in interpretation among the Chinese comrades, the general opinion is that this regime rests on a petty-bourgeois social foundation with the peasantry as its main element, and is a Bonapartist military dictatorship. (The Chinese minority is an exception, since it has already asserted that the CCP regime represents "state capitalism" or "bureaucratic collectivism.")

In the last analysis, therefore, in view of its fundamental stand on property relations, it is a bourgeois regime. Here, however, some of our comrades hold a completely opposite view. I was told by one comrade that the CCP regime is a proletarian dictatorship. Though he did not offer any reasons, I surmise that he very likely deduced this conclusion from the formula given for the YCP regime in Yugoslavia. We can find another view in the formal document which regards the CCP regime as one character-ized by "dual power."*

Since such diverse ideas prevail among our International comrades, especially among leading comrades, it is necessary, in my opinion, to undertake a thorough clarification. First of all, let us start with the notion of "proletarian dictatorship."

To determine the nature of any regime, we Marxists must check on two essential conditions: the class relations and the property relations, the latter being more decisive. We call the regime established by the Bolsheviks after the October revolution in Russia a proletarian dictatorship because power was completely in the hands of the proletariat supported by the peasant masses even though there was not yet a fundamental change in the property relations at that time. The change in the class relations sufficed for us to call it a proletarian dictatorship. We can also call the YCP regime after 1947 a proletarian dictatorship mainly because the property relationships have been basically altered, i.e., from private ownership to statization of property. Despite the fact that the YCP's power is not entirely controlled by the proletariat, and is still marked by certain bureaucratic deforma-tions, the fundamental change in property ownership suffices to qualify this regime as a *deformed* proletarian dictatorship.

But what is the real situation with the regime established by the CCP? In class relations, this regime claims to be a coalition government of four classes (workers, peasants, the petty bourgeoi-sie, and the national bourgeoisie). It is therefore very clear that this regime is not controlled or "dictated" by the proletariat. In fact, the social basis of this regime is constituted by the petty bourgeoisie, of which the peasants form the major part. Though the bourgeoisie does not have a decisive role in the government, yet in comparison with the proletariat it is still prominent (at least in appearance). In property relations, this regime not only has not abolished the private-property system, but on the con-trary has deliberately enacted laws and constitutions to protect private ownership, to develop the economy of so-called New Democracy, i.e., a nonsocialist economy. It must, therefore, be asked: on what ground can we characterize this regime as a "proletarian dictatorship"?

The argument brought forth by Comrade Germain on the "dual

* See Comrade Germain's "The Third Chinese Revolution," in the January-February 1951 issue of *Fourth International.*

character" of this new regime is in the following passage: "Whether it wished to or not, the government found itself compelled to institute a genuine *dual power* in Southern China. On the provincial and district level, the majority of the old cadres remain in place; on the local level, their class enemies, the poor peasants of the *Peasants' Associations* bid fair to seize all the actual power in carrying out the agrarian reform."[12]

Despite the obscurity in this passage, it seems to mean that power at the provincial and county level is bourgeois in character, whereas in the countryside the power is in the hands of the poor peasants. Let us assume that this is true. But we cannot conclude from this that the CCP regime in the South has a dual character, because the power of the poor peasants is not identical with proletarian power. At most it can only be considered as the most thoroughgoing petty-bourgeois peasant power. The change in the petty-bourgeois character of poor peasant power is possible only when it is under the leadership of the urban proletariat. This is precisely the condition that is lacking in the present regime, so this idea of a dual character is too inadequate to stand criticism.

To enable our comrades to recognize more concretely and more precisely the nature of this new regime, I will point out several of its important characteristics:

a. The major support of this regime is the enormous peasant army, which is entirely under the control of the already Stalinized (or bureaucratized) CCP. Hence the CCP has absolute control and decision-making power over the regime.

b. Representatives of the bourgeoisie and the top layers of the petty bourgeoisie occupy honored positions in this regime, but they have no direct decisive function. They can only indirectly affect the regime through their economic and social influence.

c. Though a handful of individuals among the workers have been appointed to participate in the government (very few in important posts), the working class as a whole remains in a subordinate position. The working masses are deprived of the fundamental right to freely elect their own representatives—such as soviets or other similar workers' representative committees, etc.—to participate in and supervise this regime. General political rights—freedom of speech, assembly and association, publication, belief, etc.—are considerably limited, and even completely forbidden (such as strikes). Consequently, though the workers are hailed as the "master" by this regime, in reality they only have the right to petition within the "bounds of law" for an improvement of their living conditions.

d. On the social and economic plane, the regime has carried out land reform on a considerable scale, and is prepared to complete it and wipe out the feudal remnants "step by step"—in line with the CCP's bureaucratic methods. This is an indeed unprecedented and great reform. But it is confined within the framework of preserving the "industrial and commercial properties" of the landlords and rich peasants, and free purchase of land, i.e., nonviolation of capitalist property relations.

e. In relation to the capitalist properties, with the exception of those properties nationalized at the outset (the so-called bureaucratic capital), which the new regime took over and transformed into nationalized properties, all other kinds of private property is being left untouched and offered protection by new laws. Despite this, through its regulations the new regime imposes relatively strict restrictions on the interests of private capital. As a result, the workers under this regime, though still remaining in the position of hired laborers, can at the same time avoid overly severe exploitation.

From these characteristics, we can clearly see that the nature of this regime is by no means very simple and normal. Since this regime is a product of the combination of exceptional historical conditions, its nature and the forms it takes are both complex and abnormal. It is scarcely possible to find another regime in modern history analogous to it. If we compare this regime to that of the Jacobins during the French Revolution, its features may be made more distinct.

The social base of the Jacobin Party was the then-urban toiling masses in general—the "sansculottes." It carried out a thorough land reform and eliminated feudal influences. The CCP regime is founded on the petty-bourgeois social base of the rural population and it is also carrying out the land reform and eliminating the feudal remnants. Both of these regimes are consummate dictatorships. From these essential aspects, these two regimes bear great resemblances to one another. But the time of the Jacobins was a period when capitalism was still in its embryonic stage. Its land reform and uprooting of feudal influences fulfilled a great historical task for the bourgeoisie, and opened the broad highway for later capitalist development. This regime was thus thoroughly revolutionary, and only the regime established by the Russian Bolsheviks has been able to match it in significance. The epoch in which the CCP exists is entirely different: it is the period of the utter decline and approaching fall of capitalism.

In this epoch, genuine revolutionary power must be founded on the social base of the proletariat (the modern "sansculottes"), even in backward countries. The realization of land reform should not and cannot clear the way for capitalist development but must immediately open the prospects for socialism. Hence it must proceed in line with the expropriation of the landlords and the private properties of the bourgeoisie. This is just what was carried out by the regime of the Russian Bolshevik Party under the leadership of Lenin and Trotsky. Since the CCP regime is proceeding in the opposite way, in the last analysis it will eventually be a stumbling block in the course of historical development, and is in essence reactionary.

In conclusion, in class relations, this new regime bases itself on the petty-bourgeois peasants and attempts to "arbitrate" between the proletariat and the bourgeoisie. In property relations, it has abolished feudal land ownership, built up the capitalist land system, and nationalized the greater part of the factories. On the other hand, it is conferring protection on capitalist private property, and seeks to "coordinate" the relationship between nationalized property and private property in order in the long run to construct a "New Democratic" economy. Therefore the regime is in itself fully charged with incompatible contradictions and high explosives. From the historical point of view, it can only be very short-lived and transitional. In the development of future events, it will be obliged to choose its social base between the proletariat and the bourgeoisie, to decide its destiny between socialism and capitalism. Otherwise, it will either be overthrown by one of these two classes, or will be crushed by both, and become only an episode in history.

The evolution of the measures taken by the new regime

To give an adequate account and criticism of the measures taken by the new regime on all economic, social, and political planes over the past two years—beginning with October 1949 when this government was formally announced—would necessitate the writing of a special document for this purpose. This report, being limited in space, and lacking sufficient data on hand, can only offer a brief description of some essential features of these measures and the most important changes that have taken place in the regime's orientation. On this count, we are prepared to supply further materials for supplementary reference.

In respect to the evolution of the regime's measures, looking at its characteristic policies and their modification over time, we can take the outbreak of the Korean War as the line of demarcation and divide the whole into two periods. During the initial months of the first period (October 1949 to June 1950), under the slogan of "Military matters first!" i.e., clearing away the remaining military influence of the KMT on the mainland, the CCP threw its whole effort on the economic plane into extracting money and food from the people to support the front and to cover the expenses of administration. The noteworthy aspects of these measures are as follows:

They levied heavy taxes on all industry and commerce; forced the buying of bonds, such as "Victory Bonds," "Front-support Bonds," "Patriotic Bonds," etc.; and appropriated foodstuffs from the countryside (the so-called voluntary contributions). The deficit in the budget was made up by issuing enormous quantities of paper currency. Land reform was suspended, and wages lowered, etc. On the political plane, the CCP assiduously conciliated the bourgeoisie, landlords, and rich peasants; and pulled toward itself all kinds of bourgeois and petty-bourgeois politicians and military men, including some of the Kuomintang bureaucrats and agents, in an attempt to disintegrate the enemy and strengthen its own power. But the regime did its best to suppress the activities of the workers and peasants. Cases were often heard of workers being arrested or even killed on account of protests and strikes.

All of these measures resulted in inflation, the lowering of the standard of living, pauperization of the whole society, and the precipitation of industrial and commercial collapse. Most factories and shops were utterly unable to sustain themselves and asked for official permission to close down, or simply closed by themselves. Even those that remained in operation could not pay salaries and wages to their employees. Consequently great anxiety and resentment were aroused among the bourgeoisie. With the lowering of wages—compared with the level during KMT rule—and the compulsory reduction of wages through buying bonds, the living conditions of the worker masses became more and more miserable. Yet they had no way to express their opinions or to demand improvements, and were universally discontented with the new regime, even complaining openly against it.

The most serious consequences, however, occurred in the countryside. As a result of the interruption of land reform, the broad peasant masses were not in the least benefitted but on the contrary were forced to contribute endless taxes and food. At the same time, the landlords and rich peasants transferred the greater part of their own burdens onto the shoulders of the peasant masses and even "contributed" the last handfuls of grain used for seed crop, required for their livelihood.

Robbed of their means of living, filled with fury, and further provoked by the landlords, rich peasants, and KMT agents, a segment of the peasants were driven to acts of open rebellion. These included refusal to "contribute," forming groups to plunder "public" foodstuffs, and even rallying to the anticommunist guerrilla bands. This reaction objectively revived the influence of the Kuomintang anticommunist guerrillas.

In the spring of 1950 this situation reached a crisis point. At that time the CCP's leading organ was compelled to admit:

At present the feudal system of the vast countryside has still not been eliminated, the wounds of war are not yet healed, and in addition to the unbalanced and unfair appropriation of state foodstuffs last year, the lawless landlords exploit this opportunity to transfer their own burdens. As a result the peasants in many regions are destitute of food and seeds, and can hardly proceed with the spring farming. In the regions ravaged by drought and flood, conditions are much more grave. At the same time there are a few special agents of the enemy, the bandits, who use threats to make people organize revolts, plunder state food, attack revolutionary groups and individuals, create social confusion, and sabotage the orders of production . . . to throw productive relations and the social order into a chaotic and dangerous state.*

The *Yangtze (Ch'ang-chiang) Daily*, the official paper published in Hangkow, summarized this critical situation in the following conclusion: "The essence of the immediate crisis lies in this: whether the peasants follow the Communist Party and the People's Government, or the country autocrats and the Kuomintang agents."

Faced with this crisis and pressure from all sides, especially from the peasant masses, the industrialists, and the merchants, the regime was obliged to make a turn in its policy. This turn first appeared with the announcement of the resumption of land reform, at the beginning of March 1950. This was the so-called land reform by stages. It was proposed to begin with the redistribution of land north of the Yangtze, while in the South

* See the announcement of the Military and Political Committee of the Central-South Area, published in the Hong Kong *Wen-hui Pao*, March 6, 1950.

(not including the Northwest and Southwest) to proceed first of all with the struggle "against the vicious autocrats" and with the "reducton of rents and interest." The regime also revised the Food Appropriation Act. These measures served as palliatives to appease the peasants' resistance. At about the same time, it proclaimed the Financial Coordination Act, which has more or less alleviated the weight of taxes while unifying and standardizing taxation on a national level. This has to a certain extent pacified the resentment of the tax contributors and comparatively stabilized finances. Inflation has also slackened.

The principal measure taken to maintain industry and commerce was the universal organizing of "Labor and Capital Consultative Conferences." Under the government's supervision and arbitration, the outcome of these "consultations" was always unfavorable to the workers. In order to maintain the factories and shops, the workers and employees were obliged to lower or even forfeit their wages, or else to resign "voluntarily" in order to take part in "farm labor in their native counties." Sometimes they were called on to "voluntarily" prolong their worktime with the aim of reducing production costs. The industrialists and merchants, of course, were quite pleased with these results, while the workers became more and more resentful.

All of these urgent measures were then discussed, amended at the meeting of the Political Consultative Conference in May 1950, and concretized into various laws and acts—such as the Land Reform Law, the Trade Union Law, etc.—which were ratified by the government and became decrees. In addition, there was a Report on Financial and Economic Coordination also adopted by the conference, ratified by the government, and put into practice. The following points in the new acts deserve our attention:

First the new Land Reform Law is generally in the same vein as the former Land Law, except that it emphasizes the "necessity of preserving landlords and rich peasants' industrial and commercial properties" (according to Liu Shao-ch'i's report), and strictly forbids all violence: beatings, killings, arrests, and the parading of criminals in high hats (contained in the Ministry of Public Affairs directives). This is obviously designed to prohibit the spontaneous organization by the masses to use their own revolutionary methods to punish the landlords, the country gentry, and the autocrats. It aims to submit all kinds of struggle to the procedure of law and appeal to law, this being termed by the regime "rational struggles."

Second, in the economic field, it supported the industrialists by means of low-interest loans; or by allotting what is called extra works, whereby the administrators of the state enterprises offer raw materials, consign extra labor, and allocate a certain amount of profits to the private enterprises; or by buying the commodities of the private enterprises; or by giving extra facilities in buying raw materials, fuel, and transportation. With this aim it also reduced state commerce to oblige private business. In the Trade Union Act, it recognizes the workers' right to demand improvements in their living conditions within the limits of the law. So the workers remain helpless if the "law does not consent." In addition, the compulsory buying of bonds was stopped.

In brief we can say that this turn in the CCP's policy springs from its feeling the danger of the pressure from the peasant masses and the bourgeoisie, who have become the main beneficiaries of the turn and gained certain concessions from the regime. The working class, especially the workers in private enterprises, have not only scarcely benefitted but in many respects have been its victims.

In the second period, from the outbreak of the Korean War up to the present, the regime's measures have generally proceeded according to the orientation fixed in May by the Political Consultative Conference. However, during the "Aid Korea, Resist America" campaign, and particularly under compulsion to undertake a broad mass mobilization for participation in the Korean War, the CCP has once again had to modify its policy, or make another turn.

On the economic plane, following the blockade by American imperialism, the supply of certain industrial raw materials and machines has declined day by day. And since its own finances have faced greater and greater difficulties, aid to private enterprises has also been decreased and limited. Consequently, the relative revival of private enterprise has relapsed into stagnation and decline. The government attempts to concentrate its energy on the development of the state sector of industry and stresses the building up of a "self-sufficient heavy industry." But owing to the extreme lack of capital and equipment, it has made very little progress. In the field of commerce, particularly in foreign trade, it has more or less resumed control over private business, and hence causes a stagnation of commerce.

Since the regime has won support from the huge peasant masses for the "Aid Korea" campaign, it has certainly accelerated the pace and enlarged the scope of agrarian reform. To a certain extent it has even relaxed its control over the peasants and strengthened its support among the poor peasants. The obvious examples in recent months have been its emphasis on the role of the peasants, especially the importance of the poor-peasant movement; its attempt to correct right-opportunist deviations in the land reform movement; and the penalties inflicted on some cadres who are directly responsible for the execution of land reform, when they violate the "will of the masses," employ "bureaucratic methods," or are corrupted. But this does not signify that the CCP has full confidence in the peasant masses and will permit them to freely exercise their revolutionary initiative, to spontaneously organize the distribution of the land and carry out the revolutionary struggle against the landlords and rich peasants. In fact, the fundamental line of "protecting the industrial and commercial properties of the landlords and rich peasants," or "the gradual execution of land reform," and of "rational struggle" still holds sway. It is only in the practical execution of these policies that control is less strict than before.

Because of its need for support in the Korean War, the regime has made some improvements in the workers' living conditions. Recently it has gradually raised the wages of workers in the state enterprises and is more inclined than before to listen to the workers' opinions about technical production. But the executive power of production is still in the hands of the manager or the committee appointed by the higher echelons. Under the slogan of competition to increase production, on the one hand the labor of the already overburdened average worker is further intensified, while on the other hand a group of labor aristocrats (the Stakhanovists) is created and weighs upon the general working masses, dividing the workers' ranks.[13]

The regime is much more tolerant than before in its attitude toward workers' struggles in private enterprises. It permits the trade unions, "on the condition of not fundamentally hampering production," to engage in a "legal struggle" with capital for improving living conditions. Henceforth, the lowering of wages and the firing of workers at will is more tightly controlled than in former times. Although the recently adopted Labor Assurance Law is still a half-measure, generally speaking it has indeed resulted in a considerable improvement in the position and life of the working masses. But the essential rights of the working class in politics and in production—namely the rights of participation and control in government and factory administration—are still denied.

Since the outbreak of the Korean War, the activities of all the reactionary elements have revived. This has forced the CCP to more or less modify its former political line of conciliation. This new turn is manifested in the tempestuous drive to "suppress the counterrevolutionaries." In this campaign thousands of reactionary landlords and rich peasants (the "vicious local autocrats," as they are labeled), labor traitors, and KMT bureaucrats and agents have been imprisoned, exiled, and executed. In addition a great number of "affiliated" elements and followers of Li Chishen and the "Democratic League" have suffered the same fate. This, however, marks a considerable progress within certain limits. But this drive has not touched a single hair of the real spokesmen of the bourgeoisie, such as the actual leaders of the Kuomintang Revolutionary Committee, represented by Li Chishen, and the heads of the Democratic League.

On the other hand, under the same pretext of suppressing "counterrevolutionaries," the more advanced and discontented elements among the workers and peasants, especially the Trotskyists, are repressed, imprisoned, and killed. This only demonstrates that, even while carrying out certain limited progressive measures, this regime still drags behind it the reactionary specter of Stalinism.

In its international relations, the regime has really made important progress. After its establishment, it won a large measure of political independence from imperialism—such as taking back the customs houses and canceling the stationing of foreign armies in China. We must say that this has opened a new phase in modern Chinese diplomatic history. But in the economic sphere, it still assures "protection to the properties of all foreigners in China," and attempts to engage in conciliation with imperialism by its implicit consent to the preservation of the concessions of Hong Kong, Kowloon, and Macao. With the outbreak of the Korean War the CCP's foreign policy has shown certain further developments.

In retaliation against the economic blockade and freezing of Chinese property in the United States, the CCP regime has taken over American banks and enterprises, and seized all the schools, hospitals, and similar institutions formerly operated by foreigners. Moreover, as a countermeasure against the appropriation of a "rebellious" oil ship by the Hong Kong government, the People's Government declared its "appropriation" of all the capital of the Asia Oil Company in China. Although these progressive measures have not altered the fundamental line of "protecting all foreign properties in China," they have at least driven the regime to encroach more or less on the inviolable foreign properties.

Another result of the CCP's direct intervention in the Korean War and the measures that flowed from that is a great decline in the possibility of compromise with American imperialism—the chieftain of the capitalist world. Mao's regime, in fact, has become the government most hated by the American imperialists in Asia.

From the very beginning, because of its historical origins and its geographical and economic ties, this regime has tended to be dependent and submissive in its relations with the Soviet Union. This attitude was clearly reflected in the Sino-Soviet Mutual Aid Agreement signed in February 1950. This agreement was first of all aimed at pacifying the Chinese people's indignation toward the Soviet Union. (There have been very strong and hostile reactions among broad layers of the Chinese people, especially among the workers of Manchuria, ever since the USSR seized Port Arthur and Dairen under the provisions of the Yalta Agreement, and after it acquired many other privileges, such as joint control of the Chungtung and Ch'ang-ch'un railways, and especially after it destroyed or moved away the majority of the industrial and mining installations in Manchuria.)

Also, made wiser by the bitter lessons of the Yugoslav events, the Soviet bureaucracy has learned to pay its "respects to the sovereignty and independence of the Chinese People's Government," and has promised to restore the two ports and control over the railroads in Manchuria no later than 1952. Whether this promise will be kept, or carried out by that date, is still an open question.

On the economic plane, the trade agreements and the so-called Sino-Soviet partnership mostly favor the Soviet Union. They are quite similar to the treaties signed with the Eastern European countries. Especially after the outbreak of the Korean War, the new regime's dependence on the Soviet Union has become deeper and more unshakable. That is to say, the Soviet Union's actual control over the Chinese government has become more solid and irremovable. Viewed simply from this angle, the Korean War is like a set of chains binding the CCP regime to the Soviet Union's war chariot and dragging it along independent of its will.

It is true that the regime's intervention in the Korean War has greatly increased its weight on the international arena, as well as raising its standing and prestige among the people in the country. But the grievous damage incurred in this war, in both men and material resources, has strewn more difficulties in the path of social and economic construction in China, even for the limited goals set by the CCP, inasmuch as such construction was already overwhelmed by difficulties. Meanwhile, these sacrifices have also stirred up discontent and complaints among the masses. If the war should continue, future evils can scarcely be calculated. From the standpoint of these considerations taken alone, the government would probably have to withdraw from the war or scale down its participation. But if the Kremlin should persist in its intention to use the war to weaken the CCP, the war might be further prolonged.

Over the past two years, pushed and pulled by powerful and complex influences at home and abroad, the new regime's policies, both domestic and foreign, have been constantly and empirically changing. In general, it is moving in a "leftward" direction. But its fundamental opportunist orientation and bureaucratic administrative methods—the "revolution by stages" line, New Democracy, and class collaboration—and the systematic and well-planned control over all mass activities from above are still completely preserved. Therefore the basic contradictions and explosiveness contained in the regime—indicated in the previous section—are far from attenuated or diminished by the measures taken. They have even become more acute with the logical development of events.

The perspectives for China

With the CCP's victory, a brand-new situation has unfolded in China—the beginning of a deformed third Chinese revolution. But having absorbed into itself all the profound and sharp contradictions in social and economic relations, class relations, and international relations, this situation can only be transitory. It will be channeled into one or the other of the following perspectives.

A. *Relapse into the reactionary rule of the bourgeoisie*

Given all the objective factors and conditions—the protection of capitalist property relations in the cities and countryside, maintenance of a certain political power and influence by the bourgeoisie, the frustration and repression of the proletariat in political and economic life, and the despotic state apparatus built on a petty-bourgeois social basis, inclining to corruption—we cannot exclude the possibility of retrogression to the reactionary rule of the bourgeoisie. But this could only be achieved through a most brutal counterrevolutionary bloodbath. However, as long as the CCP has full authority over a potent peasant armed force, this perspective is out of the question.

But in the event that both internal and international events were to develop unfavorably at the same time, the possible structural disintegration of the CCP regime would favor restoration of bourgeois rule. Particularly if a future world war were to break out and the proletarian revolution in other countries was unable to rise in time to intervene energetically in Chinese events, American imperialism, after striking a military death-blow to the Soviet Union, could turn around and lead the armies of Japan and Taiwan to attack the Chinese mainland. This would bring about the inevitable ruin or split of the CCP regime, with some of the bourgeois and petty-bourgeois elements surrendering to American imperialism. Then a reactionary bourgeois reign would reappear on the political stage of China.

Of course, this is the worst perspective and it is merely a possibility. But it is not wise to absolutely exclude this worst variant. Only by recognizing and comprehending this worst of perspectives, by our precaution and alertness, and through our subjective revolutionary efforts, can we prevent its appearance and development.

B. To the road of revolutionary proletarian dictatorship

The progressive measures already instituted have objectively laid a favorable basis for a revolutionary development. These include the gradual extension of the land reform; the widespread purge of feudal remnants; the nationalization of a great part of the enterprises and properties, such as the main industries and mines, means of transport, big banks, etc.; the liquidation of the reactionary forces represented by Chiang's groups; the considerable rise of broad peasant masses; the regrouping of the urban working class, in the national trade union organization; and a gradual lifting of the general cultural level and political consciousness of the worker and peasant masses (indicated by the universal literacy campaign and the legalization of reading the works of Marx, Engels, and Lenin).

The chief obstacle on the revolutionary path is the tenacious opportunism and tyrannical bureaucratism of the CCP. But in the favorable unfolding of future events at home and abroad, the worker and peasant masses would be able by their own strength to push the CCP forward. They could deliver blows to the reactionary influences of the bourgeoisie, and by securing certain prerequisites for revolutionary development, such as certain democratic rights, proceed step by step on the road of revolution.

Even in the event of the third world war, if there should be an upsurge of revolutionary movements in the world, the Chinese worker and peasant masses, stimulated by the strong impetus of revolutions abroad, could possibly assail the CCP's opportunism and bureaucratism, bring about a split, and create a revolutionary left wing in this party. They would thus free themselves from the yoke of Stalinism, and then join the current of the Trotskyist movement. This would lead the revolution straight to proletarian dictatorship, which would complete the third Chinese revolution and open a future of socialist construction.

Yet I must point out that this perspective would not be a reproduction of the Yugoslav events, but a more advanced and deeper revolutionary development. There is very little possibility for such a repetition, simply because China is a very different country from Yugoslavia, both in its internal and external conditions, particularly after the outbreak of the Korean War. (On this point, I could offer further explanations, if need be.)

C. Assimilation into the Soviet Union

The two perspectives set forth above deal with only the most fundamental outcomes of the possible developments in the Chinese situation. But, in view of the opportunist bureaucratic deformations of the CCP leadership and its present intimate relations with the Kremlin, these two perspectives will meet frantic resistance, since either one of them would be fatal for this leadership. Consequently, it will consciously or unconsciously choose a third road—the road of gradual assimilation into the Soviet Union. That is to say, under the ever-increasing menace from bourgeois reactionary forces allied with imperialism and the ever-growing dissatisfaction and pressure of the masses, the CCP would empirically by gradual steps exclude the bourgeois parties and cliques from the political field.

Through purges and fusions it would annihilate these factions, and with them, the coalition government. It would then form a one-party dictatorship in name and in content, which would conform to what they would call the "transformation from people's democratic dictatorship to proletarian dictatorship."

On the economic plane, it would carry out a gradual process of expropriation of bourgeois private property and the concomitant expansion of nationalized property, in keeping with the formula, "progression from the New Democratic economy toward the socialist economy."

On the other hand, while carrying out these political and economic measures, the CCP would make certain concessions to mass pressure to gain a weapon in the suppression of reactionary influences. But it would never basically loosen its tight bureaucratic grip upon the revolutionary activities of the masses, especially of workers and poor peasants, lest they pass over the permitted boundaries or interfere with its basic line.

This line may be called that of "East Europeanization." But an essential difference exists between the two processes. The "assimilation" of the buffer states of Eastern Europe was accomplished entirely under the Kremlin's military control and through its directly designated Stalinist bureaucrats in those countries. In China, because of the vastness of the territory, the huge population, and the powerful influence of the CCP, and in the absence of the Soviet Army, and especially taking into account the experience in Yugoslavia, the Kremlin can rely only on its general economic and military superiority and its control over Manchuria and Sinkiang to threaten and pressure the CCP. However, in appearance, it would still pay certain respects to the "independence and sovereignty" of the CCP regime and allow it to proceed on its own "initiative."

In the main, this assimilation depends exclusively on the CCP's own subjective intentions. But we should not overlook the important role that can be played by the subjective will of a party already in power, which holds in its hands immense material forces—including a powerful peasant army—at least under particular circumstances and for a certain period of time. (The role of Stalin and his group in the Soviet Union is a conspicuous example.)

Prior to the outbreak of a new world war, and in the absence of other revolutionary upheavals in the world, the course of CCP assimilation into the Soviet Union is the most probable and realistic. To reject its likelihood would be unwise as well as harmful in the field of practical politics. But as soon as the third world war breaks out or a new revolutionary movement arises in other countries, this process of assimilation of the CCP will immediately be interrupted, and the whole situation in China will be forced to head in one of the two directions indicated above.

We should also point out that this process of assimilation will by no means have a smooth and even course. Parallel with the development of the situation, the profound and acute contradictions inherent in the new regime, and the conflicts between the interests of the Chinese revolution and the diplomatic interests of the Kremlin, would inevitably erupt and gather into fierce billowing disturbances or tragedies.

In general, the development of the Chinese situation will be slow-paced and drawn out, and will hardly undergo decisive change before the explosion of the coming great war. Therefore we may say that the destiny of China will only be ultimately solved in the course of the third world war and a gigantic upsurge of world revolution. There is therefore still time enough for us to prepare before the advent of such a solution.

Our fundamental attitude and orientation

Following the above analyses and appraisals, we must openly admit that a new revolutionary situation has not only begun, but has already attained certain achievements, and will possibly go forward. Hence we reject all sectarian and passive criticisms. We must integrate our organization in the main current of this movement, join in the mass struggles, and make the utmost effort to push this movement onto a really victorious road. At the same time, we must realize that, because the bureaucratic and opportunist leadership of the CCP is distorting this revolution, continuously imposing injuries and obstacles on its course, and leading it to the edge of a precipice, we must reject all naive and overoptimistic illusions.

Our fundamental attitude, confronted with this living reality, is that, with all the perils and hardships, we must point out to the masses the tremendous contradictions and crises imposed on this movement by the bureaucratic and opportunist line of the CCP. With patience and persistence, we shall convince the masses, encourage them, and help them to overcome these contradictions and crises through their own efforts and achieve a victorious outcome.

Our fundamental orientation in pushing this abnormal revolution on to a genuine victory is as follows:

a. Thoroughly carry out the land reform, exterminate all the feudal remnants, and nationalize the land. Meanwhile, expropriate all of the bourgeoisie's private property, and complete the statization of these properties as a basis for socialist construction.

b. Do away with the class-collaborationist coalition government; end the Bonapartist military dictatorship; establish a dictatorship of the proletariat leading the poor peasants; and in this way achieve genuine national unity under democratic centralism.

c. Declare the abolition of all unequal treaties; take back all settlements and concessions (such as Hong Kong, Kowloon, Macao, etc.); confiscate all imperialist properties in China; and cancel all privileges held in China by the Soviet bureaucracy—in order to attain complete and genuine national independence.

To struggle for carrying out these fundamental points of orientation, our party should formulate a concrete and inclusive program of action, in which we must emphasize that we support every progressive measure of the CCP, but criticize any reactionary measure. At all times and places we must wage the best fight we can to win basic democratic rights for workers and peasants— such as freedom of speech, publication, assembly, association, belief, strikes, etc.—and fight for the right of workers' participation, supervision, and control in administration and production. We must also seek to establish representative committees (soviets) of workers, peasants, and soldiers.

As our organization is at present still very weak and suffering the most brutal persecutions from the new regime, it is far from able to intervene directly in this movement and affect events. But since we know that our Trotskyist line of the permanent revolution is the line most suited to the objective logic of revolutionary developments in China, if we stand resolutely and courageously within this movement, within the struggles of the masses, cautiously and patiently explaining to them in order to convince them, the evolution of events will help us step by step to win the confidence of the masses. With a new conjuncture, in a new rise of the revolutionary tide, we will be lifted to the leading position and direct the masses on the road to victory.

Finally, I should add that the events in China have wrought important effects in the Far East and even in the whole international situation that deserve our special attention—and not simply because of the vast territory and the enormous population. We should further understand that of all the backward countries, China is the most typical in its manifestation of the law of uneven and combined development.

In the past half century a series of great events have broken out in this country—two revolutions, several prolonged civil wars, and foreign wars, and the third revolution still at its beginning.

During these twenty-five years, Trotsky and the Chinese Trotskyists under his leadership have directly participated in the greater
part of these events, and have therefore accumulated a rich
experience. Therefore, a correct solution of the Chinese question
will not only have decisive significance for the future of the
Chinese Trotskyist movement, but will be a precious guide for our
International in orienting and directing the movements in Asia
and in all other backward countries, and even in advanced
countries. That is why I repeat once more: I hope that our
International comrades, in discussing the Chinese question, will
not be constrained by any formalistic analogies and abstract
concepts, but will seriously employ the Marxist method in
analyzing the objective reality in order to arrive at a satisfactory
conclusion.

November 8, 1951

Some Supplementary Remarks
and Corrections to the
"Report on the Chinese Situation"

Having analyzed the most recent facts relating to the development of the Chinese situation and after a study of the evolution of Yugoslavia and the Eastern European countries, I feel it is necessary to make some supplementary remarks and corrections to the analysis and appraisal of the character of the CCP and its regime in my previous "Report on the Chinese Situation." This will provide the next IEC with more concrete material on this question so that it can arrive at correct conclusions.

On the problem of the character of the Chinese CP

On this question, in view of the fact that after the defeat of the second Chinese revolution the CCP completely abandoned the workers' movement in the cities, turned toward the countryside, absorbed a great number of peasants into the party, and concentrated on the peasant guerrillas, Trotsky and the Chinese Trotskyists declared that this party had gradually degenerated and become a petty-bourgeois party based on the peasantry. But some comrades have their doubts on this point and say that even if Trotsky had expressed this opinion he was wrong. That is why I think it is necessary first to give some explanations in the context of certain facts.

In judging the character of a party, we Marxists base ourselves on two fundamental factors: the party's composition and its political tendency. If workers comprise the majority of the party, and the party truthfully represents the fundamental interests of the working class, this party can be called a healthy or revolutionary workers' party. If the workers comprise the majority of the party and its political leadership is of a petty-bourgeois or opportunist reformist type, we still call it a workers' party, but it is a deformed or degenerated workers' party. If the petty bourgeoisie predominates in its social composition and if the leadership is also opportunist, even if it pretends to be a workers' party, we can only designate it a petty-bourgeois party.

Regarding the evolution and the composition of the CCP, in the last period of the second Chinese revolution it had approximately 60,000 members, according to the report to the party's Fifth Congress, in April 1927 (not including the Communist Youth, which had a larger membership than the party). Industrial workers accounted for 58 percent of the membership. But after the disastrous defeats of this revolution and several adventuristic insurrections, particularly after the great defeat of the Canton uprising, most of the workers were sacrificed or left the party. Proletarian membership declined to 10 percent in 1928 and to 3 percent in 1929 (see "On the Organizational Question" by Chou En-lai). It fell to 2.5 percent in March 1930 (*Red Flag*, March 26, 1930), and to 1.6 percent in September of the same year ("Report to the Third Plenum of the CC of the Party" by Chou En-lai).

The October 10, 1931, issue of *Bolshevik* openly admitted that "the percentage of workers had already fallen to less than 1 percent." After most of the workers' branches of Shanghai were won over to the Left Opposition "Trotskyist Group," *Red Flag* complained on October 23, 1933, that in Shanghai, the largest industrial city of the country, "There is not a single real workers' branch." But in the same period they said that the number of members had risen to over 300,000. This is adequate proof that the CCP had an almost exclusively peasant composition. Precisely because of that, Trotsky drew the conclusion:

"The Chinese Stalinists . . . in the years of the counterrevolution . . . passed over from the proletariat to the peasantry, i.e., they undertook that role which was fulfilled in our country by the SRs [Social Revolutionary Party] when they were still a revolutionary party. . . . The party actually tore itself away from its class. . . ."

And further:

the causes and grounds for conflicts between the army, which is peasant in composition and petty bourgeois in leadership, and the workers not only are not eliminated but, on the contrary, all the circumstances are such as to greatly increase the possibility and even the inevitability of such conflicts. . . .

Consequently our task consists not only in preventing the political-military command over the proletariat by the petty-bourgeois democracy that leans upon the armed peasant, but in preparing and ensuring the proletarian leadership of the peasant movement, its "Red armies" in particular. [Trotsky, in a letter to the Chinese Left Opposition and postscript to this letter, September 22 and 26, 1932.—P'eng.[14]]

When the CCP was obliged to flee from the South to the North, to Yenan, the number of its worker members dropped still further because the conditions there were still more primitive. The only possible recruitment of worker elements came from village artisans. Consequently the petty-bourgeois peasant atmosphere enveloped the entire party and was formally crystallized in the "theory of the revolutionary peasantry." Mao Tse-tung in the theses "On New Democracy" openly declared:

> Stalin has said that "*in essence*, the national question is a peasant question." This means that the Chinese revolution is essentially a peasant revolution. . . . Essentially, the politics of New Democracy means giving the peasants their rights. The new and genuine Three People's Principles [Mao pretends that his New Democracy contains the "real" Three People's Principles inherited from Sun Yat-sen so as to distinguish them from the "false" principles espoused by Chiang Kai-shek] are essentially the principles of a peasant revolution.[15]

These words of Mao Tse-tung establish that the CCP was a petty-bourgeois party not only because of its peasant composition but also in its ideology. Consequently, during the entire Anti-Japanese War, the CCP, by supporting the KMT's leadership, not only insisted on class collaboration in its propaganda but showed openly in its practice that "the workers should increase production to aid the government in the common resistance against Japan." It rejected the "exorbitant demands" presented by the workers to the national bourgeoisie, charging that the Trotskyist policy of class struggle was a "policy of betrayal to aid the enemy," thus slandering the Trotskyists as "traitors." Naturally, in the workers' real struggles the CCP was always on the side of the national bourgeoisie and against the workers' reasonable demands, even sabotaging these struggles.

At the same time, the CCP did everything possible to encourage the most active elements of the working class to leave the struggle in the cities and join the peasants in the countryside. It was for precisely this reason that while the CCP considerably increased its armed peasant forces during the Resistance War, its influence remained extremely weak among the worker masses of the cities.

After the Anti-Japanese War it is true that the CCP once again joined the workers' movement in the cities, recruiting cadres among the workers and building an organization. But its main aim was to obtain the workers' support to pressure Chiang Kai-shek into accepting the CCP's compromise with him in a "coalition government." Therefore, in that period the CCP's policy toward the workers was always to lead the mass of the workers into a compromise with the national bourgeoisie, hoping through the national bourgeoisie to put pressure on Chiang Kai-shek to successfully conclude its negotiations with him. As a result, the CCP's influence among the workers was very feeble.

Finally, when the CCP was obliged to carry on a general counteroffensive against the Chiang government and to occupy the big cities, not only did it not make any appeal to the mass of the workers to carry on some form of struggle, but it did its best to curb their activities. Its only appeal was to call upon them to "protect production and watch Chiang Kai-shek's bandits who are sabotaging it." When the CCP occupied the cities it imposed severe restrictions on all activity or spontaneous organization of the working class.

When the workers went out on strike to demand wage increases or to resist oppressive conditions, it was brutal in its repressions, going to the point of massacres. For example, the strikers in several factories in Tientsin were arrested and executed. The workers of Shen Hsin factory number 9 (which employed 8,000 workers) were attacked with machine guns because they refused to leave the city with the factory; there were more than 300 casualties. At the Ching Hsing coal mines in Hopeh Province, when the workers revolted against the cruelty and arrogance of the Soviet advisers and specialists,* the CCP sent a large number of troops to suppress the revolt. There were more than 200 dead or wounded workers and more than a thousand were expelled and exiled to Manchuria or Siberia (this happened in May 1950).

All of this demonstrates this petty-bourgeois party's attitude toward the working class, an attitude of distrust, hostility, and even murderous rage. That partially confirms the prediction and the warning made by Trotsky nineteen years ago. If the worker masses of the cities had been more united under the leadership of another revolutionary force (the Trotskyists), it is very probable that the CCP would have had recourse to civil war to beat the

* Since this mine produces a better grade of coal which can be used in steel making, the Soviet Union had sent advisers and specialists to control the mine so as to appropriate its production for the USSR. This arrangement has probably been modified by the Sino-Soviet Mutual Aid and Assistance Agreement.

workers down. As Trotsky said, "they will incite the armed peasants against the advanced workers."[16]

From these historic facts the question of whether Trotsky and the Chinese Trotskyists were right in their estimation of the nature of the CCP can be left to the reexamination of those comrades who have doubts on the matter. If the comrades have adequate facts and correct theoretical reasons to demonstrate that the estimation of the CCP made by Trotsky and the Chinese Trotskyists was incorrect, we are ready to abandon our estimation and adopt the new one.

*   *   *

There is one other aspect of this question. It is true that the CCP, through its change in composition, gradually degenerated into a petty-bourgeois party based on the peasantry. It adopted as its ideology Mao Tse-tung's theory that "the Chinese revolution is essentially a peasant revolution. . . . the politics of New Democracy means giving the peasants their rights." But I should stress that because of its historic origin as a section of the Communist International, because of some working-class traditions remaining from the second revolution, because of its close relations with the international Stalinist party (which, as degenerated as it is, still remains a workers' party), and because of its general support of Marxism-Leninism, of the dictatorship of the proletariat, and of the perspective of communism, etc., we have to admit that even when it had degenerated into a peasant party there remained a certain inclination in the party toward the workers. But this tendency was curbed and repressed during the long years of peasant guerrilla war.

When this party entered the cities and came into contact with the mass of the workers, and especially when it had an urgent need of the support of the working class to resist the threats of the bourgeoisie and imperialism, the worker tendency, long hidden and repressed, had the opportunity to emerge and to place some pressure on the leadership of the party. It demanded the transfer of the party's base from the peasantry to the working class and called for certain concessions to the demands of the worker masses. The events of the last two years, and particularly of the last six months, have clearly reflected this tendency.

The CCP decided to stop the recruitment of peasants into the party and emphasized the need for rapid recruitment of workers. The editorial in the July 1, 1950, *People's Daily*, on the twenty-ninth anniversary of the founding of the CCP, stressed a reform in party composition, i.e., the absorption of workers into the party. It also said that in the recent period, among the 6,648 new members in Tientsin, 73 percent were workers, and out of 3,350 in Peking, more than 50 percent were workers.

To sum up, according to these concrete facts, there have been quite a considerable number of workers recruited by the CCP in the last two years in the large industrial cities and in the mines in the Northeast, in Shanghai, and in Wuhan. Of course, if consideration is given to the composition of the entire party (according to the same editorial in the *People's Daily*, there are some 5 million members in the party), the number of workers is still very small. (Kao Kang, secretary for the Northeast District, admitted in a January 10 speech to party heads that "working-class elements are still not very numerous in our party." This was given as the principal reason to explain the present crisis over the emergence of a right-wing tendency in the party and widespread party corruption.)

But the CCP's turn toward insisting on working-class recruitment in order to change its composition has unquestionably had an important effect on the class nature of the party.

This turn is more or less reflected in the process of carrying out the agrarian reform. According to the plan for agrarian reform adopted by the Political Consultative Conference of the CCP and other organizations and parties in May 1950, special emphasis is placed on "the protection of the commercial and industrial property of the landlords and the rich peasants." The decree of the minister of the interior severely prohibits "excessive actions" by the poor peasants toward the landed proprietors and rich peasants. Consequently, when this project was first implemented, not only were the industrial and commercial properties of the landlords and the rich peasants generally protected, but in numerous areas they obtained the best and the largest share of the land, and even preserved local power (such as head of the Peasants' Association or of the village, etc.). But then, when the masses of the poor peasantry gradually awakened in the course of the movement, the lower cadres, under the demands and pressure of the poor peasants, considerably altered the agrarian reform project and even upset it. That is to say, a great number of industrial and commercial properties of the landlords and rich peasants were subjected to severe penalties from the poor peasantry. (Recent reports on the agrarian reform in Chinese newspapers often reveal these facts.)

In face of the "left" tendency of the lower cadres to upset the party's guidelines and take their places in defense of the interests of the masses, the CCP leadership not only has not retaliated for these expropriations but on the contrary it has in general acquiesced. Although the CCP has not fundamentally changed its policy of protecting the industrial and commercial properties of the landlords and rich peasants, there is nevertheless a tendency to defend the interests of the poor peasants, which manifests itself strongly in the lower cadres and in the party ranks. This is particularly worthy of our attention.

In the campaign of recent months carried on against corruption, waste, and bureaucratism, an antibourgeois, working-class tendency is clearly being revealed in the CCP ranks. The principal reason for this campaign is that an extremely serious phenomenon of corruption, waste, and bureaucracy is manifesting itself among the CCP's responsible cadres in the state apparatus, the army, and mass organizations, and, in particular, in the industrial and commercial section and the cooperatives dealing with finances and the economy.

These cadres not only fatten themselves by pilfering state funds under their control or wasting public funds to assure a comfortable life, but in addition they associate with the bourgeois elements "to sell commercial information, state resources, and raw materials, to cut the working force and to raise [production—Tr.] costs in order to assure supplementary profits to the capitalists. The capitalists do not hesitate in providing necessary sums to corrupt these corrupted elements." (See Kao Kang's report cited above.)

On the one hand, this situation has caused enormous financial and economic losses to the various state institutions, and on the other hand it has aroused mass discontent, especially of the workers in the ranks of the party. (See Comrade Fang Hsing's report on this campaign.)

In order to maintain itself, the CCP leadership is obliged to organize this campaign to expel certain rotten cadres and to attack certain bourgeois elements as a means of appeasing the discontent in the party ranks and especially of the mass of the workers.

The corruption and degeneration of the CCP cadres at various levels is due primarily to the opportunist policy of class collaboration and to bureaucratic practice in violation of workers' democracy. This campaign against corruption, waste, and bureaucratism does not fundamentally alter the CCP's opportunism and bureaucratism; it is carried out by bureaucratic methods. The tendency toward corruption in the party will of course not be eliminated in this way. Nevertheless, the antibourgeois, working-class tendency within the CCP is strongly fortified in this campaign.

Because of this movement, the main CCP leadership insists, although only verbally, on "the necessity of recognizing the corrosive influence of bourgeois ideology on the party and the harm caused by the right-wing tendency in the party." They also say that "to base oneself on the bourgeoisie signifies only to abandon the working class, the popular masses, and the role of the party and the country" (see Kao Kang's report cited above). In fact, they have more or less accepted the appeal and the demands of the working masses.

For example, they now publish in all the newspapers descriptions of the oppression and exploitation of workers in the state enterprises in recent years at the hands of CCP cadres. This is in addition to reports made now under the pretext of showing a "violation of decrees" which expose the various methods of exploitation and oppression used by private capitalists. Such things were rarely mentioned previously and it was prohibited to denounce them openly. CCP public opinion recognizes this and considers it necessary to make certain improvements.

From the facts cited above regarding the social composition of the CCP, we can say that although the peasants and other petty-bourgeois elements still predominate (more than 90 percent of the 5 million members), the worker elements have increased in number in the last two years. The working-class tendency has been strengthened during the agrarian reform and the campaign against corruption, etc. That is why up until now the CCP has had a dual character. From the point of view of the tendency of its composition, keeping in mind the systematic acceleration in the recruitment of workers and the halting of peasant recruitment, the party is in a transitional stage toward a workers' party.

From the point of view of ideology, we can see three different tendencies in the CCP: the right tendency representing the upper strata of the petty bourgeoisie of the cities and the rich peasants; the left tendency representing the workers and the poor peasants; and the centrist tendency in the middle represented by the top leadership. Naturally, these three tendencies, and in particular the right and left, are still obscure and far from having been crystallized. But in the subsequent development of the class struggle, these tendencies toward the right and the left will gradually crystallize and will lead to an organizational differentiation. Finally, when the international and national situation reaches a serious, decisive stage, this party will tend inevitably toward a split.

On the character of the new regime

If we reevaluate the character of the party as being of a dual nature, this duality naturally affects the character of the new regime which is controlled by the party. In light of the importance of the nationalization of enterprises, the dual character of this regime is even more manifest.

Of course, the new regime under the control of the CCP is quite different from the dual power referred to by Lenin after the Russian February revolution, and the classic form of dual power. It is a special kind of dual power created by exceptional circumstances. This duality is analogous to that of the transition period in Yugoslavia and in the countries of Eastern Europe. Consequently, the new regime established by the CCP can only be a transitory form which will either move in the direction of the dictatorship of the proletariat—normal or not—or will move backward to the dictatorship of the bourgeoisie. But in the view of the present tendency, it is moving in the direction of a deformed dictatorship of the proletariat. Therefore, so far as its perspectives are concerned, I retain my previous position.

May 10, 1952

SOME COMMENTS ON THE
DRAFT RESOLUTION ON
"THE THIRD CHINESE REVOLUTION"

The following remarks concern what I feel are important mistakes or imperfections in the draft resolution which should be amended or supplemented.[1] Other minor mistakes, defects, or factual errors will be pointed out in the final discussion in the International Secretariat or at the International Executive Committee meeting.

1. In the section entitled "The Significance of Mao Tse-tung's Victory," the draft resolution states:

> The Third Chinese Revolution has begun, not through the alliance with Chiang Kai-shek, but through the breaking of this alliance. Thus the Trotskyist theory of the permanent revolution, implacably defended for 25 years by the Chinese Trotskyists and the world Trotskyist movement, has found confirmation for one of its fundamental theses.

I feel that this passage has misinterpreted Trotsky's permanent revolution.

The fundamental concept of Trotsky's permanent revolution is that in the backward countries (such as Russia, China, India, etc.) the thoroughgoing solution of the delayed bourgeois-democratic tasks is possible only when the proletariat, leading the peasant masses, proceeds to conquer power and establish the proletarian dictatorship. Once the proletarian dictatorship is established, however, it cannot be limited solely to solving democratic tasks such as land reform, national unity, and independence, etc. It must also pose the tasks of the socialist

---

This article, written in June 1952 in reply to a draft resolution on China by the International Executive Committee of the Fourth International, was circulated to the leadership bodies of the Fourth International in manuscript form but has not previously been published.

revolution, i.e., the expropriation of the private property of the urban and village bourgeoisie. This fundamental conception of the permanent revolution was repeated over and over again in Trotsky's *The Permanent Revolution* and in many other works. It is this that has been "implacably defended for 25 years by the Chinese Trotskyists and the world Trotskyist movement."

What Mao Tse-tung has presented in the course of this third Chinese revolution is just the opposite. He relied entirely on the peasant armed forces isolated from the urban worker masses. Although he conquered power under the exceptional conditions created by the Second World War, he did not establish a proletarian dictatorship, but formed a "coalition government" with the national and democratic bourgeoisie; he has not expropriated the private property of the bourgeoisie, but rather protected it. This is obviously an artificial and obstinate distortion of the natural development of the permanent revolution in China by applying the extremely reactionary Menshevik theory of "revolution by stages" (as represented by the "New Democracy" of Mao Tse-tung). If we were to admit that in Mao Tse-tung's victory over Chiang Kai-shek one of the fundamental theses of the permanent revolution "has found confirmation," that would amount to a distortion of the permanent revolution under the dazzling light of Mao Tse-tung's victory.

To say that "the Third Chinese Revolution has begun, not through the alliance with Chiang Kai-shek, but through the breaking of this alliance" has nothing to do with "confirmation" of the permanent revolution. With the defeat of the second Chinese revolution and Chiang's seizure of power, Chiang had already become the principal target of the revolution. Besides, although Mao broke with Chiang, he has not broken with the whole bourgeoisie. On the contrary, he established an "alliance" with the national or democratic bourgeoisie against Chiang.

The key question of the theory of permanent revolution is the proletarian dictatorship. Therefore Trotsky said:

> The Chinese revolution contains within itself tendencies to become permanent insofar as it contains the possibility of the conquest of power by the proletariat. To speak of the permanent revolution without this and outside of it, is like trying to fill the cask of the Danaides. Only the proletariat, after having seized the state power and having transformed it into an instrument of struggle against all the forms of oppression and exploitation, in the interior of the country as well as beyond its frontiers, gains therewith the possibility of assuring a continuous character to the

revolution, in other words, of leading it to the construction of a complete socialist society.[2]

What does this have in common with the draft resolution's words "thus the Trotskyist theory of the permanent revolution . . . has found confirmation for one of its fundamental theses"?

It goes without saying that we should never proceed from the programmatic norm of the permanent revolution to deny the important significance of the third revolution begun by Mao's party. But neither should we permit the objective significance of Mao's victory to draw us into depreciating the theory of the permanent revolution, nor into accommodating to the victory by misrepresenting it in the name of the permanent revolution. Our attitude should be, on the one hand, to understand the objective facts and diverse causes of Mao's victory, and, on the other, to analyze from the standpoint of the permanent revolution how this victory was distorted by the theory of "revolution by stages," resulting in its present deformed shape, the obstacles arising from this deformation, and the perspectives of its possible development. Our fundamental task is to stand on the program of the permanent revolution in order to defend, to push forward, and to complete the revolution, bringing it to final victory.

Here I must point out to the author of the draft resolution that the agrarian revolution in China is different from the one in Russia and has its own characteristics. These characteristics are that "China has no landed nobility; no peasant estate, fused by community of interests against the landlords. The agrarian revolution in China is aimed *against the urban and rural bourgeoisie*."[3] However, the land reform is now being carried out by Mao's party on the basis of protecting the interests of urban and rural bourgeois private property. This deserves special attention, and should be emphatically pointed out in the resolution.

2. In the section on "The Causes of Mao's Victory," the explanation of the diverse causes is not only inadequate, but is in some cases distorted. I have outlined in detail the causes of Mao's victory in the "Report on the Chinese Situation," so it is not necessary to repeat them here. I would only like to pose one question about the following passage: "The policy of the Soviet bureaucracy, far from promoting this transformation of the practical orientation of the Chinese CP, did everything to perpetuate the old position," and offer a brief criticism. The draft

resolution enumerates five ways the Soviet bureaucracy perpetuated the old positions of the CCP:

"(a) By the conclusion of the 1945 agreement with Chiang Kaishek." This is of course a fact. But this took place in 1945 not 1946, the year of the turn in the CCP's policy. The Sino-Soviet Agreement of 1945 was signed in the midst of the Kremlin's greatest effort to effect a compromise with imperialism and Mao's arduous attempt to collaborate with Chiang Kai-shek and establish a coalition government. Therefore, Mao's party was in full support of this agreement and hailed it as a "great achievement."

"(b) By the seizure and dismantling of industry in Manchuria, which paralyzed the workers' struggle there during the decisive stage of the civil war." This is indeed true and is the capital crime of the Kremlin bureaucracy. But this criminal activity was enthusiastically supported by Mao's party. In fact, when a section of the Chinese masses held protest demonstrations against the dismantling of industrial equipment in Manchuria by the Soviet bureaucracy, the CCP did its best to sabotage this movement and energetically defended the activity of the Soviet bureaucracy in the newspapers, magazines, and platforms under its control, causing vehement controversies.

"(c) By the technical aid accorded Chiang (the departure of the Russian troops from the vital centers of Manchuria was delayed until the arrival of the Kuomintang troops)." I do not know anything about "technical aid." We never saw or heard anything like this in China. But that "the departure of the Russian troops from the vital centers of Manchuria was delayed until the arrival of the Kuomintang troops" was entirely in accord with the provisions of the Sino-Soviet Agreement so enthusiastically applauded by Mao's party.

"(d) By the pressure exerted upon the Chinese CP to maintain the tactic of guerrilla warfare, and not to attack the big cities." The CCP maintained the tactic of guerrilla warfare and did not attack the big cities, not because of "pressure" exerted by the Soviet bureaucracy, but because of its own relationship of forces and especially its lack of heavy arms and equipment. As soon as the troops were armed with the heavy weapons of the Japanese army that had been captured by the Soviet Union (as in the case of Lin Piao's Fourth Division), they started to "attack the big cities" and this offensive was practically carried out under the direction of Soviet officers.

"(e) By the efforts undertaken by Soviet diplomacy for the constitution of a Chiang-Mao coalition goverment." This was true

from the end of the Second World War until the end of 1946. But
when Chiang categorically rejected any conciliation with Mao
and unleashed a violent military offensive against him, the
Soviet Union not only completely dropped this kind of "diplomacy," but in fact assisted the CCP in its preparations for a
general counteroffensive. It helped, for instance, to speed the
advance of Lin Piao's troops, to transport munitions from Port
Arthur and Dairen to aid the CCP army in the provinces of
Shantung and Hopeh, etc.

From the above facts, I believe that the draft resolution's
efforts to portray the turn in the CCP's policy as "outside the
leadership given by the Kremlin" are in vain. There is no
evidence to place the "turn" in the CCP's policy on the same level
with the "turn" in the Yugoslav CP's policy. On the contrary, one
has to see the CCP's turn in regard to Chiang as part of the turn
in the Kremlin's policy in regard to imperialism (the so-called
cold war), i.e., one has to view the first as being inspired by the
second.

3. In the section on the "Character of Mao's Power," the CCP is
characterized as an "opportunist workers' party." In my supplementary report[4] I have already supplied detailed explanations
and corrections concerning my original views of this question and
I do not intend to repeat it all here. However, I would like to ask
the author of the draft resolution to explain whether Trotsky's
assertion that since the defeat of the second Chinese revolution
the CCP gradually degenerated into a petty-bourgeois party, the
"Chinese Social Revolutionary Party," is wrong. I would also like
to ask whether the assertion of the Seventh Plenum of the
International Executive Committee that "from the social point of
view, the CCP is a bipartite party" is correct. Without a lucid
explanation of these questions, it would be difficult for the
Chinese comrades to assimilate the draft resolution's definition.

Regarding the dual character of Mao's regime, I have stated my
views in my supplementary report and am in general agreement
with the draft resolution on this point. But I feel that the
characterization of this government as a workers' and farmers'
government is doubtful. This use of the term does not conform to
the interpretation of the "workers' and farmers' government" in
the Transitional Program drafted by Trotsky and adopted by our
International at its First World Congress. The Transitional
Program explains that the slogan for a "workers' and farmers'
government" is employed by us "only in the sense that it had in
1917 with the Bolsheviks": to demand "that the SRs and Men-

sheviks break with the liberal bourgeoisie," i.e., as an antibour-geois and anticapitalist slogan. In no case do we use it "in that 'democratic' sense which the epigones later gave it, transforming it from a bridge to socialist revolution into the chief barrier upon its path."[5]

But the Mao Tse-tung regime today not only has not broken with the "liberal bourgeoisie" (the national or democratic bour-geoisie as he calls it), but has on the contrary established a "coalition government" or "People's Democratic Dictatorship" in alliance with it. If we accept the present Mao regime as a "workers' and farmers' government," it is obviously not in the spirit the Bolsheviks used the slogan in 1917, but rather in the "democratic" sense later given to it by the epigones. Not only are there three vice-presidents and several ministers in the central government, as well as dozens of governmental members, who are representatives of bourgeois parties or organizations, but in addition there are bourgeois representatives participating in the provincial and district governments, and former Kuomintang generals are the governors of several provinces (for instance Hunan, Yunnan, Szechuan, etc.). It is precisely due to this situation that we should raise the demand, "systematically addressed to the old leadership [the CCP in this case]—'Break with the bourgeoisie. . . .'" and establish a "workers' and farmers' government" as "an extremely important weapon for exposing the treacherous character" of the CCP.[6] At the same time, this demand serves as a powerful slogan for a revolutionary mobilization of the worker and peasant masses against the bourgeoisie and against capitalism. Therefore, the chief task in the present conditions in China is not to characterize Mao's regime as a workers' and farmers' government, but to demand that the CCP break with the national or democratic bourgeoisie and establish a workers' and farmers' government in order to arrive at a genuine proletarian dictatorship.

4. The last section of the draft resolution, "Perspectives of the Chinese Revolution," is not clear enough, and is too optimistic regarding the evolution of the CCP. The draft resolution asserted:

The CP entered upon the Third Chinese Revolution as a Stalinist party empirically freeing itself from the direction of the Kremlin. The interna-tional and national social forces which act upon it will determine its transformation from a highly opportunist workers' party into a centrist party going forward along the road of the completion of the revolution.

In reality, the CCP was not emancipated from the leadership of the Kremlin when it began the third Chinese revolution, and it is still acting within the bounds set by the Kremlin. Hence its opportunism and bureaucratism still maintain their original Stalinist nature. Although under the impact of the collision of contradictions at home and abroad it might turn more to the left in an empirical manner, and might even be transformed into a centrist party, this does not mean it would be able to lead the Chinese revolution to its ultimate completion. The Yugoslav CP became a centrist party long ago. But since then it has regressed towards the right. This is a very instructive example of the transformation of a Stalinist party into a centrist party. Therefore, in my opinion, even if the CCP turns further left under the impact of international and national conflicts, without the impulse of an upsurge of the world revolution, i.e., a revolutionary victory in several important countries outside of the control of the Kremlin, it would hardly be possible for the CCP to rid itself of its deep-rooted opportunism and bureaucratism. If victorious revolutions, beyond the control of the Kremlin, took place in important countries, a differentiation and even split would be inevitable within the ranks of the CCP. Only a revolutionary wing that emerged in the course of this differentiation and split could return to genuine Bolshevism and form a real revolutionary leadership by joining the current of Trotskyists to thoroughly complete the Chinese revolution and march on the road of socialist construction. This is the perspective the Chinese Trotskyists should strive to win. Only then can the Chinese Trotskyist organization, entering the CCP and the movement under its leadership, have a clear revolutionary outlook. Otherwise, without discerning our own perspective, the Chinese Trotskyists would be entangled in confusion and would finally be dissolved under the influence of the CCP.

June 2, 1952

THE CASE OF THE CHINESE TROTSKYISTS

Open Letter to the Central Executive Committee of the CCP

In the past two years I have repeatedly received news from comrades on the mainland, reporting the incessant persecutions your party has inflicted on our comrades—the steady pursuit and surveillance, searches, arrests, imprisonment, and even killings by your secret agents. For instance, in the fall of 1949 several dozen comrades were arrested in Shanghai and Wenchow. Two of them were executed. In 1950, a similar group in the cities of Kweilin and Liuchow of Kwangsi Province, Chunsan district and other parts of Kwangtung Province were arrested, and several of them shot. Even I, too, was threatened with assassination by secret agents of yours who came to my home January 22, 1952.

The detailed report received recently is particularly shocking: In the dead of night last December 22 and January 8 of this year, your party launched wholesale arrests of Trotskyists simultaneously in Shanghai, Canton, Peking, Chungking, and other regions, and the number of arrests reached several hundred!

Even the wives, brothers, sisters, relatives, friends, and sympathizers of the comrades were not spared. As in previous instances, these wholesale arrests were carried out without juridical sanction. The victims have never appeared in court. Once arrested, they disappeared completely. No one knows their fate.

I am thus obliged to lodge the strongest possible protest with your party on behalf of the Chinese Trotskyists.

First of all, I must ask: By what right or under what "charges" do you so brutally and systematically attack and persecute the Trotskyists? And, even if you had any shred of "proofs" which obliged you to "suppress the Trotskyists," you were duty bound to proclaim them to the masses and the public, to proceed with open arrests and trials, so that the arrested and persecuted could exercise their right of appeal and defense. Why do you deal with them in utter secrecy? Since taking power, your party has become the ruling party and has enacted innumerable laws. Why have you not proceeded according to your own laws?

Judging from your consistent attitude and propaganda toward us, it seems that you assume that the Trotskyists' ideas and views differ greatly from yours, are "extremely dangerous," even "counterrevolutionary," and "should be especially severely suppressed."

Of course, I would never deny that since the defeat of the second revolution (1925-27)—whether in regard to the lessons of this defeat, or the fundamental attitude toward the bourgeois Kuomintang and imperialism, or the relationship between the democratic revolution and socialist revolution in China (i.e., the theory of the permanent revolution versus the theory of revolution by stages), or the problems of strategy in a number of important events (such as the Resistance War against Japan and the Second World War)—serious differences still exist.

But as to who was right and who was wrong, historical fact has determined. In certain respects, under pressure of objective circumstances, you, acting empirically, have made important changes and revisions.

For instance, after Japanese imperialism capitulated and the Second World War came to an end, the extremely corrupt Chiang Kai-shek government was actually already tottering. The conjuncture was most favorable for mobilizing the broad worker and peasant masses under a revolutionary program in preparation for the overthrow of Chiang's government and the establishment of a revolutionary power.

But your party had entirely given up the revolutionary program, including agrarian reform, the eight-hour day, national independence, etc. Under the blandishments and persuasion of American imperialism, represented by Marshall, you engaged in continuous and prolonged compromise peace negotiations with Chiang Kai-shek, this counterrevolutionary butcher, in hope of establishing a "coalition government" and thus moving toward "construction of a New China."

Meanwhile, we criticized and warned you that your opportunist compromise policy not only would lead nowhere, but would let slip the revolutionary conjuncture and help Chiang Kai-shek gain time to stabilize his shaky position and plot his military preparations to launch an all-out attack on your party. (Read "Our Views on the Present Situation," published in December 1945.) Unfortunately, the development of the events completely verified our criticism and warning.

Later, when the peace negotiations failed completely and Chiang Kai-shek had already started his military offensive, you were obliged to once more propose land reform, and finally overthrow Chiang Kai-shek's reactionary regime on the mainland by military means. This is indeed a tremendous political turn for your party since your "second collaboration" with the Kuomintang beginning in 1937. The victory of today is precisely due to this turn. We consider your "revision" of your previous compromise policy with Chiang Kai-shek not only a decisive turn in your party's politics but also a historical leap in the development of the Chinese revolution.

Yet, after your party had overthrown Chiang Kai-shek's regime, you did not proceed directly to the establishment of a worker-peasant soviet government of the proletariat leading the peasants, relying on the revolutionary forces of worker and peasant masses—but, on the contrary, with all the other bourgeois and petty-bourgeois political parties and factions except Chiang's clique you formed a "united front" (in the form of the "Political Consultative Conference"), established the so-called coalition government or "People's Democratic Dictatorship" with the participation of workers, peasants, petty bourgeoisie, and national bourgeoisie. This is entirely in violation of the essential teachings of Marxism-Leninism and the tradition of the October revolution.

On the land problem, you have carried out confiscation of the land and distributed it to the peasants. You have also secured considerable political independence from imperialism. These are important gains on the revolutionary road. But, through your decrees, landlords and rich peasants are still legally entitled to preserve their "industrial and commercial properties," and you have openly declared that imperialist properties in China will be protected. Not only is this not thoroughgoing; it has become a great obstacle to further development of the revolution.

Above all, since you did not immediately confiscate and nationalize the means of production and bourgeois private property as the first step in the direction of socialism, but instead granted them legal protection, this has made it possible for the bourgeoisie to sabotage the realization of national economic construction today. Moreover, the bourgeoisie is left with a material basis that can enable it to restore its counterrevolutionary rule.

Most important and decisive for revolutionary perspectives is the following fact: Your party, which claims to represent the workers and the peasants, and which particularly exalts the worker as its "master," has in practice done its best to restrict the workers and peasants and limit their democratic rights, especially the revolutionary activities of the worker masses.

They are not allowed to directly elect their own representatives to form councils or a congress of workers and peasants to supervise and control the state administration and all organizations of production. Even the representatives of trade unions and peasant associations are for the most part appointed. In addition, the workers are deprived of the right to defend themselves by strike action against capitalist exploitation. Hence the current bureaucratic abuses and despotism. This situation will inevitably sap the revolutionary initiative and the vigor of the worker and peasant masses and act as a brake to the further development of the revolution toward ultimate victory.

Notwithstanding all the serious differences in our views as stated above, we Trotskyists, conscious of our revolutionary responsibilities, approve and support to the best of our ability the revolutionary conquests which you have already arrived at, such as the overthrow of the Chiang Kai-shek regime and the agrarian reform.

We have participated in all the progressive movements and campaigns initiated by your party, such as the campaign to liquidate the remaining forces of Chiang Kai-shek, the land reform movement, the campaign against American aid to Korea, etc. And we are ready to defend with all our might these same revolutionary conquests against aggression from any imperialism, especially American imperialism and its lackey, Chiang Kai-shek.

To undertake our responsibilities to the revolution regardless of differences in political opinion—that is our attitude. This can be proved by examining the practical activity in the past years of the comrades you have arrested. Not a few of them have been openly praised in your papers on account of their hard work and self-sacrifice in various campaigns and movements. It is likewise clearly demonstrated by the public position and actions of the various sections of the Fourth International.

In the United States, where there is no section of the Fourth

International, the Trotskyists of the Socialist Workers Party and the Trotskyist paper, the *Militant*, have incessantly opposed American imperialism in its support of Chiang Kai-shek and its aggression in Korea. The American Trotskyists publicly demand that the United States recognize your "People's Government." They oppose the preparations for a third world war aimed at the Soviet Union and China, etc.

The Trotskyists in Ceylon have not only been propagandizing in general in favor of and in support of the revolutionary movement you head, but their representatives in parliament have further proposed to the Ceylon government that it reach a trade agreement with your government, and are vigorously pressing this move ahead to success. At your Peace Conference in Peking last November, their delegates openly and resolutely called on the worker and peasant masses of all countries to defend the revolution headed by you against aggression from imperialism.

Here, I must call your attention particularly to the following facts: For these twenty-five years, we Trotskyists have carried through the most resolute struggle for the national independence of China, for the liberation of the proletarian and peasant masses, for a socialist perspective—against the imperialist invasion, against the reactionary rule of the Kuomintang, and against capitalist and landlord exploitation and oppression of the workers and peasants.

It is precisely because of this struggle that our comrades suffered the most brutal persecution from all reactionary forces. Many of them were killed by the imperialists, especially the Japanese, by Chiang Kai-shek and Wang Ching-wei. Many other comrades passed long, painful years together with your comrades in the prisons of our common enemies. Comrade I K'uan, whom you arrested two years ago, and Comrade Cheng Ch'ao-lin, just recently arrested, are among those who were imprisoned together with your comrades for a number of years in Chiang Kai-shek's dungeons. And I, too, once spent three years in the same cell in the prison at Nanking where your comrade Niu Lan (then deputy of the Comintern to China) was held.[1] Even today, we have not a few comrades still imprisoned by Chiang Kai-shek on the island of Taiwan.

While you are at present engaged in a decisive battle with American imperialism and its puppet Chiang Kai-shek, against the reactionary landlords, and partially against the capitalists, by what reason are you justified in so ruthlessly persecuting the most resolute fighters on the same front, the Trotskyists?

Let me remind you in particular that your party is now agitating for a "united front" against the aggression of "American imperialism and Bandit Chiang." This "united front" includes all bourgeois and petty-bourgeois political parties and factions (such as those collected in your "Political Consultative Conference"). Further, even such hangmen of the second revolution as Li Chi-shen, Yang Hu, and the partisans of Chiang Kai-shek's reactionary rule such as Ch'eng Ch'ien and Lung Yün are placed in top posts in your government.

At the same time you are especially intolerant of revolutionary Trotskyists. You refuse to permit them to serve the revolution and to struggle for the interests of the vast worker and peasant masses within the movement that is under your leadership.

How explain this grotesque phenomenon? If it is not aimed at injuring the revolutionary left wing to please the reactionary right opportunists, it only demonstrates that you are consciously or unconsciously reflecting the pressure of the Kremlin. What cutting irony this presents in the movement under your leadership!

Since Lenin's death, Stalin has eliminated step by step the whole generation of Old Bolsheviks and massacred the first great leaders of the October revolution. He was particularly hostile to the revolutionary thought and positions represented by Trotsky, and hence would not spare any means to calumniate, to smear, to frame him up with the most hideous "counterrevolutionary crimes" in order to persecute him and his partisans and supporters. The atmosphere of extraordinary hostility thus created still prevails in the USSR and the Communist parties of various countries. Your previous and present hostility and persecution toward our comrades is undoubtedly fruit of this vicious and poisonous tradition of Stalin's bureaucracy.

However, in the brief period since Stalin's death, under pressure of the increasingly acute international situation and the accumulating dissatisfaction of the masses, his successors, beginning to feel uneasy about the criminal persecutions under Stalin's rule for which they bear guilt, have even openly exposed the charges against the fifteen doctors previously arrested by the Ministry of Public Security* as complete frame-ups and have

---

*At the end of 1952 a number of prominent Soviet doctors—almost all Jews—were arrested and charged with plotting assassinations and other acts in collusion with Jewish organizations and U.S. intelligence.

also revealed the persecutions inflicted on the workers by the party and Bureau of Public Security in Georgia.

This signifies that Stalin's successive big trials in the past were all frame-ups concocted to eliminate his adversaries. It also reveals that the whole GPU regime created by Stalin is beginning to collapse. All this deserves your special attention and should prompt you to correct your position.

All the conquests which you have already obtained in this revolution—the overthrow of Chiang Kai-shek's reactionary rule, the carrying out of land reform, the struggle for national independence . . . are really great and monumental. You should be proud of them. But you must also be clear and alert to the fact that these achievements are still far from the goal of ultimate triumph.

Obstructions bar the way. The influence of the bourgeoisie in the country is still generally intact. The greater part of the national borders are still surrounded by mercenary armed forces of imperialism. Above all the third world war is being prepared at accelerated speed by American imperialism with the USSR and China as main targets.

In this situation, to overcome all internal and external dangers and obstacles, to resist and crush the coming general offensive of American imperialism, you should be extremely calm and watchful and consider all the fundamental problems of the revolution without prejudice.

You should stand on the fundamental position of the historic interests of the Chinese proletariat and poor peasant masses and the world socialist revolution. You should free yourselves immediately from the yoke of the Kremlin bureaucracy.

First of all it is necessary to change entirely the present bureaucratic centralist system and replace it with genuine proletarian democracy. It is necessary to trust and rely unreservedly on the revolutionary initiative of the worker and peasant masses. They must have complete freedom to fully express their own opinions and aspirations, to carry out their revolutionary struggles to the fullest extent, and to democratically elect without delay their own representative organizations—soviets (councils) to replace the present four-class "coalition government." (The univerally elected people's conference of all classes now being prepared by you is not able to create a genuine democratic centralist system.) It is necessary to confiscate all the means of production now held by the bourgeoisie as a step forward on the road to socialist construction.

On the international plane, you should discard whatever sectarian attitude you have, support and unite with all workers' revolutionary parties and organizations in different countries in the struggle to overthrow the rule of reaction and to conquer power in these countries as the alternative to today's "peace" campaigns. Only if the revolutionary struggle of the working class and all the exploited throughout the world, and especially in the advanced capitalist countries, grows and wins victory can the outbreak of the third world war possibly be prevented, or the attempted aggression of American imperialism be smashed in the course of the war.

Free all the arrested Trotskyists! Let the Trotskyists and all other parties organized in the name of the workers have complete democratic freedom to express revolutionary ideas and to criticize your current policy in order to push the revolution forward.

Personally, I, together with some comrades among you, was responsible for carrying out Stalin's opportunist policy in the second revolution. This resulted in the most tragic defeat. It is precisely from that bitter experience that I have since understood most profoundly the disastrous effects of a revolutionary defeat, and its lessons. For this reason, I am not willing to see the present revolution under your leadership wrecked midway, and the worker and peasant masses shed blood in vain.

If you could cast off Stalin's bureaucratism and opportunism and return to the position of Marxism-Leninism and the tradition of the October revolution, I would exert all my efforts to support you and cooperate with you in pushing this revolution forward to ultimate completion.

April 14, 1953

THE THIRD CHINESE REVOLUTION AND ITS PERSPECTIVES

On the basis of the deepgoing changes that have taken place within China, and their tremendous impact on relations in the Orient and internationally, it is not an exaggeration to describe the third Chinese revolution as the biggest event since the October revolution in Russia in 1917. Because of this importance, its consequences at home and abroad and its perspectives deserve special attention and examination, whether or not one approves of the revolution.

Unfortunately, up to now, there have only been blind attacks from its opponents and superficial accounts and eulogies from its supporters. There are very few people who are able to give a penetrating account of the revolution and an analysis of the causes of its victory, its achievements, and its contradictory elements, and arrive at a balanced evaluation. Therefore I will try to provide a general account and analysis of the causes of the victory of the third Chinese revolution, its gains, its inherent contradictions, and its perspectives, all based on a number of indisputable facts, in order to offer international readers a point of reference for their research and understanding.

Diverse causes of the revolution's victory

Although it overthrew the Ch'ing dynasty, the first Chinese revolution (1911), under the leadership of Sun Yat-sen, the representative of the bourgeoisie, left the most fundamental national and democratic tasks completely untouched—tasks such as national independence, agrarian reform, liberation of the minority nationalities in the country, etc. Moreover, the revolu-

---

This article was written at the end of 1954 for publication in German by the Swiss Trotskyist organization. It has not previously appeared in English.

tion led to a situation in which the country was torn apart by struggles between the old and new warlords, and incessant warfare among them plunged the people into the depth of misery.

The second revolution (1925-27) was led by the Chinese Communist Party, representing the Chinese proletariat. By then this party was completely controlled by Stalin and the Soviet bureaucracy, who replaced the Bolshevik line of the proletariat leading the peasantry in independent struggle, substituting the Menshevik line of the "bloc of four classes" (workers, peasants, petty bourgeoisie, and national bourgeoisie). Stalin forced the Chinese CP to join the Kuomintang and to become the accomplice of the bourgeoisie in deceiving the masses, to the fatal detriment of the struggle for power of the proletariat leading the peasantry. This revolution was tragically defeated. Chiang Kai-shek's counter-revolutionary military dictatorship was erected on the blood of the worker and peasant masses. Under this dictatorship the entire country was dragged to the brink of ruin after the invasion by Japanese imperialism.

The third Chinese revolution, under the leadership of the Chinese Communist Party, has destroyed Chiang Kai-shek's reactionary rule on the mainland, secured national independence on the international arena, and has generally carried out the agrarian reform. These are enormous achievements.

However, the CCP, which led this revolution to victory and obtained these tremendous successes, still remains a Stalinist or opportunist party. It has proceeded along the basic line of the "bloc of four classes," abandoning its own role as a proletarian leadership leading the peasants on the road of insurrection and power. Instead, it relied entirely on the peasant armed forces to attack the cities and win its victory. This appears to be in opposition to the revolutionary theory of Marxism and in contradiction to all the other experiences in the modern history of revolutions. For this reason, the Chinese revolution has caused great confusion, bewilderment, distortions, disputes, and strange interpretations among revolutionary and radical groups both in China and internationally.

In order to clear away the various strange ideas and correctly understand the nature of this revolution, I believe one must first explain the diverse causes that contributed to its victory.

On the basis of Mao Tse-tung's opportunist line of class collaboration and the purely military actions of the peasant army isolated from the urban proletariat, one cannot find any revolutionary doctrine or experience that would explain this victory.

The defeat of the second Chinese revolution and the successive debacles of the attempts to form the "Red Army" in the country-side (peasant armed forces) to attack the cities has amply illustrated this.

What, then, were the causes of the victory of this revolution led by the CCP? The explanation lies in the extremely complex and exceptional situation created by the Sino-Japanese War and the Second World War. This situation is expressed by the following characteristics as far as China is concerned:

1. The decay and disintegration of Chiang Kai-shek's rule

Because Chiang's regime represented the counterrevolutionary interests of the Chinese bourgeoisie, from the very beginning it was marked by Asiatic arbitrariness, corruption, and impotence. All these traits were developed to an extreme during the eight years of resistance to the Japanese invasion. This not only provoked intense hostility and resentment among the masses, but it even caused deep dissatisfaction and despair on the part of the great majority of the bourgeoisie, which had previously supported the regime but now began to desert it and go over to the opposition. This situation was manifested in the Kuomintang, the government, and the army, resulting in the formation of anti-Chiang cliques that tore the Kuomintang apart, paralyzed the government, and disorganized the army.

On the other hand, because of the total absorption of financial resources by the prolonged Resistance War, inflation assumed unheard-of proportions, bankruptcies or stagnation swept the major part of industry and commerce, and an economic crisis was precipitated. This in turn drove the great mass of the population, including Chiang's lower-level functionaries, toward famine and death, further intensifying their resentment against Chiang's government. In short, at the end of the Second World War, Chiang's regime was already rotten from top to bottom and was disintegrating. Its sole base of support during its death agony was American imperialism.

2. American imperialism finally deserts Chiang Kai-shek

As a result of the Second World War, Japanese imperialism was completely wiped out as a foreign influence in China. British imperialism, due to its weakness, also withdrew from the Chinese political arena, maintaining its influence only in Hong Kong and Kowloon. American imperialism alone had the ambition to monopolize the Chinese market through its support of Chiang's government, and it wanted to establish a stronghold against the Soviet Union. To this end it furnished enormous material aid to Chiang's government and rearmed Chiang's army at the end of the Second World War. When U.S. imperialism saw the extreme decay of Chiang's regime and the ever-growing menace of the CCP's forces, it sent Gen. Marshall to China on a special mission to attempt to persuade Chiang Kai-shek to carry out some reforms against corruption as preventative measures and to seek a temporary compromise with Mao in order to gain time to prepare for his extermination.

But Chiang's stupidity, ignorance, and stubbornness, representing the interests of the reactionary bourgeoisie and landlords, rendered any reform whatsoever impossible, and his categorical refusal to engage in any compromise with Mao doomed Marshall's mission to complete failure. All that was left for American imperialism was to exercise direct control over Chiang's government and launch a military offensive against the CCP on its own. But the exceptional situation created by the Second World War did not permit American imperialism to adopt that course of action. It would have drawn the entire armed forces of the U.S. into the swamp of China and would run the risk of provoking a new world war, which the U.S. was not yet prepared for. Such a course would, moreover, have encountered strong opposition from its British imperialist ally. For these reasons, when Mao's party began its counteroffensive against Chiang's regime, American imperialism was forced to finally abandon the regime and adopt a "wait and see" attitude, hoping for better times to come.

3. The extraordinary growth of the peasant armed forces of Mao's party

Mao Tse-tung's original strength derived from the armed peasant forces that developed during the peasant insurrections after the defeat of the second revolution. These peasant armies suffered many attacks by Chiang's forces and were compelled to retreat from the South to the North in a greatly weakened state. They finally showed their submission to Chiang's government by abandoning the name "Red Army" and the call for "soviets," giving up the agrarian revolution, and accepting the lead of Chiang's government in their participation in the Resistance War against the Japanese invasion. During and after the war the utter incapacity, despotism, and rottenness of Chiang's government and the hatred fermenting in the general population and especially in the peasantry afforded major new opportunities for

Mao's peasant armed forces to develop once again. This peasant army became a huge force within a brief period of time.

However, Mao's party's political line, which was still one of class collaboration in hopes of achieving a compromise with Chiang and establishing a "coalition government," contributed to slowing down and even paralyzing the class struggle of the working class and poor peasants. But due to the extreme suffering and misery of the masses and the lack of a genuine revolutionary party to lead them, Mao's party, which made certain criticisms of Chiang's government and proposed some democratic reforms, became a pole of attraction in which the common people, especially the petty-bourgeois and peasant masses, placed their hopes. This was the source of this party's political capital. This "political capital" plus the "peasant armed forces" constituted the subjective strength of Mao's party. But without the aid of the Soviet Union the victory of that party would still have been quite uncertain.

4. *The Soviet Union's aid to Mao's party*

Although the Soviet bureaucracy was extremely fearful of a revolution under the virtual leadership of the working class in alliance with the peasantry in China, and although its postwar diplomacy aimed at conciliation with American imperialism in order to maintain "peaceful coexistence," nevertheless in order to maintain its own privileges and resist the extreme threat of a U.S. imperialist offensive, the Soviet bureaucracy would not hesitate to support Mao's party as long as it could control it.

For example, although when the USSR occupied Manchuria (the biggest center of heavy industry in China) it destroyed all the productive organizations, paralyzed the struggle of the working class there, and transferred the big cities and mines to Chiang Kai-shek, at the same time it also tried to prevent Chiang from using the Manchurian industry and mining enterprises, and it armed Mao's troops with the mass of weapons taken from the captured Japanese army. These weapons enabled Mao's army to beseige these big cities and mining districts, forcing Chiang Kai-shek to tie down a large portion of his armed forces to defend these centers. This involved tremendous financial expenditures and was nothing less than a fatal blow to Chiang's regime. Moreover, with its control over Mukden and Dairen, the Soviet Union cut the main maritime communications link between Chiang's government and Manchuria, while using these cities as bases to supply Mao's army in Shantung and Hopeh and to furnish them with technical military personnel from the Soviet Union and from among the Japanese captives. The backward peasant armed forces, originally very badly equipped in terms of modern weapons, especially heavy weapons, was suddenly transformed into a modernized army. The former peasant army, which had been limited to guerrilla warfare, was now capable of coping with large-scale regular battles and attempting offensives on the large cities. This factor undoubtedly played a decisive role in assuring the victory of Mao's party, which relied entirely on the peasant army in conquering the cities.

The facts above provide a clear picture: the bourgeois-landlord power of Chiang Kai-shek was undergoing complete economic, political, and military collapse, and in the end had been deserted even by American imperialism, which had previously supported it. The peasant armed forces, having the support of the peasants and the petty bourgeoisie and especially having received enormous arms aid from the Soviet Union in the form of captured Japanese weapons, had become a giant army with modern equipment. All these objective and subjective factors resulted in the extraordinary victory of Mao's party, which counted entirely on the peasantry in its offensive on the cities.

This victory would have been impossible if even one of these exceptional conditions had been missing. If, for example, American imperialism had been able to undertake direct military intervention in the face of Mao's party's counteroffensive against Chiang's regime, as it was able to do in Korea, China would inevitably have been the arena of a prolonged international war. In that case Mao's party could at most have controlled part of the North of the country.

Similarly, if the Soviet Union had not occupied Manchuria during the Second World War, and if Chiang Kai-shek had been allowed to control this whole area under the direction of the U.S. army, utilizing the industrial base and the huge quantity of arms taken from the Japanese army, and cutting off contact between Mao's party and the Soviet Union, it would not only have been impossible for Mao's party to conquer the whole country, but even its control of the North would have been questionable.

Precisely because all these exceptional conditions existed at the same time, the opportunist CCP, which had entirely given up mobilizing the urban working class and relied on the peasant army, succeeded in overthrowing Chiang's regime and established its "People's Government" or "People's Democratic Dictatorship." Precisely for this reason, this *third Chinese revolution has suffered extraordinary deformations;* in other words, it differs from all classical revolutions, and *it contains very deep contradictions that seriously affect all political and economic measures carried out by Mao's party and distort and hamper the natural development of the revolution, sowing nearly insurmountable difficulties and crises for its future.*

The composition and character of the new regime

In order to understand the internal organization of Mao's regime and the political and economic measures it has carried out, it is necessary to briefly examine Mao's opportunism.

The clearest and most systematic expression of Mao Tse-tung's opportunism can be found in his work "On New Democracy." The doctrine of "New Democracy," which is derived from Stalin's adoption of the Menshevik theory of "revolution by stages," artificially divided the Chinese revolution into two historical stages: the stage of the bourgeois-democratic revolution and the later stage of socialist revolution. According to this schema, the so-called democratic revolution restricts itself to carrying out agrarian reform and proceeding with the struggle for national independence, without trying to overthrow the whole bourgeoisie, expropriate its private property, or establish a dictatorship of the proletariat. On the contrary, the schema calls for collaborating with the bourgeoisie in establishing a coalition government, and protecting its property and guaranteeing its "lawful profits."

Only after completing the first stage can one proceed on with the socialist revolution, i.e., expropriation of bourgeois property and establishment of the proletarian dictatorship. This doctrine runs counter to the Marxist concept of the permanent revolution, and it flies in the face of the historical experience of the Russian October revolution.

The experience of the October revolution has vividly demonstrated that the revolutionary road in the backward countries must of necessity be the road of intransigent struggle by the proletariat leading the peasantry against the bourgeoisie. This leads to the insurrection, the destruction of the bourgeois regime, and to the establishment of a proletarian dictatorship. In this way the revolution, in the natural course of its development, solves the democratic tasks and at the same time puts the expropriation of bourgeois private property, the first step on the road to socialist construction, on the agenda. This is the concrete and living expression of the theory of permanent revolution.

But because Mao Tse-tung counterposes his "New Democracy" or "revolution by stages" to the theory of permanent revolution, even after the overthrow of the Chiang regime Mao persists in maintaining a "united front" with the national or democratic bourgeoisie as the first step in the realization of his "New Democratic" politics. This "united front" is embodied in the so-called Political Consultative Conference, which is composed of representatives of the Chinese Communist Party, various bourgeois and petty-bourgeois parties, trade unions and peasant organizations, etc. It becomes the supreme body in defining the general policy of the state. The composition of the new regime is thus not the product of the election of representatives of workers' and peasants' committees (in the sense of soviets), but is determined by the Political Consultative Conference. For this reason this regime, which includes representatives of the CCP, the trade unions and peasant associations, and bourgeois and petty-bourgeois parties and groups, is called a "coalition government" of the four classes (workers, peasants, petty bourgeoisie, and national bourgeoisie) or a "People's Government."

In both the Political Consultative Conference and the "coalition government" the Chinese CP undoubtedly holds the final decision-making power in its own hands, especially maintaining complete control of the army and police. However, the bourgeoisie can exercise some influence on the policy of the Political Consultative Conference and the "People's Government" through its superiority in property relations and in society as well as through its representatives who still hold important positions in the People's Government on different levels. Three vice-presidents and several ministers and vice-ministers of the central government, for example, are representatives of the bourgeoisie. In addition, three presidents of provincial governments are their representatives.

On the other hand, the working class and poor peasants not only do not have their own representative councils to directly elect their representatives to participate in the government, but they further suffer great restrictions in expressing their opinions and in their activity (such as being deprived of the right to strike, etc.). At most they have to be content with the CCP's naming its own trusted delegates from the trade unions and peasant associations to participate in the different levels of government.

The regional and provincial People's Congresses that have been held since the beginning of this year (1954) and the various levels of the People's Government formally elected by the National People's Congress held in September do not change the essence of the former provisional People's Governments. Since the election of the People's Congresses is based on so-called universal suffrage, all the "national or democratic bourgeoisie" and the petty bourgeoisie are eligible to vote and to be elected. And in fact, all the representatives to the People's Congresses were designated or nominated beforehand by the CCP and the various bourgeois and petty-bourgeois parties or factions. Consequently the population could merely vote for those appointed "candidates," and the People's Governments that emerged from the People's Congresses, especially the central government, were scarcely different from their predecessors. The National People's Congress held this year has only added a legal coating to the original provisional People's Government.

The basic policy of this People's Government also contains great contradictions. Its famous slogan is "mutual consideration for both state and private property, equal benefits for both labor and capital." This means that on the one hand the property of the "bureaucratic bourgeoisie" is confiscated by the state and operated on the basis of the state-controlled planned economy, while on the other hand the private property of the so-called national bourgeoisie is protected and allowed to secure "legal profits" subject only to the condition of "coordination" in production. The working class is honored as the "master," but at the same time it remains the employee of the capitalist, who only has to observe certain limits on his exploitation.

In view of the composition of the new regime and its political line, as described above, this regime certainly is no longer a bourgeois dictatorship. But it cannot be characterized as a proletarian dictatorship either. Rather it is a distorted form of dual power that is in transition between the bourgeois and proletarian dictatorship. This dual power has very little in common with the classic form as it appeared after the February revolution in Russia. In fact it has no historic precedent. Nevertheless, it has some features that are essentially similar to the regimes that existed in the postwar Eastern European countries (with the exception of Yugoslavia) up to 1947. This regime is not stable. It has a tendency either to move forward and become a proletarian dictatorship, or to slide back to a bourgeois dictatorship.

Tremendous achievements of the agrarian reform and the hidden dangers

The agrarian reform carried out by Mao's party has gone through successive stages and is therefore officially characterized as an "agrarian reform in stages." Actually the regime was forced to proceed with the land reform empirically and step by step under the twofold pressure of the reactionary forces and peasant masses.

Early in 1946, under the pressure of Chiang's military offensive and the insistent demands of the peasants, Mao's party began a limited land reform in some of the areas under its control in order to strengthen its military forces for resistance to Chiang. In 1948, as part of the preparations for a counteroffensive against Chiang Kai-shek, the agrarian reform was extended to all the "old liberated areas," and to the Northeast, "Manchuria." As soon as Chiang's regime was overthrown, the agrarian reform was halted and officially postponed until 1950. But beginning in 1950, especially with the outbreak of the Korean War, the CCP was compelled to carry out a nationwide agrarian reform when faced with serious discontent among the general peasant masses and the raging counterrevolutionary forces of the landlords and rich peasants.

This agrarian reform was largely completed on a national scale at the end of 1952, except in regions inhabited by national minorities (Inner Mongolia, Sinkiang, Tibet, and certain national minority areas in the Southwest). The surplus land belonging to landlords and rich peasants was expropriated and distributed to the landless or land-hungry poor peasants and tenants. This reform destroyed the semifeudal agrarian system that had survived more than two thousand years in China, and it eliminated the whole landlord class along with the system of exploitation. Over 200 million poor peasants and tenants have received their piece of land. The productive forces in the countryside have experienced the first stage of emancipation, and the preconditions for a general rise in the peasants' standard of living are now present. Rural power has been transferred from the landlords and rich peasants into the hands of the poor and middle peasants. The most backward and reactionary rituals, habits, and traditions, which had long dominated the countryside, have been swept away. This is an extremely important and deepgoing reform, an expression of social revolution. It is one of the greatest and most progressive achievements in modern Chinese history.

However, alongside the tremendous achievements of the agrarian reform, the seeds of new dangers have been sown in the countryside. This is due to the CCP's opportunist policy of "maintaining the industrial and commercial properties of landlords and rich peasants" contained in the agrarian reform law, and the policy of allowing "free purchase and sale of land" after the completion of the reform.

Because of the "industrial and commercial property" they retain, the landlords and especially the rich peasants naturally occupy a superior position in the rural economy. The new regime's encouragement of the peasants to "enrich themselves," and other measures protecting the rich peasants in the name of raising rural productivity, have furnished the rich peasants with a good opportunity to rapidly flourish. Today the better-off middle peasants have become rich peasants (called "new rich peasants") and, joining the original rich peasants, are the dominant economic force in the countryside. Rural handicrafts, cultivation of industrial raw materials, and the majority of retail trade have fallen into their hands.

On the other hand, the lower layers of the middle peasants have gradually degenerated into poor peasants. Among the poor peasants and tenants who got their share of land, a number of them are again sinking into poverty and are gradually being dragged down the old path of despair due to a lack of the tools that are indispensable for rural production and the resulting extremely low productivity. Because of this situation, in an attempt to aid the poor peasants and as a bridge toward the collectivization of agriculture, the People's Government has promoted and even compelled peasants to join "mutual-aid teams" (which means collective farming by the individual farmers who then share the fruits according to the amount of labor and farming tools they contributed) and "agricultural cooperatives." But since the share of the harvest in the "mutual-aid teams" is proportional to the farming tools and labor expended in the course of collective farming, the rich peasants who possess tools such as cows, horses, and carts, which the poor peasants don't have, naturally get the larger and better portion of the share. The agricultural cooperatives, which distribute their benefits in proportion to the capital invested, also favor the rich peasants. As a result, the agricultural policy of the People's Government has led to the growth of the rich peasants and the pauperization of the poor ones.

Usury and land concentration are again emerging in the countryside, particularly in the "old liberated areas" of North and Northeast China. According to incidental revelations in the *People's Daily*, the official organ of the Chinese Communist Party, in some rural areas up to 20 percent of the poor peasants sell all or part of their land to rich peasants. Usury has become a more and more prevalent phenomenon. The most startling point is that in some districts in the Northeast, rural CCP members who are engaged in commercial enterprises, in land purchasing, and in usury are asking to withdraw from the party. This phenomenon has become so general that Kao Kang, the head of the CCP in the Northeast, acceded to their demands, asking only that they be "good citizens in the political sense."

On the other hand, while rural political power is generally in the hands of the poor and middle peasants, this does not mean that it is in the hands of representatives elected by committees of the poor and middle peasant masses. Actually political power is monopolized by elements coming from the poor and middle peasants who enjoy the confidence of the CCP and are designated by it. These elements have become the privileged bureaucrats in the rural districts and are gradually isolating themselves from the life of the broad poor peasant mass, who, under the economic pressure of the rich peasants and because of their discontent with the new bureaucracy, are becoming increasingly passive and often refuse to attend any kind of assemblies.

To sum up, despite the fact that the agrarian reform has thoroughly swept away the semifeudal landholding system and has established new land ownership on the basis of small-scale production, the opportunist policy of "protecting the industrial and commercial property of landlords and rich peasants" and the freedom to buy and sell land have raised serious dangers: reconcentration of landholding, growth of usury, rapid growth of the position of the rich peasants (i.e., capitalist economy), degeneration of the poor peasants, polarization of the middle peasants, and usurpation and monopoly of rural political power by bureaucratic elements.

The only way to overcome these dangers is to nationalize the land, restrict land purchases, expropriate all industrial and commercial properties of the landlords and rich peasants, and organize representative councils of poor and middle peasants in order to permit them to elect their own representatives to rural governmental bodies, thus replacing the current bodies that are monopolized by a few privileged elements in the countryside. But this transformation is only possible if the whole opportunist political line of the CCP is changed.

Economic construction and the contradictions involved

If the CCP has empirically carried out a social revolution in the countryside by overturning the property of the landlord class, it still lags far behind in the cities because of its basic line of class collaboration. This is fully revealed in its protection of the national bourgeoisie's private property.

Because of its desire to protect the national bourgeoisie's private property and legal interests, all the regime's economic measures and construction plans must deviate from the natural tendencies of economic development. This has created insurmountable contradictions.

On the one hand the state has confiscated the property of the "bureaucratic bourgeoisie" (which, in fact, for the most part are already state properties) and has proceeded with large-scale national economic construction. This has had considerable results. The currency has been stabilized, there is efficient control of foreign trade, the old industrial enterprises have been reorganized and modified, new industries have been created, the state operates some of the principal commodity markets (cereals, cotton, cloth, iron and steel, coal, wood, oil, etc.) in order to control the domestic market, the state dominates a large portion of retail commerce, etc. All these achievements have helped national industry and commerce to rapidly overcome the previous stagnation and ruin and to develop considerably. There is no question on this score.

But on the other hand, for the sake of protecting the property and legal interests of the national bourgeoisie, the new regime is deprived of the means to proceed with the full-scale planned economic construction that is required to cope with the needs of the national economy and to rapidly raise the standard of living of the working class and the masses in general. It is unable to move in the direction of socialist reconstruction of the economy.

Although it attempts to take advantage of the superiority of the state enterprises to control or coordinate the private enterprises (by means such as the restriction of loans to private enterprises from state banks, extra or supplementary orders sent by state enterprises to private ones, etc.), the state has not been able to resolve the fundamental contradictions between the state enterprises and private enterprises or to avoid the corrosive influence and sabotage of the private enterprises on the state sector. This situation has been fully exposed in the course of the "Three Anti" and "Five Anti" campaigns.[1]

Because of the existence of the private sector of the economy, the state economy must yield to the workings of all the capitalist economic laws (market laws of supply and demand, prices and wages, the law of profits, the law of an average rate of profit, etc.). This has a number of serious consequences.

For instance, in order to raise productivity and lower the costs of production, the state enterprises must compete with the private enterprises to secure the highest rate of profit. This competition not only intensifies the fundamental conflicts between the state and private enterprises, but it also seriously damages coordination among the various state enterprises and their mutually complementary functions. Meanwhile, the intensity of labor is strained to the limit, working hours are prolonged, wages are reduced, sanitary and safety equipment is neglected, etc. All this forces the workers to live with nervous tension, physical fatigue, and pain.

Along with a universal practice of piecework wages (the most brutal form of exploitation in capitalist society), propaganda is launched in favor of "labor heroes" and "model workers" (synonyms for Stakhanovists) to encourage the intensification of labor productivity and to serve as models for all workers, who are sometimes pushed by force to emulate them. Consequently, not only are the worker masses exhausted, and not only are the rates of accidents, illness, injury, and death increased, but a layer of privileged worker-aristocrats is artificially created within the working class, leading to divisions inside the class. These things all run entirely against the basic interests of the emancipation of the working class and are contrary to rational socialist economic reconstruction.

In addition to the contradictions and problems caused by the coexistence of state and private enterprises, bureaucratism causes grave injuries to the carrying out of economic measures and industrial construction. Because the CCP completely excludes the working class from directly controlling and managing state production, all productive organizations are run by purely bureaucratic and administrative commands. This expresses itself first of all in the gap between goals fixed by the production plans and the actual possibilities for their achievement.

For example, at the end of the first half of last year, which was the first year of the five-year plan announced in 1953, only 30 percent of the goals established by the plan were fulfilled (since the whole plan has never been published, only the first year figures are known). This reveals the blind chasing after figures that characterize this plan. Even the 30 percent of this plan was not accomplished through normal development based on real possibilities. Rather it proceeded through an uneven and feverish race for speed, employing labor contests in production. "Complete the plan by means of special measures stimulating productivity of labor" has become a universal slogan and phenomenon. This destroys the equilibrium and harmony of production and replaces it with a vicious cycle of production by forced measures, and results in a decline in the quality of production, a rise in unusable goods, damage to the means of production, and injuries and accidental deaths of workers.

At the same time the bureaucrats, ignoring the everyday needs of the masses and putting particular emphasis on the importance of building up heavy industry, have neglected light industry. This does harm to the organic relationship between heavy and light industry, leads to great shortages in necessities for the masses, and causes a soaring of prices that seriously affects the standard of living of the population.

These contradictions and harmful consequences will remain completely unresolved without the expropriation of all the bourgeoisie's private property and without the replacement of the present bureaucratic administration by representatives directly elected by the working class to control and manage production.

The new regime's foreign policy

In addition to the agrarian reform, another of the regime's major accomplishments is the restoration of Chinese control over tariffs and the abolition of all extraterritorial privileges for the imperialists, such as the right to station imperialist armies in China and the right to free navigation on inland waters, which has resulted in the considerable extension of national sovereignty. Without formally proclaiming the expropriation of all imperialist properties in China, since the outbreak of the Korean War the government has been obliged to take over certain enterprises and cultural institutions that belonged to imperialists, especially American imperialists. All these measures have great economic as well as political significance.

Moreover, the People's Government was compelled to participate in the Korean War and has won glorious successes in it. It has also given enormous aid to the Vietminh in its war against French imperialism. These measures have increased the weight of China internationally, have seriously undermined the imperialist position and hold in Asia, and have greatly modified the relationship of forces between world imperialism and the anti-imperialist camp.

Despite all of this, the fundamental attitude of the new regime toward world capitalism is nevertheless wavering, opportunist, Stalinist. Because of the Korean War it has had to stress the struggle against American imperialism. But it has always adopted a compromising attitude toward the other imperialists, especially the British imperialists. It has still not called for the return of Hong Kong and Kowloon to China. In fact, this regime is subordinate to the leadership of the Kremlin bureaucracy's diplomacy, which attempts to ally itself with the non-American imperialists, especially British imperialism, and other capitalist countries like India, in order to stand up to American imperialism, *in hopes of reaching a compromise with it that can lead to "peaceful coexistence of socialism and capitalism." Needless to say, this policy runs contrary to the interests of the genuine emancipation of the Chinese and international working class and all oppressed nationalities.*

Because of the Stalinist tradition of Mao's party and the considerable support it got from the Soviet Union in the course of its fight to overthrow Chiang's regime and after taking power, the relationship between the new regime and the Soviet Union has been very close. This does not mean, however, that genuine equality and harmony exist between them.

The Chinese People's Government is quite different from those of the Eastern European countries (except Yugoslavia) in the sense that Mao Tse-tung created his own party and army in the course of a prolonged struggle and because, thanks to its immense size and population, China has played an important role in Asia. Rather than being servile and docile in its relations with the Kremlin, China maintains considerable independence. On the other hand, under the pressure of the Soviet Union's preponderant superiority on the economic and military planes, the government is obliged to follow the Kremlin's lead in order to obtain its support and protection. Therefore it must consult with the Kremlin on the political and economic measures it takes at home, and on its foreign policy.

In the past five years the Soviet Union, besides offering limited economic and financial support and military aid to Mao's government (for example, its participation in the Korean War), has sent tens of thousands of "advisers and specialists" to all parts of China, penetrating deep into the Chinese army, government institutions, party, factories, transport, commerce, cooperatives, and cultural organizations. These advisers and specialists have certainly made considerable contributions in the military arts and the technical side of industrial construction. At the same time, however, their penetration contributes to strengthening the Kremlin's influence and control over Mao's regime. In any event, the Soviet bureaucracy's support and respect for the independence of Mao's government is conditioned by the extent of its capacity to control it. What comes from the Soviet bureaucracy is in the long run more harmful than helpful to the general interests of the Chinese revolution. This reflects the incompatibility between the fundamental revolutionary interests of the Chinese working class and the privileges of the Soviet bureaucracy.

China's future

Since the natural course of this last Chinese revolution has been greatly distorted by the "New Democracy" schema imposed on it by Mao's party, and by the Menshevik-Stalinist theory of "revolution by stages" instead of the Marxist theory of "permanent revolution," this has led to tremendous contradictions in all economic and political aspects and it indicates the most probable tendency of development in the near future.

On the basis of existing conditions and the fundamental line laid out by Mao's party, we can make the following predictions: It is probable that even before either a new world war breaks out or a proletarian revolution is victorious in one or several advanced capitalist countries, *Mao's party will follow the path taken by the Eastern European countries. Under the pressure of class contradictions, both internal and from abroad, Mao's party will step by step eliminate the bourgeois representatives from the new regime, do away with the "coalition government," and establish a regime controlled by a single party, i.e., establish a "regime in transition from a people's democratic dictatorship to the proletarian dictatorship." In parallel fashion it will gradually annex or expropriate the bourgeois private enterprises to the state in a "transition from the New Democratic economy to the socialist economy."*

In this way China will resemble the deformed workers' states of

Eastern Europe in all essential features. If this happens, China will have to go through a political revolution to achieve genuine socialist construction, just as the Eastern European countries and the Soviet Union itself must.

If a new world war breaks out in the near future, or a proletarian revolution is victorious in any of the advanced capitalist countries, this would affect the evolution along the lines indicated above, and the destiny of China would then be decided in the course of the development of this war and the emerging revolutionary situation.

As a final word, the author expects that all revolutionary working-class parties and groups around the world will stand firm on the basic interests of the world socialist revolution and to the best of their ability will defend the successes and achievements of the Chinese revolution against any aggression by imperialism, particularly American imperialism. At the same time they must unreservedly criticize the opportunist policy and bureaucratism of Mao's party in order to help awaken the Chinese working class and enable the working class to consolidate its forces in gradually freeing itself from the hold of Mao's party's opportunism and bureaucratism, as a step toward the final triumph of a socialist revolution.

December 1, 1954

A CRITICISM OF THE VARIOUS VIEWS SUPPORTING THE CHINESE RURAL PEOPLE'S COMMUNES

What Our Attitude Should Be

The rural People's Commune movement was propelled by the Chinese Communist Party on an immense scale and at a ferocious tempo. Productive relations in agriculture were upset; personal lives of 500 million peasants were thrown into turmoil. Not only were the masses in all of China affected, especially the peasantry, in whom it aroused fright, anxiety, illusory hopes, and opposition; it became a worldwide issue. Landowners, capitalists, and imperialists, especially the Americans and the gangster Chiang and Company, vehemently denounced the movement. Bureaucrats in the Soviet bloc outside of China, and Stalinists the world over, exhibited the reticence that goes with great uneasiness. On the other hand, among petty-bourgeois circles abroad, especially among intellectuals far from China, it appeared that an ideal world had been realized in the People's Communes. They accepted them naively, and praised them lavishly.

Faced with something of such extraordinary and bewildering complexity, revolutionary Marxists, i.e., Trotskyists, require careful and detailed study to reach a correct objective estimate. We find ourselves compelled to utilize Marxist method and theory as a guide, and especially to recall the theory and strategy of Engels and Lenin in regard to the peasantry. To reach a correct position

---

This article was written in August 1959 as part of a discussion within the Fourth International and within the Socialist Workers Party over the Chinese government's decision the previous year to reorganize China's collective farms into huge agricultural "People's Communes."

171

on the communes we must consider the experience and lessons of agricultural reconstruction in Russia for the forty years since the October revolution and in the Eastern European countries for the past ten years. In addition, in our analysis and synthesis, we must collect the most dependable facts available on the Chinese commune movement itself. If we confine our approach merely to an abstract principle, to a one-sided formula, or to the propaganda of the CCP, or make a hasty appraisal and decision as to what our standpoint and attitude toward the communes should be, we inevitably risk being careless and arbitrary, and can even stumble onto the road of compromise with Stalinism and betrayal of Marxism. Differences in opinion have appeared over the Chinese communes, as is evident in the documents that have been published so far (mainly those of the Chinese and American comrades). If these differences deepen and develop to their logical conclusion, they can involve principles and lead to unfortunate consequences. It is my hope that through full and democratic discussion internationally we can clear up the differences and arrive at a common policy. I believe that the truth will emerge in a serious discussion and gain the approval of the majority.

Superiority of large-scale farming and the principle of voluntary peasant participation

Among the arguments presented in support of the People's Communes, the most powerful is the "superiority of large-scale farming." This stems from the axiom in Marxist political economy that "large-scale production is superior to production by small units."

A systematic exponent of this idea is our Chinese Comrade Ma Chi. In his long article *The People's Communes* he writes:

characteristic of the People's Communes are their "large scale" and "collective ownership." The so-called large scale is obtained through the merger of many cooperatives. . . . Ninety-nine percent of the peasantry at present have joined the People's Communes. There are 26,000, each including an average of 5,000 peasant households, over 10,000 laborers and 60,000 mu [six mu equal one acre]. . . . The agricultural economists tell us that in agriculture as well as in industry large-scale production is superior to production by small units. . . . [Ma Chi, *The People's Communes*, p. 4. The article has not been translated into English.—P'eng]

That large-scale production is superior to production by small units in agriculture as well as in industry is a general principle of economics that is undoubtedly true. That is why all socialists adhering to Marxism maintain that individual peasant farming must give way to agricultural collectives. Only as the scattered, less-productive small-peasant economy is superseded by cooperative ownership can the peasant become integrated into highly productive socialist economy. But this "economic principle" is closely related to and inseparable from the "political principle"— the "voluntary participation" of the peasants in large-scale units or collectives. If we only take the "economic principle," while the "political principle" is overlooked or abandoned, then, instead of advantages, damage and even worse can occur to the work of socialist construction.

Obviously—at least from the Marxist viewpoint—the difference between the peasants and the workers is qualitative. The peasants represent a transitional formation left over from precapitalist society that has not been assimilated by the capitalist system (but which undergoes continuous differentiation under the influence of capitalism). A portion of them have declined gradually, becoming hired peasants or laborers—the proletariat of rural areas. A smaller portion have become big peasants or rich peasants—rural capitalists. Engels pointed out in "The Peasant Question in France and Germany":

"This small peasant, just like the small handicraftsman, is therefore a toiler who differs from the modern proletarian in that he still possesses his instruments of labour; hence a survival of a past mode of production."[1]

In the same article, Engels analyzed in detail the gradual decline of the small peasant under the pressure of capitalist large-scale production and concluded: "The common possession of the means of production is thus set forth here as the sole principal goal to be striven for. Not only in industry, where the ground has already been prepared, but in general, hence also in agriculture."[2]

Engels pointed out the superiority of large-scale production from the economic viewpoint, and the necessity for the common possession of the means of production in agriculture, the replacement of small individual peasant holdings by collective ownership. But at the same time he declared:

it is just as evident that when we are in possession of state power we shall not even think of forcibly expropriating the small peasants (regardless of whether with or without compensation), as we shall have to do in the case of the big landowners. Our task relative to the small peasant consists, in the first place, in effecting a transition of his private enterprise and private possession to cooperative ones, not forcibly but by dint of example and the proffer of social assistance for this purpose. And then of course we shall have ample means of showing to the small peasant prospective advantages that must be obvious to him even today.[3]

We of course are decidedly on the side of the small peasant; we shall do everything at all permissible to make his lot more bearable, to facilitate his transition to the cooperative should he decide to do so, and even to make it possible for him to remain on his small holding for a protracted length of time to think the matter over, should he still be unable to bring himself to this decision.[4]

Engels thus dialectically combined the "economic principle" with the "willingness of the peasant." That is, he combined the principle of large-scale production in agricultural collectives with the principle of voluntary participation by the peasant, in this way establishing a basic norm governing the attitude of the proletariat toward the peasantry. This determines the strategic direction for agricultural reconstruction and the alliance between the workers and peasants. Since then, all revolutionary Marxists have accepted this as their guiding principle in action. The Bolsheviks, after the seizure of power and the establishment of the Soviet government following the October revolution, under Lenin's leadership applied the principle laid down by Engels. For example, Lenin said in his speech to the First Congress of Agricultural Communes and Agricultural Artels:

Of course, from all the activities of the Soviet government you know what tremendous significance we attach to the communes, artels, and all organizations generally that aim at transforming and at gradually assisting the transformation of small, individual peasant farming into socialised, co-operative, or artel farming. You are aware that the Soviet government long ago allotted the sum of one thousand million rubles to assist efforts of this kind. The Statute on Socialist Agrarian Measures particularly stresses the significance of communes, artels, and all enterprises for the joint cultivation of the land, and the Soviet government is exerting every effort to ensure that this law shall not remain on paper only, but shall really produce the benefits it is intended to produce.

The importance of all enterprises of this kind is tremendous, because if the old, poverty-stricken peasant farming remains unchanged there can be no question of building up a stable socialist society.[5]

In the above paragraph, immediately after emphasizing the significance of the aim of transforming small, individual peasant farming into communes, artels, and similar enterprises for common cultivation of the land, Lenin illustrated methods of carrying out this aim.

Only if we succeed in proving to the peasants in practice the advantages of common, collective, co-operative, artel cultivation of the soil, only if we succeed in helping the peasant by means of co-operative or artel farming, will the working class, which wields state power, be really able to convince the peasant that its policy is correct and thus secure the real and lasting following of the millions of peasants. It is therefore impossible to exaggerate the importance of every measure intended to encourage co-operative, artel forms of farming. We have millions of individual farms in our country, scattered and dispersed throughout remote rural districts. *It would be absolutely absurd to attempt to reshape these farms in any rapid way, by issuing an order or bringing pressure to bear from without. We fully realise that we can influence the millions of small peasant farms only gradually and cautiously and only by a successful practical example,* for the peasants are far too practical and cling far too tenaciously to the old methods of farming to consent to any serious change merely on the basis of advice or book instructions. That is impossible, and it would be absurd. Only when it has been proved in practice, by experience comprehensible to the peasants, that the transition to the co-operative, artel form of farming is essential and possible, shall we be entitled to say that in this vast peasant country, Russia, an important step towards socialist agriculture has been taken.[6]

Lenin states very clearly in the above paragraph that to prove "the advantages of common, collective, co-operative, artel cultivation of the soil," it is absolutely forbidden to use compulsive measures; we can only convince the millions of small peasants by practical example, and only in this way bring them to the side of the working class. This policy is not limited to Russia, but holds also in the advanced capitalist countries. In his "Preliminary Draft Theses on the Agrarian Question" for the Second Congress of the Communist International, Lenin wrote:

In most capitalist countries, however, the proletarian state should not at once completely abolish private property; at all events, it guarantees both the small and the middle peasantry, not only the preservation of their plots of land but also their enlargement to cover the total area they usually rented (the abolition of rent).

A combination of such measures with a ruthless struggle against the bourgeoisie fully guarantees the success of the policy of neutralisation. The proletarian state *must effect the transition to collective farming with extreme caution and only very gradually, by the force of example, without any coercion of the middle peasants.*[7]

The "principle of voluntary peasant participation," namely, the objection to coercive measures to force the peasants into collectives, Lenin stressed particularly, concretely, and in detail in his "Report on Work in the Countryside" delivered at the Eighth Congress of the Russian Communist Party in 1919:

> We must particularly stress the truth that here by the very nature of the case coercive methods can accomplish nothing. The economic task here is an entirely different one. . . . *Here coercion would ruin the whole cause.* Prolonged educational work is required. We have to give the peasant, who not only in our country but all over the world is a practical man and a realist, concrete examples to prove that the "communia" is the best possible thing. . . .
> On this question we must say that we do encourage communes, but they must be so organised *as to gain the confidence of the peasants. . . . Nothing is more stupid than the very idea of applying coercion in economic relations with the middle peasant.*[8]

> When it is stated that *we must strive to gain the peasants' voluntary consent, it means that they must be persuaded, and persuaded by practical deeds.* They will not allow themselves to be convinced by mere words, and they are perfectly right in that. It would be a bad thing if they allowed themselves to be convinced merely by reading decrees and agitational leaflets. *If it were possible to reshape economic life in this way, such reshaping would not be worth a brass farthing.*[9]

> We must live in peace with him. In a communist society the middle peasants will be on our side only when we alleviate and improve their economic conditions. If tomorrow we could supply one hundred thousand first-class tractors, provide them with fuel, provide them with drivers— you know very well that this at present is sheer fantasy—the middle peasant would say, "I am for the communia" (i.e., for communism). But in order to do that we must first defeat the international bourgeoisie, we must compel them to give us these tractors, or so develop our productive forces as to be able to provide them ourselves. This is the only correct way to pose this question.[10]

It was because of his resolute objection to forced collectivization, and insistence on model examples to persuade the peasants in agricultural reconstruction, that Lenin considered collectivization or cooperation to be absolutely impossible of accomplishment hastily or even within a brief time. Consequently he said in his essay "On Co-operation": "But it will take a whole historical epoch to get the entire population into the work of the co-operatives. . . . At best we can achieve this in one or two decades."[11]

According to Lenin, if Russia, with all its backwardness, was to eventually arrive at socialism (including agricultural collectivization), one condition was absolutely essential, namely electrification. He gave the following explanation:

> If we construct scores of district electric power stations . . . and transmit electric power to every village, if we obtain a sufficient number of electric motors and other machinery, we shall not need, or shall hardly need, any transition stages or intermediary links between patriarchalism and socialism. But we know perfectly well that it will take at least ten years only to complete the first stage of this "one" condition; this period can be conceivably reduced only if the proletarian revolution is victorious in such countries as Britain, Germany or the U.S.A.[12]

I have patiently quoted examples of Lenin's repeated emphasis on the correct principle in agricultural collectivization—the need for the voluntary consent of the peasants. I have done this not only because the bureaucrats in the Stalinist parties have violated this principle, but also because quite a few Trotskyists, deluded by the current Chinese rural People's Communes, have also forgotten or neglected it.

In the period following Lenin's death, Stalin, compromising with the rich peasants, abandoned, or, at least, delayed agricultural collectivization. The growth of the rich peasants was facilitated, leading to a serious food famine. Beginning in 1929, under the threat of the mounting influence of the rich peasants, Stalin jumped from one extreme to the other, forcing all peasants by decree to join collectives despite their resistance. He even mobilized the Red Army and the GPU to suppress the opposition of the rich peasants and the great majority of the middle peasants. The tragic results of the forced collectivization are well known to us; they testify that violation of the will of the peasants leads to dire consequences.

Forced collectivization in Eastern Europe after World War II provided fresh evidence that such measures create dissatisfaction among the peasants, and lead to stagnation and even retrogression in agricultural production. Chronic food shortages forced Tito and Gomulka to readjust and even dissolve some collectives in order to allay the crisis.

In the struggle between Trotsky and Stalin, agricultural collectivization became an important issue. Trotsky fully accepted the principle established by Engels and Lenin of respecting the will of the peasants in agricultural collectivization. When Stalin made his compromise with the rich peasants and delayed collectivization in 1926, the Left Opposition led by Trotsky called for a policy of collectivization. Later when Stalin introduced forced collectivization in the face of peasant resistance, Trotsky relentlessly attacked it as adventurism that would lead to disaster. Finally, in the Transitional Program of the Fourth International Trotsky summarized as the guiding strategy for the alliance of workers and peasants Engels's and Lenin's principles for the nationalization of land and collectivization, and drew the tragic lesson of its malpractice in Russia under Stalin.

> The program for the *nationalization of the land and the collectivization of agriculture* should be so drawn that from its very basis it should exclude the possibility of expropriation of small farmers and their compulsory collectivization. The farmer will remain owner of his plot of land as long as he himself believes it possible or necessary. In order to rehabilitate the program of socialism in the eyes of the farmer, it is necessary to expose mercilessly the Stalinist methods of collectivization, which are dictated not by the interests of the farmers or workers but by the interests of the bureaucracy.[13]

Now let us turn to the Chinese communes. Were they formed with the voluntary consent of the peasants, or as the CCP propaganda puts it, with the enthusiastic support of the peasant masses? Ma Chi, who supports the communes, made the following judgment:

> The commune movement as a whole was largely compulsory in character. . . . Though the CCP agrees in words with the principle of voluntary consent by the peasants, it has not complied with it in deeds. The People's Communes started as an experiment in April 1958, but the documents concerning them were first published in August 1958. Then in a period of not more than two months, 99 percent of the rural population was organized into the communes. In such a short period, the superiority of the communes could not be proved by an increase in production and by an improvement in the standard of living of the people. Also there was insufficient time for discussion among the masses on how to form the communes. . . . All was decided simply by decree in this hastily organized movement.[14]

In fact, the CCP inherited the traditional Stalinist practice and policy in agricultural production. For a relatively long time after taking power, the CCP, compromising with the landlords and rich peasants, suppressed its program of nationalization of the land and its intention of collectivizing agriculture. Even the urgent task of confiscating the land of the rich peasants and distributing it to the poor peasants was postponed. Later, during the Korean War, after encountering the resistance of the landlords, rich peasants, and bourgeoisie, the CCP was forced to solve the problem of distributing the land to the poor peasants, but still hesitated to project a policy of agricultural collectivization. In 1955, jumping from one extreme to the other as Stalin did in 1929, the CCP suddenly announced agricultural collectivization. In less than a year all Chinese peasants had joined the cooperatives. This forced collectivization inevitably aroused the resentment of the peasants, causing general unrest, chaotic conditions, and even riots in the rural areas during 1957. Some cooperatives were dissolved by the peasants themselves. To meet this awkward situation, the CCP repressed the dissatisfaction and resistance of the peasants under the guise of an "antirightist" campaign. In an attempt to turn the peasants' attention away from resistance, it forced them, under the slogan of a "Great Leap Forward," to work doubly hard to increase production. The move into People's Communes carried the "Great Leap Forward" to its culmination.

The utter violation of Engels's and Lenin's principles on the agrarian question and agricultural reconstruction, and hence the violation of the strategy of the alliance of workers and peasants, is amply proved by the extreme inconsistency with which the CCP dealt with the agrarian question—the abrupt shift from right to left in agricultural reconstruction, as indicated above. We are justified in saying, therefore, that the cooperative movement in 1955 and the general establishment of People's Communes in September 1958 were "dictated not by the interests of the farmers or workers but by the interests of the bureaucracy."

Comrade Ma Chi acknowledges the validity of the principle of voluntary peasant participation in agricultural collectivization. He says:

> The commune, no doubt, is vastly superior, but since it signifies a great change in productive relations and social life, an experimental stage and concrete examples are necessary to obtain the full understanding and hearty support of the masses. Otherwise, the imprudent forced communization will encounter mass resistance. Moreover, the lack of tested planning and experiment loads the new system with defects which bring much unnecessary suffering and great inconvenience to the masses, increasing their misgivings and opposition. That is why all Marxists insist on the principle of voluntary consent by the peasants in agrarian collectivization.[15]

If Comrade Ma Chi had actually insisted on "the principle of voluntary consent by the peasants in agrarian collectivization" and if the "imprudent forced communization" mentioned by him above is a fact, then his support in general of the CCP's handling of the communes is not only self-contradictory, but signifies abandonment of his insistence on the principle of voluntary consent by the peasants.

Why does Comrade Ma Chi take such a contradictory position on such an important issue, an issue which is so basic to the alliance of the workers and peasants and which affects the daily life of 500 million peasants? It is obvious that by insisting one-sidedly on the "superiority of large-scale agrarian production" and by falling victim to a delusion in which he sees the commune as "vastly superior," he overlooks the ominous result of the "imprudent forced collectivization."

Consequently, he fails to understand the decisive role played by the "principle of voluntary consent" in "agricultural collectivization" about which Lenin warned us: "We must particularly stress the truth that here, by the very nature of the case, coercive methods can accomplish nothing." "Here coercion would ruin the whole cause" and "nothing is more stupid than the very idea of applying coercion in economic relations with the middle peasants." Comrade Ma Chi forgets or neglects, in addition, the painful lesson of Stalin's forced collectivization and the fresh experience of forced collectivization in Eastern Europe during the past ten years.

If Comrade Ma Chi will make a careful study of Lenin's writings and the experience of the forced collectivizations in Russia and in Eastern Europe, I believe he will come to the following conclusion:

"Large-scale agrarian production is superior to production by small units"; "the commune is vastly superior"; but in view of the "lack of an experimental stage and concrete examples" to "obtain the full understanding and hearty support of the masses," "imprudent forced communization" is adventurism. "Coercive methods can accomplish nothing"; "coercion would ruin the whole cause"; therefore, communes of this type "are dictated not by the interests of the peasants or workers but by the interests of the bureaucracy."

Let us leave aside for the moment the principle of voluntary peasant participation. We remain with "the superiority of large-scale agrarian production." But this is not something all power-ful. As Comrade Ma Chi observes: "The superiority of large-scale production has its limitation; namely, increasing a farm's size hinges on the agrarian technical level, to overdo it has disadvantages."[16]

This is especially true where agrarian technology is at such a low level as in China—not only are modern machinery and draft animals lacking, but the greater part of farming is done by primitive means, depending virtually on human labor alone. On the other hand, the communes were set up on a grandiose scale—averaging 60,000 mu with 5,000 households, quite a few ranging from a hundred thousand to several hundred thousand mu with 15,000 to more than 30,000 households.[17]

The readily apparent contradiction between such extraordinarily large-scale farms and the low technology can only be overcome by agrarian mechanization and electrification. These absolutely cannot be achieved in a short period of time.

Though Lenin held the superiority of large-scale agrarian production in high esteem and insisted on practicing collectivization, he emphasized at the same time the principle of voluntary peasant participation, pointing out in particular that collectivization must be carried out gradually, in combination with mechanization and electrification. He said, as we noted, that it "will take a whole historical epoch to get the entire population into the work of the cooperatives. . . . At best we can achieve this in one or two decades."

Disregarding for the time being the item of "unnecessary suffering and great inconvenience to the peasants"—which increases their "misgivings and opposition"—purely from the viewpoint of production, the commune is unprofitable. A real increase in agrarian productivity depends on the general application of modern technology (tractors, chemical fertilizers, electrification, etc.). If an increase rests solely on lengthened hours and increased intensity, dependent in turn on the rigid or militarized organization of labor, the increase in production at best can be only temporary; it cannot make up for the backwardness of the agrarian technology. Consequently it remains open to question whether the communes have increased productivity and, if they have, by how much. (I will return to this point later.)

Another argument raised in support of the communes is that large-scale communes facilitate huge irrigation projects and public works such as opening up new acreage to irrigation, dredging rivers, erecting flood controls, etc. Comrade Ma Chi declares: "The commune movement developed large-scale irrigation projects which are greatly needed." This is the same as saying that in order to undertake large-scale irrigation projects and other public works, large-scale communes must be set up. Such a statement is not only absurd in theory, it is unrealistic in practice.

Let us follow Comrade Ma Chi more closely in his remarks about accomplishments in irrigation:

"Less than 20 percent of the farmland in China was irrigated in 1952; now it has increased to 55 percent, 30 percent of which was accomplished at the high tide of the advanced cooperative movement in two periods: from the winter of 1955 to the following spring and from the winter of 1957 to the following spring."[18]

This indicates that the 30 percent of the land newly brought under irrigation can be credited to the advanced cooperatives before the establishment of the communes. The communes can be credited with only 5 percent.

Liu Shao-ch'i, now chairman of the Chinese government, in his report to the second session of the CCP's Eighth Congress in May 1958, said:

In agriculture, the most striking leap took place in the campaign of the co-operative farmers to build irrigation works. From last October to April this year, the irrigated acreage throughout the country increased by 350 million *mou*, that is, 80 million *mou* more than the total added during the eight years since liberation. . . .[19]

What Comrade Ma Chi and Chairman Liu Shao-ch'i say comes to the same thing; namely, without large-scale communes large-scale irrigation was achieved within the original framework of cooperatives. This discredits the theory that only large-scale communes can handle large-scale irrigation projects.

Actually, the construction of really large-scale irrigation projects such as big reservoirs, high dams, river dredging, especially controls on the Yellow, Yangtze, and Pearl rivers cannot be carried out on a commune, or even provincial scale, but only on the level of the state power. This stands to reason. Immense human power, a large quantity of machine equipment, and high industrial technology are required to build large-scale reservoirs, floodgates (such as the Yellow River floodgate now under construction), and to dredge rivers. In the past, the controlling of the Huai River and some large-scale floodgates and reservoirs (such as the Tungling Dam near Peking, etc.) required the support of the state power.

In a word, it is completely in violation of the basic principles of Engels and Lenin on the agrarian question and agricultural collectivization to separate the superiority of large-scale farming from voluntary consent by the peasants and to use the former as an argument to support the communes. It is absurd to claim that the construction of large-scale irrigation and public works depends upon the construction of communes.

The "Great productive increase in farming" and "From enslavement of women to equality"

Besides the "superiority of large-scale farming," the two suppositions most convincing to those who support and glorify the "advantages" of the People's Communes are the "Great productive increase in farming" and "From enslavement of women to equality." For instance, Comrade Liang in his commentary on the "Draft Resolution on Chinese Communes" submitted by the Secretariat of the Socialist Workers Party held that "the progressive character of the Communes as superior forms of socio-economic organization [is] proven by the great productive increases already achieved and the smashing of outworn social and family relationships."[20]

Liang's suppositions are also contained in "The Communes in China (Draft Resolution Proposed by NC Members in Los Angeles)"; they constitute the chief reasons advanced for supporting the communes.[21] The "great productive increases in farming" of the communes is described in the draft resolution of the Los Angeles comrades as follows:

"The economic advantages deriving from the communes have already been proven. The 1958 cotton crop and the early rice crop were double that of 1957. The wheat crop was up 60 per cent. Work teams opened up 69 million acres to new irrigation. . . . These and derivative accomplishments are due to the advantages of the new productive form of the commune. . . ."[22]

The draft resolution also emphasized: "This economic yardstick is for historical materialists the basic measure of progress."[23] This statement is absolutely correct. Unfortunately these productive increases in farming and derivative accomplishments have no, or little, connection with the communes.

The communes began to spread in the early part of September 1958 (after the "Resolution on Establishment of People's Communes in the Rural Areas" was announced by the Political Bureau of the Central Committee of the CCP, August 29, 1958). Wheat was harvested in the middle of June, the early rice crop between July and August, while cotton, raised in the summer, was ripe for harvest by the time the communes were established.

These, therefore, harvested a crop raised by the cooperatives. It is surprising that the author of "The Communes in China" could commit such a blunder as to credit the communes with achievements of the cooperatives. Evidently he is uninformed on the harvest time for early rice, wheat, and cotton. This alone is sufficient to demonstrate the author's carelessness.

As to "work teams" opening up "69 million acres to new irrigation," this likewise does not correspond to the facts. On this, as we see from the report of Comrade Ma Chi, out of the 35 percent increase in new areas opened to irrigation since the CCP took power, 30 percent was accomplished before the establishment of the communes. To credit the communes before they were organized for opening up new areas to irrigation astonishes us.

We must understand that the great increase in farm production in 1958 was neither an achievement of the communes nor a "miracle" attributable to the cooperatives (due to lack of agricultural machinery, electricity, chemical fertilizers, insecticides, etc., a "miracle" is not possible), but is the direct result of the increase in hours and the increase in intensity of labor ruthlessly forced on the peasants by the CCP in the "bitter battle" against nature.

Since the winter of 1957, particularly after the general line in agriculture was announced at the second session of the Eighth Party Congress in early May 1958, the peasants, under the slogan of the "Great Leap Forward," have worked day and night—twelve hours, fifteen hours, even eighteen hours; carrying out deep plowing, building and repairing dams and canals, collecting fertilizer, opening up areas to new irrigation, etc.

Farm production increased tremendously under the extraordinary intensity of labor. Even Comrade Ma Chi, who supports the communes, admitted: "A big part of the increase in farm production is due to the extreme intensity of labor (men, women, aged, and children engaging in the 'bitter battle' day and night)."[24] This is not a normal development in agriculture, since the length of the workday and the intensity of labor cannot be kept up over a long period, while such primitive methods of obtaining fertilizer and opening up new areas to irrigation are limited. Fertilizer collected by peasants consists mostly of dirt dug from sewers and ponds or the earth from the walls of old dismantled houses, etc. Such sources, like the scrap iron collected for blast furnaces, cannot be tapped for long. The new areas opened up for irrigation are mostly front yards or backyards, or fallow land along river and forest edges—areas again which are limited.

Even with land reform and collectivization, the heightening of farm production will proceed at a slow tempo if there is no general application of machinery, electric power, chemical fertilizers, insecticides, and if the voluntary participation of the peasantry is lacking. This has been proved by the Chinese experience itself. In his "Report on the Work of the Government" to the Second National People's Congress, April 18, 1959, Chou En-lai said:

As a result of the fulfilment and overfulfilment of the First Five-Year Plan, the total value of our industrial and agricultural output in 1957 amounted to . . . an increase of 68 percent compared with 1952. . . . The total output value of industry reached . . . an increase of 141 percent over 1952 . . . ; and that of agriculture reached . . . an increase of 25 percent over 1952. . . .[25]

Let us, for the time being, grant that Chou's report coincides with fact. (In reality, CCP official reports always exaggerate. The great food shortage this year disproves the reported doubling of farm products last year.) Thus the average yearly rate of increase in industry in the five years of the first plan can be put at 19.2 percent; agriculture at 4.5 percent. It is beyond reasonable dispute that the development of agriculture occurred at a slow tempo during the five years prior to 1958, which can be taken as relatively normal. The tremendous increase reported this year is abnormal (the value of agricultural output in 1958 is claimed to be 64 percent greater than in 1957).[26] This is the result of the extraordinary increase in intensity of the peasants' labor.

The rate of increase in 1958 absolutely cannot be maintained by simply depending on what peasant labor can accomplish under the whip. The frenetic increase in labor time and intensity to increase the rate of production will inevitably engender its opposite. All the facts that have become evident since the establishment of the communes have tended to prove this. After their entry into the communes, the peasants were forced to continue working "energetically," the intensity of labor was increased even more, the great majority of women were put to work at the same intensity as men.

This exceedingly harsh drive, neglecting the well-being of the masses, soon met with bitter resistance and resentment from the peasants. Hence the CCP was compelled to prescribe last December in a "Resolution on Some Questions Concerning the People's Communes" a minimum of "eight hours' sleep and four hours for meals and recreation daily"; that is, the working day should not exceed twelve hours. (In fact, it still exceeds twelve hours.)

A twelve-hour day cannot be kept up indefinitely, for, due to the lack of machinery and draft animals, almost all farm work means physical labor. The peasants dig the earth with simple hoes, stoop to transplant young rice plants, and sow seeds, carry fertilizer and grain on their shoulders with a pole, use hand power for irrigation through a water-lifting apparatus, etc. All this réquires endurance beyond that of horses and oxen, if the twelve-hour day is continued for long.*

Thus the growing peasant dissatisfaction eventually reaches open opposition. First, general sabotage, which damages crops, decreases production, and lowers the rate of expansion. The CCP has been compelled to acknowledge many instances of this. For example, T'ao Chu, the first secretary of the Kwangtung Provincial Committee of the Communist Party, said in his report on the "Investigation of the Hu-men Commune": "There is sabotage, waste, and lack of enthusiasm among the masses."[27]

The "lack of enthusiasm among the masses" means passive sabotage due to overwork. This exists not only in the Hu-men Commune; it is a general phenomenon in the great majority of the communes. Consequently, for the past half year the *People's Daily* continually speaks of absenteeism and inefficiency among some members of the communes, and calls for enforcement of the "production responsibility system." (the so-called fixed quota system) and the "incentive penalty system."

The so-called production responsibility system gives each unit a fixed production target; the "incentive penalty system" penalizes absenteeism and lack of enthusiasm. (T'ao Chu recommends docking two days' pay for each day's absence.) But this increasingly severe forced labor with its penalty system not only cannot raise production, it will further arouse passive resistance among the masses. Even during the autumn harvest a year ago, when the communes were first established, mass sabotage had already shown what serious effect it could have. Vice-premier Teng Tzu-

---

*The Los Angeles draft resolution on "The Communes in China" states: "As with all forced marches, hardships are inevitable." How should this sentence be interpreted by the Chinese peasants? Even if they agreed that the American Trotskyists are not defenders of the CCP, they would surely blame them for utter lack of understanding of how they are overworked and for indifference to their unbearable suffering in a "bitter battle" indescribably damaging to their health.

hui admitted at the Second National People's Congress in 1959: "Last year we reaped less in spite of a fine crop." This means that at the autumn harvest great waste and loss occurred as a result of sabotage among the peasantry. This occurred again in the summer harvest this year according to reports in recent issues of the *People's Daily*. Precisely because of this passive resistance of the peasantry, the CCP had to admit further:

> In order to get high yields we need tractors, large amounts of chemical fertilizers, modern agricultural machinery, and effective insecticides. At present our country does not have these prerequisites. Consequently, farm production is very uneven; we can have a bumper harvest one year and a poor harvest in another. . . . This year some communes have scored an increase in unit-area yield, but total sowing areas were much less than last year. Thus, there was actually no increase and in some cases even decreases were reported.[28]

After reaching the conclusion that the "great productive increases in farming" were not the "accomplishment" of the communes, as I sought to point out, and then reading the acknowledgment by the CCP that "farm production is very uneven" due to the lack of modern farming "prerequisites," and that "this year . . . there was actually no increase and in some cases even decreases were reported," I wonder what the authors of "The Communes in China" think.

This "form of socioeconomic organization," put into practice on such a large scale, had not been subjected to testing. Instead of crediting it for an increase in production accomplished before it came into existence, we should have retained cool heads and analyzed carefully its productive possibilities and contradictions so as to arrive at a conclusion or judgment subject to the test of events and criticism. Only by a serious attitude of this kind in dealing with an important issue can we lay claim to being "historical materialists." Otherwise, the so-called economic yardstick becomes a mere caricature.

We also find in "The Communes in China": "The advance by the way of such collectives is . . . from enslavement for women to equality."[29] This statement is further explained: (*a*) "The communes have plowed up and pulverized the crust of outworn social and family relations . . ." (p. 39) and (*b*) ". . . they have accelerated the liberation of women from domestic slavery, opened up new avenues of cultural development, and are narrowing the age-old cultural gulf between city and country" (p. 40).

Here, *a* apparently refers to the equality of women with men through liberation from the bonds of the feudal or patriarchal family, while *b* refers to the liberation of women from "domestic slavery" and their stepping into "new avenues of cultural development."

What *a* and *b* refer to is surely epoch-making. But the question remains: Have the communes actually led to this kind of "liberation" for women? First, let us investigate the facts. As everyone knows, Chinese women, before the third Chinese revolution, had been recognized by law to have equal status with men. This included the right of inheritance, equal rights in education, participation in social and political spheres, and freedom in marriage. Of course, this legal equality was far from being realized in reality, especially in the rural areas. But it is undeniable that the Chinese women had won a preliminary stage in their liberation from patriarchal relations. Because of this relative freedom a great many women participated in revolutionary activities. After taking power, the CCP proclaimed further measures establishing legal equality for women, such as equal pay for equal work, complete freedom in marriage and divorce, etc.

And by participating in all kinds of social movements such as the land reform, agricultural cooperatives, etc., Chinese women, especially those in rural areas, have, no doubt, broken with the traditional patriarchy and obtained equality with men. This is certainly an important contribution, made by the CCP after it took power, toward the liberation of women. It was noted in "The Third Chinese Revolution and Its Aftermath" that the revolution "destroyed the Asian relations in the family and swept away other feudalistic rubbish."[30] All this was accomplished a few years before the establishment of the communes and has no connection with them. The authors of "The Communes in China," crediting the communes for bringing women "from enslavement . . . to equality," again get their facts chronologically out of order as they did in doubling farm production (crediting the communes with an early rice crop, wheat crop, etc., which were actually due to the cooperatives).

Undoubtedly, only liberation from "domestic slavery" will make it possible for women to win genuine, thoroughgoing liberation. But the general establishment of community kitchens and nurseries as prerequisites for the complete liberation of women, which every communist stands for, is conceivable only under highly developed material and cultural conditions. At present, neither the Chinese rural areas nor the advanced Western countries have achieved these.

Under such unfavorable material and cultural conditions, the CCP's reckless and forcible replacement of family life with collective life unavoidably brings innumerable inconveniences and suffering to the masses. Comrade Ma Chi, a supporter of the communes, especially their community kitchens and nurseries, has to say this when confronted with the undeniable facts:

Just as in the commune movement as a whole, this great leap [meaning the community kitchens established to liberate women—P'eng] was made with too much ferocity and compulsion, hence the cadres went overboard in many things. For instance, by sudden order everybody had to eat in the mess halls; all stoves in private homes were dismantled or centralized; and no food rations were issued to individuals. Yet the meals in the mess halls are insufficient and bad in quality. There is rice but no hot water; no special care for the aged, children, and sick ones. Though called community kitchens, actually there is no mess hall; people eat in the open or take meals home on rainy and windy days. . . . Worst of all is the fact that the cadres have their own small mess halls![31]

In the above paragraph, Comrade Ma Chi gives just a bare sketch of the communal kitchens without analyzing their many serious shortcomings and contradictions. Yet it is enough to prove that they are unbearable. I am sure that except for a few, who never had enough to eat, the great majority of the peasantry harbor resentment against the communal kitchens. They at least find them inconvenient.

The situation in the nurseries is not much better. Too many children are crowded into small rooms without any nursery equipment and placed in charge of illiterate or disabled old women. Under these conditions, how can the children be well cared for? That is why mothers are "physically in the field, while their minds are back home." (The mothers worry about their children all the time.)

What is the actual situation of the women liberated from "domestic slavery" and precipitated into social production? Comrade Ma Chi, who supports this kind of "liberation of women," gives us the following description and explanation:

"equality" with men has been demanded of women in physical output since communization; they work on farms, dams, highways, mines, and factories—day and night in the "bitter battle," even during menstruation, pregnancy, and after giving birth . . . the customs and prejudices of thousands of years cannot be broken at one stroke; the masses see things differently. This plus these shortcomings in the process of practicing the new system explain why the suspicion and resentment of the masses are growing to such a large extent. After the plenary session of the Eighth Central Committee of the CCP, these shortcomings became the target for investigation in the checkup of the communes. But these shortcomings can only be resolved thoroughly when genuine proletarian democracy is fully realized in the communes and in the country as a whole.[32]

Here we can draw a conclusion from Comrade Ma Chi's description and explanation: "Before genuine proletarian democracy is fully realized in the communes and in the country as a whole," the sufferings (Comrade Ma Chi called them "shortcomings") of women liberated from the family to participate in productive labor cannot be "thoroughly solved." The problem here is reduced to how to "realize genuine proletarian democracy" in "the communes and in the country as a whole."

Comrade Ma Chi has also provided us with sufficient material to answer the questions I posed before: (*a*) "the meals in the mess halls are insufficient and bad in quality . . ." which proves that they are worse than those at home; the same goes for the nurseries. (*b*) Since communization, "'equality' with men has been demanded of women in physical output day-and-night in the 'bitter battle'. . ." which is harder and more harmful to their bodies and minds than "domestic slavery." This is the logical conclusion to forcibly replacing family life with collective life. The main aim of this CCP policy is not the thoroughgoing liberation of women but the mobilization of maximum labor power in pushing the Great Leap Forward in agriculture. Hence the brilliant idea of pushing all the women in the rural areas out of their home responsibilities and into the greatly needed labor force, there to work them with the same intensity as men. From "domestic slavery," the women are simply thrown into "social slavery."

I should like to repeat: to feed an entire population, especially a rural population, in community kitchens; to place all children in nurseries; and to liberate all women from "domestic slavery" and include them fully in social production is conceivable only under highly developed socialism, after the full victory of the world proletarian social revolution.

And even after the full victory of the world proletarian social revolution, in the advanced countries with highly developed material resources and culture, the whole people should not be forced to join community kitchens at once, nor the children forced into nurseries at one stroke. This is stupid and absurd. First, let us establish model community kitchens and nurseries so that the people can see for themselves that this is preferable to home-cooked meals and to keeping the children at home. Gradually they will join voluntarily. By then socialist collective life will be closely linked in reality with its name.

We should understand that the disappearance of the family system, a heritage of thousands of years, and the full participation of women, freed from "domestic slavery," in social production on a basis of equality with men marks not only the complete liberation of women, but also humanity's entrance into the ideal society of genuine freedom, equality, and happiness. Even after the complete victory of the world socialist revolution, it can be gradually achieved only over a relatively long period. Since the family was gradually formed during the dissolution of primitive communist society, it can only die gradually with the development of the future communist society.

Under primitive material and cultural conditions such as exist in China's rural areas and under an objective situation in which the world socialist revolution is still far from victory, with no planning and within a few months, the CCP with unprecedented rudeness and arbitrariness forced the whole peasant mass to suddenly abandon family life for the "socialist collective life." Besides discrediting the perspective of communes and socialist collective life, the result was inevitably to give today's communes a bad name among the masses and to sow distrust and hatred against the urban proletariat (which has not been communized), thereby dealing a heavy blow to the alliance of workers and peasants.

It can safely be predicted that the community kitchen and nursery cannot be maintained for a long period. Under compulsion of necessity, in the not too distant future, they will be reorganized or the great majority of them will be disbanded. The return from "collective life" to "family life" means the complete bankruptcy of the communes. If, in disregard of the unwillingness and opposition of the peasants, the CCP seeks to maintain this collective life represented by the communal kitchen and nursery in order to prove the absolute correctness of the commune policy of the CCP and Chairman Mao, then the communal kitchen and nursery, together with the unbearable forced labor, will become centers of a highly explosive situation within the communes, which can touch off a disaster.

Is "voluntary peasant cooperation" evident in the communes? Are they "adminstered by elected councils, not by bureaucratic edict"?

Comrade Liang, in criticizing the "Draft Resolution on Chinese Communes," which had been submitted by the Secretariat, wrote:

> On Page 7 of the draft, Par. 4, our support of the Communes is made to depend, not on their essentially progressive character, but on "the readiness of the peasants to accept them." How and by whom is this "readiness" to be determined? It might be recalled that we supported, with great consistency, the collectivization of farming in the Soviet Union *despite peasant resistance*. What we opposed was the rude and violent *forcing* of the peasantry by the Stalin regime. In the case of China's Communes, there is *no evidence* so far of mass coercion by the Peking government, but considerable evidence of voluntary peasant cooperation. . . .
>
> The fact that the Communes are administed by *elected councils*, not by bureaucratic edict, is an important fact demanding a place in the resolution.[33]

The idea expressed here by Comrade Liang was fully supported by the National Committee members in Los Angeles in their proposed draft resolution, "The Communes in China" (see page 40 of the *SWP Discussion Bulletin* containing this document). This point was supported and defended with special vigor by Comrade Swabeck (see page 5 of his article, "The Third Chinese Revolution and Its Communes," in *SWP Discussion Bulletin*, vol. 20, no. 13, June 1959). Since this is one of the main arguments they offer in advocating support and sanction of the communes, discussion of it is in order.

First, I should like to point out that Comrade Liang does not cite evidence. He simply makes the statement that "considerable evidence" exists of "voluntary peasant cooperation" in the communes and asserts it as a "fact" that "the communes are administered by *elected councils*, not by bureaucratic edict." If he has "considerable evidence" and "fact," he should share it with his readers. Otherwise they may feel inclined to challenge his unsupported assertions.

A great amount of coercion was used in forming the communes. . . . The masses had no chance to consider all the practical problems. These were decided simply by the CCP cadres and passed on as orders to the peasants.

The above was written by Ma Chi in his piece, *The People's Communes*. He lives nearby to mainland China, follows all the CCP official newspapers and documents in Chinese, and reads the reports of foreign visitors to the mainland. Among the supporters of the communes, Comrade Ma Chi's account can be taken as at least more trustworthy than that of such comrades as Liang and Swabeck, who are far away from China, who are unable to read official publications in the original Chinese, and who depend heavily on reports of certain foreign visitors to China. Let us now consider the communes in the light of theory and facts, leaving aside for the time being Comrade Ma Chi's account.

1. Ninety-nine percent of the rural population are in the communes (500 million). Is it conceivable that within the short space of three months (September to December 1958) such tremendous numbers of the rural population would of their own volition and not under compulsion join the communes and start living collectively? That is, for all of the women to leave the family circle, to join the men in work teams, eat in community kitchens, and by these acts alone bring an end to the system of private property.

I cited at some length above the attitude of Lenin on the peasant question. He emphasized that the peasant is conservative and realistic: "They will not allow themselves to be convinced by mere words." "We have to give the peasant, who not only in our country but all over the world is a practical man and a realist, concrete examples to prove that the 'communia' is the best possible thing." Consequently, "it will take a whole historical epoch to get the entire population into the work of the cooperatives . . . At best we can achieve this in one or two decades."

Instead of showing the masses "concrete examples to prove that the commune is the best possible thing," the CCP set tasks to accomplish in a few months that should require a historical period, or at best one or two decades. They supposedly organized 99 percent of the peasants into communes without "mass coercion." If this is what actually happened, then not only is Lenin's whole theory on the peasant question and his fundamental policy in regard to agricultural collectivization completely overturned, but the lessons to be drawn from the experience in collectivizing agriculture in Russia (forty years) and the Eastern European countries (ten years) become meaningless!

The only conclusion we can draw is that the Chinese peasants are completely different from those in the rest of the world; they are not "realists," but "born communists," or they are "especially inclined to collectivization." As soon as the call for collectivization and communization was announced, they unhesitatingly, or, as CCP propaganda puts it, "enthusiastically," joined up! I would like Comrade Liang, Comrade Swabeck, and the others to consider the implications of such a "conclusion"!

2. Are the Chinese peasants "born communists" or "especially inclined to collectivization"? Let us check some facts that have appeared in official CCP publications.

The *People's Daily* of September 24, 1958, revealed that in setting up communes in the environs of Hangchow, "The poor and middle peasants thought that since a rational distribution of products is difficult, peasant enthusiasm in production is not likely to be encouraged; while the upper-middle peasants vacillated, worried that the communes, on such a large scale and with such an enormous membership, could not work out."

Li Chun-hua, first secretary of the Ho-p'u county committee of the CCP in Kwangtung province, and Ho Wen-li, a section head of the Ho-p'u County Cooperative, reported in the Canton *Southern Daily* in October 1958:

Capitalist ideology and behavior is still dominant among the upper-middle peasants. This includes some party members and some lower cadres who come from the upper-middle peasants. They loathe and oppose the communes. A minority of them lack enthusiasm in production. They eat and drink heavily, hide their property and reserve of food, dig green vegetables from their private plots of land, and slaughter their domestic animals and poultry.

Political Study, no. 10, 1958, published in Peking, pointed out:

In the movement of the People's Communes, quite a few peasants still intend to go back to capitalism; they do not welcome, but oppose, the communes whose aim is to eliminate the remnants of the private property system. [The reference is to taking over the peasants' private plots of land, private orchards, domestic animals and poultry, homes, and private bank deposits.—P'eng] Even some party cadres, due to their particularist ideology, oppose this elimination of the remnants of the private property system. Hence they become an obstacle to setting up and consolidating the People's Communes.

Ta Kung Pao, a newspaper published in Peking, revealed December 8, 1958: "A general loss of grain, cotton, tobacco, and hemp occurs on the way to the storehouses. No one kept an eye on more than ten parcels of cotton left on the highway for four or five days."

A report published by *Yang Ch'eng Evening Post* in Canton, December 20, 1958, informed us: "Peasants in Kwangtung province have rushed into the city recently to avoid communization. This was considered by the city authorities as not only increasing difficulties in city management and security, but also as affecting the consolidation of the communes and the peasants' enthusiasm in production."

Red Flag, a theoretical journal published in Peking, in its issue no. 12 in 1958 reported:

Since the People's Communes were set up in such great haste and on such a large scale, and with the complete elimination of private property, the ideological preparation of the cadres could not keep pace with it. The ideological struggle between two tendencies [for or against the communes—P'eng] among the masses has found receptive soil among some cadres; they doubt that "communism will raise labor enthusiasm" and are returning to the ideology of localism and individualism. Some of them have even led the masses in hiding property to keep it from being included in the communes.

Such bits of information were disclosed either accidentally or purposefully by the officials. The actual reaction of the peasants toward the communes has certainly not been reported in detail or systematically, and what we have been given is most certainly distorted. Yet it is sufficient to show that the Chinese peasants are neither "born communists," nor "especially inclined to collectivization." Like peasants elsewhere in the world, the Chinese peasants are "realists," imbued with "capitalist ideology and behavior," and afraid of "the elimination of the remnants of the private property system." Consequently they did not welcome but opposed the communes. Their general way of opposing the communes is through "sabotage": i.e., "lack of enthusiasm in production," "damaging farm products," "slaughtering domestic animals and poultry," "cutting down fruit trees," "fleeing to the cities," etc. Moreover, these ideas and acts have also "found receptive soil among some cadres."

The "lack of enthusiasm in production" will, of course, reduce the rate of agricultural production. "Damaging farm products" is reflected in last year's "lower harvest in spite of a fine crop" (admitted by Vice-premier Teng Tsu-hui) and "slaughtering of domestic animals and poultry" has caused a shortage of nonstaple foods in the whole country and a scarcity of meat in the cities.

In spite of the daily exhortations of the *People's Daily* to the peasants to raise plenty of livestock, pigs, etc., the shortage of nonstaple foods and meat is getting worse and worse.

Here we come to a very important question: How did it happen that the CCP, despite the opposition of the peasants (at least a part of them), could successfully organize 500 million people in the communes within a few months and yet claim that no "rude and violent" methods were used as in Stalin's time? In reaching an answer, the following considerations should be borne in mind:

1. In the cooperatives, the distribution of products was based mainly on the workday. Some poor peasants with large families, few of them able to work, could barely maintain the lowest standard of living and often went hungry. They raised both hands at the beginning in favor of the communes when they were told about "free meals" in the community kitchen.

2. The CCP strove through its cadres among the peasants to propagandize the "advantages" of the communes. For example:

The People's Communes are the best form for the transition from collective ownership to ownership by the people as a whole. They contain the first shoots of communism . . . such as the communal kitchens, nurseries, and sewing facilities to emancipate women from the household; and a wage system, namely, basic wages plus awards paid directly to the members. Members get food and clothing allowances, housing and child-birth care, education and medical treatment, weddings and funerals.[34]

Offered such beautiful pictures, quite a few peasants, especially the young ones, found it easy to accept the communes and even gave them naive and enthusiastic support.

3. Beginning in the autumn of 1957, the CCP waged an extensive antirightist "socialist construction campaign" in the rural areas. Under the "antirightist" slogan, the CCP attacked not only the rich peasants, but also the middle peasants who were dissatisfied with the CCP's policy of collectivization. The hardest blows fell above all on Left elements who dared to criticize the CCP's policy openly. (They were sent to border regions or labor concentration camps for reform.) Having just experienced such a severe "antirightist" campaign, the peasant masses naturally feared to publicly defy the CCP's order to set up the communes.

4. A great part of the twelve million members of the Young Communist League were stationed in the rural areas when the communes were established. These organizations hold full power over rural economic, financial, political, military, and social affairs. It was clear to every peasant from the beginning that if

he openly opposed setting up the communes, he would face very harsh reprisals.

Under such beguilement and intimidation, the peasants unwillingly accepted the party's order to form the communes. They could only resort to anonymous acts of sabotage such as "lack of enthusiasm in production," "slaughtering domestic animals and poultry," "cutting down fruit trees," "damaging farm products," or "fleeing to the cities," etc. Comrade Ma Chi had the following to say about this:

> The CCP's policy on the People's Communes, though compulsory, was carried out, as in so many other dealings with the peasants, mainly through an organizational drive instead of by force. Through pseudodiscussion, the CCP manages to stampede the masses into accepting its policy. The masses lack not only an independent organization, but also a political staff to clarify and systematize their dissatisfaction with the CCP. Consequently, their enthusiasm for socialism has often been manufactured and their opposition to the CCP's policy remains uncrystallized.[35]

The explanation that "the CCP's policy on the People's Communes, though compulsory, was carried out . . . mainly through an organizational drive instead of by force" is factually correct. But to make the policy compulsory and carry it out by means of an "organizational drive," though different from the "rude and violent" methods used by Stalin, is still "coercion." As Lenin said: "It would be absolutely absurd to attempt to reshape these farms [today it is the communes in China—P'eng] in any rapid way, by issuing an order or bringing pressure to bear from without."

Moreover, one must understand that the reason why the CCP has not adopted Stalin's "rude and violent" methods in setting up agricultural producer's cooperatives and the People's Communes is that it learned some lessons from the tragedy of collectivization in the Soviet Union and has sought to avoid the same gross mistakes in China. Similarly the coercive collectivization in the postwar East European countries was also accomplished mainly "through an organizational drive instead of by force." Can we, therefore, permit ourselves to conclude: "There is no evidence so far of mass coercion by the governments of the East European countries"?

From the above facts and accompanying theoretical analysis, it is beyond reasonable dispute that the establishment of the People's Communes by the CCP leadership did not occur through voluntary acceptance by the peasantry but by mass coercion. In the light of this, how could a Trotskyist, inheriting Engels's and Lenin's traditional principle that collectivization is conditional on voluntary acceptance by the peasantry, support and glorify the CCP's policy of coercive communization?

The draft resolution on the Chinese communes submitted by the Secretariat stated: "Our support of the 'rural People's Communes' must, therefore, be governed by the readiness of the peasants to accept them." This is completely correct. For it is based not only on Engels's and Lenin's traditional standpoint of voluntary collectivization, but also follows faithfully the position on agricultural collectivization in our Transitional Program.

But Comrade Liang is clearly in conflict with this program. This is sufficient to show that on the problem of the Chinese People's Communes he has departed from Trotskyism. He even openly declared: "We supported, with great consistency, the collectivization of farming in the Soviet Union despite peasant resistance." I must ask, whom does this "we" include? We Trotskyists? No, absolutely not! The Left Oppositionists (the Trotskyists) stood unanimously with Trotsky in severely criticizing and resolutely opposing Stalin's policy of collectivization, which coerced the peasants into collectives "despite their resistance." Trotsky expressed this viewpoint not only in many articles at the time, but also in the Transitional Program as follows:

"In order to rehabilitate the program of socialism in the eyes of the farmer, it is necessary to expose mercilessly the Stalinist methods of collectivization, which are dictated not by the interests of the farmers or workers but by the interests of the bureaucracy."[36]

Consequently, I can assert that at that time (1929-32) those "who supported, with great consistency, the collectivization . . . in the Soviet Union despite peasant resistance" were not we Trotskyists, but the Stalinists in every country.

Comrade Liang bases his support of the communes on their "essentially progressive character." According to him, whether peasant resistance exists or not has nothing to do with the "essentially progressive character" of the communes. In other words, in order to support the "essentially progressive character" of the communes, he disregards opposition by the peasants to the communes. This is a revision of Engels's and Lenin's principles on agricultural collectivization, which insist that when the proletariat proceeds to agricultural collectivization after taking power, this be a voluntary matter among the peasants themselves. If Comrade Liang denies the validity of Engels's and Lenin's principle of letting the peasants decide when to join, he should state this openly. (When Stalin forced the peasants into the collectives in 1929 he publicly declared that Engels's principle of leaving it up to the peasants was "too cautious" and did not fit the situation in the Soviet Union.)

Moreover, if Comrade Liang continues to insist on this stand, he should further propose the revision of the points on the nationalization of land and collectivization of agriculture in our Transitional Program, for there it is unambiguously stated: "The program for the nationalization of the land and collectivization of agriculture should be so drawn that from its very basis it should exclude the possibility of expropriation of small farmers and their compulsory collectivization."[37]

If Comrade Liang is faithful to the logic of his own thinking, the words "should exclude" in the program should be revised to read "should *not* exclude."

How do the "councils" administer the communes?

Comrade Liang says: "The fact that the Communes are administered by *elected councils*, not by bureaucratic edict. . . ." In other words the administration and the internal life of the communes are entirely democratic. But what is "the fact"? How are the "councils" elected? These questions are related to the basic problem of a democratic system, and Comrade Liang is obviously not interested in this aspect. As soon as he heard about "elected councils," he concluded that a democratic system had been realized in the communes and that "bureaucratic edict" no longer existed.

Was this what really happened? Let us determine the facts. When the communes were organized all over the country, they incorporated previously existing organizations, on the rule that "the upper structure was changed while the lower structure remained unchanged." The "commune committee" was formed by combining local "people's committees" and the "[agricultural] cooperative committees." This was the so-called "merger of township government and commune into one."

The "Resolution on the Establishment of People's Communes in the Rural Areas" (August 29, 1958) states: "The township governments and the communes should become one, with the township committee of the Party becoming the Party committee of the commune and the township people's council becoming the administrative committee of the commune."[38]

In carrying out the resolution and setting up the communes, what this specifies is that the township chief becomes the commune chief; the township party secretary becomes the commune party secretary; the township People's Congress becomes the Commune Congress; and the township People's Council becomes the administrative committee of the commune. No election was held at the time. After the communes were set up generally, elections were held in some communes and commune councils were elected by the peasants to administer the economic, financial, political, military, police, educational, and other affairs of the communes.

The election of these "councils" was conducted in the same way as that of the "People's Congress." As a rule, the township party secretary or the commune party secretary (some township party secretaries became commune party secretaries after the communes were set up) proposed a list of candidates, always nominating party leaders or cadres. The peasants, having gone through the procedure of voting for the township People's Congress in the past, were quite familiar with this kind of election. They knew very well that their only right was to approve, not oppose, the list of candidates. When the election was held, they cast their votes or raised their hands in favor of the "candidates' list." This was how the so-called "commune councils" were elected. Consequently "the merger of township government and commune into one" actually was "the merger of party and commune into one." For the commune chief is, in most communes, the first secretary of the commune party committee and the members of the commune council are members of the commune party committees. It is well known that all the economic, financial, political, military, police, and educational affairs are controlled by the party, especially the first secretary of the party.

There is a common saying in the communes: "The party secretary commands all," meaning that all the important affairs of the commune are handled and decided by the party secretary. Hence the commune party secretary is the dictator of the commune, just as Mao Tse-tung is the dictator of the central government. (It is true that Mao has nominally resigned the chairmanship of the central government, but he is, in fact, still the dictator.) So it can be said that every commune is a miniature replica of the central government.

Let us ask Comrade Liang if these "councils," created by such elections, are fully in accord with democracy. Can such "elected councils," in conducting the administration of the communes, represent the interests and wishes of the masses, rather than the interests of the bureaucracy? Or as Comrade Swabeck puts it: "It looks more like a reasonable form of democracy"![39]

If Comrades Liang and Swabeck really believe what they assert, then not only the communes, comprising 500 million peasants, but also every level of government in China is a reasonable form of democracy, since every level of the People's Congress is "elected by the people" the same way as in the communes. So what we have is not the dictatorship of the bureaucracy but proletarian or socialist democracy in China. This not only completely reverses our assessment of the nature of the CCP and its regime, but also repudiates the resolution "The Third Chinese Revolution and Its Aftermath"—which was approved by Comrades Liang and Swabeck—passed by the SWP in 1955. After all, that resolution asserts that the CCP is a Stalinist party and its governmental regime is a bureaucratic dictatorship that must be overthrown in a political revolution.

Furthermore, to extend the logic implied in the thinking of these two comrades, proletarian or socialist democracy has also been achieved in the Soviet Union as well as in the East European countries, since the "soviets" in the Soviet Union and the "people's councils" in the East European countries also claim to be "elected by the people" or to be approved in accordance "with universal electoral rights." From this you can see how a false judgment or concept, followed to its logical end, finally brings us to an amazing conclusion. A Chinese proverb says: "A hair's difference; a thousand-mile gap."

Trotsky told us: "The bureaucracy replaced the soviets as class organs with the fiction of universal electoral rights—in the style of Hitler-Goebbels."[40] If Comrades Liang and Swabeck have not yet forgotten the meaning of Trotsky's words, they should seek to understand what the "elected councils" of the present communes are. Actually the commune "councils" are copies of the former township "people's councils" or "people's committees." The Chinese "people's councils" are patterned after those in the East European countries. And the "people's councils" in the East European countries are a variation of Stalin's "soviets." Whoever does not understand this will become totally confused trying to understand the problem of the Chinese regime and will fall into irreparable errors.

Certain definite conditions are required to realize socialist democracy. First of all, the worker and peasant masses must enjoy complete freedom of speech, press, assembly, association, and belief. The secret ballot must exist at every level during elections. Finally, and most important of all, the legality of every workers' party that accepts socialism must be guaranteed.

But in China today, as well as in the East European countries, these conditions are absent. The communes, consequently, cannot be isolated and administered democratically just by themselves. Their "councils," both in form and content, are not different from the former township "people's councils," and as a result are run only by "bureaucratic edict." Such things as arbitrarily increasing the hours of labor (from twelve to fifteen, and even to eighteen hours a day), compelling women to do the same amount of intensive work as men, forcing the peasants to dismantle their stoves and leave home to eat in the communal kitchens, etc., are enough to prove the ruthlessness of the bureaucracy.

Are the communes a "superior type of socioeconomic organization," or an effective instrument in the hands of the CCP for exploiting and controlling the peasants?

I quoted above Comrade Liang's words on the "progressive character of the Communes as superior forms of socioeconomic organization proven by the great productive increases already achieved. . . ." The phrase "superior forms of socioeconomic organization" in Comrade Liang's statement was adopted in "The Communes in China (Draft Resolution Proposed by NC Members in Los Angeles)," with the following explanation:

The communes are . . . a superior type of socioeconomic organization, surpassing any yet installed in a predominantly peasant country. The large-scale utilization of cooperative labor and the resulting production of agricultural surpluses can serve to speed up the accumulation of capital imperatively needed for China's industrialization. In this way the communes can make an indispensable contribution to the building of the economic basis for socialism.[41]

That "the communes are a superior type of socioeconomic organization" is a sociological evaluation. According to Marxist sociology, whether a "socioeconomic organization" is "a superior type" depends on the harmony of its inner structure; i.e., that there is no contradiction between the productive forces and the relations of production, and coordination among the various branches of production. The present People's Communes are described as "a basic social organization for the all-round development of agriculture, forestry, animal husbandry, side occupations, and fishery, as well as for the all-round combination of economic, political, cultural, and military affairs where industry, agriculture, trade, education, and military affairs merge into one."[42]

Thus the communes, pictured as self-contained and self-supported social units, are represented as utopias. Yet they are rife with contradictions. It is absolutely impossible to achieve rational division of labor and cooperation among the various branches of production, together with the specialization necessary in each of the branches of production, inside the communes, despite their large size (the average is about five thousand households, and the largest about thirty thousand). This is due to the fact that they engage simultaneously in numerous branches of production such as agriculture, forestry, side occupations, animal husbandry, fishery, and industry. This kind of setup in production must inevitably lead to chaos, backwardness, and primitiveness. First, it weakens the commune by dissipating its forces into so many branches of production. Thus the diversion from concentration in agricultural production. Everybody knows that the communes were ordered to set up various kinds of industry, even a steel industry (for example, the blast furnaces), in this way not only introducing confusion into the state industrial plan but placing demands on the communes far beyond their own capacity. Only if they were fully equipped with modern machinery could the commune industries compete with other industries and maintain their own existence. Lacking this prerequisite, the communes can only set up a few handicraft workshops (most of them were transferred from the cooperatives). This testifies that the commune industries are backward, outmoded, and incompatible with modern industry. Consequently, judged by its mode of production, the commune is not "a superior type of socioeconomic organization," but a backward or conservative type.

The utopianism of the commune manifests itself in such fantasies as attempts to eliminate the difference between city and country, worker and peasant, mental and manual labor through the all-round development of industry and agriculture; attempts to supersede the system of pay according to work by a system of rationing through the communal kitchen plus other collective benefits.

Until the communes have been in existence for a relatively long period of time it is premature, if not careless arbitrariness, to assert that they are "a superior type of socioeconomic organization."

If we consider the commune as "a superior type of agricultural cooperative" (the fact is that its actual foundation of production is agriculture), then due to its large scale and the huge labor force available, it is possible that it can increase agricultural production through the "large-scale utilization of cooperative labor" and "can serve to speed up the accumulation of capital imperatively needed for China's industrialization," if the following conditions prevail:

1. That the peasants join the commune voluntarily. Their living conditions should gradually be improved in order to raise their enthusiasm in their work and to increase production.

2. That genuine democracy is observed in commune management. The administrative committee should be elected by secret ballot among the entire membership; officials should be subject to recall at any time; important planning in production and distribution should be based on the real interests of the peasant masses and discussed freely and thoroughly among all the membership and then decided by majority vote.

3. That taxes and prices set for the purchase of agricultural products by the government are reasonably applied. Industrial products should be made available as rapidly as possible to the peasants at reasonable cost.

4. That the government provides the technology and large amount of capital necessary to construct agricultural machinery plants, electric power stations, vehicle manufacturing plants (such as truck factories), and so on, to gradually equip the peasants with modern agricultural implements so as to lessen heavy physical labor and steadily increase productivity.

In the absence of the above conditions, the communes, dependent simply on sheer size and a huge labor force, will find it difficult to increase productivity. Moreover, the dissatisfaction aroused among the peasants decreases production. Poland's latest experience confirms this. Gomulka reported at the Eighth Plenum of the Central Committee of the United Workers Party of Poland on October 20, 1956, that after six years' collectivization, the value of agricultural products per hectare of land owned by individual farmers was 621.1 zlotys; while that of the cooperatives was 517.3 zlotys. In other words, the value of production on large-scale collective farms was 16.7 percent less per hectare than that of individual farms.

As I indicated above, the majority of peasants were coerced or inveigled into joining the communes in China. Living conditions for the majority of them have not improved but deteriorated. First of all, working hours and intensity of labor have been greatly increased; a great segment of the women are put to work with the same intensity as men; food supplies in the communal kitchens are neither sufficient nor good in quality; small amounts of wages are continually in arrears; the health of the peasants is deteriorating and they are frequently sick, while medicines are in extremely short supply. All these conditions have greatly dampened the peasants' enthusiasm in production.

Since the administration of the communes is in complete violation of democracy, the peasants naturally become more passive—everything is decided by "bureaucratic edict."

Government taxes on the communes are far above those placed on the agricultural cooperatives. The latter were taxed 15 percent, and, at most, 25 percent of their total income. No quota is fixed for the communes; it is said, "Let them decide for themselves." This actually means that the communes pay as high a tax as possible. Consequently the tax on the communes is often more than 30 percent. For example, the Red Star People's Commune of Sui County, Hunan province, paid out 32 percent of its total income in taxes.

Prices paid for agricultural products are variable and not set by the government, although it purchases almost everything not consumed in the communes themselves. Often prices are set by the local government agents or cadres. To please the upper bureaucrats, they always make prices very low. On the other hand, industrial products supplied to the communes by the government are either insufficient or poor in quality and at prices always higher than those in the open market.

The commune bears the administrative, military, education, and production expenses (developing various branches of production for self-sufficiency and self-support): these, plus the accumulation fund, quite often amount to 50 percent of the total income. For example, in the Ch'eng Nan People's Commune of Heilungkiang province, the accumulation fund and expenses are 48 percent of total income; in other communes they even reach 60 percent. So, in general, only 20 percent remains of the total income (after deducting 30 percent for taxes, and 50 percent for the accumulation fund and administrative expenses). How can the communes maintain their members except on the lowest of standards?

Though the CCP has widely publicized great improvements in

agricultural techniques, little has actually been done. The state budget for 1959 provides ample evidence for this conclusion. Li Hsien-nien, the finance minister, reported at the Second National People's Congress that agricultural investment for 1959 is one billion yuan; that is, 3 percent of the total budget. How effective can this small amount be in meeting the agricultural needs of such a vast country? According to the CCP, the improvement of agricultural technique is the business of the peasants and they "must rely mainly on their own accumulations to expand their economy."[43]

This is why the communes are continually urged by the official CCP newspapers to reconstruct and make their own agrarian tools, collect fertilizer, practice deep plowing, etc.

The policy toward the peasants in the period of agricultural cooperatives was basically to increase production by intensifying peasant labor to the utmost, to exploit the peasants' surplus labor by collecting taxes, to purchase agricultural products at low proces and raise the prices of industrial products. The aim of this policy was to meet the expenses of the huge bureaucratic apparatus and to "speed up the accumulation of capital imperatively needed for China's industrialization."

But the cooperatives were small and scattered, therefore difficult to control. So, Mao Tse-tung, on inspecting several experimental People's Communes in Hunan province in August 1958, declared immediately that "it is better to set up the communes, because it is easier to lead by merging industry, agriculture, exchange, culture and education, and military affairs into one." Here the euphemistic "easier to lead" obviously means "easier" for the bureaucrats to arbitrarily exploit and control the peasant masses. Events since then have confirmed this.

The large labor force of the peasants has been concentrated and expanded; the former through the merger of the cooperatives and the latter through the liberation of women from "domestic slavery" via communal kitchens, etc. Thus, by practicing "large-scale utilization of cooperative labor," "production of agricultural surpluses" can be increased. Also, it is easier, through the communes, to apply higher taxes to the peasants, to lower what is paid for their products, and to raise the price of industrial products which they must buy. Is this not enough to show that *the communes have become the most convenient instrument for the CCP to exploit the surplus labor of the peasants*?

Intensification and exploitation of the peasants' labor to the utmost will inevitably arouse the resentment and resistance of the peasants. Therefore, strict organization, constant supervision, and tight control become absolute necessities. This is why the policies of "getting organized along military lines," "working as if fighting a battle," and "living the collective way" were invented. In order to carry out these policies thoroughly, the CCP put special emphasis on the organization of the militia as the communes began. On this point, Comrade Ma Chi, a supporter of the communes, has made the following rather profound analysis:

> The main purpose of widely developing the militia at the beginning of the commune movement was obviously to administer production and private life in the commune by means of military organization and discipline. The CCP's policy was not to gradually substitute the militia system for the nonproductive regular army. Serving as the assistant to and reserve for the regular army, the militia is provided with the most backward weapons manufactured by local arsenals. Militiamen are divided into two groups: basic and ordinary. The Communist Party maintains "absolute guidance" of the militiamen and all the weapons are issued to the most "reliable elements." From past experience we know that those who criticize official policies are classified as "unreliable" elements and the Left opposition as "rightist elements."

> Mao's words that "the militia is a combination organization for labor, education, and gymnastics" became, in fact, the principle in organizing and directing the militia. The members of the commune are organized into units such as regiment, battalion, company, etc., for the purpose of military training and similar activities. In correspondence with the policies of "getting organized along military lines," "working as if fighting a battle," and "living the collective way," the work of production and the private life of the peasants are supervised by the commanders of the military units to which they belong. This militia system has assumed virtual control of every aspect of the peasants' life and has eliminated completely any individual freedom by imposing the harshest military discipline. Its military significance becomes secondary.[44]

It is true that the CCP, "having felt the general dissatisfaction among the masses," in the words of Comrade Ma Chi, announced last December at the Sixth Plenary Session of the Eighth Central Committee of the party: "The leading bodies of the militia and production organizations should be separated," and "it is absolutely impermissible to impair one iota of the democratic life in the communes and in the militia organization on pretext of 'getting organized along military lines.'" But these official statements have not changed the essence of "getting organized along military lines," "working as if fighting a battle," and "living the collective way." The peasants continue to be organized in production teams: big, medium, and small (equal to the regiment, battalion, and company, etc.). The chief of each team decides when and where the peasants gather and march to work. He directs, supervises, and speeds up the peasants' work with a megaphone. Also he arbitrarily decides the working hours of the group and extends them whenever he thinks it necessary. After work, the peasants march back to the community kitchen for supper. Isn't this a militarized labor organization?

Moreover, the peasant is deprived of the freedom to change his work assignment, or to move from one section of the commune to another, or, even, to a different commune. For instance, he cannot refuse to transfer to a remote place even though it means being separated from his wife for a period of time; and he cannot get a job, food, and living quarters elsewhere if he does not get a permit issued by the head of the commune to which he belongs. Bound to the communes, the peasants bear resemblance to the serfs of the Middle Ages.

Still another item is worthy of attention: the recruiting of labor forces to meet the needs of the city factories. This is in the hands of the communes, whose chiefs arrange such assignments. In the eyes of the peasants, to work in the city is considered very lucky. Those considered the most active are certainly in line for first choice for these assignments. Thus, freedom to work in the city is excluded.

These actual facts of life under the slogans of "getting organized along military lines," "working as if fighting a battle," and "living the collective way" have never been seen in any "type of socioeconomic organization" in modern times except in labor concentration camps.

Consequently, we can say that despite their "progressive character," the present People's Communes, due to the contradictions, chaos, coercion, and deprivation of peasant freedom, can hardly be termed "a superior type of socioeconomic organization," but only *an effective instrument for the CCP to exploit and control the peasants*. The communes cannot "make an indispensable contribution to the building of the economic basis for socialism"; instead they arouse the distrust and resentment of the peasants toward "socialism" and damage the cause of socialism. As Lenin said:

For the name "agricultural commune" is a great one; it is associated with the conception of communism. It will be a good thing if the communes show in practice that they are indeed seriously working for the improvement of peasant farming; that will undoubtedly enhance the prestige of the Communists and the Communist Party. But it has frequently happened that the communes have only succeeded in provoking a negative attitude among the peasantry, and the word "commune" has even at times become a call to fight communism.[45]

The general food shortage that began earlier this year, and the current elimination, as I write these lines, of communal kitchens in many communes, have been verified by various sources. The food shortage shows in a negative way that the CCP was unreliable when it announced the doubling of food production last year. Why has the shortage of food become so acute that the food quota of commune members has been reduced to two-thirds, or even one-half, and city residents can hardly get enough food? Any other explanation is unlikely except that the bumper figures on the harvest last year were fake.

The communes were set up in accordance with two principles— "large scale" and "collective ownership." The communal kitchen is a concrete illustration of "collective ownership." Now, many of them, along with nurseries, at least those in Kwangtung province, have been disbanded. From social production women have been returned to "domestic slavery." On this, Vice-premier Teng Tzu-hui has openly admitted "the failure of the community kitchens," and proclaimed that "in the future the socialization of households in the countryside should be on a voluntary basis." This shows that one of the fundamental principles upon which the communes were established is being abandoned. Thus, the communes have begun to expose their bankruptcy "in principle."

The general shortage of food and the forced abandonment of a number of communal kitchens are undoubtedly evidence of a serious crisis due to the CCP's use of coercion in setting up the communes. Various clues indicate that Mao and Company are now meeting to consider this crisis.

Perhaps in the near future the CCP will once again "adjust" its policy toward the communes as it did at the Sixth Plenary Session of the Eighth Central Committee of the party last year. That is to say, under pressure of growing discontent among the peasant masses all over the country, the CCP will again empirically make certain changes in the communes by way of appeasement. But to save face, they will never admit that their commune policy is fundamentally wrong; nor will they give up their basic policy of exploiting and controlling the peasants. Consequently the communes will be maintained, as will the recurring crises.

In the future, when the authors of "The Communes in China (Draft Resolution Proposed by NC Members in Los Angeles)" witness a certain change in the communes, they probably will say that this is exactly what they predicted in their draft:

> Their organization and operation will very likely undergo further modifications. But such revisions, and even a retreat from their present status, would not vitiate the progressive character of the communes any more than the retreat from collectivization in Poland has negated the progressive character of collective farms over private proprietorship and individual production.[46]

This statement separates the "progressive character of the communes" from the principle of voluntary consent by the peasants and uses the former as the sole criterion in evaluating the communes. I pointed out the error in this above in criticizing Comrade Liang's position. Here I would like to discuss in particular the reference to the change in the policy of collectivization in Poland.

Gomulka, in pointing out that the value of production per hectare in the collective farm was 16.7 percent lower than that on the individual farm, stated that this lag was due to the policy of coercive collectivization. So after coming to power, he reorganized or disbanded certain immature collective farms and discontinued forced collectivization. But he did this not because forced collectivization had "negated the progressive character of collective farms over private proprietorship and individual production," but merely because he thought that the consent of the peasants together with mechanization in agriculture were prerequisites for the successful realization of collectivization and increased production in agriculture. This viewpoint was clearly evident in his report "The Central Task of Polish Agriculture from 1959 to 1965" at the Second Central Committee of the United Workers Party of Poland, June 22, 1959.

In his report, Gomulka emphasized the importance of planning and "the decisive significance of increasing the actual wages and income of the rural population" in the development of agriculture. Therefore: "The total investment in agriculture in 1959-65 is put at 13 billion zlotys, of which 9 billion zlotys is allocated to improving production, that is, in mechanization, improvement of soil, and the construction of 1,200,000 buildings both for housing and production."

He particularly emphasized the manufacture of 112,000 tractors between 1959 and 1965 to increase production and to promote collectivization in agriculture. His conclusion was:

> The party insists on the program of socialist reconstruction in the countryside, and is fully aware that the completion of this program can only be realized under the condition of large-scale agricultural economy, i.e., the collectivization of production. The aim of this reconstruction is, first of all, the enlargement of agricultural production. And the *collective peasant economy can be established only through the consent of the peasants.* [Emphasis added]

The proposals and conclusions emphasized by Gomulka in his report could not be taken as evidence that the "retreat" in agricultural policy in Poland had "negated the progressive character of collective farms over private proprietorship and individual production"; but they do underline the need to pay more attention to the actual interests and the voluntary consent of the peasants; that is, the need to abandon Stalin's coercive methods and return to, or at least approach more closely, Lenin's point of view in the nationalization of land and collectivization of agriculture.

The authors of "The Communes in China" describe the Polish policy in agriculture as not having "negated the progressive character of collective farms. . . ." But this approach misses the essence, and reveals that these authors adopt the same incorrect viewpoint in approaching the change in Polish agrarian policy as they do in the problem of the Chinese communes. Here is a demonstration that an incorrect viewpoint in one set of events often becomes the basis for a similar approach to comparable phenomena.

We Trotskyists should understand that despite holding the Stalinist viewpoint on certain issues, Gomulka's latest policy in nationalization of land and agricultural collectivization is correct in principle. He is the first one to abandon Stalin's coercive methods and to turn toward Lenin's viewpoint. In this, he is much more correct than Mao Tse-tung.

The present Chinese People's Communes have already exhibited all kinds of contradictions and are in serious crisis. In order to halt the extension of the crisis and a possibly disastrous outcome, the Polish experience should be accepted as a pattern and China should undertake a similar bold "retreat," that is, from ultra-adventurism back to Lenin's viewpoint. The communes, on the basis of the actual interests and voluntary participation of the peasants, should undergo complete change, following thorough investigation. I will return to the point more specifically in the final section of this article.

A few more words on Comrades Liang and Swabeck

In the foregoing I criticized the main data on which Comrades Liang and Swabeck based their support of the communes. Here I wish to deal with the attitude and basic tendency which they reveal in their study of the communes.

In stating his judgment on the communes in his commentary on the [SWP Secretariat's] "Draft Resolution on Chinese Communes," Comrade Liang presents neither our basic theory nor historical examples. For instance he simply says: "The draft largely repeats the sins and errors of the Roberts article."[47] But what are the "sins and errors" of the Roberts article, "The Chinese Communes"? Liang doesn't specify. With one stroke, through an unsupported assertion, he wipes away another comrade's opinion. To me, the general viewpoint of Roberts's article, especially its conclusion, is basically correct, and even the facts cited by him are tentatively correct and able to withstand criticism. At least they are more dependable than those cited by Comrade Liang.

Another special reason advanced by Comrade Liang for supporting the communes deserves comment: "The continuing drumfire of hostile comment on the Communes by capitalist propagandists places us squarely before the need to take a clear-cut position on what, essentially, is a *class-struggle issue:* FOR or AGAINST the Communes?"[48]

According to the formula of a "class-struggle issue" advanced here by Comrade Liang, we should be for something if the "capitalist propagandists" give it "hostile comment" and we should be against it if they favor it. This is ultramechanical formal logic, having nothing in common with Marxist dialectics.

All of us remember the continued and vigorous attacks on Stalin's bureaucratic dictatorship by all the "capitalist propagandists." According to Comrade Liang's "logic," we should have supported the former. But Trotsky, instead of supporting it subjected it to penetrating criticism. The difference was that the "capitalist propagandists" considered Stalin's bureaucratic dictatorship to be the product of Bolshevism and socialist property relations; Trotsky considered it to be the result of the betrayal of

Bolshevism and hence a hindrance to the rational development of socialist relations.

A fresh example occurred when all the "capitalist propagandists" furiously attacked Russia for putting down the Hungarian revolution with tanks. At the time we Trotskyists did not give up our relentless criticism of the Kremlin's role in this event. The difference was that the "capitalist propagandists" criticized it from the viewpoint of bourgeois nationalism as an "intervention of Russian imperialism", while we criticized it as a betrayal by the Kremlin of the interests of the Hungarian working class and the world socialist revolution. And at that time the "Trotskyists" who "took a clear-cut position" were the Marcyites, who later left our movement.[49]

Today the reason for the continuous and vigorous attacks on the communes by the "capitalist propagandists" is that they see them eliminating the remnants of the holy private-property system and the holy family system connected with it. We see the forcible introduction of the communes within a short period by the CCP as adventurism and as against the peasants' will. We hold to this view because China today does not have the material and cultural prerequisites for eliminating the remnants of the private-property system and superseding family life with the collective life of socialism; and because, therefore, the CCP policy is very harmful to the alliance of workers and peasants and to socialism. Superficially our criticism sounds the same as that of the "capitalist propagandists," but the substance and class position represented by us is the exact opposite. As the French proverb puts it: "One tongue, two languages."

Comrade Swabeck, in his article "The Third Chinese Revolution and Its Communes," quoted quite extensively from the reports of a few foreigners who had visited China (leaving aside the truthfulness of these reports) to defend his position on the superiority of the communes. Unfortunately, the facts quoted by him either have no connection with the communes or have been proclaimed bankrupt by the CCP. For instance:

1. "No less significant is the vast public projects made possible by the Communes. . . . As one concrete example that witnessed by the Montreal reporter can be mentioned: A huge dam and reservoir near Peking, completed in the phenomenally short time of 160 days by 400,000 'volunteers.'"[50]

The "huge dam and reservoir," i.e., the Tungling Dam near Peking, was completed before the communes by the great mass of workers and suburban peasants of Peking mobilized by the central government.

2. "In addition to the demonstrated economic gains, cultural advance is symbolized by an increase of primary school pupils from 64.3 million in 1957 to 84 million in September 1958."[51]

The fact cited here (granting that it is true) was also achieved before the communes. They began in September 1958. A further example is the "homemade" or "backyard" blast furnaces, highly extolled by Comrade Swabeck as the "most celebrated" of the small and medium industrial enterprises initiated by the communes. These in fact ended, unfortunately, in a fiasco. They had been abandoned long before Swabeck's article was published, although the CCP did not formally discontinue them until July 1959. I wonder how Comrade Swabeck will explain this.

Comrade Swabeck devoted considerable discussion in the last part of his article to the problem of the permanent revolution in China. I can only state that his interpretation of this problem is incorrect. (Unfortunately I don't have space here to go into it.) He had not one word to say about the CCP's foreign policy, "peaceful coexistence" (i.e., the "Five Principles" stipulated by Chou En-lai and Nehru of India).[52]

The sudden shift from right to left of Mao's internal policy originates from this extremely reactionary foreign policy which, inherited in toto from the Stalinist theory of "socialism in one country" (now Mao has developed it into his theory of "communism in one country"), contravenes the permanent revolution. Mao neither believes in nor understands the decisive role that the victory of the world socialist revolution, particularly the victory of the proletarian revolution in the advanced countries, would play in bringing the Chinese socialist revolution to victory. To maintain his own power, Mao started by compromising in all possible ways with the bourgeoisie and landlords, in an attempt to build the "New Democracy" social system (i.e., nonsocialist, noncapitalist) within a few decades.

Later, under pressure of imperialist intervention (especially the American intervention in Korea) and the counteroffensive of the domestic bourgeoisie and landlords, he pragmatically jumped from ultraright opportunism to ultraleft adventurism. Thus, he sought to exploit to the utmost the surplus labor of the workers and peasants in an attempt to facilitate industrial development and to build socialism in one country. And his reckless introduction of the communes within a short period is the culmination of adventurism in the application of the theory of "socialism in one country" or "communism in one country."

In addition, in the articles by Comrades Liang and Swabeck discussing the Chinese rural communes, which concern the lives of 500 million peasants, there is not one word about the principle developed by Engels, Lenin, and Trotsky on the nationalization of land and voluntary peasant participation in agrarian collectivization. It is very significant, for it indicates how they have neglected the traditional Marxist position on the agrarian question and our position on the alliance of the workers and peasants set forth in our Transitional Program.

It is because of this complete disregard of the traditional Marxist position that their position on the communes is the same as that of the revisionist Pablo, or at least, very close to it.

Jean-Paul Martin, who speaks with complete authority for Pablo, wrote an article, " 'Uninterrupted' Revolution in China," which was published in *Quatrième Internationale* in November 1958. Besides acclaiming that "China is at present in a state of 'uninterrupted' revolution," and praising the stupendous development of its industry and agriculture, the main point of his article is the great significance to China of the communes in the rural areas. For example, he said:

All this is not simply boasts, hypocrisy, or infantilism; it is pride, the immensity of her stature confronting the world of the twentieth century. China feels in herself unlimited forces awakening. Her vision of the world, quite different from that of any other power, is a mixture perhaps of infantilism—normal for a country still sleeping yesterday in the past, now entering with such impetuousity and such fury into the atomic age— and real gigantism.

Besides such abstract eulogies as above, Martin declared: "The administrative committees of the communes are in reality 'popular town councils,' soviets." This political appraisal of the communes is almost identical with that of Comrades Liang and Swabeck; namely, "the communes are administered by *elected councils*, not by bureaucratic edict."

Having appraised the nature of the CCP and its regime in the light of Pablo's revisionism, it is not strange for Martin to have such an appraisal of the communes. It is the logical development of Pabloite revisionism. Comrades Liang and Swabeck, who opposed Pablo's revisionism in the past, have arrived at almost the same political conclusion on the People's Communes today as Pablo. This is worth some thought on their part.

Finally, I should point out in passing that the errors of Comrades Liang and Swabeck on the issue of the People's Communes go far beyond those of Comrade Ma Chi. Comrade Ma Chi does not paint up the communes, but gives them serious criticism in light of the facts; his error is that he places too much weight on the superiority of the communes' large-scale production and neglects the principle of voluntary peasant consent. This is not an error in principle, but a bias and is easy to correct. But the errors of Comrades Liang and Swabeck intersect with principles, and if not recognized in time, can lead them into the swamp of revisionism.

Our attitude toward the communes

1. We have always held to and persistently maintained the necessity for nationalization of the land and agrarian collectivization, considering it to be the only possible form through which the scattered individual peasant economy can be brought to socialist relations. But at the same time we hold to the principle put down in our Transitional Program by Trotsky: "The program for the *nationalization of the land and collectivization of agriculture* should be so drawn that from its very basis it should exclude the possibility of expropriation of small farmers and their compulsory collectivization.[53]

That is to say, in the practice of agrarian collectivization, it is necessary to convince the peasants by concrete example, bringing them to believe that collectivization is in fact beneficial to them, hence calling forth their voluntary participation.

Therefore, we severely criticized Stalin's forced collectivization and, together with Trotsky, considered it to be "dictated not by the interests of the farmers or workers but by the interests of the bureaucracy."[54]

2. Taking the Chinese rural communes as a case of large-scale agrarian collectivization, and considering it in the light of the general principle of collectivization, we are for it; but, at the same time, in view of the fact that since the collectivization is on such a large scale and combines the practice of collective life in all rural areas (substituting the communal kitchen and nursery for family life), we consider it an absolute necessity to use concrete examples to win the voluntary participation of the peasants.

The policy practiced by the CCP toward the communes at present has greater compulsory character than CCP policy toward the former agricultural cooperatives. Consequently it is adventuristic and is dictated not by the interests of the farmers or workers but by the interests of the bureaucracy.

3. Forced entry into the communes—all the peasant masses are forced into "getting organized along military lines," "working as if fighting a battle," "living the collective way"—and the extraordinary increase in the intensity of labor has brought not only numerous dislocations, suffering, and ill health to the peasants, but the intensification of contradictions, lower agricultural production (as the current shortage of food and daily necessities in the cities shows), and injury to the alliance of workers and peasants. If persisted in, it will end in chaos and even cause uprisings in the rural areas, setting back the future of socialism.

4. In confronting this very serious situation, for the benefit of the majority of the peasant masses and the strengthening of the worker-peasant alliance, we advocate the following policy toward the present communes:

a. We call for an immediate and full democratic discussion on the communes among the workers and peasants of China. This should be done in each commune. A secret ballot should be taken. Those communes approved by the members, or a majority of them, will, of course, be maintained. Those not approved should be dissolved into the precommune cooperatives. In addition, farm tools and land should be distributed to those peasants who want to join neither the communes nor the co-ops.

b. The administrative committees of the remaining communes should be elected through secret ballot by the members, with the provision that inefficient officials can be recalled at any time. Production, distribution, and the important welfare planning of the communes should be decided beforehand by majority opinion through open discussion among all the members. The communal kitchen and nursery should be based on the principle of voluntary participation. All this should apply also to the cooperatives.

c. The agricultural tax should be applied rationally to the communes, cooperatives, and individual peasant households—a maximum of not more than 20 percent of their total income. Prices of agricultural products purchased by the government should be determined reasonably (i.e., according to the general market price). The peasants should be supplied with industrial products at reasonable prices.

5. This important measure—the People's Communes—involving the lives of 500 million peasants and the alliance of the workers and peasants has not been openly discussed by the worker and peasant masses nor by the membership of the CCP.

With Mao's word—"Communes are better"—at the beginning of August 1958, every local section of the CCP acted at once as if it had received an imperial edict, ample proof that the CCP acts politically not only as a one-party dictatorship, but also as a Stalinist-type personal dictatorship. In order to end this personal dictatorship with its vicious results, China needs freedom of speech, press, assembly, association, and belief among the workers and peasants. To guarantee these freedoms and rights to the worker and peasant masses and to effectively correct the wrong policies which run counter to the interests of the peasants and workers, the existence and activities of working-class parties adhering to socialist principles should be made legitimate. Only through such means can the dictatorship of a party, a group, or a person be avoided and socialist democracy achieved.

6. In order to carry out the measures indicated above, the fantasy propagated by the CCP that communism will be realized in the rural areas within a few years (or several decades) must be rejected. Instead it should be proclaimed that the actual fulfillment of collectivization—increased farm production, guaranteed real improvements in the lives of the 500 million peasants, and industrialization of the country—can only become a possibility with assistance from the proletariat in the advanced countries upon the victory of the world socialist revolution. Hence the theory of "socialism in one country" or "communism in one country," and the illusion of "peaceful coexistence" related to it, must be rejected entirely. The main aim of foreign policy should be to aid the world proletarian socialist revolution; first of all, the Japanese and Indian proletarian revolutions. Just as Comrade Roberts said:

Successful working-class revolutions in Western Europe and the United States, leading to the elaboration of a world socialist economic plan, would enable China to take the great leap forward in the shortest possible time. . . .

A socialist overturn in Japan alone would transform China's prospects overnight. The economies of the two countries would gear together naturally. Japan would be able to mass-produce power-driven pumps, plows, carts, trucks, lift forks, and dredges for China's farms . . . while making equipment available for industrial development.[55]

August 19, 1959

POSTSCRIPT

Three weeks after finishing the above article, I received the *People's Daily* of August 27, in which appeared the "Communiqué of the State Statistical Bureau of China on the Revision of 1958 Agricultural Figures" and the "Resolution on Developing the Campaign for Increasing Production and Practicing Economy" passed by the Eighth Central Committee of the CCP at its Eighth Plenary Session. I will quote below some excerpts from these two documents and make brief criticisms as a postscript to my article.

The "Communiqué of the State Statistical Bureau of China on the Revision of 1958 Agricultural Figures" states:

China reaped a bumper harvest in 1958 unmatched before in its history. Owing to lack of experience in estimating the output of such an unprecedented bumper harvest, the agricultural statistical organs in most cases made overassessments. At the same time, during the bumper autumn harvest, manpower was not very well arranged, and the harvesting, threshing, and storage were somewhat inadequate. As a result there were some losses and the harvest did not conform to the estimated figures. After repeated checkups and verifications in the first half of this year, it was found that some of the 1958 agricultural statistical figures previously released were higher than the actual amount gathered. The revised 1958 agricultural statistical figures are as follows: Total grain output, 500 billion catties [250 million tons], 35 percent more than in 1957; total cotton output, 42 million tan [2.1 million tons], 28 percent more than in 1957.[56]

From the figures quoted in the above "communiqué" (the truthfulness of which is still in question), the following points are worth our attention:

1. The statistics in industry and agriculture published by the CCP were not compiled after production to record the actual amount of increase, but were advance estimates, an "assessment" or prediction. Here, for the first time, the secret statistical methods of the CCP are revealed. Of course, this revelation was forced from them by the resentment and dissatisfaction of the masses, aroused by the general food shortage when the so-called bumper harvest proved in fact to be not so large. Hence, we can see what little reliance can be placed in the production figures put out by the CCP for industry and agriculture!

2. How did it happen that after the establishment of the communes "the manpower was not very well arranged and the harvesting, threshing, and storage were somewhat inadequate"? Obviously, the great majority of peasants were forced to join the communes, which is why they vented their feelings by sabotaging and damaging the autumn harvest.

3. The increase for grain was 35 percent over 1957, not double or 100 percent as had been claimed; the increase for cotton was 28 percent over 1957, not 60 percent. What a big difference between the actual figures now reported and those figures about "the great productive increases in farming" quoted by the authors of "The Communes in China"! This especially deals a great blow to the arguments of Comrade Swabeck, because he had emphasized:

In this manner China has revolutionized the feeding of its millions. Food grain production in 1958 reached the astounding total of 375 million tons, doubling the 1957 output of 185 million tons. With this the teeming, crowded population has advanced from the malnutrition and famines of yore to a living diet today. This is confirmed by Lord John Orr, world authority on food and population, who declared upon return from his recent visit, that China is solving its food problem.[57]

According to the revised statistics published by the CCP, the doubling of the 1958 output, which was so highly praised by Comrade Swabeck, is declared false, and a question mark is placed on the "confirmation" by the highly recommended "Lord John Orr, world authority on food and population."

4. In my article, I said that the CCP official reports on the increase in agricultural production were exaggerated and that the CCP's widely proclaimed doubling of the 1957 output was unreliable, as proved negatively by the general food shortage. My distrust of the official CCP reports stemmed from general distrust of the acts and words of Stalinist bureaucrats. The revised statistics now published by the CCP not only show that our distrust of official CCP reports is completely justified, but prove that the discrepancies far exceeded what we had imagined, since the difference between the two reports on the actual increase in amount of grain gathered was 65 percent. What a hard lesson for those who only depend on the official reports to study and judge the development of Chinese agriculture, especially for Comrade Swabeck who blindly believes the official CCP reports!

Following are several points which are worth taking up here in the "Resolution on Developing the Campaign for Increasing

Production and Practicing Economy" adopted by the Central Committee of the Chinese Communist Party at its eighth plenary session on August 16, 1959.

1. The resolution states: "During the check-up, the principles of management and business accounting at different levels, of 'to each according to his work' and more income for those who do more work have been implemented."[58]

This signifies the elimination, "in principle," of the "rational system" originally prescribed for the communes of "to each partly according to his needs," and the abandonment, "in principle," of marching toward communism by gradually replacing the system of "to each according to his work." Here the utopia of the CCP, under the merciless lesson of circumstances, has demonstrably been returned to its starting point. It is also evident that the CCP, in order to fulfill the aims of the "Great Leap Forward," is attempting to put pressure on a part of the peasants—those with the greatest capacity for work—with the material incentive of "more income for those who do more work." This attempt will inevitably have two bad results: first, a detrimental effect on the peasants' health; and second, a widening of the differentiation at the two poles; i.e., rich and poor peasants in the communes.

2. On ownership in the communes: "It has been decided that at the present stage a three-level type of ownership of the means of production should be instituted in the people's communes. Ownership at the production brigade level constitutes the basic one. Ownership at the commune level constitutes another part. . . . A small part of the ownership should also be vested in the production team."[59]

To go by the decision that "ownership at the production brigade level constitutes the basic one" in this three-level type of ownership of the means of production, the commune has actually turned back to the former producers' cooperative, inasmuch as the production brigade is the same size as the former producers' cooperative, and was reorganized from the latter. On this, the CCP has officially admitted: "In the present People's Communes . . . *ownership is basically the same as that of the original production brigade in the advanced cooperative.*"[60]

Thus, in production, distribution, and especially in "ownership," the commune actually has almost dissolved into the original producers' cooperative. It is time now for Comrades Ma Chi, Liang, etc., to reexamine their opinions on the communes. (Ma Chi praises highly the "superiority of large-scale production" of the commune and Liang paints it as a "superior type of socioeconomic organization.")

3. I pointed out that the community kitchens, because they were forced upon the peasants, absolutely could not be kept up— "in the not too distant future, they will be reorganized or the great majority of them will be disbanded." Now the CCP resolution states:

> With regard to the community dining-rooms in the rural areas, the principle of making vigorous efforts to run them well and voluntary participation should be adhered to; grains should be distributed to each family on the basis of a fixed allocation for each individual; a food ticket system should be introduced in the community dining-rooms, with unconsumed food being returned to the person who saves it.[61]

This open admonition to adhere to "voluntary participation" in the dining rooms is the same as admitting "in principle" that the former measures forcing the peasants to participate in the community kitchens were wrong and absurd. Also, it is the same as permitting women "in principle" to return home to do the cooking. Thus, the women are going back to "domestic slavery." This fact should prove sobering to Comrade Liang and the others who highly praised the way the communes freed women from "domestic slavery."

4. On future grain targets: "In light of the verified figures on last year's agricultural output . . . the Eighth Plenary Session of the Eighth Central Committee recommends that the State Council submit to the Standing Committee of the National People's Congress a proposal for appropriate readjustment of the 1959 plan . . . grain, about 10 per cent above last year's verified output of 500,000 million *jin* (250 million tons). . . ."[62]

The target for grain in 1959 was originally 500 million tons. Now the readjusted targets are cut to almost half the original goal. This indicates how arbitrary the planning is in agricultural production under the CCP bureaucracy led by Mao Tse-tung, and to what depths they have descended in their ignorance, confusion, impudence, and self-contradiction.

The readjusted target also testifies to the correctness of our judgment that due to the lack of modern mechanization and chemical fertilizers, etc., the raising of farm production will still proceed "at a slow tempo." Here is a little victory for Marxist analysis.

5. On criticism and opposition: "The Eighth Plenary Session of the Eighth Central Committee of the Chinese Communist Party calls on the whole Party and the people of all nationalities of the country, under the leadership of the Central Committee of the Party . . . [to] overcome the right opportunist sentiments among some unstable elements. . . ."[63]

But who holds "right opportunist sentiments"? Those who are "sceptical of the Great Leap Forward, the People's Communes. . . ."[64] And those who consider the Great Leap Forward and the People's Communes to represent "petty-bourgeois fanaticism."[65]

The CCP's call for a fight to uphold "the superiority of the People's Communes" against "right opportunists" and "rightist ideas and sentiments," as proclaimed in the *People's Daily* editorial "Oppose Right Deviation. . . ." shows that criticism and opposition to the Great Leap Forward and the People's Commune movement among the broad masses of workers and peasants have become very effective and widespread. The opposition even attacks this movement as "petty-bourgeois fanaticism." In his report, Chou En-lai has publicly admitted that "This kind of thinking and sentiment has grown in the past two months."[66] This shows that the masses of workers and peasants, from practical experience in life, have already sensed the dire consequences of the adventurism in the policies forced upon them by the CCP.

To allay this resentment and criticism by the masses, the CCP on the one hand makes some concessions (as shown in the resolution); and, on the other hand, it increases repression under guise of a fight against "right opportunists." But until the "petty-bourgeois fanaticism" evident in these adventurist policies is finally eliminated, the resentment and criticism by the masses will continue to develop. Consequently, we have reason to predict that the commune movement will prove unstable and crises will continue to break out. Only by carrying out the proposals indicated in the section of my article headed "Our attitude toward the communes" can this outcome be avoided.

September 15, 1959

ON THE NATURE OF THE CHINESE COMMUNIST PARTY AND ITS REGIME—POLITICAL REVOLUTION OR DEMOCRATIC REFORM?

The distorted permanent revolution

In my article "A Criticism of the Various Views Supporting the Chinese Rural People's Communes," I criticized the assertion by Comrades Swabeck and Liang that the "communes are administered by elected councils, not by bureaucratic edits." Carrying their position to its logical conclusion, I made the following comment:

If Comrades Liang and Swabeck really believe what they assert, then not only the communes, comprising 500 million peasants, but also every level of government in China is a reasonable form of democracy, since every level of the People's Congress is "elected by the people" the same way as in the communes. So what we have is not the dictatorship of the bureaucracy but proletarian or socialist democracy in China. This not only completely reverses our assessment of the nature of the CCP and its regime, but also repudiates the resolution "The Third Chinese Revolution and Its Aftermath"—which was approved by Comrades Liang and Swabeck—passed by the SWP in 1955. After all, that resolution asserts that the CCP is a Stalinist party and its governmental regime is a buraucratic dictatorship that must be overthrown in a political revolution.

Less than four months after I wrote the above, Comrades Liang and Swabeck came out with another article, "The Third Chinese Revolution, the Communes and the Regime." In this new article they certainly followed the logic of their position to its ultimate conclusion. They openly called on the SWP to abandon its

---

This article was written in April 1960 for the internal discussion in the Fourth International. It was first published in English in 1961.

"present basic position"—that is, the position that "the CCP is a Stalinist party and its regime a bureaucratic dictatorship necessitating political revolution"—passed by the SWP in its resolution of 1955, and adopt the new line offered by them as the correct position—the CCP is not a Stalinist party and its regime is not a bureaucratic dictatorship, therefore "the program and slogan of the political revolution is invalid for China."[1] What is required in China today is "a program of democratic demands."[2]

If this "new line" is adopted, not only must the "present basic position" of the SWP be overturned from the bottom up, but it is inevitable that our attitude toward North Korea, North Vietnam, Yugoslavia, Poland, and even Russia must also be changed. This would constitute an epochal change in the strategy of the world Trotskyist movement toward the countries in the Soviet bloc, a change of decisive effect on the future of our movement. Hence it is incumbent on every Trotskyist to give the problem serious consideration and to probe the facts and the theory involved with the closest attention in order to reestablish our position.

The nature of the CCP — Is it still a Stalinist party or has it departed from Stalinism?

The main grounds advanced by Comrades Swabeck and Liang in proposing that the SWP abandon its "present basic position" is "changing reality," especially in the agricultural sphere — the development of mutual aid groups into "the superior type of socioeconomic organization" represented by the communes. They attempt to demonstrate that the "basic position" reached by the SWP in 1955 has become outdated and no longer entirely corresponds with this "changing reality." Actually, the "new line" they propose is not based on "changing reality," but on their reappraisal of the nature of the CCP and its regime. The so-called changing reality is only a pretext for overturning the "present basic position" of the SWP.

For instance, they say:

The resurgence in 1947-49 triumphed when the CCP engaged in a struggle for power by revolutionary means, disregarding Stalin's policy of coalition with Chiang Kai-shek. *By this action the Chinese Communist Party departed from Stalinism in the properly accepted sense of this term and proved itself an adequate instrument for the historic task.*[3]

If this judgment is correct, then the CCP when it took power back in 1949, was not a Stalinist party, having already "departed from Stalinism." Therefore, the resolution passed by the SWP in 1955, and approved by Comrades Swabeck and Liang, was basically incorrect and it is not necessary to argue against it in terms of "changing reality" since then. Why didn't Comrades Swabeck and Liang frankly go to the heart of the question? Apparently, under guise of appealing to the "changing reality," they want to back out of their responsibility for supporting the SWP resolution in 1955.

Let us begin by considering the question in the form in which it has been raised by Comrades Swabeck and Liang—whether or not the nature of the CCP changed.

To say that the nature of the CCP changed during its struggle for power in 1947-49 is not something new. Early in 1951 Germain offered the following opinion:

> Our movement has traditionally conceived the outstripping of Stalin-ism by the masses as involving profound splits inside the Communist parties. The Yugoslav and Chinese examples have demonstrated that, placed in certain exceptional conditions, entire Communist parties can modify their political line and lead the struggle of the masses up to the conquest of power, while passing beyond the objectives of the Kremlin. Under such conditions, these parties cease being Stalinist parties in the classical sense of the word.[4]

In this Germain is defending "theoretically" the revisionism that Pablo had begun to display toward Stalinism. (Pablo at that time had already begun to publish his revisionist views; i.e., that under mass pressure Stalinist parties can take the revolutionary path that leads the masses to power, the establishment of proletarian dictatorship, and socialist reconstruction.) Concerning this, I offered the detailed facts and analysis in my "Report on the Chinese Situation," emphasizing the following few points:

> First, since the CCP withdrew from the cities to the countryside in 1928, it established a quite solid apparatus and army (the peasant army). For these twenty years it used this army and power to rule over the peasant masses—as we know, the backward and scattered peasants are the easiest to control—and hence a stubborn and self-willed bureaucracy took shape, especially in its manner of treating the masses. Even toward the workers and students in the KMT areas, it employed either ultimatistic or deceitful methods instead of persuasion.

> Second, in ideology the CCP has further fortified and deepened the theory of Stalinism through its treatment of a series of important events:

the defeat of the second revolution, the peasant wars, and the Resistance War against Japan, etc. This was especially true in its rejection of the criticism of its concepts and policies by Trotsky and the Chinese Trotskyists. (I should call the comrades' attention to the fact that Trotsky's critique of Stalinism was more extensive on the Chinese question than for any other country except for the Soviet Union.)

Mao Tse-tung's "systematic" and dogmatic "New Democracy" is nothing but an ideologically and politically deepened and crystallized expression of Stalinism; i.e., it is the expression of obstinately holding onto the "revolution by stages" in direct challenge to the permanent revolution.

Third, over these two decades the CCP has received special attention from the Kremlin, and it follows that its relations with the latter are particularly intimate. After the Soviet Union occupied Manchuria and rearmed the CCP with weapons taken from the Japanese captives, the Kremlin's control over the CCP became more rigorous than ever.[5]

My conclusion was that

the most important turns the CCP underwent in the past were entirely the result of pressure from the Kremlin, and in violation of the will of the masses. Even the present "turn" toward the seizure of power was not a product of its yielding to mass pressure and going against the Kremlin's objectives, but, on the contrary, resulted from the mortal pressure of Chiang Kai-shek, and was taken in complete agreement with the Kremlin.

Precisely because of Chiang's uncompromising policy and under peril of his attack, the CCP, in order to survive—and with the consent of Stalin—was compelled to counterattack and take the road to power. Therefore, the CCP has certainly not departed from Stalinism so that it "ceases being a Stalinist party." This opinion, which I expressed, has demonstrated its durability; it has not been refuted by either Germain or Pablo or anyone else.

Eight years pass (1951-59) and Comrades Swabeck and Liang pick up the old opinion of Germain defending Pablo's revisionism, which they had opposed. (By approving the SWP resolution in 1955 that the CCP is a Stalinist party, Swabeck and Liang put themselves on record against Germain and Pablo's position.) They now use this old opinion of Germain's as a major argument to challenge the SWP's "present basic position." This demonstrates that to oppose an incorrect view or to accept a correct one without deep consideration and understanding opens the door to undue susceptibility to the influence of immediate events and even impressionism.

In order to counter such a capricious appraisal of the nature of the CCP, I feel that a reinvestigation of the nature of the CCP factually and theoretically is needed.

First, let me make a simple explanation of what Stalinism is in general or what "the distinctive and exclusive characteristic of Stalinism" is (Comrades Swabeck and Liang's words).[6] As we all know, Stalinism was formed in the process of degeneration of the first workers' state in a backward and isolated situation. Its social base is the petty-bourgeois bureaucratic caste. Due to the specific privileges of this caste, its ideology is conservative, compromising, and opportunistic in nature. In face of disastrous defeat or rejection by an opponent, its opportunistic policy turns to the other extreme—adventuristic or imprudent action. And when this adventuristic action proves unsuccessful, it reverts to its original position. Sometimes, a combination of adventurism and opportunism occurs. The highest expression of its opportunism is the theory of "socialism in one country" from which is derived the line of "peaceful coexistence" between socialism and capitalism in place of the strategy of international world revolution.

Organizationally, Stalinism substitutes bureaucratic centralism for proletarian democratic centralism—and this is concentrated in an omniscient faultless leader. By stifling all party democracy, conditions are prepared for a dictator given to arbitrary orders and indulgence in the cult of the individual. This organizational method is applied to the masses; persuasion is replaced by commands or ultimatums and even deceitfulness; in the state apparatus, police or GPU absolutism appears; the revolutionary opposition is met with slander, smear, and persecution (including murder, frame-ups, liquidation, etc.).

Here it is not necessary for me to recall the domestic and foreign policies (opportunism and adventurism) carried out by Stalin after he usurped power, nor to recall how the Communist parties in every country were converted into diplomatic instruments of the Kremlin. In the case of the Chinese Communist Party, it, too, was deeply poisoned by the opportunistic policies of Stalinism and suffered a tragic defeat in the course of the second revolution. Then the surviving revolutionary forces were buried in adventurism. They became ideologically and organizationally Stalinized—the image of the beloved Stalin. Before being forced to struggle for power, it was a genuine Stalinist party, as even Comrades Swabeck and Liang have admitted. Now the question is: Do the facts show that it has departed from Stalinism since coming to power?

Let us consider some major facts to see what generalization can be reached:

1. Under the peculiarly favorable situation created by the Second World War, the CCP overthrew the landlord-bourgeois regime of the Kuomintang. Nevertheless it still continued to practice the opportunistic policy of class collaboration or four-class bloc. Thus a "coalition government" of the workers, peasants, petty bourgeoisie, and national bourgeoisie was formed. It decreed the protection of bourgeois property, "equal consideration to state and private industry," and "equal benefit to labor and capitalist." To compromise with the landlords and rich peasants, it even postponed the acutely needed agrarian reform demanded by the peasants.

2. On the other hand, except in permitting the workers to join unions, it prohibited any independent organization of the workers, any strikes—even strikes against private capitalists to improve living standards. Peasants were permitted to fight gangsters, and to fight for reduction of high rents and interest, but not for the expropriation of land from the landlords or the elimination of interest on loans.

3. Its foreign policy not only completely followed the Stalinist "peaceful coexistence" line; it even openly declared the sanctity of foreign property in China.

4. It arbitrarily arrested, imprisoned, and even shot down revolutionists who disagreed with such policies, especially its political opposition, the Trotskyists.

5. It not only practices absolute bureaucratic centralism in the party; in addition, it holds up Mao as the "Eastern Sun," the Chinese Stalin. He, like Stalin, is the only interpreter and elucidator of Marxism in China and the only person who decides the policy of the state and the party. His "New Democracy" ideology has been defined in the party constitution (passed by the CCP's Seventh Congress) as "the guiding principle of all its work" and the foundation on which the party members "endeavour to raise the degree of their consciousness."

The second paragraph of the programmatic section of the CCP's constitution reads: "The CCP takes the theories of Marxism-Leninism and the combined principles derived from the practical experience of the Chinese revolution—the ideas of Mao Tse-tung—as the guiding principles of all its work. . . ."[7] In the section on membership this same document declares: "Party members shall perform the following duties: (*a*) Endeavour to raise the degree of their consciousness and study the basic ideas of Marxism-Leninism and of Mao Tse-tung's thought."[8] (Any policy decided by Mao and any speech uttered by him are for the membership to study and obey and absolutely cannot be criticized or opposed.)

These indisputable facts show the character of the CCP in the period from its coming to power to the outbreak of the Korean War. Isn't this enough to prove that the CCP not only did not depart from Stalinism during the struggle for power, but still remained a Stalinist party in the period after taking power (1949-51)?

Maybe Comrades Swabeck and Liang will argue that at least after the outbreak of the Korean War, particularly after 1953, the CCP departed from Stalinism, since it not only armed itself against American imperialism, suppressed the counterattack of the domestic bourgeoisie, landlords, and rich peasants (such as the "Five anti Movement"), but also abandoned the New Democracy policy, adopted the "general line of socialist construction" (proclaimed in the beginning of 1953), and began the five-year plan of industrialization, agricultural collectivization, and even communalization.

Yes, after the outbreak of the Korean War, under the mortal threat of the attack of the imperialists from abroad and the counterattack of the domestic bourgeoisie and the landlords, just as in face of Chiang's all-out attack, the CCP again was forced to take a big step forward by abandoning the reactionary illusion of New Democracy and adopting a series of revolutionary measures. But this does not equal departure from Stalinism. This was an empirical jump to the left within the frame of Stalinism.

The CCP started gradually expropriating bourgeois property instead of protecting it (through both state and private operation), but it still allows the capitalists to draw "fixed interest," and also allows the bourgeois and petty-bourgeois parties to exist legally and partly participate in the regime. Its foreign policy in particular still follows "peaceful coexistence" as developed in the "Five Principles" of Chou En-lai and Nehru. On the other hand, it still limits the democratic rights of the worker and peasant masses and still suppresses the revolutionary Trotskyists and other revolutionary elements. Bureaucratic centralism in the CCP and absolutism in the state regime are flourishing. Its practice of industrialization depends on the administrative lash; agrarian collectivization and communalization especially are carried out by administrative decree, amply manifesting their adventurism. We must not forget that Stalin practiced state industrialization and agricultural collectivization without departing from Stalinism. In carrying out these policies, Stalin used administrative decrees shot through with adventurism and intended not for the benefit of the workers and peasants but for the benefit of the bureaucracy. The CCP policy of industrialization and collectivization is a copy of Stalin's, with certain modifications but the same in nature.

Here I must specifically stress that if a party, deeply rooted in Stalinism, wishes to depart from Stalinism and return to Marxism and Leninism, this cannot conceivably be done without a serious internal struggle—an unlimited open discussion on the basic revolutionary theory of the present epoch and on political and organizational questions within the party. The thorough elimination of the opportunism, adventurism, and bureaucratic centralism characteristic of Stalinism as well as the elimination of obstinate Stalinists has to be achieved in the process of discussion. But within the CCP, neither before coming to power, nor in the process of taking power, nor in its turn to the "general line of socialist construction" after it was in power, has there been any such purge of Stalinist ideology.

In fact, just the opposite. When Stalin was still alive, the CCP ordered its members, the cadres in every organization, teachers and students in school, etc., to study Stalinist ideology—in the pattern of the "Study Stalinist ideology movement" after the Nineteenth Congress in the Soviet Union. After Stalin died, in his funeral oration, Mao said:

"All the writings of Comrade Stalin are immortal Marxist documents. His works, *The Foundations of Leninism, The History of the CPSU (Bolsheviks)*, and his last great work, *The Economic Problems of Socialism in the USSR*, are an encyclopedia of Marxism-Leninism, the summation of the experience of the world Communist movement in the past hundred years."[9]

The writings mentioned here by Mao embody precisely the "essence" of Stalinism and the "crystallization" of his betrayal of Marxism and Leninism and his falsification of the history of the Bolshevik Party. The Central Committee of the CCP, following the line of this speech, immediately mobilized the "Study Stalinist ideology movement" on the largest scale, forcing all members of the party and youth organization, teachers and students in the schools, cadres in organizations of all levels, and officials in all mass bodies to participate. This movement lasted for some months, every participant having to listen to numerous reports and discuss them.

After Khrushchev's liquidation of Stalin's cult and admission of some of his fantastic errors and crimes at the Twentieth Congress of the Soviet Union, the CCP, although compelled to admit that some errors were committed by Stalin in his old age, still did everything to defend him and praise his great contributions to fortifying the Soviet Union, building socialism, and eludidating Marxist-Leninist ideology. (See *On the Lesson of Proletarian Dictatorship* put out by the CCP.) Mao said at a Central Committee meeting of the CCP: "We have to defend the dead Stalin." That is to say, the "glory," the "achievements," and the ideology of Stalin have to be defended.

Finally, after the outbreak of the Hungarian revolution, the CCP, defending the interests of the Stalinist bureaucracy, not only did not show any sympathy but did all it could to smear it— denouncing it as a counterrevolution. At the same time, they praised and gave resolute support to the merciless policy of the Kremlin in suppressing this revolution.

From the facts cited above, we have adequate reason to conclude that the assertion of Comrades Swabeck and Liang that the CCP "departed from Stalinism in the properly accepted sense of this term" is baseless. Facts speak just the contrary. And judging from their extreme abhorrence of the Hungarian revolution, and the "Study Stalinist ideology movement" they have undertaken, Stalinism in the CCP, or at least in its leading cadres, has become strengthened and more stereotyped.

The contrast between the CCP regime and the Stalin regime in the Soviet Union

If we acknowledge that the CCP is a Stalinist party, then the nature of its regime is naturally settled. But Comrades Swabeck and Liang maintain that the CCP departed from Stalinism during its struggle for power. Hence they assert that "the Peking regime is not a Stalinist-type regime."[10] In defending this new idea they cite a great deal of material and theory. So I am forced to follow them in the process of further investigation.

Comrades Swabeck and Liang themselves raised the question in the first place: "Can the regime be defined by simple allusions to its training in the school of Stalinism, or by reference to

Stalinist characteristics alien to socialism?" And they answered it themselves: "Such references are not very helpful for serious study. . . . We should analyze carefully both the similarities and the contrasts of Chinese development with those of the Stalin regime in the Soviet Union."[11] They think that the CCP's "training in the school of Stalinism" and the "Stalinist characteristics alien to socialism" are irrelevant and "not very helpful for serious study." According to their theory, then, "training in the school of Social Democracy," or reference "to Social Democratic characteristics alien to socialism" are "not very helpful for serious study" of a Social Democratic party. Thus they completely forget Lenin's most important teaching: "Without revolutionary theory, there is no revolutionary action." Here, I leave aside temporarily the relation between revolutionary theory and action; that is, the nature of action decided by theory (including the nature of the regime). Let us take a look at "the similarities and the contrasts of Chinese development with that of the Stalin regime in the Soviet Union." On this, Comrades Swabeck and Liang tell us:

We have always attributed the rise of the Stalinist bureaucracy, and its crystallization into a privileged caste, to the conditions of a particular historical juncture. Basically, its rise was due to the world situation and a special correlation of internal factors and forces. Mention need be made here only of such outstanding factors as the economic backwardness of the country and its isolation in a hostile capitalist world.[12]

It is true that in the Soviet Union we attributed "the rise of the Stalinist bureaucracy and its crystallization into a privileged caste to the particular conditions of a historical juncture. Basically, its rise was due to . . . the economic backwardness of the country and its isolation in a hostile capitalist world." But Comrades Swabeck and Liang are mechanical in their approach to the "similarities" and "contrasts." They say: "The third Chinese revolution unfolds in a distinctly different historical period and under different historical conditions" and so China cannot undergo "the rise of the Stalinist bureaucracy and its crystallization into a privileged caste."[13] However, taking a dialectical approach, we must consider the following fundamental points:

1. If the "economic backwardness" of Russia is taken as the most basic objective condition for "the rise of the Stalinist bureaucracy, and its crystallization into a privileged caste," then the economy of China is more "backward" than Russia, a fact

that is acknowleged by Comrades Swabeck and Liang. For instance, they say: "To be sure, the new China started out from a position even more economically backward than did the young Soviet state. . . ."[14] And: "Bureaucratism arises from the need to apportion an insufficient national product. The poorer the society that issues from a revolution, the more dangerous is bureaucratism to socialist development."[15]

This means that in China objective conditions for the formation of "Stalinist bureaucracy and its crystallization into a privileged caste" are more favorable than they were in Russia.

2. Only with direct aid (including military, economic, cultural, and technical aid) from the victorious working class in the advanced capitalist countries can "the rise of the Stalinist bureaucracy, and its crystallization into a privileged caste" be avoided. No such condition exists in China today, just as it did not exist in Russia in its time.

It is true that Comrades Swabeck and Liang argue that "the Chinese revolution, in its development, has been able to draw assistance from the now well advanced resources of the Soviet Union, both military and economic."[16] But they forget that despite the "now well advanced resources" Russia has today, it is still a degenerated workers' state under a Stalinist bureaucratic dictatorship. Its "military and economic" assistance to China can, of course, help the latter to resist the invasion of imperialism (as in the Korean War) and build a socialist-type industry; but on the other hand, by bringing the CCP under its control and making it more dependent, the Kremlin bureaucracy facilitates the growth of the Chinese "Stalinist bureaucracy and its crystallization into a privileged caste." A concrete example of this was the influx along with the "military and economic assistance of Russia" of thousands of military, political, economic, and cultural advisers and all kinds of specialists or technicians, etc. Being of the bureaucratic caste, they bring with them to China the bureaucratic method in their work and the habit of granting special privileges to the new generation of bureaucrats in China.

On the international side, the period and the conditions facing the CCP are greatly different from what they were in the Soviet Union in its time. But there is one basic similarity. Since the Second World War, just as after the First World War, the working-class movement in the advanced countries (Germany and France) has suffered defeats. The nationalist movement in the Far East, Near East, and even North Africa is rising. But with the exception of North Korea and North Vietnam, the regimes fall into the hands of the native bourgeoisie, who form so-called democratic parliamentary regimes (as in Ceylon, India, Burma, Indonesia, etc.) or military dictatorships (as in Egypt, Iraq, etc.). These bourgeois-democratic regimes or military dictatorships can neither inspire the Chinese working class nor counter the growing bureaucracy; instead they strengthen the myth of "peaceful coexistence," the foreign policy of the Chinese bureaucracy, by providing the screen of neutralism. There is still another important factor: the only advanced capitalist country in the Far East—Japan—is entirely under the control of American imperialism. By using Japan as a base and tying South Korea, Taiwan, and South Vietnam together, American imperialism has set up a blockade or encirclement that threatens China.

3. The Russian Bolshevik Party took power through an uprising in which the working class under Lenin and Trotsky led the peasants. Due to the backwardness of Russia and a series of defeats of the working-class revolution in the advanced Western countries, the revolution became isolated; this led to the degeneration of the most revolutionary party and the loss of state power to the bureaucracy. But the CCP from the very beginning was under the leadership of a Stalinist, Mao Tse-tung, who not only did not mobilize the workers to lead the peasants through an uprising in the cities to overthrow the landlord-bourgeois regime, but who instead suppressed to the utmost the activities of the working class, relying solely on the peasant armed force to attack the cities. It was only because of the exceptionally favorable conditions created by the Second World War that the CCP was able to come to power. Therefore, the CCP from the beginning organized a Stalinist regime.

Precisely because the regime in the Soviet Union was a proletarian dictatorship established after a victorious armed uprising by the working class, which was led by a genuinely revolutionary party, the usurpation of power and conversion of the regime into a bureaucratic dictatorship by the Stalinist bureaucracy was met by stormy resistance (the Left Opposition led by Trotsky). Finally, through Thermidor,[17] the Stalinist bureaucracy, to use the words of Comrades Swabeck and Liang, "had to strangle the Leninist party and destroy physically the whole generation that led the revolution to the victory under Lenin and Trotsky."[18] Since the CCP regime began as "a Stalinist-type regime" it develops in accordance with its own logic without the necessity of going through "degeneration" and "Thermidor."

The few points analyzed above are sufficient to prove that the attempt by Comrades Swabeck and Liang to conclude "theoretically" that there is a basic difference between the regime of the CCP and that in the Soviet Union—that "the Peking regime is not a Stalinist-type regime"—lacks sound basis. The cause of their error is the substitution of mechanical "contrast" for dialectical analysis.

When Trotsky explained the "conditions for omnipotence of the bureaucracy," he wrote:

> The scarcity in consumer goods and the universal struggle to obtain them generate a policeman who arrogates to himself the function of distribution. Hostile pressure from without imposes on the policeman the role of "defender" of the country, endows him with national authority, and permits him doubly to plunder the country.[19]

This explanation is fully applicable to China under the rule of the CCP today.

Of course, "the rise of the Stalinist bureaucracy and its crystallization into a privileged caste" "is not likely to be reproduced elsewhere under different historical conditions." But in a certain area and under certain conditions, where the influence of the Soviet Union reaches or where a Communist Party under Kremlin control comes to power, then "the rise of the Stalinist bureaucracy and its crystallization into a privileged caste" can be inevitably reproduced. Conditions in Eastern Europe demonstrate the former; China, North Korea, and North Vietnam testify to the latter.

The shaping and development of the privileged caste— their enjoyment of special privileges

In my "Report on the Chinese Situation," written in 1951, I pointed out that even before the CCP took power, a stubborn and self-willed bureaucracy had taken shape in the rural area it occupied. After taking power, this bureaucracy, because of the monopoly and concentration of all political, economic, military, and cultural organizations and power, rapidly crystallized into a privileged caste. Along with the expansion of these organizations and aggregation of power, the newly shaped privileged caste attracted into its ranks a large number of the petty bourgeoisie, especially intellectuals, a part of the labor aristocracy (the so-called labor hero, model worker, or Stakhanovite), even a few members of the bourgeoisie (through cooperation between the bureaucracy and the bourgeoisie). In this way, a huge privileged caste formed. Its number is estimated as much greater than that of the Soviet Union under Stalin's rule. (Due to limited space I will not attempt to analyze here the component parts and approximate number in the Chinese bureaucracy. Generally speaking, it resembles the Soviet bureaucracy as analyzed by Trotsky in *The Revolution Betrayed,* pp. 135-39.)[20] This privileged caste, like its counterpart in the Soviet Union, forms a pyramid of several strata. At the bottom are the vast masses of oppressed workers and peasants and all the poor people; at the pinnacle stands the chairman of the party, Mao Tse-tung. The strict division of strata in the pyramid is clearly reflected in the formation of the officers' ranks—lieutenant, colonel, general, and marshal in the Chinese army, in complete imitation of the Red Army in the Soviet Union.

The consequence of the formation and development of this privileged caste is surely the enlargement and deepening of social inequality, the deterioration of the worker and peasant masses' living conditions, and the growth of prerogatives among the privileged caste.

It seems to me that nobody has ever denied the low standard of living of the Chinese worker and peasant masses (even Mr. Clark, the Canadian reporter whom Comrades Swabeck and Liang praise highly as an "objective observer," admitted as much in his book *Red China Today*).[21] What is in dispute is whether the ruling stratum of the CCP enjoys privileges and maintains a police system that protects its privileges. In respect to these questions Comrades Swabeck and Liang explain as follows:

> However, granting the existence of bureaucratic tendencies does not at all justify the characterization of the Peking regime as the rule of a privileged caste in the sense that we have always understood it—a hardened social formation of a parasitic nature, standing above the people, consuming an inordinate share of the national income and concerned primarily with the protection of its own powers and privileges against the masses. There is no evidence for such an assumption. Nor is there any evidence of an omnipresent police system which would be required to protect such a caste.
>
> Townsend mentions a certain degree of social differentiation, the only example in his whole book of about 400 pages,[22] Cadres who drew their provisions from the government would eat in "bigger kitchens," or "little kitchens." To the former came department heads, ministers and those of similar rank. Their fare contained more meat than was served in the more common "little kitchens." But Townsend adds: "After searching for those

riotously living Communists of whom one sometimes hears, I came on none who qualified for the description."

More recent verification is contained in Gerald Clark's book. "Mao Tse-tung, Chu Teh and Chou En-lai lead austere, almost monastic existences, dedicated to the building of a nation; and millions follow suit," he reports.[23]

The above-cited "facts" on the nonexistence of the privileged caste in China as presented by Comrades Swabeck and Liang are specially important, so it is worthwhile to check them. If their argument is correct and the facts observed by Townsend and Clark are reliable, then China would be entirely different from the Soviet Union, in that whereas a privileged caste exists in the USSR, China has only a group of incorruptible and honest officials who serve the country in the interests of the worker and peasant masses and for the sake of building socialism.

Do the facts really testify to this? In contrast to the observations of Townsend and Clark, let me cite, as extensively as space permits, some of the more concrete facts in a book entitled *Ten Years of Storm* written by Chow Ching-wen in Hong Kong. Chow was a standing member of the Central Committee of the China Democratic League, which cooperates with the CCP, and was a member of the Committee on Political and Legal Affairs of the Government Administration Council. (Tung Pi-wu and P'eng Chen, members of the Political Bureau of the CCP, are respectively the chairman and vice-chairman of this committee. The task of this committee is to lay out the systems and regulations in state administration and jurisprudence.) He was also a delegate to the National People's Congress. He participated in the CCP's regime for eight years (1949-56) until his departure for Hong Kong in December 1956. (It is said that his departure had Mao's permission.) This voluminous book contains nearly 600 pages.[24] The following are citations from it describing the privileges enjoyed by the CCP bureaucracy.

The Communists boast that they themselves have heroic personalities. Stalin even said a Communist is made of special material. Before seeing their ways of living and behaving, I also had the illusion for quite a time that members of a revolutionary party should "grieve before anybody, and rejoice after everybody." Although I did not agree with Communist ideology and methods, I did respect them. But after working together with them for nearly eight years in which I learned how they live, my respect for them evaporated.[25]

As to the way of living among the Communists, I could write a book dealing exclusively with this, but since there is no space here I can only sketch it on the basis of some concrete facts. Also I should like my readers to bear in mind that today's China is neither a capitalist country like the USA with an abundance of goods, nor is it a Soviet Union which claims to have reached socialism thirty years after its revolution, but a poverty-stricken country emerging from the Second World War and the civil war. Most people in China still live in old and decrepit houses. In densely populated Shanghai the average person occupies a living space of only two square meters. People eat mostly rice products and wear coarse cotton clothes; in the poorer areas they even eat distiller's grains, leaves, weeds, and wild fruits and wear indescribably tattered garments. . . . This is the real picture of the Chinese people. Bearing this in mind, we shall see how astonishing are the living conditions of those so-called revolutionaries who call for improvement in the people's standard of living![26]

The material life of a human being consists mainly of clothing, food, housing, transportation, and recreation. In the following, I shall describe living conditions among the Communists along these lines.

First is their housing. Prior to 1948 the top party leaders lived in caves in Yenan. In 1949 they moved into imperial palaces in Peking, and the cadres (big and small) took over the best buildings in all the cities which once belonged to the capitalists. Dissatisfied with the original furniture and decorations, which were in fact quite nice, they had them redecorated and bought new and better furniture. They wanted specially designed carpets, comfortable sofas, imported bathtubs and basins, splendid gardens, and to be served by many servants. If you happened to visit such a mansion, you would say that it is not in poverty-stricken China, but rather the villa of a New York millionaire.[27]

But the original buildings were not enough for the party men. New mansions with modern decorations have been erected in all the big cities to meet the demand of the new aristocracy. As a result, a newly constructed residential area in any city is where the new aristocrats live.[28]

Mao Tse-tung, Liu Shao-ch'i, Chou En-lai, Chu Te, etc., built their new villas in the western suburbs of Peking. The provincial and municipal leaders followed suit. So socialist construction started by building beautiful residences for top leaders, then the apartments, dormitories, auditoriums, dance halls, etc., for the enjoyment of party functionaries.[29]

New hotels were also built in many cities, with the exception of Shanghai where there are many good buildings left by Westerners for the use of important guests and top men. All these places are exclusively reserved for foreign visitors and top cadres. No ordinary people are allowed to stay in them. This includes the Peking Restaurant, Peace House, Liu Kuo Restaurant, Tsineman Restaurant, West Village Guest House, New Overseas Chinese Restaurant . . . in Peking; the Ching Restaurant and Broadway Building . . . in Shanghai; the original Sun Le

Teh Restaurant and the Tai Li Restaurant in Tientsin.[30]

Next let us talk about how and what the new aristocracy eats. . . . People in other countries know only that there are three kitchens; namely, the little kitchen, the middle kitchen, and the big kitchen for the top, middle, and low cadres respectively. The little kitchen cooks special and delicious food for high-class leaders; the middle kitchen is for the middle-class cadres; while the big kitchen cooks ordinary meals for lower cadres and the rank and file.

[Translator's note: Comrades Swabeck and Liang erroneously put them in reverse order. See *SWP Discussion Bulletin*, vol. 21, no. 2.]

This distinction among kitchens has roughly told us the division of three classes. But if you enter the place behind the curtain, you will discover that the top and middle-rank "chiefs" not only live in magnificent mansions, they also enjoy delicacies from the hills and sea. At least all the ministers whom I have visited live this kind of life. Everyone has a famous cook, who in the old days used to serve imperial officers or mandarins. I have tasted at a leader's residence both Chinese and Western dishes prepared by a cook who used to serve P'u-yi, the last emperor of the Ch'ing dynasty. Well-known cooks of big restaurants are transferred to serve top men. Whenever I dined at a chief's home, I often heard the host boasting about what a big person the cook used to serve or what big restaurants they were transferred from. Judging from the fact that cooks are called in to serve the top men at their residences, you can see that what they eat is not rice and salt vegetables, but chicken, duck, goose, fish, and delicacies from far and near.

Doesn't a ration system for meat and edible oil prevail in China? The hierarchy enjoys exceptional rights. They have special permits to buy extra meat and oil. When the markets open, cars and jeeps are lined up. Their cooks buy the best portions of meat and leave the bones and skins for the ordinary people. The chiefs are not confined to enjoying good meals at home; they give big banquets all the year around, some of them attended by over a thousand guests. Peking Restaurant, Peace House, New Overseas Chinese Hotel, and Huai Jen Hall . . . are places where big banquets are usually given. You can see over six hundred cars parked in front of the Peking Restaurant at dinner time almost every evening. Those who have never been in Peking could hardly believe it; but those who have been in Peking are accustomed to such scenes.[31]

The ruling class enjoys a lot of privileges. Fattened chickens and ducks are sent directly to their residences without passing through the market. Special farms and vegetable gardens for the top men grow special food which can never be enjoyed by the ordinary people. First-class apples grown in Manchuria are reserved for the top men. . . . When the harvest season for Peking peaches arrives, the government will buy all the first-class ones for the top men and distinguished visitors. . . . Watermelon which grows in Harin, Sinkiang; lichee which grows in Kwangtung; and all the other best fruits of the country are transported by air to Peking, giving priority to the taste of the top men.[32]

Let us now turn to the means of transportation. In the countryside people either walk on foot or ride donkeys or horses. . . . In the city, there are street cars and buses. Only the new aristocracy is permitted to ride in automobiles. It is interesting to see that the CCP distributes automobiles according to the rank and position of the officers. First-rank personages such as Mao Tse-tung, Liu Shao-ch'i, Chou En-lai, Chu Te, etc., ride first-class Russian cars. Ministers of the central government ride second-class Russian cars. Middle-rank officials ride American cars. Each governmental department has special buses for its employees. . . . But ordinary people have no right to share these privileges. . . . As a result, there is every indication in the city that those who ride in automobiles must be top men or middle-rank functionaries.

These cars are not confined to officers' use. Wives and children of the new aristocracy also ride in cars to the theaters or schools. A long line of cars can be seen every night in front of theaters. In the hot summer, dust flies in the street when a car of the new aristocracy passes by; while in winter a cold chilly wind blows dust in people's faces.[33]

Now I shall describe in a few lines what the Communists wear. When the Communists marched into the cities in their shabby clothes, the city dwellers praised them for austerity. Therefore, everybody followed suit. . . .

While the country earnestly copied the austerity of the Communists, the top leaders, however, changed their clothing from shabby outfits to new ones: woolen uniforms, fox or sable overcoats, sealskin collars, and otter fur hats. Then all the high-rank and middle-rank Communists followed suit. . . . Their wives also did not want to lag behind and began to wear woolen clothing and so do their sons and daughters. As a result, those who shop in the department stores or patronize big restaurants are mostly the Communist chiefs and their families.[34]

As for recreational institutions there were no commercial dance halls in the past few years, but there were movies, folk music, and local dramas. However, every organization, no matter how big or small, holds evening parties every Saturday or holiday, mostly for dancing, but sometimes for drama. Hwai Jen Hall [Translator's note: where the delegates of the National People's Congress meet] and the auditorium of the Political Consultative Conference give evening parties all the time. Whenever there is an evening party, thousands of cars of the top men roll into the place like flowing water. . . .

Here is something worth mentioning. During the meetings of the Political Consultative Conference in the spring of 1958, Mao Tse-tung dropped a remark about Chou Hsin-fang, a well-known Peking opera actor, then performing in Shanghai. Ch'en I, the vice-premier, guessed that the "chairman" wanted to see the performance of Chou Hsin-fang and his group; so he telephoned Shanghai and asked Chou's group to be sent immediately to Peking. As a result we had a chance to see Chou's performance the third day after the call.

The most lively recreational activity among the Communists is the evening party. The most colorful and enjoyable one is the dancing party held at the Violet Light Pavilion in Peking. It is exclusively for the chiefs of the central government. There the music is superb, furnishings splendid, service best, women extraordinarily pretty, food delicious, and atmosphere soft and fascinating. Present are high-ranking chiefs, such as Liu Shao-ch'i, Chou En-lai, Chu Te, and other political and military chiefs in the party.[35]

The Communist top men usually go to summer resorts such as Peitaiho and the seaside resorts in Tsingtao and Dairen in the North, and Lu Mountain Resort and Hwang Mountain Resort in the South. In the old days these places were where foreigners, politicians, and capitalists went during the summer, and where they built villas and modern-style resorts. . . . Now the owners of these resorts are the Communists, who in addition built many more splendid ones. But in order to show that the party is for the working class, the new aristocracy selected a few common buildings and also built a few in warehouse style as workers' sanatoriums; it is these that appear in the newspapers and not the splendid resorts of the new aristocracy.

The top men go to the summer resorts as soon as summer comes. They and their families take chartered trains with cooks, nurses, doctors, attendants. So those enjoying themselves in the mountains and at the seashores are the top men in the party and the administration. Their lives are comfortable and they are spendthrifts. They have everything, but the ordinary people who feed the former have neither enough to eat nor enough to wear but watch with sad faces the enjoyments of the new aristocracy.[36]

This extravagant and rotten way of living started first among the top party leaders, then spread among the middle-rank party officials, and then even to some degree among its lower cadres.[37]

How does this privileged caste of the CCP cover the cost of their extravagant way of life? Chow Ching-wen tells us: "Although the wage system has been adopted in recent years, the Communists, besides wages, can get what they want in the name of public expenses."[38] The so-called public expense is an "expenditure from the state treasury."

I don't have to mention that Mao Tse-tung, Chou En-lai, and the other high-ranking leaders naturally get their expenses from the state treasury, but so do the other elements of the privileged class—the party members and officials. Therefore, there is no distinction between public and private expenses. The upper- and middle-rank officials have official residences, special cars, and attendants. When they travel, they have first-class transportation and their expenses—private and public—are paid by the state treasury. Even the lower cadres also share these privileges, though to a lesser degree. Take a regimental commander for example: he has sufficient salary, an official residence, a radio, an automobile, first-class transportation when traveling, and a first-class room in the hospital in case of sickness.[39]

The Communist regime is an unprecedented, huge organization containing over ten million party members, two or three million armed forces, over twenty million functionaries. . . . This parasitic class, from top to bottom, enjoys luxurious living rendered possible only by its unhampered control over the economic system.[40]

The luxurious life of the CCP privileged caste, described above, is sometimes referred to in official CCP publications. For instance, when the party center attacks some dissident functionaries, it often accuses them of being extravagant and wasteful in their way of living. Especially at the peak of the "Hundred Flowers" campaign (April to June 1957),[41] a number of articles appeared in the *People's Daily, Ta Kung Pao,* and *Kwang-ming Daily,* listing many facts concerning the privileges and extravagant lives of the CCP bureaucracy. This testifies, from another angle, to the reliability of Chow Ching-wen's report. Chow, a petty-bourgeois democrat and a self-styled socialist, favors the nationalization of big enterprises but disagrees with Marxist theory and its fundamental policies, and considers the CCP to represent Marxism and Leninism. Therefore his criticism of the CCP's policies, from the theoretical viewpoint, is always incorrect and reactionary. But the factual exposition of the arbitrariness and the privileges enjoyed by the CCP, and the low living standards and miserable conditions of the workers and peasants in China, is based on reality. This is due to his participation in the CCP regime for nearly eight years, to his close relations with the top and middle bureaucrats, and to several missions to rural areas to interview peasants and investigate their conditions. This presented him with first-hand material.

Now we can say that the detailed and concrete facts mentioned by Chow Ching-wen not only suffice to discount the "observations" made by Townsend and Clark, but also prove that Clark's claim that "Mao Tse-tung, Chu Teh and Chou En-lai lead austere, almost monastic existences, dedicated to building of a nation; and millions follow suit" is an entirely false myth. Chow's report fully confirms the accuracy of the "characterization of the Peking regime as the rule of a privileged caste in the sense that we have always understood it—a hardened social formation of a parasitic nature, standing above the people, consuming an inordinate share of the national income. . . ." Now the remaining question is whether or not there is any "evidence of an omnipresent police system which would be required to protect such a caste."

The "evidence of an omnipresent police system"

After the defeat of the revolution in 1927, the CCP started to organize a secret police. Its main purpose was to protect the party cells from destruction by Kuomintang agents. Later, when Mao Tse-tung set up the "Chinese Soviet government" in Kiangsi, this secret police organization was moved there also and became the local secret police. After Mao and Company moved to Yenan in 1935, this secret police system continued to exist and develop with the participation of the GPU of the Soviet Union. As soon as the People's Republic was established in Peking during 1949, the secret police network spread immediately all over the country as the official public security organization. Russian GPU experts were invited in as advisers to help set up plans and train new agents to complete this public security police system. Now let us turn to Chow's description of the CCP "police system."

The most general and penetrating machine of suppression utilized by the Communists for control of people is the police. The chief policeman is Lo Jui-ch'ing, the minister for public security. His men are sent out to every province, city, county, and district to suppress the people. . . . The Communist agents have excellent capacities in their work. They live among the people and as a result constantly watch and control every activity of the latter.[42]

As for the policy system of the Communists, at the top level there is the Ministry for Public Security; at the municipal level, the Bureau for Public Security; in the districts, the branches of the Public Security Bureau; and at the bottom, the basic police station which directly governs and controls the people. Police stations are scattered among the residential areas. Each station controls a certain number of families and, of course, their activities. For instance, each police station is in charge of the population records in its governing area. Any person who wants to go to another place, even temporarily, has to report to the police station about his destination, the purpose of his trip, and the date of return. Likewise if a family has a visitor, within three days he has to be reported to the police station in that area as to his personal history, the purpose of his trip, etc.

Under the guise of a population survey, a policeman can enter any home at any time (day or night) to ask any question about something he suspects. If one buys things for private use he has to register them at the police station. If he receives money from a source other than his job, he should also put the amount he received in the "family register record" for the inspection of the police.[43]

Besides the police station, there is a street committee under the direction of the police. Its responsibilities are to know every family's status and to mobilize the people for contributions, campaigns, and demonstrations. To carry out its functions it either calls a meeting or visits the family in which it is interested. Like a policeman, the member of the street committee has to report in time to the police station on the general situation. The main task of the street committee is to uncover secret agents of the Kuomintang and suspicious elements. . . . In addition to the police station and the street committee, everyone, every family, especially those considered by the police station as activists, have special assignments. That is, for an individual to watch other members of his family; for a family to watch its neighbors and relatives. If one finds anything suspicious, he or she should immediately report to the police station. Consequently, everyone and every family is under constant watch and has the possibility of being the target of investigation. Under Communist police rule, people can't trust each other, not even husband and wife, father and son, brother and sister, relatives and neighbors. Amid the black cloud created by the Communists, everybody lives in the terror of uncertainty and everybody suspects the others as being his or her enemy or a police agent. As a result, to avoid getting into any trouble one has to be very discreet in words and deeds.[44]

In calling the Communist regime a police state we not only mean its police organization, but also include its entire police network. Living amid this network, who would not be horrified, terrified, and compliant? Those who are in government administration, factories, enterprises, schools, etc., are handled by the Communists with the same method mentioned above. Many visible or invisible shadows are behind everybody's back; every word and action are under constant watch and an unsuitable sentence is often the target for report and criticism; everybody is a watcher in the eyes of the others. Disturbed, everybody either keeps his mouth shut or cautiously utters Marxist terminology and the political line endorsed by the top leadership. Thus, every organization is a prison, and its members the prisoners.[45]

We can cite many specific instances that testify to the truthfulness of Chow's description of the "police system." On account of limited space, I will mention only two examples experienced by our Trotskyists:

1. Within a year of taking power, the CCP, through the surreptitious activities of its secret agents, had thoroughly

investigated all the leaders, members, sympathizers, and friends of our organization. In the autumn of 1950 all the leading comrades in Shanghai, Wenchow, and Kwangtung were arrested simultaneously and some of them murdered afterward. On December 22, 1952, and January 10, 1953, all our comrades, sympathizers, their relatives, and friends in Shanghai and elsewhere were imprisoned.

2. In the spring of 1955 our Comrade Chin visited a friend of his while touring Canton. Within five minutes after his arrival, a special agent from the street committee walked in and stayed to listen to their conversation until he left.

The above two facts sufficiently prove the existence of "the omnipresent police system of the Peking regime." Therefore we can say that the police system of the Peking regime is, if not more severe, at least equivalent to the GPU under Stalin's rule. If Comrades Swabeck and Liang deny both Chow's reports and our judgment, they should submit concrete facts by way of refutation.

Is the election of the National People's Congress "remarkably similar to the elections to the All-Russian Congress of Soviets at the time of the Bolshevik revolution?"

In order to glorify the democratic system of the Peking regime, Comrades Swabeck and Liang not only deny the existence of a privileged caste and police system, but also beautify as much as possible the National People's Congress which sets up the government. Under the subtitle "How About Popularly Elected Government?" the following lines appear.

This body [the People's Political Consultative Conference—P'eng] was later superseded by the National People's Congress. Says Townsend: ". . . by 1953 the votes cast by electors in villages, city lanes and other 'cells' had replaced the hitherto supreme organ of the United Front . . . with a government elected in accordance with 'democratic centralism' whereby the lower electoral bodies elected representatives to those a step higher, which in turn elected representatives to those immediately above."

Describing the first such regular election in Peking, Townsend points out that representatives were elected directly from large factories, from universities and from city wards; smaller units could combine to elect joint representatives. "All were subject to recall at the elector's demand." This is remarkably similar to the elections to the All-Russian Congress of Soviets at the time of the Bolshevik Revolution.[46]

Basing themselves merely on Townsend's sketchy report of the election of the National People's Congress in Peking and completely neglecting the necessary conditions and concrete steps in carrying out a socialist democratic election, Comrades Swabeck and Liang assert that "This is remarkably similar to the elections to the All-Russian Congress of Soviets at the time of the Bolshevik Revolution." This is even more lightminded and incoherent than the assertion they made that "the communes are self-governing" when they heard about "elected councils" in the communes. In criticizing their misjudgment on the "elected councils" of the communes, I pointed out:

Certain definite conditions are required to realize socialist democracy. First of all, the worker and peasant masses must enjoy complete freedom of speech, press, assembly, association, and belief. The secret ballot must exist at every level during elections. Finally, and most important of all, the legality of every workers' party that accepts socialism must be guaranteed. But in China today, as well as in the East European countries, these conditions are absent.[47]

In China today the necessary conditions for realizing socialist democracy are not only absent, but, under the strict control of the police system, it is just as impossible to hold a democratic election for the People's Congress as it is in the communes. However, "the fiction of universal electoral rights—in the style of Hitler-Goebbels" (see the *Transitional Program*) is maintained in elections at all levels in the People's Congress and commune committees. A list of candidates appointed by the CCP is given to every electoral unit for the people, or representatives of the people, to vote for or to circle. It is a familiar fact known to everyone in China. Now let us bring Chow Ching-wen forward as our witness, since he personally participated in the election of the National People's Congress in 1953, particularly the election in the Peking District People's Congress. The following is his description of the elections at all levels of the People's Congress and the government administration:

The lists of representatives at all levels of the People's Congress are handpicked by the CCP. Likewise with the lists of candidates in all the governmental committees. That is, the representatives of the village People's Congress are appointed by the Communist Party; the village administrative officials elected in the village People's Congress are also selected and appointed by the Communist Party. The so-called election is the party appointing someone for the masses or representatives of the masses to be approved by the raising of hands or voting. This also holds true in the *hsien* People's Congress and *hsien* governmental committee and even the provincial and central government People's Congress and its committee. . . .

The list of candidates decided on by the party beforehand is given to each electoral unit for election. For example, in the election of the more than one thousand delegates to the National People's Congress, about half of the candidates are chosen by the Central Committee of the CCP from the officials and personnel of CCP headquarters, the Central People's Government, and other organizations in Peking; the remainder are chosen by provincial party committees and submitted for approval to the Central Committee of the CCP. The candidates are then "elected" in the provinces as delegates. The same procedure is followed in electing delegates to the People's Congress on all levels. One part of the delegates to the provincial People's Congress is chosen by the provincial party committee, the other part by the *hsien* party committee with the approval of the provincial party committee, then the list is submitted for election by the *hsien* People's Congress. The candidates for the *hsien* People's Congress are decided on by the *hsien* party committee for election in the villages.

Administrative officials at all levels in the government are named by the party and passed by the People's Congress. These candidates for office at all levels of the People's Congress are always passed. The number of candidates always equals the number of delegates to be elected, so that voting is only a question of whether or not to put a circle around the names of the candidates. In brief, the names on the list given to you are all to be elected; if you disapprove of certain persons, all you can do is not circle their names, but they will be elected just the same because the majority of the electors put circles around every name on the ballot. And also before the election the Communist Party mobilizes persuasion in order to pass unanimously the names it has appointed. In fact, this kind of list is always passed by a big majority vote if not unanimously at all levels of the People's Congress.[48]

The above description of the elections at all levels of the People's Congress and governmental administrative committee fully proves that Townsend's report of "a government in accordance with democratic centralism" is completely false. In fact it is precisely what Trotsky called "the fiction of universal electoral rights—in the style of Hitler-Goebbels." I have said before: "The Chinese 'people's councils' are patterned after those in the East European countries. And the 'people's councils' in the East European countries are a variation of Stalin's 'soviets.'" To say, as Comrades Swabeck and Liang do, that the election of the National People's Congress in China is "remarkably similar to the election to the All-Russian Congress of Soviets at the time of the Bolshevik Revolution" is the same as saying that "the elections to Stalin's soviets" is "remarkably similar to the election to the All-Russian Congress of Soviets at the time of the Bolshevik Revolution"!

Since we all know the democratic conditions and election procedures in "the All-Russian Congress of Soviets at the time of the Bolshevik Revolution," I need not repeat them here. However, it is necessary particularly to point out that the soviets at the time of the Bolshevik revolution absolutely excluded electoral rights to all exploiters. But the Chinese People's Congress has granted by law the participation of bourgeois elements and their political representatives (such as the Democratic League, the Revolutionary Committee of the Kuomintang, etc.) in the elections with full right to run and to be elected. Therefore, in the past two National People's Congresses and at all levels of the People's Congress, political representatives of the bourgeoisie and capitalists were elected and even designated as committeemen in all levels of the government administration. This reveals that the class content of the Chinese People's Congress is different in essence from that of the soviets at that time. It is astonishing to read the assertion of Comrades Swabeck and Liang that the Chinese People's Congress, which includes bourgeois elements, is remarkably similar to that of the soviets which excluded all exploiters!

The distorted permanent revolution and the distortion of the theory of permanent revolution

After asserting that the CCP has departed from Stalinism, has no privileged caste and no police system for the protection of the privileged caste, and after praising the election to the National People's Congress which forms the national government, Comrades Swabeck and Liang proceed to describe the whole process of the third Chinese revolution, concluding as follows:

Subsequently [that is, after the outbreak of the Korean War—P'eng] the CCP leaders put forward their general line of the transition to socialism. Where private capitalist enterprise had previously been encouraged to develop under government control, it was now to be restricted and gradually transformed in order to attain "the step by step abolition of systems of exploitation and the building of a socialist society." At the end of 1952 the first Five Year Plan was launched. Industrialization now became a prime objective.

In agriculture the march of events proceeded from the early mutual aid groups to producers cooperatives and collectives, culminating in the socialist type of socioeconomic organization—the Communes. Unfolding side by side with industrialization, this powerful combination constitutes the motive force for the whole newer culture, while providing a material foundation for the socialist transformation of society.

Thus, regardless of the misconceptions, empirical improvization and opportunism of the CCP leaders, the uninterrupted development of the Chinese revolution stands out clearly and conclusively. Each new stage has been firmly anchored in the preceding one, each stage elevated society to qualitatively higher levels in which the socialist direction is unmistakable. What this signifies is a striking confirmation of the theory of permanent or continuous revolution.[49]

To picture the third Chinese revolution as "a striking confirmation of the theory of permanent or continuous revolution" constitutes the highest praise. It almost equals saying that the third Chinese revolution is a model example of the democratic revolution proceeding successfully into socialism. If this is the fact, then we cannot criticize but only unconditionally support the CCP policy. But the "facts" singled out above by Comrades Swabeck and Liang do not correspond either with the theory of the permanent revolution or the historical experience of the October revolution. What they noted belongs to the sphere of socialist economic reconstruction and they completely overlooked the most decisively significant political factor of the theory of permanent revolution. The great adventurism of the CCP in carrying out economic reconstruction—industrialization and collectivization—directly violates the theory of permanent revolution.

Since the beginning of the third Chinese revolution, great confusion, involving all kinds of misunderstandings and distortion of the theory of permanent revolution has been evident in the Trotskyist movement. Therefore, I consider it a special need to investigate the development of the third Chinese revolution in the light of Trotsky's own explanation of the theory of the permanent revolution as well as the historical experience of the October revolution.

Trotsky wrote in the preface to the Russian edition of *The Permanent Revolution*, November 30, 1929:

To dispel the chaos that has been created around the theory of the permanent revolution, it is necessary to distinguish three lines of thought that are united in this theory.

First, it embraces the problem of the transition from the democratic revolution to the socialist. This is in essence the historical origin of the theory.[50]

The theory of the permanent revolution, which originated in 1905, declared war upon these ideas and moods. *It pointed out that the democratic tasks of the backward bourgeois nations lead directly, in our epoch, to the dictatorship of the proletariat and that the dictatorship of the proletariat puts socialist tasks on the order of the day. Therein lay the central idea of the theory.* While the traditional view was that the road to the dictatorship of the proletariat led through a long period of democracy, the theory of the permanent revolution established the fact that for backward countries the road to democracy passed through the dictatorship of the proletariat. Thus democracy is not a régime that remains self-sufficient for decades, but is only a direct prelude to the socialist revolution. Each is bound to the other by an unbroken chain. Thus there is established between the democratic revolution and the socialist reconstruction of society a permanent state of revolutionary development.[51]

This "central idea" of the theory of the permanent revolution, stated by Trotsky in 1905, was fully confirmed by the October revolution. That is: in the midst of the democratic revolutionary tide flowing from the February revolution, the Bolshevik Party established the proletarian dictatorship by overthrowing the bourgeois power through an uprising in which the working class led the peasants (armed peasants in uniforms). Immediately after announcing the transfer of land to the peasants and the right of internal nations to self-determination (these were the democratic tasks of Russia at the time), the socialist task of expropriating private property was put on the agenda by the Bolshevik Party. This is precisely the model of the democratic revolution developing uninterruptedly toward socialism.

What was the attitude of the CCP toward this "central idea" of the theory of permanent revolution? It took the cities with armed peasant forces (not through an uprising with the proletariat leading the peasants). After the overthrow of Chiang's regime, instead of establishing a proletarian dictatorship, it did just the contrary. "Cooperating" with the democratic or national bourgeoisie, it set up a "coalition government," the "People's Democratic Dictatorship." Instead of placing the socialist task of expropriating the bourgeoisie on the agenda, it declared that "private capitalist enterprise has been encouraged to develop under government control" and it promoted "equal consideration of private and state industry" and "equal benefits to workers and capitalists." It even postponed the burning land problem and protected foreign property (the land problem and the expropriation of foreign property were the democratic tasks in China). All this was Mao's New Democracy policy. Mao's policy was formally passed by the "Political Consultative Conference" in which the CCP, bourgeoisie, and petty bourgeoisie participated, and it became the "Common Program" for building the state. The period for realizing this program was the so-called New Democracy stage. Though the CCP did not formally state how long this stage would endure, it was understood to be for a long time. Chow reports that in one meeting it was said that the New Democracy period would last twenty years. In other words, the passing over from the democratic or "New Democratic" revolution to socialist tasks would take a "very long period" and the "New Democracy" was able to become a "self-sufficient regime" (Mao called it a "New Democracy regime") for several decades before proceeding to the socialist revolution. Doesn't this sound like an application of the typical Menshevik theory of "revolution in stages"?

But the class struggle has its own logic which is precisely the dynamic of the permanent revolution. Even before the Korean War, but especially after its outbreak, the peasants in many areas displayed great resentment and unrest due to postponement of agrarian reform, oppression by the landlords, exploitation by rich peasants, and all kinds of excessive taxes levied by the new regime. On the other hand, the landlords, rich peasants, and commercial-industrial capitalists in the cities took advantage of the advance of the imperialists to mobilize a counterattack. (For instance, cheating in both labor and material in filling government orders, upsetting the market through black market manipulations, corrupting the CCP cadres with bribes, etc.) In addition the remnants of Chiang's regime were very active.

So, under the twofold menace—the advance led by American imperialism and the domestic counterattack of the united forces of landlords and bourgeoisie—the CCP was forced to revise its New Democratic policy empirically, once again undertaking agrarian reforms against the landlords and rich peasants, pushing forward the "Five Anti Movement" against the bourgeoisie, severely suppressing counterrevolutionary elements, etc., in order to satisfy the land hunger of the peasantry and gain the workers' support by allaying their dissatisfaction. Following this, at the beginning of 1953, the CCP also announced the "general line of the transitional period" of building socialism and it began the First Five-Year Plan of industrialization. All this demonstrates that the CCP under the irresistible pressure of the class struggle was forced to relinquish its completely reactionary New

Democracy policy of "revolution in stages" and adopt some progressive measures corresponding to the development of the permanent revolution.

But in adopting these progressive measures the CCP put great limitations on them. They did not announce the expropriation of bourgeois property and were not ready for collectivization of agriculture. This is apparent in the resolution passed by the CCP in March 1955 that the "general line of the transitional period" was to be fulfilled in several decades or half a century. According to this resolution, socialist reconstruction will be accomplished in several decades or half a century through the establishment within the national boundaries of a self-sufficient socialist economic system. This, once again, is in evident violation of another basic concept of the theory of permanent revolution—internationalism.

Trotsky wrote in the above-cited preface of the Russian edition of *The Permanent Revolution*:

The international character of the socialist revolution, which constitutes the third aspect of the theory of the permanent revolution, flows from the present state of economy and the social structure of humanity. Internationalism is no abstract principle but a theoretical and political reflection of the character of world economy, of the world development of productive forces and the world scale of the class struggle. The socialist revolution begins on national foundations—but it cannot be completed within these foundations. The maintenance of the proletarian revolution within a national framework can only be a provisional state of affairs, even though, as the experience of the Soviet Union shows, one of long duration. *In an isolated proletarian dictatorship, the internal and external contradictions grow inevitably along with the success achieved. If it remains isolated, the proletarian state must finally fall victim to these contradictions. The way out for it lies only in the victory of the proletariat of the advanced countries. Viewed from this standpoint, a national revolution is not a self-contained whole; it is only a link in the international chain.* The international revolution constitutes a permanent process, despite temporary declines and ebbs.[52]

Precisely because of the decisive significance of "international socialism," Lenin, right after the victory of the October revolution, proclaimed that this revolution was only the "prelude of the world revolution." He even said in April 1918: "Our backwardness has put us in the forefront, and we shall perish unless we are capable of holding out until we receive powerful support from workers who have risen in revolt in other countries.[53]

A resolution of the Seventh Congress of the Bolshevik Party in March 1918 also declared: "The Congress considers the only reliable guarantee of consolidation of the socialist revolution that has been victorious in Russia to be its conversion into a world working-class revolution."[54]

In order to convert the revolution "into a world working-class revolution," or to convert the "prelude of the world revolution" into world revolution, the Bolshevik Party led by Lenin and Trotsky sought with all its might to establish the leading organ of the world revolution—the International. At that time all the foreign policies and activities of the Bolshevik Party centered in pushing forward the world revolution. Precisely this is the concrete expression of the internationalism of the theory of permanent revolution.

After the death of Lenin, Stalin, on usurping Bolshevik leadership, published his "theory" of "socialism in one country," a thorough betrayal of internationalism, and a development in a new situation of the Menshevik theory of "revolution in stages." On the basis of this "theory," Stalin converted the Bolshevik policy of pushing forward the world revolution into the line of "peaceful coexistence," a line contrived for compromise with world capitalism so as to help build socialism in one country.

Under the theory of "socialism in one country," Stalin at first compromised with the rich peasants to the utmost and postponed industrialization and collectivization. Later, threatened by the rich peasants, he turned to the opposite extreme, disregarding the interests of the workers and peasants, accelerating industrialization and collectivization with the administrative lash. Concerning this, Trotsky wrote in the introduction to the German edition of *The Permanent Revolution* (March 29, 1930):

We must gain [say the Stalinists] economic "independence" as speedily as possible with the aid of the speediest possible tempos of industrialization and collectivization!—this is the transformation that has taken place in the economic policy of national socialism in the past two years. Creeping and penny-pinching was replaced all along the line by adventurism. The theoretical base under both remains the same: the national socialist conception.[55]

After "creeping" for two years (1953-55), the CCP "general line of the transitional period" came to a turn at the end of 1955. The collectivization of agriculture was proposed and the transformation of all private industry into "state and private" was also announced almost at the same time. This turn was facilitated under pressure of the rapid differentiation of the peasants in the mutual aid groups toward opposing poles and the obstruction of economic planning by private industry. The turn represented, certainly, great progress, and it corresponds in a way to the law of uninterrupted development of the revolution. But in carrying out collectivization, the CCP forced the peasants to join the producers' cooperatives regardless of their willingness. And so all the peasants were forcibly collectivized in less than a year. On the other hand, under the name of "state and private operation," the property rights of the private capitalists were retained through payment of "fixed interest" and they have been allowed to participate continuously in the administration of production. At the same time, the workers are given the whip to speed up production in order to overfulfill the plan.

Under the slogan of a "Great Leap Forward" in 1958, this kind of speedup in pushing industrialization and collectivization almost reached a maniac pitch. The most concrete expressions were the "steel production by the whole nation" movement (producing steel in backyard furnaces) and the commune movement. This was nothing but replacing "creeping and penny-pinching . . . all along the line by adventurism. The theoretical base under both remains the same: the national socialist [Mao further develops it into a national communist] conception." Utilizing a "national socialist or communist conception" to accelerate industrialization and collectivization is far from "a striking confirmation of the theory of permanent revolution"; in fact, it is the exact opposite of this theory.

Trotsky, in the above-cited introduction to the German edition of *The Permanent Revolution*, stated the difference between the Left Opposition and the Stalinists in basic standpoints on industrialization and collectivization as follows:

Industrialization is the driving force of the whole of modern culture and by this token the only conceivable basis for socialism. In the conditions of the Soviet Union, industrialization means first of all the strengthening of the base of the proletariat as a ruling class. Simultaneously it creates the material and technical premises for the collectivization of agriculture. The tempos of these two processes are interdependent. The proletariat is interested in the highest possible tempos for these processes to the extent that the new society in the making is thus best protected from external danger, and at the same time a source is created for systematically improving the material level of the toiling masses.

However, the tempos that can be achieved are limited by the general material and cultural level of the country, by the relationship between the city and the village and by the most pressing needs of the masses, who are able to sacrifice their today for the sake of tomorrow *only up to a certain point.* The optimum tempos, i.e., the best and most advantageous ones, are those which not only promote the most rapid growth of industry and collectivization at a given moment, but which also secure the necessary stability of the social régime, that is, first of all strengthen the alliance of the workers and peasants, thereby preparing the possibility for future successes.

From this standpoint, the decisive significance is the general historical criterion in accordance with which the party and state leadership direct economic development by means of planning. Here two main variants are possible: (*a*) the course outlined above toward the economic strengthening of the proletarian dictatorship in one country until further victories of the world proletarian revolution (the viewpoint of the Russian Left Opposition); and (*b*) the course toward the construction of an isolated national socialist society, and this "in the shortest possible time" (the current official position).[56]

The two antithetic basic positions on industrialization and collectivization in the Soviet Union pointed out by Trotsky are not only of profound theoretical value and great historical significance, but also bear the most realistic political significance, particularly for China today. The starting point of the position represented by the Left Opposition, led by Trotsky at that time, was internationalism as expressed in the theory of permanent revolution, and the position represented by Stalin was national socialism expressed in the theory of revolution in stages.

Stalin's domestic and foreign strategy and tactics, flowing from this "theory and ideology of national socialism," brought unprecedented damage in human and material resources by ruthlessly forcing the peasants into collectivization; brought an imbalance between heavy and light industry, shortages in daily necessities, intensification of labor, and the decline of working-class living standards as industrialization was speeded up under the administrative goad; the destruction with rare ferocity of the whole generation of Old Bolsheviks and revolutionary youth; the undermining of the revolutions in China, Germany, Spain, etc., which had big chances of success. What terrible sacrifices were placed on the workers' state when the internationalism of the theory of permanent revolution was violated!

The "general line" in the industrialization and collectivization of China, which is highly praised by Comrades Swabeck and Liang today, is in its nature a copy of Stalin's national socialism as practiced and developed on Chinese soil. The "strategy and tactics" flowing from this "general line" is unavoidably a mixture of opportunism and adventurism. It has been proved beyond reasonable dispute that the acceleration in production and communalization (the so-called Great Leap Forward) represented adventurism, matching the opportunism of the "Five Principles" of "peaceful coexistence" in foreign policy.

The damage caused by such domestic and foreign "strategy and tactics" is beginning to appear (as can be seen in the great shortages in daily necessities, the extreme intensity of mass labor, the decline in living standards and the semihunger of the peasant masses, the breakdown of the alliance of peasants and workers, etc.). And more ominous consequences still lie ahead!

In general, the basic policy practiced by the CCP in the process of the third Chinese revolution is not "a striking confirmation of the theory of the permanent or continuous revolution," but the distortion of this theory. When the dynamics of the continuous revolution become objectively irresistible under the pressure of internal and external contradictions, the CCP is empirically forced to make a "turn" and proceed a step forward. This certainly reflects objectively the correctness of the theory of permanent revolution.

But the step forward taken by the CCP becomes either a half step (as in the turn in the general line to a "transitional period" in 1953) through suppression of the natural tendency for the revolution to continue uninterruptedly, or a blind scramble under the impulse of adventurism (as in the collectivization in 1956 and the "Great Leap Forward" in industrialization and communalization in 1958). We are able to say, therefore, that the power of the theory of permanent revolution is surely revealed in the process of the third Chinese revolution which, through a series of turns, forces the CCP to compromise with it for its own survival. But due to the deep-rooted Stalinism (the opportunism and adventurism inherent in the theory of revolution in stages), the uninterrupted development of the revolution is distorted at every "turn," resulting in the deformation of the whole process of revolution. Hence the creation of great confusion in the uninterrupted development of the revolution, which in turn leads to distortion and confusion involving the theory of permanent revolution.

Early in 1951, Pablo reached the opinion that "Mao practices permanent revolution in China." (I heard this from people close to him.) In 1952, the draft resolution on the "Third Chinese Revolution," written by Germain under the influence of Pablo, stated that "the Third Chinese Revolution has begun, not through the alliance with Chiang Kai-shek, but through the breaking of this alliance. Thus the Trotskyist theory of the permanent revolution, implacably defended for 25 years by the Chinese Trotskyists and the world Trotskyist movement, has found confirmation for one of its fundamental theses."[57]

I wrote several critical comments on the draft resolution regarding its distortion of the theory of permanent revolution, but these were suppressed by Pablo and not published.

Liu Shao-ch'i, in his May 1958 report to the second plenary session of the CCP Central Committee elected at the Eighth Party Congress, asserted that "the Central Committee of the Communist Party and Comrade Mao Tse-tung have always guided the Chinese revolution by this Marxist-Leninist theory of permanent revolution."[58]

Inspired by Liu's revelation, Jean-Paul Martin, an author whose thought always parallels that of Pablo, wrote an article, "Uninterrupted Revolution in China," in which he proclaimed: "China is currently in a state of uninterrupted revolution." (See *Quatrième Internationale,* November 1958.) Actually the CCP Central Committee and Mao have practiced the theory of "revolution in stages" in opposition to the theory of permanent revolution for the past thirty years. The sudden proclamation by Liu Shao-ch'i in May 1958 that the CCP practices permanent revolution is aimed at no more than defending the adventurism in the "Great Leap Forward" which Mao was pushing full speed at the time in order to accelerate industrialization and prepare for communalization. Similarly, Lominadze, Stalin's representative in China, suddenly proclaimed in November 1927, after the defeat of the revolution, "China is in a situation of permanent revolution." He did this to defend his adventurous policy of uninterrupted uprisings. In praising the CCP's practice of permanent revolution, Pablo was only echoing Liu Shao-ch'i.

Comrades Swabeck and Liang, in praising the development of the Chinese revolution as "a striking confirmation of the theory of permanent revolution," only follow Pablo in distorting Trotsky's theory of permanent revolution to defend CCP adventurism in industrializing and collectivization.

In criticizing the draft resolution on the "Third Chinese Revolution," I said:

It goes without saying that we should never proceed from the programmatic norms of the permanent revolution to deny the important significance of the third revolution begun by Mao's party. But neither should we permit the objective significance of Mao's victory to draw us into depreciating the theory of the permanent revolution, nor into accommodating to the victory by misinterpreting it in the name of the permanent revolution. Our attitude should be, on the one hand, to understand the objective facts and diverse causes of Mao's victory, and, on the other, to analyze from the standpoint of the permanent revolution how this victory was distorted by the theory of "revolution by stages," resulting in its present deformed shape, the obstacles arising from this deformation, and the perspectives of its possible development. Our fundamental task is to stand on the program of the permanent revolution in order to defend, to push forward, and to complete the revolution, bringing it to final victory.[59]

I still consider this opinion, written eight years ago, to be correct and effective. Here I only add: It is still necessary for us Trotskyists, basing ourselves on the theory of permanent revolution, to criticize the CCP in its turn from the New Democracy policy toward a socialist policy, especially its practice of industrialization and collectivization. Our basic position toward industrialization and collectivization in China today is at bottom the same as that of the Left Opposition in the Soviet Union as I have sought to indicate above.

Political revolution or democratic reform?

In light of the above analysis of the CCP regime and its Stalinist characteristics, and in view of the existence of a privileged caste protected by a police system under CCP rule, as proved by the facts, the need for political revolution follows logically. I can say, therefore, that no matter how "reality" has "changed," the basic position of "the Third Chinese Revolution and Its Aftermath," the resolution passed by the SWP in 1955—for political revolution—is still correct and effective. Its correctness is reflected not only by its theoretical analysis and prognosis, but also by the facts and the tendency that came to light in the "Let a hundred flowers bloom, let a hundred schools of thought contend" campaign of 1957.

After the liquidation of the Stalin cult at the Twentieth Congress of the Soviet Communist Party and the outbreak of the Hungarian revolution, the CCP found itself under heavy mass pressure. Revolutionary elements, inside as well as outside the party, reacted with sympathy to the Hungarian events. In response to this threat the CCP was compelled to launch the "Hundred Flowers" movement, inviting other parties and factions, as well as the people as a whole, to express their opinions, to criticize the "three harms" within the CCP—"bureaucratism, commandism, and subjectivism"—and to help in "rectifying" and reforming the party. This was intended to prevent the outbreak of a Hungarian-type revolution on Chinese soil.

Before launching the "Hundred Flowers" campaign, Mao said: "Certain people in our country were delighted when the Hungarian events took place. They hoped that something similar would happen in China, that thousands upon thousands of people would demonstrate in the streets against the People's Government."[60]

This proves that the CCP felt threatened by the sympathy of revolutionary elements in the country for the Hungarian revolution.

At the high tide of the "Hundred Flowers" movement (April to June, 1957), facts about the arbitrariness and special privileges enjoyed by the CCP bureaucracy poured in from all corners among the masses, especially young students and revolutionary intellectuals (including members of the CCP and its youth organization). Liu Shao-ch'i, the second leader of the CCP, openly admitted: "There is serious bureaucracy. . . . Mass criticism is spreading to every corner of China, including factories, farms, schools, and other organizations. The target of criticism is the leadership."[61]

The revolutionary tendency of this movement was reflected in the opinions expressed by Lin Hsi-ling, student-movement leader and member of the CCP youth organization, and Tai Huang, reporter for Hsinhua and member of the CCP. Lin declared that "the present upper strata of China does not correspond with the property system of common ownership" because "the party and state apparatus has become a set of bureaucratic organs ruling people without democracy." Therefore she proclaimed "not reform but a thoroughgoing change." Tai Huang proposed to build a new party and "to realize democracy, freedom, and the eradication of a privileged class." Doesn't this revolutionary tendency, reflected in the "Hundred Flowers" movement—calling for "not reform but a thoroughgoing change" and "to realize democracy, freedom, and the eradication of a privileged class"—mean the junking of the bureaucratic dictatorship of the privileged caste and the realization of a socialist democratic political revolution?

Precisely because of the threat to CCP rule from the revolutionary tendency opposing bureaucratic dictatorship, which was revealed in the "Hundred Flowers" movement, the CCP immediately discontinued this movement (in the middle of June 1957) and vigorously counterattacked all the criticizers. Under the label of an "antirightist" campaign all the Left revolutionary elements were ruthlessly suppressed! Thousands upon thousands were forced to recant, were suspended from their posts, placed under surveillance, and even arrested and sent to the labor camps. Thousands upon thousands of party and youth organization members, besides suffering expulsion, were fired from their jobs, dismissed from school, placed under surveillance or arrested, etc. Accordingly, those who had been invited to criticize the CCP now became sacrificial goats because of their criticism. Once again it was proved that a Stalinist party and its dictatorial regime cannot undergo self-reform. Their nature is to represent the interests of the privileged bureaucracy.

But Comrades Swabeck and Liang insist:

> The answer to bureaucratism is not a call for *the overthrow of the present Peking regime—which would be regarded by the masses as counterrevolutionary*—but a program of democratic demands designed to curb and break down bureaucratic arbitrariness through ever greater popular participation in, and control over, all phases of the national life.[62]

> Our support of these revolutionary developments must of necessity be critical of all bureaucratic manifestations and emphasize demands for specific democratic measures without which the road to socialism cannot be assured. These should include democracy in the party with free opportunity for all members to criticize and to control policies and leadership. Similarly, democracy in all the organs of government, through the various levels from the local to the national, requires full powers of control in the hands of the people. In the economic domain democratic control by the masses of working people of state planning in production and distribution at all levels is essential to enable timely review of results in the light of actual experience, and to reduce inequalities to the minimum. *Implicitly and explicitly our position should include the idea that in China such measures can be attained by means of reform.*[63]

The above "program of democratic demands" or "demands for specific democratic measures" raised by Comrades Swabeck and Liang is attractive and exciting and worth approving—if it can be realized. But they completely forget or fail to take note of the facts and lessons of the "Hundred Flowers" movement of 1957.

1. At that time those who proposed the "overthrow of the present Peking regime" were not Trotskyists, but revolutionary elements, even members of the CCP and its youth organization such as Lin Hsi-ling, a member of the youth organization, and

Tai Huang, member of the party, etc., who represented the interests of the masses and their thinking.

2. At that time the CCP members who attempted "to criticize and to control policies and leadership" met with expulsion from the party and youth organization, dismissal from all posts, and even merciless punishment—arrest and imprisonment.

3. Those who expressed the view that "democracy in all the organs of government, through the various levels from the local to the national, requires full powers of control in the hands of the people" met with all kinds of punishment (including forced recantation, dismissal from jobs, surveillance, and transfer to labor camps for reform).

4. From this it must be concluded that it is quite impossible to achieve "in the economic domain democratic control by the masses of working people of state planning in production and distribution at all levels."

In the light of the lesson drawn from the historical facts, let me ask Comrades Swabeck and Liang: How do you expect to achieve your "idea that in China such measures can be attained by means of reform"? Will you ask the CCP leadership to achieve it? They have answered this question to the negative in the "Hundred Flowers" movement. Would you propagate and inspire among CCP members and the worker-peasant masses realization of your idea?

That is equivalent to calling them to rise in a political revolution against the CCP. My dear comrades, in the fact of reality, your idea of "democratic reform" ends in a blank wall.

For a time (at least before 1953), I had hoped CCP rule in China could be reformed through democratic measures, just as I entertained similar hopes about Russia under Stalin before 1933. But at present in China, as in Russia, the Eastern European countries, North Korea, and North Vietnam, it is impossible to carry out democratic reforms. The right road, and the only possible one, is political revolution. The following program for political revolution should be proposed by us:

1. End the special privileges of the bureaucracy. Down with the new aristocracy (including the "labor hero" or "model worker") and its rankings. Greater equality in wages for all forms of labor. Strict observance of the eight-hour day. Greater efforts to raise the living standard of all laborers.

2. Fight for freedom of choice in union and factory committees, freedom of assembly, and freedom of the press.

3. In line with the interests and the will of the peasants,

thorough reorganization of the communes. (This point is spelled out in detail in the section "Our attitude toward the communes" in the article "A Criticism of the Various Views Supporting the Chinese Rural People's Communes.")

4. Abolish the "fixed interest" given the capitalists, readjust the economic plan according to the interests of the producers and consumers. Establish the right of factory committees to supervise production. Form committees through democratic means in all the state stores, regional stores, and consumers' cooperatives to check quality and prices.

5. Replace the "People's Congress" with worker, peasant, and soldier soviets, excluding not only bourgeois elements but the bureaucratic aristocracy, limiting the delegates in the soviets to workers, peasants, and soldiers.

6. Ban all parties and factions of the bourgeoisie. All parties that accept socialism must be granted legal recognition and the right to conduct political activities.

7. Abrogate the foreign policy of the "Five Principles of Peaceful Coexistence"; substitute the strategy of pushing forward the world revolution.

8. Together with the worker-peasant masses in the Soviet bloc, overthrow the system of Stalinist bureaucratic dictatorship and restore or establish socialist democracy.

In fighting for the above program of political revolution, we Trotskyists, standing with the masses, resolutely and unconditionally defend the existing socialist property and planned economy against imperialism, particularly any intervention or invasion of China engineered by American imperialism.

Long live socialist democracy!

Long live the world revolution!

Where are Comrades Swabeck and Liang headed?

In discussing the communes, I pointed out: "But the errors of Comrades Liang and Swabeck intersect with principles, and if not recognized in time, can lead them into the swamp of revisionism."[64] Since then, Comrades Swabeck and Liang not only failed to recognize their errors in time, but went further in their original errors, sinking deep in the swamp of revisionism, as is clear from their recent article, "The Third Chinese Revolution, the Communes and Regime."

Their revisionism is obvious in the following items: On the issue of agricultural collectivization, they revise the principle of "nationalization and agricultural collectivization" as set down in our Transitional Program by departing from the transitional position of Engels and Lenin. On the nature of the CCP, disregarding "the training in the school of Stalinism" and "Stalinist characteristics alien to socialism," and singling out this or that measure which the CCP felt compelled to adopt for a time, they judge that the CCP has broken with Stalinism. On the nature of the CCP regime, entirely overlooking the essence of Stalinism implicit in its whole policy, and depending only on the electoral form of "universal electoral rights," they assert that it is a regime of socialist democracy. On the theory of permanent revolution, they distort it, neglecting the decisive significance of the internationalism at its core. Due to this series of violations of the principles of Marxism-Leninism and their revision of Trotskyism, they have reached the point on the Chinese question where, as in the case of "birds of a feather," they find themselves in Pablo's revisionist flock.

What is the objective force that brought Comrades Swabeck and Liang into revisionism on the Chinese question? It is mainly the influence of the "Great Leap Forward" in production which the CCP has boasted about since 1958, particularly the "success of the communalization." Affected by the idealization of the People's Communes current among petty-bourgeois intellectuals who live far away from China, they unconsciously departed from their original position. This is clearly reflected in the change and development of their stand following the growth of the commune movement. For example, when informed that "elected councils" exist in the communes, they asserted that the communes are "self-governing political-economic units." Later, in accordance with their logic, they concluded: "The Peking regime is not a Stalinist-type regime." Also, the subtitle of their article, "the Communes and the Regime," and the attractive description of the communes under this heading, clearly show that their reappraisal of the nature of the CCP and its regime is closely connected with their appraisal of the communes. In other words, their reappraisal of the CCP and its regime is deduced from their formula, "the communes are self-governing. . . ." If Pablo's departure from Trotskyism and arrival at revisionism came in response to the expansion of Stalinist influence after the war, expecially after the surprising victory of the CCP, then the fall of Comrades Swabeck and Liang into the swamp of revisionism was due to the blinding brilliance of the "Great Leap Forward" in Chinese industrialization, and especially communalization.

Another reason for the fall of Comrades Swabeck and Liang into revisionism is their methodology in studying questions. They stress, of course: "The position taken in the 1955 resolution can be maintained only by sacrificing the materialist principle and dialectical method that constitute the heart of Marxism."[65]

But in fact, *they* are "sacrificing the materialist principle and dialectical method" and applying the mechanism of formal logic and even idealism in dealing with problems and establishing and defending their new position. For example:

1. Disregarding the exceedingly low level of material, technical, and cultural conditions in China today, as soon as the propaganda of the CCP came to their attention about a "doubling" of agricultural production and the "liberation of women from domestic slavery" after the general establishment of the communes, they responded with the belief that "China has revolutionized the feeding of its millions,"[66] and asserted that the communes "have accelerated the liberation of women from domestic slavery, opened up new avenues of cultural development, and are narrowing the age-old cultural gulf between city and country."[67]

Such an obviously idealistic pronouncement could be made only "by sacrificing the materialist principle."

2. Seeing the "Great Leap Forward" in Chinese industrialization and communalization, but completely ignoring the adventurism and the grave harm it signified to the worker-peasant masses, they gave it unconditional praise and support. In this they manifested mechanical thinking, sacrificing materialism.

3. Hearing about "elected councils," they did not ask how such "councils" are elected, or what their concrete content might be. They drew the conclusion of formal logic: "The communes are self-governing political-economic units." Likewise they judge the "People's Congress" by the form of the elections.

4. Comrade Liang declares: "The continuing drumfire of hostile comment on the Communes by capitalist propagandists places us squarely before the need to take a clear-cut position on what, essentially, is a *class-struggle issue*. FOR or AGAINST the Communes?[68]

To raise a question in this way is purely "ultramechanical formal logic," as I pointed out in my article discussing the communes.[69]

5. They emphasize that we "must become genuine partisans of the Chinese revolution and give unqualified support to its positive gains."[70] But they denounce those who criticize CCP

policy as "critical commentators with a factional axe to grind."[71] They do not understand that it is possible for us to "become genuine partisans of the Chinese revolution" only if we hold firmly to a Marxist-Leninist viewpoint and to Trotsky's program of permanent revolution, seriously criticize the Stalinist policy of the CCP, and do everything possible to arouse the masses to recognize the error of this policy in order finally to bring their power to bear to change it. This is nothing else but flexible application of dialectically uniting "support" and "comment" or "criticism."

In the final analysis, Comrades Swabeck and Liang sacrifice "materialist principle and dialectical method" because of their impressionism, as is indicated by the following:

A few fundamental questions remain to be considered, particularly the question of our own methodology. If we agree that reality is ever changing and always manifested concretely, then our thinking must reflect these same characteristics, and be likewise concrete and change-able, for only the application of this method can assure a reasonably correct position.[72]

In appearance this declaration seems above criticism. But on deeper consideration, it is revealed as the root of impressionism. They completely left out by what principle or law we should investigate "reality" and its "change." They stress only "that reality is ever changing and always manifested concretely . . . our thinking must reflect these same characteristics. . . ." All impressionists disdain principle, paying particular attention to "ever changing reality" which they "reflect" or accept as "con-crete" or new phenomena. But as soon as a new "change" occurs in this "changing reality," they fall prey to other "concrete" or "new" phenomena. The impressionist, therefore, forever changes with the changing reality, lacking a consistent principle of his own. It was that way with Pablo and Max Shachtman. Now our Comrades Swabeck and Liang prove to be no exceptions.

On the eve of the outbreak of World War II, Shachtman saw the signing of the "Soviet-German pact," followed by the Soviet army attack on Finland, etc. He thereupon decided that the nature of the Soviet Union had changed and was not worthy of uncondi-tional support.

On seeing the expansion of Stalinist influence and the victory of the CCP, etc., after World War II, Pablo saw the possibility of the self-reform of Stalinist parties and therefore no need for political revolution in the Soviet Union. Confronted by CCP industrialization and collectivization, especially the "changing reality" of communalization, Comrades Swabeck and Liang assert that the CCP has departed from Stalinism, "the Peking regime is not a Stalinist-type regime," and the political revolution is outdated. This series of examples demonstrates that impressionists, unable to maintain principles firmly, disdaining theory, and relying only on the "concreteness of events," or "new reality," or "changing reality," depart inexorably from a principled stand and fall into revisionism.

The revisionist position of Comrades Swabeck and Liang on the Chinese question has now reached its culmination. If they proceed in accordance with the logic they are following, they will inevitably arrive at revising the basic Trotskyist position toward the Soviet Union. But I hope that in the light of comradely criticism they will reconsider their position. I believe that subjectively, with their long record of faithful service, they are loyal to the Trotskyist movement. After serious self-investigation, in the light of the criticism of their facts that has been called to their attention, it should be possible for them to reestablish their original authentic Trotskyist position.

April 1960

TWO INTERVIEWS ON THE "CULTURAL REVOLUTION"

First interview: June 1966

The recent events in China, such as the dismissal of P'eng Chen from his key party post,[1] are the result of a struggle inside the Chinese Communist Party that began almost a decade ago. In order to understand what is happening now we must take into account the whole evolution of the struggle and the opposition led by Teng T'o.

We should start from around 1957 when Mao Tse-tung initiated the "Let a hundred flowers bloom and let a hundred schools of thought contend" movement, inviting the intellectuals and the people as a whole to speak their mind, to criticize the "three harms" within the CCP—"bureaucratism, commandism, and subjectivism"—and to help in "rectifying" and reforming the party. Within a very short time this movement became very large with many deepgoing criticisms of the leadership being brought into the open.

Much of the important criticism was published in such papers as the *People's Daily,* the official organ of the party. Teng T'o, editor-in-chief at the time, encouraged criticism from the people and even wrote some articles of sharp criticism himself.

At the high tide of the "Hundred Flowers" movement (April to June 1957), facts about the arbitrariness and special privileges enjoyed by the CCP bureaucracy poured in from all corners, especially from young students and revolutionary intellectuals.

These interviews on the unfolding of the "Cultural Revolution" were obtained in Europe in June 1966 and on January 20, 1967, by Antonio Farien (David Fender). The first, in article format, was written by Farien from his notes, then submitted to P'eng for correction. The second appears in question-and-answer form. The bottom-of-the-page footnotes are by David Fender. Source citations have been incorporated in the editor's notes at the back of the book.

Members of the CCP itself and its youth organization also responded. By June the movement had developed to such an extent that it seemed that the Hungarian revolution of 1956 might be transplanted to Chinese soil. (There was a rebellion, for example, by more than 3,000 students in a high middle school— the equivalent of high school in the U.S.—in Hanyang, one of the three cities that make up the Wuhan complex.)

The leadership became frightened at such a possibility and immediately discontinued the movement—in the middle of June— and vigorously counterattacked all its critics. The Left revolutionary elements were ruthlessly suppressed under the blanket charge of being "rightists." Thousands upon thousands were forced to recant, were suspended from their posts, placed under surveillance, and even arrested and sent to labor camps. Many party and youth organization members, besides suffering expulsion, were fired from their jobs, dismissed from school, placed under surveillance, or arrested, etc. Teng T'o was removed from editorship of the *People's Daily*.

The opposition was accused of being headed by rightist elements, representatives of the bourgeoisie, and large landlords, etc., similar charges to those leveled by the CCP at the present time against victims of the purge. However, close examination of some of the facts that have slowly sifted out since, shows that this accusation does not seem to have been justified in many cases. For example, in *Red Flag*, the ideological journal of the CCP's Central Committee, it was reported that Teng T'o "vigorously supported the rightists attacking the party. The extreme rightist Lin Hsi-ling was his most intimate friend."[2] But if anything, Lin Hsi-ling, a student movement leader and member of the CCP youth organization, reflected in her writings the revolutionary tendency of this movement. Lin Hsi-ling, who was purged in 1957, had written that "the present upper strata of China does not correspond with the property system of common ownership" because "the party and state apparatus has become a set of bureaucratic organs ruling people without democracy." Therefore, she proclaimed "not reform but a thoroughgoing change."

The statement in *Red Flag* about Lin Hsi-ling also sheds light upon the political thinking of Teng T'o. Since she was identified as being so close to Teng T'o, one can probably surmise that their political positions were not much different. Also in speaking of Teng T'o, she said that he was not an orthodox Marxist. In other words, Teng T'o did not agree with everything the infallible Mao

Tse-tung said, or rather, Teng T'o was not a Maoist Marxist.

An example of what is meant by orthodox Marxism in China is to be found in the June 10 issue of *Peking Review:*

> No one who dares to oppose Chairman Mao, to oppose Mao Tse-tung's thought, to oppose the Central Committee of the Party, the dictatorship of the proletariat and the socialist system can escape denunciation by the whole Party and the whole nation, whoever he may be, whatever high position he may hold and however much of a veteran he may be. The only possible result is the total loss of his standing and reputation.[3]

In 1958, after crushing the "Hundred Flowers" movement, the CCP adopted an adventuristic policy in order to rationalize its forceful suppression of the so-called rightist opposition. Around May, the Central Committee of the CCP adopted the slogan of the "Great Leap Forward." Under this slogan a program was initiated to make steel in small backyard furnaces. Around 100 million people were mobilized to carry out this program. Almost all students as well as professors, workers, peasants, and even housewives had to make steel. This program lasted about one year—June 1958 to July 1959.

A little later, in August 1958, Mao gave the order that every peasant must enter the People's Communes as quickly as possible. Three months later 99 percent of the peasants were in the People's Communes. The CCP ordered the privately owned land, stored grain, animals, etc., to be turned over to the communes; all peasants were to eat in the commune's kitchens; the children must attend the commune nurseries, etc. This policy was designed to communalize all the peasants within a five-year period.

The peasants were given no choice in the matter. They were forced to join and to give up all their holdings to the commune. This resulted in wide dissatisfaction among the peasants. At least half of the peasants—there were approximately 500 million at the time—were against such measures and opposed the communes actively by committing acts of sabotage, such as killing their animals, cutting down fruit trees, or destroying crops. This precipitated a tremendous scarcity of non-staple foods, and the situation became very serious in the summer of 1959. At the same time the failure of the backyard steel-making program became clear—three million tons of steel had been made, but little of it met minimum standards in quality.

The bankruptcy of these two policies which had been bureaucratically imposed by Mao and the top leadership of the CCP became quite evident to everyone, and mounting dissatisfaction was very apparent among the masses. They referred to Mao and his policies as "petty-bourgeois fanaticism." This dissatisfaction made inroads into the cadres of the CCP. Many top leaders in the Central Committee, the army, and government administration were also in sympathy with the masses. Among the leaders voicing dissatisfaction was P'eng Te-huai, minister of defense.

As early as the spring of 1959 he criticized the policies of the party; i.e., he criticized Mao Tse-tung. This precipitated a crisis inside the party. The Central Committee along with Mao called a plenum in August 1959 to deal with it. This meeting became known as the Lushan conference.

At the plenum a serious dispute took place among the top leaders. Although the actual proceedings have never been released, two important measures were adopted: (1) P'eng Te-huai was relieved of his position along with Huang K'o-ch'eng, chief of staff of the army, and many other members of the Central Committee also disappeared. (2) A resolution was passed which made certain concessions to the peasants; i.e., the People's Communes would be reorganized.

A short while after the plenum, Teng T'o formed a small group. His closest collaborator in the group was Wu Han, a leading historian and vice-mayor of the Peking municipal government. In June 1959, before the plenum, he had written an article called "Hai Jui Scolds the Emperor." Hai Jui was governor of Nanking under the Ming dynasty. (Peking was the capital.) The emperor was a bad one, unjust to the people, so Hai Jui sent him a letter criticizing him. Wu Han used this historical analogy to describe the present situation; i.e., "P'eng Te-huai Scolds Mao Tse-tung."

After the plenum Wu Han wrote a drama called *Hai Jui Dismissed from Office.* When Hai Jui was governor he carried out a few token reforms. One of these was a small land reform in which he took some unjustly acquired land from the big landowners and returned it to the small peasants from whom it had been taken. The big landowners became furious and complained bitterly to the emperor, who promptly dismissed Hai Jui from his governorship. The people were very angered at this turn of events. Hai Jui was very popular, becoming known as an honest official. Here too, Wu Han utilized the historical analogy to describe and criticize the present situation; i.e., *P'eng Te-huai Dismissed from Office.*

The drama was openly published in January 1961 in the Peking daily papers, and afterward it was performed on the stage in Peking. It received an exceptionally enthusiastic reception from the people and many critics gave it high praise.

The third closest collaborator in the secret group organized by Teng T'o was Liao Mo-sha, head of the United Front Work Department in the Peking Municipal Party Committee. He along with Wu Han and Teng T'o—from 1961 to the end of 1962—wrote many articles which appeared in the *Peking Daily, Peking Evening News,* and *Frontline.* The *Peking Daily* and the *Peking Evening News,* the daily newspapers of the Peking Municipal Party Committee, were also controlled by Teng T'o. Since he was the secretary of the Secretariat in the Peking Municipal Party Committee, he had the power to control and direct all the cultural institutions of the city, including the newspapers.

Some of these articles were published under the titles "Notes from Three-Family Village" and "Evening Talks at Yenshan." Later they were published in book form under the same titles. The authors used old fables, parables, historical analogies, satire, etc., in their articles to criticize the leadership, its program, and the situation at the time.

Teng T'o, for example, wrote an article which included a poem that was supposed to have been written by a small boy:

> The Heaven is my Father,
> The Earth is my Mother,
> The Sun is my Nurse,
> The East wind is my Benefactor,
> The West wind is my Enemy.

Teng T'o criticized the poem saying that it was only hot air— "great empty talk." This was an indirect criticism of Mao's famous slogan: "The East wind prevails over the West wind."

Teng T'o wrote in one article, "The wisdom of man is not unlimited. If anyone should want to know everything and possess unlimited wisdom, he would be a fool. People who think of themselves as being omniscient, despise the masses" and "attempt to win victory by devious means. Such people, if they do not correct their faults, will be defeated in the end." The passage refers to Mao; i.e., Mao is foolish for acting as though he were infallible and using bureaucratic means to maintain his power, because in the end he is going to be defeated if he doesn't change.

In another article entitled "Special Treatment for 'Amnesia,'" he accused the leadership of suffering from "amnesia," because they "quickly forget what they have seen and said . . . go back on their own word, fail to keep faith. . . ." He then prescribes that the leadership should "say less and take a rest when time comes for talking."

"Speak Big Words" was the title of another article in which he says that big words are not always useful and can even be damaging. In the essay, "The Theory of Treasuring Labor Power," he accuses the leadership of wasting the people's time and labor power—"we should . . . take care to do more in every way to treasure our labor power." Both of these were indirect references to the "Great Leap Forward," i.e., the program has been a failure and even harmful and wasteful.

Teng T'o wrote another article entitled "Cheng Pang-ch'iao and His Style" in which he quoted this famous artist, who said that one must become a master and not a servant. In other words, the people must control the leaders of the revolution and not just become the servants or slaves of the Maoist bureaucracy.

There were around 150 such articles written by Teng T'o and the group around him, all of which were indirect criticisms of the policies handed down by Mao and the top leadership. These articles also reflected criticisms coming from the masses. In 1961-62 the economic situation in China had become serious: food was scarce and during the summer of 1962 alone more than 100,000 persons fled to Hong Kong.

At the end of 1962 the economic situation started to improve to a certain degree, so the leadership—feeling more secure—adopted stronger measures to better control the peasants. Measures were also taken in order to control the intellectuals and students—many were sent to the countryside to work and be "reeducated."

In face of the more and more aggressive policy of the CCP leadership, which included blocking publication of their articles, Teng T'o and his group started to retreat.

In November 1965, in an article published in the *Wen Hui Pao* and then in the *People's Daily* and many other newspapers, the CCP for the first time openly criticized Wu Han's drama *Hai Jui Dismissed from Office*.[4]

After that the campaign against Wu Han's *Hai Jui Dismissed* spread throughout the country. Every day the *People's Daily*, and especially the *Liberation Army Daily*, plus many other papers all over China carried articles criticizing Wu Han.

Between November 1965 and April 1966, however, there were a few writers, mainly in Peking and Shanghai, who wrote articles defending him. Wu Han also wrote an article which, while admitting he had made some mistakes in the drama, defended himself and his work.

However, since April the situation has changed radically in many ways: (1) Up to then Wu Han was said to have only made some mistakes and to be revisionist in his thinking. Now he is accused of being antisocialist, antiparty, and even counterrevolutionary—supporting the bourgeoisie, and trying to restore capitalism.* (2) The papers stopped publishing articles by Wu Han and his supporters. (3) More and more people came under attack and Teng T'o was made the central target. As a result, parts of "Notes from Three-Family Village" and "Evening Talks at Yenshan" were published in the *People's Daily* with commentary as proof of his counterrevolutionary objectives.⁵ (4) The newspapers and the journals edited and controlled by Teng T'o and his group came under attack from such publications as the *Peking Daily, Peking Evening News, Frontline,* and, beginning in May, *Peking Literature and Art, Kweichow Daily,* and the *Yunnan Daily.* (5) High party officials like P'eng Chen, the mayor of Peking, became targets.

Since the beginning of the Sino-Soviet dispute, around 1960, the CCP has not only criticized Khrushchev's revisionism, but also his repudiation of Stalinism at the Twentieth Congress of the CPSU. Since then they have carried on a systematic campaign to establish a worldwide cult of Mao Tse-tung similar to that of Stalin. Since November 1965 this campaign has been greatly stepped up. For example, the *People's Daily,* a six-page paper, now devotes an average of four pages daily to this task. Each day a slogan such as: "One must study the thinking of Mao Tse-tung and raise higher the red banner of Mao's thought," "The people must study Mao's books, hear his words, and work according to his instructions," or "Mao's thought is the beacon of revolution for the world's people" appears on the front page. In other words, Mao's thought has become a panacea and his writings a *bible.* A typical example of the articles is one in the May 16, 1966, issue. A musical concert that took place in Shanghai is reported. In conjunction an article describes how Mao's thought influenced the concert.⁶

---

*Red Flag, according to the May 17, 1966, *New York Times,* "asked why they [the Peking newspapers] had never mentioned that Professor Wu 'is willing to be a slave of the U.S. and is guilty of scheming and planning for the reactionary Kuomintang clique?'"

A similar article was sent in by a cook. After a satisfied customer asked him how he cooked so well, he sat down and wrote an article explaining the secret of his success—he used Mao's method.

In the University of Peking an English teacher told his class that in order to learn English, they must use Mao's method. (Mao knows no foreign language except a few words of English.) Such stories are not the exception but the rule.*

The attempt to establish the cult of Mao is connected with the present purge. Because of Mao's many mistakes his standing is low among the intellectuals. It is understandable why they are opposed to deifying him. They favor an intelligent and fruitful discussion of the problems which continue to haunt China and her development.

The increasing difficulties and failures of Mao's foreign policy have also undoubtedly played a great role in the present purge if nothing more than in its timing and fierceness.

The disastrous role of Moscow's opportunism is undeniable. However, the extremely sectarian position taken by Peking in rejecting a united front against U.S. imperialism—especially in regard to the Vietnam War—has not only weakened the struggle against imperialism, but has heightened the danger of an attack on China herself and increased the possibilities of a nuclear war.

This sectarian position has also led to the increasing isolation of China in the socialist world. Many of the workers' states that leaned toward China at the beginning of the dispute, such as Korea and Vietnam, are now leaning more toward Moscow. Also, the defeats suffered by the colonial revolution and the failure of Chinese diplomacy in the "Third World" have led to increased isolation for China and to demoralization of Peking's followers all over the world.

The crushing of the Communist Party in Indonesia (PKI) with hardly a fight stands out as one of the greatest defeats and tragedies for China.** D. N. Aidit, whose policies were almost identical to those followed by the Khrushchevists, spoke many times in China; his books were translated into Chinese and he

---

*For information on how Mao Tse-tung's teaching in *On Contradiction* can lead to higher sales of watermelons, see *Hsinhua*, May 19, 1966.

**The PKI was the largest Communist Party in the capitalist world. It had a membership of three million and more than ten million organized sympathizers. Between September 1965 and now [June 1966—Ed.], between 250,000 and 500,000 have been slaughtered.

was highly praised by the leadership of the CCP, who held up the PKI as a model Communist Party, and one to be emulated by the other Communist parties in the world. In other words, the responsibility for the tragedy of the PKI and the Aidit leadership falls directly on the CCP, and especially on Mao.

Because of such events, the people, and especially the intellectuals, placed an even bigger question mark over Mao's leadership. The intellectuals, such as Teng T'o and his group, who were already voicing doubts, base their opposition around three main points: (1) They are against the bureaucracy and its arbitrariness and want more freedom of thought, criticism, etc. In other words, they want a program such as the "Hundred Flowers" movement to be the norm. (2) They are against the adventurism of the CCP with its programs like the "Great Leap Forward" and its wasting of the people's labor in such things as the backyard steel-making and forced collectivization of the peasants into the People's Communes, which they claim have not been successful and have even been damaging. (3) They oppose the idea that Mao is omniscient and infallible, and they are against making a cult of his personality.

From Mao's point of view the opposition of the intellectuals to his regime is intolerable and must be ended. The present situation reminds Mao and the leadership too much of the 1956 Hungarian revolution as can be seen from their references to the "literary men of the Petöfi Club who acted as the shock brigade in the Hungarian events. The turbulent wind precedes the mountain storm."[7] But Mao does not even want the wind to blow, let alone allow it to get turbulent. He has not only attacked those intellectuals and party leaders who looked upon the gentle breeze as a breath of fresh air but even those who only tolerated it.

At the beginning of May, the leadership of the CCP raised the general slogans: "Great Leap Forward in the Ideological Field" and "The Great Revolution of Socialist Culture" in order to eliminate the "poisonous weeds" of the "bourgeoisie" and "feudalists," i.e., to eliminate all differing tendencies and elements. However, in order to carry out the purge, Mao has mainly utilized the army, because even the party cannot be trusted to any great extent, as the Peking Municipal Party Committee so well demonstrates.

In March 1966, Lin Piao, minister of defense, gave instructions to the army that it must take a strong position against the "antiparty and antisocialist" tendency. The army cadres were mobilized for the campaign and since then the most vicious articles attacking the opposition have come from the *Liberation Army Daily*, which has already gone so far as to suggest the physical elimination of the opposition.

The campaign has been carried on to create an atmosphere of terror in order to stifle criticism from the intellectuals and to assure maintenance of control over the masses who feel likewise. They publish continual reminders of what happened to those who dared criticize the party during the "Hundred Flowers" movement. "Your fate cannot be better than that of your forerunners and brothers-in-crime!" "Your days are numbered."

Nor is this intimidation directed only against the intellectuals in Peking or the upper echelons. It involves intellectuals in every field, along with officials and cadres in the party and government at all levels and all over China. (It is also safe to assume that each of the prominent figures who have been attacked represents a larger group.* From all appearances, however, they seem to be very loosely and poorly organized.) While at first, there may only be slanderous attacks in the press plus removal from posts, it is most likely that arrests with long prison terms will follow or possibly worse in some cases.

The fierce action taken by the party against those who dared to question Mao's infallibility and criticize the policies of the party

---

*P'eng mentioned two other well-known figures who have been denounced whom I failed to include in the above text. One is the very famous playwright T'ien Han, chairman of the National Drama Association. He also wrote a play like Wu Han's which came under fire last February . The second is the famous historian Chien Po-tsan, who has been a professor in many of the universities in Shanghai and head of the history department at Peking University. Others not mentioned in the above article who have been denounced or purged include: Chou Hsin-fang, a famous actor and head of the Shanghai Opera Company; Lu P'ing, secretary of the Peking University party committee, and his deputy secretary, P'eng P'ei-yun; Sung Shuo, deputy director of the Peking Municipal Party Committee's Universities Department; Li Chi, a director in the party's Peking municipal branch; Hsia Yen, noted playwright who was vice-minister of culture from 1954 to last year; Wang Hsiao-chuan, propaganda chief for the Kweichow Provincial Party Committee and editor of the *Kweichow Daily;* Li Meng-wei, editor of the *Yunnan Daily* in Yunnan province; and Fan Chin, a woman who is director of the *Peking Daily* and vice-chairman of the All-China Journalists' Association.

leadership set the stage in which Kuo Mo-jo, China's most noted scholar, made his speech of self-criticism in order to protect himself from the onslaught.

The purge of the opposition, represented by Teng T'o and Wu Han, reflects a serious contradiction inside the CCP—a contradiction which developed from the suppression of the "Hundred Flowers" movement. By suppressing progressive intellectuals and others, Mao may be able for the time being to silence the oppositional mood but he cannot suppress the objective conditions which gave rise to it in the first place. And in the future it will undoubtedly again challenge the bureaucracy. As Teng T'o put it, "People who think of themselves as being omniscient, despise the masses" and "attempt to win victory by devious means. Such people . . . will be defeated in the end."

The victory, however, will not be scored by reaction or by the procapitalists who are undoubtedly to be found in the administration, and in very high posts at that. The victory will be won by those seeking proletarian democracy based on the conquests of the revolution. That victory will reinforce those conquests and assure China a genuine great leap forward, not only at home but internationally.

Second interview: January 20, 1967

Question: Because of all the news accounts of the events in Peking and Shanghai, and especially in Nanking, during the last two weeks, there has been much speculation that China might be on the brink of a civil war. What do you think about this possibility?

Answer: The struggle between the two main factions—pro-Mao and anti-Mao—has developed to a very critical stage in the last few weeks. Such things as the recent strikes by the workers in the cities of Peking, Shanghai, Canton, and many other places, especially the fierce clashes in Nanking, where it has been reported that more than fifty people were killed and several hundred were injured, demonstrate quite clearly the seriousness of the conflict between the two factions.

If this news is true, then it is certain that the struggle inside the party has become much more critical and is finding expression in the toiling masses outside the party. If such a situation continues, it is of course possible that it will lead to a civil war. However, in order to speak about the possibilities of a civil war, it is necessary to look at the evolution of Mao's so-called Cultural Revolution over the past several months.

Q. Could you outline some of the most important aspects of that evolution?

A. In order to explain the recent developments it is necessary to recall the previous interview I had with you last June. In that interview I explained the development of the present divisions in the party which began at the time of the failure of the "Great Leap Forward" program, when many intellectuals, and even a few top party leaders, openly expressed discontent and were critical of many domestic and foreign policies arbitrarily instituted by Mao; and they even went so far as to call into question Mao's leadership capacities. This, then, was the origin of the factions as they are more or less presently constituted.

What seems to have precipitated the present crisis and heightened it, however, was the question of foreign policy—the continuing isolation of China in general, and the defeat in Indonesia in particular.

Just after the Indonesian coup d'etat there was a meeting of high officials of the party. At this meeting it was reported that P'eng Chen said "everyone is equal before the truth" and that if Chairman Mao has made some mistakes, he should also be criticized. It seems that Mao suffered a setback at this meeting.

It was shortly after this that Mao left Peking for Shanghai—the end of October or the beginning of November 1965—where he immediately began to secretly organize the "Cultural Revolution."

During the period when Mao was in Shanghai—about six months—he was out of public view, and it was at this time that the press began to speculate a lot about his health. It seems that Mao chose Shanghai as his base of operations because he thought the party officials there were loyal to him. Mao began by attacking many cultural leaders, especially writers, such as Wu Han and Teng T'o, who had written many unfavorable things about him and his programs in the past. The campaign increased in intensity until finally P'eng Chen and the whole Municipal Party Committee of Peking were purged and the committee was reorganized. This was followed shortly by the purge of Lu Ting-i and Chou Yang—who were respectively heads of the Propaganda Department of the party and minister of culture—along with other high officials of the state and party in the cultural field.

Mao ordered all the universities and middle schools (high schools) closed, and many famous educators, such as the presidents of Peking University, Wuhan University, Nanking University, and others, were purged.

Such large-scale actions and purges aroused many of the top leaders such as Liu Shao-ch'i and Teng Hsiao-p'ing, along with many regional leaderships, and caused new antagonisms among the different tendencies.

Mao carried out his actions and purges by relying on the army, led by Lin Piao. For example, Lin Piao sent troops at the end of April 1966 to occupy the offices of the Peking Municipal Party Committee in order to remove P'eng Chen and the other leaders.

Under such conditions Liu Shao-ch'i and other leaders felt the situation to be very serious, and they began to unite against Mao's so-called Cultural Revolution.

Q: Are there any concrete facts which prove that some of the top leaders began to organize at this time against Mao and the "Cultural Revolution"?

A: Yes, there are. However, in order to be able to see it clearly, I must explain a little about the structure of the leadership in the party. The decision-making body of the CCP is the Political Bureau of the Central Committee. In addition to this bureau there are six regional bureaus—the North Bureau, the Central South Bureau, the East Bureau, the Northeast Bureau, the Northwest Bureau, and the Southwest Bureau. Each of these bureaus directs several provinces or administrative areas. Each is very powerful. They are in charge of the direction of the party, the local governments, and the army in their region.

The leaders of two of these six bureaus, that is the first secretaries, such as Li Hsueh-feng of the North Bureau and Liu Lan-t'ao of the Northwest Bureau, have in the past collaborated very closely with Liu Shao-ch'i.

Li Ching-ch'üan, first secretary of the Southwest Bureau, and Sung Jen-ch'iung, first secretary of the Northeast Bureau, are close to Teng Hsiao-p'ing.

The removal of P'eng Chen from office by Mao, with the help of the army, caused these bureau leaders, along with Liu Shao-ch'i and Teng Hsiao-p'ing, to be worried that they might suffer a similar fate, and they began to unite their forces against Mao. The leaders of the Northwest and Southwest bureaus in particular took a passive attitude toward Mao's "Cultural Revolution," and at times even actually resisted it. For example, when P'eng Chen was dismissed at the beginning of last June, Mao organized a central Cultural Revolution Group. Mao made his former private secretary, Ch'en Po-ta, the chairman of the group, and his wife, Chiang Ch'ing, first vice-chairwoman.

This group sent representatives to the provinces in order to organize the "Cultural Revolution." However, many groups were resisted by the provincial leaderships, especially in the four bureaus I mentioned earlier. This resistance was attacked in an editorial of the *People's Daily*, July 1, 1966.

The most important event, however, occurred in June-July 1966. During this time Mao left Peking for south China. In his absence, Liu Shao-ch'i, as first vice-chairman of the party, prepared to call an emergency meeting of the Central Committee in order to decide anew the policies of the "Cultural Revolution," to put pressure on Mao and possibly to remove him from the leadership of the party. At about the same time P'eng Chen was sent to the Northwest and Southwest bureaus to talk with the leaders there about the current situation, and about the emergency meeting of the Central Committee.

Around July 10, P'eng returned to Peking with the members of the Central Committee from these bureaus for the emergency meeting, the date of which had been set by the Political Bureau for July 21. Mao, who was still in south China, sent a message to the Political Bureau asking them to delay the emergency meeting in order that he might be able to attend. At the same time, Lin Piao surrounded Peking with troops, and it was under this threat that Liu Shao-ch'i and Teng Hsiao-p'ing retreated by rescheduling the Central Committee meeting for the first of August.

Lin Piao's army remained just outside the city during the plenary meeting of the Central Committee, and it was at this time that the decisions "Concerning the Great Proletarian Cultural Revolution" were adopted. The plenum also took decisions to organize the "Red Guards" and to reorganize the Standing Committee of the Political Bureau. It was through this reorganization that Mao was able to gain firm control of the Standing Committee by selecting and placing on it three of his closest supporters. They were T'ao Chu, Ch'en Po-ta and K'ang Sheng. (The Standing Committee carries on the day-to-day work of the party. Five members in all are reported to have been added at this time. The other two were Ch'en I and Li Fu-ch'un.)

Mao, along with Lin Piao, also opened up a fierce attack on Liu Shao-ch'i, and they removed him from his post of vice-chairman. Lin Piao took over as first vice-chairman.

This plenum gave the "Cultural Revolution" a furious boost, and outlined as its objective "to struggle against and crush those persons in authority who are taking the capitalist road."[9]

Q: Why didn't Mao organize the purge through the party and its youth group instead of organizing the Red Guards?

A: This is a very important question, and it should be given special attention and clearly explained. The CCP is very large. The membership of the party and its youth group, for example, is almost equal to the whole population of France. There are approximately 50 million altogether—20 million in the party, and 30 million in the youth group. If there really existed a procapitalist tendency in the party, as Mao claims, and if he had any confidence at all in the masses of the party, he would organize a democratic discussion inside the party which would, it seems, resolve the question very easily.

However, the reality is the opposite, that is, no procapitalist tendency exists. It is even unimaginable that the same leaders of the party who struggled so many years against capitalism are, after conquering power, now struggling for capitalism.

The fact is that those people whom Mao accuses of taking the procapitalist road are against Mao because they believe that many of his policies, arbitrarily taken on many foreign and domestic issues, have endangered the prospects of socialism.

Many cadres of the party, such as Teng T'o and Wu Han, whom I talked about in the last interview, are good examples and reflect the opinions of most of the rank and file in the party and youth. They feel that Mao has made some mistakes and that it is absolutely necessary to correct them in order that China might continue her development toward socialism.

If Mao organized any discussions in the party, he would place himself in great danger; and therefore he has tried to suppress all criticism. This is the reason Mao has utilized the army since the beginning of the "Cultural Revolution."

The decisions taken by the August plenum were only formalities. Mao was able to obtain them because of his bureaucratic control of the top bodies. But in reality he has completely avoided the party, and has employed the Red Guards in order to carry out his purge, or as he calls it, the "Cultural Revolution."

Q: What has been the result of the actions of the Red Guards?

A: We must first understand who the Red Guards are. They are primarily youth. About 60 percent of them are lower-middle-school students, that is, between the ages of 13 and 16. About 30 percent are high middle-school students between the ages of 16 and 20. Only about 10 percent of them are university students. Because the overwhelming majority of the Red Guards, especially the lower-middle-school students, are so young, they have had no previous political experience, and do not possess any great understanding of politics.

For this reason it is very easy to understand why such elements can be organized behind the campaign to build the cult of Mao, leading to many outlandish and absurd actions, even to attacks upon local party headquarters and officials.

Most of the university students went along at first with the "Cultural Revolution," but as it developed, these students, because of their greater political understanding, began to become divided among themselves.

The first actions of the Red Guards were to destroy the "Four Olds"—old ideas, old culture, old customs, and old habits—and to establish the "Four News." This became a slogan: "Destroy the Four Olds and Establish the Four News."

They later continued with such actions as destroying Buddhist sculpture, making people remove Western clothing and jewelry, and even invading people's homes and destroying any modern furniture, among other things, which they found.

They changed the names of almost everything in their path, such as streets, stores, buildings, and even cemeteries. This and more was all done in the name of carrying the revolution forward against the feudalists, the bourgeoisie, the revisionists, and the imperialists. The *People's Daily* even commented in an editorial August 28, 1966, that the spiritual face of the country had been changed as a result of Mao Tse-tung's thought.

There were, nevertheless, some progressive slogans and demands raised by some elements of the Red Guards. One of them was the demand to eliminate the interest payments to the remaining capitalists and to confiscate all their properties. These progressive slogans, however, have not been carried out.

Since the beginning of September the actions of the Red Guards have changed their complexion. At a large meeting of the Red Guards in Peking on August 31, 1966, Lin Piao gave a speech, substituting for Mao, in which he emphatically told the Red

Guards that the main aim of the "Cultural Revolution" was to isolate and purge those party officials who are taking the capitalist road. It was after this speech that the Red Guards began to attack many provincial leaders by name in wall posters.

It was in retaliation against these attacks that some of the provincial leaders began to organize the party functionaries and cadres and even some of the workers and peasants, and they proceeded to set up their own Red Guards. These were the organizations that Mao's Red Guards soon began to clash with.

The *People's Daily* has referred many times to these clashes. On September 12 it said, "Some responsible leaders in some locals have suppressed the mass movement under many and different pretexts, and they have agitated many of the workers and peasants against the revolutionary students." That is to say, they organized the masses against the Red Guards and the "Cultural Revolution."

Many of these conflicts ended with hundreds of casualties. For example, in Ch'ing-tao there were more than 140 killed and injured. In Canton there were over 50, and in Lin-wu more than 300.

On September 15, at the third large meeting of the Red Guards in Peking to be reviewed by Mao, Lin Piao made a speech in place of Mao. What he told the Red Guards, in effect, was that they must attack all those officials who are resisting Mao's thought, and that they must have no fear since the army was supporting them.

It was after this speech that the Red Guards began to be much bolder and even unrestrained. In the wall posters in Peking, leading party members were named and accused of taking the capitalist road. The first secretaries of the Southwest, Northwest, and North bureaus—Li Ching-ch'üan, Liu Lan-t'ao, and Li Hsueh-feng (who had also become first secretary of the Peking party in place of P'eng Chen) are only three examples.

Simultaneously, officials of the state began to come under attack. Ch'en I, foreign minister, Li Hsien-nien, minister of finance, and especially Po I-po, minister of industry and communications, are only a few examples. Finally Liu Shao-ch'i, president of China, and Teng Hsiao-p'ing, secretary of the party, also came under attack.

In the latter part of October a special, very important meeting was held. This meeting lasted for seventeen days. It was during this meeting that Liu Shao-ch'i and Teng Hsiao-p'ing were forced to make their self-criticisms after being severely attacked by many of the participants. It was just after this meeting that P'eng Chen and Lu Ting-i, head of the Central Propaganda Department, were arrested.

It seemed that Mao thought he had beaten the opposition. On December 26 a large victory celebration of the Red Guards was held in Peking, and publications such as *Red Flag* proclaimed the victory of the "Cultural Revolution." At this celebration, the self-criticisms of Liu and Teng were revealed for the first time. Nevertheless, we can see by the events from the first two weeks in January that the opposition was far from being broken.

Q: Since the beginning of the year the newspapers have reported very confusing accounts as to what has been happening in such places as Nanking and Shanghai. Can you clarify at all what has actually been taking place?

A: First of all, it must be noted that the events in these cities mark a new stage in the development of the struggle. Before, everyone considered these cities to be under the strict control of Mao and Lin's forces. However, the events there have shown the existence of a very powerful resistance.

Shanghai and the surrounding area make up the most industrialized section of China, and Nanking is also an industrial city. It was the party in these cities that organized the opposition, and it has, of course, a very large base in the working class. By granting the workers more pay and more welfare benefits, it has organized the workers against many of the slogans of the "Cultural Revolution," such as "Grasp revolution and promote production."

This presents a big problem for Mao. The only means he has to suppress such a force is the army. However, it would be very dangerous for him at this time to actively use it. From this angle, then, Mao is very weak. His strategy in Shanghai has been to try to gain control of the workers' organizations by occupying the offices of the trade unions and other workers' institutions. After the occupation of these offices, the leaderships of the organizations were reorganized and Mao placed his own followers in charge. Mao, as far as I know now, seems to have been successful in doing this in the dockers, railway, and bus workers' trade unions, and it is this that his faction refers to when speaking about the victories it has made in the working class in Shanghai.

In Nanking the situation was a little different. The party in this city was able to control the police and army as well as to organize the workers. It appears that Mao has been unable to make any headway whatsoever there, and the whole city, therefore, remains under the control of the opposition.

Q: Then it seems very important, if one is to consider the possibilities of a civil war, to examine the strength of both factions in the party and in the army.

A: Yes, especially the army. At this point we can very briefly draw a balance sheet as far as the party is concerned. As I stated earlier, the leaders in the Northwest, Southwest, and Northeast bureaus can be considered to stand pretty firmly in the camp of the opposition. The leaders of the North Bureau in general seem to be in support of the opposition. However, there are some leaders who support Mao.

The Central-South Bureau has been considered a stronghold of Mao and Lin, although now we have to consider the situation in light of the recent attacks against T'ao Chu, the new chief of the party's Central Propaganda Department, because before assuming his new post he had been the first secretary of the Central-South Bureau for many years, and he is still very influential there. The new first secretary of the bureau, Wang Jen-chung, has also been attacked, which demonstrates that Mao and Lin are not completely in control.

As far as the East Bureau is concerned, the events in Nanking and Shanghai demonstrate that Mao and Lin have even less control than in the Central-South Bureau. It is possible to say, then, that a large majority of the party either supports or sympathizes with the opposition.

It is more difficult to judge the relationship of both factions to the army. Nevertheless, if we take into consideration some historical aspects of the army, it makes the situation much easier to judge.

The original People's Liberation Army was divided into several parts. After victory, and Chiang Kai-shek's flight to Taiwan, the different sections of the army were led into a number of different regions by their commanders. The army led by Lin Piao went from the Northeast to the region now controlled by the Central-South Bureau. The army led by P'eng Te-huai went to the region now under the Northwest Bureau. Liu Po-ch'eng led his army to the area under the Southwest Bureau.

When Lin Piao left the Northeast, he left behind the native guerrilla army. It is now under the control of the Northeast Bureau. Ch'en I's army occupied the whole area under the control of the East Bureau. In the Northern Bureau the army was constructed by combining many regional armies under the direct leadership of the North Bureau. As I said earlier, the leadership in each bureau controls that particular army, and therefore we can say generally that the influence in the army of both factions is similar to their relationship in the party. Of course, it is possible that certain local army leaders are in disagreement with the bureau leaderships.

There are, however, some other factors we have to take into consideration concerning the army. There are figures such as P'eng Te-huai, minister of defense from December 1954 to September 1959, Lo Jui-ch'ing, the chief of staff from 1959, and especially Chu Te, the historical leader of the whole army, and Ho Lung, who is also a historical leader of the army, all of whom wield tremendous influence in the army. All of these figures have been attacked—Chu Te and Ho Lung only recently—by the Mao-Lin Piao faction, which indicates that these leaders have differences with it.

From this we can judge that the position of Mao in the army as a whole is not too favorable. It is precisely because of his weakness that he has attempted to reorganize the army by introducing into it the "Cultural Revolution Committee." This committee sent representatives to the different armies for two main reasons. One was to find out what strength the opposition had in the army and on what parts of the army Mao himself could depend. The other was to try to win certain elements in the army to its side, by such methods as bribing certain leaders with promises of promoting them to high posts.

In my opinion, this cannot change the situation very much in Mao's favor. Of course, the delegates are met and dealt with very diplomatically, and they show their enthusiastic agreement with the sixteen-point program adopted by the Central Committee on August 8, 1966. Yet in reality it seems most of them are waiting, if not preparing, for a showdown with Mao in the future.

There is one other force which is also of importance and this is the security forces, both public and secret. This organization was formed right after the CCP took power by Lo Jui-ch'in with the assistance of many specialists from the GPU of the USSR. When he resigned from that post in 1959 in order to become chief of staff, Hsieh Fu-chih—who had worked under the leadership of

Teng Hsiao-p'ing for almost twenty years—took over his post as head of the Ministry of Public Security. Both of these men have been attacked by the Red Guards, and Lo Jui-ch'ing has even been arrested by the Mao-Lin faction because, as it seems, the police force as a whole, or at least the greater part, are under the influence of the opposition. Recently it seems that Hsieh Fu-chih, under tremendous pressure, especially that of Lin Piao's army surrounding Peking, made a compromise with the Mao-Lin Piao faction and this explains the statement of Mao's wife, Chiang Ch'ing, that the Red Guards should no longer attack him.

I must also say a few words about Chou En-lai, who represents somewhat of a third major tendency between the two opposing factions. This tendency is very weak as it has no mass base and is not itself actually struggling for power. The strength it does have comes from its control of the government ministries.

To understand the position of this group, it is necessary to describe its leader, Chou En-lai. Politically, he is very weak and has continually, throughout his career, leaned toward the stronger groups when there has been a struggle in the party. Yet, organizationally, he is very capable, and he is valued by the whole party for his abilities in this field.

At the present time with Lin Piao's army surrounding Peking and his ministries, he has made a compromise with Mao and is trying to play more or less the role of a compromiser. If the opposition should begin to show its power, however, there is no doubt that he would change his position accordingly. What the future holds, then, still depends on many factors, domestic and foreign. However, we can make an overall judgment now, that Mao's forces are in a minority and that Mao and Lin Piao will not—unless they take an adventuristic course, or are forced to—launch a civil war at this time.

Q: If Mao is in a minority, as you explain, how has it been possible for him to seemingly control the party and carry on with the "Cultural Revolution"? For example, how was he able to get the party to adopt the sixteen-point program of August 8, 1966?

A: First of all we must not underestimate Mao's influence in the party and in all of China. The CCP conquered power under his leadership as chairman of the party. Therefore, in the eyes of the masses he is the great symbol of the victory of the revolution. There is no doubt that even now he still commands respect among a portion of the masses.

However, with the failure of the "Great Leap Forward," his influence was weakened, and the many obvious mistakes in his policies since then, such as his positions on literature and art, education, on the Vietnamese War, and especially on the Indonesian CP, have further tarnished his reputation in the party and among the masses.

Most of Mao's so-called victories have taken place in Peking, such as the adoption of the sixteen-point program you mentioned by the Central Committee. These "victories" have been almost completely dependent upon one factor—the army of Lin Piao. It is with the army and the threat of the army that Mao removed P'eng Chen, secured the adoption of the sixteen-point program, forced self-criticisms of leaders such as Liu Shao-ch'i, forced Hsieh Fu-chih to compromise, etc.

Q: Mao accuses his opponents of being capitalist restorationists, revisionist, etc. Yet no one seems to know for sure what the program of Mao's opposition is and whom this opposition represents. Can you clarify the nature of the opposition?

A: The CCP is something like its sister party in the USSR. There is no democratic discussion inside the party; all decisions are handed down from above and must be carried out and obeyed by the cadres and the rank and file. Even in the top bodies such as the Central Committee and the Political Bureau there is generally little discussion. Only on very critical questions such as the "Great Leap Forward," the People's Communes, and the defeat of Indonesia, has any real discussion taken place inside the top bodies. The oppositions which have developed and attempted to criticize Mao and his programs have in the past been expelled. I have already spoken about P'eng Chen, for example, and in the first interview, about P'eng Te-huai.

Under these conditions it is very difficult to learn what the specific program of the opposition in the party is. However, we can get an idea of the opposition's general attitudes from the documents published by the CCP itself criticizing the opposition, as well as from the writings for which many intellectuals in the party have been attacked. I will point out what seem to be the main points of disagreement with Mao's faction.

1. They considered Mao's economic programs like the "Great Leap Forward"—especially the formation of the People's Communes—to be adventuristic.

2. In literature and art they have felt that Mao's ideas are too

strict, and that they put a straitjacket on any creative writing, etc.

3. Almost all educators, professors, teachers, and university students opposed Mao's policies in the educational field because of their interference with freedom of study, and they felt it was a waste of time for them to be sent into the countryside or into the factories. They felt that Mao's policies on the whole had disrupted the educational system.

4. The position of the opposition on international questions is much more difficult to determine because there is much less material. It is probably safe to assume that there is general agreement with Lo Jui-ch'ing on the question of how to defend China in case of a possible attack from the U.S. Lo Jui-ch'ing does not seem to have been in disagreement about politics being in command in the army. Rather, it was his position that one must recognize the importance of today's type of warfare, especially the role of nuclear weapons. Therefore, he felt that the break with the Soviet Union on the state level had endangered China's capacity to defend herself militarily against a probable imperialist attack.

5. Finally on one point they make themselves very clear. There is general disgust with Mao's omniscience and they demand more discussion in the party on important questions.

These five points give us a general picture of the ideas and opinions of the opposition. It is impossible, of course, for us to give a comprehensive explanation of their program, and I doubt that they have one that is systematic and formal. But we can say that these make up the most important disagreements with Mao to be found among the various members of the opposition.

To understand fully the differences between the two groups, I should say something about some particular points in Mao's own program. Since the stated objectives of Mao's formal program do not correspond to the development of the "Cultural Revolution" itself, it is more enlightening to examine the way in which Mao has actually implemented the "Cultural Revolution." I have already described at some length what Mao is doing when I discussed the struggle and its evolution. Briefly, Mao is trying to carry out a purge in the most undemocratic way, and in fact a coup d'etat. He has tried to make himself a living god and to make his very word law.

It seems that in the recent events another very important disagreement has arisen between the two factions. The opposition, in order to win over and organize the workers, has granted many concessions in some localities, and has taken measures to raise their standard of living. Mao, with the "Cultural Revolution," has continually and strongly opposed such measures.

Q: Does the opposition, then, represent a democratic force, and what do you think about the idea which seems to be the most widely accepted, that is, that the main opposition to Mao is Khrushchevist?

A: The opposition is not homogeneous but is composed of many tendencies. We are able to distinguish three main currents. The first is found among the top leaders like Liu Shao-ch'i, Teng Hsiao-p'ing, and many leaders of the bureaus. This tendency in general represents a bureaucratic group inside the party which is in control of a considerable sector of the party's apparatus. The political traditions of this group organizationally and politically are those of Stalinism.

The second current can be referred to as a "liberalizing" tendency, and is made up of second rank or middle cadres in the party, of which Teng T'o and Wu Han are good examples.

The third current is much more difficult to define because there doesn't seem to be any single leader, or any well-known cadres for that matter, who represent it. But we can say almost with certainty that this group represents, if not a revolutionary, then a quasi-revolutionary tendency, and is made up primarily of rank-and-file party members.

The third current would, of course, represent a sector of the masses and express most vividly the feelings of the population as a whole. The middle layers of the party have much more contact in their work with the rank and file, and would therefore be more likely to reflect the attitude of the masses.

It is with sectors of the middle layers that the top leaders have the most contact in their day-to-day party work. For example, Teng T'o was directly under P'eng Chen, who was one of the top leaders. It would have been impossible for Teng T'o to carry on the work that he did without at least the tolerance, if not the approval, of P'eng Chen. It was Liu Shao-ch'i's close personal relationship with P'eng Chen that probably thrust him into the leadership of the present opposition faction.

In the very top leadership, Mao tolerated no disagreement, and every opposition was expelled. However, because of the past experience of the top leaders in working with the masses, and their connection with the middle layers, some of them reflect in some measure the movement of the masses. While the middle layers represent the tendency in the party for reform, it is probably safe to assume that the need for reform is also recognized by top leaders who are, nonetheless, more conservative, and who still wish to maintain a tight control over the party.

The question of Khrushchevism is very important. We must first understand what is meant by Khrushchevism, and especially what Mao means by Khrushchevism.

There are two different aspects of Khrushchevism: one is political revisionism, which is reactionary; and the other is de-Stalinization, which is progressive.

Mao does not distinguish between these two aspects. He lumps them together under the label of revisionism. Both are reactionary from his point of view, and he has said that Khrushchev's policies have restored capitalism in the USSR.

We must understand, then, that anyone agreeing with any aspect of Khrushchevism is, according to Mao, a revisionist, and wants, or is attempting, to restore capitalism. From what I have said earlier, you can see that the opposition desires in its own way similar reforms to those carried out under Khrushchevism during de-Stalinization, and of course these reforms are directed at Mao.

In Mao's opinion, then—if he actually believes his own propaganda—such reform measures will lead to a capitalist restoration.

As far as the politically revisionist side of Khrushchevism is concerned, we must recognize that in practice Mao's own policies have not proved to be substantially different, as the events in Indonesia so well demonstrate. It seems that Mao's main objection to the revisionism of Khrushchev has been de-Stalinization. There is no evidence I know of that the opposition is in any way in disagreement with the official policy of exposing the political revisionism of Khrushchev. Therefore, at least on the question of de-Stalinization, the stand of the opposition is the more progressive. In general, the opposition shades from currents that are really Maoist to tendencies that are quite revolutionary.

Q: What, in your opinion, will be the final outcome of the struggle?

A: Taking into consideration the relationship of forces on each side as I have already outlined, it is clear that the odds are against Mao, especially if the organization and mobilization of the peasants and workers, which we have seen in recent events, continues.

If Mao should nevertheless be victorious, I think a sweeping purge comparable to the one in the Soviet Union during the 1930s, if not larger, could occur and the defense of the Chinese revolution would be placed in grave danger. However, if the opposition should win, the most likely result would be a few concessions of a liberalizing nature as well as a shift away from the ultraleft sectarian positions taken by Mao. For example, it is possible they would set up some kind of united front with the other workers' states against U.S. imperialism.

There is another important prospect if the opposition should win. If the masses have entered into motion, it will not be so easy for the bureaucracy to stop them or to contain them within the prescribed limits. In that case, a real massive struggle for workers' democracy could open up.

OPEN LETTER TO THE MEMBERS
OF THE CHINESE COMMUNIST PARTY

Dear Comrades,

In May 1966, in the *Liberation Army Daily*, the chairman of your party, Mao Tse-tung, launched the so-called Cultural Revolution. Since then, and especially since the organization of the Red Guards in August 1966, a storm has arisen over China, and a series of extraordinary events have taken place which have greatly shocked some of the most devoted friends and supporters of the Chinese revolution. In particular, these events have included such things as the dismissal, arrest, and imprisonment of top leaders in your party and government like P'eng Chen, Lu Ting-i, and Lo Jui-ch'ing, without any recourse to the laws of the state or the regulations of the party. These same people have also been so insulted and abused, and even humiliated by being paraded through the streets by the Red Guards, that some of them have attempted suicide. Hundreds of other well-known leaders and cadres in the cultural and educational fields, such as Chou Yang, Wu Han, Teng T'o, T'ien Han, Hsia Yen, Yang Han-sheng, Li Ta, Lu P'ing, Kuang Ya-ming, P'eng Kang, etc., have been purged. Even Liu Shao-ch'i, a vice-chairman of the party and president of the People's Republic of China, and Teng Hsiao-p'ing, the general secretary of the party, have been openly attacked by the Red Guards and obliged to make self-criticisms. Moreover, in recent weeks, Mao Tse-tung has used the army to take over the government and party apparatuses in certain provincial capitals such as Taiyuan in Shansi, Nanchang in Kiangsi, and Hofei in Anhwei.

All these events taken together demonstrate that your party not only finds itself in the grave crisis of an open split, but that the country itself could be on the brink of a civil war. If this situation is not corrected in time, the outcome will be catastrophic and socialist China will be led into an impasse. For the sake of the perspectives of socialism in China, the fundamental interests of the workers and peasants, and the fate of thousands of militants inside and outside the party, I can no longer remain silent. Therefore, I am addressing this letter to you in order to express my views on the crisis in the party, and to offer my ideas on how that crisis can be resolved.

First of all I would like to ask you to notice that all the top leaders of the party, as well as the leading cadres in the cultural and educational fields, have been purged or attacked for the "crime" of being "antiparty," "antisocialist," and opposed to "Mao Tse-tung Thought," and they have been accused of being "capitalist restorationists" and of "taking the capitalist road." But, one must demand, what evidence is there to support such extreme charges as being "antisocialist" and "taking the capitalist road"? We must say that absolutely no such evidence has been offered, and that these charges are very clearly nothing but a frame-up. They are similar to the ones Stalin employed thirty years ago when he eliminated his political opponents by accusing them of being "enemies of the people."

As far as I am concerned, I am not in agreement with the fundamental political positions and organizational methods of those leaders of your party who have been purged. Nevertheless, I feel that these leaders cannot be accused of being antisocialist, nor are they taking the bourgeois road and trying to restore capitalism.

I am personally acquainted with Liu Shao-ch'i. I know him very well since I was a co-worker with him in the party from 1920 to 1927. Since he joined the Communist movement in the autumn of 1920, he has actively and wholeheartedly participated in revolutionary activities. After the defeat of the second Chinese revolution, our ways parted politically (Liu supported the position of Stalin, while I turned in the direction of Trotsky). However, at that time I still considered him to be a revolutionary. As far as your party is concerned, Liu has made a very great contribution. During the "White Terror" of Chiang Kai-shek, he worked in the underground under very difficult and dangerous circumstances in order to overthrow Chiang Kai-shek's bourgeois regime and to put China on the road to socialism. It is absurd and absolutely impossible to believe that such a person as Liu Shao-ch'i, who enjoys the high post of head of state, would, seventeen years after the victory of the revolution, now turn against socialism and work for the restoration of capitalism.

Teng Hsiao-p'ing, P'eng Chen, Lu Ting-i, Lo Jui-ch'ing, and others, in the cultural and educational fields—who all have a history similar to that of Liu Shao-ch'i—have also been labeled "antisocialist" and accused of "taking the capitalist road." Such absurd accusations can only be described as slanderous. Are these not almost the same accusations as those used by Stalin when he accused Trotsky, Zinoviev, Kamenev, and their supporters of being "capitalist restorationists" and "enemies of the people"? How could such base and absurd slanders find their way into your party? This is the central question that now confronts you, and which you must try to understand and resolve.

Your party refers to itself as "Marxist-Leninist," and has stated in its statutes that it bases itself on democratic centralism. But as you know only too well, in reality there is no democracy in your party, but only a bureaucratic centralism in which the power is centered in the hands of the party's chairman, Mao Tse-tung. All the important decisions taken by the party are arbitrarily decided by Mao Tse-tung himself, and the party must accept them as being infallible. If anyone did not agree with or criticized Mao's opinions, he would be accused of being "antiparty," "antisocialist," and "anti-Mao Tse-tung Thought," and would almost certainly be purged. These procedures, which violate democratic centralism, are the source of the grave crisis in which your party presently finds itself.

If your party actually operated on the basis of democratic centralism, such slanders would be impossible. The method of democratic centralism practiced by the Bolsheviks placed all important questions before the entire membership, and allowed them to freely present their own ideas and to criticize anyone's position, including that of the top leaders. The final decisions were taken at the party congresses, and it was after these decisions that the party became united. The minority had to obey the majority decision, although it had a right to maintain its ideas, and to ask the party, at any time it felt necessary, to reconsider them. The minority was at no time punished for its ideas. This, then, was the democratic centralism instituted by the Bolsheviks under the leadership of Lenin.

During the period of Lenin's leadership of the Soviet party and government, the congresses of the party were held each year, and emergency congresses were even called when urgent and important issues arose. It is only by such practices that the opinions of the rank and file can find expression. This is the embodiment of democratic centralism.

In the Soviet party, then, all important issues, such as the Brest-Litovsk Treaty and the New Economic Policy, were decided upon only after a full and free discussion.[1] After the decisions were taken, the minorities were able to maintain their political position. It was only mandatory that they unite with the rest of the party to help carry out the majority decisions. The leaders of the minorities, such as Bukharin and Radek, who continued to maintain their minority position concerning the Brest-Litovsk Treaty, were not only not punished, but they retained their official posts in the party and in the government. This is a concrete example of democratic centralism in practice.

After the death of Lenin, Stalin usurped the leadership of the party and turned the democratic centralism practiced by the Bolsheviks into bureaucratic centralism without democracy. He took all the power into his own hands and made himself into a dictator. Under these conditions, all the important issues concerning the party and state were arbitrarily decided by Stalin himself, and as a result, neither free discussion within the party nor regular scheduled party congresses were any longer necessary. (After the Sixteenth Congress, when Stalin established his rule, there were only three congresses of the party until his death in 1953—a period of twenty-three years.) Those who did not agree with Stalin and criticized him were purged as being "rightist," "antiparty," and "enemies of the people." It was for this reason that the entire generation of the Old Bolsheviks, as well as numerous newer, young revolutionaries, were liquidated under Stalin's dictatorship.

Since your party took power in 1949, none of the important questions has been decided upon at a party congress following a democratic discussion. For example, the "Great Leap Forward" policy—especially the People's Communes, involving the lives of 500 million peasants—and the current "Proletarian Cultural Revolution" policy, were never democratically discussed by the party or decided upon by a party congress, nor were they even discussed and decided upon by your Central Committee. These and all other important questions have been decided by your party's chairman, Mao Tse-tung, and he has merely given the party orders to carry them out. The Central Committee of your party only meets to ratify Mao's decisions, often after they are already being carried out. For example, Mao Tse-tung arbitrarily instituted the People's Communes in the beginning of August 1958, and then an enlarged meeting of the Political Bureau at the end of August 1958 had to ratify his decision. And again in May

1966, Mao organized the "Cultural Revolution," and it was not until August 1966 that the plenum of the Central Committee, which adopted the resolution on the "Great Proletarian Cultural Revolution," took place.

During the seventeen years that your party has been in power, there has only been one party congress—the Eighth Congress in 1956. Therefore, the conditions of your party resemble those of the Soviet party under Stalin, if in fact they do not duplicate them. Hence, if your party continues in the same way, it will engage in a purge comparable to the one carried out by Stalin in the 1930s. The present purge of P'eng Chen, Lu Ting-i, Lo Jui-ch'ing, and the others is only a prelude to a much greater tragedy.

The most serious and dangerous condition which has so far presented itself is your Chairman Mao's ordering the army to intervene in the struggle taking place inside the party. He has used the army, as well as the Red Guards, in order to take over, step by step, the offices and administrative powers of the party and state throughout the country, in order to establish his Bonapartist military dictatorship. By doing this he has ignored and violated all laws (these are laws which were initiated and passed by your party and government). Mao has gone beyond the actions of Stalin. This situation will inevitably lead to a large-scale civil war if it is not countered in time.

As you already know, the Mao-Lin Piao faction is a very small minority among the rank and file of the party. Except for Peking and the capitals of Kwangtung, Shansi, Kiangsi, Anhwei, and Heilungkiang provinces, where the Maoist forces claim they have control—even in these places the Maoist forces have had to depend upon the army and the Red Guards for their power—the rest of the country remains under the control of the opposition or neutralist elements. If Mao Tse-tung continues to insist upon occupying the rest of the country, he will undoubtedly meet strong resistance from the opposition and neutralist elements, who will be forced to unite to protect themselves in many areas, and especially in the Southwest, Northwest, and in Inner Mongolia; in such an event, a great civil war will be unavoidable. Who can say what amount of economic destruction would take place in the event of a civil war, or how much suffering it would bring to the people, and how many would meet their death? It is impossible to say. Yet, there is one thing which can be predicted: a civil war would set China back many years, her energy would be exhausted, and the cause of socialism would receive a very, very damaging blow. There is even a strong possibility that American imperialism would be influenced to take this opportunity to strike. In the event of such developments it is impossible to predict what the fate of China would be.

My dear comrades, the present situation is so serious that not only is your party endangered, but the fate of socialist China itself is at stake. The time has come for you to rise up and begin to struggle.

It is claimed that your party has around twenty million members, and the youth organization around thirty million. The party is unique because of its huge mass membership, and because of the real and potential power it possesses compared to all other forces in China. With such masses and power, any and almost all obstacles should be easily overcome. Except for a minority of corrupt bureaucrats, case-hardened Stalinists, and Maoists, I believe that the majority of the party is made up of militants who are loyal to socialism and concerned that China remain on the socialist road, and who are willing to sacrifice themselves in the interest of the worker and peasant masses. Therefore, I would like to put forward the following proposals as a means to overcome the present critical situation.

I

You must immediately make an appeal to the whole party and its youth, calling on them to intervene with practical action. First you must demand that your chairman, Mao Tse-tung, comply with the following measures:

1. Immediately stop using the army to remove the party and government officials throughout the country. The leadership of the party must be elected by the members of the party through democratic procedures. As regards the government, it should be democratically elected by soviets (councils) of the workers, peasants, and soldiers.

2. Immediately dissolve the Red Guards, because the majority of them are completely controlled by Ch'en Po-ta (Mao's ex-secretary) and Chiang Ch'ing (Mao's wife) through the Cultural Revolution Group, and because they have been used as an instrument to slander and physically attack the opposition. Their activities have been contrary to democratic procedures, and are hence reactionary.

3. Immediately release all the party opposition leaders and cadres who have recently been arrested and imprisoned, and restore them to their original positions. At the same time, release

all those political prisoners who have been arrested in the past and who believe in socialism, and let them freely express their opinions and participate in political activities.

4. All the organs of the party, as well as other journals and radio broadcasts, must immediately stop their slanders against the oppositions—the use of such epithets as "antiparty," "antisocialist," and "capitalist restorationist"—and stop the absurd propaganda relating to Mao's personal cult. Substitute in their place the actual political positions of the different tendencies, and launch a public discussion on all important questions.

5. Immediately establish a consulting committee made up of representatives of all the different tendencies in the party. Its task should be to prepare a party congress and to launch a democratic discussion inside the party on all the essential questions on which differences have arisen, such as the failure of the People's Communes and the "Great Leap Forward"; the different ideas on literature, art, and education; the personal cult of Mao Tse-tung; democratic centralism in a Bolshevik party; the reasons for the tragic defeat of the CP in Indonesia; and especially the question of a united front with the other socialist countries to oppose U.S. imperialism in Vietnam. The many different tendencies should be allowed to express their opinions and submit their resolutions on the issues stated above, and then a final decision should be adopted at the party congress.

These proposed measures, if carried out, would make it possible to avoid a civil war, and would restore peace.

II

If Chairman Mao fails to comply with the measures outlined above, it would demonstrate that he has absolutely no respect for your opinions, and that by using the Red Guards and the army he is bent on taking the power and destroying any and all opposition in the party and government in order to establish his own Bonapartist military dictatorship. This, then, will inevitably lead to a civil war which could lead socialist China into a blind alley.

In such circumstances, you not only have the full right but a duty to split with him and openly appeal to the worker, soldier, and peasant masses, calling on them to struggle in defense of the socialist conquests and for the reunification of the country, that is, to transform the present factional struggle into a revolutionary struggle against bureaucratic dictatorship.

As a program in this struggle, I urge you to consider the following proposals:

1. It is absolutely necessary to defend the conquests of the revolution and the socialist property relations, and to resolutely attack all attempts at capitalist restoration led by the remaining bourgeois elements, rich farmers, and corrupt bureaucrats who might try to take advantage of the present situation. The payment of interest to the remaining capitalists must be stopped, and they must be removed from their high positions in the factories, etc.

2. It is necessary to form a united front with all socialist-minded groupings in order to do away with the dictatorship by one faction or by one party. At the present time your party is divided into two uncompromising factions—pro-Mao and anti-Mao—but in reality it is already split into two parties. In addition to this, there are several tendencies in the opposition. There are also many revolutionaries who are outside the party, such as those people who were expelled after the crackdown on the "Hundred Flowers" movement. All these revolutionary tendencies must be allowed to form their own independent party or grouping, and every group or party claiming to be fighting for socialism must be allowed to present its political position and program in an attempt to win the support of the masses. These different socialist groupings and parties must then unite in one common front to oppose the Mao-Lin Piao faction and prevent it from establishing a Bonapartist military dictatorship—thereby preventing a tragedy similar to that of Stalin's purges in the 1930s—and in order to establish a truly democratic socialist regime.

3. To establish a democratic socialist regime, it is necessary to work among the worker and peasant masses, to call on them to struggle, to encourage them to form soviets and elect their soviet representatives by secret ballot, and to form a government based on soviets, in place of the present government which obtained power by fraudulent elections. The organization of soviets is not only one of the best ways to mobilize the masses for struggle, but it is the only type of structure that can lead to a democratic socialist government.

4. The present militias must be expanded and reorganized, and their commanders elected through secret ballot by those who belong to the militias. This organization must take the place of the public and secret police in maintaining social order, and if

necessary, it should be used to defend the democratic socialist government against its enemies.

5. Workers' committees must be democratically formed by secret ballot in every factory and mine in order to direct production in cooperation with the technicians, and administrative committees must be formed in every commune, through the same democratic methods, in order to manage production and distribution. As for the communes themselves being reorganized, this question should be resolved only after a complete and thorough discussion among the whole peasantry.

6. It is necessary to improve the living standards of the masses by such means as increasing wages and cutting working hours for the workers, and increasing the incomes of the peasants while doing away with their excessive work loads. Improving the material benefits of the working masses and developing their initiative through democratic procedures is the only way to increase production and to mobilize the masses for struggle. At the present time, Mao's faction considers any material improvement for the masses to be "economism." This only reflects the psychology of those in the top bureaucratic layer who themselves enjoy privileges, including luxurious material benefits.

7. In the history of China, the antagonisms between national minorities have led to many civil wars. Resolving the question of the national minorities, therefore, has become a very important factor in unifying the nation and stabilizing society as a whole. In 1922 the Chinese Communist Party decided to acknowledge the right of self-determination of the national minorities, which meant they had the right to establish their own independent government in such places as Tibet, Inner Mongolia, and the Muslim community in Sinkiang. This decision was taken in order to win the sincere collaboration of the national minorities and to unify the nation on the basis of equality.

Since your party took power in 1949, it has yet to solve the problem of the national minorities on the principles practiced by Lenin. Formally the party has established the autonomous regions of Tibet and Inner Mongolia, yet, in practice the national minorities are still ruled in the tradition of the great Han race, and they have never enjoyed the right of self-determination, let alone the right to establish their own independent government. It is for this reason that old antagonisms still lie just beneath the surface and could possibly foment a crisis of still another civil war. Already in the present crisis of the party, the problem of the national minorities has again erupted.

To unify the nation, then, it is absolutely necessary to acknowledge, both in word and deed, the right of the national minorities to form their own independent parties and governments in Tibet, Inner Mongolia, and among the Muslims in Sinkiang. Only in this way will it be possible to win the sincere collaboration of the national minorities, and to form a Soviet Union of China, that is to accomplish the socialist unification of the nation. It is imperative, then, that the recognition of self-determination for the national minorities be an important point in any socialist program.

8. It is necessary to adopt a revolutionary foreign policy, and in order to do this, it is necessary to draw the lessons of the tragic defeat in Indonesia. As you have all personally witnessed, the leader of the Indonesian Communist Party (PKI), D. N. Aidit, visited China several times, and each time he talked with Chairman Mao. Aidit also made several speeches in which he supported the NASAKOM of President Sukarno.[2] These speeches were reprinted in the *People's Daily*, the organ of your party, not only without criticism, but even with much praise; the Indonesian CP was held up as a great Marxist-Leninist party, and D. N. Aidit as its great revolutionary leader. Mao encouraged the PKI to lend its support to Sukarno in order that Mao himself might win Sukarno for his own diplomatic interests. He also encouraged Aidit to practice the same revisionist policies of Khrushchev in order to win Aidit to his side in the dispute with Khrushchev. The result of these policies was the great October tragedy in which the blood of hundreds of thousands of Indonesian Communist militants, workers, and peasants was spilled. This gigantic defeat has dealt a serious blow to your party and to the cause of socialism in China and all of Asia.

The tragedy of the PKI is a repetition of the disastrous setback dealt to the Chinese revolution in the years 1925-27. Mao's encouragement of the PKI's support of NASAKOM—support which was the very reason for the defeat of the PKI—echoes the way Stalin forced the Chinese CP in the 1920s to support Chiang Kai-shek and his continuation of the "Three People's Principles," the program of Sun Yat-sen. The only difference is that the defeat in Indonesia was a still greater calamity. From this we have to learn an important lesson: the policy of class collaboration, embodied in the theory that a bloc of four classes—working class, peasantry, petty bourgeoisie, and national bourgeoisie—is required to carry out a national democratic revolution before coming to the stage of a socialist revolution, is a policy which dooms the revolution to a catastrophic defeat. This lesson must be clearly presented in any program seeking to promote the world revolution, especially in the backward countries of the world.

9. At present, Chariman Mao Tse-tung accuses all his opponents of being Khrushchevists, that is, modern revisionists, and this has caused considerable confusion in the party. Mao has even said that there can be no unity with the Khrushchevists, and has in practice tried to break off all relations with the USSR. Therefore, it is necessary to clarify the question of Khrushchevism.

First of all one must define Khrushchevism. In general, there are two different aspects of Khrushchevism. One is the political revisionism, i.e., the policy of peaceful coexistence between socialist countries and capitalist countries, and the perspective of a peaceful transition to socialism. This is, of course, complete opportunism, and must be rejected and exposed. The other aspect is de-Stalinization, i.e., the partial repudiation of Stalin's personal cult, and the partial exposing of his personal dictatorship and horrendous crimes. However limited the de-Stalinization has been, it is nonetheless progressive, and must be supported with the necessary criticisms of its inadequacies.

Mao lumps both of these two quite different aspects together, attacking them both as "revisionist." It is even being said in official party publications that under the leadership of Khrushchev the Soviet Union is becoming a capitalist state. This is absolutely absurd, because the socialist property relations remain intact. One must differentiate between the socialist property relations and the bureaucratic political dictatorship. Every Marxist must defend the former against the latter.

Mao's own political policies have not differed much from those of Khrushchev, as the Indonesian affair demonstrates. Consequently, when Mao speaks against revisionism, he is for the most part attacking de-Stalinization, and he attacks de-Stalinization in order to maintain his own personal dictatorship and cult.

As far as the relationship between the socialist countries is concerned, it must be pointed out that the ideological struggle must not interfere at the state level nor interrupt the advancement of the country by hindering such things as commerce, military aid, etc., despite the fact that the ideological struggle must still be carried on against the revisionists.

10. Since U.S. imperialism began its systematic escalation of the war in Vietnam and its savage bombing of the Democratic Republic of Vietnam, it has inflicted immense suffering upon the

people. Not only has the Vietnamese war of resistance been endangered, but China herself is being threatened, and there is even a possibility of a nuclear war. The only way these perils can be overcome is for the socialist countries to unite in a common front to oppose the aggressive might of U.S. imperialism. However, Chairman Mao has refused to join in any united front, under the pretext of opposing revisionism. Objectively, such a sectarian position only helps U.S. imperialism in the end. It is absolutely clear that the Soviet bureaucracy, with its line of peaceful coexistence, is not resolved to help the Vietnamese people win their struggle against imperialism. On the other hand, because of the pressures from the people of the USSR and the other socialist countries, the Soviet bureaucracy has been forced to take certain steps to aid the Vietnamese people, and even to adopt the position of agreeing to a united front with the other socialist countries. China has no alternative but to accept the united front proposals, and to join in common action with the other workers' states to oppose U.S. imperialism in Vietnam.

Should the Soviet bureaucracy then reject the united front, they would expose themselves before the whole world as insincere. If they accepted the united front but then sabotaged it in practice, it would be much easier to expose them and their treacherous policies. The possibility of such an exposure might be enough to prevent them from even attempting such sabotage. The result would be to enormously strengthen the Vietnamese people. For these reasons, it is necessary to counter Mao's sectarian policy with the policy of joining in a united front so that the Vietnamese people can carry their struggle forward to victory.

The program outlined above can be condensed into the following slogans:

Struggle against the restoration of capitalism and defend socialist property relations.

Down with the personal cult and dictatorship of Mao, and establish a democratic socialist regime.

Advance the world revolution by replacing all class-collaborationist policies with revolutionary Marxism.

A united front with the socialist countries and all revolutionary and democratic-minded forces to defend the Vietnamese revolution.

February 15, 1967

THE RELATIONSHIP AND DIFFERENCES BETWEEN MAO TSE-TUNG AND LIU SHAO-CH'I

Question: Since my last interview with you the development of events has become more and more serious. The struggle between the two factions—anti-Mao and pro-Mao—has become more and more violent.

On the one hand, since Mao openly called on the army to intervene in the struggle to help the Red Guards to seize power, the Maoists have occupied the government and party offices in Shanghai and in the capitals of Shansi, Heilungkiang, Kwei-chow, Fukien, Kiangsi, and Kwangtung. This struggle for power has now extended into the provinces of Honan and Szechwan, as well as many other cities and districts, such as Ch'ich'i, Heilung-kiang; Suchow, Kiangsu; Pinghsiang, Kiangsi; etc. The situation in Honan and Szechwan is of special significance, since according to *Le Monde* of June 14, 1967, during the night of June 7-8, a large-scale, bloody clash took place in Szechwan in which over three hundred were killed and several thousand wounded. In Honan similar clashes were supposed to have taken place, and the opposition captured the key positions of power. It was reported over the Honan radio that the oppositionists openly supported the positions of Liu Shao-ch'i. These events demonstrate that the possibility of the struggle between the two factions breaking out into a national civil war is becoming increasingly greater. In fact, the present clashes already constitute civil war on a local scale.

On the other hand, immediately following the publication of an article in *Red Flag* by Tse P'eng-yu (April 1, 1967), huge demonstrations of Red Guards took place in Peking, Shanghai, and

---

This interview was obtained by Antonio Farien (David Fender) on July 6, 1967.

other cities against Liu Shao-ch'i, openly accusing him of being "the top party person in authority taking the capitalist road," and shouting the slogans "Down with Liu Shao-ch'i!" "Down with the Chinese Khrushchev!" "Down with Liu Shao-ch'i, Teng Hsiao-p'ing, and T'ao Chu!" and "Bury the Black Dynasty of Liu's Family!" These and other such slogans were spread about as widely as possible by the Maoists. The Peking radio even broadcast newpaper articles attacking Liu Shao-ch'i by name, and reported all the news about the demonstrations and meetings which were held in order to denounce him. Judging from these events, it seems that Mao had decided to prepare public opinion for the removal of Liu, Teng, and other opposition leaders from their posts. This development is, of course, not surprising, since it stems logically from the earlier developments. However, many people who are interested in China and concerned with her fate find it difficult to understand why and how these two factions have reached such irreconcilable positions. In other words, it is very difficult to understand just what the basic political differences are that separate the two factions, making all compromise between Mao and Liu impossible. Can you explain these differences and how they developed?

Answer: Because of the Stalinist traditions of the Chinese Communist Party, the nature of all essential differences is kept secret, and it is very difficult for anyone outside of the party to understand these differences. However, owing to the wall posters and the many newspapers of the Red Guards, which in recent months have openly attacked Liu Shao-ch'i, we can see much more clearly what the essential differences between Liu and Mao are. For example, two articles—"See the Ugly Face of Liu Shao-ch'i," published in the Red Guard newspaper, *Chingkang-shan* (reprinted in *Ming Pao Monthly*, January 18 and 19, 1967), and "The Crimes of Liu Shao-ch'i," published in *Red Guards in the Capital* (February 22, 1967)—despite the most malicious attacks on Liu and his past activities, reveal some important facts that may be used to judge the underlying historical differences between Mao and Liu. (It should be pointed out here that some of the facts revealed in the Red Guard newspapers have never before been known outside of the ruling echelons of the party. Therefore, it is quite evident that these articles were written, if not by, then under the direction of, some very high officials close to Mao, directing the "Cultural Revolution," such as Ch'en Po-ta, Chiang Ch'ing, K'ang Sheng, etc.)

However, before one can understand the present differences between Liu and Mao, one should first know a little about their past, that is, their different posts and activities, both inside and outside the party, as well as the two men's past relationships.

After attending the founding congress of the CCP in 1921, Mao was sent to Hunan as the secretary of the provincial committee, where he was active for about two years. In 1923 he was elected to the Central Committee at the Third Congress of the party, and was assigned to the post of organizational secretary. It was during this period that the Comintern ordered members of the CCP to join the Kuomintang and to collaborate with it, and Mao was appointed a member of the Kuomintang's Shanghai Municipal Committee, where he did all of his work, neglecting his work in the CCP.

In the autumn of 1924 Mao returned to Hunan and participated in the peasant movement, after which he went to Canton and began to work in the headquarters of the Central Committee of the Kuomintang as a secretary of the Propaganda Department and as editor of the Kuomintang's magazine *Political Weekly*. Toward the end of 1926 he again returned to Hunan, and it was during this time that he gathered the information for his famous article on the peasant movement.

In the spring of 1927 Mao became the president of the Provisional National Federation of Peasant Associations. He held this post until the defeat of the revolution in July 1927, when the members of the CCP in Wuhan were purged from the Kuomintang.

Liu Shao-ch'i's work during this same period is quite different. After returning to China from Moscow in the summer of 1922, all of his work was done in the workers' movement. His first activities were among the coal miners in Anyuan, where he and Li Li-san led huge strikes and organized several trade unions, and Liu became one of the most important leaders.

In the summer of 1925 Liu went to Shanghai, where he participated in the May Thirtieth Movement and helped in the organization of trade unions. In the latter part of the year he was sent by the party to Tientsin to help in the organization of the workers' movement there.

In the spring of 1926 Liu went to Canton, where he organized, together with Li Li-san and Teng Chung-hsia, the Third Congress of the National General Labor Union and he was elected secretary of the congress and a member of the NGLU executive committee. After this Liu became well known, and one of the most important leaders in the trade union movement.

At the end of 1926 Liu went to Wuhan as a delegate from the NGLU in order to lead the workers' movement. He remained there until July 1927, when the Kuomintang purge took place.

From the above brief descriptions of the two men one may say that, generally speaking, up to mid-1927 Mao's main area of work was in the Kuomintang and with the peasant movement, while Liu's work was entirely in the working-class movement. Therefore, we can say that during this period there was no direct working relationship between Mao and Liu.

After the defeat of the 1925-27 revolution, the policies of the Comintern changed from opportunism to adventurism. It was during this turn that Mao began to play an important role in carrying out the party's line by organizing the peasants into guerrilla units and carrying out the "Autumn Harvest Uprising." After the failure of the uprising he became one of the most important leaders of the guerrilla and soviet movement in Kiangsi until 1934. Nevertheless, during this period, Mao was still under the leadership of Ch'u Ch'iu-pai, Li Li-san, and Wang Ming—ideological leaders of the Central Committee of the CCP—who criticized him very severely, especially the Wang Ming group, which dealt him a very severe blow after the Central Committee moved to the soviet base in Kiangsi in 1933. All of Mao's powers were, in reality, taken away from him, and he was left with only the name of "Chairman of the Soviet Government," while the vice-chairman, Hsiang Ying, took over almost all the responsibilities.

The situation only changed for Mao at the meeting of the Central Committee of the CCP held in Tsun-i during the Long March, where Mao took over the leadership of the party. Yet, he did not control the whole party and the army, because the followers of Wang Ming captured many leading posts, and because a part of the army remained behind in Kiangsi, Anhwei, and Chekiang led by Hsiang Ying, who was a follower of Wang Ming and refused to accept Mao's leadership. It was not until the Seventh Congress of the CCP in 1945 that Mao was able to gain complete supremacy over the party.

This same period (1928-45) found Liu Shao-ch'i in much different circumstances. After 1928 Liu's work was mainly inside the party. Until about 1931 he worked in Peking and Manchuria, and then in 1932 he was sent to the soviet area in Kiangsi, where he was assigned to the workers' movement. (In reality, he had no work there, since there was no workers' movement in the soviet areas.) He arrived just about the time when Mao lost all of his powers.

In the autumn of 1934 Liu was sent north, where he again began to work for the party in Peking, and became the secretary of the party's Northern Bureau. It was during his work at this time that he helped to launch the anti-Japanese movement of September 9, 1935. It was from this movement that Liu, along with P'eng Chen and others, was able to win many new, young, and talented recruits to the party, such as Liu Lan-t'ao, Chiang Nan-hsiang, Lu P'ing, Teng T'o, etc.

At the beginning of 1938 Liu was recalled to Yenan to participate in the work of the Central Committee and Political Bureau of the CCP, where for the first time he collaborated closely with Mao Tse-tung.

In 1938 Liu, as secretary of the newly created Central Plains Bureau, was sent as a special representative from the Central Committee to the region occupied by the New Fourth Army (NFA). This army had been organized out of the many small guerrilla units in the South which had not made the Long March. The commander of this army was Yeh T'ing, and the vice-commander and political commissar was Hsiang Ying.

At this time there was a dispute taking place between Mao and Wang Ming over the question of collaboration with the Kuomintang, and since Hsiang Ying was in agreement with Wang Ming, it was Liu's mission to try and reduce the influence of the Wang Mingists in the New Fourth Army.

In January 1941 the New Fourth Army was attacked by Chiang Kai-shek's forces, and Yeh T'ing was captured and imprisoned by Chiang; Hsiang Ying was killed in action. Afterward, Ch'en I took over as commander while Liu Shao-ch'i took Hsiang Ying's place as political commissar. Liu also dissolved the Southeastern Bureau, of which Hsiang Ying had been the secretary, and incorporated its jurisdiction under the Central Plains Bureau, of which he himself was secretary. Liu then became the party's most important leader in those areas under the influence of the Kuomintang and those areas occupied by Japanese imperialism. During this time he greatly expanded the influence of the party throughout these areas, and at the same time increased the numbers of the New Fourth Army, destroying in the process all the influence of Wang Ming's group. In other words, he brought the entire NFA under Mao's direction, since before, while under the influence of the followers of Wang Ming, the NFA had not always obeyed Mao's directives. This was a great contribution to Mao and his position, and there followed a very close collaboration between Liu and Mao.

In the autumn of 1942 Liu returned to Yenan to work in the Political Bureau, and he became recognized as the party's number-two leader after Mao.

During the next few years Liu helped Mao to discredit Wang Ming and his supporters in the Central Committee. He also helped Mao prepare several documents, such as the "Resolution on Some Questions in the History of Our Party" (adopted by the Seventh Plenum of the Central Committee in April 1945) and "The New Statutes of the CCP" (adopted at the Seventh Congress of the CCP, April-June 1945).

In the first document, all the defeats which the CCP had suffered were blamed on Ch'en Tu-hsiu, Ch'ü Ch'iu-pai, Li Li-san, and especially Wang Ming and his group. Ch'en Tu-hsiu was blamed for the defeat of the 1925-27 revolution; Ch'ü Ch'iu-pai and Li Li-san were blamed for the defeats during the adventurist period; and Wang Ming was held responsible for the defeat of the Red Army in Kiangsi, which was followed by the Long March. The Comintern was never singled out for any rebuke whatsoever. This document justified Mao's work as always having been correct, and praised Liu for his position from 1928 to 1932.

The second document, which was probably written by Liu Shao-ch'i and which was reported on by him at the Seventh Congress, stated in the preamble: "The CCP takes the theories of Marxism-Leninism and the combined principles derived from the practical experience of the Chinese revolution—the ideas of Mao Tse-tung—as the guiding principles of all its work."[1]

Liu's whole report was along this very line, praising Mao's thought as the supreme guide of the Chinese revolution.

The congress ended by electing Mao as the supreme leader of the party, and Liu as one of its top leaders, while almost all of Wang Ming's followers were either removed from the Central Committee or set back to candidate status. (Of the forty-four members and nineteen candidates in the new Central Committee, Wang Ming and a close collaborator of his were elected members in the next-to-last and last positions.)

Following the congress, Mao and Liu collaborated closely in the struggle against Chiang Kai-shek. With the victory of the CCP in 1949, Mao became the chairman of the People's Republic of China, and Liu its vice-chairman; the ensuing close collaboration between Mao and Liu is well known.

Q: When did the differences between Mao and Liu develop, and over what questions?

A: There were, of course, no major political differences during the period I have just described. According to some recent news, major differences became apparent over the question of the agricultural cooperative movement. For example, the newspaper *The Red Guards in the Capital* reported that in 1955-56 "Liu Shao-ch'i openly and frankly dared to sabotage the movement of cooperativization. In 1955 he helped Teng Tzu-hui [then head of the CCP's Rural Work Department] to cut off the formation of 200,000 cooperatives." This accusation is, of course, far from concrete. Yet it is sufficient to demonstrate that a major difference between Mao and Liu developed in 1955.

Mao proposed his plan of agricultural cooperativization in 1955, and insisted that it be completed in a very short time. His plan called for the completion of 850,000 cooperatives before the end of the year. Liu Shao-ch'i, Teng Tzu-hui, and others, probably basing themselves on some of the past experiences of the Soviet Union, as well as on some of Lenin's ideas concerning collectivization, advocated a much more prudent policy of long-term collectivization (Liu was reported by a Red Guard newspaper to have said, in a speech given at the conference of national propaganda workers in 1951, that "some comrades think that socialism in the countryside can be realized through the peasant mutual aid groups and cooperatives. This is, however, impossible. It is the utopian idea of 'agricultural socialism.' The realization of socialism in the countryside, i.e., collectivization, without industrialization, is absolutely impossible." This statement tends to indicate that Liu has studied some of Lenin's works on collectivization and industrialization.)

Liu, Teng, and their supporters were able to secure the majority of the National People's Congress for a program that called for the completion of cooperativization only in 1967. Mao was against this decision, and over the head of the NPC he called a conference of municipal, provincial, and regional party secretaries which decided that the agricultural collectivization should be completed in 1957.[2]

This was the first major difference between Liu and Mao, and it is clearly and closely connected with the later differences over the "People's Communes."

Q: In previous discussions you have stated that the most important difference was over de-Stalinization. You explained that while Mao was opposed to de-Stalinization, Liu seems to have been in agreement with it. Are there any facts to substantiate this?

A: Yes, it is true that this is the most serious difference between Mao and Liu. The Maoists have openly called Liu the "Chinese Khrushchev." The origin of this label is precisely over the question of de-Stalinization. The article recently published in the Red Guard newpaper *Chingkang-shan*, entitled "See the Ugly Face of Liu Shao-ch'i," stated that at the Eighth Congress of the CCP in September 1956 Liu revised the statutes of the party, changing the sentence from the preamble which I quoted earlier: "The CCP takes the theories of Marxism-Leninism and the combined principles derived from the practical experience of the Chinese revolution—the ideas of Mao Tse-tung—as the guiding principles of all its work." In the 1956 party constitution this read simply: "The Communist Party of China takes Marxism-Leninism as its guide to action."[3]

Thus, any reference to Mao and his thought was deleted. The author of the article in the Red Guard journal considered this to be proof that Liu was in most malicious opposition to the great leader, Chairman Mao.

The Eighth Congress of the CCP not only revised the party constitution, removing the reference to Mao, but also emphasized the prohibition of any personality cult. This can be seen very clearly in Teng Hsiao-p'ing's report on the revision of the party constitution:

The Twentieth Congress of the Communist Party of the Soviet Union has thrown a searching light on the profound significance of adhering to the principle of collective leadership and combating the cult of the individual, and this illuminating lesson has produced a tremendous effect not only on the Communist Party of the Soviet Union but also on the Communist parties of all other countries throughout the world.[4]

And: "An important achievement of the Twentieth Congress of the Communist Party of the Soviet Union lies in the fact that it shows us what serious consequences can follow from the deification of the individual."[5]

And: "Of course the cult of the individual is a social phenomena with a long history, and it cannot but find certain reflections in our Party and public life. It is our task to continue to observe faithfully the Central Committee's principle of opposition to the elevation and glorification of the individual. . . ."[6]

Teng, who became the general secretary of the party at this congress, has, along with Liu, been attacked as one of the "top leaders in the party who are taking the capitalist road."

It is very clear that under the impact of the Twentieth Congress of the CPSU and de-Stalinization, the majority of the Central Committee accepted the ideas of opposition to the personality cult; hence the removal of the reference to Mao and his thought from the party constitution and the prohibition of his personal cult.

It is necessary to point out that Teng's words about the personality cult reflecting the society and the party are very important, as this was in direct reference to Mao Tse-tung himself. Since the Seventh Congress in 1945, and especially since the CCP took power in 1949, Mao Tse-tung has deliberately established his personal cult, and has considered himself as "the Sun in the East," and "the Chinese Stalin." For example, there is a song, "The East Is Red," which has the following verse:

> The east is red,
> The sun rises.
> China has brought forth a Mao Tse-tung.
> He works for the people's happiness,
> He is the people's great saviour.[7]

After Mao's talks with Stalin in Moscow in 1950, a new song was composed, "Mao Tse-tung and Stalin Are Like the Sun Shining in the Sky." These two songs have been scored for orchestration, and at the beginning of important meetings, especially when Mao was in attendance, one or both of these songs were played, while everybody stood and afterward shouted, "Long Live Chairman Mao Tse-tung!" This became almost a religious ceremony. After the beginning of de-Stalinization in the USSR, however, this ceremony was discontinued in China.

The effects of de-Stalinization in China constituted, without a doubt, a severe personal blow to Mao, and under the pressure of existing conditions Mao was obliged to make certain concessions, tolerate the changes—if only for the time being—and wait for more favorable circumstances in order to reassert his own cult.

At the Eighth Congress Mao made a speech in which he declared:

At its Twentieth Congress held not long ago, the Communist Party of the Soviet Union formulated many correct policies and criticized short-comings which were found in the Party. It can be confidently asserted that very great developments will follow on this in its work. . . . In transforming China from a backward, agricultural country into an advanced, industrialized one, we are confronted with many strenuous tasks and our experience is far from being adequate. So we must be good at studying. We must be good at learning from our forerunner, the Soviet Union. . . .[8]

This demonstrates that Mao at this time could not oppose the anticult atmosphere, and that it was only against his will that he tolerated the anticult actions of the party.

If one compares the Seventh and Eighth congresses of the CCP one can see clearly the decline of Mao's prestige. At the Seventh Congress, Mao made the political report, and with Liu's help Mao's "thought" was incorporated into the party constitution, thus establishing his personal cult. At the Eighth Congress, however, the political reporter was Liu, Mao's "thought" was removed from the constitution, and measures were taken to prohibit his personal cult. This shows what a tremendous effect Khrushchev's de-Stalinization has had, and it is clear why Mao became so hostile toward Khrushchev, as well as toward Liu Shao-ch'i and Teng Hsiao-p'ing.

Q. Earlier, you stated that the differences between Mao and Liu on the cooperative movement were closely connected to the differences concerning the People's Communes. Could you explain this?

A: Until recently, Liu was thought to have been a supporter of the People's Communes idea launched by Mao. However, the recent facts have revealed that this is not true. In the article, "The Crimes of Liu Shao-ch'i," it was stated:

At a meeting called by the Central Committee, which was attended by seventy-eight cadres in January 1962, he [Liu Shao-ch'i] made a revision-ist report. He violently attacked the "Three Red Banners" and exagger-ated to the utmost errors and mistakes in our work.[9] He felt that the temporary economic difficulties were due to these errors and mistakes— 30 percent due to natural disasters, 70 percent due to artificial disasters. He attacked the 1959 struggle against the rightists as being excessive and even said, in an attempt to rehabilitate the rightists, that the struggle itself was a mistake. He maliciously said that the party lacks democracy, and that party life is a "brutal struggle" and a "pitiless fight," attacking Chairman Mao's correct leadership of the Central Committee.

From the many attacks against Liu, one can conclude the following:

1. Liu opposed the "Three Red Banners" policy, that is, he opposed the People's Communes launched by Mao. This stems logically from his opposition to Mao's cooperativist movement.

2. Liu considered the economic difficulties as mainly the result of artificial disasters; that is, he felt that the economic troubles from 1960 were a result of the People's Communes and Great Leap Forward policies.

3. Liu's opinion that the party was mistaken in the struggle against the rightists of 1959, and in the purging of Defense Minister P'eng Te-huai, Huang K'o-ch'eng, and others, means that he felt their criticism of the People's Communes was correct, and therefore he felt they should be rehabilitated.

4. Liu's charges that the CCP lacked democracy, that party life was a "brutal struggle" and a "pitiless fight," mean that Liu felt that Mao's purge of P'eng Te-huai and the others was a very dangerous symptom.

These four points show that very serious differences existed at that time between Liu and Mao.

Following the failure of the People's Communes and the economic disaster, Mao let Liu take over the reins of the party and deal with the serious difficulties. Liu, along with Teng Hsiao-p'ing, put into effect a rectification campaign which included many reforms, such as reestablishing private plots, a free market, personal ownership of livestock, and doing away with most of the public kitchens, public nurseries, etc. All the reforms met with a very favorable response from the great majority of the people, and therefore Liu won their respect and support, as well as that of most of the party cadres.

Q: Are there, or have there been, any differences between Mao and Liu over questions of literature, art, and education?

A: Differences between Mao and Liu do exist over these questions. Your interview with Chen Pi-lan explained some of the differences which exist between Mao and the opposition as a whole.[10] The fact that Chou Yang was one of the main leaders of the opposition in the cultural field shows that it was under the influence of Liu Shao-ch'i. One can find proof of this in an article in the *People's Daily*, April 25, 1967, entitled "Crush the Counter-revolutionary Program of Peaceful Transition—Expose the Words of the Chinese Khrushchev Concerning the Problems of Writers." In this article it was stated that in March 1953 Liu Shao-ch'i asked Chou Yang and others to discuss with him questions concerning the writers. During these discussions Liu was supposed to have advocated the necessity of writers having more time to study, allowing them to write freely, and not interfering with their creative freedom.

These same ideas were expressed by Liu in his political report to the Eighth Congress of the CCP, September 1956, and the congress adopted a resolution based on Liu's report. This resolution stated: "In order to ensure the full flowering of science and art, we must steadfastly give effect to the policy of 'letting flowers of many kinds blossom and diverse schools of thought contend.' It is wrong to impose restrictions and arbitrary measures on science and art through administrative channels."[11]

This shows that Liu's ideas on these questions are much different from those of Mao.

When Liu took over the reins of the party (in 1960) he carried out a much more moderate policy in the fields of literature, art, and education, allowing much more freedom to the artists and writers. As a result, the work in the cultural fields improved to a certain degree under Liu's direction of the party. This, combined with the improvement in the economy, rallied to Liu's side most of the cultural workers, as well as the party cadres. The Peking Municipal Party Committee, led by P'eng Chen, is a good example. This turn of events led to the increasing isolation of Mao, and he even felt that his leadership position had been brought into question.

Q: What was Mao's reaction to this situation?

A: Mao saw the hopelessness of waging a struggle inside the party; he therefore turned toward the army. After 1960 Mao, through Lin Piao, Lo Jung-huan, and Hsiao Hua, launched a broad movement in the People's Liberation Army to study "Mao Tse-tung Thought," under the pretext of "correcting the mistaken line of P'eng Te-huai and Huang K'o-ch'eng."

Lin Piao proposed to the Central Military Committee a resolution entitled "The Correct Handling of Four Questions in the Political Fields of the Army." In this resolution Lin placed his emphasis on the importance of the role of man, politics, and thought. Some time later, the Military Committee adopted a "Resolution Concerning Political Work in the Army." This resolution set forth fourteen provisions. The first one stated that "it is necessary that Mao Tse-tung Thought be in command in all spheres of the army." Before this, the slogan had been "Politics in Command," but now openly, and probably for the first time, this was spelled out clearly to mean "Mao Tse-tung Thought" in command.

It was following the adoption of this resolution that Lin Piao demanded: "Everyone must read Chairman Mao's books, listen to Chairman Mao's words, work according to Chairman Mao's instructions, to become a good fighter of Chairman Mao."

An editorial published on January 1, 1966, in the *Liberation Army Daily* even stated that "every word of Chairman Mao is truth. . . . We must firmly support and carry out everything conforming to Mao Tse-tung's thought and we must firmly resist and oppose anything which does not conform to Mao's thought." The reasoning behind such statements is very clear. No longer were the directives of the Central Committee, headed by Liu Shao-ch'i, to be followed, if they did not correspond to Mao's own personal thinking.

Mao also attempted to purge Liu's supporters in the party. In September 1963 Mao proposed a resolution entitled "Some Current Problems Raised in the Socialist Education Movement in the Rural Areas" (the twenty-three article document). This resolution was not adopted by the Political Bureau; nevertheless, it was circulated throughout the party. This document then formed the basis of the "Four Clean-ups Movement," i.e., the Socialist Education Movement to clean up politics, ideology, organization, and economy. The main purpose of this movement was to purge those cadres who supported Liu, but the movement met with strong resistance, and in many places was sabotaged. The movement had no great effect except for the purging of some lower ranking cadres in the People's Communes and the district party committees. Therefore, Mao became even more dependent upon the army, and put forward a theory to carry on the struggle outside the party. The foundation of this theory was the idea that the class struggle continues after the victory of the proletariat and is reflected inside the party.

In a plenum of the Central Committee in September 1962 Mao put forward the slogan "We must not forget the class struggle!"

This same plenum issued a communiqué, on Mao's insistence, which said:

throughout the historical period of transition from capitalism to communism . . . there is class struggle between the proletariat and the bourgeoisie and struggle between the socialist road and the capitalist road. . . . This class struggle inevitably finds expression within the Party. . . . While waging a struggle against foreign and domestic class enemies, we must remain vigilant and resolutely oppose in good time various opportunist ideological tendencies in the Party. The great historic significance of the Eighth Plenary Session of the Eighth Central Committee held in Lushan in August 1959 lies in the fact that it victoriously smashed attacks by right opportunism, i.e., revisionism, and safeguarded the Party line and the unity of the Party.[12]

Here we can see that Mao is directly attacking Liu's defense of P'eng Te-huai and Liu's suggestion that those who had been purged should be rehabilitated.

During 1963 and 1964 the Central Committee of the CCP published nine articles criticizing the CPSU. The ninth article was entitled "On Khrushchev's Phoney Communism and Its Historical Lessons for the World" (July 14, 1964). This article maintained that under the leadership of the revisionist Khrushchev the USSR had been transformed from a socialist to a capitalist state. The implication was, of course, that it was necessary to unleash a struggle inside the party against all revisionists, otherwise China herself would "change color."

At a meeting of the All-China Federation of Literature and Art Circles in June 1964 Mao made an address in which he warned that

In the past fifteen years, these associations and most of their publications have for the most part failed . . . to carry out the policies of the party. . . . In the recent years, they have even verged on revisionism. If they do not make serious efforts to remold themselves, sooner or later they are bound to become groups of the Hungarian Petöfi Club type.

These words were a frank warning to those cadres working in the cultural fields under the influence of Liu's leadership.

All the arguments elaborated by Mao, such as those mentioned above, were a preparation for the purge of "those people in power who are taking the capitalist road," which was to follow.

Recently, *Red Flag* and the *People's Daily* published an article entitled "A Great Historic Document" in which they stated:

> Lenin saw that after the proletariat seized power, the defeated bourgeoisie still remained stronger than the proletariat and was always trying to stage a comeback. . . . In order to cope with this counter-revolutionary threat and overcome it, it was therefore necessary to strengthen the dictatorship of the proletariat over a long period of time. There was no other way. However, Lenin died before he could solve these problems in practice. Stalin was a great Marxist-Leninist who actually cleared out a large number of counter-revolutionary representatives of the bourgeoisie who had sneaked into the Party, including Trotsky, Zinoviev, Kamenev, Radek, Bukharin, Rykov and their like.[13]

These words not only demonstrate that Mao tries to justify his purge of the opposition led by Liu Shao-ch'i and Teng Hsiao-p'ing on the basis of Lenin's theory, but also justifies his purge on Stalin's famous frame-up trials in the 1930s. From this, one can see clearly what Mao has in mind for Liu, Teng, and the rest of the opposition.

Q: Are there any differences between Mao and Liu on foreign policy?

A: In the last interview I pointed out that the position of the opposition on foreign policy questions is much more difficult to determine, since there is less material from which to judge, and up to now I have been unable to find any new facts. Nevertheless, the position of Liu on foreign policy is different from Mao's extremely sectarian attitude. Foreign policy is almost always an extension of domestic policy. Therefore, in my opinion, Mao is responsible for China's extremely sectarian foreign policy, which would be in agreement with his extremely sectarian domestic policies. Liu, on the other hand, probably advocates a more moderate foreign policy, in line with his domestic policy. Since Lo Jui-ch'ing has been attacked as one of Liu's strongest supporters, we can almost certainly say that Liu's attitude towards the USSR and the united front with the various socialist countries over the Vietnam War is identical with that of Lo.

Q: You have explained how reference to Mao's thought was included in the party statutes at the Seventh Congress, and how it was removed at the Eighth Congress, as well as the campaign carried out in the army on how everything was to be done under the guidance of Mao's thought. Now, in the "Cultural Revolution," Mao's thought stands out as one of its most prominent characteristics. Other than the personality cult aspect, can you briefly describe what Mao's thought actually is?

A: Broadly speaking, Mao's thought boils down to nothing more than the practical application in China of Stalin's theories. The essence of Stalinism consists of opportunism and adventurism, the revolution by stages, socialism in one country, and bureaucratic centralism, which finds its most pronounced form in personal dictatorship. All these things can not only be found in Mao's theoretical works, but also in his actions. Here I will only give a few examples.

You will recall some of the things I have already said about the "Resolution on Some Questions in the History of Our Party," adopted by the Central Committee in April 1945, in which Mao laid all the blame for all past defeats on Ch'en Tu-hsiu, Ch'ü Ch'iu-pai, and Li Li-san. Mao never analyzed or even pointed out the opportunist or adventurist policies of the CCP during and after the 1925-27 revolution, which had been forced on the CCP by Stalin. That is, Mao accepted Stalin's role and policies of opportunism and adventurism as being correct.

Mao's most important theoretical work is "On New Democracy." When the party adopted the new statutes at the Seventh Congress in 1945, which stated that Mao's thought should be the guide to all the party's actions, the party congress was basing itself on this work, written by Mao in January 1940. At this congress, Lin Po-ch'ü, an important member of the Political Bureau at that time, said: "The theory of 'New Democracy' is the most brilliant manifestation of the universal truth of Marxism-Leninism combined with the concrete revolutionary practice in China. This theory is the sharpest weapon the party and the Chinese people have in the struggle for victory."

Chou En-lai said: "We are dependent on the brilliant leadership of our party's leader and comrade Mao Tse-tung. He has shown us the direction to follow in 'New Democracy.'" With such praise, we should examine the contents of Mao's "New Democracy."

According to Mao, after the October revolution in Russia the national democratic revolution in the colonial and semicolonial countries was a "new bourgeois-democratic revolution." In this revolution, the national bourgeoisie remained a revolutionary class, and hence it was necessary to carry out the "united front" of workers, peasants, petty bourgeoisie, and national bourgeoisie—the bloc of four classes—in order to destroy the imperialists and feudal forces, and to establish a "New Democratic Republic." That is to say, Mao advocated the establishment of a coalition government of four classes, as well as a "New Democratic economy."

The "New Democratic economy" meant the nationalization only of "the big banks and the big industrial and commercial enterprises" by the state; "but the republic will neither confiscate capitalist private property in general nor forbid the development of such capitalist production as does not 'dominate the livelihood of the people'....A rich peasant economy will be allowed in the rural areas."[14]

All this is, of course, self-explanatory, and demonstrates clearly Mao's opportunism.

In Indonesia, where Mao applied the theory of revolution by stages, the revolution has suffered a greater disaster than did the second Chinese revolution, which Stalin led to defeat with the same theory.

Here it should be pointed out that Mao's "On New Democracy" is still considered as the center of Mao Tse-tung's thought. The "Sixteen Point Decision" adopted by the Central Committee in August 1966 put "On New Democracy" as the first work to be studied in studying Mao's thought. The *Liberation Army Daily* published some articles explaining the contents of "On New Democracy," encouraging all the cadres in the army and the party to study it.

As far as Mao's methods are concerned, one can really find no difference between him and Stalin. Mao has always imposed his own opinions upon the party, and the present "Cultural Revolution" is the best example of Mao's bureaucratic methods against the great majority of the party in order to maintain his own personal dictatorship.

Q: What has been your personal relationship with Mao and Liu, and what is your personal appraisal of the two men?

A: Because my work and posts in the party were different from Mao's I did not have much of a working relationship with him. I did have some personal contacts with him, however, only two of which I will describe.

In May 1926, after Chiang Kai-shek's coup d'etat of March 20, I went to Canton as the Central Committee's representative to discuss with Borodin, the Comintern representative. During my stay Mao visited me twice. One time he asked me to address his peasant school. The other time he brought an article he had written on the different strata among the peasantry, on which he asked my opinion. In his article he had divided the peasantry into many different strata according to the amount of land they owned. I then told him that in Lenin's opinion the peasants were divided mainly into three categories—rich, middle, and poor— depending upon the amount of land they were able to farm and what they needed in order to maintain their families. Mao did not reject my criticism and seemed to have accepted it.

In June 1927 I saw Mao for the last time in Wuhan. At that time he was very disappointed with the revolution, although he never discussed with me how the revolution could be rescued from the dangerous situation which existed. He was only concerned with finding a safe place for his family, and he asked my wife, Ch'en Pi-lan, if she could help him.

My contact with Liu Shao-ch'i is somewhat different. In Shanghai in 1920 I studied Marxism and Russian together with Liu, and our relationship was quite close. In 1921-22 we studied together in Moscow, during which time I was able to recruit him to the party.

After returning to Shanghai from Moscow in August 1924 all my work was in the party itself, and especially in the Political Bureau, as head of the Propaganda Department. I therefore had no real working relationship with Liu, although I saw him several times during my stay in Canton, and again in Wuhan during the summer of 1927. The last time I saw Liu was in the summer of 1929. At this time Ch'en Tu-hsiu and I had started to organize the Left Opposition. Liu, of course, understood my position in relation to the party, yet nevertheless he visited me at my home. During this visit we discussed the party's policy, and I criticized the party's present policy of adventurism as well as the bureaucratic organizational methods of the leadership. I also pointed out that during the workers' and peasants' uprising in the spring of 1927 the party should have then organized soviets in preparation for the taking of power. With all these criticisms Liu expressed his agreement, but could not bring himself to join the Left Opposition and struggle against the leadership. Liu was considered in the party at that time a "conciliator."

As far as my personal appraisal of the two men goes, I would say from a political point of view that both of them are Stalinists. After the defeat of the second Chinese revolution, neither of them accepted the lessons of the defeat, and they remained in the Stalinized CCP following Stalin's line on all fundamental questions. Nevertheless, from the point of view of character and personal experience, the two men are quite different. While both men are very strong willed, Mao is very arbitrary while Liu is much more considerate.

Due to Mao's experiences of working in the Kuomintang, and especially his work in organizing the peasants and guerrilla warfare, his arbitrary character has been reinforced. Hence, upon coming to power in 1949, regardless of the opinions or well-being of the majority, Mao deliberately established his personal cult and personal dictatorship. The cooperativization, the Great Leap Forward, the People's Communes, and the present Cultural Revolution, as well as China's sectarian foreign policy, are all the result of Mao's arbitrariness.

Liu's life work, however, has mainly been among the working masses, and at times under very difficult circumstances, such as after the defeat of the 1925-27 revolution when he worked for the party in the underground during the reactionary rule of Chiang Kai-shek. These environmental conditions reinforced his basic thoughtfulness, since he was obliged to listen to the opinions of other cadres in the party and workers' movement who reflected the opinions and aspirations of the masses. Hence, in his dealings with people, he is more capable of reaching a balanced solution, and this is the origin of his personal differences with Mao on cooperativization, People's Communes, etc., as I have already explained.

Q: What, in your opinion, will be the future of China under the leadership of the two men respectively?

A: The above analysis of Liu and Mao shows clearly that Mao represents a more hardened and extreme form of Stalinism. Regardless of the circumstances or the will of the masses he has carried out his adventuristic and sectarian domestic policies. On the other hand, Liu represents a much more moderate and reformist tendency in the party. He attempted to a certain degree to correct Mao's extremist policies, in order to avoid the catastrophic consequences.

In my opinion this same analysis is valid in the present struggle between the two men. If Mao should win, it would be at the expense of all the Left and revolutionary elements, and he will commit China to a most reckless and cataclysmic course, in which the Chinese revolution would be placed in grave danger. If Liu should win, China's domestic course will most likely be similar to that carried out when the party was under Liu's leadership, with China's foreign policy becoming less sectarian and possibly resulting in a united front with other socialist countries, including the USSR, to aid the Vietnamese and their struggle.

In a China under Liu's leadership there would definitely be more freedom in the party and society, although the overall question of the Stalinist bureaucracy would not be solved. Nevertheless, Liu's victory could be a first phase in the development of a real revolutionary struggle for socialist democracy.

THE MAY FOURTH MOVEMENT AND THE "GREAT PROLETARIAN CULTURAL REVOLUTION"

We are now at the fiftieth anniversary of the May Fourth Movement, a movement that had a tremendous impact on modern Chinese history.[1] *Ming Pao Monthly*'s preparation of a special commemorative issue on May Fourth is a very important event. Although the movement took place a half century ago, it has still not received the recognition and analysis it deserves. On the contrary, the significance of the May Fourth Movement has been arbitrarily distorted and deliberately rewritten, especially by Chinese Communist historians, to a point beyond recognition. For that reason, if the special issue offers authentic historical data, serious analysis, and objective evaluation of the movement, it will make an important contribution to modern Chinese history.

Ming Pao Monthly has asked me to write about my recollections of the May Fourth Movement and I gladly agreed. In my opinion, however, while that kind of personal recollection has some value, it is far more worthwhile to discuss the meaning and contribution of the movement to the development of Chinese thought and culture. From that kind of discussion the young generation can get a true historical picture of the movement and can learn lessons from it as well.

In essence the May Fourth Movement was an enlightenment movement of the Chinese bourgeoisie. In other words, it was the Chinese bourgeoisie's cultural revolution. It we compare it with the "Great Proletarian Cultural Revolution" of the last three

---

This article contrasting the mass cultural radicalization of 1919, the May Fourth Movement, with Mao's Cultural Revolution was written in April 1969 for the Hong Kong liberal magazine Ming Pao Monthly. *It has not previously been published in English.*

years on the mainland, this comparison can only show the important contribution made by the former and the unparalleled destruction and lamentable consequences of the latter on Chinese culture. Therefore, rather than writing the personal recollection originally planned, I shall discuss "The May Fourth Movement and the Great Proletarian Cultural Revolution" in hopes that such a discussion will serve a greater purpose.

Twenty-three years ago I wrote an article entitled "On the Epoch-making Significance of the May Fourth Movement" (published in the May 1, 1946, issue of *Searching for Truth*). At that time, in addition to pointing out the significance and contributions of the movement, I also provided a very detailed description and analysis of it, which I based on the important articles by Ch'en Tu-hsiu, Hu Shih, Li Ta-chao, and others in *Hsin ch'ing-nien*, the ideological "center" of the movement. Therefore, in this article I will not repeat all that has been written before. Instead I will simply summarize the important points and conclusions of my earlier article in order to present my evaluation of this great movement.

The article began by saying:

The May Fourth Movement, in its immediate sense, was a political movement that resisted the external Japanese imperialist aggression and opposed the internal treachery of the Anfu dictatorship.[2]. . . The students of Peking, who spontaneously and with great courage went into action, held strikes and marches that directly attacked the lair of the treacherous bureaucrats (Chao-chia-lou Street), and they punished the traitors with their own hands (for instance burning down Ts'ao Ju-lin's house and beating up Chang Tsung-hsiang).[3] Throughout the country there was sympathy for and a response to the Peking students. For instance, students, workers, and merchants went on strike on a national level, and a campaign to boycott Japanese goods was organized. Even the stubborn and reactionary Anfu clique had to dismiss several traitors (Ts'ao, Lu, Chang) and announce that the government had refused to sign the Versailles Treaty.[4]. . . All of these are significant historical facts that deserve emphasis. However, the epoch-making significance of the May Fourth Movement is not just restricted to its political implications. Rather, it had an even greater impact on Chinese culture and thought. In other words, the real meaning of the May Fourth Movement lies in its having been the Chinese bourgeois enlightenment movement. And, in the course of the movement, the foundations of the enlightenment movement of another class [the proletariat] were also laid.

Acceptance of Western radical democracy, on the basis of which all aspects of Chinese feudal traditions were thoroughly repudiated (by Ch'en Tu-hsiu); adoption of the colloquial language in place of the classical Chinese of the gentry (by Hu Shih); and lastly introduction of the highest development of Western culture—scientific socialism—into China (Li Ta-chao): the synthesis of these three themes crystallized the epoch-making significance of the May Fourth Movement.

My article concluded by pointing out:

The May Fourth Movement was a real epoch-making movement in Chinese history. It unleashed vehement criticisms and a full-fledged denial of the validity of the old ethical system that had dominated Chinese spiritual life for over two thousand years (for example, the use of Chinese classical books as texts). The movement bravely and resolutely attacked Confucianism, toppling the idol of the "supreme saint," the "teacher of the ages," which is almost the equivalent of destroying the idolatry of Jesus Christ in Europe. Similarly the movement deserted the classical language, which had been regarded as the "orthodox" and "pure" Chinese language by the educated classes, and replaced it with the vernacular language spoken by the masses. This is quite similar to the replacement of Latin with the vernacular languages in Europe in the Renaissance.[5] Finally, the movement introduced to China the world view of Western culture developed to its highest level—scientific socialism (Marxism)—in a serious way for the first time in Chinese history. Moreover, the movement immediately applied the method of analysis of Marxism to interpret the change of thought in modern China, especially the transformation of Chinese ideology during the movement. Our past enlightenment movements had not raised, nor even thought of raising, these epoch-making changes.

Therefore, we can say that if the Enlightenment movement of eighteenth century France is typical of the enlightenment movements in advanced Western countries, our May Fourth Movement is then the model of enlightenment movements for backward Oriental countries. . . .

Because of the achievements of the May Fourth Movement, the minds of our generation were thus freed from the chains of Confucianism and thus we could think, believe, and criticize freely. In addition our pens were liberated from the fetters of the classical language and we could thus express our own feelings and ideas and create our own literature. Moreover, we became familiar with the method and viewpoint of scientific socialism, which enabled us to study the historical development of humanity, to examine the inner relations of the whole world, to anticipate the future development of society, and finally to seek the programs and strategy to enable us to change and reshape it. In particular, the movement's courageous and critical spirit that stood up to the old traditions and outmoded thoughts, its serious and sober attitude toward new ideas and new theories, and its burning thirst for truth were all spiritual reflections of an epoch that was making radical progress. Our next generation should treasure this valuable heritage.

The synthesis of democratic ideas and the use of the colloquial language, under the encouragement of the May Fourth Movement, has given birth to a new literature and art. New writers, novels, poems, dramas, prose, and translations of first-rate literature from the West prospered and flourished. Through the May Fourth Movement a new road opened up for Chinese literature and art. In addition, the introduction of new schools of thought, the study of the Russian revolution, the debates over capitalism versus socialism, science versus metaphysics, and Marxism versus anarchism, and especially the research and controversies among young people regarding social problems were not carried out only in tiny groups. Rather this took place in all kinds of new magazines and newspaper supplements. It reflected a rapidly growing and immense intellectual ferment.

At about the same time young people who believed in Marxism were quickly attracted to the Communist groups formed by Ch'en Tu-hsiu and Li Ta-chao. These groups culminated in the formal establishment of the Chinese Communist Party in 1921, and it was this party that organized the great 1925-27 revolution.

All of these things were the products of the May Fourth Movement in the spheres of culture and thought.

Forty-seven years after the May Fourth Movement, Mao Tse-tung opened up the "Great Proletarian Cultural Revolution" (the slogan was first advanced in May 1966) and organized the struggles which drew all of China into a storming whirlpool. Now, almost three years later, the effects of the Cultural Revolution in the field of culture can be clearly shown. We are now able to examine it, judge it, evaluate it, and learn from its negative aspects.

The real purpose of Mao's "Great Proletarian Cultural Revolution" was to "bring down the capitalist-roaders in power in the party." That is, it aimed to seize the party leadership from Liu Shao-ch'i, Teng Hsiao-p'ing, P'eng Chen, and others, and to mobilize the people to suppress and defeat them once and for all. Armed struggles, bloody conflicts, and regional civil wars took place all over the country and resulted in the sacrifice of the lives of several hundred thousand students, workers, and peasants. It also had "great results" (as the Maoists boast) on the cultural side. The main "results" are as follows:

1. All members and cadres responsible for cultural work in the Chinese CP and the government, ranging from the minister of the Central Cultural Department, its deputy minister, the minister of education, all the leading figures in all other cultural and

educational departments or branches, provincial and regional leaders and workers in the same field, the overwhelming majority of the presidents, professors, and teachers in the universities, specialized colleges, and senior middle schools, and also almost all the writers and artists (musicians, painters, film directors, and even actors), and almost all the scholars and researchers in various specialized fields have been purged. Some of them were even driven to commit suicide (such as Lao She and Fu Lei, etc.).

2. All over the country the publication of all literary, artistic, and academic periodicals, of all literary works, including translations and textbooks, was stopped or prohibited. Instead, the printing presses and paper in the country were used to print Mao Tse-tung's *Selected Works* and *Quotations*. Even the printing of the complete works of Marx, Engels, and Lenin came to a halt. They were to be replaced by the *Selected Works* and *Quotations* of Mao.

3. All over the country the universities, specialized colleges, and secondary schools were suspended for nearly three years. Although classes have recently been reopened, *normal classes* still have not been restored. The army and "Mao Tse-tung Thought workers' propaganda teams" were sent to every campus to carry out the "struggle, criticize, transformation" movement, which caused tremendous confusion and disruption in the schools. Millions of secondary and university students were forced to go to work in the countryside, factories, mines, and border regions in order to "reform through labor." It has further been announced that an "educational revolution" will be put into effect. Although details have not yet been disclosed, it can be seen from articles in the *People's Daily* that courses other than the sciences and engineering will either be canceled or greatly curtailed, and will be replaced by the teaching of the *Selected Works of Mao Tse-tung* and the learning of "Mao Tse-tung Thought." This is similar to the schools the churches ran in medieval Europe, the only difference being that the *Selected Works* take the place of the Bible and Mao's thought replaces theology.

4. Today in China "Mao Tse-tung Thought" is already regarded as the supreme, absolute, and sacred guiding ideology (the so-called Mao Tse-tung Thought in command). Mao himself has become god of the secular world, a new "saint of saints," and the "teacher of all ages." His *Selected Works* are regarded as an encyclopedia, his *Quotations* are glorified as the Bible—"Chairman Mao's sayings are true in every word," "Everyone should

read Chairman Mao's books, hear Chairman Mao's sayings, and act according to Chairman Mao's guidelines." Thus Mao takes upon himself the duties both of Pope Innocent III in the Middle Ages and the ancient Chinese emperor Ch'in Shih Huang. How wonderful it is! Unprecedented in the past, never to be surpassed in the future.

What I described above is a sketch of the "Great Proletarian Cultural Revolution," a microcosm of terrifying events. If we compare its results with the fruits of the May Fourth Movement, it is not difficult to see how different the two are: The May Fourth Movement destroyed Confucius—the "saint of saints," the "teacher of all ages," while the Cultural Revolution created a new idol in Mao Tse-tung—the "great teacher, the great helmsman, and the great leader." The May Fourth Movement created an entirely new literature and art, and nourished thousands of writers and scientists, while the Cultural Revolution stopped the publication of all literary works and dealt a deadly blow to the writers and intellectuals of a whole generation.

The May Fourth Movement introduced Marxism as a revolutionary theory into China. People could study it freely and believe in it, while the Cultural Revolution replaces Marxism with "Mao Tse-tung Thought" (a Chinese version of Stalinist ideology) as a religious dogma that people are forced to learn and to believe superstitiously. "Everybody must listen to Chairman Mao's words, read Chairman Mao's writings, and do everything according to Chairman Mao's directives." It also aims to make the Chinese people live like the naive Christians of the Roman Church in the Middle Ages, like the subjects of the feudal oppressors; whenever people disagree or doubt Mao's thought, they will be immediately persecuted as the "heretics" of the Middle Ages were.

After reading the above analysis and comparison, one naturally would ask how a ridiculous and absurd phenomenon like the "Great Proletarian Cultural Revolution" could take place in a country that was established through a revolution and is on its way to socialism? Could it be that those who initiated and carried out the Cultural Revolution completely lost their heads and were in a complete state of hysteria? Or could it be, as columnist Joseph Alsop maintained, that the "commander" of the revolution is a "madman"? No, it is not that simple. The mad and absurd expressions of the "Great Proletarian Cultural Revolution" have deep-rooted causes that stem from the economic and political relationships in present Chinese society. In other words, the Cultural Revolution is the sharp, changing, and distorted reflection of the irreconcilable contradictions between the economic base and the political superstructure of present Chinese society. That is the reason why both the events and the people involved exhibit a sort of madness.

Since the creation of the state-private mixed enterprises in 1956, and after the nationalization of all the means of production—the preconditions for speeding up production and raising the living standards and cultural development of the people— China began to move toward socialism in terms of its economic base. However, if China were to develop its society harmoniously, a democratic political system of a socialist character was definitely required. But on top of China's socialist economic base was a totalitarian bureaucratic dictatorship that was not subject to any control from below, and on top of that bureaucracy stood the self-adulating dictator. This is the absolutely irreconcilable contradition between the base and the superstructure of Chinese society.

Under the impact and pressure of various changes inside and outside of the country, the contradictions inevitably sharpened and deepened and came close to erupting. The exposure of Stalin's personality cult and personal dictatorship at the CPSU's Twentieth Congress in 1956; the revolutionary movements toward de-Stalinization and antibureaucratic uprisings in Poand and Hungary in the same year, the opening and then suppression of the 1957 "Hundred Flowers Bloom" movement in China; and the great disaster that resulted from the "Great Leap Forward" and the adventuristic policy of the People's Communes in 1958: all these fit into a context that dealt a heavy blow to the Chinese bureaucratic dictatorship in general, and to Mao's personality cult and dictatorship in particular. Even Mao had to tactically and temporarily retreat behind the scenes and place Liu Shao-ch'i "in power" in order to redress the deteriorating situation.

Faced with the extreme discontent among most of the workers, peasants, and intellectuals, and under the pressure of their demands for change, Liu introduced some mild economic and cultural reforms that temporarily quieted the critical situation. However, as Mao saw it, Liu's reforms and their outcome threatened and damaged Mao's personality cult and dictatorship. In order to restore them, Mao had to throw out those "in power." This is the explanation of Mao's launching of the "Great Proletarian Cultural Revolution" in November 1965.

Mao Tse-tung has successfully used the "Great Proletarian Cultural Revolution" to destroy the Liu-Teng leadership. He is now convoking the Ninth National Congress of the CCP in order to consolidate his victory and rebuild the party in such a way that his dictatorship can be strengthened. Whatever the results of the Ninth Congress, one thing is clear: the once seemingly unshakable CCP, which had enabled Mao to impose his dictatorship earlier, was completely shattered by the Cultural Revolution, and the rebuilt party can never be tightly united and stable. The party carries within itself too many contradictions: contradictions between the army and the party cadres, contradictions within the army, contradictions between the party's old and new cadres, and between the rank and file and the upper levels. All of these are destined to intensify as a result of changes inside and outside the country.

Moreover, the thousands and thousands of young students, intellectuals, and low-level cadres who were sent to work in the villages, mines, factories, and border regions will surely communicate their discontent, grievances, and rebellious sentiments to the masses of workers and peasants, and this will finally fuse with the already existing discontent and anger of the workers and peasants. The result will be that a flood of anger will sweep the country, pull down the bureaucratic caste, and put an end to the arbitrary rule of a dictator. This is a political revolution which, based on the maintenance of socialist property relationships, establishes democratic institutions of socialism. Only such a democratic system can provide sufficient democratic rights, freedom, and equality for all workers, peasants, poor urban strata, and prosocialist intellectuals. Only through such a political revolution can the creativity and active initiative of the masses be fully developed, can industrial and agrarian production be rapidly increased, and can the standard of living and cultural attainment of the people be raised to a higher level. In short, only in this way can China move smoothly toward socialism.

The spirit of the May Fourth Movement remains strong and alive a half-century after its inception. Chinese culture and thought, suppressed during the past nineteen years of CCP domination and disrupted by the Cultural Revolution, have been nearly ruined. Therefore, the "May Fourth spirit"—the demands for democracy, freedom, equality, free discussion, free research, and especially the courageous critical spirit—is bound to be the indispensable moving force if Chinese culture and thought are to be saved and revived. History shows that the deepest darkness always announces the approaching dawn. Therefore we have reason to believe that in the near future the "May Fourth spirit" will be revived and will criticize and eliminate "Mao Tse-tung Thought" and its dictatorship.

April 9, 1969

THE FALL OF LIN PIAO

Question: What was the significance of the "Cultural Revolution"?

Answer: You should ask: Why did Mao need the Cultural Revolution? The fact is that at a certain point he was in a minority in the Political Bureau. In 1957-60, in a completely personalistic and dictatorial way, Mao launched a campaign for agricultural cooperatives. He forced the peasants to join them, just as Stalin did around 1929. This resulted not only in massive resistance among the peasants but also in dissatisfaction among large strata of the rest of the population (workers, students, and intellectuals).

This resistance became apparent in 1957 when the Chinese leadership was forced to begin the "Hundred Flowers" campaign. This liberalization coincided roughly with the Hungarian revolution of 1956. But the campaign took on more and more the character of resistance to the entire party bureaucracy. In Wuhan, for example, a huge opposition developed. Mao was forced to suppress all opposition.

As usual, this Left opposition was portrayed as a "right deviation." Hundreds of thousands of people disappeared from the youth movement, but the feeling of dissatisfaction continued to exist, especially among the intellectuals.

Mao understood very clearly that he had to take measures to

These are excerpts from a two-part interview obtained by Igor Corne- lissen and published in the January 15 and 29, 1972, issues of the Amsterdam weekly Vrij Nederland, *translated in the* Intercontinental Press, *June 5 and 12, 1972. Published here are the sections of the interview dealing with the Cultural Revolution and the disappearance in September 1971 of Defense Minister Lin Piao. The other sections of the interview concerned the early years of the CCP.*

quiet the peasantry. In 1958, he started another big campaign, the campaign for the so-called People's Communes. All small private ownership of land was eliminated. The free market was done away with. Mao also launched the Great Leap Forward, the experiment in which millions of people were forced to produce steel in their backyards. This was a horrendous failure.

As a result, there was a further decline in Mao's position. Now not only the peasants opposed him but also the party leadership, at least the majority of it. In July-August 1959, Mao was forced to call a special meeting of the party Central Committee. Minister of Defense P'eng Te-huai opened the meeting with a sharp attack on Mao, and he was supported by the chief of staff of the army and other members of the Central Committee.

The outcome of the meeting, however, was that P'eng Te-huai and his immediate associates were ousted from their posts. But behind the scenes, Liu Shao-ch'i, the vice-chairman of the party, as well as Marshal Chu Te, had supported P'eng. Mao's position had also been weakened by the secret speech that Khrushchev gave about Stalin in 1956. Liu and Teng Hsiao-p'ing, the general secretary of the party, were in agreement with Khrushchev, at least as regards his criticism of Stalin. Mao on the other hand did not agree with Khrushchev but at that time he could not openly say so.

All these factors together determined the situation in the party in those years.

Mao was forced to take a step backward. In 1959, he had to give up his position as head of state to Liu Shao-ch'i. Many concessions were made in the areas of education and the communes, and the people were given more freedom to express themselves. The opposition to Mao continued to exist. Pamphlets were even circulated demanding his resignation. The Cultural Revolution began in November 1965, when Lin Piao wrote an article on this theme in the army paper. He directed his fire against *all* opposition tendencies.

It is important to keep in mind that Lin Piao had supported Mao earlier, when Liu Shao-ch'i came to the fore as the head of state. *Lin Piao saw this as a threat to his position as Mao's heir.* Mao knew very well that almost the entire intelligentsia supported Liu Shao-ch'i and Teng Hsiao-p'ing, who in turn controlled the party apparatus. On the local level, in Canton, Sinkiang, Manchuria, Shanghai, and many provinces the party opposed Mao.

According to the statutes, at that time Mao should have opened a discussion and called a congress. But he knew that would have meant his downfall. Therefore, Mao had to use the army, but he could not rely on the loyalty of all the units. So, he resorted to using the high school and university students (as the Red Guards). *In fact, power was then taken out of the hands of the party and even of the government.*

Although many party leaders were attacked, they still held their posts. Then Mao ordered the army to support the Red Guards. The conflict that followed was reminiscent in some places of a civil war. In Kwangsi province, several hundred persons, probably several thousand, were killed. Many houses were destroyed. The situation took an especially dangerous turn when the Red Guards also attacked some army commanders (in July 1967), as in Wuhan, where the officer corps was split. At that time, the Cultural Revolution Group—whose core was made up of Ch'en Po-ta (Mao's secretary), Chiang Ch'ing (Mao's wife), K'ang Sheng (a Politburo member), and Wang Li (director of the Central Committee's Propaganda Department)—felt that the army endangered the goals of the Cultural Revolution. This group wanted to launch an attack on the army leadership. *But Lin Piao remained loyal to the military command.*

After this Mao Tse-tung was forced to make concessions to the army leaders. Mao purged the "ultraleftists," such as Wang Li, the writer Ch'i Pen-yu, and also the deputy chief of staff of the army, Yang Ch'eng-wu. This part of the Cultural Revolution Group was purged *under the pressure of the army command.*

All this shows how great the contradiction was between Lin Piao and Mao Tse-tung. Facing the pressure of the military leaders, it was *primarily* Mao who made the concessions. In the period after 1967, Revolutionary Committees arose in almost all localities and were controlled by the military.[1] This conflict between the army and the party became permanent, and through the defeat of Mao's Cultural Revolution the party was also wrecked. Power in the country was now unquestionably in the hands of the army. In this situation, in August 1970, Ch'en Po-ta was purged, no one knows how or by whom.

Lin Piao and his army controlled the entire party. At the beginning of 1968, Lin Piao replaced General Yang Ch'eng-wu, the deputy chief of staff, with Huang Yung-sheng, from Canton. From the moment he took this post, Huang began placing *his* closest associates in important positions, for example, Wu Fa-hsien, the minister of the air force, who also became a member of the Political Bureau. The same thing happened in the navy and in the logistics sections. Everywhere followers of Huang Yung-sheng turned up in important posts.

Q: What happened to Lin Piao?

A: What happened to him physically, we don't know, but politically he is dead. Huang Yung-sheng and all his followers have disappeared. *For months I heard him every day on Radio Peking, since I follow it very closely. But since mid-September I have heard nothing more about him. A lot of months have gone by. It goes without saying that the party members and the military want to know what is going on, but nothing has been disclosed, nothing explained. A big development is being kept secret.*[2]

In my opinion, the purge of the Lin Piao group means that Mao's own position has been enormously weakened. Lin Piao was Mao's heir. That was even emphatically declared in the party constitution. In the party's highest body, the present Political Bureau Standing Committee, Mao still has the support only of Chou En-lai. The other members—Ch'en Po-ta, Lin Piao, and K'ang Sheng—are dead or purged.

How was Mao able to defeat Lin Piao? In my opinion, because he had the support of Chou En-lai. Their common interest was to preserve the party in order to be able to control the army. Of course, Chou En-lai does not have mass support in the army but he knows enough commanders to have an influence. It is important in this connection that Chou was head of the party Military Committee before 1949.

The most important man in the army, and perhaps in all of China, in my opinion, is now Marshal Yeh Chien-ying (member of the Central Committee since 1945, chief of staff of the People's Liberation Army in 1945-47, and a member of the Political Bureau since 1967). In practice, Yeh Chien-ying is acting as minister of defense. When you make a quick survey of the situation, you get the following picture. After the purge of the Lin Piao group, the army has become weaker. Yeh Chien-ying does not have the same kind of influence in the army as a Chu Te (commander in chief 1946-54), a Lin Piao, or a Ch'en I (recently deceased) had. The army may break up into many factions; it may disintegrate.

The same kind of picture is presented by the party. No one has any authority. How can the members have any confidence? No one trusts anyone. I think that many cadres in the army and the party are demoralized. Therefore, it is my opinion that a militarily dangerous situation has arisen. I think that the trend in China now is toward political revolution; there is no other way out.

THE "CRITICIZE LIN, CRITICIZE CONFUCIUS" CAMPAIGN

Question: Since the beginning of 1974, the media in Europe and the United States have reported on the campaign in China to "criticize Lin Piao" and "criticize Confucius." What is the significance of this campaign, which is directed against two historical Chinese figures who are separated by so many centuries in time?

Answer: This campaign is complicated and difficult to understand. The media's attempts to explain it only add to the confusion. Not only Westerners sense the contradictions involved; the Chinese themselves are left in a fog about it. In order to explain the campaign, we must first determine the origin of the conflict between Mao Tse-tung and Lin Piao. This examination must begin with the outcome of the Cultural Revolution movement. I have described in general the origins of this conflict in an interview which was published in January 1972 in the Amsterdam weekly *Vrij Nederland*.[1] In this interview I pointed out that the friction between Lin and Mao was extreme, stemming from the developments of the so-called Cultural Revolution. Lin intervened in the Cultural Revolution with the armed forces under his command. The military controlled almost all the power in the center and the localities.

Through his position, Lin gained great respect in the party, the armed forces, and the government. In the military apparatus, for example, the Defense Ministry, the office of the chief of staff, and the commanders of the air force and navy were controlled by Lin or by members of his faction. Even in such top policy-making bodies as the Standing Committee of the party's Political Bureau, Lin's faction had a powerful influence. In the provinces, munici-

---

This interview was obtained by a correspondent of the New York weekly Intercontinental Press *and published in its January 12, 1976, issue.*

palities, and localities the power was almost totally controlled by army personnel influenced by Lin. This was because in the latter part of the Cultural Revolution, all the governmental bodies in the local areas had been replaced by the Revolutionary Committees. Most of these committees were under the control of military people because they had been commanders in such places as Wuhan, Nanking, Canton, Kwangsi, Fukien, and Manchuria.

At the same time, Lin Piao was the first vice-chairman of the party and the vice-premier of the government. Mao's personal dictatorship was threatened by this situation. To overcome this unfavorable situation, Mao united with Chou En-lai, determined to destroy Lin's faction and recover his personal dictatorship. Mao raised the slogan: "The party must command the gun, not the gun command the party." In order to retain its power, Lin's faction was forced to counterattack, even to the extent of preparing a political coup d'etat to destroy Mao. Lin's coup failed. It was later alleged that Lin's daughter told the Maoist authorities about the plot in order to save her husband's life, and her revelation of the plot caused Lin and his followers to try to escape by plane to the Soviet Union. The plane was reportedly shot down over Outer Mongolia and they lost their lives.

It was ironic, to say the least, that the conflict between Mao and Lin reached the point that Mao had to have Lin and his followers killed. Even before the Cultural Revolution, the armed forces controlled by Lin had supported Mao. From the time Lin became minister of defense in 1959, he propagated "Mao Tse-tung Thought" inside the armed forces.

Lin did all this to establish the cult of Mao in the armed forces before the Cultural Revolution in 1966. At the same time, the Maoists raised the slogan, "The people must learn from the army," as they had used the earlier slogan, "Power springs from the barrel of a gun." They had used these slogans to enhance the position of the armed forces, and as a result this position was very high. The people were supposed to learn from the armed forces, especially during the Cultural Revolution.

In the Cultural Revolution, at first, the Red Guards, helped by Lin's armed forces, destroyed Liu Shao-ch'i's faction, thereby winning for the Mao–Lin faction the commanding position in the party and the government. Then the Red Guards became more radical and split into two major factions, fighting each other to the point of civil war in many localities, with some of them against Mao and Chou. Mao and Chou at this point decided to stop the Red Guard movement. But these millions of young people were not so easily stopped. The result was bloody battles in places like Canton, Kwangsi, and Szechuan. Before, Mao had used the Red Guards to destroy the Liu Shao-ch'i faction; now he used the armed forces to destroy the Red Guards and to stop the Cultural Revolution, establishing the Revolutionary Committees under armed-forces leadership.

Because Mao had used the armed forces to stop the Red Guards, sending almost all of them to the countryside, power was now centered in the Revolutionary Committees, but the Revolutionary Committees were controlled by Lin's faction. Mao was once again threatened by a faction, as he had been before by Liu Shao-ch'i and the Red Guards.

Q: With Lin dead, was his faction destroyed?

A: Even though Lin and his main followers were killed, the survivors of his faction had great potential force in many different organizations within the party, the armed forces, and the government. The reason for the continued influence and potential threat to Mao of Lin's faction was that for many years Lin was considered by Mao to be his "comrade-in-arms" and his legal successor, his heir. This was even written into the CCP's constitution, which was adopted at the party's Ninth Congress in 1969. The constitution read: "Comrade Lin Piao has consistently held high the great red banner of Mao Tse-tung Thought and has mostly loyally and resolutely carried out and defended Comrade Mao Tse-tung's proletarian revolutionary line," and designated Lin as "Mao Tse-tung's close comrade-in-arms and successor."[2]

Now, if Lin was so highly praised and had so consistently "held high the great red banner," and was the legal successor and heir to Mao, how could he betray Mao and attempt a coup d'etat against Mao?

If Lin was such a bad person, a rotten egg, why didn't Mao understand this from the beginning, rather than elevate Lin to be his close "comrade-in-arms and successor"? It was impossible for Mao to explain this. Therefore, for a long time after the death of Lin in September 1971 he never attempted to explain it. Neither did the newspapers controlled by the CCP. Why the silence? Because Mao had no explanation!

For a long time the newspapers attacked Lin indirectly, referring to him only in the phrase "Liu Shao-ch'i and other swindlers." This was, of course, very abstract. No attempt was made to mention the important charges against Lin, or to state the facts of the case openly. There were a few reports, especially from Taiwan, that Lin had tried to launch a coup d'etat against Mao. This plan was called the "Outline of Project 571." This secret plan was first published in Taiwan. It was very difficult to believe the reports from Taiwan, since it was likely that they had come from Chiang Kai-shek's agents. I was very skeptical, but then Mao's newspapers confirmed them. They quoted from this document in their attacks against Lin.

During that time, Mao was cautious in his attacks on Lin because it was still difficult for him to explain his past high esteem for Lin. How could the Maoists explain to the ranks that Lin, who was second only to Mao, had become a counterrevolutionary? The obvious next question would be raised, was this also true of Mao?

Q: What were the contents of the "Outline of Project 571"?

A: I do not have the document at hand. However, some of the articles attacking Lin Piao in the *People's Daily* indicate the contents of the document.

For example, the *People's Daily* repeatedly attacked Lin for allegedly saying that the "May 7 Cadre Schools" were a maneuver to strip the cadres of their posts and jobs in the party, to take away their livelihood.[3] It was also claimed that Lin had said that "the intellectuals were sent to the mountains and countryside for reform through forced labor." He was supposed to have described the Cultural Revolution as a failure.

The August 1974 issue of *October Review*, published by Trotskyists in Hong Kong, cited two particular paragraphs from Lin's "Outline of Project 571":

he [Mao] abused the trust and post given by the Chinese people, he is opposing history. In reality, he has become a current Ch'in Shih Huang.[4]

He is not a real Marxist-Leninist and uses the name Marxism-Leninism to carry out his doctrine of Confucianism-Menciusism, adopting the method of Chin Shih Huang. He is the greatest tyrant in the history of China.

These attacks against Mao expressed not only the opinions of Lin and his followers, but reflected the discontent, dislike, and hatred of the overwhelming majority of the people.

After Mao launched the Cultural Revolution in May 1966, not only the party and its youth, but the trade unions, the government at all levels, the schools, from middle school to university, and the cultural and educational institutions were thrown into great confusion. Bloody clashes took place throughout the country. Thousands and thousands of cadres who worked in the party and government institutions were attacked by the Red Guards. Most of them were purged from the party or lost their jobs and posts. Many were put in prison. Finally, the millions of Red Guards were sent to the mountains and countryside. All the people were affected by these events. They felt as if they were living in an atmosphere of terror. Naturally, they were dissatisfied with Mao; they disliked and hated him. That is why Lin Piao and his followers called Mao "the current Ch'in Shih Huang" and "the greatest tyrant in the history of China."

It is very clear that Mao was isolated both from the ranks and from his old comrades who had cooperated with him in the movement for several decades. Even his closest comrades-in-arms—Lin Piao and Ch'en Po-ta—left him, and according to the regime, made an attempt on his life.

It is necessary to point out that Lin was the only person in the central leadership who had faithfully and consistently supported Mao since the initiation of guerrilla war in Chingkangshan in 1928. Ch'en Po-ta had been Mao's private secretary since the late 1930s and helped Mao draft many documents and articles that established his personal cult. Ch'en also helped Mao, as head of the Cultural Revolution Group, during the Cultural Revolution. But both Lin and Ch'en became Mao's bitter enemies. They charged Mao with being a tyrant. This was the dangerous situation facing Mao after Lin's downfall.

Q: With the continued influence of Lin's faction, how could Mao break this deadlock?

A: Only one person could help Mao: Chou En-lai. The people had a better impression of Chou; they thought he was better than Mao. Chou seemed more moderate, more human. The general public considers Chou the best of the bureaucrats. Unlike Mao, Chou had not fostered a personal animosity against himself among party cadres, government officials, or the military. He was even liked, because in the worsening situation his reputation as a moderate led people to hope for improvements if he were put in charge.

The people had a good impression of Chou En-lai. In addition, he had a great deal of influence among those old leaders purged by Mao during the Cultural Revolution. Almost all the leaders, from the center to the provinces, were attacked by the Red Guards under Mao, and were later purged. Thus, these old leaders were dissatisfied with Mao and hated him. Chou, however, always tried to intercede with Mao in their behalf, and he sometimes even defended them against Mao's attacks. So almost all the leaders purged by Mao placed their hope in Chou.

Even though these old leaders were purged and dismissed from their posts, they still had a certain influence among the middle- and lower-level cadres. For Mao this again was dangerous; the people influenced by the purged leaders were also opposed to Mao.

Among all these people, Mao's only hope, Chou En-lai, alone still retained his influence and had connections with top military commanders in local areas.

Chou had been the leader of the party's Military Committee for a long time before the CCP took power in 1949. He was the real head of the committee, a post Mao later took for himself. Chou retained contact and influence with the military leaders after the CCP took power.

At the end of the Cultural Revolution, Mao lacked this support; he was isolated. He had almost no reliable supporters in the party, government, or the military. To break this isolation, Mao used Chou against the party and military cadres, because Chou was still influential. The result of the new Mao–Chou combination was a decision to bring party cadres together to discuss the situation. This was done with the Tenth Congress of the CCP, held in August 1973.

Q: Why did Mao have so few party cadres loyal to him?

A: At the time that Mao launched the Cultural Revolution against Liu Shao-ch'i's faction, the CCP apparatus as a whole was controlled by Liu's faction. But Mao's Red Guards and later Lin's troops attacked and purged virtually *all* the leaders in the local areas, leaving Mao without cadres. Even among those few officials who supported the Red Guards there were further purges for "ultraleftism." This was the charge aimed by Mao at those of his supporters who became too closely tied to the Red Guards. These "ultraleft" supporters of Mao continued to encourage the Red Guard movement even after some of the Red Guards had begun to turn on Mao's lower-level followers. Such Red Guards concluded that the Mao faction was just as bureaucratic as the

Liu faction had been and that they deserved to be removed from office just as much as did the opponents of Mao whom the Red Guards had been encouraged to attack.

You see, almost all the government cadres were also in the party, so when these cadres were purged, the local governing organs in the provinces were likewise purged. After this purge, when the Revolutionary Committees were established, they were composed only of members of Lin's faction and some "neutralists." Later, when Lin came to oppose Mao, all the cadres under Lin's influence were attacked or purged.

During the Cultural Revolution, all the supporters of Liu Shao-ch'i were purged from the cultural, education, and propaganda departments, where many people were employed. Ch'en Po-ta at that time used the authority of the Cultural Revolution Group to also purge a few people for "ultraleftism." These included Wang Li, Ch'i Pen-yu, Kuan Feng, and Lin Chieh. None of the top leaders of the "left" wing were purged at that time, however; Ch'en Po-ta and Chiang Ch'ing retained their official posts. In this struggle, Mao purged first the "Right" and then the "Left." He destroyed the factions of Liu and then Lin, but in the process he left himself isolated and without loyal cadres.

At the Tenth Party Congress, Mao was forced to make some changes. Most important, he made concessions to the old leaders. The situation was very clear at the congress. Chou En-lai made the political report for the Central Committee of the Party. Chou's report is very revealing. In the first part of the report, he read a list of Lin Piao's "crimes"; Lin was a "bourgeois careerist" and "conspirator"; he launched an "armed counterrevolutionary coup d'etat," including an attempt "to assassinate our great leader Chairman Mao"; he was turning the CCP into a "revisionist, fascist party," reinstating the "landlords and bourgeois classes," and instituting a "feudal-comprador-fascist dictatorship"; he was a renegade, traitor, superspy, and doubledealer connected with the Soviet revisionists, aligning with imperialism, revisionism, and reactionaries to oppose Chinese communism and revolution.[5]

Of course, this was simply slander. And what Chou said in this unbelievable report, he stated for Mao. Chou's report also slandered Ch'en Po-ta. The report said that Ch'en was the principal member of Lin Piao's antiparty clique. (Elsewhere Ch'en was accused of being an anticommunist Kuomintang element, a Trotskyist, a renegade, an enemy agent, and a revisionist.)

The Tenth Congress endorsed Chou's report, and in a meaningless gesture expelled Lin—after his death! All references to Lin, such as "Mao's close comrade-in-arms and successor," were removed from the party constitution, and a new, revised constitution was adopted. Very easy! Ch'en Po-ta was expelled from the party and dismissed from all posts outside the party. This was Chou's report for Mao; it was dictated by Mao Tse-tung. At the same time, a number of the old leaders who had been purged were rehabilitated. They included Teng Hsiao-p'ing, the former party general secretary, T'an Chen-lin, and Ulanfu. These three had all been members of the Political Bureau before the Cultural Revolution; now they were rehabilitated. Others were also rehabilitated; among them were some important and powerful military commanders, such as Hsu Shih-yu in the Shanghai-Nanking area; Ch'en Hsi-lien in Manchuria; and Han Hsien-ch'u in Fukien. They retained all their posts, remaining party first secretaries in their local areas and heads of their Revolutionary Committees. Hsu was commander in the Nanking area, which is very important because it includes Shanghai. Manchuria is another important area because it is highly industrialized and lies close to the Soviet Union. Fukien is important because it is the front with Taiwan. Quemoy and Matsu are near Fukien and they are occupied by Chiang Kai-shek's forces. So the armed forces in this area are more important than elsewhere.

There were other commanders of lesser importance who were similarly rehabilitated. Of course, this was a large concession for Mao to make.

Q: Were all these people attacked during the Cultural Revolution?

A: Yes, but in varying degrees. In Nanking in 1967, there had been some clashes between the Red Guards led by Mao's Cultural Revolution Group, and those who supported the army and the party. Hsu was attacked at that time. But Chou En-lai and even Chiang-Ch'ing stepped in to moderate the situation, which was less serious than the case in Wuhan and Canton.

In Wuhan, the commander, Ch'en Tsai'tao, was purged. This was not universal. In Canton, the commander, Huang Yungsheng, was Lin's man. He not only was not purged, but was elevated to Peking to become chief of staff. Lin Piao promoted him after Huang was attacked.

Besides smashing the factions that opposed him, and rehabilitating some of the old purged leaders, Mao also promoted a new figure, Wang Hung-wen. Wang reported to the Tenth Congress on the revision of the party's constitution. He was then elected as a member of the Central Committee and the Political Bureau, becoming third after Mao and Chou. Mao used Wang, along with Chang Ch'un-ch'iao, the mayor of Shanghai, to control the Shanghai workers during the Cultural Revolution. Wang is a young man in the CCP leadership, about forty years old. He was not a leading figure in the government or party prior to his elevation by Mao.

Q: What did Wang and Chang do for Mao in Shanghai?

A: The workers in Shanghai were influenced by the old leaders, Ch'en P'ei-hsien, the party first secretary; and Ts'ao Ti-ch'iu, the mayor. These leaders had sympathized with Liu Shao-ch'i and were later purged. From late December of 1966 to January 1967 there was a massive strike movement organized by the old leaders in the trade unions, party, and government. This strike was against the Cultural Revolution, although not openly. The workers wanted to improve their living standard, and the older leaders in the party and the government made some concessions to them. Mao sent people to Shanghai, especially the Red Guards, under the protection of the army (which was led by Lin Piao), so the old leaders there, almost as a whole, were purged. For the first time, Revolutionary Committees were established, returning power to Mao's supporters. Besides Wang, Chang Ch'un-ch'iao also opposed the old leaders and he organized a group for Mao. At the same time, a similar strike movement broke out in Nanking.

Mao used Wang and Chang against the workers to break the strike. Mao, through Wang, attacked the old leaders who were supported by the workers. Mao repaid Wang for his services by elevating him into the party leadership.

The main features of the Tenth Congress were the following: first the smashing of the faction that had been led by Lin Piao; second, the rehabilitation of purged older leaders; and third, the elevation of nonentities, such as Wang, to the leadership.

Q: If Lin Piao was so discredited by Chou En-lai at the Tenth Congress, why does Mao continue a nationwide campaign against him and against Confucius?

A: Lin was disgraced at the congress, but a certain influence still existed. This was especially true among the military commanders who maintained their posts in the most important regions such as Nanking, Manchuria, and Fukien. Also, the older leaders had been rehabilitated. A force still existed; this was not only unsatisfactory for Mao, it was a mortal threat to him. You see, even though Chou En-lai helped Mao to disgrace Lin, Chou himself became an attractive center for all the cadres who opposed Mao. In this situation, Mao must continue to struggle to suppress the opposition in order to restore his own personal dictatorship. First of all, to eliminate the powerful military commanders from their posts. With this in mind, Mao prepared a new campaign against Lin and against Confucius.

The first aim of this campaign was to remove the commanders: Hsu Shih-yu, Ch'en Hsi-lien, and Han Hsien-ch'u. All of these people were transferred to other places. This happened in December 1973. Hsu was transferred to Kwangtung; Ch'en to Peking; Han to Lanchow. Although they retained their posts as commanders in the new areas, they were not appointed to posts of first party secretaries or as chairmen of the Revolutionary Committees.

Q: Why did Mao allow these commanders to retain their posts in the military?

A: If Mao had removed them from the military positions, it would have caused discontent among the cadres in the army. After all, the commanders had not committed any crimes or made any serious mistakes. Mao proceeded slowly against them, first failing to reappoint them to all their former posts. Later, of course, he hoped to eliminate all the old commanders and replace them with newer, more pliant people who are more likely to obey Mao. But the problem for Mao was that he had no new supporters to replace the old officers. That is why the Maoists energetically propagandized that the party must control the army. In other words, the army officers must absolutely obey the party leadership, which the Maoists hoped would be wielded exclusively by Chairman Mao. In the year that followed the transfer of the commanders, however, Mao's position in the leadership deteriorated very severely.

The Maoists did their utmost to expand the urban people's militia. Especially in Shanghai and Peking, millions of militia members, who for the most part are workers, were organized and trained by the Maoists. The Maoists attempted to counterpose the people's militia to the army, pressuring the commanders of the army to give up their opposition to Mao. Of course, such a plan would not be easy to bring about, but it was not impossible. In any event, it would not be enough by itself to accomplish Mao's aims. Thus we see the continued campaign against Lin and Confucius.

Q: What then is the real aim and significance of the campaigns against Lin and Confucius?

A: The main or central task is to counter Lin's accusation that Mao is a new Ch'in Shih Huang, the greatest tyrant in Chinese history, and to "prove" that instead of a tyrant, Mao is the most progressive figure and the greatest revolutionary leader in the history of China.

With this in mind, the Maoists first of all must "prove" that Ch'in Shih Huang was not a tyrant, but the greatest, most progressive emperor in Chinese history because he destroyed "slave society" and established a "feudal society." However, Ch'in Shih Huang did not actually do this. The society that Ch'in Shih Huang destroyed was not a slave society but a classical feudal society.

This was a great step in China's historical development. Ch'in Shih Huang's actions can be compared to those taken in Europe by several monarchs in the period of the rise of capitalism, the sixteenth to the eighteenth centuries, in which they destroyed the power of the local feudal lords and established absolute monarchies. On a world scale, the best-known examples of this were England and France.

In China, prior to the unification, the ruling class was a hereditary landed nobility that passed on its property to the eldest son through the institution of primogeniture. Seven independent kingdoms existed, each at war with the other. A kingdom had its own administration, army, customs, tariffs, and written language. At that time, land owned by the kings could not be bought or sold. The peasants worked the land, paying taxes to the feudal lords. This was a feudal institution based on periodic labor service, not the buying and selling of humans as slaves.

When Ch'in Shih Huang destroyed the kingdoms, unifying China as a centralized monarchy, the first step he took was to remove all the nobility from their native kingdoms. Ch'in wanted no remnants of the prior system to exist.

After unifying the kingdoms, Ch'in Shih Huang then divided

them into thirty-six provinces. All previous borders were abolished and all officials were appointed and recalled by the central government.

Ch'in Shih Huang established a common written language and standardized the currency and measures. This was a necessary step to remove the obstacles for establishing economic commerce.

As is obvious, in this process, Ch'in Shih Huang and his supporters represented the rising new merchant and petty land-owning class, which had struggled against the feudal land-owners. The new society he built introduced money relations in place of feudal bondage. This new system created the circumstances, both economically and politically, for economic development.

As for the "criticize Confucius" campaign, according to the Maoists, Confucius represented "slave society." Therefore, all Confucianists were attempting to restore the slave society, after it was supposedly destroyed by Ch'in Shih Huang. Hence, all Confucianists were utterly reactionary. And, they assert, Lin Piao was playing a similar role. As a representative of the "landlords and capitalists," he was trying to restore "slave society." They are falsifying history on both counts.

Q: The Maoists call Lin a "Confucianist." What evidence do they produce to prove that he was such a reactionary?

A: The Maoists claim to have found a single sentence, a quotation from Confucius written by Lin on a scroll on the wall of his room. The sentence read "K'e chi fu li." Literally this means "Restrain oneself in order to restore the rites." "Rites" here is the Confucian term *li*, which refers to rationality in ethics, morality, and politics. The Maoists cite this to "prove" Lin was trying to restore capitalism in China. It is highly possible that Lin Piao wrote this sentence and hung it on his wall. Perhaps it was an expression of a wish to return to the earlier, less dangerous days of the CCP's history, right after they took power in 1949. After all, he had personally seen most of the old leaders and cadres, who fought alongside Mao during the revolution, purged, and in many cases jailed and even assassinated.

But in any event, this sentence hardly proves that Lin wanted to restore capitalism in China. Rather, it is yet another example of the Maoists slandering their opponents, pretending that anyone who disagrees with Mao wants to restore capitalism. They have thus framed up all their oppositions. It is ironic that Lin Piao had helped Mao do this before, and that the same method was used to destroy him and his followers.

It is necessary to point out that the campaign against Lin and Confucius is very widespread. In the last part of 1974, the Maoists wrote thousands of articles in newspapers and magazines. They held meetings on a massive scale in the party, armed forces, factories, schools, and other institutions. In these articles and meetings, the theme was the same: The Confucianists were reactionary elements because they wanted to restore "slave society." The Legalists (the scholars who codified Ch'in Shih Huang's reforms) were progressive because they helped the Ch'in dynasty destroy the "slave system."

Q: The Maoists have emphasized that the Confucianists were utterly reactionary and that the Legalists were progressive. What were the actual differences between these two tendencies?

A: The essential difference between the Confucianists and the Legalists centered on how to unify China, ending the continual state of warfare between the heads of the seven kingdoms. The followers of Confucius, accepting his ideas and developing them, looked back to the period of the Western Chou dynasty; there was no war and the many feudal lords obeyed the central king.

A premier of the Western Chou dynasty, Chou Kung, had developed, based on the feudal system, a code of ethics, morals, and politics. Confucius looked to this as a model, and his saying *K'e chi fu li*, proposed a return to the practices of the Western Chou dynasty.

Thus, we can say that Confucius was a reformer of feudalism, but that he looked backward to an earlier, idyllic period. In this he was both an idealist and a reactionary.

After Confucius died, his followers, such an Mencius, continued to develop his ideas along the same lines. But, another Confucianist, Hsun Tzu, broke with the backward-looking Confucian concepts and developed proposals for the reform of feudalism based on the current realities. The disciples of Hsun Tzu, such as Han Fei and Li Ssu, became the Legalists. Han Fei was a great theoretician of the Legalist school and Li Ssu became premier for Ch'in Shih Huang. Li proposed systematic changes in policy that resulted in the elimination of feudalism, growth of the petty landlord class, and the establishment of a centralized monarchy, under Ch'in Shih Huang.

The Confucianists opposed Ch'in Shih Huang's reforms. In this struggle, the Legalists played a progressive role, the Confucianists a reactionary one.

But it is not sufficient simply to outline the roles of these two tendencies. The brutal methods used by Ch'in and the Legalists left a reputation for cruelty and arbitrariness unsurpassed in Chinese history. It was not just the fact that Ch'in buried alive hundreds of Confucianists and burned books. More important is the fact that Ch'in and the Legalists were extremely brutal toward the peasants, to the point that fifteen years after the unification and centralizing of the government, the first peasant revolt in recorded history overthrew the Ch'in dynasty. In its place arose the Han dynasty—which, not unexpectedly, utilized the Confucian scholars as advisers in place of the Legalists who were used under Ch'in. However, the Confucianists did not restore the old property relations, they did not reestablish primogeniture, rebuild the landed nobility, or abolish the alienability of land.

This shows that from the time of the Han dynasty (206 B.C. to A.D. 220) no one can show that these two schools of thought represented opposing social classes. On the contrary, they differed only in the methods of their support to the landlord-merchant class that had arisen with Ch'in Shih Huang's reforms. From this point on, the Legalists were no more progressive than the Confucianists. Their differences had narrowed to the point of being analogous, for example, to those in the United States today between the "law and order" conservatives and the liberals. The first base themselves more on naked repression, while the liberals depend more on illusions and guile. The Legalists continued to stand for harsh methods, especially toward the peasantry. The role of Confucianism in maintaining the Chinese social order through its conservative mores is well known; it is enough to mention the backward status given women (subordinated first to their fathers, then to husband, and then to son).

It is, of course, the reputation for brutality of the Legalists that causes Mao to be termed a second Ch'in Shih Huang; and the modern Confucianists are those like Liu Shao-ch'i, who opposed some of Mao's more brutal policies.

Q: Confucius, then, was not a representative of a slave society, and the social system established by Ch'in was not feudalism, but rather a transitional regime from feudalism to capitalism. Can you explain this development?

A: The development of Chinese society was different from the European pattern. Europe, as Marx wrote, passed from a slave society, such as in Greece and Rome, through a feudal social system in the Middle Ages, directly to capitalism.

Based on recorded history, we know that the Shang dynasty (1787-1134 B.C.) marked the transition directly from a community of tribes to a feudal society. Following the Shang was the Chou dynasty (1122-256 B.C.), which was a classical feudal society. This was the society that Ch'in Shih Huang destroyed. The transitional regime that Ch'in established lasted almost two thousand years, from the third century B.C. to the mid-nineteenth century, when capitalism penetrated China from abroad. From this time on China declined to a semicolonial country. That is to say, the old economic form of petty-commodity relations gradually declined. Handicrafts could not compete with the modern goods and machinery introduced into China by imperialism.

The introduction of these goods brought the development of railways, factories, mines, and so on. In the process the merchants of China, working as agents (compradors) for the imperialists, became the new class, the bourgeoisie.

Slowly, China evolved from the old petty-commodity economy to the new form of capitalism. Through these stages, China's economic life became tied to world imperialism.

Q: Since Ch'in destroyed the feudal society, establishing a monarchy based on new social relations, why did China not develop capitalism in this earlier period?

A: This is a very interesting and complicated theoretical question. One could ask why capitalism did not emerge from ancient Rome, but waited until the eighteenth century, when it arose in England. This question is explained by Marx and Engels in the *Communist Manifesto*:

The discovery of America, the rounding of the Cape, opened up fresh ground for the rising bourgeoisie. The East-Indian and Chinese markets, the colonisation of America, trade with the colonies, the increase in the means of exchange and in commodities generally, gave to commerce, to navigation, to industry, an impulse never before known, and thereby, to the revolutionary element in the tottering feudal society, a rapid development.[6]

That is to say, *capitalism can be organized only on a world scale*, as the *Manifesto* said:

"Modern industry has established the world-market, for which the discovery of America paved the way."[7] That is, *without a world market, industrial capitalism could not arise.*

In China, when Ch'in destroyed the feudal system, the countries or nations surrounding China were very backward. So the China united by Ch'in remained very narrow as a market. Of course, these conditions could not give rise to capitalism. Even though for a number of years handicrafts and commerce developed to a limited extent, and limited trade relations existed with Southeast Asia and Japan, the scale of the commerce remained narrow. Therefore, China remained stagnant for a long time, about two thousand years.

Q: The Maoists have carried out a vigorous campaign against Lin Piao and Confucius for more than a year now. What are the results of this campaign?

A: The results can be seen clearly in the consequences of the Fourth National People's Congress held in January 1975. In order to understand the consequences, we must consider some of the congress's most important decisions.

First, the congress adopted a new constitution for the People's Republic of China, in which the words "the chairman of state" were removed, and "the Chairman of the Central Committee of the Communist Party of China commands the country's armed forces" were added. This means that formally all the armed forces have been put under Mao's control. On paper at least, all the armed forces' officers and soldiers must obey Mao's orders.

However, the other important decisions made by the congress show how fictitious Mao's control of the military really is. He suffered heavy setbacks at the congress. For instance, the new constitution added the words: ". . . people's commune members may farm small plots for their personal needs, engage in limited household sideline production, and in pastoral areas keep a small number of livestock for their personal needs."[8] This was a great concession to the peasants, under the pressure from the old cadres, including the supporters of Liu Shao-ch'i. This step had been carried out by Liu after the failure of the People's Communes, and was then violently opposed and prohibited by the Maoists during the Cultural Revolution.

In addition, the new Standing Committee of the People's Congress elected by this congress, the highest organ in China, was another blow to Mao. The committee's chairman, Chu Te, was reelected. Chu Te is an important and well-known old leader. He participated in and led the Nanchang uprising in August 1927. In addition, he was a longtime leader of the army prior to the CCP's taking power. He has disagreed with Mao, sometimes openly, as during the Great Leap Forward and People's Commune period. He was attacked violently by the Maoists during the Cultural Revolution.

There are twenty-two vice-chairmen of the Standing Committee of the congress. These include a number of people who were previously attacked or purged by the Maoists, such as T'an Chen-lin, Li Ch'ing-ch'üan, Ulanfu, Nieh Jung-chen, and Ch'en Yun. T'an Chen-lin and Ulanfu, as I have already stated, were former members of the party Political Bureau who were rehabilitated. Li Ch'ing-ch'üan, Nieh Jung-chen, and Ch'en Yun were also attacked and removed from their posts in the Cultural Revolution. Li was first secretary of the Southwest Region Political Bureau and a member of the CCP's Political Bureau. Nieh was minister of science and technology; atomic research and production were fields under his control. Ch'en was minister of heavy industry.

The leading members of the central governmental apparatus, the Executive Committee, are Chou En-lai, reelected as premier; Teng Hsiao-p'ing, first vice-premier and chief of staff of the People's Liberation Army; and Yeh Chien-ying, defense minister. Yeh is the oldest figure in the People's Liberation Army. He participated in the December 1927 Canton insurrection, and was chief of staff of the Eighth Route Army under Chu Te, a supporter of Chou En-lai.

Teng Hsiao-p'ing is another well-known old leader of the CCP who fell out with Mao. He participated in the Long March, rose in the Red Army, and became party general secretary. In 1966 he was attacked by the Red Guards, who considered him second only to Liu Shao-ch'i as a figure to be removed. For seven years he was out of a job, and now he has been rehabilitated by Chou En-lai.

Mao hates Teng. When Teng was purged during the Cultural Revolution, Mao in a speech accused him of having refused for a long time even to inform Mao on the work of the party center under Teng's control. And now this man is second to Chou En-lai!

With these posts, Chou and his supporters now have in their hands the central government apparatus and the armed forces.

Hence, Chou has now become the most powerful leader, the real leader in the People's Republic of China.

Mao's most important supporters, on the other hand, got only one position of any importance. That was Chang Ch'un-ch'iao, who is now *third* vice-premier and head of the Political Commission of the People's Liberation Army. Others of Mao's supporters, such as Wang Hung-wen, Yao Wen-yuan, and Chiang Ch'ing, got no important posts. Of course, Mao was designated as commander in chief of all the armed forces. But this is merely a figurehead post. The real power is in the hands of the defense minister and the chief of staff—these are Chou En Lai's men.

Thus, from the outcome of the Fourth National People's Congress, you can see that despite the furor of the campaign against Lin and Confucius, the Maoists have made no real gains, but to the contrary, have only succeeded in further isolating themselves from the old leaders and cadres, and they are further from the power than when they began the campaign. The one place the Maoists remain strongly entrenched is in the press. Their opponents permit them to talk as a way of avoiding a further disruptive struggle within the bureaucracy, but this is not where the important decisions are made. The isolation of the Maoists is one reason why Mao did not attend the Fourth National People's Congress. He knew that the outcome of the congress would not be favorable toward him.

Q: What do you think Mao will do in the period ahead?

A: There is a logic to the struggle for power in the Stalinist system; and taking this into account, along with Mao's character and methods, which have been consistent, we can say that Mao and his followers will try to recover their former authority in the party hierarchy. The bureaucracy has used Mao for so long as the symbol of its power that it will be reluctant to risk a public break with him. This gives his followers more room for maneuver than their actual strength should warrant. (This was an important factor in permitting Mao to defeat Liu Shao'ch'i.)

Just after the close of the congress, the *People's Daily* and other newspapers and magazines continued to publish articles against Lin Piao and against Confucius. In particular, *Red Flag*, the theoretical magazine of the CCP, published a "call to learn the theory of proletarian dictatorship in March 1975. This article quoted Mao as follows: "Why did Lenin speak of exercising dictatorship over the bourgeoisie? This question must be thoroughly understood. Lack of clarity on this question will lead to revisionism. This should be made known to the whole nation."

Following this quotation from Mao, the editors of *Red Flag* asserted:

It is a major matter of combating and preventing revisionism and consolidating and strengthening the dictatorship of the proletariat for the hundreds of millions of people throughout the country to study and master the Marxist theory on the dictatorship of the proletariat. The Party committees at all levels should firmly and effectively grasp the study of the theory on the dictatorship of the proletariat, more consciously implement the Party's basic line and policies, *achieve greater success in the movement to criticize Lin Piao and Confucius,* and continue the revolution under the dictatorship of the proletariat through to the end.[9] [Emphasis added.]

Following their own proposals, the editors proceeded to publish long quotations from the works of Marx and Lenin on the dictatorship of the proletariat.

This "call" to learn the theory of the dictatorship of the proletariat is clearly *a new campaign.* Its purpose is to use the Marxist theory of the proletarian dictatorship as a smoke screen, a code word for the personal dictatorship of Mao Tse-tung, and to justify all the purges of his opponents in the past as necessary and correct because they were allegedly against the dictatorship of the proletariat. It is also to warn all members of party committees that they will be severely punished or purged if they do not "firmly and effectively grasp the study of the theory on the dictatorship of the proletariat," i.e., Mao's personal dictatorship, and "consciously implement the Party's basic line and policies" as elaborated by Mao.

Following the line of the article mentioned above, Yao Wen-yuan, Mao's son-in-law, wrote an article titled "On the Social Basis of Lin Piao's Anti-Party Clique," which was published in the same issue (March 1975) of *Red Flag.* After he listed many of Lin's "crimes," such as attacking the May 7 Cadre Schools and calling Mao "a current Ch'in Shih Huang," Yao presented an analysis of the social basis of Lin's faction. He concluded that "the Lin Piao anti-Party clique represented the hope not only of the overthrown landlords and bourgeoisie for restoration but of the newly engendered bourgeois elements in socialist society for usurping power."[10]

From these words, one can see the attitude of the Maoists

toward Lin's followers and all other opponents. Every political difference is treated as coming from an enemy class. This is the method of Stalinism.

The April 1975 issue of *Red Flag* also published another article, by Chang Ch'un-ch'iao, called "On Exercising All-Round Dictatorship Over the Bourgeoisie." Chang quoted Lenin's writings from *Left-Wing Communism* that "small production *engenders* capitalism and the bourgeoisie continuously, daily, hourly, spontaneously, and on a mass scale. For all these reasons the dictatorship of the proletariat is essential."

In his article, Chang asserted that in the present Chinese situation, it is not only necessary to have a proletarian dictatorship, but necessary that the dictatorship over the "bourgeoisie" be all-sided, including in the ideological field, in order to eliminate the new bourgeois elements that continually arise "in one batch after another." Otherwise, the new bourgeois elements could convert the proletarian dictatorship into a dictatorship of the bourgeoisie and restore capitalism. Chang goes on to argue that this is what happened in the Soviet Union under Khrushchev and Brezhnev, and that Liu Shao-ch'i and Lin Piao were trying to follow in the footsteps of Khrushchev and Brezhnev in the Soviet Union, by using the same methods.[11]

From these articles in *Red Flag*, we can easily see what the next step for the Maoists will be. We should recall the experience of the purges under Stalin's dictatorship in the 1920s and 1930s, and after the end of World War II. In China, since the CCP came to power in 1949, there have been four mass purges.

First, Kao Kang, the vice-chairman of the People's Republic of China and the first secretary of the party's Northeast Bureau, and Jao Shu-shih, first secretary of the party's Eastern Bureau, along with several dozens of old cadres, were purged by Mao, Liu Shao-ch'i, and Chou En-lai in 1954. They had some differences over economic policies and personnel posts in the party and the government. Next, P'eng Te-huai, defense minister, and Huang K'o-ch'eng, chief of staff, and several members of the Central Committee were purged by Mao at the Lushan conference in 1959 because they disagreed with the adventurist policies of the Great Leap Forward and the People's Communes. Then, Liu Shao-ch'i's faction, and later Lin Piao's group, were purged by Mao, as the whole world now knows.

From this we can conclude that the Maoists will certainly continue their struggle to purge all their opponents in order to restore Mao's personal dictatorship. They will do this as long as

Mao lives. The question is whether the Maoists have the strength to achieve this goal. In my opinion, not only can they not succeed, but they will become more and more isolated. Chou En-lai and Teng Hsiao-p'ing's faction, after all, has had much experience in the past internal struggles, and will be prepared to arrange their forces to counter the Maoists' attacks.

Finally, the endless struggles and purges inside the CCP will demonstrate more clearly to the masses that what is necessary is a political revolution carried out by the masses themselves. Only through a political revolution can the bureaucratic dictatorship be overthrown and a proletarian system of socialist democracy be established. Only this can open the broad road to socialism.

THE MEANING OF THE
T'IEN AN MEN DEMONSTRATION

Question: The mass demonstration that took place in T'ien An Men Square, April 5, 1976, in Peking was noted throughout the world. Although the media reported the event, the significance of it is not yet clear. Can you describe the T'ien An Men Square demonstration and explain its meaning?

Answer: In order to explain the T'ien An Men Square incident, I must first describe events that preceded it, that is, Mao's campaign since early February, counterattacking the "rehabilitated rightist" faction.

The death of Premier Chou En-lai on January 8 of this year caused the political apparatus of the Chinese Communist Party to lose its equilibrium, which is why Mao launched the antirightist campaign so soon after Chou's death. At the Fourth People's Congress, held in January 1975, the faction associated with Chou En-lai and Teng Hsiao-p'ing gained control over all areas of the government, including the military. Mao was very disturbed with the situation, but he did not have the forces to challenge the Chou faction at that time. After the congress, Mao prepared to continue the faction struggle in his own way, the background to which I have outlined in my interview with *Intercontinental Press* published January 12, 1976.[1]

Chou En-lai's death left the Chou-Teng faction without a leader capable of maintaining power over Mao's faction. Hence, Mao quickly took advantage of Chou's death to launch a campaign to destroy his faction. It should be noted that the Chinese masses mourned Chou's death on a mass scale. Millions of people

This interview was obtained by a correspondent of the New York weekly Intercontinental Press *on July 10, 1976, and published in its September 13, 1976, issue.*

in Peking alone attended a memorial service for Chou. Young workers, soldiers, and students expressed their sorrow visibly, many even wailing and crying, as reported by Chinese and foreign correspondents. This shows that the majority of people in China had a great deal of respect for Chou En-lai.

On the other hand, the masses' response showed anxiety and fear about what effects Chou's death would have on the government. The situation was clearly dangerous for Mao, who quickly moved to restore his personal dictatorship over the party and the government.

Q: Who are the "rehabilitated rightists"?

A: These are the old leaders and cadres who were purged during the Cultural Revolution and rehabilitated at the Tenth Party Congress held in August 1973. Almost all the first secretaries and heads of the Revolutionary Committees who were purged during the Cultural Revolution are supporters of the Chou–Teng faction and were rehabilitated at the congress under the pressure of the Chou–Teng faction, creating a very dangerous situation for the Maoists. After Chou's death, Mao struck at the Chou–Teng faction by attacking Teng as the man responsible for the rehabilitation of these "rightists."

According to the constitution of the People's Republic of China, Teng Hsiao-p'ing, who was vice-premier, should have become the successor to Premier Chou En-lai. However, Mao used his post as chairman of the CCP to appoint Hua Kuo-feng as the acting premier.

Q: What are the political arguments against Teng in this struggle?

A: The Maoists say that Teng abandoned the class struggle and attempted to restore capitalism. They identify Teng as the representative of the "capitalist-roaders." In an article published in the *People's Daily* February 17, entitled "The Point Is the Restoration of Capitalism," the "capitalist-roaders" were accused of proposing to use the "Three Directives" as a program opposed to the class struggle. Teng was accused of refusing to accept the theory of the dictatorship of the proletariat. In reality, Mao proposed the Three Directives himself after the Cultural Revolution: stability and unity, development of the national economy, and class struggle. The directives were generally accepted as correct until the current campaign. Now they are counterposed to the theory of the dictatorship of the proletariat in order to brand Teng as a capitalist-roader.

On March 1, *Red Flag*, theoretical organ of the CCP, published an article called, "A General Program of Restoration of Capitalism." The article attacks the "Four Modernizations"— agricultural modernization, industrial modernization, defense modernization, and scientific and technological modernization. The Four Modernizations were proposed by Chou En-lai at the Fourth National People's Congress as the way China could overcome its backwardness in order to become a strong socialist country in the next twenty-five years. Chou is generally correct on these four steps, but overcoming China's backwardness is not simply a question of the economic system but also of the political structure. If the bureaucratic dictatorship continues, modernization of the economy is impossible. However, the masses do not understand this weakness in Chou En-lai's program.

As I said before, the Maoists did not have the strength at the Fourth National People's Congress to oppose Chou's faction. They did not openly criticize the Four Modernizations at all. Yet, immediately after Chou's death, throughout February and March, all the newspapers and magazines controlled by the Maoists repeatedly attacked Teng Hsiao-p'ing, just as they had previously attacked Lin Piao as a Confucianist and a capitalist restorationist. They claimed that the Four Modernizations would abolish the dictatorship of the proletariat and establish the dictatorship of the capitalists.

Seeing such violent attacks in the media, the people were naturally confused and afraid. The incident at T'ien An Men Square was an attempt by the masses to express their ideas and their fears about the political situation.

Q: What actually happened at T'ien An Men Square on April 5?

A: There is a traditional custom in China at the beginning of April called the Ch'ing Ming Festival, where the people pay respects to their ancestors. The people in Peking used the occasion to take wreaths to the Monument of People's Heroes to pay their respects to Chou En-lai.

The first wreaths were brought by workers from three machine factories. Then, soldiers brought wreaths. On the second, third, and fourth of April, the people continued bringing wreaths and some brought pictures of Chou En-lai. On April 4, between forty and fifty thousand people came to T'ien An Men Square to pay their respects in this manner. It is of special significance that many of the wreaths had slogans and poems attached to them. For example, one slogan was, "Respect for Premier Chou En-lai, We Will Always Remember You." Another said, "Long Live Our Respected Premier Chou, We Want to Defend Your Heroic Memory and We Will Finish Your Projected Plan." Another stated, "Beware Conspirators in the Party, Down with the Betrayers of Chou En-lai."

All these slogans not only reveal support for Chou En-lai but take a position against Mao. Other slogans such as "Down With the Dowager Empress" and "Down With Indira Gandhi" are slogans against Chiang Ch'ing, Mao's wife, who is the real leader of the antirightist campaign.[2] This activity worried and angered Mao, who ordered the police and the militia to take all the wreaths away from the monument. News of this unwise move spread quickly throughout Peking and aroused the anger and indignation of the people.

Early in the morning of April 5, the masses surged into T'ien An Men Square. They came to protest the removal of the wreaths and brought more wreaths to the Monument of People's Heroes. By the middle of the day, more than 100,000 had gathered in the square, a figure acknowledged by the *People's Daily*.

The crowd demanded return of the wreaths. Their demands turned to violence in some instances such as the following:

• When a propaganda car drove near the square, it was surrounded, the occupants were removed, and the car overturned.

• A car driven by party cadres was stopped and set on fire.

• About 3 p.m., three cars driven by secret police were emptied of their occupants and set on fire.

• It was supposed by some of the crowd that the wreaths might have been taken inside the Great Hall of the People, which was guarded by several hundred soldiers, militia, and police. A struggle ensued when the crowd demanded entrance to the building.

• Another section of the crowd supposed some uniformed officers outside a building in a nearby square had ordered the removal of the wreaths. The crowd entered the building, took books and documents, destroyed furniture, and eventually set fire to the building.

By six or seven p.m. the masses were tired and hungry and felt that they had been victorious, as their demonstration had not been suppressed. They jubilantly sang the "Internationale": "Arise ye prisoners of starvation. . . . A better world's in birth. . . . Tis the final conflict/Let each stand in their place/The international party shall be the human race."

Finally, the people sent a wreath on which a poem expressed their defiance of Mao through the following lines:

> China is no longer the China of yore,
> And the people are no longer wrapped in sheer ignorance;
> Ch'in Shih-Huang's feudal society is gone and cannot return.
> We believe in Marxism-Leninism.
> To hell with those scholars who castrate Marxism-Leninism.
> What we want is genuine Marxism-Leninism.
> For the sake of genuine Marxism-Leninism
> We fear not shedding our blood and laying down our lives.
> The day the Four Modernizations in our fields are realized
> We will come back to offer libations and sacrifices.

It means that the people will no longer accept the arbitrary rule of Mao's party, which they liken to the feudal dictatorship of Ch'in Shih-Huang. It calls for genuine Marxism-Leninism as opposed to the castrated version, Mao Tse-tung Thought. Reference to the Four Modernizations clearly shows support to Chou En-lai's economic and social programs as opposed to Mao's so-called proletarian revolutionary line, i.e., Mao's personal dictatorship.

Of course the Maoists were watching the day's events and finally ordered the militia, the police, and even the soldiers to go to the square. Around 10 p.m., most of the crowd had dispersed, but more than 3,000 of the most determined and brave young people remained. It was then that more than 10,000 police, militia, and soldiers converged on the square from all sides and attacked the people, the militia beating protesters with long wooden clubs. There are no official casualty figures, but according to some observers several hundred demonstrators were killed or wounded and many more were arrested.[3] The demonstration and protest movement of April 5 in T'ien An Men Square was suppressed in blood.

This act of suppression by Mao's bureaucratic regime is the first open attack on the people in the twenty-six years of the CCP's rule. The demonstration and its aftermath are a prelude to the political revolution against the bureaucratic dictatorship. It is similar to the situation in Hungary in 1956 when the people revolted against the Stalinist bureaucratic dictatorship in that country.

The *People's Daily* published an article on April 10 stating that the revolt involved only a handful of reactionary and antirevolutionary elements directed by Teng Hsiao-p'ing from behind the scenes. Teng was branded as the Chinese Imre Nagy.[4] Such a description is a total lie by the Maoists, who admit that 100,000 were gathered at the square. The demonstration was clearly spontaneous, from all accounts. One statement in the *People's Daily* article is true, however—Teng Hsiao-p'ing is like a Chinese Nagy. He is not a real revolutionary leader, but a reformist and a compromiser. He played a certain objective role in the demonstration because he was the focus of Mao's antirightist campaign that precipitated the whole T'ien An Men incident.

Q: What was the reaction of the people throughout the country to the T'ien An Men incident, and what measures were taken by the Maoists afterwards?

A: Most news reports of the events have been strictly censored by the government. However, some facts have been revealed by foreign and Chinese travelers who witnessed demonstrations in several cities such as Nanking, Cheng-Chou in Honan province, and K'un-ming in Yunnan province. Of course, these actions were on a smaller scale than in Peking and no details are available. As for the measures taken by the Maoists after the T'ien An Men incident, I can indicate two. First, Teng Hsiao-p'ing was formally removed from all posts inside and outside the party and the government. Second, the Maoists mobilized the police, the militia, and even the street committees to search for those who had participated in the T'ien An Men demonstration, especially the young people. An unknown number of militants were arrested. Their fate has not been revealed, but a news account in the *People's Daily* reported that a so-called public trial was held in Peking in mid-May. At this trial, five people were supposedly judged by the people. Two were sentenced to death and the other three to thirty years at hard labor.

Q: What attitude has been taken by Mao toward the late Premier Chou En-lai since the T'ien An Men incident? Has Mao continued the campaign against the "rehabilitated rightists" of the Chou-Teng faction?

A: The Maoists clearly understand that the people respect Chou En-lai and support his programs against Mao's. They have not dared to criticize Chou openly for fear of arousing more anti-Maoist sentiment. On the other hand, the Maoists will attempt to criticize Chou En-lai in order to clarify their line and explain their suppression of the T'ien An Men demonstration. This contradiction for them has meant that they only abstractly criticize the Four Modernizations, and are waiting for a better opportunity to make Chou En-lai himself a target.

Of course the Maoists continue the campaign against Teng Hsiao-p'ing and the "rehabilitated rightists." Since T'ien An Men Square, there have been numerous articles attacking them and several public meetings have been held. Yet up to now no action has been taken against these so-called rightists. The only one specifically named is still Teng Hsiao-p'ing. In some localities, such as Hunan province, the Maoists openly criticized the first secretary of the party, but they took no steps to remove him from office.

The Maoists' attitude toward the army, especially toward the commanders in the outlying areas, is one of caution. Most of these men were rehabilitated by Chou En-lai and support his ideas. No commanders have been removed from their posts, although some have been transferred. This shows that the Maoists do not have the cadres qualified to replace these men and will wait for a better opportunity in the future.

Q: The media in Europe and America call Mao's faction "radical" and Chou's faction "moderate." The Maoists call the Chou–Teng faction "rehabilitated rightists" and "capitalist-roaders." Most people think the word *radical* means *progressive* and even *revolutionary*, whereas *moderate* means *conservative* and even *reactionary*. What are the real meanings of these labels?

A: All the factions inside the CCP can be called Stalinist because they all support Stalinism theoretically and politically. In practice, however, certain differences do exist between them. An example from Mao's domestic policy is when he launched the Great Leap Forward and the People's Communes. Defense Minister P'eng Te-huai and Chief of Staff Huang K'o-ch'eng, supported by Liu Shao-ch'i, disagreed with Mao's adventurist policies. They were purged by Mao and labeled as "rightists."

Another example from the early 1960s is when Liu Shao-ch'i and Teng Hsiao-p'ing took some measures in the industrial, agricultural, and cultural fields, including certain concessions to the peasants and intellectuals, in order to correct Mao's adventurist policies. Mao accused Liu and Teng of being "rightists" and "revisionists." He launched the Cultural Revolution to purge them from the party. When Khrushchev launched de-Stalinization at the Twentieth Congress of the Soviet Communist Party, Liu and Teng welcomed it and took it as an example to be practiced in China. At the Eighth Party Congress of the CCP in 1956, Liu and Teng were responsible for removing the reference to Mao's thought from the party constitution.

The prohibition against Mao's personal cult expressed by Teng at the Eighth Congress is the principal reason for the current campaign against him.

Mao's foreign policy reveals more about his "radical" faction. During the 1960s he called on all the oppressed people throughout the world to unite to destroy American imperialism. Since the early 1970s, however, he has taken the opposite position. He invited Nixon to China, which produced the so-called Shanghai communiqué confirming the principles of peaceful coexistence between the imperialist United States and the People's Republic of China. The Maoists no longer call on the oppressed peoples to unify against imperialism but, on the contrary, call on imperialism to unify to destroy the Soviet Union.

Based on the above examples, one can see the differences between Mao and the Chou–Teng factions. If we are to call things by their right names, Mao's faction should be labeled the hard-line Stalinists and the Chou–Teng faction, the moderate Stalinists. The demonstrators at T'ien An Men Square showed sympathy for the moderates as against the hard-liners. It is very similar to the Hungarian people's sympathy for Nagy against Rákosi in 1956.

It is certain that the militants who participated in the T'ien An Men Square demonstration will draw the lessons from that struggle for the future political revolution in China. They must organize themselves into a new faction, a revolutionary party, to carry out the political revolution to overthrow the bureaucratic dictatorship and establish a system of proletarian socialist democracy. Only under the leadership of a revolutionary party can the masses be mobilized to achieve the "Four Modernizations," creating in China a modern socialist state.

BEHIND THE FALL
OF MAO'S FACTION

Question: On October 7, according to reports in the Chinese and world press shortly afterward, the four main leaders of the Chinese Communist Party who were closest to Mao Tse-tung were arrested. These included Chiang Ch'ing, Mao's widow; Chang Ch'un-ch'iao, a vice-premier of the government and chief political commissar of the People's Liberation Army; Wang Hung-wen, vice-chairman of the CCP; and Yao Wen-yuan, the main propagandist of Mao's thought. All four were members of the party's Politburo. The four were denounced by Peking's mayor, Wu Te, at a rally in T'ien An Men Square on October 24 as an antiparty clique who attempted to "usurp party and state power." If Hua Kuo-feng was hostile to Mao's protégés, why did Mao himself appoint Hua premier of the government and the first party vice-chairman in April 1976?

Answer: First, one should understand what gave rise to the conflict between the four main leaders of Mao's faction and Premier Hua Kuo-feng. Recent newspaper reports reveal that there were differences over who should fill the posts of premier and of party chairman after Mao's death. The four are said to have proposed Chiang Ch'ing as party chairman and Chang Ch'un-ch'iao as premier.

Hua, of course, disagreed with these nominations because they would remove him from his newly acquired posts. Hua therefore

---

This interview was obtained by Rose Connolly on December 7, 1976.

turned to the old leaders of the so-called moderate faction with purported evidence that Chiang Ch'ing and her supporters were preparing a coup d'etat. The old leaders, in particular Defense Minister Yeh Chien-ying, sought to use Hua to destroy the extremist Maoist faction. On the basis of his information, they immediately arrested the "gang of four."

As to why Mao appointed Hua to high posts, one must realize that Mao was like Stalin. In his own self-interest, he elevated people who would be loyal and obedient to him. Mao has never been concerned with the interests of the revolution. For example, Mao appointed Lin Piao as his successor in the party because of Lin's personal loyalty and obedience. When Lin was defense minister he propagated Mao's thought and established Mao's cult in the army, calling on everyone to "read Chairman Mao's books, listen to Chairman Mao's teachings, and act according to Chairman Mao's directives." During the Cultural Revolution, Lin used the army to help the Red Guards destroy Liu Shao-ch'i's faction. At the same time, however, Lin was building his own faction, which Mao viewed as another threat to his personal dictatorship. Mao then eliminated Lin Piao and his followers, after Lin allegedly failed in an attempted coup.

As far as Hua Kuo-feng is concerned, he never played any role either before or during the third Chinese revolution. Mao promoted him from a local cadre to vice-premier of the government and minister of security only because of his subservience. In 1955, when Hua was party secretary in Hsiang-t'an county, Mao's birthplace, he carried out Mao's adventurist policy of creating agricultural producers cooperatives. He had Mao's old home rebuilt as a shrine for visitors, and even planned to bring in a railroad line from the city to transport the pilgrims. Mao was impressed by this and promoted Hua from county secretary in Hsiang-t'an to vice-secretary of the Hunan Provincial Committee.

During the Cultural Revolution, Hua also helped the Red Guards destroy Liu Shao-ch'i's faction. When it was over, he was promoted to the posts of first secretary of the Hunan party committee and chairman of the province's Revolutionary Committee. He was elected to the CCP Central Committee at the Ninth Congress in 1969. When Mao launched the campaign against Lin Piao and Confucius in 1974, Hua helped smash the remnants of Lin's faction in Hunan, which won him the posts of vice-chairman of the government and minister of public security, the political police. After Chou En-lai's death in January 1976, Mao appointed Hua premier of the government and first vice-chairman of the party, thus naming Hua as his successor.

Q: According to press reports, Mao's lieutenants had a power-ful base in Shanghai and Peking. They controlled the leadership of the party and government in Shanghai as well as a militia of over a million. In Peking, the Chiang Ch'ing group also con-trolled the militia and the 50,000 troops who served as Mao's guards, the much-feared 8341 regiment, commanded by Mao's loyal supporter Wang Tung-hsing. The "gang of four" also controlled the central news media in Peking (*People's Daily, Liberation Army Daily, Red Flag,* and the Hsinhua news agency), as well as the cultural and educational ministries, and Peking and Tsinghua universities. This seems like an immense amount of power. Why have there been no protests from these Maoist strongholds after the arrest of the "gang of four"? How was Hua able to stage massive demonstrations against the four in Shanghai and Peking?

A: Many people inside and outside China were surprised at these events, but it is not that difficult to understand. First, during the Cultural Revolution, the Maoists occupied and con-trolled Shanghai, relying on Mao's prestige and helped by the army under Lin Piao. The Maoists never won real support; on the contrary, the masses hated them because they never improved the standard of living and they suppressed all freedom of expression. Whenever the working masses demanded a wage increase, the Maoists always rejected it, calling it a demand for "material incentives." They told the masses to "take hard work as joyful" (Mao). This naturally dissatisfied the workers, and as a result, when the "gang of four" were arrested in Peking, the masses in Shanghai immediately organized demonstrations to welcome the purge.

Second, the militias were formally controlled by the Maoists, but only at the top. The rank and file of the militias shared the working masses' dissatisfaction with the Maoists. That is why there was no response when Wang Hung-wen asked the militias for help.

Third, the army and almost all of its officers stationed in Shanghai are subordinates of the old commander Hsu Shih-yu, who was attacked by the Maoists during the Cultural Revolution and later transferred from the Nanking-Shanghai Military Re-gion to Canton. The army officers have never been satisfied with the Maoist leadership in Shanghai. When news of the arrests of the "gang of four" reached Shanghai, the officers and soldiers did not attempt to stop the demonstrations but even helped to organize them behind the scenes.

Fourth, most of the other old leaders and cadres purged during the Cultural Revolution in Shanghai are still living there. They enthusiastically welcomed the arrests and encouraged the attacks against the "gang of four."

In addition, at the end of the Cultural Revolution hundreds of thousands of Shanghai Red Guard were sent by the Maoists to the countryside, forbidden to return. All the parents and relatives of these young radicals hated these harsh measures, hated the Maoists, and even hated Mao. They have welcomed the purge with the hope of seeing their children return in the near future.

For these reasons one can clearly see why no one protested the purge of the "gang of four." On the contrary, the people of Shanghai organized demonstrations for three days that took on the character of a joyful festival. In Peking, reaction to the arrests has been even more dramatic. First, the troops of the so-called 8341 secret police supported Hua in the purge, mainly because their commander, Wang Tung-hsing, was under strong anti-Maoist pressure from the army, especially the Peking garrison. Wang completely switched his allegiance, from Mao to Hua, to protect his own position in the power struggle. This is the logical evolution of a faction based solely on personal interests rather than revolutionary principles.

While Mao was alive, supporters of his faction were rewarded with posts in the party and the government. But after the death of the dictator, these people must find a new way to maintain their privileged positions. Thus many members of Mao's faction have now deserted its leaders and surrendered or gone over openly to the other side. The head of the Peking militia, Ni Chih-fu, is one of the more prominent figures who turned his back on Mao's faction under pressure from the army. He supported the purge in order to get a good post and thus was sent to Shanghai replacing Wang Hung-wen as the second secretary of the party and vice-chairman of the Revolutionary Committee.

The media formerly controlled by the Maoists have all changed their allegiance following the dismissal of their editors-in-chief. The cultural and educational ministers were also thrown out. All the cadres who controlled Peking and Tsinghua universities were arrested. The forces of Mao's faction in Shanghai and Peking have been largely destroyed. We can say, therefore, that the

Maoist faction as a hard-line Stalinist formation within the CCP has ceased to exist. There were signs beforehand that this would happen. The Maoist faction has been completely isolated from the old leaders and cadres in the party and the army since the Cultural Revolution. Mao had very few loyal and reliable cadres, making the downfall of his faction inevitable. His death only hastened the event.

Q: Since Chiang Ch'ing and the other Politburo members were arrested, they have been denounced by the new leadership as capitalist restorationists, saboteurs, betrayers of Marxism-Leninism, and so on. Why aren't these charges leveled against Mao himself? Why are Hua and his supporters still maintaining Mao's prestige and pledging to carry out Mao's "revolutionary proletarian line"?

A: The leadership of the CCP was and still is Stalinist. The ideology and methods of the various factions have been identical. Therefore Mao's prestige can serve Hua's faction as well as it did his own. Hua Kuo-feng has no base and no prestige of his own in the party, the government, or the army. He was appointed to high leadership positions by Mao, so must continue to use Mao's authority as his political capital.

In the absence of Chou En-lai and Teng Hsiao-p'ing, the other old leaders, the so-called moderates, have neither the ambition nor the ability to build an independent leadership without utilizing Mao's authority. They do want to destroy Mao's faction, and have enthusiastically supported and encouraged the purges. The accusations that the "gang of four" are revisionists and capitalist restorationists are only deceptions used to disgrace them and destroy their influence. The "gang of four," under Mao's direction, used these same accusations against Liu Shao-ch'i, Lin Piao, and Teng Hsiao-p'ing in the past. It is, of course, ironic that Mao's chosen successor should use Mao's methods to destroy Mao's faction. The accusation that the "gang of four" betrayed Mao's ideas and violated his instructions is only a fabrication by Hua and the new leaders to escape responsibility for the purge. The historical facts indisputably prove that the four were loyal and obedient to Mao all his life.

Hua Kuo-feng is now maneuvering to separate Mao from his followers so that Mao's reputation can continue to be used as a tool to deceive and control the masses. The masses are not so easily duped, however, having seen and experienced the many purges of the last decade.

During the Cultural Revolution the Chinese people witnessed attacks against almost all the leaders and cadres who worked in the party, the government, and in cultural and educational institutions. Under attack from the Red Guards, at the direction of Mao, thousands of people were purged and lost their posts. Many were imprisoned or sent to labor camps, such as the May 7 schools. Then millions of Red Guards and "educated youths" were exiled to the countryside and to mountainous regions. This is why millions of people throughout the country hated the Maoists and participated in demonstrations to welcome the purge of the "gang of four." The masses were also celebrating the death of Mao and the downfall of his faction.

Q: How do you foresee future developments in China?

A: The death of Mao Tse-tung is the end of the rule of a personal dictator. The purge of his hard-line Stalinist faction is a victory for the so-called moderate Stalinists. Thus, to a degree, the political, economic, and cultural situation in China will change.

First, the new leadership in the CCP must reorganize itself. The highest policy-making body of the party was the Political Bureau, composed of twenty-one members elected at the Tenth Congress in August 1973. Since that time, however, five members have died: Chou En-lai, Chu Te, Mao Tse-tung, Tung Pi-wu, and K'ang Sheng. The "gang of four" has been purged. (Teng Hsiao-p'ing was also purged, in April 1976, but at the time of the Tenth Party Congress in August 1973 his "rehabilitation" was too recent for him to be put on the Political Bureau and he was elected only to the Central Committee.)

This leaves only twelve members on the Political Bureau, all of whom are weak and have no prestige or base in the party. Only Yeh Chien-ying, Li Hsien-nien, Ch'en Hsi-lien, and Hsu Shih-yu have influence in the army and the government. This means that the leadership of the party must be reorganized through a national congress, or at least through a Central Committee meeting. It seems that Hua does not want to call a national congress or a plenum of the Central Committee because he fears this could undermine the positions he presently holds—chairman of the party, premier of the government, chairman of the Military

Commission, and minister of the public security police. Even Mao himself held only two of these posts.

Hua will probably try to manage a temporary leadership through combination, maneuver, and compromise with the old leaders. First, he will probably establish a Standing Committee of the Political Bureau, making Yeh Chien-ying chairman of the National People's Congress, yielding the premiership to Li Hsien-nien, and elevating Ch'en Hsi-lien to defense minister and Hsu Shih-yu to chief of staff of the People's Liberation Army. Ch'en and Hsu are now the strongest men in the army and both played an important role in the purge of the "gang of four." The old leaders such as T'an Chen-lin, Li Ching-ch'üan, Nieh Jung-chen, and Ch'en Yun will probably become part of the Political Bureau.

If such a reshuffling of posts can be realized, the leadership in Peking could stabilize itself for a certain period. But a number of problems still face them. First, they must deal with those old leaders and cadres who were purged during the Cultural Revolution. These people include P'eng Chen, former mayor of Peking; Lu Ting-i, former head of the party Propaganda Department; Chou Yang, former head of the government's cultural ministry; Liu Lan-t'ao, former first secretary of the Northwest Bureau; Ch'en P'ei-hsien, former first secretary of the party; Ts'ao Ti-ch'iu, former mayor of Shanghai, and Teng T'o, former editor-in-chief of the *People's Daily*.

In addition, thousands of cadres who worked in the party and the government and in educational and cultural institutions were also purged during the Cultural Revolution, under Mao's direction, aided by the "gang of four." Since the four have been purged for committing crimes of revisionism and capitalist restoration, the logical conclusion would be to rehabilitate all those cadres who had been purged by them.

The rehabilitation of Teng Hsiao-p'ing, recently purged by Mao himself, poses a particular problem. Teng, next to Chou En-lai, was the most important leader of the moderate faction, possessing much more influence and experience than anyone in the current leadership. His rehabilitation would be a serious threat to Hua's position, yet Teng's role in the new situation is a problem Hua must deal with soon.

The second area of probable change will be the economy, which has steadily worsened since the Cultural Revolution. Although some officials are blaming the economic situation on the intrigues of the "gang of four," the government must seek to improve things. They have already pledged to carry out the "Four Modernizations" laid down by the late Chou En-lai, but their problem will be to find the necessary funds and technology.

The third area of change concerns the living standard of the masses, which has become intolerable since the Cultural Revolution. Wages have been frozen for the working class as a whole. That is why the workers staged a general strike in Hangchow, the capital of Chekiang province, in July 1975.

Fourth, China's education system was completely destroyed by the Cultural Revolution. Almost all presidents of universities and principles of middle schools were purged. Many professors and teachers were fired, and most were sent to the countryside for reform. Mao's supporters have carried out his "revolutionary education" instead of a regular course of study. All schools have been controlled by so-called Mao Tse-tung Thought Worker-Propaganda Teams, which conduct a continual "criticism, struggle, and transformation" of teachers and students." The schools have been in great confusion from the Cultural Revolution up to the present, making it absolutely impossible to educate the new generation in the interests of socialism, i.e., to bring China out of backwardness into the modern world.

The situation is the same in all cultural fields. Mao imposed a policy like that of Zhdanov under Stalin in the 1940s. Writers, artists, actors, painters, musicians—all were forced to stop their work or were fired. That is why there have been no worthwhile novels, plays, or poems produced in China since the Cultural Revolution. There are several so-called modern operas produced by Chiang Ch'ing for propaganda purposes, without any artistic significance. In one word, the cultural field in China today is a wasteland. Thus, the restoration and development of education and culture are urgent issues for the new leaders.

The new leadership must also deal with the estimated ten million urban youth and intellectuals who were sent to the countryside and are still living there.[1] Naturally, these people are dissatisfied and hate their forced exile, creating an explosive situation. They desperately want to return to the cities and their homes to continue school, get jobs, and see their relatives. Many have already returned illegally to the cities, causing great hardship for their parents and trouble for the authorities. An estimated 30,000 to 40,000 young people have escaped to Hong Kong, at the risk of their lives.

Finally, the relationship between China and the Soviet Union has steadily worsened since the early 1960s. The Soviet bureaucrats have sent millions of troops to the border between the two countries, which stretches for thousands of miles. Mao also sent troops. This counterposition of troops has existed for many years now and has resulted in some incidents of armed conflict. If this dangerous situation is not modified by China's new leaders, it is possible that a war could develop.

The problems outlined above, generated under Mao's leadership, cannot be resolved in a reasonable manner by the new leaders because they were created by the logic of Stalinism. To resolve these problems, the methods and ideology used by Mao must be rejected.

In the face of these pressing problems, China's new leaders are centralizing their efforts in the continued campaign against the "gang of four," accusing them of persecution of the old cadres, especially cadres in the cultural field. The personal lives of the four are exposed, with charges ranging from corruption and extravagance to the absurd charge that Chiang Ch'ing in particular is like a prostitute. Through this personal slander campaign, the new leadership is attempting to justify the purges as necessary and correct as well as appease the people's hatred for the four.

The obvious question remains: Who authorized the "gang of four" to persecute the old cadres and who permitted them to lead such corrupt and self-indulgent lives? Wasn't it the chairman of the CCP? Wasn't it Mao himself who launched the Cultural Revolution and ordered the four to purge other party leaders? The people know that Chiang Ch'ing lived with Mao as his wife for almost forty years. If her personal life was truly so ugly and corrupt, then what does this say about Mao? These are precisely the questions Hua hopes the masses will ask. By attacking the "gang of four" explicitly, he is attacking their leader, Mao, by implication. Hua is opening the door for de-Maoization in the future.

It seems the new leaders are preparing to make some concessions to the intellectuals by permitting a little more freedom of speech and press and allowing some of the prohibited literary works and films to again be produced. Some of the old leaders and cadres will probably be released from prisons and labor camps. On the other hand, the new leaders are preparing to take measures to increase the productivity of the workers through the use of "material incentives," i.e., longer hours for higher wages.

The leadership wants to introduce more machines and technology from abroad into China's industry, but the problem is lack of funds.

Peking seems to be willing to take some measures to reduce tensions in its relations with the Soviet Union, but it will not be possible for them to resolve the basic dispute because both countries are ruled by bureaucratic cliques that are based on "socialism in one country." The Peking regime is continuing its propaganda that the Soviet Union has restored capitalism and is "social imperialist."

That the new leadership has no intention of allowing the exiled young people to return from the countryside was made clear in a *People's Daily* article where Hua stated that he was very happy to have his own daughter sent to the countryside.

In short, the new leadership cannot resolve the problems discussed above. They can only appease the masses on a short-term basis by giving small concessions, but this will only cause the dissatisfied workers, peasants, and revolutionary intellectuals to press even harder their demands for an end to the present intolerable situation.

Even after the purge of the "gang of four," conflict still exists within the new leadership and undoubtedly new factional disputes will arise. Hua has organized his own faction and the beginnings of his own personality cult to strengthen his hold on his new posts and legitimize himself as Mao's successor. But the old leaders, remnants of the Chou–Teng faction and others, are dissatisfied with Hua. In particular, local cadres in the provinces do not consider Hua any more qualified than themselves to hold such high posts in the party, the army, and the government. Under these conditions, it is possible that a campaign against Hua is developing behind the scenes. If this is true it could mean a very serious struggle within the CCP in the near future.

On the other hand, the masses are expecting an improvement in their standard of living and an increase in their personal and political freedoms under the post-Mao leadership. They will be more willing than ever before to employ mass action to pressure the new leadership, because they have seen the weakness of the new group in resolving its own factional disputes. The demonstrators at T'ien An Men Square last April gave an example to the people of China of how to prepare the necessary political revolution which is long overdue. The words to the poem made famous at T'ien An Men point the way forward:

We believe in Marxism-Leninism.
To hell with those scholars who castrate
    Marxism-Leninism.
For the sake of genuine Marxism-Leninism
We fear not shedding our blood and
    laying down our lives.

These words clearly call for the downfall of the bureaucratic dictatorship in China.

AN APPRAISAL OF THE
POLITICAL LIFE OF MAO TSE-TUNG

Question: Since the death of Mao last September 9, politicians throughout the world have praised Mao as a great leader and peacemaker. What is your opinion of Mao's achievements?

Answer: To analyze Mao's achievements it is necessary to outline his ideas and actions throughout his entire life. We must "call things by their right names," as Trotsky once said.

Mao joined the Communist movement in the fall of 1920 and attended the founding congress of the Chinese Communist Party in July 1921. He was sent to Hunan to become secretary of the branch there. During his two years in Hunan, Mao was an active local leader and made certain contributions in the student and workers' movements. However, he was responsible for forcing two leading comrades, Ho Ming-fan and Li Ta, out of the party, indicating his arbitrary and bureaucratic tendencies.

Q: What was Mao's role in the 1927 revolution?

A: When Stalin, through the Comintern, ordered the CCP to join the Kuomintang in early 1923, Mao not only supported this opportunistic policy but attempted to theoretically justify it. In an article entitled "The Peking Coup d'Etat and the Merchants," Mao stated: "The present political problem in China is none other than the problem of the national revolution. . . . The revolution is the task of the people as a whole. . . . Nevertheless, the merchants [the bourgeoisie] are the ones who feel these sufferings most acutely and most urgently."[1]

This interview was obtained by Rose Connolly on March 14, 1977. The text was submitted to P'eng Shu-tse and he enlarged on his replies before its publication in Intercontinental Press *in October 1977.*

Mao also stated:

> The Shanghai merchants have arisen and begun to act. We hope that
> the merchants outside of Shanghai will all rise up and act together. . . .
> The broader the organization of merchants, the greater will be their
> influence, the greater will be their ability to lead the people of the whole
> country, and the more rapid the success of the revolution![2]

Mao then put this Menshevist line into practice, devoting all his
efforts for many years to working for China's bourgeois party,
the Kuomintang.

Mao was elected to the Central Committee of the CCP at its
Third Congress in June 1923 and given the post of organizational
secretary, but he neglected this work in favor of working in the
Shanghai headquarters of the KMT. In the autumn of 1924 Mao
abandoned his CCP post and moved to Hunan, where he tried to
launch a peasant movement, ending with failure. Then he moved
to Canton and became secretary of the KMT propaganda section
under Wang Ching-wei, and editor of the magazine *Political
Weekly*. Through the pages of this publication, Mao actively
propagated the "Three People's Principles" of Sun Yat-sen.

In March 1926, under pressure from CCP cadres, Mao wrote
"Analysis of the Classes in China," in which he seemingly
altered his rightist position. He acknowledged that "the industrial proletariat is the leading force in our revolution" but divided
the bourgeoisie into "right" and "left" wings, stating "its left
wing may become our friend. . . ."[3] Hence, he reasoned, the
policy of KMT-CCP collaboration should be maintained indefinitely.

Just after publication of Mao's article in *Peasant Monthly* in
early March 1926, the "left wing" of the bourgeoisie, led by
Chiang Kai-shek, launched the March 20 coup d'etat, expelling
all the Communists, including Mao, from the headquarters of the
KMT. Mao then went to Shanghai and was assigned by the CCP
Central Committee to lead the peasant movement.

He went to Hunan to gather facts, which he published in his
"Report on an Investigation of the Peasant Movement in Hunan." This report has been called by the Maoists a "classic
document" of CCP-led peasant struggle.[4] Some foreign scholars,
such as Benjamin Schwartz, praise this report as the starting
point of the rise of Mao.[5]

The report makes no proposals for resolving questions such as
leadership of the peasant movement and confiscation and redis-

tribution of the land, but only contains descriptions of the peasants' actions and defends their excesses against their detractors. Mao's only proposal was that "the revolutionary authority must correct all the mistakes regarding the peasant movement," the "revolutionary authority" at the time being Chiang Kai-shek, Wang Ching-wei, and T'ang Sheng-chih.

After leaving Hunan, Mao went to Wuhan, where he participated in a land-reform committee led by the KMT. He also became an officer of the Provisional National Peasants Association, but never made any formal proposals for land reform to that body or to the CCP leadership. On the contrary, Mao carried out Stalin's opportunistic line, while the situation in Wuhan became worse and worse.

In the Soviet Union, Trotsky proposed that the policy of KMT-CCP collaboration end immediately and that the CCP lead an independent movement of workers, peasants, and soldiers to form soviets and take power. Stalin opposed this, and as a result the so-called revolutionary authority in Wuhan, headed by Wang Ching-wei, expelled all the Communists from the KMT and the army and disbanded all the mass organizations, including the Provisional National Peasants Association. Thus on July 15, 1927, the second Chinese revolution was tragically defeated.

Q: Since Mao was submerged inside the KMT most of this time, when did he become prominent as a Communist?

A: Following the defeat of the 1927 revolution, Stalin changed his policy from extreme opportunism to extreme left adventurism, ordering the CCP to launch an armed struggle for power. To put the new plan into effect, the CCP leadership under Ch'ü Ch'iu-pai called an emergency conference on August 7, 1927. The conference adopted an open letter to the CCP membership, absolving Stalin of his role in the defeat and laying the blame on Ch'en Tu-hsiu. Mao completely supported this deception.

The conference adopted a resolution for initiation of a "harvest uprising" in Hunan and Hupeh. Mao was sent to Hunan to lead the uprising, which involved around 3,000 people and took place September 8-17, 1927. Hundreds were killed or wounded by KMT troops. In utter defeat, Mao escaped with his remaining people to Chingkangshan, arriving in October 1927.

Mao and his followers waited in total isolation for further direction from the CCP. Two bandit groups joined them, claiming allegiance to communism. The bandits' leaders, Yuan Wen-ts'ai and Wang Tso, pledged to struggle under Mao. However, after Mao left Chingkangshan, the bandits returned to their former activities and were later killed by peasants.

Meanwhile, an uprising of 30,000 people in Nanchang, capital of Kiangsi province, was led by the CCP under Ho Lung, Yeh T'ing, and Chu Te, under the leadership of Ch'ü Ch'iu-pai. The uprising was quickly defeated, forcing Ho, Yeh, and Chu to lead a retreat to Swatow in Kwangtung province.

In December 1927, a CCP-led uprising in Canton was tragically defeated, with the loss of more than 5,000 lives. Stalin's policy of armed struggle in China was demonstrated in blood as totally bankrupt.

A congress of the Comintern was held in Moscow in August 1928, which evaluated the situation. But rather than learning from the devastating defeats, the delegates adopted a resolution for continuing the armed struggle:

at the present time, the Party must everywhere propagate among the masses the idea of Soviets, the idea of the dictatorship of the proletariat and peasantry, and the inevitability of the coming revolutionary mass armed uprising. . . . it must consistently and undeviatingly follow the line of seizure of State power, organization of Soviets of organs of the insurrection. . . .[6]

In China, the future growth of the revolution will place before the Party as an immediate practical task the preparation for and carrying through of armed insurrection as the sole path to the completion of the bourgeois-democratic revolution and to the overthrow of the . . . Kuomintang.[7]

This resolution reached Mao at Chingkangshan in the autumn of 1928. Chu Te had already brought the remainder of his troops there from Swatow, and they were soon joined by a large army unit commanded by P'eng Te-huai, which had revolted against the KMT. All these troops were formally organized into the Red Army.

The new Red Army set out from Chingkangshan in early 1929 to expand CCP territory. They occupied a number of counties in western Kiangsi and southeast Hunan, establishing soviets, increasing the size of the army, and extending land reform wherever they went. In December 1930, the CCP called the first Congress of Soviets in Kiangsi, which established a "Soviet government" with Mao as its elected chairman. Chu Te then became general commander of the Red Army.

In response to these advances by the CCP, Chiang Kai-shek

attempted several attacks on the Soviet areas during 1931, losing thousands of troops and weapons to the Red Army. In April 1933, Chiang launched his fourth attack on the Red Army and met an even worse defeat. He lost two divisions of soldiers, and the commanders of these divisions were taken prisoner.

A representative from Moscow arrived in January 1931 in Shanghai to reorganize the CCP Central Committee there. Li Lisan was replaced in the leadership by Wang Ming. Meanwhile, many CCP members and cadres were being arrested, some of whom were executed if they didn't capitulate. For safety, Wang's Central Committee moved to the Soviet base in early 1933. All Mao's power was taken from him and chiefly delegated to Vice-Chairman Hsiang Ying. Mao retained only the title of chairman of the Soviet government—a heavy blow.

The entire Soviet area in Kiangsi and Fukien had been surrounded by more than a million of Chiang's troops imposing a total blockade and extreme hardship. Thus, Mao and Chu Te in October 1934 began the Long March to Yenan in the northeast of China. Already, when they left Kiangsi, over a million peasants had been killed or died of hunger.[8]

During the march, Mao held a Political Committee meeting in Tsun-yi, Kweichow province, at which he was elected chairman of the party and restored to leadership of the Red Army.

When the Red Army arrived in northern Shensi province in October 1935, it had been reduced from 300,000 to less than 30,000.[9] In addition, since the launching of the armed struggle, the KMT had severely suppressed CCP organizations that remained in the big cities such as Shanghai, Wuhan, Peking, and Tiensin. More than 10,000 cadres and members of the CCP and its youth affiliate had been arrested, killed, or forced to capitulate. Workers' organizations were completely destroyed. Stalin's adventurous policy of armed struggle for power, promoted by Mao and the other leaders of the CCP, was defeated. A tremendous sacrifice was paid in human life.

When the remnants of the Red Army arrived in Shensi, Mao appealed to all parties and groupings, including the KMT, to establish "a national front against Japanese imperialism," modeled after the "People's Front against fascism" line of the Comintern.

Chiang rejected Mao's proposal and sent troops led by Chang Hsueh-liang to Shensi to surround Yenan in hopes of destroying the Red Army. Chiang intended to personally supervise the attack but was arrested by a group of Chang Hsueh-liang's subordinates who had a personal hatred for Chiang for allowing the Japanese to occupy their homeland in Manchuria.

The officers intended to execute Chiang, but Stalin sent a telegram to the CCP instructing them to bargain with the captive. Mao dispatched Chou En-lai to convince Chiang to lead the resistance war against Japan. He agreed. The CCP then liquidated the soviets, abandoned land reform, and reorganized the Red Army into a national army under Chiang's command. Thus, KMT-CCP collaboration was achieved for a second time with Mao's strong support.

Q: This so-called bargain with Chiang looks like a class-collaborationist agreement in which all the concessions were made by Mao.

A: In effect, yes. After ten years of struggle, the CCP virtually surrendered to the KMT. The terms of the agreement between the CCP and KMT were contained in a manifesto published by the CCP Central Committee July 15, 1937:

(1) The *San-min chu-i* (Three People's Principles) enunciated by Sun Yat-sen are the paramount need of China today. This Party is ready to strive for their thorough realization.

(2) (This Party) abandons its policy of overthrowing the KMT by force and the movement of sovietization, and discontinues its policy of forcible confiscation of land from landlords.

(3) (This Party) abolishes the present Soviet government and practises democracy based on the people's rights in order to unify the national political power.

(4) (This Party) abolishes the designation of the Red Army, reorganizes it into the National Revolutionary Army, places it under the control of the Military Affairs Commission of the National government, and awaits orders for mobilization to shoulder the responsibility of resisting Japanese aggression at the front.[10]

Chiang had been under heavy criticism by the masses for not organizing resistance to the Japanese, and some of his officers were on the verge of revolt. Publication of the CCP manifesto gave Chiang a new lease on life and also caused great confusion among the ranks of the CCP.

Q: Was there any opposition to the manifesto within the CCP?

A: Those who understood its real meaning were very angry. Mao was compelled to write a series of articles to justify the new opportunism. In his article "Urgent Tasks Following the Establishment of Kuomintang-Communist Co-operation," Mao explained:

> Now the newly formed united front between the two parties has ushered in a new period in the Chinese revolution. There are still people who do not understand the historical role of the united front and its great future and regard it as a mere temporary makeshift devised under the pressure of circumstances; nevertheless, through this united front, the wheel of history will propel the Chinese revolution forward to a completely new stage.[11]

And further: "The present task is to restore the revolutionary spirit of Dr. Sun's Three Principles throughout the country. . . ."[12]

Mao's illusions in the KMT are evident in this quotation from his pamphlet *On the New Stage:*

> the Kuomintang and the Communist Party are the foundation of the Anti-Japanese United Front, but of these two it is the Kuomintang that occupies first place. Without the Kuomintang, it would be inconceivable to undertake and pursue the war of resistance. In the course of its glorious history, the Kuomintang has been responsible for the overthrow of the Ch'ing, the establishment of the Republic, opposition to Yüan Shih-k'ai, establishment of the Three Policies of uniting with Russia, with the Communist Party, and with the workers and peasants, and the great revolution of 1926-27. Today it is once more leading the great Anti-Japanese War. It enjoys the historic heritage of the Three People's Principles; it has had two great leaders in succession—Mr. Sun Yat-sen and Mr. Chiang Kai-shek; it has a great number of faithful and patriotic active members. All this should not be underestimated by our compatriots and constitutes the result of China's historical development.
>
> In carrying out the Anti-Japanese War, and in organizing the Anti-Japanese United Front, the Kuomintang occupies the position of leader and framework. . . . Under the single great condition that it support to the end the war of resistance and the United Front, one can foresee a brilliant future for the Kuomintang. . . .
>
> The task of the nation as a whole is to call on all people to honestly support Chiang as head of the KMT, support the national government, and support KMT-CCP collaboration.
>
> For this purpose we must promote the prestige of Chiang and the national government in order to avoid bad influences and to increase close solidarity between the KMT and the CCP. The so-called collabora-

tion will last a long time—not only for the duration of the existing war but after the end of the war, when national and international conditions will be more favorable for this collaboration.[13]

Mao's most important theoretical work, *On New Democracy*, was adopted as the basic program of the party at the Seventh Congress held in 1945 and implemented as the program of the People's Republic of China after the 1949 victory. In this article, Mao explained that after the October revolution in Russia, the national-democratic revolution in the colonial and semicolonial countries was a "new bourgeois-democratic revolution," in which the national bourgeoisie remained revolutionary. Hence it was necessary to carry out a "united front" of workers, peasants, petty bourgeoisie, and bourgeoisie—the bloc of four classes—in order to destroy the imperialists and feudal forces and to establish a "New Democratic republic." That is, Mao advocated the establishment of a coalition government with the bourgeoisie.

He also advocated a "New Democratic economy," meaning the nationalization of only "the big banks and the big industrial and commercial enterprises" by the state. "The republic will neither confiscate capitalist private property in general nor forbid the development of such capitalist production as does not 'dominate the livelihood of the people', for China's economy is still very backward. . . . A rich peasant economy will be allowed in the rural areas."[14]

Mao further explained the theory of revolution by stages in the following sentences: "The present task of the revolution in China is to fight imperialism and feudalism, and socialism is out of the question until this task is completed. The Chinese revolution cannot avoid taking the two steps, first of New Democracy and then of socialism. Moreover, the first step will need quite a long time and cannot be accomplished overnight."[15]

Then to justify their policies, Mao and the CCP launched a vicious and violent campaign against the Trotskyists, the only organized voice of opposition within the workers' movement to their policies. In his article "Tasks of the CCP in the Period of Resistance to Japan," Mao charged:

Our enemies—the Japanese imperialists, the Chinese collaborators, the pro-Japanese clique and the Trotskyites—have been trying with all their might to wreck every measure for peace and solidarity, democracy and freedom, and armed resistance to Japan. . . . From now on we must exert ourselves not only to conduct propaganda, agitation and criticism among the die-hards of the Kuomintang and the backward sections of the people, but to expose in every possible way and fight resolutely the intrigues of Japanese imperialism and its jackals, the pro-Japanese clique and the Trotskyites, for invading China.[16]

Trotskyists, particularly Ch'en Tu-hsiu and P'eng Shu-tse, were denounced as traitors in all the newspapers and magazines controlled by the CCP, despite the fact that they had pledged support to the military effort under Chiang against Japanese imperialism. The anti-Trotskyist campaign became violent to the point of madness, because the Trotskyists insisted on their right to criticize Chiang and his government. They called for the arming of the masses and proposed a program of struggle around freedom of speech, press, assembly, and association, the eight-hour day, and the right to strike. In place of the KMT government-led resistance, they raised the slogan "Convene a national assembly with full powers, elected by universal, equal, and direct suffrage."

As for Chiang, despite Mao's praises of him, he was publicly preparing to destroy the CCP's forces. In January 1941, Chiang attacked and destroyed the New Fourth Army of the CCP in Anhwei province, capturing its commander, Yeh T'ing, and killing the head of the political commission, Hsiang Ying. At the same time, a powerful KMT force led by Hu Tsung-nan surrounded Yenan. These defeats for the CCP were an ominous sign of things to come.

Q: What was Mao's relationship with Stalin at this time?

A: On the occasion of Stalin's sixtieth birthday, in December 1939, Mao gave a speech in which he said: "Congratulating Stalin means supporting him and his cause, supporting the victory of socialism, and the way forward for mankind which he points out, it means supporting a dear friend. For the great majority of mankind today are suffering, and mankind can free itself from suffering only by the road pointed out by Stalin and with his help."[17]

In 1941 at a party school in Yenan, Mao made a speech entitled "Reform Our Study" in which he said:

"Moreover, in studying Marxism-Leninism, we should use the *History of the Communist Party of the Soviet Union (Bolsheviks), Short Course* as the principal material. It is the best synthesis and summing-up of the world communist movement of the past hundred years, a model of the integration of theory and practice. . . ."[18]

Actually, *The History of the CPSU* already demonstrated the theory and practice of Stalinism: revolution by stages, "socialism in one country." It contained Stalin's adventuristic policies of collectivization, industrialization, and foreign policy of the so-called third period, and "the highest synthesis" of Marxist revisionism—the famous purges in the 1930s of all the Old Bolsheviks and other revolutionists, and the firm establishment of Stalin's cult and personal dictatorship.

Q: How did Mao explain the defeat of the 1927 revolution and the later defeats suffered under Stalin's direction?

A: In a resolution adopted at a Central Committee plenum in April 1945, Mao placed the responsibility for the defeat of the second Chinese revolution on Ch'en Tu-hsiu and responsibility for defeat of the armed struggle and Soviet campaign of 1927-37 on Ch'ü Ch'iu-pai, Li Li-san, and Wang Ming. The resolution claimed that only Mao held a correct position in the Communist movement, concluding that:

the practice of the Chinese revolution has confirmed for the last twenty-four years and continues to confirm that the line of the struggle of our Party and of the broad masses, a line represented by Comrade Mao Tse-tung, is perfectly correct. . . . Today the whole Party recognizes the correctness of Comrade Mao Tse-tung's line with unprecedented unanimity and rallies under his banner with unprecedented consciousness.[19]

The resolution contained not a word about the ultra-opportunist policy imposed by Stalin during the second Chinese revolution and the ultra-adventuristic policy after the revolution was defeated. On the contrary, Mao cited Stalin's own words to claim that Stalin's ideas on the Chinese revolution were totally correct.

Following the April plenum, Mao made a report to the Seventh Party Congress, entitled "On Coalition Government," in which he emphasized the absolute necessity of a coalition of the KMT, CCP, and other parties and groups, i.e., a government of four classes. The KMT did not respond to this proposal, however.

The congress adopted a new party constitution which contained the following sentence: "The CCP takes the theories of Marxism-Leninism and the combined principles derived from the practical experience of the Chinese revolution—the ideas of Mao Tse-tung—as the guiding principles of all its work. . . ."[20]

Thus, Mao's personal cult, modeled after Stalin's, was officially established at this congress. Since then, Mao has been referred to as "the sole great leader of the CCP," a "Stalin in China," a "sun in the East," a "messiah for the people in China." There is a famous song called "The East is Red," which contains the following verse:

The east is red,
The sun rises.
China has brought forth a Mao Tse-tung.
He works for the people's happiness,
He is the people's great saviour.

Q: What happened after the Japanese surrendered?

A: In August 1945, just after the Japanese surrendered to the United States, Mao went to Chungking, the provisional capital of the KMT government. Mao stayed for one and a half months to have secret discussions with Chiang Kai-shek on how to continue collaboration and establish a coalition government. The results of their discussions were published on October 10, 1945, in a communiqué containing a number of measures to keep peace between the KMT and CCP. At a public meeting Mao expressed his sentiments by shouting, "Long live Chiang, head of the KMT." But soon after, a series of conflicts broke out between the two parties. Chiang sent troops to attack a number of towns and villages occupied by CCP guerrillas. In an effort to moderate the impending civil war, Truman sent his special representative George Marshall to China.

Chiang Kai-shek for his part had made use of the time during the peace conference to transport his army, with the aid of American planes and warships, from the interior of China to the great cities and the strategic bases in the "recovered areas," to solidify his position. He suppressed all the newly arising mass movements, especially the student movement.

At the end of 1946, when Chiang's preparations for armed attack on the CCP were complete, the government openly barred all doors to compromise and peace parleys by holding its own National Assembly and organizing a "Constituent Government," avoiding forming a coalition with the CCP. Then a great military offensive was launched, in which Chang-chia-k'ou in Hopeh and some small cities and towns in north Kiangsu were seized.

Even yet, the CCP had not given up its efforts at conciliation.

Its delegates to the peace conference still lingered in Shanghai and Nanking, trying to reopen peace parleys with the Kuomintang through mediation of the so-called third force, the Democratic League.

Not until Chiang drove away the CCP peace delegation and succeeded in occupying the CCP capital and stronghold, Yenan, in April 1947, did the CCP finally realize the hopelessness of compromise, and only then did it muster a military defense. The CCP still did not dare raise the slogan of overthrowing the KMT government, nor did it offer the masses a program for mobilization around agrarian reform. Finally, Chiang issued a warrant for the arrest of Mao Tse-tung (June 25, 1947) and proclaimed the "Decree of Mobilization for Suppressing Revolts" (July 4). After several months of hesitation, during which the CCP seemed to be waiting for instructions from Moscow, on October 10 the CCP in the name of the "People's Liberation Army" openly urged the overthrow of Chiang Kai-shek and the building of a "New China."

Q: Some people claim that the CCP changed its position from opportunism to revolution in violation of the Kremlin's wishes in order to overthrow Chiang's regime. Do you agree with this?

A: The CCP operated with the complete agreement of the Kremlin, which had been compelled to change its line under pressure from postwar American imperialism, particularly the Marshall Plan.[21] Communist Party members had been expelled from bourgeois governments in Western Europe, so Stalin felt he had to strengthen the East European governments by carrying out land reform and nationalizations of capitalist property and the establishment of the "Cominform." In my opinion, Stalin, out of the same considerations, endorsed the decision of the Chinese Communist Party to overthrow the KMT after Chiang Kai-shek made further compromise impossible.

Q: How was the CCP able to overcome Chiang's army and take power after so many years of opportunist policies?

A: The CCP victory was due to exceptional conditions created by the Japanese invasion of China, particularly during World War II. In the period of the Resistance War, Chiang's regime became completely corrupt and so inefficient that it was unable to counter any severe attack from Japan without powerful assistance from the United States. American imperialism was unable to continue military aid to Chiang after the Japanese surrender, because American soldiers were unwilling to fight after the war was over. Modern weapons taken from the Japanese by the Soviet Red Army, which had occupied Manchuria at the end of the war, were turned over to CCP troops, primarily to the Fourth Field Army led by Lin Piao.

Had this combination of historical conditions not existed, Mao's victory over Chiang Kai-shek would have been highly improbable. If Chiang had had control of Manchuria, the most industrialized area of China, he could have cut off the economic and military aid the CCP was receiving from the Soviet Union. Similarly, if American troops had remained, Mao's party would have had little chance of victory. We need only recall the terrible defeat suffered by the peasant army in Kiangsi during 1930-34 to know the difference American and other imperialist aid meant to Chiang.

Q: Did the CCP abandon opportunism and become a revolutionary party after conquering power?

A: Mao's policies since 1949 have twisted and turned, ranging from opportunism to adventurism, but never transforming the CCP into a revolutionary party.

When the People's Republic of China was proclaimed on October 1, 1949, a coalition government of representatives of the workers, peasants, petty bourgeoisie, and bourgeoisie was established. Government officials have never been elected, but were, and are, appointed by the so-called People's Political Consultative Conference, composed of the CCP, the KMT Revolutionary Committee, the Democratic League, the Worker Peasant Party, and other groups.

The government's policies were based on Mao's "New Democracy." They did not call for confiscation of capitalist property but for its protection and the protection even of imperialist property in China. In the name of New Democracy, the government postponed the badly needed agrarian reform demanded by the peasants in order to effect a compromise with the landlords and rich peasants. Mao expected the New Democracy to last several decades, and Chou En-lai said, "The New Democracy stage of the revolution will be complete within twenty years."

The objective situation soon changed, however, with the beginning of the Korean War in 1950. Under the pretext of assisting

South Korea, the American imperialists attacked North Korea, directly threatening China. This compelled Mao to assist North Korea, first by confiscating imperialist holdings in China. The bourgeoisie and landlords of China took advantage of the American presence to mount antirevolutionary activities. Mao carried out a land reform to keep the peasantry on the side of the government and intiated the "Five Anti Movement" in order to strike out at the capitalists.

The land reform of 1952 was carried out without nationalizing the land, which meant continued buying and selling on the open market. This created a further differentiation among the peasantry—poor peasants were forced to sell their land in order to maintain themselves, and rich peasants bought it. Rich peasants were also in the business of loaning money to poor peasants at high interest rates, and some of these loan sharks were party members.

The situation was very serious, obliging the CCP to again carry out an agricultural reform in 1955—agricultural collectivization. Mao was at odds with other CCP leaders on how to carry this out, however. His plan called for completion of the collectivization before the end of the year. Liu Shao-ch'i and Minister of Agriculture Teng Tzu-hui were among those who advocated a more prudent policy, to be completed by 1967. Mao, over the heads of the Political Bureau, called a conference of the municipal, provincial, and regional secretaries, which decided that agricultural collectivization should be completed in 1957. This arbitrary maneuver by Mao violated the principles on collectivization of land and agriculture laid down by Engels and Lenin. Instead, Mao's policy was copied directly from that of Stalin during the late 1920s, and created deep dissatisfaction among the masses for years to come.

At the beginning of 1953, American imperialism blockaded China. The CCP then proclaimed its "general line of the transitional period," which included the First Five-Year Plan for economic construction and industrialization. In 1955 and 1956, in face of bourgeois sabotage of the economic plan, the New Democracy was abandoned for the policy of "state and private cooperation," aimed at the gradual abolition of bourgeois property and the beginning of socialist construction.

The evolution of the CCP's policies after taking power in 1949 until 1955 was similar to Stalin's policies from 1945 to 1948 in the East European countries occupied by the Red Army. In foreign policy, Mao followed Stalin's course of peaceful coexistence between capitalism and socialism. The "Five Principles" statement agreed upon by Chou En-lai and India's Nehru is a good example. During this time, Mao's government looked to the Stalinist regime in the Soviet Union as both model and mentor. In July 1949, Mao proclaimed the foreign policy of the New China to be "i-pien-tao," which literally translated means "to lean to one side" but in practice meant to lean on the Soviet Union. After this policy statement, Mao visited the Soviet Union in 1950 to talk directly with Stalin. The result was a series of economic, political, and military treaties between the People's Republic of China and the USSR. All these treaties were more favorable to the Soviet Union than to China, which caused Mao to later complain, "Our relationship with the Soviet Union was like the relationship between a son and a father."[22]

After the Nineteenth Congress of the CPSU, Mao ordered the CCP members and cadres to study Stalinist ideology. At the time of Stalin's death in 1953, Mao said:

All the writings of Comrade Stalin are immortal Marxist documents. His works, the *Foundations of Leninism,* the *History of the CPSU (Bolsheviks),* and his last great work, *The Economic Problems of Socialism in the U.S.S.R.,* are an encyclopedia of Marxism-Leninism, the summation of the experience of the world Communist movement in the past hundred years.[23]

The study of Stalin's ideology was enforced on all members of the CCP and its youth organizations, on teachers and students in all schools, on cadres in all mass organizations, and on officials at all levels of government. The campaign, which lasted several months, was in reality a campaign to Stalinize China.

Q: How did Khrushchev's speech, revealing many of Stalin's crimes, affect China?

A: It is ironic that at the very time the CPSU was compelled under mass pressure to strike a blow at the cult of Stalin, the CCP was engaged in a campaign to build up Stalin's reputation. At the Twentieth Congress of the CPSU in 1956, Khrushchev denounced Stalin's personal cult and exposed many of Stalin's errors and crimes. Communist parties throughout the world and particularly in China were strongly affected by the revelations. The reaction within the CCP was voiced at the Eighth Congress, held in September 1956. A resolution proposed by Liu Shao-ch'i revised the party constitution to remove the sentence, "The CCP takes the theories of Marxism-Leninism and the combined principles derived from the practical experience of the Chinese revolution—the ideas of Mao Tse-tung—as the guiding principles of all its work. . . ."

Teng Hsiao-p'ing, in a report on changing the constitution, stated:

The Twentieth Congress of the Communist Party of the Soviet Union has thrown a searching light on the profound significance of adhering to the principle of collective leadership and combating the cult of the individual, and this illuminating lesson has produced a tremendous effect not only on the Communist Party of the Soviet Union but also on the Communist Parties of all other countries throughout the world. It is obvious that the making of decisions on important questions by individuals runs counter to the Party-building principles of the political parties dedicated to the cause of communism, and is bound to lead to errors. Only collective leadership, in close touch with the masses, conforms to the Party's principle of democratic centralism and can reduce the possibility of errors to the minimum.[24]

This report represented the majority opinion of the CCP leadership. Mao did not dare to resist the revision of the party statutes and was even compelled to declare to the congress, "At its Twentieth Congress held not long ago, the Communist Party of the Soviet Union formulated many correct policies and criticized shortcomings which were found in the Party. It can be confidently asserted that very great developments will follow this in its work . . . *our experience is far from being adequate.* So we must be good at studying. We must be good at learning from our forerunner, the Soviet Union. . . ."[25]

Despite the above statement, Mao had suffered a heavy blow. After the Eighth Congress he prepared an attack on Khrushchev and the destruction of the Liu Shao-ch'i/Teng Hsiao-p'ing faction. In the autumn of 1956 the Hungarian revolution broke out. It was the first political revolution in the Soviet bloc. Soviet tanks mercilessly suppressed the masses, yet the event had global impact, eliciting support and sympathy from revolutionary-minded people throughout the world. In China, Mao was forced to speak out: "Certain people in our country were delighted when the Hungarian events took place. They hoped that something similar would happen in China, that thousands upon thousands of people would demonstrate in the streets against the People's Government."[26]

Q: What did Mao do to prevent an outbreak of a Hungarian-type revolution on Chinese soil?

A: Mao sought to alleviate discontent by launching a campaign around the slogan "Let a hundred flowers bloom, let a hundred schools of thought contend." This campaign invited every party, every faction, and any individual to express opinions and criticism of the so-called Three Harms—bureaucratism, commandism, and subjectivism. Mao hoped to appease dissatisfaction and hostility to his personality cult by giving the people a few concessions and freedom of expression. During the Hundred Flowers movement (April-June 1957), criticism of the party and government and the privileges of the CCP bureaucrats were criticized. Liu Shao'chi admitted, "There is a serious bureaucracy of the CCP and its youth organization. The arbitrariness of the government and the privileges of the CCP bureaucrats were criticized. Liu Shao-ch'i admitted, "There is a serious bureaucracy . . . much criticism is spreading to every corner of China, including factories, farms, schools, and other organizations. The target of the criticism is the leadership."[27]

The opinions of the masses were most notably expressed by Lin Hsi-ling, a member of the youth and a leader of the student movement, and by Tai Huang, a member of the party and a reporter for Hsinhua, the official press agency. The former stated, "The present upper stratum of China does not correspond with the property of common ownership because the party and state apparatus has become a center of bureaucratic organs ruling the people without democracy." Therefore, she proclaimed, "Not reform but thoroughgoing change." The latter proposed to build a new party and "to realize democracy, freedom, and the eradication of the privileged class."[28] In the middle of June 1957, more than 3,000 middle-school students in Hanyang, near Hankow, demonstrated, destroying the police stations and occupying the offices of the party and the city government. The rebellion was a repeat of the Hungarian revolution on a small scale.

Mao was quick to respond, by launching a counterattack against those he had so recently invited to help reform the party and government. Now these people were labeled as rightists and counterrevolutionaries and punished ruthlessly. More than 50,000 were expelled from the party and the youth organizations. People were dismissed from schools, jobs, and public posts. Many were arrested and imprisoned or sent to labor camps.

Q: Instead of restoring his personality cult, Mao seems to have worsened the situation.

A: The masses regarded the Hundred Flowers Movement as a cruel trick and a trap to identify and eliminate dissidents. Mao was temporarily disappointed with the results of the campaign but soon launched his next project—the Great Leap Forward and the People's Communes. At a plenum of the Central Committee of the CCP held in May 1958, Mao proposed the Great Leap Forward, in hope of creating a miracle in agriculture and industry. What the plan amounted to was production of steel in backyard furnaces. The effort lasted for about a year, mobilizing around 100 million people. Students, professors, workers, peasants, and even housewives made steel in their backyards. Over three million tons of steel were produced in this manner, and not one pound was usable! This tremendous waste of labor and materials demonstrated Mao's utter ignorance in the field of technology.

In early August 1958, after visiting an experimental People's Commune in Honan, Mao personally ordered that every peasant must immediately enter a commune. The Political Bureau of the CCP was forced to order the communalization of all privately owned plots of land, including private gardens, stored grains, animals, and fruit trees. The aim was "to abolish all remnants of private property." All peasants were to eat in communal kitchens and children were to attend communal nurseries, thus allowing women to work a twelve- to fourteen-hour day in the fields. In the short period of three months, 99 percent of China's peasants were compelled to enter the People's Communes. This method of forced collectivization violated the fundamental Marxist principles as laid down by Engels, Lenin, and Trotsky.[29] Most peasants opposed the communes by committing acts of sabotage, such as killing their animals, cutting down fruit trees, or destroying crops, which of course brought about a great scarcity of food. The situation became critical in the summer of 1959, at the same time the failure of the backyard steelmaking scheme became clear. The whole country was dissatisfied. Many cadres and top leaders of the party spoke out against the People's Communes, including Liu Shao-ch'i, vice-chairman of the party and the government; Chu Te, commander in chief of the People's Liberation Army; P'eng Te-huai, defense minister; Huang K'o-ch'eng, army chief of staff, and several other members of the Central Committee.

P'eng Te-huai openly criticized the People's Communes policy as "petty-bourgeois fanaticism." He wrote a letter to Mao on July 14, 1959, in which he said that the Great Leap Forward had been executed in such haste that all rational proportions in economic development had been destroyed and that 20 billion Chinese dollars (approximately equal to US$9 billion) had been wasted. P'eng claimed that, "The People's Communes were set up too early, which set back agricultural production." P'eng's demand that the People's Communes be reorganized had widespread support, particularly in the army. Mao responded by calling a plenum of the Central Committee of the CCP at Lushan in August 1959. After a sharp debate, the now-famous meeting— known as the Lushan Conference—adopted a resolution calling for the reorganization of the People's Communes. The resolution declared the producers cooperative to be the basic level of ownership—i.e., a return to the form of production before the Great Leap Forward. The plenum also took measures to reorganize the dissidents within the government. P'eng Te-huai's position as defense minister was taken over by Lin Piao, Huang K'o-ch'eng was dismissed from his post, and several other Central Committee members disappeared from public life.

Mao himself, in an effort to cover up his blunders, had resigned as head of state in December 1958, proposing that his position be taken over by Liu Shao-ch'i. Liu was formally appointed to the post in April 1959. Now responsibility passed to him for undertaking measures to rectify the serious economic situation and the mass discontent.

Q: Was Liu able to make any reforms in his new position?

A: Liu, along with Teng Hsiao-p'ing, general secretary of the party, and P'eng Chen, mayor of Peking, initiated a rectification campaign, including the ending of backyard steelmaking, restoration of private plots of land and personal ownership of livestock, restoration of the free market in the countryside, and abolition of most communal kitchens and nurseries. The great majority of the people, especially the peasants, greeted these reforms with enthusiasm. Production was increased and the extreme shortages of vegetables and meats lessened. From 1960 to 1961 an actual famine existed, attributable to the People's Communes, but by the beginning of 1963, agricultural production was restored almost to the level before the launching of the communes.

For those working in education and culture, Liu permitted a certain freedom of expression and independence in their work. This immediately brought forth many newspaper and magazine articles and some new plays. Wu Han, vice-mayor of Peking, wrote a play called *Hai Jui Dismissed from Office*, in obvious reference to the recent purge of P'eng Te-huai. The play was published in the *Peking Daily* in January 1961 and performed on the Peking stage. It met with an exceptionally positive response from the public and critics alike, both for its artistic and political content. Teng T'o, secretary of the Peking Municipal Committee, Wu Han, Liao Mo-sha, head of the United Front work in Peking, wrote a great many articles published in Peking's newspapers and magazines. They published two pamphlets, *Notes from Three-Family Village* and *Evening Talks at Yenshan*, using old fables, parables, historical analogies, and satires to criticize Mao.

At a meeting held in Dairen in August 1962, writers from all over China expressed their dissatisfaction with the Great Leap Forward, the People's Communes, and Mao's policies in literature and art. One said, "The life of the peasants is getting worse and worse." Chou Yang, vice-minister of the Cultural Department, said, "The People's Communes are adventurist. The Great Leap Forward represents subjective idealism." These comments illustrate the deep discontent among literary people.

Reform of education was initiated with the publication of "Sixty Points of Higher Educational Reforms," issued by the Central Educational Department. These reforms aimed at encouraging students to study in their fields of interest and gave them the necessary time to do so, which they had not had during the Great Leap Forward. Liu's reforms won him great respect and support from the people, particularly the peasants and intellectuals—a situation very unfavorable to Mao. Liu made a speech at a meeting called by the Central Committee on February 22, 1962, in which he said:

The temporary economic difficulties were due to the serious errors and mistakes in our work—30 percent were due to natural disasters and 70 percent due to artificial disasters. The attacks against the rightists at Lushan in 1959 [P'eng Te-huai] were excessive, even though termed an attempt to rehabilitate them. The struggle was mistaken. . . . The party lacked democracy. Party life was a brutal struggle and a pitiless fight.

This speech, published during the Cultural Revolution in *Red Guards in the Capital,* was an attempt to discredit Liu but in fact did him the service of explaining his views to the public. It was Liu's first attempt at reforming party life and rehabilitating P'eng Te-huai and others.

Meanwhile, Mao was preparing to reestablish his cult and to retaliate against his opposition. First he used Lin Piao, newly appointed defense minister, to propagate his thought and establish his cult within the army. In the early 1960s, Lin Piao proposed a resolution to the Central Military Committee entitled "The Correct Handling of Four Questions in the Political Fields of the Army," in which he emphasized the role of the individual in politics and thought. When the resolution was adopted, Lin declared, "Everyone must read the books of Chairman Mao, listen to the words of Chairman Mao, work according to the instructions of Chairman Mao." At a work conference of the Central Committee in September 1963, Mao raised the slogan "We must not forget the class struggle." This same conference issued a communiqué saying:

During the transitional period from capitalism to socialism . . . the struggle between the proletariat and the bourgeoisie still exists. The struggle between the two lines of socialism and capitalism still exists. This struggle is inevitably reflected inside the party. . . . We must take heed in time and we must firmly struggle against the different types of opportunist tendencies. The significance of the Eighth Plenum of the Central Committee in August 1959 at Lushan was the crushing victory over the rightist tendency. That is, the crushing of the attack by the revisionists.

These sentences were a warning to Liu Shao-ch'i that he and his opposition would be crushed like P'eng Te-huai if they continued with their so-called revisionist tendency. Since then, the labels "revisionist" and "opportunist" have been frequently repeated against any of Mao's opponents within the party. At a meeting of the All-China Federation of Literature and Art in June 1964, Mao stated: "In the past fifteen years this association and most of their other publications have for the most part failed. . . . They have even verged on revisionism. If they do not remold themselves, sooner or later they are bound to become groups of the Hungarian Petöfi type."

Mao was issuing a warning to those in cultural fields who were influenced by Liu, but these words referring to the Hungarian revolutionists were also a sign of the coming Cultural Revolution.

Q: Why did Mao launch the Cultural Revolution?

A: The Cultural Revolution in China was precipitated by the tragic events in Indonesia in October 1965. The Indonesian Communist Party had been the largest in the capitalist world, with 3 million members and 10 million sympathizers. Since early 1960 Mao had tried desperately to win this party to his side in the Sino-Soviet dispute. Mao invited Indonesian CP leader D. N. Aidit to Peking many times for discussions, during which Mao proposed CP cooperation with the Sukarno government, modeled upon the CCP-KMT collaboration during the second Chinese revolution. The Indonesian CP adopted this opportunist policy, which paved the way to a coup d'etat in October 1965, during which 250,000 to 500,000 Communists and militants were slaughtered, including Aidit. This tragedy horrified the entire world and dealt a heavy blow to the credibility of the Chinese Communist Party and Mao himself. Many leaders in the CCP were dissatisfied with Mao's policies at that juncture, which compelled Mao to call a special meeting of the CCP in September-October 1965. At the meeting, some party leaders blamed the Indonesian defeat on the CCP's influence. One speaker, P'eng Chen, said, "Everyone is equal before the truth, and if Chairman Mao made some mistakes he should be criticized."

After this setback, Mao left Peking for Shanghai to regroup his forces, among them Chang Ch'un-ch'iao, director of the Shanghai Cultural Board, and Yao Wen-yuan, editor of *Wen Hui Pao*. Yao Wen-yuan, under Mao's direction, wrote a criticism for his paper of the play *Hai Jui Dismissed from Office*, the publication of which can be considered the first "shot" fired in the Cultural Revolution. A campaign to propagandize Mao's thought was begun in the *Liberation Army Daily* under the direction of Lin Piao, using such slogans as, "One must study the thinking of Mao Tse-tung and raise high the banner of Mao's thought," and "Mao's thought is the beacon of revolution for the world's people." An editorial on January 1, 1966, stated, "Every word of Chairman Mao is truth. . . . We must firmly support and carry out everything conforming to Mao Tse-tung's thought and we must firmly resist and oppose everything which does not conform to Mao's thought." This message was aimed against the authority of Liu Shao-ch'i and the Central Committee.

A few writers in Peking and Shanghai continued to defend Wu Han against his detractors until Lin Piao gave orders for an all-out assault on the "antiparty" tendency. The *Liberation Army Daily* was used to wage this campaign, which went so far as to suggest physical elimination of the opposition. Army cadres were mobilized. Even after Wu and his supporters stopped writing, Mao continued to accuse them of "antisocialist," "antiparty," "counterrevolutionary," and "capitalist restorationist" activity—all of which left Wu thoroughly disgraced. In April, Yao Wen-yuan wrote another article condemning *Notes From Three Family Village* and *Evening Talks at Yenshan.* Soon after, Teng T'o and the other authors of these articles were expelled from the party.

At the end of April, Lin Piao sent troops to occupy the office of the Peking municipal government. Mao returned to Peking from the South and formally proclaimed the "Great Proletarian Cultural Revolution." He also established the Cultural Revolution Group (CRG) with Ch'en Po-ta as first chairman and Chiang Ch'ing as second chairman. The Peking municipal government, headed by P'eng Chen, was formally dismissed in early June 1966. Lu Ting-i, head of the party's Propaganda Department, Chou Yang, vice-minister of culture, and other high-ranking cadres in cultural institutions were removed. Lo Jui-ch'ing, chief of staff, was arrested and by mid-June all schools from elementary to university level were closed in the name of the Cultural Revolution. Almost all presidents and principals of universities and middle schools, as well as many teachers and professors, were attacked by their students under the direction of the CRG headed by Ch'en Po-ta and Chiang Ch'ing.

Liu Shao-ch'i and Teng Hsiao-p'ing attempted to reverse the course of events by calling an emergency meeting of the Central Committee. But Mao refused to attend, since his plan for purging Liu and Teng was not yet complete. When Mao returned to Peking, he ordered Lin to surround the city with army troops. Then he called a special plenum of the Central Committee in early August, which adopted "A Decision Concerning the Great Proletarian Cultural Revolution." The major points were: "to struggle against and crush those persons in authority who are taking the capitalist road" and to reorganize the Standing Committee of the Political Bureau. Thus Liu Shao-ch'i was removed from his post of first vice-chairman of the party and replaced by Lin Piao. The plenum also called for all the students in the country to be organized into the Red Guards. Their first project was a campaign to destroy the "Four Olds"—old ideas, old culture, old customs, and old habits—and to establish the "Four

News." At the end of August, at a mass rally in Peking, Lin Piao instructed the Red Guards "to isolate and purge those party officials who are taking the capitalist road." Demonstrations and wall posters attacking local leaders poured forth.

Some local leaders organized their own Red Guards to counter Mao's forces, resulting in violent clashes in several areas of the country. On September 15, Lin Piao, acting for Mao, made a speech to a large gathering of Red Guards, in which he assured them of the army's support in their attacks on those officials who resisted Mao's thought. This speech removed all restraints. The Red Guards unleashed a wall poster campaign in Peking, naming leading party members and accusing them of "taking the capitalist road." They singled out regional leaders such as Li Ch'ing-ch'üan, first secretary of the Southwest Bureau; Liu Lan-t'ao, first secretary of the Northwest Bureau; and Li Hsueh-feng, secretary of the North Bureau. Officials of the state were also attacked, and finally the accusations were leveled against Liu Shao-ch'i, chairman of the People's Republic of China, and Teng Hsiao-p'ing, general secretary of the CCP. In the latter part of October a special seventeen-day meeting was held where Liu and Teng were forced to make self-criticism. After the meeting P'eng Chen and Lu Ting-i were arrested.

Q: Did this mean Mao had succeeded in crushing his opponents?

A: Mao thought so. On December 26 a large victory celebration of the Red Guards took place in Peking, and journals like *Red Flag* proclaimed the triumph of the Cultural Revolution. Subsequent events revealed that the opposition was far from broken, however.

In the autumn of 1966, a powerful group of Red Guards was organized by Chang Ch'un-ch'iao, Yao Wen-yuan, and Wang Hung-wen to attack the local Shanghai authorities. The Shanghai party and government, led by Mayor Ts'ao Ti-ch'iu and First Secretary of the Municipal Committee Ch'en P'ei-hsien, responded by offering concessions to the workers to win their allegiance. By the first week of January 1967, the antagonisms were so intense that a general strike broke out, which Mao recognized as directed against the Red Guards and the Cultural Revolution as a whole. The party Central Committee, under Mao's orders, instructed the "left" Red Guards to seize power in Shanghai. This enabled a part of the army, under Lin Piao, to suppress the strike. Mao then purged the entire leadership of the party and the government, and cadres in Shanghai's factories, trade unions, and educational and cultural institutions. The wage increases and working conditions so recently won were rescinded, and the entire economic structure of the city was paralyzed. Chou En-lai intervened with a proposal to establish a Revolutionary Committee, made up of army cadres, Red Guards, and a few of the original Shanghai public officials. This so-called Triple Alliance was the first Revolutionary Committee established to replace the old governmental system. The party and the government in Shanghai were firmly in the hands of Chang Ch'un-ch'iao, Yao Wen-yuan, and Wang Hung-wen (recently branded as members of the "gang of four"), who kept Shanghai a stronghold of Mao's faction until Hua Kuo-feng's purges last fall.

Meanwhile, a serious clash between rival Red Guards took place in Nanking. Approximately fifty people were killed and more than a hundred were wounded. Mao was unable to support his Red Guards with the army because the opposition Red Guards were backed by the local Nanking officials, as well as the army commander Hsu Shih-yu. Again Chou En-lai intervened and worked out a compromise. In Honan province, the Red Guards who called themselves the "February 7 Commune" attempted to follow the Shanghai example by proclaiming the seizure of power. The local authorities followed the Nanking example and resisted, with support from the army. The struggle for power lasted from February to June 1967, and many were killed and wounded. The "February 7 Commune" was defeated and some army officers purged, but power remained in the hands of the original authorities.

The most dramatic episode took place in Wuhan in July when a strong Red Guard group, supported by the Peking CRG, attempted to seize power. The local authorities organized a resistance force calling itself "A Million Brave Troops." They were backed by Ch'en Tsai-tao, the area army commander. The Maoist Red Guards had to ask Peking for assistance, and the CRG sent Hsieh Fu-chih, minister of public security, and Wang Li, acting head of the party Propaganda Department. They arrived in Wuhan on July 14 and condemned the army for supporting the "conservatives." They were promptly arrested by the army.

Lin Piao arrived with warships to deliver an ultimatum that the Wuhan authorities must surrender and release their prisoners or face an armed assault. The authorities were forced to surrender, after which many party and government leaders were dismissed, including Ch'en Ts'ai-tao. The "Million Brave Troops" were dissolved. It seemed a victory for Mao but again, the situation was far from stable.

Q: Did the Red Guards ever unite the campaigns against government officials or did they continue to physically battle among themselves?

A: Following the events in Wuhan, Mu Hsing and Wang Li, under the direction of Chiang Ch'ing and Ch'en Po-ta, wrote an article in *Red Flag* ordering the Red Guards to attack "a handful of the military" and "to seize the weapons from military arsenals." This forced a counterattack by military officials, who joined with local party and government people in organizing their own Red Guards.

An account of these events was given by Ch'en Pi-lan at the 1969 world congress of the Fourth International:

Since Mao organized the Red Guards to seize power in early January 1967, no part of China has been spared the spectacle of huge and brutal clashes between the different factions and tendencies. It is specifically these clashes which characterize the dramatic new stage in the so-called Cultural Revolution. The high point of these sanguinary events took place between April and July, 1968, mainly in the provinces of Kwangsi, Kwangtung, Yunnan, Tibet, Sinkiang, and Fukien. The scale of these clashes could in reality be considered as a local civil war.

For example, in Kwangsi, the Red Guards were divided into two different groups. One called itself "The 22nd of April Rebel Army," the cadres of which were composed of students, a few workers and some army units, and was under the direct leadership of the Cultural Revolutionary Group in Peking. The other referred to itself as the "Kwangsi United Rebel Headquarters," the cadres of which were composed mainly of workers and peasants, army units, party functionaries, and students. This latter group was organized and controlled behind the scenes by the First Kwangsi provincial secretary, Wei Kuo-ch'ing, as well as by a top army commander. The struggle between these two groups reached the crucial stage in a clash during May in Wuchow. The most modern weapons were used—from modern rifles and machine guns to heavy artillery and tanks—by both sides, which left thousands of dead and wounded from each group. According to reports published in the *Angry West River Tide* (Hsi Chiang Nu Ch'ao) put out by the "22nd of April Rebel Army" group, their side suffered several thousand killed and wounded, more than 3,000 captured, of whom 317 were executed. They also reported that over 2,000 homes were destroyed. Similar battles also took place in other Kwangsi cities, such as Nanning, Liuchow, and Kweilin, as well as in those provinces I noted earlier. For example, in the province of Yunnan, the Kunming (capital of the province) army commander Tang Fu-jen said on July 3, 1968, in his personal report to Mao in Peking that over 30,000 had been killed throughout the province of Yunnan. Mao replied that he estimated the number to be closer to 80,000. "According to the local papers," Mao said, "160,000 were killed. This is perhaps exaggerated. I would judge that at least 80,000 have been killed" (*People's Daily*).

As a result of the serious situation I have just described, Mao was forced to take certain measures to alleviate his precarious position. First, on July 3, 1968, an emergency order was published, and then, on July 24, an emergency appeal was issued. These demanded immediate cessation of all struggles between the different Red Guard and workers' groups. At the same time, army detachments from Peking were sent to such areas as Kwangsi, Yunnan, Fukien, and Sinkiang in order to intervene in the struggle. It was only in this way that Mao was able to put a stop to the local civil-war situation. Mao also demanded that revolutionary committees be established in the five remaining provinces of Kwangsi, Yunnan, Tibet, Fukien, and Sinkiang, as well as in their principal cities.[30]

It should be noted that the Revolutionary Committees, the so-called Triple Alliances, were controlled by the military because most often the chairman of the committee would be the local army commander. The Red Guards were forced to return to school or work and many of them were sent to the countryside. Official figures state ten million young people were exiled in this manner.

Q: The Red Guards were certainly a powerful tool for Mao while they lasted.

A: Yes. However, things did not always work out according to Mao's plan. For instance, in January 1967, just after the seizure of power in Shanghai and the purge of the entire leadership, several prominent old leaders—T'an Chen-lin, agricultural minister; Yeh Chien-ying, vice-chairman of the Central Committee's Military Commission; Nieh Jung-chen, head of the Science and Technology Committee; and Li Fu-ch'un, head of the Planning Committee—all members of the party Political Bureau, openly criticized the Cultural Revolutionary Group for instigating the purge. The Maoists labeled their influential critics the "February adverse current." It was only through the intervention of Chou En-lai that a compromise ended the stalemate between Mao and the old leaders. T'an Chen-lin, agricultural minister, was removed from office, but otherwise the old leaders scored a minor victory.

Another event concerned the "May 16 Army Corps," a group of Peking Red Guards under Ch'i Pen-yu, Wang Li, and the CRG. They waged a campaign against ministers in the central government in hopes of replacing them with Mao's supporters. Chou En-lai led a stiff resistance to this maneuver, in direct conflict with Chiang Ch'ing and Ch'en Po-ta. Mao was forced to retreat and remove from the CRG Ch'i Pen-yu, Wang Li, and his other handpicked replacements.

In Hunan in the summer of 1967, a powerful group of Red Guards called the *Sheng-wu-lien* (Proletarian Revolutionaries Great Alliance) attacked local officials and seized weapons from the army. They even occupied some factories and financial institutions. Backed by Chiang Ch'ing and Ch'en Po-ta, they issued a proclamation called "Whither China?" which attacked the Revolutionary Committee as a bureaucratic apparatus of the "new bourgeoisie" and called Chou En-lai a representative of the "new bourgeoisie." They called for the formation of genuine "People's Communes" in China as the only revolutionary perspective for the country.

Despite their confused and ambiguous ideas, the Red Guards reflected a revolutionary tendency among the masses. For this reason Chiang Ch'ing and Ch'en Po-ta abandoned them. Mao sent a representative of the Politburo Standing Committee, K'ang Sheng, to disband the "Proletarian Revolutionaries Great Alliance," which was branded as counterrevolutionary, and cruelly suppressed by the Hunan authorities (including Hua Kuo-feng).

A fourth event which got out of Mao's control occurred in August 1968. A struggle in Canton broke out between Red Guards backed by the CRG in Peking and Red Guards backed by Kwangtung's local authorities and the military commander Huang Yung-sheng. Huang was Lin Piao's man and was thus immune from direct attack by the CRG. In fact, he was elevated to chief of staff in Peking.

Q: Can the mass mobilizations during the Cultural Revolution be considered a revolutionary movement against the bureaucracy?

A: This question has been in dispute among radicals and even some Trotskyists for the last ten years. The answer lies in how the Red Guards were organized and what methods were used to fight the bureaucracy. The following excerpt from an article by George Novack and Joseph Hansen supplies some of this information:

> Schools were shut down and millions of youth turned loose. They were then offered a special privilege that would be attractive even in a wealthy capitalist country; namely, taking a trip at government expense to Peking [in fact, to anywhere in China—P'eng]. Transportation, free lodging and free meals were provided to a large proportion of these prospective candidates for the new organization.
>
> The policy was to line up these youth on the side of one of the contending factions by such means and inveigle them into adopting its factional platform without being informed of what was intended, without giving the opposition currents an opportunity to present their views in a fair debate, and, in fact, with the opposition smeared and branded from the beginning without a hearing as disloyal and even counterrevolutionary, a "miserable handful" of monsters, demons and ghosts. . . .
>
> The real "crime" of the accused leaders is not that they have been plotting to bring back capitalism but that they have serious differences with the Mao-Lin faction. Their views are falsified to discredit them in the eyes of the masses and to destroy them politically, if not physically.
>
> These polemical methods, which Mao and his men learned in the school of Stalinism, were first applied against the Trotskyists, later against the Khrushchevists and their allies, and now invoked against some of their oldest comrades-in-arms. There are no innovations in the pattern beyond peculiarities of style in applying it and even these are not very novel.[31]

I would only add that Mao organized the Red Guards to aid in destroying the Liu Shao-ch'i/Teng Hsiao-p'ing faction. When the faction was destroyed, Mao quickly dispersed the Red Guards, with the aid of the army under Lin Piao. Then Lin himself became Mao's next target.

Q: What was the overall outcome of the Cultural Revolution?

A: Chinese society was thrown into utter turmoil, as if from a devastating war. The CCP and its youth organization were smashed to pieces. Mao's orders and quotations replaced party statutes and governmental laws. The central government maintained its outward appearance; yet government at all levels had been transformed. The newly established Revolutionary Committee wielded state power under the control of military officers, except in a few cities like Shanghai and Peking. Almost all the old leaders who had struggled alongside Mao before and during the third Chinese revolution had been betrayed and suffered severe attack at the hands of the Red Guards. Most were purged and some were sent to labor camps and prisons. The educational system and cultural life of the country had been destroyed. Thousands of educators, artists, and writers had been purged from the party and dismissed from their jobs.

Millions of rebel Red Guards had been exiled to the countryside and the mountains. The economy was in a state of stagnation, productivity having drastically declined. Workers, peasants, technicians, and party cadres who had participated in the Cultural Revolution or who had associated with anyone who had been purged, were themselves purged.

Mao's foreign policy became extremely sectarian, as evidenced by the fact that he refused to join a united front with the other workers' states against U.S. imperialism in Vietnam. On the other hand, he permitted Red Guards in Peking to storm the British and Soviet embassies. In the wake of the Cultural Revolution, China became extremely isolated in the eyes of the world. This isolation and China's devastating internal crises were the backdrop to the Ninth Congress of the CCP.

Q: What happened at the Ninth Congress?

A: The congress, held in April 1969, was attended by 1,512 delegates, appointed, not elected by the Local Revolutionary Committees. From the outset, the congress was dominated by those who had newly come to prominence in the Cultural Revolution.

Lin Piao made a political report speaking for the Central Committee, most of whose members had been purged. Lin praised Mao for launching the Cultural Revolution and praised the army for carrying it through. He never mentioned any of the resultant problems nor did he offer proposals for rebuilding the economy and the people's morale. His report was a stream of abstract slogans:

Grasp revolution, promote production. . . .

. . . to develop relations of friendship, mutual assistance and co-operation with socialist countries on the principle of proletarian internationalism; to support and assist the revolutionary struggles of all the oppressed people and nations; to strive for peaceful coexistence with countries having different social systems on the basis of the Five Principles. . . .

Bury U.S. imperialism, Soviet revisionism and their lackeys. . . .[32]

Lin did propose that all cadres who made mistakes in the past be rehabilitated for party or government work if they would admit their errors. This proposal was designed to rebuild the ranks of the Mao–Lin faction, but cadres did not flock back to the party under these terms. The most important victory for Mao and Lin at the congress was the adoption of a new party constitution, which restored the references to "Mao Tse-tung Thought" that had been omitted by the Eighth Party Congress:

Mao Tse-tung Thought is Marxism-Leninism of the era in which imperialism is heading for total collapse and socialism is advancing to worldwide victory.

For half a century now . . . Comrade Mao Tse-tung has integrated the universal truth of Marxism-Leninism with the concrete practice of revolution, inherited, defended and developed Marxism-Leninism and has brought it to a higher and completely new stage.

Comrade Lin Piao has consistently held high the great red banner of Mao Tse-tung Thought and has most loyally and resolutely carried out and defended Comrade Mao Tse-tung's proletarian revolutionary line. Comrade Lin Piao is Comrade Mao Tse-tung's close comrade-in-arms and successor.[33]

The congress elected a new Central Committee of 170 members, with military men taking 30 percent of the seats. Nine military men were elected to the twenty-one-member Politburo. Military people held a majority of the posts in the new government, with the offices of defense minister, army chief of staff, commander of the air force, and head of the Political Commission of the navy, all under the influence of Lin Piao. Lin also controlled the military men who headed the Revolutionary Committees.

Q: What caused the conflict between Mao and Lin?

A: After the Ninth Congress, Mao, feeling greatly threatened that the country's military apparatus was under Lin's control, proclaimed a new slogan: "the party must command the gun, not the gun command the party." Lin responded to this indication of Mao's change of attitude toward him by organizing his own faction. Mao began the elimination of his new opponents with the purge of Ch'en Po-ta in August 1970 from his post as chairman of the CRG and member of the Standing Committee of the Political Bureau. It was not clear at the time why Ch'en had disappeared from public life, but later, at the Tenth Party Congress, Chou En-lai labeled Ch'en as a principal member of Lin Piao's "antiparty" group. After Ch'en was purged, Lin was forced to reveal his plans. In a document called "Outline of Project 571," he stated:

he [Mao] abused the trust and post given [him] by the Chinese people. . . . In reality he became a current Ch'in Shih-Huang. . . . He is not a real Marxist-Leninist and uses the name Marxism-Leninism to carry out his doctrine of Confucianism-Menciusism, adopting the method of Ch'in Shih-Huang. He is the greatest tyrant in the history of China.[34]

These charges against Mao made it clear that Lin was preparing a coup d'etat. However, he was betrayed by his own daughter before he could act. Mao's government later claimed that Lin and his main followers attempted to escape to the Soviet Union, but their plane was shot down over Outer Mongolia. All passengers were killed.

Mao was left in a desperately isolated position, having eliminated by one means or another so many of the party's leaders. It was impossible for him to publicly explain his conflict with Lin; therefore Mao needed the assistance of Chou En-lai. The Mao–Chou combination attempted to clear the air at the Tenth Party Congress in August 1973. Chou gave a political report in the name of the Central Committee in which he labeled Lin as a "bourgeois careerist" and a "conspirator" who "launched [a] coup in a wild attempt to assassinate our great leader Chairman Mao." Lin was accused of trying to turn the CCP into a "revisionist, fascist party," reinstating the landlords and the bourgeois classes.

Internationally, they wanted to capitulate to Soviet revisionist social-imperialism and ally themselves with imperialism, revisionism and reaction to oppose China, communism and revolution.

Lin Piao, this bourgeois careerist, conspirator and double-dealer, engaged in machinations within our Party not just for one decade but for several decades.[35]

Most of Chou's report was pure slander, but it served to establish reasons why Lin had betrayed Mao. All references to Lin were removed from the party statutes. A number of old leaders such as Teng Hsiao-p'ing, T'an Chen-lin, and Ulanfu were rehabilitated. Some military commanders such as Hsu Shih-yu, Ch'en Hsi-lien, and Han Hsien-ch'u were also rehabilitated. Wang Hung-wen was promoted to vice-chairman of the party. A nationwide campaign to criticize Lin Piao and Confucius was launched from autumn 1973 to the end of 1974, during which the remnants of Lin's faction were attacked and purged and military commanders were transferred from their bases of support. Hsu Shih-yu was transferred from Nanking to Canton, Ch'en Hsi-lien from Manchuria to Peking, and Han Hsien-ch'u from Fukien to Lanchow. Mao assumed all these changes would secure his personal dictatorship once again, but a new powerful figure stood in his way—Chou En-lai.

Q: Did Chou have his own faction?

A: Since the demise of the Liu Shao-ch'i and Lin Piao factions, Chou had become a magnet for dissatisfied leaders and cadres. Chou's rising power was evidenced at the Fourth National People's Congress in January 1975, which unanimously adopted his proposal for the Four Modernizations—in industry, agriculture, defense, and science and technology. Most of the newly elected members of the Standing Committee were Chou's people, including its chairman Chu Te, one of Mao's arch foes. Chou En-lai was reelected premier, Teng Hsiao-p'ing became first vice-premier and army chief of staff. Yeh Chien-ying became defense minister. The only post taken by a member of Mao's faction was third vice-premier and head of the Army Political Commission, to which Chang Ch'un-ch'iao was elected. In short, Chou En-lai became the real leader of the People's Republic of China and Mao was now merely a figurehead.

After the congress, Mao launched a new campaign aimed at Chou's faction. An editorial in the March 1975 *Red Flag* stated:

Millions of millions of people must learn and grasp Marxism concerning the theory of the dictatorship of the proletariat, which is the most important thing in consolidating and strengthening the proletarian dictatorship. All members of party committees must learn and grasp the theory of the proletarian dictatorship in order to carry out consciously the basic line and all policies and advance to carry out the anti-Lin, anti-Confucius [i.e., anti-Chou—P'eng] campaign.

Mao used the theory of the dictatorship of the proletariat as a smoke screen for the dictatorship of Mao Tse-tung, and justified all past purges as necessary for the defense of Marxist principles. Mao was also warning "all members of the party committees" that they will be severely punished or purged if they do not "grasp" Mao's personal dictatorship and carry out Mao's "basic line and all policies."

The Maoists wrote a series of articles indirectly charging Chou with being a traitor. They compared him to the famous character Sung Chiang in the novel *Water Margin*, who had turned traitor. In addition to the public slanders, the Maoists caused great physical discomfort to Chou En-lai in his final illness, hoping to hasten his death. They had his personal physician transferred out of Peking so he could not care for Chou. Wang Hung-wen forced Chou to accept a telephone call from Mao while he was undergoing medical treatment in the hospital. Chou's close supporter, Education Minister Chou Jung-hsin, was driven to suicide under an onslaught of public criticism. And these are only a few of the harassments perpetrated against Chou on his deathbed.

Q: Did Mao ever attack Chou openly?

A: No. After Chou's death on January 8, 1976, Mao focused the campaign on Chou's legal successor, Teng Hsiao-p'ing, who was called a "rehabilitated rightist" and a "capitalist-roader." Chou's Four Modernizations were also attacked. Mao's response to Chou's death led directly to the huge demonstration in Peking's T'ien An Men Square, April 5, 1976. The demonstrators' violent actions, including burning police cars and a military barracks, were a direct challenge to the CCP regime headed by Mao. For the first time, Mao's "thought" was publicly denounced as "castrating Marxism-Leninism." The action foreshadowed the revolutionary movement needed to overthrow the bureaucracy when the participants declared, "We fear not shedding our blood and laying down our lives." After the Hungarian revolution, Mao had remarked that certain people "hoped that something similar would happen in China." In April 1976, thousands upon thousands of Chinese people did precisely what Mao feared—demonstrated against the government. Despite the fact that Mao mercilessly suppressed the demonstrators, their defiant and determined spirit will remain as a specter haunting China, just as the *Communist Manifesto* welcomed the "specter haunting Europe." In fact, after Mao witnessed this specter, he died and went to the kind of "hell" history reserves for dictators and tyrants.

Q: Did Mao's death spell the death of his faction?

A: Mao's personal dictatorship ended in a fitting manner, with the purge of his most faithful followers, Chiang Ch'ing, Chang

Ch'un-ch'iao, Wang Hung-wen, and Yao Wen-yuan—all purged by Mao's handpicked successor, Hua Kuo-feng. The scenario parallels the purges of Malenkov and Beria by Khrushchev after Stalin's death. In reviewing Mao's political career, it is indisputable that his ideas were inherited directly from Stalin—class collaboration, revolution-by-stages, socialism in one country, and peaceful coexistence between capitalism and socialism. Mao loyally and systematically propagated Stalin's ideology throughout his life, from the opportunist KMT-CCP collaboration to the adventuristic armed struggle for power after the 1927 defeat. Mao closely followed Stalin's example of purging the entire generation of Bolsheviks and young revolutionists of the 1920s, '30s, and '40s as he established his own personal cult and bureaucratic dictatorship in China.

Mao strove to be the greatest Stalinist in the world. He became a true Stalin in China, his character and methods almost identical to those of his Soviet hero. Mao attempted politically, if not physically, to destroy anyone who questioned his policies or who had authority with the masses in their own right—Liu Shaoch'i, Teng Hsiao-p'ing, Lin Piao, and Chou En-lai, to name a few. It is true that Mao was a modern-day Ch'in Shih-huang, a Chinese Nero, to whom Trotsky's words so aptly apply: "Nero, too, was a product of his epoch. Yet after he perished his statues were smashed and his name was scraped off everything. The vengeance of history is more terrible than the vengeance of the most powerful General Secretary [or chairman—P'eng]. I venture to think that this is consoling."[36]

Q: Why did Mao receive so much praise after his death, by bourgeois politicians and radicals alike?

A: Bourgeois politicians like Gerald Ford and UN Secretary General Waldheim praised Mao because he had completely abandoned the world revolution in favor of peaceful coexistence with capitalism. He denounced the Soviet Union as social-imperialist and called on the capitalist world to overturn the gains of the October revolution. Needless to say, the bourgeois politicians were delighted at Mao's betrayal of socialism and found no difficulty calling him a "great leader" and "peacemaker." Some Trotskyists misread Mao's political history and claimed he was not a Stalinist. They considered him to be a "bureaucratic centrist" because he zigzagged between a revolutionary and antirevolutionary course, finally going so far as to nationalize capitalist property and institute an agrarian reform. Yet Stalin carried out similar measures in Eastern Europe, and certainly Stalin remained a Stalinist.

Trotskyists have always maintained that Stalin was a counter-revolutionary despite the fact that he overturned capitalist property relations in Eastern Europe; since he established totalitarian bureaucratic dictatorships in these countries in conflict with the socialist economic base. This served as a brake on the development of the East European and the world revolution. Leon Trotsky could have been talking about Mao in China when he predicted the overturn of private property in Soviet-occupied Poland at the beginning of World War II:

The primary political criterion for us is not the transformation of property relations in this or another area, however important these may be in themselves, but rather the change in the consciousness and organization of the world proletariat, the raising of their capacity for defending former conquests and accomplishing new ones. From this one, and the only, decisive standpoint, the politics of Moscow, taken as a whole, completely retains its reactionary character and remains the chief obstacle on the road to world revolution.[37]

APPENDIX

An Interview with Ch'en Pi-lan on the "Cultural Revolution"

Question: In my interviews with P'eng Shu-tse, who analyzed the situation in China in some detail, I have gotten a fairly clear idea of the origins and subsequent evolution of the "Great Proletarian Cultural Revolution," the different and contrasting positions of the Maoists and anti-Maoists, and the possible future perspectives of the struggle. In the first stage of the "Cultural Revolution," the people who were attacked were artists, writers, scholars, and educators. Therefore, I would like to ask you some questions about the differences of opinion on questions of literature, art, education, etc. First of all, may I ask you to describe and analyze the differences between the two factions on these questions, as it seems these differences can be most important and give us a much clearer and better understanding of the general lines and positions of the two contending factions.

Answer: Yes, this is true. If one understands the differences on these questions, one can get a very good idea as to what the general struggle between the two factions is about.

In reality, when Mao launched the "Cultural Revolution" movement, he began by attacking Wu Han's drama *Hai Jui Dismissed from Office*, T'ien Han's drama *Hsieh Yao-huan*,[1] and Teng T'o's writings *Evening Talks at Yanshan* and *Notes from Three-Family Village*. In other words, Mao began by attacking

---

The following interview with Ch'en Pi-lan was obtained by Antonio Farien (David Fender) in the summer of 1967. It was first published in World Outlook *in its July 14, 1967, issue.*

the leading cadres in the cultural fields, which, of course, gave rise to the name "Cultural Revolution."

We all know that under Stalinist dictatorial regimes, there is no political freedom, and, under these conditions, there is much dissatisfaction among the people. Dissatisfaction of this kind is usually reflected in literature and art since most artists and writers are very sensitive to the world around them. They observe the daily life of the people and see their plight as well as their hopes and aspirations. Through the means of literature and art, then, they mirror what they have observed—the bad as well as the good. It is for just this reason that Stalinist policies have always severely restricted the cultural fields, in order to keep the bad side from being exposed, including the bureaucratic regime. Literature and art were no longer allowed to reflect the actual reality but became mere propaganda to praise the policies of the bureaucrats as well as them as individuals. It is very clear that such a situation existed under Stalin's regime; and the policies elaborated by Zhdanov on literature and art are typical examples.

The policies elaborated by Mao in this respect have been in no way different, except perhaps they have been more restrictive and harsher. The result in China has been an almost constant resistance in the field of literature and art to Mao's policies. The present purge of people in this field is by no means the first, although it is the largest and most serious.

Q: Could you briefly tell us when Mao began to purge these people in the cultural fields and why?

A: Mao's policy of restricting literature and art began in May 1942 during the Yenan period. It was during this time that Mao made his well-known "Talks at the Yenan Forum on Literature and Art" which were given in preparation for the purge of a well-known writer. In these long discourses, except for a few quotations from Lenin, whom he cited as his authority, Mao demanded that literature and art serve only the workers, peasants, and soldiers in line with the political policies of the party; and he was against any exposures or satires of his Yenan regime. The writers were only supposed to praise the Communist New Democracy, revolutionary heroes, etc.; and he pointed out that there were many defects in the field of literature and art and that it was necessary to launch a movement in order to purge them.

During this time, there were several writers who had written some articles exposing the real life in Yenan, such as the famous woman writer Ting Ling, who wrote an article entitled "Impressions of the March Eighth Celebration"; the famous poet Ai Ch'ing, who wrote an article entitled "One Should Understand and Respect the Writers"; and Wang Shih-wei, who wrote a series of articles entitled "Wild Lilies." These last were the sharpest exposure of certain aspects of Yenan. He criticized the lack of democracy and contrasted the privileged life of the bureaucracy to that of the rank and file. These articles attracted much attention among the people and especially among the young Communists. Mao could not tolerate such criticism and for this reason called a meeting to discuss the questions of literature and art where he gave his talks. These meetings and talks not only prepared for the purge which followed; they also laid the foundations for the basic line of Communist Party policy in questions concerning literature and art.

Not long after these discussions and meetings, a special meeting was called to purge Wang Shih-wei. Many of the party's officials, such as the heads of the Central Propaganda Department and the Organization Department and the president of the Central Research Institute, as well as cadres working in the field of literature and art, and other writers, took part in this meeting. One might wonder why it was of such a serious nature. The reason is simple. Wang joined the party in 1926. This made him an old party member and one of the most important members of the Central Research Institute. Wang had translated into Chinese more than two million words of the works of Marx, Engels, and Lenin. He was, as well, a very capable writer and was respected by almost everyone, especially the youth. Thus the purge of Wang Shih-wei was a most important event in the Yenan period.

The meeting lasted sixteen days, during which Wang expressed and defended his opinions in the face of vigorous attacks by the leading cadres and officials of the party. There were a number of cultural workers who agreed with Wang's opinions and sympathized with him. Yet, due to his being condemned as antiparty, anti-Marxist, and a Trotskyist by some of the party leaders, and especially by Ch'en Po-ta—who is now the leader of the present Cultural Revolution Group but who at that time was Mao's private secretary—who criticized Wang most maliciously, they became fearful and retreated. Nevertheless, Wang, from beginning to end, remained strong in defending his ideas as correct. The meeting finally ended by condemning him as being antiparty, anti-Marxist, and a Trotskyist. He was expelled from the party, thrown into prison, and tortured. Finally, he acknowledged that he was a Trotskyist; and hence he was killed.

We should take special note of the fact that Wang Shih-wei's book *Wild Lilies* has exercised great attraction and has interested many youth, including members and sympathizers of the CCP as well as its youth organization. The book has circulated throughout China by means of handwritten copies passed on and on, time after time. The original copy that I read was borrowed from a sympathizer of the CCP and was of this type. Because of the bravery and boldness of Wang's resistance against the vicious attacks and his insistence on the correctness of his own position, he became very famous. His name is to be found in most histories of this period.

Q: Were there any other purges after Wang?

A: After the CCP took power in 1949, Mao's cultural policies were put into effect for the nation as a whole. The first to resist and criticize them was Hu Feng, who was a very famous left theoretician on literature and art. He considered Mao's "Talks at Yenan" to be mechanistic and therefore he said that "mechanism has controlled literature and art circles for the last ten years . . . this ideology of literature and art has been sterilized . . . when one speaks they must employ Mao's thought which causes people more than enough trouble."[2]

He held that truth is the highest principle of art. He was against what he regarded as the oversimplified policy of having literature and art serve only political ends and was against the limitation of themes as proposed by Mao. Thus he insisted that all writers should have the right to choose their own subjects. The ideas and opinions of Hu Feng, as I have indicated, are, of course, based on principles which everyone should be able to accept. However, from Mao's point of view, such ideas were out of bounds and in 1955 he began a campaign against Hu Feng and his followers. This campaign lasted several months and was carried out on a national scale.

No only were Hu Feng's followers attacked and criticized, but many people in the universities, middle schools, and cultural organizations who only sympathized with him were also attacked and purged. According to reports published at the time, more than 130 Hu-Fengists were imprisoned or put in labor camps. Since that time there has been no news of him or his followers.

Almost immediately after the Hu Feng purge came the "Let a hundred flowers bloom and a hundred schools of thought contend" movement, April to June 1957. It was during this period that a number of Left writers criticized Mao's policies on literature and art, such as Ting Ling, Ai Ch'ing and Feng Hsüeh-feng, the most famous contemporary theoretician of literature and art. These three were all leaders of the party in the cultural fields, especially Ting Ling and Feng Hsüeh-feng, who were respectively chairwoman and vice-chairman of the National Association of Literature and Art Workers.

In June, when Mao began to suppress the "Hundred Flowers" movement, they came under attack.

For example, in September a special meeting was held in Peking to purge Ting Ling. There were around one hundred participants in this meeting, including many high officials of the party in the cultural fields, such as the minister and vice-minister of culture, Shin Yen-ping[3] and Chou Yang. This meeting, like the one held in Yenan to purge Wang Shih-wei, lasted sixteen days and was very exhausting for Ting Ling as she was subjected to one attack after another, accusing her of being a rightist and a reactionary. Attacks against her which appeared in the *People's Daily* made a connection between her and Wang Shih-wei and accused her of being like him. Shortly after the meeting, Ting Ling, Feng Hsüeh-feng, Ai Ch'ing, and many others were imprisoned or sent to "reeducation camps." As with Hu Feng and his followers, nothing further has been heard about their fate.

Concerning Ting Ling, I should say a few more words. In 1923-24, she was a classmate of mine in Shanghai University where we lived in the same home. We became very close friends, so I know her very well. She had a very strong character and was very democratic minded.

Also during the "Hundred Flowers" movement, we should take notice of the position taken by Shen Yen-ping. In a meeting called by the Central United Front Department on May 16, 1957, Shen Yen-ping expressed his own views on literature and art. He said, "In regard to literature and art, it must be considered a special field. By only depending on some of the party's basic texts and without any special knowledge in this field, it is impossible to resolve concrete problems concerning literature and art. . . . What then should be done? There is the short road which is dogmatism and commandism." It is very clear that Shen was criticizing the whole apparatus of the cultural department. Shen considered that in literature and art, there existed a "general phenomenon" of "monotony" and "repetitiousness." He explained that the "sickness" of repetition was due to reducing everything to formulas and to the lack of variety in themes. In short, these sicknesses were due to not carrying out the policy of the "Hundred Flowers" movement.

All the criticisms of Shen Yen-ping no doubt implied that Mao's policies on literature and art restricted the creative initiative and freedom of the writers; hence the monotonous and repetitious works which were devoid of any liveliness or creativity.

Q: Since Shen Yen-ping was the minister of culture, that is, the highest leader in the cultural field, why is it that he spoke out against Mao's policies and why was he not purged with the others?

A: In order to answer this question, it is necessary to give a short resumé of Shen's personal history. He joined the CCP in 1921 and at that time he was already the author of several articles and the editor of the large magazine, *Novel.* After the defeat of the revolution of 1927, he left the CCP. However, he continued to write and published several books under the pen name of Mao Tun, some of which became very celebrated and he himself became very well known. It was for this reason that he became minister of culture after the CCP took power in 1949. He held this post until January 1965 when he requested that he be allowed to retire.

As to the reasons why he criticized Mao's policies and why he was not purged, we must note that first of all, his speech was made during the peak of the "Hundred Flowers" movement; second, Shen was not a member of the party; and, third, the Ministry of Culture was really controlled by Chou Yang. According to some recent reports, however, Shen has been arrested in the current purge. It is most probable that he was arrested because of the position he expressed in his speech of 1957. During the 1925-27 revolution, I had quite a bit of personal contact with Shen, and so I also knew him very well. He was an extremely cautious man and most likely, in my opinion, he has probably not made any criticism of Mao's policies since 1957.

Q: Since you said that it was really Chou Yang who controlled the Ministry of Culture and since Chou Yang himself has recently been attacked, what were his ideas and did they conform with those of Shen Yen-ping?

A: Chou Yang's opinions on literature and art are not only similar to those of Shen Yen-ping, they are much more profound. If we turn only to the article by Yao Wen-yuan, recently published in the *Red Flag*, no. 1, 1967, "On the Counterrevolutionary Double-dealer Chou Yang," attacking Chou Yang, we can see what his position is. For example, Yao Wen-yuan very clearly states:

Chou Yang, like Hu Feng, repeatedly advocated the propaganda that "the highest principle of art is truth," and he was against the "oversimplification and vulgarization," the conditions placed on writers, and the role of literature as propaganda. Chou Yang considered that "dogmatism" and "sectarianism" and the harsh attitude towards artists and writers has seriously restricted their freedom. . . .

As to the "question of making literature and art serve politics," there was narrow, one-sided, and incorrect understanding. [Consequently, Chou advocated that] "there should be no limits on subjects and that we should help people see the diversity of the world, the laws of history, and the complex nature of life. . . . Regardless of the subject, it can reflect the spirit of the present period."

In another article, Chou Yang is quoted as saying:

It is better to describe the intellectuals, technicians, and others from the point of view of the proletariat. However, the working class should not be sectarian; that is, it should not only write about the workers and peasants. The idea that proletarian literature is only about workers and peasants is not correct.[4]

Chou Yang was especially against literature and art serving only politics. He also said, "The writers should not only write about current affairs and should not follow the policy put forward today and then follow a different policy that might be put forward tomorrow."[5] Commenting on this article in *Wen Hui Pao*, the Hong Kong liberal *Ming Pao Monthly* concluded:

In a word, Chou Yang considered that writers should write what they themselves see and according to what they themselves feel, even if what they see and feel does not correspond to the ideas and policies of the party. The writer must be loyal to the facts, to the truth, and to the objective conditions, and write freely what he believes.[6]

Therefore, Chou Yang advocated assuring freedom in the sphere of writing.

Q: If Chou Yang disagreed with Mao's policies, why was he allowed to remain as vice-minister of culture, being in fact the real head of the ministry, to carry out Mao's policies?

A: This is an important question and it is very necessary that it be answered. Under the personal dictatorship of Mao, many leaders and cadres of the party disagreed with his policies, but nevertheless they were forced to carry out Mao's decisions. Chou Yang was only one of many such cadres and leaders. He often found himself in a contradictory situation, that is, not believing in Mao's policies and even speaking and writing about his differences, but nevertheless forced to carry out Mao's line in practice. For example, before the purge of Hu Feng in 1955, during a discussion meeting on Hu Feng's case, Chou Yang said, "Hu Feng's general political position is in agreement with the party."[7] In other words, Chou Yang did not want the case of Hu Feng to become too serious. When Mao ordered Hu Feng to be purged as a reactionary, Chou was obliged to carry out his orders.

In 1957, when Ting Ling, Feng Hsüeh-feng, Ai Ch'ing, and the others were attacked, Chou Yang was forced into the same contradictory position as in the case of Hu Feng. It was for this reason that Yao Wen-yuan accused him of being a "double-dealer" or "two-faced counterrevolutionary." In reality, then, under the pressure of Mao, many cadres were obliged to carry out policies with which they did not agree. This reflects the contradiction between Mao and the cadres of the party of which the present crisis is only a culmination, reaching the point of explosion.

Q: Can Chou Yang's opinions be considered as exemplary for most of the cadres in the cultural fields?

A: Yes, it seems as though Chou Yang's opinions reflect most of those of the rank and file. For example, the two other vice-ministers of culture, Hsia Yen and Lin Mo-han, as well as the secretary of the party group heading the All-China Federation of Literature and Art Circles, Yang Han-sheng, all shared the same opinions as Chou Yang. Yang Han-sheng's opinions were even more radical than Chou's, however, and it was for this reason that he has been subjected to harsher criticism than many of the others.

Q: Could you give us some idea of Yang Han-sheng's opinions?

A: Yes, I can, but first I should give you a few details about his personal history. Yang Han-sheng was also a classmate of mine at Shanghai University in 1923-24. He was at that time a member of the party and was a very active participant in the revolutionary movement. After the defeat of the revolution in 1927, he remained in Shanghai and was active in the underground, and it was during this time that I had much contact with him and his wife. Beginning in 1928, he wrote several novels and afterwards became a very important party cadre in the cultural work of the party.

Because he remained loyal to certain traditions of the party during the second Chinese revolution, he disagreed with the many restrictions which Mao placed upon writers and artists and criticized them very harshly. For example, in 1962, at a meeting of playwrights and actors in Canton, he said:

The party's policy on literature and art [that is, Mao's policy] is equal to ten ropes binding the hands and feet of writers. These ten ropes prove to be five obligations: (1) one must write about important subjects; (2) one must write about heroes and outstanding figures; (3) one must participate in collective writing; (4) one must finish his work in a certain amount of time; (5) one must always have the OK from the party leadership. From these five obligations arise five prohibitions: (1) to write about the contradictions among the people, especially between the masses and the leaders; (2) to write any satirical dramas; (3) to write any tragedies; (4) to write about the defects and failures of a hero; (5) to write about the weaknesses of any of the party's leaders. All of this leaves a writer in despair and makes it difficult for him to write, and even when he does write, his work is only repetitious.[8]

In conclusion, he advocated that "it is necessary to do away with all restrictions and to break out of all limitations. We must respect the rule of creativity, that is, freedom for the writers."

Yang Han-sheng was severely attacked by the Maoists for the above opinions as well as for many other things. In 1957, Yang and T'ien Han went to the USSR for the anniversary of the October revolution. While they were there, they saw many plays, such as *The Infinite Perspective* and *The Bluebird*. These two dramas were exposures of the personal cult of Stalin and the purges of his opponents. They portrayed Stalin's rule to be "like that under the tsars," and pointed out that "the USSR no longer needs the period of terror." When Yang Han-sheng and T'ien Han returned to China, Yang said that the actors of the USSR were very "bold"; "we are very timid. We should make the utmost effort to reform, to be bold and creative."⁹ For these things, the Maoists accused Yang of being a "counterrevolutionary revisionist"; yet, in reality, he was only expressing agreement with the de-Stalinization taking place in the Soviet theater. It was this which Mao could not tolerate.

Q: Wu Han, Teng T'o, and T'ien Han are some of China's most famous writers who not only have been among the first to be attacked but also among those who have been the most severely attacked by the Maoists. Have they ever expressed their opinions on literature and art?

A: Wu Han, Teng T'o, and T'ien Han have, of course, differences with Mao's policies, but these have never been expressed openly as far as I know. They have, however, written plays and articles in which they have indirectly criticized Mao's policies and his personal cult and dictatorship. The two plays, *Hai Jui Dismissed* by Wu Han and *Hsieh Yao-huan* by T'ien Han, which use historical plots in order to criticize Mao and his policies, are good examples. Teng T'o also wrote many articles in which he indirectly attacked the policy of the People's Communes as well as Mao's infallibility. But this was explained in your interview with P'eng Shu-tse, and so it is not necessary for me to repeat it. Here, I would only like to point out that even those who attacked Mao indirectly could not be tolerated by Mao.

Q: Were any of the leaders in the cultural fields, such as Chou Yang, against any of Mao's other policies?

A: Almost all of those who disagreed on questions of literature and art were also in disagreement with Mao's overall policy. Since the leaders and cadres working in the cultural fields have frequent contact with writers and artists working directly with the masses, they learn from them the feelings and aspirations of the masses. For example, in a meeting held in Dairen, August 1962, of writers from all over the country, the overwhelming majority of them expressed their dissatisfaction with and criticized the "Great Leap Forward" policy and especially the People's Communes, as well as Mao's policies on literature and art. They felt that "the life of the peasants is getting worse and worse," and "the general line is the psychology of an upstart." Similarly, "the Great Leap Forward is like a stimulant," and "the People's

Communes are adventurism." Chou Yang himself said, "The Great Leap Forward represents subjective idealism." Again, "the People's Communes have been established too early." He even said, "It is good to let the peasants have their own plots," and he advocated "opening the free market" in the countryside.[10]

The criticisms of the "Great Leap Forward" and the People's Communes by Chou Yang and the other writers are echoes of the criticism advanced by P'eng Te-huai in 1959. Therefore, in a meeting of the All-China Federation of Literature and Art Circles in June 1964, Mao made an address in which he said that

in the past fifteen years, these associations and most of their publications [a few were said to be good] had for the most part failed . . . to carry out the policies of the party . . . and failed to reflect the socialist revolution and construction. In recent years, they had even verged on revisionism. If they did not take serious steps to remold themselves, sooner or later, they were bound to become organizations of the Hungarian Petöfi Club type.[11]

From what Mao said, it is clear that he feared the intellectuals in the cultural fields and it is easy to understand why he began the Cultural Revolution and a purge of all those who opposed him. Mao feared an actual development such as the Hungarian revolution of 1956 in China itself, started by similar groups as the Petöfi Club and it is for this reason that he began his purge by singling out these cadres in the fields of literature and art.

Q: Why is it that many of the famous educators such as Lu P'ing, president of Peking University, Li Ta, president of Wuhan University, K'uang Ya-ming, president of Nanking University, etc., have been purged? Did they have differences, and possibly refused to carry out Mao's policies in education?

A: These educators were against Mao's policies on education. But this is a complicated and difficult question. It would make it much clearer if I would first outline Mao's attitude toward education.

Since the CCP took power in 1949, Mao has based his educational policies on the principle that "education must serve politics." Mao often stressed the idea that "students and professors should remold their thought." Mao compelled the students to attend political lectures and to participate in political discussions and physical work. In other words, his policy was to make Communists out of all the students and to get them to accept and support the party's policies. The learning of other subjects, Mao does not regard as being important; or, at best, it is only a secondary consideration. Because of such policies, the standards of education have greatly diminished.

In the "Great Leap Forward" program of 1958, Mao put forward the idea of an "educational revolution." He stressed the idea that "education must be accompanied by productive work." Under this slogan, the professors as well as the students were sent to the countryside to participate in the work of the People's Communes, while others were sent to work in the factories, still carrying on their political studies and activities. These conditions led to almost a standstill in the students' regular studies. This was the situation in 1958-59.

Mao's policies and their results aroused much dissatisfaction among the professors, teachers, and students. For example, Li Ta said:

> The Educational Revolution has destroyed the educational process. The fundamental courses have been torn asunder. The quality of education has been lowered, the methods of teaching and studying have been disorganized. All the schools controlled by the party have become anarchic. The relations between teachers and students, between the young and old, and between the masses and the party have worsened to the greatest degree.[12]

He also said, "The Educational Revolution in 1958 caused a very bad situation. It destroyed the activities of the intellectuals and hampered their self-respect."

The crisis described by Li Ta represents the common opinion of the overwhelming majority of educators, professors, teachers, and students. Li Ta was one of the founding members of the CCP and was one of the twelve who attended the founding congress in 1921. He was elected to the Central Committee of the party and became the head of the Central Committee's Propaganda Department. Sometime afterward, he left the party because he disagreed with the decision that the members of the CCP should join the Kuomintang, although he remained a Marxist. He translated many Marxist books and propagandized the ideas of Marxism in many of his own articles. It is evident that he helped the Marxist movement when he was outside the party.

Since he was a professor and had studied education from a Marxist point of view, including the educational system in the

USSR, he became very well known as a Marxist educator. This was why the CCP, after taking power, appointed him as the president of Wuhan University. It was because of his profound knowledge as an educator that he realized the dangers of Mao's educational policies and criticized them very severely.

Mao's policy of "educational revolution" met with bankruptcy following the failure of the "Great Leap Forward." At the beginning of 1960, Mao was no longer able to maintain his policies and so he temporarily sat back while Liu Shao-ch'i and Teng Hsiao-p'ing took on the responsibility of dealing with the situation. Educational policies, then, were somewhat changed and corrected. First of all, the Central Educational Department published the "Sixty Points of Higher Educational Reforms." The chief reforms were aimed at encouraging the students to study in their special fields and to make sure that they had the necessary time to do so. The students were supposed to participate in physical work and political activities; however, these things were not supposed to interfere with or be done during the time set aside for study and class. A regular system of teaching and studying was to be reestablished as well as a disciplined relationship between the students and professors. In order to raise the quality of education, examinations were also to be reinstituted. Many of the students were to be encouraged to take up studies in the scientific fields as well as foreign languages. The schools were no longer supposed to interfere in the love life of the students, nor were they supposed to apply any other inappropriate pressures. Attention was also to be brought to the health of the students and to their welfare in general.

The Peking municipal government, headed by P'eng Chen, carried out these new reforms very enthusiastically and elaborated a series of concrete measures to implement them. For example, it was stated that

> students and teachers should not be demanded to learn politics too quickly, nor should any time be taken away from their regular studies for political activities. The teachers must know and teach their subjects as well as possible and the students must learn their lessons as well as they can. The use of abstract political ideas and terms, empty preaching, and long political reports must be avoided.

The president of Peking University, Lu P'ing, from 1961 completely abandoned the "educational revolution" policy and turned the university into an experiment for the new education reforms. He lowered the amount of time required for physical labor and political activity and made sure the students had adequate time to study their particular subjects. Hence the students of Peking University were much better off after 1961-62.

Lu P'ing also advanced the slogan, "Learn from the USSR," that is, China should also try to copy some of the educational policies in some of the Western countries; and he advocated inviting the old professors who had been expelled in the past years to return to their teaching posts. Li Ta, K'uang Ya-ming and many of the other educators carried out similar reforms. Thus the universities and colleges succeeded in returning to normal and constructive educational practices. This educational reform, in the eyes of Mao Tse-tung, was an absolute negation of his own policies of "education serving politics" and "education combined with productive labor," and he considered it to be a "revisionist educational line" or the "restoration of bourgeois educational policies." With this he deliberately prepared to purge those who were responsible for these reforms.

On June 13, 1966, Mao published a notice in the name of the Central Committee of the CCP and the State Council. This document is a concrete manifestation of the purge in the educational field and contains two major points:

1. All universities and middle schools were ordered closed for six months in order to "carry out thoroughly the Cultural Revolution." In reality, this meant to "carry out thoroughly" a purge in all the universities and middle schools. Following publication of the notice, there was a furious struggle and all Mao's opponents in the universities and middle schools came under attack and were purged.

2. Almost all opponents were attacked by the students as they carried out Mao's orders, resulting in the purge of such people as Lu P'ing; Li Ta; K'uang Ya-ming; P'eng Kang, president of the University of Communications in Sian; Ho Lu-ting, president of the Music College in Shanghai; and Chiang Nan-tsen, president of Tsinghua University in Peking. As for the professors, the purge is difficult to estimate; however, from all reports, it seems as though the number would run into many thousands.

The *People's Daily* held that the most important question was to see "whether we shall pass on Mao Tse-tung's thought from generation to generation." This is comparable to the religious attitude towards the Bible, and Mao's "cultural revolutionary educational" reforms come close to paralleling the educational methods of the Catholic Church during the Middle Ages.

Q: What, in your opinion, will be the outcome of the "Cultural Revolution"? That is, what do you think will be the overall influence and effect of Mao's "Cultural Revolution" on Chinese culture?

A: Mao's purge has included almost all those cadres working in the Central Propaganda Department, the Central Cultural Ministry, the All-China Federation of Literature and Art Circles, the All-China Union of Stage Artists, National Federation of Film Workers, and the National Federation of News Workers, as well as writers, musicians, painters, educators, professors, etc., who are the embodiment of China's culture. To purge them means to destroy China's culture. I will only point out here two indisputable examples of what Mao's "Cultural Revolution" means concretely to Chinese culture.

1. Since Mao launched the "Cultural Revolution" in May 1966, most writers have not dared to write anything. The publication of most cultural magazines has stopped, film-making has almost come to a standstill; the publication and republication of many books of foreign origin and even many by Chinese authors has been terminated; many cinemas and theaters have ceased to operate. In other words, almost all cultural activities no longer exist.

2. Since all the middle schools and universities were closed in June 1966, not one university has reopened and it was only last March that a part of the middle schools began to reopen in such places as Peking and Tientsin. Even before the "Cultural Revolution" and Mao's purge, there was a great lack of teachers and professors; now, of course, there are even fewer. The worst part is that from the elementary schools to the universities there is a chronic shortage of textbooks, since almost the whole printing establishment has been given over to printing the works of Mao Tse-tung. For example, in the last half year, fifteen million *Selected Works of Mao Tse-tung* have been produced, each containing four large volumes, as well as eighty million *Quotations from Mao Tse-tung*. In addition to this, another eighty million copies of the *Selected Works* have been scheduled for publication this year. Nearly all other books, therefore, such as

textbooks, literature, and even the works of Marx, Engels, and Lenin have ceased to be printed. Generally, then, I can say that not only have cultural activities stagnated since Mao launched his "Cultural Revolution," but China's culture is being destroyed to the point of disaster.

Finally, I would like to say that the "Proletarian Cultural Revolution" is theoretically absurd. When the proletariat takes power in a country, its greatest task is to overthrow the remaining capitalists in the world and complete the socialist revolution. Before the world capitalist class has been destroyed, it is impossible to construct a real proletarian culture. However, after the world socialist revolution has been completed, the proletariat itself will begin to disappear; that is, classes and, of course, class antagonisms will begin to disappear. It is at this point, then, that socialist culture will begin naturally to establish itself. Therefore, it is in no way necessary to establish a proletarian culture. Mao's launching of the "Cultural Revolution" is not only theoretically absurd, it is also foolish from a practical point of view. The socioeconomic base in China is so backward that there are many areas which remain in a state of primitive production. As for culture, the majority of the peasantry remain illiterate along with almost half the working class. If under these conditions, to launch a "proletarian cultural revolution" in order to establish "Four News"—new culture, new ideas, new habits, and new customs—does not display ignorance, then it reveals illusions and foolish idealism.

If Mao really intended to raise the cultural level of the workers and peasants, he should have started by eliminating the illiteracy of the masses. In order to achieve this, it would, first of all, be necessary to increase the standard of living of the masses, that is, increase their pay and decrease their hours of work. It would be necessary to let them have time and energy to study and to participate in cultural activities. Mao's policy is, however, just the contrary, demanding that the workers and peasants work longer hours with no improvement in their living standards. Mao's recent campaign against "economism" and his refusal to grant any concessions to the working class show his attitude quite clearly; that is, the working class should serve only as instruments of production in the interests of the bureaucracy.

In reality it can be said that Mao utilized the label of "proletarian" only in order to rationalize his attack and to purge his opposition under the accusation of "taking the capitalist road."

However, we can see that Mao has not attacked the real capitalist and bourgeois elements still existing in China. This in itself is enough to prove that Mao's "Great Proletarian Cultural Revolution" is nothing more than a purge which he is carrying out in order to maintain his own bureaucratic rule and personal cult.

NOTES

INTRODUCTION: Looking Back Over My Years with P'eng Shu-tse—by Ch'en Pi-lan

1. From the early years of the nineteenth century, Britain sought to exploit the China market by the forcible importation of opium from India. In 1839 the Chinese government destroyed large quantities of British opium at Canton. In retaliation the British launched the Opium War, which ended in the reduction of China to the status of a semicolony. It began with the arrival of British warships in Hong Kong in June 1840 and led to the bombardment of the South China coastal ports in 1842. China capitulated with the signing of the Treaty of Nanking in 1842, ceding Hong Kong to Britain as a colony, opening five ports to British trade, and agreeing to pay $21 million in indemnities. The so-called Boxer Rebellion (this name is not used in China) was a mass anti-imperialist movement led by the I-ho Ch'üan (Righteous and Harmonious Fists) secret society in 1899-1900. The supporters of the I-ho Ch'üan organized attacks on imperialist personnel in China and on their Chinese collaborators. In June 1900 a force of 140,000 from this movement occupied Peking. The imperialist powers retaliated by sacking Peking in August 1900, using an eight-power expeditionary force including troops from the United States, France, Britain, Germany, Austria, Italy, Russia, and Japan. The Ch'ing government was compelled to pay reparations to the imperialist governments after the uprising was suppressed.

2. The May Thirtieth Incident in 1925 marked the beginning of the Chinese revolution of 1925-27. Twelve students were killed by British troops while protesting the murder of a Chinese worker at a Japanese-owned factory in Shanghai. This touched off a general strike that spread throughout the country under the name of the May Thirtieth Movement.

3. Fengtien was a province in Manchuria that has since been renamed. The leader of the Fengtien military clique was the Manchurian warlord Chang Tso-lin. His troops were expelled from Shanghai by the somewhat more liberal Sun Ch'uan-fang in October 1925. During the continuing fight between Chang and Sun, the Japanese government, which backed Chang, sent troops to Manchuria in December 1925 allegedly to protect Japanese railroad concessions. This prelude to the full-scale invasion of Manchuria in 1931 was strongly protested by the CCP and the Shanghai labor movement. During the warlord struggles for control of North China,

General Feng Yü-hsiang, who was then allied with the KMT, blockaded the Taku forts on the outskirts of Tientsin in early March 1926. The imperialist powers protested that this interfered with the foreign access to the port and violated the Boxer Protocol of 1901. Eight foreign powers delivered an ultimatum to China's nominal government in Peking demanding immediate reopening of the port at Tientsin. On March 18, Chinese students led by the CCP held a demonstration in T'ien An Men Square in Peking to protest this encroachment on Chinese sovereignty. Government guards fired on the demonstration, killing as many as 200 persons.

4. On March 20, 1926, Chiang Kai-shek organized a military coup in Canton in which he took over as head of the KMT. More than fifty members of the CCP were arrested and the Russian guards disarmed. Chiang afterward proposed to continue to work with the CCP only if the CCP would accept severe restrictions on its activities inside and outside the KMT.

5. The Northern Expedition to defeat the warlord regimes was first publicly projected by Sun Yat-sen in the spring of 1921, when his local Canton government disavowed the legitimacy of the military regime in Peking. It was finally begun in July 1926. The petty warlord states rapidly collapsed as the National Revolutionary Army of the KMT moved north, sparking a wave of peasant and worker uprisings.

6. In December 1926 the KMT, over Chiang Kai-shek's objections, moved its government from Canton to Wuhan. After Chiang's April 1927 coup in Shanghai he established a rival KMT government with its capital at Nanking. The "left" KMT regime at Wuhan, headed by Wang Ching-wei, maintained the policy of collaboration with the CCP until July 1927, when it too staged an anticommunist purge. The two wings of the KMT reunited in the fall of 1927.

7. The uprising in Canton was ordered from Moscow to coincide with the Fifteenth Congress of the Russian Communist Party. Its aim was to refute the charge of the Left Opposition that Stalin's line was responsible for the defeat of the Chinese revolution. Armed units led by the CCP took over Canton the morning of December 11, 1927. By December 13 the rising had been crushed. More than 5,000 Communists and workers were killed in the repressions that followed.

8. These documents are available in *Leon Trotsky on China* (New York: Monad Press, 1976).

9. Liu Shao-ch'i had been reelected as China's head of state in January 1965, the year this article was written. He was purged during the "Cultural Revolution," in 1967.

10. In November 1933 the KMT's Nineteenth Route Army rebelled against the Chiang Kai-shek regime and set up a "People's Revolutionary Government" in Fukien province. The revolt had been provoked by Chiang's failure to resist the Japanese advances (the Nineteenth Route Army had made a serious stand against the Japanese attack on Shanghai). Initial discussions of possible united military action between

the Fukien rebels and the CCP collapsed and the Fukien revolt was suppressed by Chiang in January 1934.

11. On August 22, 1939, the Soviet Union signed a nonaggression treaty with Nazi Germany. This freed Hitler's hands for the invasion of Poland on September 1, 1939, the beginning of World War II. Until the German invasion of the Soviet Union in June 1941 Moscow and the Communist parties that supported Stalin refrained from criticizing fascism.

12. "Pabloism Reviewed" was completed on January 1, 1955, for discussion within the International Committee of the Fourth International, one of two public factions formed in the international split of 1953-54. It is available in the Education for Socialists bulletin *The Struggle to Reunify the Fourth International (1954-1963)* (New York: Pathfinder Press, 1976), vol. 1. "Where Is Healy Taking the Socialist Labour League?" was directed at the sectarian British Trotskyist organization led by Gerry Healy, which refused to participate in the reunification of the Fourth International in 1963. It was published in the *International Information Bulletin* (New York: Socialist Workers Party), May 1963. The documents by P'eng on China mentioned above are reprinted in this volume.

13. *King Richard the Second,* Act 1, Scene 3, John of Gaunt.

The Theory of Permanent Revolution and the Underdeveloped Countries

1. V. I. Lenin, *Collected Works* (Moscow: Foreign Languages Publishing House), vol. 9, p. 112.

2. Leon Trotsky, *The Permanent Revolution and Results and Prospects,* 3rd ed. (New York: Pathfinder Press, 1974), p. 71, emphasis in original.

3. Ibid., p. 80, emphasis in original.

4. The proletariat, the peasantry, the petty bourgeoisie, and the national bourgeoisie (as distinguished from the compradore, presumably more proimperialist, bourgeoisie). This is the origin of Mao Tse-tung's slogan of the "bloc of four classes."

5. The Canton/Hong Kong Strike Committee led a general strike in Canton and in the British colony of Hong Kong following the May Thirtieth Incident in Shanghai in 1925. Involving some 250,000 workers, the strike was the longest in Chinese history, tying up British shipping from June 1925 to October 1926. In the course of the strike, the strike committee took on many functions that paralleled soviet forms of organization.

6. "Second Letter to Radek," March 4, 1927, *Leon Trotsky on China* (New York: Monad Press, 1976), p. 124.

7. April 3, 1927, in ibid., p. 142.

8. Ibid., pp. 145-46.

9. Ibid., p. 161.

10. Trotsky is expanding here on an analogy in the Communist press between the French revolution of 1848 and the Chinese revolution of 1925-27. Chiang Kai-shek had been compared to Louis-Eugéne Cavaignac (1802-1857), a French general and a leader of the moderate bourgeois republicans in 1848. Despite his republican credentials, Cavaignac, as war minister in the French cabinet, ordered the execution of 3,000 Paris workers after the June 1848 uprising. Trotsky points to the role of the French liberals in paving the way for Cavaignac. Alexandre Auguste Ledru-Rollin (1808-1874) was a leader of the liberal republicans in the 1848 revolution; he supported the crushing of the workers' movement. Louis Blanc (1811-1882) was a utopian socialist and pacifist, and a member of the provisional government established by the February 1848 revolution. In place of leading the workers in struggle, he sought compromises with the capitalists that led to the defeat. At the time Trotsky was writing, Aleksandr Martynov (1865-1935), a Menshevik who had joined the Soviet CP only in 1923, was the leading Stalinist theorist of the "two-stage revolution" and is regarded as the author of the slogan of the "bloc of four classes."

11. "The Chinese Revolution and the Theses of Comrade Stalin," *Leon Trotsky on China*, pp. 169-70, emphasis in original.

12. Ibid., p. 171.

13. Ibid., p. 176.

14. Ibid., p. 195.

15. "Second Speech on the Chinese Question," May 1927, in *Leon Trotsky on China*, pp. 234-35, emphasis in original.

16. Trotsky's criticism of Stalin and Bukharin's 1928 draft program for the Communist International is published in full in his book *The Third International After Lenin* (New York: Pathfinder Press, 1970). The chapter on China is also included in *Leon Trotsky on China*.

17. Leon Trotsky, *The Permanent Revolution and Results and Prospects*, 3rd ed., pp. 276-79, emphasis in original.

18. The "Five Anti" campaign of 1952 was proclaimed to stamp out bribery, tax evasion, fraud, theft of government property, and theft of state economic secrets. This was the first significant move against those industrialists who had remained in China after the defeat of Chiang Kai-shek in 1949. Some 500,000 private concerns of various size were investigated by the government.

19. This article was written in 1960 during the several years of severe food shortages in China following the collapse of Mao's Great Leap Forward. Even in the late 1970s, however, most foods remained strictly rationed, with meat in extremely short supply.

20. "The Revolution in India, Its Tasks and Dangers," May 30, 1930, *Writings of Leon Trotsky (1930)* (New York: Pathfinder Press, 1975), p. 244.

21. Ibid., pp. 245-46, emphasis in original.

22. This was the putsch at Madiun in September 1948. The Sukarno regime crushed the rebellion, arresting 36,000 members and sympathizers

of the Indonesian CP. In December of that year the army executed without trial eleven of the party's most prominent leaders.

23. This prediction was borne out when the Indonesian army turned on the CP in October 1965 in one of the most terrible bloodbaths of modern times. As many as 1,000,000 members and supporters of the CP were murdered. To the end the CP declared its loyalty to Sukarno and refused to organize any serious resistance to the slaughter.

24. This refers to the liberal Arbenz government of March 1951–June 1954.

25. The Castro government took power as a coalition between revolutionists and liberals such as Manuel Urrutia. In their first year and a half in office, the forces grouped directly around Castro moved to the left, breaking with one after another of their procapitalist fellow travelers. The decisive step in the creation of a workers' state did not come until the great bulk of Cuban capitalist property was nationalized in October of 1960, only a few months after this article was written.

26. "The Death Agony of Capitalism and the Tasks of the Fourth International," in *The Transitional Program for Socialist Revolution* by Leon Trotsky, 3rd ed. (New York: Pathfinder Press, 1977), pp. 137-38, emphasis in original.

The Causes of the Victory of the Chinese Communist Party Over Chiang Kai-shek, and the CCP's Perspectives

1. The "gold yuan" was a currency reform announced by the KMT government on August 19, 1948. At that time the Chinese dollar was exchanging on the black market at a rate of 10 million to US$1. The "gold yuan" was a supposedly gold-backed currency, pegged at 4 to the US $1. The old currency was withdrawn, but military defeats in Manchuria set off a further wave of financial panic that destroyed the parity of the gold yuan by the end of November.

2. The figures mentioned here, all high-ranking KMT leaders, went over to the CCP toward the end of the civil war and were rewarded with posts in the Mao regime.

3. In January 1949 Chiang Kai-shek was forced into retirement as a result of the KMT defeats in Manchuria. The presidency of the Republic was assumed by Li Tsung-jen until after the KMT's flight to Taiwan.

4. E. Germain (Ernest Mandel), "What Should Be Modified and What Should Be Maintained in the Theses of the Second World Congress of the Fourth International on the Question of Stalinism?" *International Information Bulletin* (New York: Socialist Workers Party), April 1951, p. 9.

5. The "yellow trade unions" were organized by the KMT following the suppression of the CCP in 1927 as government-controlled rivals to the Communist-led "Red unions." The yellow unions were government agencies for policing the working class rather than actual trade unions.

6. The "third period" theory was first formally adopted by the Commu-

nist International at a plenum of its Executive Committee in July 1929. This theory divided the post–World War I epoch into three periods: the first period, of revolutionary upheaval, was said to have run from 1917 to 1923; the second, of capitalist stabilization, had lasted from 1924 to 1928; the Comintern maintained that the "third period," beginning in 1928, would see steadily rising mass struggles on a world scale, ending with the final collapse of capitalism. The Stalinists used this theory to justify refusing to cooperate with other tendencies in the workers' movement— denouncing all other workers' parties as "social fascists." Several Asian CPs, including the Chinese, adopted a course of rural guerrilla warfare. Stalin retreated from the "third period" ultraleftism after 1933, when his refusal to permit the German Communists to seek a united front against fascism led to Hitler's rise to power.

7. The Sian Incident occurred in December 1936, when Chiang Kai-shek was detained for fourteen days by the Manchurian troops in Shensi province engaged in the KMT's campaign against the CCP forces.

8. These articles were published in the *International Information Bulletin* (New York: Socialist Workers Party). The March 1952 issue of the bulletin contained: "The Third Chinese Revolution and the Tasks of the Revolutionary Communist Party," signed "by the Editors of the Chinese Party's Organ," and "Why Is this Civil War Called a Revolution and the Importance of this Recognition," by Ma Ki. The April 1952 issue of the bulletin contained: "The Problem of the So-called 'Revolutionary Situation,'" by Chung Yuan, and "The Rule of the Chinese CP and the Tasks of Our Party," by Lin, Wang, Chi, Tin, Chian, and Tao.

9. Harold R. Isaacs (1910-   ) became a Trotskyist in China in 1934 and joined the American Socialist Workers Party on his return to the United States in 1936. The first edition of his book *The Tragedy of the Chinese Revolution*, still the most authoritative account of the Chinese revolution of 1925-27, was published by Secker & Warburg in London in 1938. Trotsky had gone over the manuscript and provided an introduction for the book. Isaacs broke with Marxism during World War II and published two subsequent editions of his book, in 1951 and 1961, which deleted Trotsky's introduction and politically revised the text to give it an anticommunist slant.

10. "The Third Chinese Revolution," resolution of the Seventh Plenum of the International Executive Committee of the Fourth International, April 1949, *International Information Bulletin* (New York: Socialist Workers Party), June 1949, p. 29, emphasis in original.

11. Trotsky's discussion of the social role of two-class "worker-peasant" parties can be found in his "Summary and Perspectives of the Chinese Revolution" (June 1928), in *Leon Trotsky on China* (New York: Monad Press, 1976), pp. 327-36.

12. Ernest Germain, "The Third Chinese Revolution," *Fourth International*, vol. 12, no. 1, January-February 1951, p. 19, emphasis in original.

13. The term *Stakhanovist* is derived from the Russian coal miner

Alexei Stakhanov, who was publicized in the Soviet press of the 1930s for prodigious feats in overfulfilling his labor quotas. In 1935 an official "Stakhanovite Movement" was launched, in which substantial material rewards were offered to workers who would act as pacesetters in introducing speedup in Soviet industry.

14. Leon Trotsky, "Peasant War in China and the Proletariat," *Leon Trotsky on China*, pp. 526-27, 531.

15. Mao Tse-tung, "On New Democracy" (January 1940), *Selected Works* (Peking: Foreign Languages Press, 1967), vol. 2, p. 366, emphasis in original.

16. Trotsky, "Peasant War in China and the Proletariat," *Leon Trotsky on China*, pp. 529-30.

Some Comments on the Draft Resolution on "The Third Chinese Revolution"

1. "The Third Chinese Revolution" was the title of a resolution adopted by the International Executive Committee of the Fourth International in May 1952. It was published in the July-August 1952 issue of *Fourth International* (New York), vol. 13, no. 4.

2. "The Chinese Question After the Sixth Congress" (October 4, 1928), in *Leon Trotsky on China* (New York: Monad Press, 1976), p. 349.

3. Leon Trotsky, "Three Letters to Preobrazhensky" (March-April 1928), *Leon Trotsky on China*, p. 281, emphasis in original.

4. See "Some Supplementary Remarks and Corrections to the 'Report on the Chinese Situation,'" appended to the previous article in this volume.

5. These quotations come from the section entitled "Workers' and farmers' government" in "The Death Agony of Capitalism and the Tasks of the Fourth International," commonly referred to as the Transitional Program. It was adopted as its founding programmatic document by the Fourth International in 1938. It is contained in the collection of Trotsky's writings *The Transitional Program for Socialist Revolution*, 3rd ed. (New York: Pathfinder Press, 1977). These citations appear on pp. 133-35.

6. Ibid., p. 134.

The Case of the Chinese Trotskyists

1. Niu Lan was a pseudonym for a Czechoslovak Comintern representative.

The Third Chinese Revolution and Its Perspectives

1. The "Three Anti" campaign was launched early in 1952 to eliminate "waste, corruption, and bureaucratism." Its aim was to purge cadres from

the CCP ranks, particularly in the rural areas, who had become so corrupted that they were unresponsive to the directives issued by the party center. More than 10 percent of the party membership was expelled in the "Three Anti" campaign. It was followed later in the year by the "Five Anti" campaign directed at the bourgeoisie.

A Criticism of the Various Views Supporting the Chinese Rural People's Communes

1. Marx and Engels, *Selected Works* (Moscow: Foreign Languages Publishing House, 1951), vol. 2, p. 383.

2. Ibid., p. 387.

3. Ibid., p. 393.

4. Ibid., pp. 394-95.

5. "Speech Delivered at the First Congress of Agricultural Communes and Artels," December 4, 1919, *Collected Works* (Moscow: Progress Publishers), vol. 30, p. 195. Artels are a traditional Russian association of laborers for collective work.

6. Ibid., pp. 195-96, emphasis added.

7. "Preliminary Draft Theses on the Agrarian Question," June 1920, *Collected Works*, vol. 31, p. 157, emphasis added.

8. "Report on Work in the Countryside," March 23, 1919, *Collected Works*, vol. 29, pp. 210-11, emphasis in original.

9. Ibid., p. 212, emphasis added.

10. Ibid., p. 214.

11. "On Co-operation," January 4, 1923, *Collected Works*, vol. 33, p. 470.

12. "The Tax in Kind," April 21, 1921, *Collected Works*, vol. 32, p. 350.

13. Leon Trotsky, "The Death Agony of Capitalism and the Tasks of the Fourth International," in *The Transitional Program for Socialist Revolution*, 3rd ed. (New York: Pathfinder Press, 1977), p. 127, emphasis in original.

14. Ma Chi, *The People's Communes*, pp. 17-18.

15. Ibid., p. 17.

16. Ibid.

17. Hsinhua News Agency dispatches, October, 1958, *People's Daily.*

18. *The People's Communes.*

19. Liu Shao-ch'i, "Report on the Work of the Central Committee of the Communist Party of China to the Second Session of the Eighth National Congress," May 5, 1958, *Second Session of the Eighth National Congress of the Communist Party of China* (Peking: Foreign Languages Press, 1958), p. 31.

20. Liang, "The Draft Resolution on the China Communes—A Commentary," in *SWP Discussion Bulletin* (New York: Socialist Workers Party), vol. 20, no. 8, May 1959, p. 35.

21. The Socialist Workers Party began to discuss the issue of the

Chinese People's Communes at a meeting of its Political Committee in New York on March 3, 1959. On April 6, the party's Secretariat, a subcommittee of the Political Committee, issued its "Draft Resolution on Chinese Communes." This document was criticized by a number of SWP National Committee members resident in Los Angeles and on April 21, 1959, the Los Angeles NC members submitted their counterdocument, discussed here by P'eng. The Los Angeles Draft Resolution stressed the positive features of the People's Communes and saw them as an important step forward for the Chinese revolution; the Secretariat draft was more critical. Though unsigned, supporting correspondence indicates that the Los Angeles NC group included Arne Swabeck, James P. Cannon, and George Novack. Their position was supported by Liang, who sometimes signed his articles John Liang. The document "The Communes in China (Draft Resolution Proposed by NC Members in Los Angeles)" was submitted to the SWP Political Committee on April 29, 1959. It was rejected by a vote of eight to one. The discussion of the commune question was then taken to the SWP's Eighteenth National Convention, held in New Jersey, June 26-28, 1959. There a three-point resolution was adopted which proposed (1) to take no final position on the nature of the Chinese communes, but to open a written discussion after the convention adjourned; (2) that treatment of the communes in the party press "shall begin with a positive, unambiguous statement of the progressive character of the communes as a new stage and step ahead in the economic and social development of China to which we, as partisans of the Chinese revolution, give our support"; and (3) that the party's 1955 resolution defining the Mao government as a Stalinist regime that must be overthrown by China's workers should be reaffirmed. In August, Swabeck and Liang submitted a further article on the communes to the party press, moving toward the position of offering critical support to the Mao leadership as a revolutionary current in the workers' movement. This article provoked the breakup of the Los Angeles NC group that had sponsored the April draft resolution. Swabeck and Liang pursued the line of proposing "critical support" to Mao, while this was opposed by Cannon, Novack, and the rest of the central party leadership. In 1963 Swabeck began to move toward full endorsement of Maoism; this ended his collaboration with Liang. Swabeck's views were presented to and defeated at three party conventions (1960, 1963, and 1965).

22. "The Communes in China (Draft Resolution Proposed by NC Members in Los Angeles)," *SWP Discussion Bulletin,* vol. 20, no. 8, May 1959, p. 40.

23. Ibid.

24. Ma Chi, *The People's Communes,* p. 15.

25. Chou En-lai, *Report on the Work of the Government to the First Session of the Second National People's Congress,* April 18, 1959 (Peking: Foreign Languages Press, 1959), p. 3.

26. Ibid., p. 5.

27. *People's Daily,* February 25, 1959.

28. Ibid., June 11, 1959.

29. "The Communes in China," SWP Discussion Bulletin, vol. 20, no. 8, May 1959, p. 39.

30. "The Third Chinese Revolution and Its Aftermath," resolution adopted by the 1955 SWP convention, in *The Chinese Revolution and Its Development* (New York: Education for Socialists Bulletin [distributed by Pathfinder Press], 1969), p. 3.

31. Ma Chi, *The People's Communes,* p. 10.

32. Ibid.

33. *SWP Discussion Bulletin,* vol. 20, no. 8, May 1959, p. 36, emphasis in original.

34. "The Advantages of the Communes," *Red Flag,* no. 8, 1958.

35. Ma Chi, *The People's Communes.*

36. Leon Trotsky, *The Transitional Program for Socialist Revolution,* 3rd ed., p. 127.

37. Ibid.

38. "Resolution of the Central Committee of the Chinese Communist Party on the Establishment of People's Communes in the Rural Areas" (August 29, 1958), in *People's Communes in China* (Peking: Foreign Languages Press, 1958), pp. 3-4.

39. Arne Swabeck, "The Third Chinese Revolution and Its Communes," *SWP Discussion Bulletin,* vol. 20, no. 13, June 1959, p. 5.

40. Leon Trotsky, *The Transitional Program for Socialist Revolution,* 3rd ed., p. 145.

41. *SWP Discussion Bulletin,* vol. 20, no. 8, May 1959, p. 40.

42. *Red Flag,* August 1958.

43. Peking Review, no. 17, 1959, p. 29.

44. Ma Chi, *The People's Communes,* p. 2, emphasis added.

45. "Speech Delivered at the First Congress of Agricultural Communes and Agricultural Artels," December 4, 1919, *Collected Works,* vol. 30, p. 198.

46. *SWP Discussion Bulletin,* vol. 20, no. 8, May 1959, p. 40.

47. At the time the discussion over the Chinese communes opened in the SWP Political Committee in March 1959, Daniel Roberts, a long-time party leader, had submitted an article entitled "The Chinese Communes" to the American Trotskyist quarterly journal *International Socialist Review.* Although the article reflected the majority opinion in the PC, because the discussion was still in its early stages the party leadership in New York decided to recommend the article to the *ISR* editors as an individual contribution, not necessarily representing the final viewpoint of the SWP. On March 13, the Los Angeles NC group sent a telegram to New York stating that they considered the PC's tentative position on the communes "hypercritical," and requested to see the text of the Roberts article before it was published. After seeing the draft, the Los Angeles NC members requested that the article be withdrawn. At that time the Spring

1959 issue of the *ISR* was in the stage of page makeup, so the typeset pages were removed and the article was ultimately printed in the party's *Discussion Bulletin,* vol. 20, no. 8, May 1959.

48. *SWP Discussion Bulletin,* vol. 20, no. 8, May 1959, p. 36, emphasis in original.

49. Sam Marcy led a faction within the SWP that propounded the theory that the division of the world into "two class camps" (the then-Soviet bloc and the imperialist powers) predominated over the events of the class struggle in particular countries. The Marcyites interpreted the antibureaucratic uprising of the Hungarian workers in October 1956 as merely a weakening of the Soviet Union's "camp" vis-à-vis imperialism. Consequently they supported the crushing of the Hungarian workers by the Soviet army. They split from the SWP early in 1959 and in March 1959 launched the *Workers World* newspaper. Their general adaptation to Stalinism was expressed also in their attitude toward the Chinese communes. The first issue of *Workers World* carried a front-page article under the title "Hail the Communes!" which said in part: "The Communes are a new and higher stage of the Chinese Revolution. . . . Hail the revolutionary energy of the Chinese youth! Hail the brave emancipation of the courageous Chinese women! Hail the devotion of the young students and intellectuals who labor in field and factory side by side with the tillers of the soil in the most back-breaking labor!"

50. *SWP Discussion Bulletin,* vol. 20, no. 13, June 1959, p. 3.

51. Ibid.

52. The "Five Principles of Peaceful Coexistence" were first announced in a joint communiqué signed by Chou En-lai and Indian Prime Minister Nehru in New Delhi in June 1954. Later that year they were incorporated into the first constitution of the People's Republic of China as the basis of Chinese foreign policy. They are: (1) mutual respect for territorial integrity and sovereignty, (2) nonaggression, (3) noninterference in each other's internal affairs, (4) equality and mutual benefits, and (5) peaceful coexistence.

53. Leon Trotsky, *The Transitional Program for Socialist Revolution,* 3rd ed., p. 127, emphasis in original.

54. Ibid.

55. Daniel Roberts, "The Communes in China," *SWP Discussion Bulletin,* vol. 20, no. 8, May 1959, p. 9.

56. Hsinhua News Agency, August 27, 1959.

57. "The Third Chinese Revolution and Its Communes," *SWP Discussion Bulletin,* vol. 20, no. 13, June 1959, p. 3.

58. *Peking Review,* September 1, 1959, p. 7.

59. Ibid., pp. 7-8.

60. *People's Daily,* August 29, 1959, emphasis added.

61. *Peking Review,* September 1, 1959, p. 10.

62. Ibid., p. 8.

63. Ibid., p. 11.

64. Chou En-lai, "Report on the 1959 Economic Plan," August 26, 1959, at the plenum of the Standing Committee of the Second National People's Congress, *Peking Review,* September 1, 1959, p. 18.

65. "Oppose Right Deviation and Make an All-Out Effort to Fulfill the Principal Targets of the Second Five-Year Plan This Year!" editorial in the *People's Daily,* August 27, 1959.

66. "Report on the 1959 Economic Plan," *Peking Review,* September 1, 1959, p. 18.

On the Nature of the Chinese Communist Party and Its Regime—Political Revolution or Democratic Reform?

1. Arne Swabeck and John Liang, "The Third Chinese Revolution, the Communes and the Regime," *SWP Discussion Bulletin,* vol. 21, no. 2, January 1960, p. 29.

2. Ibid.

3. Ibid., p. 24, emphasis in original.

4. E. Germain (Ernest Mandel), "What Should Be Modified and What Should Be Maintained in the Theses of the Second World Congress of the Fourth International on the Question of Stalinism?" *International Information Bulletin* (New York: Socialist Workers Party), April 1951, p. 5.

5. See "The Causes of the Victory of the Chinese Communist Party over Chiang Kai-shek, and the CCP's Perspectives—Report on the Chinese Situation to the Third Congress of the Fourth International" (1951), earlier in this volume.

6. *SWP Discussion Bulletin,* vol. 21, no. 2, January 1960.

7. "Constitution of the Chinese Communist Party" (June 11, 1945), in *A Documentary History of Chinese Communism,* Conrad Brandt, Benjamin Schwartz, and John K. Fairbank (Cambridge, Mass.: Harvard University Press, 1952), p. 422.

8. Ibid., p. 424.

9. Mao Tse-tung, *Tsui weitati Yu-i* (The Greatest Friendship) (Peking: 1953). A section of this article, including the portion quoted here, is available in English in Stuart R. Schram, *The Political Thought of Mao Tse-tung* (New York: Frederick A. Praeger, 1963), p. 295.

10. "The Third Chinese Revolution, the Communes and the Regime," *SWP Discussion Bulletin,* vol. 21, no. 2, January 1960, p. 29.

11. Ibid., p. 22.

12. Ibid.

13. Ibid., p. 23,

14. Ibid.

15. Ibid., p. 27.

16. Ibid., p. 23.

17. In the Great French Revolution, which broke out in 1789, a sharp shift to the right took place with the arrest of Robespierre, the principal

leader of the radical Jacobins, on 9 Thermidor (July 27), 1794. By analogy Trotsky referred to Stalin's crushing of the Bolshevik Party as the Thermidor of the Russian revolution.

18. *SWP Discussion Bulletin*, vol. 21, no. 9, January 1960, p. 23.

19. Leon Trotsky, *In Defense of Marxism* (New York: Pathfinder Press, 1973), p. 7.

20. Leon Trotsky, *The Revolution Betrayed* (New York: Pathfinder Press, 1972). The pages referred to are a section of the chapter on "The Growth of Inequality and Social Antagonisms" entitled "The Social Physiognomy of the Ruling Stratum."

21. Gerald Clark, *Impatient Giant: Red China Today* (New York: David McKay Co., 1959).

22. The reference here is to Peter Townsend, *China Phoenix: The Revolution in China* (London: Jonathan Cape, 1955).

23. *SWP Discussion Bulletin*, vol. 21, no. 9, January 1960, p. 28.

24. This refers to the Chinese edition, from which P'eng quotes. A substantially condensed English edition was published by Holt, Rinehart & Winston (New York) in 1960.

25. Chow Ching-wen, *Ten Years of Storm* (Chinese edition), p. 112.

26. Ibid., pp. 112-13.

27. Ibid., p. 114.

28. Ibid.

29. Ibid., p. 300.

30. Ibid., p. 114.

31. Ibid., p. 116.

32. Ibid., p. 302.

33. Ibid., pp. 117-18.

34. Ibid., pp. 118-19.

35. Ibid., pp. 122-23.

36. Ibid., pp. 304-5.

37. Ibid., p. 299.

38. Ibid., p. 300.

39. Ibid., pp. 305-6.

40. Ibid., p. 306.

41. In the spring of 1957 the CCP, following the initiative of the Russian CP the previous year in criticizing Stalin, opened a "mass campaign" to solicit criticisms of its regime, under the slogan "Let a hundred flowers bloom, let a hundred schools of thought contend." Genuine oppositional currents rapidly surfaced throughout the country. Under this pressure, the CCP permitted extremely critical articles to appear in the press, particularly in May. In mid-June the party leadership counterattacked, denouncing the oppositionists as "poisonous weeds." An "antirightist" campaign was launched that reached its height in the fall of 1957, in which many thousands of people who had dared to speak out were fired from their jobs and deported to the countryside or imprisoned in labor camps. In June 1978, after Mao's death and the collapse of his faction, it was reported that 110,000 persons who had been imprisoned

since the Hundred Flowers episode had just been released from prison (*New York Times*, June 6, 1978).

42. *Ten Years of Storm* (Chinese edition), p. 98.

43. Ibid., pp. 98-99.

44. Ibid., pp. 99-100.

45. Ibid., p. 100.

46. "The Third Chinese Revolution, the Communes and the Regime," *SWP Discussion Bulletin*, vol. 21, no. 2, January 1960, p. 22. The quote from Peter Townsend appears on page 216 of *China Phoenix*.

47. This is from the immediately preceding article in this volume, "A Criticism of the Various Views Supporting the Chinese Rural People's Communes."

48. *Ten Years of Storm* (Chinese edition), pp. 415-16.

49. *SWP Discussion Bulletin*, vol. 21, no. 2, January 1960, p. 25.

50. Leon Trotsky, *The Permanent Revolution and Results and Prospects*, 3rd ed. (New York: Pathfinder Press, 1974), p. 131.

51. Ibid., p. 132, emphasis added.

52. Ibid., p. 133, emphasis added.

53. V. I. Lenin, "Speech in the Moscow Soviet of Workers', Peasants' and Red Army Deputies," April 23, 1918, *Collected Works*, vol. 27, p. 232.

54. "Resolution on War and Peace," Seventh Congress of the Russian Communist Party, March 6-8, 1918, in V. I. Lenin, *Collected Works*, vol. 27, p. 119.

55. Leon Trotsky, *The Permanent Revolution*, p. 155.

56. Ibid., p. 145, emphasis in original.

57. "The Third Chinese Revolution," resolution adopted by the International Executive Committee of the Fourth International, May 1952. Published in *Fourth International* (New York), July-August 1952, p. 113.

58. Liu Shao-ch'i, "Report on the Work of the Central Committee of the Communist Party of China to the Second Session of the Eighth National Congress," May 5, 1958, *Second Session of the Eighth National Congress of the Communist Party of China* (Peking: Foreign Languages Press, 1958), p. 40. This official English-language version of Liu's speech uses the term "uninterrupted revolution" in place of *permanent revolution*. There has been much discussion in English of the distinction between Mao's theory of uninterrupted revolution and Trotsky's theory of permanent revolution. In Chinese, however, the two terms are identical—*pu-tuan ko-ming*—and P'eng is correct in his attributing the words *permanent revolution* to Liu and Mao. *Pu-tuan ko-ming* has been the standard phrase used in Chinese throughout this century for translating the words *permanent revolution* in the works of Marx, Lenin, and Trotsky, and in all discussion of them.

59. This quotation is from "Some Comments on the Draft Resolution on 'The Third Chinese Revolution,'" which appears earlier in this volume.

60. Mao Tse-tung, *On the Correct Handling of Contradictions Among the People*, speech given on February 27, 1957, at the Eleventh Session of

the Supreme State Conference (Peking: Foreign Languages Press, 1960), p. 13.

61. Speech at a reception for representatives of the Ceylonese Lanka Sama Samaja Party, *People's Daily*, May 19, 1957.

62. "The Third Chinese Revolution, the Communes and the Regime," *SWP Discussion Bulletin*, vol. 21, no. 2, January 1960, p. 29, emphasis added.

63. Ibid., p. 30, emphasis in original.

64. From the article "A Criticism of the Various Views Supporting the Chinese Rural People's Communes."

65. "The Third Chinese Revolution, the Communes and the Regime," *SWP Discussion Bulletin*, vol. 21, no. 2, January 1960, p. 26.

66. Arne Swabeck, "The Third Chinese Revolution and Its Communes," *SWP Discussion Bulletin*, vol. 20, no. 13, June 1959, p. 3.

67. "The Communes in China (Draft Resolution Proposed by NC Members in Los Angeles)," *SWP Discussion Bulletin*, vol. 20, no. 8, May 1959, p. 40.

68. Liang, "The Draft Resolution on the China Communes—A Commentary," in ibid., p. 36, emphasis in original.

69. See "A Criticism of the Various Views Supporting the Chinese Rural People's Communes."

70. Swabeck and Liang, "The Third Chinese Revolution, the Communes and the Regime," *SWP Discussion Bulletin*, vol. 21, no. 2, January 1960, p. 30.

71. Ibid., p. 15.

72. Ibid., p. 28.

Two Interviews on the "Cultural Revolution"

1. P'eng Chen, one of the top ranking CCP leaders and mayor of Peking from 1951, disappeared from public activity at the end of March 1966. On June 3 it was announced that he had been removed from his position as first secretary of the Peking Municipal CCP Committee.

2. "A Criticism of the Bourgeois Position Taken by *Frontline* and the *People's Daily*," *Red Flag*, issue no. 7 in 1966.

3. "New Victory for Mao Tse-tung's Thought," editorial from the June 4, 1966, *People's Daily*, reprinted in *Peking Review*, June 10, 1966, p. 4.

4. This article, "On the New Historical Play *Hai Jui Dismissed from Office*," by Yao Wen-yuan, was published in the November 10 issue of the Shanghai daily *Wen Hui Pao*, and is generally regarded as the opening gun in the Cultural Revolution. Mao, at that time at odds with the majority of the central party leadership in Peking, had gone to Shanghai to rally support and strongly promoted this article. After Mao's death, Yao was arrested in October 1976 as one of the "gang of four"; the play *Hai Jui Dismissed from Office* was rehabilitated and reopened in Peking

two years later (see "Call for Rehabilitation of Wronged Writers and Their Works," Hsinhua, December 24-25, 1978).

5. The two main articles directed against Teng T'o and his group were "On 'Three-Family Village'" by Yao Wen-yuan, which appeared in the May 10, 1966, Shanghai *Liberation Daily* and *Wen Hui Pao*, reprinted in the May 27, 1966, *Peking Review*; and "Teng T'o's 'Evening Chats at Yenshan' Is Anti-Party and Anti-Socialist Double Talk," compiled by Lin Chieh, Ma Tse-min, Yen Chang-kuei, Chou Ying, Teng Wen-sheng, and Chin Tien-liang, *Kwangming Daily*, May 8, 1966.

6. For the English version of this article, see *Peking Review*, May 27, 1966, p. 18.

7. "A Great Revolution that Touches the People to Their Very Souls," quoted from the *People's Daily* in the June 10, 1966, *Peking Review*, p. 9. The Petöfi Club, or Petöfi Circle, was founded in Budapest early in 1956 by reform-minded Communist Party intellectuals and youth. (It was named for Sándor Petöfi [1822-1849], Hungarian poet and patriot, killed in the revolution of 1849.) This organization began simply as a free-speech forum, but in the course of the year raised more and more deepgoing reform demands that had a profound echo among the Hungarian workers. It was a demonstration of students called by the Petöfi Club on the evening of October 23 that touched off the Hungarian revolution. Troops ordered to suppress the demonstration went over to the protesters, leading to the creation of the Imre Nagy government. The revolution was crushed by Soviet troops on the night of November 3-4, 1956.

8. The speech was made April 14, 1966, to the Standing Committee of the National People's Congress, of which he is a vice-chairman. (See Hsinhua, May 7, 1966.)

9. "Decision of the Central Committee of the CCP Concerning the Great Proletarian Cultural Revolution," *Peking Review*, no. 33, August 12, 1966, p. 6.

Open Letter to the Members of the Chinese Communist Party

1. The Treaty of Brest-Litovsk, signed by Germany and the Soviet government of Russia in March 1918, formalized Russia's unilateral withdrawal from World War I. The Bolsheviks had pledged themselves to halt Russian participation in the war, but a sharp struggle over the terms of the treaty broke out within the Bolshevik Party because of the predatory territorial demands insisted on by the German side. Bukharin and Radek led a faction that called for rejecting the treaty and waging a revolutionary war against Germany; Lenin led a minority faction calling for immediate acceptance of the German terms; Trotsky, the chief Soviet negotiator at Brest-Litovsk, initially proposed to stall for time, but then went over to Lenin's position to guarantee him a majority against Bukharin. The New Economic Policy (NEP) was adopted by the Soviet government in 1921 to replace the strict centralization and rationing of

the civil war period. Aimed at promoting an economic revival, the NEP encouraged private trade, permitted a certain amount of private small business side by side with state-owned firms, and offered concessions of Soviet natural resources to foreign businesses in exchange for investments and access to advanced technology. The NEP was decided in substance, although not using that name, at the Tenth Congress of the Russian Communist Party in March 1921. It was opposed at the congress by the Workers Opposition faction, led by Aleksandr Shlyapnikov and Alexandra Kollontai.

2. Prior to the anticommunist military coup of October 1965, Indonesia's President Sukarno had succeeded in drawing the PKI into a class-collaborationist alliance with his regime, under the slogan of NASAKOM (Nasionalist-Agama-Komunis), or unity between the forces of nationalism, religion, and communism. This "unity" was to be realized under Sukarno's system of "Guided Democracy," a euphemism for his dictatorial rule.

The Relationship and Differences Between Mao Tse-tung and Liu Shao-ch'i

1. "The Constitution of the Chinese Communist Party" (June 11, 1945), in Conrad Brandt, Benjamin Schwartz, and John K. Fairbank, *A Documentary History of Chinese Communism* (Cambridge, Mass.: Harvard University Press, 1952), p. 422.

2. On July 30, 1955, China's nominal government, the National People's Congress, adopted a resolution on the 1953-57 Five-Year Plan that specified that by the end of 1957, two years later, only ". . . about one-third of all the peasant households in the country will have joined the present agricultural producers' cooperatives of elementary form" (*First Five-Year Plan for Development of the People's Republic of China in 1953-1957* [Peking: Foreign Languages Press, 1956, p. 119]). Twenty-four hours after the congress adjourned, on July 31, Mao called the meeting of local and provincial party secretaries where he delivered his speech "On the Question of Agricultural Cooperation," which called for immediate, wholesale collectivization. The speech was not published in China until October 1955, but by December of that year, 63 percent of all peasant families had been enrolled in the producers' cooperatives, and in 1956 all individual title to the land was abolished.

3. *The Constitution of the Communist Party of China / Report on the Revision of the Constitution of the Communist Party of China* by Teng Hsiao-p'ing (Peking: Foreign Languages Press, 1956), p. 9.

4. Ibid., p. 74.

5. Ibid., p. 82.

6. Ibid., p. 83.

7. This is the official Chinese government translation, published in *Peking Review*, no. 41, October 6, 1967, p. 22.

8. Mao Tse-tung, "Opening Address at the Eighth National Congress of

the Communist Party of China" (September 15, 1956), *Eighth National Congress of the Communist Party of China* (Peking: Foreign Languages Press, 1956), vol. I, documents, p. 10.

9. The "Three Red Banners" was a slogan of the Great Leap period, the three components being the party's general line, the Great Leap Forward campaign, and the People's Communes.

10. See "An Interview with Ch'en Pi-lan on the 'Cultural Revolution,'" printed as an appendix to this volume.

11. "Resolution of the Eighth National Congress of the Communist Party of China on the Political Report of the Central Committee," adopted September 27, 1956, in *Eighth National Congress of the Communist Party of China* (Peking: Foreign Languages Press, 1956), vol. I, documents, p. 125.

12. "Communiqué of the Tenth Plenary Session of the Eighth Central Committee of the Communist Party of China," released September 28, 1962, *Peking Review*, no. 39, September 28, 1962, p. 7.

13. "A Great Historic Document," by the editorial departments of *Red Flag* and *People's Daily*, published in *Red Flag* no. 7, 1967, and in *People's Daily*, May 18, 1967, celebrating the first anniversary of the May 16, 1966, "Circular of the Central Committee of the Chinese Communist Party" initiating the Cultural Revolution. English text from *Peking Review*, no. 21, May 19, 1967, p, 11.

14. Mao Tse-tung, "On New Democracy" (January 1940), *Selected Works of Mao Tse-tung* (Peking: Foreign Languages Press, 1967), vol. II, p. 353.

The May Fourth Movement and the "Great Proletarian Cultural Revolution"

1. The May Fourth Movement dates from a mass student demonstration in Peking on May 4, 1919, protesting the decision of the Versailles Conference that ended World War I to cede to Japan Germany's territorial holdings in China. Students demonstrating outside the homes of Chinese diplomats who agreed to these humiliating conditions were arrested, which in turn touched off a nationwide sympathy strike supporting the student protest. In addition to political nationalism, the May Fourth Movement was a deepgoing cultural radicalization. Its intellectual leades were Ch'en Tu-hsiu, Li Ta-chao, and Hu Shih, all professors at Peking University. The leading voice of the movement was *Hsin ch'ing-nien* (New Youth) magazine, founded by Ch'en Tu-hsiu in 1915. It championed the ideas of Western science and democracy against traditional Chinese Confucianism, Taoism, and Buddhism. In addition, it advocated, and practiced, the use of *pai-hua*, or vernacular, writing in place of the traditional classical Chinese written forms. Politically, the May Fourth Movement succeeded in forcing the Chinese government to withdraw its signature from the Versailles Treaty. Intellectually it spurred a sweeping cultural radicalization that produced most of the important Chinese

literary figures of the 1920s and 1930s, and helped to create the mass base for both the Kuomintang and the Communist Party. (Hu Shih became the most famous intellectual in Kuomintang China, while by 1920 both Ch'en Tu-hsiu and Li Ta-chao were won to Marxism and became founding leaders of the CCP.)

2. After the Chinese Republic, created in 1911, fell under the control of General Yüan Shik-k'ai, Yüan ruled through the Peiyang military party. Following Yüan's death in 1916, Tuan Ch'i-jui took over the Peiyang military party, adopting a pro-Japan position in exchange for Japanese arms for use in a war against dissident generals in South China. This North-South war precipitated a split in the Peiyang forces into an anti–Tuan Ch'i-jui group known as the Chihli clique and Tuan's supporters, known as the Anfu clique. The Anfu clique was the strongest force in North China until 1920, when it was defeated in a major war with the Chihli clique.

3. The student demonstration on May 4, 1919, assembled at Peking's T'ien An Men Square. About 3,000 demonstrators marched to the Legation Quarter, but were refused meetings with the representatives of any of the foreign embassies. Then they went to 2 Chao-chia-lou Street, the home of Ts'ao Ju-lin, the minister who had negotiated China's concessions to Japan, where a secret meeting was taking place among the diplomats of the Peking government. Ts'ao escaped through a window, but the demonstrators found Chang Tsung-hsiang, Chinese ambassador to Japan, and beat him. They then burned down the house.

4. Ts'ao Ju-lin, Chang Tsung-hsiang, and Chang's predecessor as ambassador to Japan, Lu Tsung-yü, were dismissed from their posts on June 10, 1919.

5. Classical Chinese, which was overwhelmingly predominant in printed materials until 1918, differs from the vernacular, or *pai-hua*, in a number of important respects. It was highly condensed, frequently using one Chinese character for words that in common speech were made up of two characters (and therefore two syllables). It was filled with literary sayings and allusions drawn from the Confucian classics, the point of which would be unintelligible to a reader who was unfamiliar with the books referred to. And it used a large number of "literary" words, never used in the spoken form, in place of more common words. The shift to *pai-hua*, championed particularly by Hu Shih, sought to make printed works conform as closely as possible to the actual spoken forms of Chinese so that literate adults without a classical education could understand them.

The Fall of Lin Piao

1. The Revolutionary Committees were established in 1967 as local and provincial organs of government, controlled by the Mao faction and the military, to replace the street committees, People's Congresses, and other municipal and province-level administrations. They were dissolved after Mao's death and the purge of the "gang of four."

2. In July 1972, six months after this interview, the Chinese embassy in Algiers announced that Lin Piao was dead, but this was not reported inside China, nor were any details provided. It was only at the Tenth Party Congress in August 1973 that Lin Piao was first denounced by name. At that time the government's official version of Lin's death was made public—through a leak to the Western press. It was claimed that Lin had attempted to assassinate Mao and stage a coup d'etat on the night of September 12, 1971. It was alleged that when this coup failed, Lin, his wife, and several of the military high command, including Huang Yung-sheng, tried to escape to the Soviet Union. They were said to have been killed in a plane crash in Mongolia.

The "Criticize Lin, Criticize Confucius" Campaign

1. See the immediately preceding article in this volume.

2. *The Constitution of the Communist Party of China*, adopted by the Ninth National Congress of the Communist Party of China on April 14, 1969 (Peking: Foreign Languages Press, 1969), pp. 5-6.

3. The May 7 Cadre Schools were "reeducation" centers for cadres who were attacked by the Mao faction. Cadres would spend from a few months to more than two years in these schools, which were located in the countryside and whose main curriculum consisted of manual labor and the study of Mao's works.

4. The reference is to China's first tyrant emperor, the founder of the Ch'in dynasty, to whom Mao liked to compare himself.

5. Chou En-lai, "Report to the Tenth National Congress of the Communist Party of China," delivered August 24 and adopted August 28, 1973, in *The Tenth National Congress of the Communist Party of China (Documents)*, special supplement to *China Reconstructs*, November 1973.

6. Karl Marx and Frederick Engels, *The Communist Manifesto* (New York: Pathfinder Press, 1970), p. 17.

7. Ibid., p. 18.

8. "The Constitution of the People's Republic of China," adopted January 17, 1975, by the Fourth National People's Congress, first session, *Peking Review*, vol. 18, no. 4, January 24, 1975, p. 14.

9. In addition to *Red Flag*, this article appeared in the *People's Daily*, February 22, 1975, and was reprinted in English in *Hsinhua Weekly* (Hong Kong branch), March 3, 1975, p. 3, under the title " 'People's Daily' Carries Quotations from Marx, Engels and Lenin on Dictatorship of Proletariat."

10. Yao Wen-yuan, "On the Social Basis of the Lin Piao Anti-Party Clique," English version in *Hsinhua Weekly* (Hong Kong branch), March 10, 1975, p. 3.

11. An English translation of this article appears in *Hsinhua Weekly*, April 7, 1975.

The Meaning of the T'ien An Men Demonstration

1. See the previous article in this volume.

2. Indira Gandhi, then India's prime minister, had instituted her personal dictatorship in June 1975. The Dowager Empress Tz'u Hsi (1835-1908) was the de facto ruler of China from 1862 until her death and is remembered as a reactionary opponent of the reform movement of 1898.

3. From the report by Hua Lin, based on a compilation of eyewitness accounts, in the April 16, 1976, issue of *Huang Ho* (Yellow River), published in Hong Kong by former Red Guards.

4. The point of the comparison was that Imre Nagy (1896-1958), although a long-time Stalinist leader of the Hungarian CP, by his policy of concessions to the mass radicalization during his term as premier in 1956 helped objectively to usher in the Hungarian antibureaucratic revolution. After the revolt was crushed by Soviet troops, Nagy was arrested and executed by the new regime.

Behind the Fall of Mao's Faction

1. This is a conservative estimate made by Chou En-lai in his speech to the Fourth National People's Congress in January 1975. Later reports in the Chinese press put the total of "rusticated" youth at 14 and even 17 million.

An Appraisal of the Political Life of Mao Tse-tung

1. Mao Tse-tung, "The Peking Coup d'Etat and the Merchants," *Hsiang-tao*, no. 31-32, July 11, 1923. An extract in English, including the lines cited here, appears in Stuart R. Schram, *The Political Thought of Mao Tse-tung* (New York: Praeger, 1963), p. 140.

2. *Hsiang-tao*, July 11, 1923, and Schram, *Political Thought of Mao*, p. 141.

3. *Selected Works of Mao Tse-tung* (London: Lawrence and Wishart, 1955), vol. 1, p. 20.

4. Hu Ch'iao-mu, *Thirty Years of the Communist Party of China: An Outline History* (London: Lawrence & Wishard, 1951), p. 22.

5. See Benjamin I. Schwartz, *Chinese Communism and the Rise of Mao* (New York: Harper & Row, 1967), pp. 73-78.

6. "Theses on the Revolutionary Movement in the Colonies and Semi-Colonies," adopted by the Sixth World Congress of the Communist International, September 1, 1928, *International Press Correspondence*, vol. 8, no. 88, December 12, 1928, p. 1670.

7. Ibid., p. 1672.

8. Edgar Snow, in his book *Red Star Over China*, based on interviews with the CCP leadership shortly after the Long March, reported that the KMT government admitted the figure of one million deaths in Kiangsi

and suggested that the CCP believed the figure should be higher. (New York: Garden City Publishing Co., 1939, p. 174.)

9. This figure is confirmed by Hu Ch'iao-mu in his *Thirty Years of the Communist Party of China*, p. 40.

10. "The CCP's Public Statement on KMT-CCP Co-Operation," *A Documentary History of Chinese Communism*, Conrad Brandt, Benjamin Schwartz, and John K. Fairbank (Cambridge, Mass.: Harvard University Press, 1952), p. 246. This document is sometimes referred to as dated September 22, 1937, from the day of its publication in the KMT press. It was drafted July 4 and formally submitted to the KMT leadership by the CCP Central Committee representatives on July 15, 1937.

11. September 29, 1937, *Selected Works* (Peking: Foreign Languages Press, 1967), vol. 2, pp. 37-38.

12. Ibid., p. 42.

13. *Lun Hsin Chieh-tuan* (On the New Stage), (Yenan: Chieh-fang She, 1939). This is Mao's report to the Sixth Plenum of the CCP's Sixth Central Committee, October 1938. Mao published it in 1939 but later stopped its distribution (only a small excerpt appears in his *Selected Works*, under the title "The Role of the Chinese Communist Party in the National War").

14. "On New Democracy," January 1940, *Selected Works*, vol. 2, p. 353.

15. Ibid., p. 358.

16. "The Tasks of the Chinese Communist Party in the Period of Resistance to Japan," May 1937, *Selected Works* (London: Lawrence and Wishart, 1955), vol. 1, p. 264.

17. "Stalin, Friend of the Chinese People," December 20, 1939, *Selected Works* (Peking: Foreign Languages Press, 1967), vol. 2, p. 335.

18. Ibid., vol. 3, p. 24.

19. "Resolution on Some Questions in the History of Our Party," adopted by the Seventh Plenum of the Sixth Central Committee of the CCP, April 20, 1945. This was published as an appendix to the International Publishers edition of Mao's *Selected Works* (New York: 1956), vol. 4, pp. 171-218 (this quotation is taken from pp. 217-18). It was dropped from later English-language editions of Mao's works.

20. "Constitution of the Chinese Communist Party," June 11, 1945, in Brandt, et al., *A Documentary History of Chinese Communism*, p. 422.

21. The Marshall Plan, named after the then–U.S. Secretary of State George C. Marshall, was proposed in June 1947 and instituted in April 1948 as a massive U.S. aid program to rebuild the war-torn economies of Western Europe as a bulwark against communism. The U.S. government dispersed $12 billion in Marshall Plan aid between 1948 and the end of the program in 1952.

22. Remarks made at the Supreme State Conference, October 12, 1957.

23. *Tsui wei-ta ti Yu-i* (The Greatest Friendship) (Peking: 1953). English text in Schram, *The Political Thought of Mao Tse-tung*, p. 265.

24. Teng Hsiao-p'ing, "Report on the Revision of the Constitution of the Communist Party of China," *Eighth National Congress of the Commu-*

nist Party of China (Peking: Foreign Languages Press, 1956), vol. 1, documents, p. 192.

25. Mao Tse-tung, "Opening Address at the Eighth National Congress of the Communist Party of China," in ibid., p. 10, emphasis added.

26. *On the Correct Handling of Contradictions Among the People* (Peking: Foreign Languages Press, 1960), p. 13.

27. Speech at a reception given for representatives of the Lanka Sama Samaja Party of Ceylon, *People's Daily*, May 19, 1957.

28. *Kwangming Daily*.

29. See the opening section of "A Criticism of the Various Views Supporting the Chinese Rural People's Communes," earlier in this volume.

30. Ch'en Pi-lan, "The New Developments in the Chinese Situation," *International Information Bulletin* (New York: Socialist Workers Party), no. 8, May 1969, p. 9.

31. George Novack and Joseph Hansen, "The Upheaval in China—An Analysis of the Contending Forces," in *Behind China's "Great Cultural Revolution"* (New York: Pathfinder Press, 1967), pp. 47-48, 52.

32. *Peking Review*, April 30, 1969, p. 33.

33. Ibid., p. 36.

34. Cited by the Hong Kong Trotskyist monthly *October Review*, August 1974.

35. *Peking Review*, September 7, 1973, p. 20.

36. Leon Trotsky, *Stalin* (London: Panther Books, 1969), vol. 2, p. 202.

37. Leon Trotsky, *In Defense of Marxism* (New York: Pathfinder Press, 1973), p. 19.

Appendix: An Interview with Ch'en Pi-lan on the "Cultural Revolution"

1. The heroine of T'ien Han's play, Hsieh Yao-huan, during the reign of the Empress Wu Tse-t'ien of the T'ang dynasty denounces the estrangement of a once-popular ruler from the people.

2. This quotation appears in the hostile article "On the Counterrevolutionary Double-dealer Chou Yang," by Yao Wen-yuan, published in *Red Flag*, no. 1, 1967.

3. Shen Yen-ping is better known under his pen name, Mao Tun.

4. This quotation appears in an article attacking Chou written by Li Chi-kai and others in the July 31, 1966, Shanghai *Wen Hui Pao*.

5. Ibid.

6. "A Reevaluation of Chou Yang," *Ming Pao Monthly*, August 1966.

7. Quoted by Yao Wen-yuan, "On the Counterrevolutionary Double-dealer Chou Yang," *Red Flag*, no. 1, 1967.

8. Quoted in the hostile article "Criticism of Yang Han-sheng's Ten Ropes," *People's Daily*, December 29, 1966.

9. Quoted in "Yang Han-sheng as a Propagandist of the Revisionist Literature and Art," *Workers Daily* (Peking), February 27, 1967.

10. These quotations appear in the article by Li Chi-kai, et al., in the July 31, 1966, Shanghai *Wen Hui Pao.*

11. Quoted by Yao Wen-yuan in his article "On the Counterrevolutionary Double-dealer Chou Yang," *Red Flag*, no. 1, 1967.

12. Quoted in *Ming Pao Monthly*, no. 12, 1966, p. 37.

ACKNOWLEDGEMENTS

"Looking Back Over My Years with P'eng Shu-tse," by Ch'en Pi-lan, from *Intercontinental Press*, November 2, 9, 16, and 23, 1970. Copyright 1970 by *Intercontinental Press*. Reprinted by permission.

"The Theory of Permanent Revolution and the Underdeveloped Countries," from *International Socialist Review*, May 1972. Copyright 1972 by International Socialist Review Publishing Association. Reprinted by permission.

"The Causes of the Victory of the Chinese Communist Party over Chiang Kai-shek, and the CCP's Perspectives—Report on The Chinese Situation to the Third Congress of the Fourth International," from *International Information Bulletin*, New York, Socialist Workers Party, February 1952. Reprinted by permission.

"The Case of the Chinese Trotskyists: Open Letter to the Central Executive Committee of the CCP," from the *Militant*, November 2, 1953. Reprinted by permission.

"A Criticism of the Various Views Supporting the Chinese Rural People's Communes," from *SWP Discussion Bulletin* New York, Socialist Workers Party, vol. 21, no. 1, January 1960. Reprinted by permission.

"On the Nature of the Chinese Communist Party and Its Regime: Political Revolution or Democratic Reform?" from *SWP Discussion Bulletin*, New York, Socialist Workers Party, vol. 22, no. 4, March 1961. Reprinted by permission.

"Two Interviews on the 'Cultural Revolution,'" from *World Outlook*, August 12, 1966, and February 10, 1967. Copyright 1966 and 1967 by *World Outlook*. Reprinted by permission.

"Open Letter to the Members of the Chinese Communist Party," from *World Outlook*, March 24, 1967. Copyright 1967 by *World Outlook*. Reprinted by permission.

"The Relationship and Differences Between Mao Tse-tung and Liu Shao-ch'i," from *International Information Bulletin*, New York, Socialist Workers Party, no. 2 in 1968. Reprinted by permission.

"The May Fourth Movement and the 'Great Proletarian Cultural Revolution,'" from *Ming Pao Monthly*, Hong Kong, May 1969.

"The Fall of Lin Piao," from *Intercontinental Press*, June 5 and 12, 1972. Copyright 1972 by *Intercontinental Press*. Reprinted by permission.

"The 'Criticize Lin, Criticize Confucius' Campaign," from *Interconti-*

GLOSSARY

Chinese personal names are given in the Chinese order, with the surname first. The Wade-Giles romanization system is used, but the newer pinyin system of spelling adopted by the People's Republic of China is added in parentheses (with the exception of a few entries such as Chiang Kai-shek and Sun Yat-sen, for whom the name they are known under in the West differs from their actual Chinese names and there is no pinyin equivalent). Where a separate entry exist for an individual or organization mentioned under another entry this is indicated by the initials *q.v.* in parentheses (quod vide—which see).

Ai Ch'ing (Ai Qing) (1910-   )—One of China's best-known modern poets. He was part of the circle of writers around Lu Hsun in the early 1930s. Imprisoned by the French in Shanghai, 1932-35. He moved to the CCP's capital at Yenan in 1941 and became a prominent CCP cultural-literary figure. In 1953 he was elected to the National Committee of the All-China Federation of Literary and Art Circles. He was attacked as a "rightist" in the fall of 1957, dismissed from his posts in 1958, and in 1959 deported to a state farm in Sinkiang province, where he was held for sixteen years and prohibited from publishing. He was rehabilitated in late 1978 and his poetry has been reprinted.

Aidit, D. N. (1924-1965)—joined the Communist Party of Indonesia (PKI) in 1943. He was elected to the Central Committee in 1947 and to the Politburo in 1948. He became the party's central leader in 1951, implementing a policy of collaboration with the capitalist government of Sukarno. He was executed without trial during the military bloodbath against the PKI at the end of 1965.

Bolsheviks—The majority faction formed in the Russian Social Democratic Labor Party at its Second Congress (1903). Led by Lenin. The Bolsheviks (the word in Russian means majorityites) became a separate party from the Mensheviks (q.v.) in 1912, and organized the October revolution in 1917 that established the first workers' state. The party changed its name to Russian Communist Party (Bolsheviks) in 1918.

Borodin, Michael M. (1884-1951)—Stalin's chief representative in China (September 1923–July 1927). He later served as editor of the Moscow *Daily News*. Borodin was arrested in 1949 and died in a concentration camp.

Bukharin, Nikolai I. (1887-1938)—Joined the Bolsheviks in 1906. In 1918 he was the spokesman of the "Left Communists" but after Lenin's death he became the chief theoretician of the right wing of the CPSU. He was president of the Comintern (1926-29), during which time he was in a bloc with Stalin against Trotsky. In 1928 he formed the Right Opposition to Stalin. He capitulated in 1929. Bukharin was a defendant in the March 1938 Moscow frame-up trial. He "confessed" and was shot.

Chang Ch'un-ch'iao (Zhang Chunqiao) (1910?-   )—A CCP journalist in Shanghai from the 1930s. Chang headed the CCP propaganda department in Shanghai and was director of the Shanghai *Liberation Daily* at the outbreak of the Cultural Revolution in 1966. A strong supporter of the Mao faction, he rose to become party first secretary of the city and mayor, and was elected to the Central Committee and to the Politburo for the first time at the Ninth Congress (April 1969). At the Tenth Congress (August 1973) he was advanced to the Politburo Standing Committee. Arrested as one of the "gang of four" in October 1976.

Chang Hsueh-liang (Zhang Xueliang) (1898-   )—The son of the Manchurian warlord Chang Tso-lin (q.v.), from whom he inherited control of Manchuria in 1928. He joined the KMT in December 1928. Chang is best known for arresting Chiang Kai-shek at Sian in December 1936. After the CCP's intervention secured Chiang's release, Chang Hsueh-liang was imprisoned by Chiang, first in China and later in Taiwan. He was given a nominal amnesty in 1961 but is still restricted to Taiwan.

Chang Kuo-t'ao (Zhang Guotao) (1897-   )—One of the twelve who attended the founding conference of the CCP (1921). Chang was a labor leader during the 1920s and headed the Oyüwan Soviet area after 1931. He commanded a section of the Long March in 1935 but clashed with Mao Tse-tung and took his troops into Southwest China, not north to Shensi. He quit the CCP in 1938 and joined the KMT. Ceased political activity after 1949.

Chang Tso-lin (Zhang Zuolin) (1873-1928)—Militarist who gained control of Manchuria in 1919 and captured Peking in 1924. Chang opposed the KMT regime and his overthrow was one of the aims of the Northern Expedition. He

was assassinated by Japanese officers and was succeeded in power by his son Chang Hseuh-liang (q.v.).

Ch'en Hsi-lien (Chen Xilian) (1913?-   )—A Red Army commander since the late 1920s and a veteran of the Long March and of the Sino-Japanese War. Commander of the PLA Artillery Force, 1951-59, and of the Shenyang Military Region (Manchuria), 1959-73. Since 1973 he has been military commander of the Peking area. He was elected as an alternate member of the CCP Central Committee in 1956. He survived the Cultural Revolution and was elected a full member of the CC and a member of the Politburo at the Ninth Party Congress in 1969, posts to which he was reelected at the Tenth and Eleventh Congresses. Since the arrest of the "gang of four" he has been periodically attacked in wall posters for his responsibility in suppressing the T'ien An Men demonstration of April 1976.

Ch'en I (Chen Yi) (1901-1972)—A Red Army commander under Mao in the Chingkang Mountains and in the Kiangsi Soviet, 1929-34. Headed the New Fourth Army in the Sino-Japanese War, 1941-45, and led troops that captured the coastal provinces in the civil war. A vice-premier from 1954 and foreign minister from 1958 to his death. He was elected to the Central Committee in 1945 and to the Politburo in 1956. Ch'en was attacked by the Red Guards in the Cultural Revolution, but retained his posts after Chou En-lai's intervention on his behalf.

Ch'en Li-fu (Chen Lifu) (1900-   )—Headed the KMT's Investigation Division (political police) for about ten years after 1928. He later was minister of education (1938-44), and in 1948 became vice-president ,of the Legislative Yuan. After a brief stay in Taiwan following the KMT collapse on the mainland Ch'en retired from politics and settled in the United States.

Ch'en P'ei-hsien (Chen Peixian) (1911-   )—Participated in the Kiangsi Soviet in the early 1930s, remaining in the South after the Long March. Fought with the New Fourth Army in the Sino-Japanese War. From the early 1950s Ch'en was a municipal party official in Shanghai, becoming party first secretary in 1965. He was elected as an alternate member of the Central Committee at the Eighth Party Congress in 1956 and headed the party's East China Bureau. He was deposed in the Cultural Revolution and dropped from the CC at the Ninth Congress (1969). He was rehabilitated after Mao's death and elected to full membership in the Eleventh Central Committee (1977).

Ch'en Po-ta (Chen Boda) (1904-)—Joined the CCP in 1927, leaving that year for Moscow, where he studied until 1930. On his return to China he worked as a propagandist and journalist for the CCP in Fukien province and in North China. In 1937 he went to Yenan, where he became Mao Tse-tung's secretary and headed the Propaganda Department's Research Section. He was prominent in the persecution of Wang Shih-wei (q.v.). Ch'en was elected to the Central Committee in 1945 and to the Politburo in 1956. He was best known in the 1950s for his many articles eulogizing Stalin and Mao. In 1958 he became the editor of the CCP's theoretical journal *Red Flag*. In 1966 he was elevated to the Politburo Standing Committee and placed in charge of the Cultural Revolution Group, which headed the purge of the followers of Liu Shao-ch'i and Teng Hsiao-p'ing (qq.v.). He was in turn arrested in 1970. After a long silence the Mao government denounced Ch'en as a cohort of Lin Piao (q.v.). He has not been rehabilitated by the post-Mao regime.

Ch'en Shao-yü (Chen Shaoyu) (1904-1974)—Under the name Wang Ming was the leader of the Russian returned student group led by Pavel Mif that defeated Li Li-san (q.v.) and took over the CCP leadership in an inner-party struggle in 1930-31. He was the CCP's representative to the Comintern, 1931-37. His faction was defeated by Mao at the

Tsun-i conference during the Long March in 1935, where Mao won the party chairmanship. From the 1940s onward he was blamed by the Maoist historians for the defeat of the Kiangsi Soviet areas. He continued to hold nominal posts in the CCP hierarchy into the 1950s, but in the middle of that decade he went into exile in Moscow, where he was living at the time of his death.

Ch'en Tu-hsiu (Chen Duxiu) (1879-1942)—Took part in the bourgeois revolution of 1911. He founded *Hsin ch'ing-nien* (New Youth) magazine in 1915, the most influential journal of cultural and political radicalism of its day. He was one of the central figures of the May Fourth Movement in 1919. He and Li Ta-chao (q.v.) were the two most important founders of the CCP and Ch'en became the party's first general secretary. He was the central leader of the CCP in the revolution of 1925-27, but was deposed at Stalin's order at the August 1927 CCP CC rump Emergency Conference. Shortly afterwards he was won to the support of Trotsky's positions by P'eng Shu-tse and the two were expelled from the CCP in November 1929. He was a founding leader of the Chinese Left Opposition. Imprisoned by the KMT (1932-37), he developed differences with Trotsky while in jail and broke with the Chinese Trotskyist organization, the Communist League of China, in 1941.

Ch'en Yen-nien (Chen Yannian) (1898-1927)—Son of Ch'en Tu-hsiu (q.v.). He helped to establish a CCP branch in France in 1922, then studied in Moscow. From 1925 to early 1927 he headed the CCP's Kwangtung Regional Committee. He was elected to the Central Committee at the CCP's Fifth Congress, April-May 1927, but was captured and executed in Shanghai in June while carrying out underground work there following Chiang Kai-shek's April massacre.

Ch'en Yun (Chen Yun) (1900?-)—Joined the CCP in 1924. During the revolution of 1925-27 he was a leader of the Shanghai General Labor Union. He was elected to the Central Committee in 1934, spent two years in Moscow, then headed the party's Organization Department in Yenan. From the mid-1940s he emerged as one of the CCP's top economic planners. At the Eighth Party Congress in 1956 he was elected to the Standing Committee of the Politburo and was ranked fifth in the party hierarchy. He clashed with Mao over the Great Leap Forward and steadily lost ground in the party apparatus until the Cultural Revolution, when he came under heavy attack and lost all of his governmental responsibilities. He remained a full member of the Central Committee through the Ninth, Tenth, and Eleventh congresses without a definite assignment. In July 1979 he was one of three previously disgraced economic planners presented to the National People's Congress by Teng Hsiaop'ing to head up China's economic construction.

Cheng Ch'ao-lin (Zheng Chaolin) (1901-   )—Joined the CCP in France in the early 1920s, then studied in Moscow, 1923-24. On his return to China he became secretary of the CCP's Propaganda Department. Following the defeat of the revolution of 1925-27 he worked underground in Shanghai as editor of the party's newspaper *Bolshevik*. In this period he was won to Trotskyism and was expelled from the CCP in 1929 along with Ch'en Tu-hsiu (q.v.) and P'eng Shu-tse. In 1931 he was elected to the Central Committee of the Left Opposition group, but was arrested that same year and imprisoned by the KMT until 1937. On his release he participated in the anti-Japanese resistance in Shanghai, and translated many Marxist works into Chinese. In 1942 he split from the official Chinese section of the Fourth International, the Revolutionary Communist Party, to found the International Communist Workers Party. He remained in China after 1949, and was arrested by the Mao regime in December 1952. He was imprisoned for twenty-

seven years, the first twenty in solitary confinement. Cheng was released in June 1979 in Shanghai.

Ch'i Pen-yu (Qi Benyu)—Maoist ideologue and an editor of the CCP's theoretical journal *Red Flag* in the early period of the Cultural Revolution. Ch'i first became prominent in the spring of 1966 and later that year was made a member of the ruling Cultural Revolution Group. He was associated with the most extreme xenophobic and repressive wing of the Mao faction represented by Wang Li (q.v.). He signed many of the most slanderous articles against Liu Shao-ch'i, published in the spring of 1967. Along with Wang Li he called for a purge of the army in the late summer of 1967, and was accused of helping to instigate the burning of the British embassy in Peking in August. He was purged early in 1968 and accused of supporting the "May 16" group, which the Maoists later claimed was an anti-Mao plot headed by Lin Piao.

Chiang Ch'ing (Jiang Qing) (1914-   )—Joined the CCP in Tsingtao in 1933. Later that year she moved to Shanghai where she worked as a stage and film actress and belonged to CCP cultural groups led by T'ien Han and Chou Yang (q.v.). In the summer of 1937 she left Shanghai for Yenan, the CCP's rural capital. In 1939 she married Mao Tse-tung. Chiang did not take an active role in party affairs until 1964, when she became prominent in film and cultural work. In 1965 she was instrumental in dismissing most of the leading actors, playwrights, and film directors from the Central Steering Committee for the film industry. In May 1966 she was appointed to the Cultural Revolution Group, where, with Ch'en Po-ta and Lin Piao (qq.v.) she served as one of the central leaders of the Mao faction in crushing the forces around Liu Shaoch'i (q.v.). She was elected to the Central Committee for the first time at the Ninth Party Congress (1969) and also to the Politburo. Reelected at the Tenth Congress in 1973, she was the most prominent member of the "gang of four" arrested in October 1976 following Mao's death.

Chiang Kai-shek (1887-1975)—Joined Sun Yat-sen's personal following in Japan in 1913. He became operations officer of Ch'en Chiung-ming's Kwangtung Army in 1918, but supported Sun against Ch'en when they clashed in 1922. Chiang was appointed chief of staff of Sun's Canton headquarters in 1923, and was assigned by the First National Congress of the Kuomintang (January 1924) to head the Whampoa Military Academy. He became the principal military leader of the KMT after Sun's death in March 1925. He blocked with Wang Ching-wei and Borodin (qq.v.) at the January 1926 KMT congress to defeat the right-wing Western Hills faction. On March 20, 1926, he staged a coup in Canton, ousting Wang Ching-wei and imposing strict conditions on the CCP to remain in the KMT. During the Northern Expedition, Chiang organized a bloody coup against the Shanghai workers on April 12, 1927. At that time he organized a rival KMT government in opposition to the official KMT regime at Wuhan. He headed the reunified KMT after March 1928 and the Nationalist government established in October 1928. He fled to Taiwan in December 1949 following the CCP victory on the mainland, and ruled the island until his death.

Ch'in Shih Huang (Qin Shi Huang) (259?-210 B.C.)—Founder of the Ch'in dynasty and the first unifier of China. (Originally named Prince Cheng, his reign title means literally First Emperor of the Ch'in). He acceded to the throne in 246 B.C., when the kingdom of Ch'in was only one of several warring states. Breaking with the hereditary landed aristocracy, he was the first to establish a system of state administration based on an appointed bureaucracy and sustained by direct taxation in place of periodic tribute from the nobility. Drawing on these increased sources of income he created a permanent standing army which rapidly defeated the part-time soldiers of the rival states. In 221 B.C. he succeeded in unifying China and establishing a centralized absolutist state on the pattern that endured until the revolution of 1911. Ch'in Shih Huang standardized the writing system, unified weights and measures, and ordered the building of the Great Wall. He also won fame as one of the greatest tyrants in Chinese history. In 213 B.C. he ordered the burning of all Confucian books. Oppressive taxation led to a peasant revolt after Ch'in Shih Huang's death that destroyed the dynasty in 206 B.C.

Ch'ing dynasty (1644-1911)—China's last dynasty before the republican revolution of 1911 was established by the conquest of China by invading Manchu peoples from the border kingdoms of the Northeast, toppling the indigenous Ming dynasty. Ch'ing, or Manchu, rulers were regarded by the Chinese as foreigners, although over time they learned to speak Chinese and were largely culturally assimilated to Chinese ways.

Chou En-lai (Zhou Enlai) (1898-1976)—Joined the CCP in France in 1922. He served as KMT political commissar at the Whampoa Military Academy under Chiang Kai-shek, 1924-26. Chou was a leader of the Shanghai workers' uprising in March 1927, then worked underground in Shanghai for several years before accompanying the central CCP leadership to the Kiangsi Soviet area in 1931. He was Li Li-san's chief lieutenant until January 1931, and then supported Wang Ming, going over to support to Mao Tse-tung only at the Tsun-i meeting during the Long March in 1935. For many years Chou was the CCP's leading diplomatic representative, acting as its chief negotiator in the Sian Incident in 1936 and in the postwar discussions with the KMT over the CCP's proposal to form a coalition government. He was a member of the CCP Politburo from 1927 and served as premier of the People's Republic of China from its founding in 1949 until his death.

Chou Yang (Zhou Yang) (1908-)—Studied literature in Shanghai and Japan in the late 1920s and early 1930s. Joined the CCP in the early 1930s and became one of its main representatives in Shanghai literature and art circles. Was secretary-general of the League of Left-Wing Writers, 1931-36. Chou, supported by T'ien Han and Hsia Yen (qq.v.), sought to use literature to convey the CCP's current political line, which brought him into a sharp clash with more independent left-wing writers such as Lu Hsun and Hu Feng (q.v.). In 1937 Chou moved to Yenan where he headed the CCP's Education Department. He led the campaign against dissident writers in Yenan, particularly Wang Shi-wei (q.v.). After the CCP's victory, Chou served as deputy director of the party's Propaganda Department, 1951-66, but was in effect the most powerful figure in those years in setting party line on literature and art and in imposing it on intellectuals. He directed the campaigns against Hu Feng and Ting Ling (q.v.) in the 1950s. Chou began to come under attack by the Mao faction in 1964 for his reservations on the Mao cult and their anti-intellectualism. He was purged in the summer of 1966 and denounced as a counterrevolutionary. This verdict was reversed after Mao's death. Chou was brought back into public activity early in 1979 and is today one of the CCP's most prominent spokesmen on cultural affairs.

Chow Ching-wen (Zhou Jingwen) (1908-)—Former president of Northeastern University in Manchuria and a leader of the liberal bourgeois Democratic League (q.v.). Chow participated in the coalition government set up by the CCP after 1949, serving as a member of the Committee on Political and Legal Affairs of the Government Administration Council. In 1957 he broke with the Mao regime and fled to Hong Kong, where he wrote a highly critical book, *Ten Years of Storm*.

Ch'ü Ch'iu-pai (Qu Quibai) (1899-1935)—Went to the Soviet Union as a reporter in late 1920, and, while there, joined the CCP in 1922. He returned to China early in 1923 and was elected to the Central Committee at the Third Party Congress, in June of that year. He became vice-chairman of the Propaganda Department, where he wrote a number of pamphlets and translated materials from Russian. He sided with the Comintern representatives against Ch'en Tu-hsiu and after the defeats at Shanghai and Wuhan in 1927 was chosen by Lominadze (q.v.) to replace Ch'en as acting head of the CCP at the August 7, 1927, Emergency Conference. Ch'ü was made a scapegoat for the failures of the ultraleftist putschist course that followed and was deposed at the CCP's Sixth Congress, held in Moscow, June-July 1928. During the early 1930s he worked underground in Shanghai as a leader of the League of Left-Wing Writers. He spent 1934 at Juichin in the Kiangsi Soviet area. He was left behind because of ill health when the Long March began, was captured by the KMT, imprisoned, and then executed.

Chu Te (Zhu De) (1886-1976)—A republican soldier from 1911. Chu joined the CCP in 1922. He participated in the Nanchang Uprising of August 1, 1927, from which the founding of the Chinese Red Army is dated. He combined forces with Mao Tse-tung at Chingkangshan in the spring of 1928. He became commander of the Fourth Red Army, and was the principal military leader of the Kiangsi Soviet Republic. He was the CCP's chief military figure in the Long March, the Sino-Japanese War, and the civil war with Chiang. Chu criticized Mao's Great Leap Forward in 1958. He was attacked by the Maoist Red Guards in the Cultural Revolution, but retained his membership in the Politburo at the Ninth Congress (1969), although he was dropped from the Standing Committee. He was reelected to the Standing Committee at the Tenth Congress in 1973, although by that time he was in effect in retirement.

Cominform—The Cominform, or Communist Information Bureau, was organized by Stalin in 1947 to unite the world Stalinist parties in response to Washington's cold war. It succeeded the Communist International, which Stalin had dissolved in 1943 as a gesture to his imperialist allies in World War II. The Cominform was in turn dissolved in 1956.

Confucius (551-479 B.C.)—China's most famous ancient philosopher (in Chinese his name is K'ung Fu-tse, or Master K'ung). Born into an impoverished family in the state of Lu, located in present-day Shantung province, Confucius was not a religious teacher but an ethical and political reformer. He sought to ameliorate the brute power of the landed nobility by urging them to promote education, to value virtue and ability over hereditary power, and to seek out capable ministers. While he condemned superstition, he did place strict individual subordination to the extended family at the center of his system. Throughout his life he sought appointment to a high post where he could implement his ideas. He failed in this, and left the state of Lu in his mid-fifties to wander throughout China for more than a dozen years. His teachings were preserved by his disciples and became ossified into a system of Chinese statecraft and moral precepts that retained tremendous influence until the May Fourth Movement of 1919.

Democratic League—Chinese bourgeois-liberal party formed in October 1944 as an outgrowth of the previous Federation of Chinese Democratic Parties. The Democratic League's formal program called for the prevention of civil war between the CCP and KMT and the formation of a democratic government. It was suppressed by Chiang Kai-shek in October 1947, but revived with the CCP conquest of power. It and

the Kuomintang Revolutionary Committee (q.v.) were the best known of seven or so minor bourgeois parties included by the CCP in its post-1949 coalition government. It disappeared in the Cultural Revolution, but some of its old leaders made public appearances in the name of their party following the death of Mao and rehabilitation of Teng Hsiao-p'ing. Since 1949 it has carried out no independent political activity and has adopted the CCP's positions on all questions.

Feng Hsüeh-feng (Feng Xuefeng) (d. 1976)—Born around the turn of the century in Chekiang province, Feng became known in the 1920s as a poet and essayist. He joined the CCP in 1927 and became a close associate and confidante of Lu Hsun, China's most famous twentieth century left-wing novelist and short story writer. Feng was a leader of the League of Left-Wing Writers in Shanghai in the early 1930s. He participated in the Long March. He later returned to Shanghai, where he supported Lu Hsun against the more rigidly Stalinist group of CCP writers led by Chou Yang (q.v.). After 1949 Feng became editor of the CCP's most important cultural periodical, the *Literary Gazette*. In 1954 he was attacked for his defense of non-CCP interpretations of classical Chinese literature, although he supported the party center in the campaign against Hu Feng (q.v.). He was purged along with Ting Ling (q.v.) in the "Antirightist" movement in the fall of 1957. He was rehabilitated in 1979 and his poems featured in the July 1979 issue of *Poetry*.

Feng Yü-hsiang (Feng Yuxiang) (1882-1948)—North Chinese warlord known as the Christian General. Feng headed a personal army, the Kuominchün. He was persuaded by Borodin (q.v.) to join the KMT in the spring of 1926, and was for a time presented in the Stalinist press as a revolutionary people's general. In June 1927 he sided with Chiang Kai-shek against the Wuhan regime and against the CCP. In October 1929 a war broke out between Feng and Chiang in western Honan province; Feng was defeated in October 1930. He held minor posts in the KMT regime until 1947 when he announced his support to the Kuomintang Revolutionary Committee (q.v.). He was killed in a shipboard fire while returning to China.

Germain—Pseudonym of Ernest Mandel.

Gomulka, Wladyslaw (1905-   )—Polish Stalinist leader. Helped to found the Polish Workers (Communist) Party and was secretary of its Central Committee, 1943-49. Served as deputy premier of Poland, 1943-49. Purged in 1949 and arrested in 1951 for alleged support to Tito. Released in 1954, he was readmitted to the CP in 1956. He became first secretary of the party in October during an upsurge of popular opposition to Moscow. He was forced to resign in 1970 following workers' riots to protest rising prices.

Han Hsien-ch'u (Han Xianchu) (1908-   )—Joined the CCP in the late 1920s or early 1930s. By 1933 was a regimental commander in the Fourth Front Army in Szechwan province. Participated in the Long March under Chang Kuo-t'ao's (q.v.) command, but his unit eventually rejoined the main CCP forces at Yenan. He fought in Manchuria and in the sweep through South China during the civil war. He was a leader of the Chinese forces in Korea, 1950-52. In 1960 he became commander of the Foochow Military Region. He was elected an alternate member of the Central Committee at the second session of the Eighth Congress in 1958, and became a full member at the Ninth, Tenth, and Eleventh Congresses.

Healy, Gerry (1915-   )—Joined the British Trotskyist movement in 1937. Broke from the Fourth International movement that year to participate in founding the Workers International League, which boycotted the Founding Congress of the Fourth International in 1938. Participated in the fusion of the WIL and the British section in 1944 to form the Revolutionary Communist Party. After the RCP entered the British Labour Party in 1949 Healy became the central leader of British Trotskyism. He broke with the Fourth International in 1963 to head a rump International Committee of the Fourth International. In the 1960s his politics were ultraleft and sectarian. By the 1970s he had moved far to the right, supporting capitalist governments in Libya and elsewhere in the Middle East.

Ho Lung (He Long) (1896-1969)—After killing a local magistrate, Ho became an outlaw in 1916, then a local commander in a warlord army in Hunan. He joined the KMT in 1925. A CCP sympathizer, he was, with Yeh T'ing (q.v.), one of the central leaders of the August 1, 1927, Nanchang Uprising, the first episode in the turn to putschism ordered by Stalin after the defeat of the 1927 revolution in Shanghai and Wuhan. Ho was a prominent CCP military leader in the Long March and in the Sino-Japanese War and civil war. He joined the CCP late in 1927, was elected to the Central Committee in 1945, and to the Politburo in 1956. He was arrested by the Mao faction in the Cultural Revolution and reportedly starved to death. He was posthumously rehabilitated after Mao's death and the fall of the "gang of four."

Ho Meng-hsiung (He Mengxiong) (1903-1931)—A founding member of the CCP in Peking, and a prominent labor organizer in the 1920s. Around 1930 he moved to Shanghai where he came to head the Kiangsu Provincial Party Committee. Ho clashed with the Li Lisan leadership throughout 1930, defending a position opposing the Comintern's ultraleftism and reflecting the influence of the workers of Shanghai. He was stripped of his leadership posts in September 1930. After Li was called to Moscow in December 1930, Ho Meng-hsiung renewed his opposition to the succeeding Wang Ming leadership. Ho along with Lo Chang-lung, a leader of the All-China General Labor Union, waged a fight against the Wang Ming group at the Fourth CCP Plenum, held in Shanghai in January 1931. Ho and Lo were expelled, after which they set up a rival CCP. An informer betrayed them to the British police, who turned them over to the KMT. Ho was executed on February 7, 1931. (Lo Chang-lung was imprisoned for a period, then became a professor. He remained in China after 1949 but made no public political appearance until June 1979, when he was made a delegate to the People's Political Consultative Congress.)

Ho Ming-fan (He Mingfan)—A founder of the Communist group in Hunan. Left the CCP after clashes with Mao, but continued to propagate communist ideas. Ho helped to establish a peasant association in Shaoyang, his native hsien. After the 1925-27 revolution he was arrested and imprisoned for many years.

Hsia Yen (Xia Yan) (1900-   )—Well-known playwright and film writer, Hsia was a founder of the League of Left-Wing Writers in Shanghai in 1930. From that time on he was closely associated with Chou Yang (q.v.) and supported Chou in the clashes with Lu Hsun in the late 1930s. He wrote a number of famous plays about the Sino-Japanese War and from 1932 headed the CCP's film team, becoming a vice-minister of culture after 1949 with special responsibility for writing and supervising films. He was removed from his post in 1965 and publicly humiliated by the Mao faction in the summer of 1966 as one of the "Four Villains" in the cultural field (Chou Yang, T'ien Han, Yang Han-sheng, and Hsia Yen) (qq.v.). He was officially rehabilitated in February 1979 and has since resumed his role as a CCP spokesman on cultural questions.

Hsiang Ying (Xiang Ying) (1898-1941)—A CCP labor leader in the 1920s, Hsiang Ying was elected to the Politburo in 1928. He was elected chairman of the All-China General Labor Union in November 1929, at a time when that organization was in sharp decline. In mid-1930 Hsiang was appointed by the party leadership, then led by Wang Ming and the Russian-returned students, to head the Revolutionary Military Committee of the Kiangsi Soviet area, in effect to remove Mao Tse-tung from control over the Kiangsi Soviet administration. Hsiang was left behind when the Long March took place in 1934. He became the effective head of the New Fourth Army when it was established in 1938 under Yeh T'ing's (q.v.) nominal command. Hsiang was killed in the New Fourth Army Incident in January 1941, when Chiang Kai-shek violated the terms of the class-collaborationist agreement of 1937 and attacked the main units of the New Fourth Army in Anhwei province.

Hsiao Hua (Xiao Hua) (1914-   )—Joined the CCP in 1929 in the Kiangsi-Fukien area then held by Mao's troops. He was assigned to youth work through the period of the Long March. In the Sino-Japanese War and civil war he served as a political officer under Lin Piao. In 1950 he became deputy director of the General Political Department of the People's Liberation Army, succeeding to the directorship in 1964. He was elected to the Central Committee in 1956. He was closely associated with Lin Piao and Chiang Ch'ing, and particularly with the "ultraleft" Maoists Ch'i Pen-yu and Wang Li (qq.v.) in the early stages of the Cultural Revolution. He joined with Ch'i and Wang in sharp attacks on the old officer corps of the PLA in the spring and summer of 1967, leading Lin Piao to repudiate him in August 1967. He disappeared early in 1968.

Hsieh Fu-chih (Xie Fuzhi) (1898-1972)—Joined the CCP sometime in the 1930s and is believed to have participated in the Long March. Was a political officer in the Red Army and People's

Liberation Army in the Sino-Japanese War and civil war. He was first party secretary in Yunnan province, 1953-59, while concurrently holding military posts in that area of South China. He was elected to the Central Committee in 1956. In 1959 he was appointed minister of Public Security, the secret political police. He was elected to the Politburo at the August 1966 Central Committee plenum, which Mao had packed with his supporters in his campaign against Liu Shao-ch'i and Teng Hsiao-p'ing. Hsieh was made head of the Peking Municipal Revolutionary Committee when it was set up by the Mao faction during the Cultural Revolution, in April 1967. After Mao's death Hsieh was posthumously denounced as an ally of the "gang of four."

Hsien—Chinese political district roughly equivalent to a county.

Hsu Shih-yu (Xu Shiyou) (1906?-)—Born into a peasant family in Hupeh, Hsu joined the CCP guerrilla forces in the Hupeh-Honan-Anhwei border area in the early 1930s. He went with Chang Kuo-t'ao (q.v.) in the split in the Red Army during the Long March, but eventually rejoined Mao's forces in north Shensi in 1937. He was commander of the Shantung Military District at the time of the CCP victory in 1949. By 1954 he was transferred to East China, where he became head of the Nanking Military Region, a post he held until early 1973 when he was transferred to head the Kwangtung Military Region. He was elected an alternate member of the Central Committee in 1956 and survived the Cultural Revolution, becoming a Politburo member at the Ninth Congress in 1969. He retained his seat on the Politburo at the Tenth and Eleventh Congresses. He is reputed to be a supporter of Teng Hsiao-p'ing.

Hu Ch'iao-mu (Hu Qiaomu) (1911?-)—Born into a wealthy landowning family in Kiangsi province, Hu studied physics in Peking, 1930-32. In 1933 he moved to Shanghai, where he became a

CCP propagandist and joined the party sometime before 1937. In 1937 he went to Yenan where he headed the Mao Tse-tung Youth Cadre School and, toward the end of the Sino-Japanese War, became Mao's political secretary. In the early years of the People's Republic he was a deputy director of the CCP's Propaganda Department and for several years was in charge of the *People's Daily*, Radio Peking, and the Hsinhua News Agency. In the mid-1950s he was active in all the party campaigns to curb dissident intellectuals. He is best known as the author of the only Maoist history of the CCP ever published, *Thirty Years of the Chinese Communist Party* (1951). Hu was elected to the Central Committee in 1956. His book was withdrawn during the Cultural Revolution and Hu disappeared—he was dropped from the Central Committee at the Ninth Congress in 1969. He reappeared only in the fall of 1978, when the Chinese press began to refer to him as the president of the Chinese Academy of Social Sciences. He was coopted to the Central Committee in December 1978.

Hu Feng (Hu Feng) (1903-)—Well-known left-wing literary critic and essayist, who became the central target in the anti-intellectual campaign of 1955. He was briefly a member of the Communist Youth League while a student in Nanking before the revolution of 1925-27, but is believed never to have joined the CCP. He spent the years 1928-33 in exile in Japan. In 1934 he returned to Shanghai and joined the League of Left-Wing Writers. Hu in the 1930s was close to Lu Hsun, the League's founder and most prominent member, and in sharp conflict with the CCP fraction in the League led by Chou Yang (q.v.). In 1949 after the CCP victory Hu was elected to the National Committee of the All-China Federation of Literary and Art Circles. Although he helped promote the Mao cult, Hu also retained enough independence in literary style to come under criticism in 1951 in the CCP's literary magazines. In July 1954 he made a report to the CCP Central Committee protesting the party's "thought remolding" of writers and calling for a loosening of restrictions on style and subject matter. In November 1954 the party launched a bitter attack on Hu that ran through June 1955. In July he was arrested and imprisoned. He was rehabilitated in the summer of 1979.

Hu Shih (Hu Shi) (1891-1962)—One of twentieth-century China's most prominent bourgeois intellectuals. Raised in Taiwan and in rural Anhwei province, Hu went to Shanghai in 1904 for his education. He studied in the United States (1910-17), where he came under the influence of the pragmatist philosopher John Dewey, whose disciple he became. From later 1917 until 1927 he worked as a professor at Peking University. Immediately on his return to China he became a regular contributor to Ch'en Tu-hsiu's (q.v.) radical journal *Hsin ch'ing-nien* (New Youth), through which he became known as an outspoken advocate of adopting the written use of colloquial Chinese or *pai-hua* in place of the difficult classical forms. He propagated the liberal ideas of science and democracy, and Dewey's experimentalist variety of pragmatism, in opposition to Confucianism and traditional Chinese thought. Hu strongly opposed Marxism, and came out against revolution in general, including the nationalist revolution advocated at that time by the Kuomintang. In 1937 he left China for the United States, where he lived most of the rest of his life. He served for a time as ambassador of the KMT regime to the United States, returned to China briefly in 1946-48 to serve as chancellor of Peking University, then lived in New York in semiretirement until 1958, when he moved to Taiwan to head the Academia Sinica.

Hua Kuo-feng (Hua Guofeng) (1920?-)—Joined the CCP in his native Shansi province in the 1940s. Served as a county-level party secretary and political officer of a military unit in Yang-chu hsien, Shansi, 1947-49. Hua worked as a party official in Hunan province, 1949-71. From 1951 to 1955 he was assigned to Hsiang-t'an hsien, Mao Tse-tung's home county. He became head of the CCP United Front Department for Hunan in 1957, when he headed the section of the "Antirightist" campaign directed at national minorities, religious believers, and former members of bourgeois parties. Hua became province vicegovernor in 1958 and province party secretary in 1959. He was first elected to the Central Committee at the Ninth Congress in 1969, and was transferred to Peking in 1971 after the fall of Lin Piao (q.v.) to help carry out the purge of Lin's followers. At the January 1975 National People's Congress Hua was appointed minister of Public Security (head of the political police). He was appointed acting premier in February 1976, following the death of Chou En-lai, and confirmed as premier after the April 1976 T'ien An Men demonstrations. He was made chairman of the CCP in October 1976, holding this post concurrently with that of premier and chairman of the CCP's Military Affairs Committee.

Huang K'o-ch'eng (Huang Kecheng) (1902-)—A member of the first class of the Whampoa Military Academy, 1924-25. Huang joined the CCP in 1927 and participated in the Autumn Harvest uprising led by Mao Tse-tung in September 1927. He was a member of the initial nucleus of the CCP's Red Army at Chingkangshan. From late 1928 he worked under P'eng Te-huai (q.v.). Elected as an alternate member of the Central Committee at the Seventh Congress in 1945, he was elected to full membership in the CC at the Eighth Congress in 1956 and in 1958 appointed chief of staff of the People's Liberation Army. Huang supported Defense Minister P'eng Te-huai's criticisms of Mao's Great Leap Forward at the August 1959 Lushan plenum of the Central Committee and in September was stripped of all his posts. Huang disappeared for six years, reappearing in 1965 as vice-governor of Shansi province. He disappeared again in the Cultural Revolution and was not seen again until December 1978, when he was coopted to the Central Committee and placed in charge of a special committee to review false charges placed against former party leaders.

Huang Yung-sheng (Huang Yongsheng) (1905?-1971?)—A KMT soldier in a unit that defected to the CCP during the Autumn Harvest uprisings in September 1927. Made his way to Chingkangshan in 1928. Huang participated in the Long March. He served under Lin Piao in the Sino-Japanese War, becoming a long-term supporter of Lin. In 1951 he was made commander of the Kwangsi Military District, then was transferred to Kwangtung that same year. In 1954 or 1955 he became commander of the Canton Military Region. He was elected an alternate member of the Central Committee at the Eighth Party Congress in 1956. He was appointed chief of the General Staff during the Cultural Revolution and elected to the Politburo at the Ninth Congress in 1969. He disappeared along with Lin Piao in September 1971 and the Chinese press later claimed that he was killed in the plane in which Lin allegedly crashed over Mongolia (Soviet officials who found the plane claimed that medical examinations showed that no one aboard was more than fifty years old, which, if true, would exclude both Huang and Lin).

I K'uan (Yi Kuan)—Went to France in 1920 on a work-study program. He was a founder of the Socialist Youth in France in 1921 along with Chou En-lai and Ch'en Yen-nien (qq.v.). He became secretary of the French branch of the CCP in 1923. I K'uan went to Moscow in 1923. He returned to China in 1924, becoming secretary of the Shantung CCP. In 1926 he was transferred to Shanghai, becoming a member of the Shanghai Regional Committee in

charge of propaganda. After the April 1927 Shanghai coup, I K'uan went to Wuhan, where he was prominent in propaganda work. After the July 1927 anticommunist purge in Wuhan, he worked as CCP branch secretary in Anhwei and then transferred to Shanghai. In December 1929 he met the Chinese students who had recently returned from Moscow, where they had been won to Trotskyism. I K'uan introduced them to P'eng Shu-tse. He was a member of the first group of the Left Opposition faction in the CCP and became a member of the faction's provisional executive committee. In 1931 he was arrested. He served seven years in prison. On his release in 1937 or 1938 he went to Shanghai. He was elected to the Politburo of the Revolutionary Communist Party, the Chinese Trotskyist organization, at its 1948 convention (the other members were P'eng Shu-tse, Ch'en Pi-lan, Chin, and Liu Chia-liang). I K'uan remained in Shanghai when the CCP took power. He was arrested in 1952 along with Cheng Ch'ao-lin (q.v.) and has not been heard from since.

Jao Shu-shih (Rao Shushi) (1901?-   )—Joined the CCP in 1925 and worked as a labor organizer in Wuhan until the break with the Wuhan government in the summer of 1927. A political officer of the New Fourth Army during the Sino-Japanese War. Elected to the Central Committee at the Seventh Congress in 1945. Headed the CCP's East China Bureau after 1949, with jurisdiction over Shantung, Kiangsu, Anhwei, Chekiang, and Fukien provinces. In 1952 he was transferred to Peking to head the CCP's Organization Department. He disappeared early in 1954 and was officially denounced at a CC plenum in March 1955 along with the head of the party's Northeast Bureau and head of the State Planning Commission, Kao Kang (q.v.). The issues in the purge of Jao and Kao have never been fully revealed. They were accused of refusing to accept central party direction and using their regional posts to create "separate kingdoms."

Kamenev, Lev B. (1883-1936)—Joined the Russian Social Democracy in 1901. He headed the Bolshevik fraction in the Duma before World War I. With Zinoviev (q.v.) he opposed the October 1917 insurrection, but was reconciled with the Bolshevik leadership after it had taken place. After Lenin's death he joined with Zinoviev in forming a ruling triumvirate with Stalin aimed at excluding Trotsky from leadership of the Soviet state and the CPSU. Later broke with Stalin and along with Zinoviev formed the United Opposition with Trotsky, 1926-27. Kamenev was expelled from the Soviet CP in December 1927. He recanted and was readmitted, but was made a defendant in the first Moscow show trial, in 1936, where he "confessed" and was executed.

K'ang Sheng (Kang Sheng) (1899-1975)—Joined the CCP in 1924. He worked as a labor organizer in Shanghai in the revolution of 1925-27. After Chiang Kai-shek's April 1927 massacre, K'ang worked in the underground in Shanghai, where he became one of the CCP's top intelligence and secret police specialists. He was reportedly elected to the Politburo in 1931. He underwent training in Moscow by the Soviet secret police, 1933-37, going from there to Yenan in 1937. He is believed to have headed the CCP security office, the Social Affairs Department, from the late 1930s to about 1946. He served for several years as Shantung party first secretary after 1949, then was assigned to Peking by the end of 1954. His most prominent assignment was as liaison officer for meetings with foreign Communist Party delegations. He was a strong supporter of Mao in the Cultural Revolution and at the time of his death was one of the five vice-chairmen of the CCP. He has been denounced in wall posters since the arrest of the "gang of four" but has not been officially attacked.

Kao Kang (Gao Gang) (1902?-1954?)—Joined the CCP in North China in Shensi province in 1926. In the early 1930s he helped to establish a guerrilla base on the Shensi-Kansu border which became the destination of the Long March after the fall of the Kiangsi Soviet in the South in 1934. Kao headed the CCP's Northwest Bureau from 1940 to the end of the Sino-Japanese War. He was elected to the Central Committee at the Seventh Congress in 1945. Later that year he was transferred to Manchuria, where he rose to head the CCP apparatus for the region. In 1949 he became secretary of the CCP's Northeast Bureau and commander of the Northeast Military Region. In November 1952 he became chairman of the newly established State Planning Commission, set up to oversee the nationalization of capitalist industry and the inauguration of the First Five-Year Plan the next year. He disappeared in January 1954 after veiled public criticisms of him in the Chinese press (he was not denounced by name until March 1955). Purged along with Kao was Jao Shushih (q.v.), head of the CCP's Organization Department and of its East Bureau. The two were accused of using their regional authority to establish "separate kingdoms" aiming at taking over the leadership of the CCP. Kao was also accused of proposing placing decision-making authority in the hands of factory managers as opposed to Mao's insistence that the party committees have final say. The government reported that Kao committed suicide after he was denounced.

Kuo Mo-jo (Guo Moruo) (1892-1978)—Trained as a medical doctor in Japan during and after World War I, Kuo returned to China in 1923. Living in Shanghai, he soon established his reputation as a poet, translator, novelist, and essayist. In 1925 he joined the KMT. He moved to Canton in 1926 and participated in the Northern Expedition as a KMT propagandist. When the break with the CCP took place in 1927 Kuo sided with the CCP and may have briefly joined the party. Early in 1928 he fled to Japan where he spent the next ten years engaged in literary work. He returned to China after the outbreak of the Sino-Japanese War in July 1937. He worked in the KMT areas throughout the war, initially on the KMT's propaganda staff, during which time he wrote prolifically on the anti-imperialist struggle and on literary questions. After 1949 he was the most prominent literary figure associated with the CCP regime's central hierarchy. He became president of the Academy of Sciences in 1949, a post he held until his death. He was elected a vice-chairman of the National People's Congress at its first meeting, in 1954. He participated in all of the party campaigns against intellectuals, such as the attacks on Hu Feng and Ting Ling (qq.v.). During the Cultural Revolution, in April 1966, Kuo made an abasing self-criticism in a speech to the National People's Congress in which he said that all of his works should be burned because they did not sufficiently reflect Mao's thought. His writings were suppressed in the Cultural Revolution but he was not purged.

Kuomintang (Guomindang) (KMT— Nationalist Party)—Bourgeois nationalist party founded by Sun Yat-sen in August 1912 as an outgrowth of the earlier T'ung-meng-hui (Alliance Society), an underground anti-Manchu organization Sun had formed in exile in Japan in 1905. After being forced out of the republican government at Peking by Yüan Shih-k'ai (q.v.) in 1913, Sun's KMT sought a military base in South China. It captured Canton in 1917 with the help of a local warlord. At first Sun hoped to reform the Peking regime, but he turned to a perspective of revolution in 1921, disavowing the legitimacy of the Peking regime and calling for a Northern Expedition to overthrow it. Forced into the underground by a clash with Kwangtung warlords, the KMT recaptured Canton in July 1925, shortly after Sun's death, establishing its first

strong government. Under Chiang Kai-shek, who won control of the party after April 1927, the KMT became the ruling bourgeois party in China, defeating the warlords in the North and creating a nationwide regime in October 1928. Defeated in the civil war with the CCP (1946-49), the KMT remains the ruling party in Taiwan.

Kuomintang Revolutionary Committee—One of the splinter "democratic parties" allied with the CCP. It was formed by Li Chi-shen and Soong Ch'ing-ling (qq.v.) in November 1947 and included in its founding committee figures such as Feng Yü-hsiang and T'an P'ing-shan (qq.v.). Its original aim was to reconcile the KMT and CCP in a coalition government. Most of its leaders remained in China after the CCP victory and were given nominal posts in the new government. It disappeared during the Cultural Revolution, but its surviving members were once more presented as evidence of the CCP's "united front" policy after the fall of the "gang of four."

Lao She (Lao She) (1899-1966)—Pen name of Shu Ch'ing-ch'un (Shu Qingchun), under which he is best known. His most famous work is *Lo-t'o Hsiang-tzu* (Hsiang-tzu the Camel) published in an English translation under the title *Rickshaw Boy*. Born in Peking, Lao She lived in England, 1924-29, where he wrote his first three novels. On his return to China in 1930 he lived first in Tsingtao, then in Hankow. In 1938 he was elected head of the All-China Anti-Japanese Writers Federation. He lived in the United States in the late 1940s, returning to China after the CCP victory. In 1953 he became vice-chairman of the Union of Chinese Writers. He is generally regarded as one of twentieth-century China's greatest novelists. He committed suicide in October 1966 under persecution from the Maoist Red Guards. He has been posthumously rehabilitated, and his works, which were banned during the last decade of the Mao regime, have been republished in China.

Li Chi-shen (Li Jishen) (1886-1959)— Participated in the revolution of 1911 as chief of staff of the Twenty-second Division of the Revolutionary Army in Kiangsu province. Went to Canton in 1921 where he became a military leader of the KMT. Became commander of the Fourth Army of the National Revolutionary Army in 1925. Participated in the campaign against the CCP forces led by Ho Lung and Yeh T'ing (qq.v.) after the Nanchang Uprising in August 1927. Was the leader of the Fukien rebellion against Chiang Kai-shek, November 1933-January 1934. Li led a second abortive revolt against Chiang in 1936, but the two were reconciled after the opening of the Sino-Japanese War in 1937 and in 1938 Li was restored to membership in the KMT. In early 1947 he issued a statement calling for unity between the CCP and KMT. This led to his expulsion from the KMT and in November of that year he founded the Kuomintang Revolutionary Committee (q.v.). He participated in the CCP regime after 1949, becoming a vice-chairman of the Standing Committee of the National People's Congress in 1954.

Li Fu-ch'un (Li Fuchun) (1899-1975)—As a work-study student in France Li participated in founding the French branch of the CCP in 1921-22. He studied briefly in Moscow in 1924, returning to China by early 1925, when he became active in the KMT in Canton. He participated in the Northern Expedition as a political officer in the KMT army. He fled to Wuhan after Chiang Kai-shek's April 1927 coup in Shanghai. Later he worked in the Shanghai CCP underground. In 1932 he transferred to the Kiangsi Soviet area. He was put on the CCP Central Committee in 1934. Li took part in the Long March. By the early 1940s he began to specialize in economic work. In 1950 he was appointed head of the Ministry of Heavy Industry. He became chairman of the State Planning Commission in 1954

after the purge of Kao Kang (q.v.), and was elected to the Politburo in 1956. After Ch'en Yun (q.v.) clashed with Mao over the Great Leap Forward he was supplanted by Li as the country's top economic planner. Li was promoted to the Politburo Standing Committee at the August 1966 Eleventh Plenum of the CC, which Mao and Lin Piao had packed with their supporters. But by the Ninth congress in April 1969 he was dropped from the Politburo, although not from the Central Committee. He was not restored to Politburo membership at the Tenth Party Congress in 1973, the last held before his death.

Li Hsien-nien (Li Xiannian) (1907?-   )—Joined the CCP in 1926 or 1927 as a peasant soldier in Hupeh province. He was active in the Oyüwan (Hupeh Honan-Anhwei) Soviet area in the late 1920s and early 1930s. He participated in the Long March, then served as a commander with the New Fourth Army in Hupeh during the Sino-Japanese War. He was elected to the Central Committee in 1945 at the Seventh Party Congress. In the early years of the People's Republic he was the central party leader in Hupeh. Li became minister of finance in 1954 and has been one of the CCP's main economic planners since that time. He was elected to the Politburo in 1956, survived the Cultural Revolution and remains today a Politburo member and one of the party vice-chairmen.

Li Li-san (Li Lisan) (1889- ?)— Joined the Chinese Communist student group in France in 1920. Was a labor organizer in Hunan during the early 1920s. Li was elected to the Politburo at the Fifth Congress, held in Wuhan, April-May 1927. He was one of the leaders of the Nanchang Uprising, August 1, 1927, which marked the birth of the CCP's Red Army. Li attended the Sixth CCP Congress, held in Moscow, June-July 1928. There Ch'ü Ch'iu-pai (q.v.) was removed as party general secretary and replaced by Hsiang Chung-fa, a colorless figurehead whom

Li Li-san soon displaced as de facto head of the CCP. Li came under attack by the Comintern in the fall of 1930 as a scapegoat for the failure of Stalin's line of seizing major cities. He was called to Moscow in December 1930 and formally deposed at the Fourth Party Plenum, held in Shanghai at the beginning of 1931. Li remained in exile in Moscow until 1945. After his return to China he was given minor posts in the CCP regime, and made a public self-criticism at the CCP's Eighth Congress in 1956. He was once again attacked in the Cultural Revolution and reportedly committed suicide.

Li Ta (Li Da) (1890-1966)—After going to college in Japan, Li returned to China in time to participate in the May Fourth Movement in Peking in 1919. He attended the founding conference of the CCP in Shanghai in 1921 and was the first head of its Propaganda Department. In 1923 he returned to his native Hunan, where he became a lecturer at Hunan University. He left the CCP after clashes with Mao Tse-tung. Li remained a Marxist and taught at colleges and universities in Shanghai and other parts of China in the 1930s and 1940s. After the establishment of the People's Republic Li served on the council of the Chinese Philosophical Society and of the All-China Congress of Workers in the Social Sciences. In 1953 he was appointed president of Wuhan University. He was killed by the Maoist Red Guards in the Cultural Revolution, who submitted him to "struggle sessions" and refused to allow him to have medical treatment.

Li Ta-chao (Li Dazhao) (1889-1927)—With Ch'en Tu-hsiu, one of the two principal founders of the CCP. Born into a peasant family in Hopei province, Li studied in Tientsin and later attended Waseda University in Tokyo, 1913-16. While in Japan he began to write articles for the Chinese left-nationalist press. He returned to China in 1916, and in 1918 was appointed head of the library at Peking University. From early in 1916 Li was a member of the editorial staff of Ch'en Tu-hsiu's *Hsin ch'ing-nien* (New Youth), the best-known journal of the cultural and political radicalization. He won a national reputation during and after the May Fourth Movement of 1919, when *Hsin ch'ing-nien* extended its influence into very broad circles. In 1919-20 he was converted to Marxism. He helped set up the first Communist group in Peking in the fall of 1920. After the formal founding of the CCP in July 1921, Li became its main leader in North China. He was forced to go underground in March 1926 after police crushed a mass demonstration in Peking's T'ien An Men Square. After the capture of Peking by Chang Tso-lin (q.v.) in December 1926, Li took refuge in the Soviet embassy. Chang's police raided the embassy on April 6, 1927, arrested Li Ta-chao, and executed him along with nineteen other CCP members on April 28, 1927.

Li Tsung-jen (Li Zongren) (1890-1969)—Joined the T'ung-meng-hui (Alliance Society), a predecessor organization to the Kuomintang, sometime before the revolution of 1911. Joined the army of Kwangsi warlord Lu Jing-t'ing in 1916. After 1921 he headed his own army as an independent militarist. Joined the KMT in December 1924, bringing Kwangsi under KMT control. Supported Chiang Kai-shek in the April 1927 split in the KMT. As head of the so-called Kwangsi clique, Li was expelled from the KMT in March 1927, then staged an unsuccessful military revolt against Chiang Kai-shek, November 1929–September 1931; this ended in reconciliation after the Japanese invasion of Manchuria. Li succeeded in maintaining Kwangsi as his private domain until after the beginning of the Sino-Japanese War, when he was compelled to accept a military assignment in Suchow in Kiangsu. In 1948 Li was elected vice-president of the KMT government. When Chiang Kai-shek was forced into temporary retirement in January 1949, Li became president, and he directed the KMT withdrawal from the mainland in its final collapse. In December 1949 Li left China for the United States, where he remained until 1965. In July of that year he and his wife returned to live in the People's Republic of China where they were given a state welcome by Chou En-lai.

Liang, John—A member of the United States Socialist Workers Party from the 1930s and a long-time member of its National Committee. In 1959 he formed a tendency with Arne Swabeck (q.v.) proposing that the SWP take a favorable attitude toward the newly organized "People's Communes" in China. By late 1959 Swabeck and Liang proposed that a general stance of critical support to Maoism be adopted. The Swabeck-Liang tendency broke up in 1963 when Swabeck became an unqualified endorser of Maoism. Liang remained in the SWP after Swabeck was expelled from the party in 1967.

Liao Mo-sha (Liao Mosha)—A member of the Shanghai League of Left-Wing Writers in the early 1930s. Known as a journalist and minor novelist. In 1961 Liao was appointed head of the United Front Department of the Peking Municipal Party Committee. He is best known for his coauthorship with Teng T'o and Wu Han (qq.v.) of the critical satirical column "Notes from Three-Family Village," which appeared in the Peking Municipal Party Committee's journal *Frontline* between October 1961 and July 1964. Liao was viciously attacked by the Mao faction in April 1966 as part of the purge of Teng T'o, Wu Han, and Peking Mayor P'eng Chen (q.v.). Liao was imprisoned for a period, then exiled to a rural village until the summer of 1979, when he was rehabilitated.

Lin Hsi-ling (Lin Xiling) (1936-)—Served in the People's Liberation Army, 1951-53, then became a student at the People's University in Peking. A Member of the Communist Youth League, she won national attention in May 1957 for a series of speeches she gave at Peking University at the height of the "Hundred Flowers" campaign. Lin demanded the abolition of special privilege on the part of the bureaucracy, called for an end to party control over literature, and for the establishment of a genuine, egalitarian socialist society. In particular she championed the establishment of a legal system guaranteeing citizen's rights, and took up the vigorous defense of the imprisoned writer Hu Feng (q.v.). Lin disappeared in the purges of the "Antirightist" campaign in the fall of 1957.

Lin Piao (Lin Biao) (1907-1971)—Raised in a village near Wuhan, Lin joined the Communist Youth League in Shanghai shortly after the May Thirtieth Incident in 1925. He studied at the Whampoa Military Academy in Canton, October 1925–June 1926, when he took part in the Northern Expedition in Yeh T'ing's (q.v.) Independent Regiment of the Fourth Army. He participated in the Nanchang Uprising on August 1, 1927, from which the founding of the CCP's Red Army is dated. After the uprising was defeated Lin managed by early 1928 to join with Mao Tse-tung's forces at Chingkanshan. By June 1930 Lin was put in command of the Red Army's Fourth Army. Lin was one of the central military leaders of the Long March (1934-35). In the Sino-Japanese War he commanded the 115th Division of the Eighth Route Army. In the spring of 1938 he was wounded and spent the next three years in Moscow undergoing medical treatment, returning to Yenan early in 1942. For the remainder of the war with Japan he divided his time between negotiations with the KMT in Chungking and troop training in Yenan. He was first elected to the Central Committee at the Seventh Party Congress in 1945. In the civil war, which began in 1946, Lin resumed direct command, heading the CCP's Fourth Field Army in Manchuria, where the most decisive battles of the war with Chiang Kai-shek were fought. After the military victory over the KMT, Lin headed the

CCP's Central-South Bureau (Honan, Hupeh, Hunan, Kiangsi, Kwangtung, and Kwangsi). He was apparently ill and out of activity during most of the first eight years of the People's Republic, but was elected to the Politburo at a plenum in 1955. He began to take an active part in party affairs again in 1958, and in 1959 was made defense minister when he supported Mao against the criticisms of the Great Leap Forward made by P'eng Te-huai (q.v.). In 1966 Lin used the PLA to back up Mao in the Cultural Revolution and was presented at the Ninth Party Congress in April 1969 as Mao's heir. He was killed in September 1971 after a split with the Mao faction, allegedly dying in a plane crash over Mongolia while trying to flee to the Soviet Union.

Lin Po-ch'ü (Lin Boqu) (1886-1960)— A founding member of Sun Yat-sen's Tung-meng-hui (Alliance Society) in 1905, the predecessor of the Kuomintang. Participated in revolutionary work against the Ch'ing dynasty before the revolution of 1911. While an official of the KMT, Lin also became a secret member of the CCP late in 1921. He served as head of the Political Department of the Hunanese Sixth Army during the Northern Expedition, but left the army before it captured Nanking in order to participate in transferring the KMT government from Canton to Wuhan. After the expulsion of the CCP from Wuhan in July 1927, Lin took part in the Nanchang Uprising, August 1, 1927. When the uprising failed Lin made his way to Moscow early in 1928 where he studied for two years, then taught at the Far Eastern Industrial University in Vladivostok, returning to the Kiangsi Soviet area in late 1932. He made the Long March, then became chairman of the Shensi-Kansu-Ninghsia Border Region Government. After 1949 he was secretary-general of the Central People's Government Council. Lin was a member of the CCP Central Committee from 1938 and of the Politburo from 1945.

Liu Chia-liang (Liu Jialiang)

(1909?-1950)—Joined the Trotskyist movement while a university student in Peking in 1931 or 1932. He transferred to Shanghai in 1933 or 1934. He was soon arrested and he remained in prison until the outbreak of the Sino-Japanese War in the summer of 1937. He was made a member of the Central Committee of the Communist League of China, then the name of the Chinese Trotskyist organization, and served on the CC from 1938-1948. He worked as a writer and translator, and is known as the translator of Harold Isaacs' *Tragedy of the Chinese Revolution.* Liu accompanied P'eng Shu-tse and Ch'en Pi-lan to Hong Kong at the end of 1948 and went with them to Vietnam in 1949. He was seized by the Vietnamese CP in January 1950 and died shortly afterward in a VCP prison.

Liu Lan-t'ao (Liu Lantao) (1904-   )— Joined the CCP at least by 1928 in north Shensi, where he participated under Kao Kang (q.v.) and Liu Chih-tan in establishing the guerrilla base that became the destination for the Long March. Elected as an alternate member of the Central Committee in 1945 at the Seventh Party Congress. When the CCP took power in 1949 he was the third secretary of the party's North Bureau. He was elected to full membership in the CC in 1956. Around 1961 he was made first secretary of the newly revived CCP Northwest Bureau, headquartered in Sian. Liu was purged in January 1967, when he was paraded through the streets of Sian wearing a dunce cap. After that he disappeared for twelve years, resurfacing only in June 1979, when he was announced as the secretary general of the Chinese People's Political Consultative Conference (CPPCC). (At the first session of this CPPCC, held in February 1978, Liu had not been listed as a member of its National Committee.)

Liu Shao-ch'i (Liu Shaoqi) (1898-1969)—Joined the Socialist Youth League in Shanghai in 1920. In 1921 he went to Moscow where he studied at the

University of the Toilers of the East; while there he joined the CCP, returning to China early in 1922. Liu was a labor leader in the 1920s. In 1925 he was elected a vice-chairman of the All-China General Labor Union. He was first elected to the CCP Central Committee in 1927. After the crushing of the 1925-27 revolution, he worked underground as a CCP and labor organizer in Wuhan, Shanghai, and Manchuria. He was elected to the Politburo in 1932. Late that year he went to the Kiangsi Soviet area, where he became chairman of the All-China Federation of Labor. He participated in the Long March but left it midway to become secretary of the CCP's North China Bureau, working underground in Peking and Tientsin. He spent the late 1930s at the CCP's capital, Yenan. Liu served with the New Fourth Army from late 1939 until 1942, becoming its political commissar after the New Fourth Army Incident of January 1941. In the early years of the Poeple's Republic he was active primarily in the government and trade union apparatuses, rather than in the party, emerging as the CCP's third most important government functionary after Mao and Chou En-lai. He presented the report on the state constitution to the First National People's Congress, held irf 1954. By 1956 he began to move into party work also, presenting the keynote report to the Eighth Party Congress. In April 1959 in the wake of the initial setbacks of the Great Leap Forward Liu succeeded Mao as chairman of the People's Republic, the post of head of state. He became the central target of Mao's Cultural Revolution from the time of the August 1966 plenum of the Central Committee. He began to be attacked openly late in 1966 and by then had been effectively stripped of his posts, although he was not formally expelled from the CCP until a CC plenum in October 1968. His death in 1969 was only reported in 1974 and at that time no circumstances were given. His wife, Wang Kuang-mei, who was pilloried along with him and then imprisoned for many years, was rehabilitated by Hua Kuo-feng at the beginning of 1979.

Lo I-nung (Luo Yinong) (1901-1928)— Joined the Socialist Youth League in its inception, August 1920. Studied in the Soviet Union, 1921-25. Lo returned to China to work as a labor organizer in Canton. He was a leader of the Shanghai general strike of March 1927 that brought the CCP to power. He worked underground in Wuhan as head of the CCP's Yangtze River Bureau for seven months following the July 1927 anticommunist coup. Lo was arrested in the International Settlement in Shanghai in April 1928, turned over to the KMT and executed.

Lo Jui-ch'ing (Luo Ruiqing) (1906?- 1977)—Attended the Whampoa Military Academy in Canton in 1926, taking part in the Northern Expedition later that year. Joined the CCP in 1926 or 1927, and participated in the Nanchang Uprising of August 1, 1927. Made his way to Chingkangshan by 1928, where he became a soldier in the Red Army. In 1934 he became director of the Political Security Bureau for Lin Piao's First Army Corps, the beginning of a long career as a secret police official. Took part in the Long March. A political officer of the Eighth Route Army in the Anti-Japanese War. He became minister of Public Security, the political police, in 1949 when the People's Republic was formed. He headed the Public Security ministry until 1959, during which time he was instrumental in setting up China's labor camp system. He became an alternate member of the Central Committee in 1945 and a full member in 1956. He became the first vice-minister of defense in 1959 following the purge of P'eng Te-huai and Huang K'o-cheng (qq.v.), also becoming chief of staff of the PLA at that time. He disappeared in 1965 at the beginning of the Cultural Revolution. He was accused of supporting Liu Shao-ch'i and of seeking to commit China to more extensive support of Vietnam in the war with the U.S. He attempted to commit suicide while under arrest by jumping out of a window, and was dragged before Red Guard rallies with a leg in a cast. He was rehabilitated at the Eleventh Party Congress in August, 1977, when he was made a full member of the Central Committee.

Lo Jung-huan (Luo Ronghuan) (1902-1963)—Joined the CCP in 1927 in Canton. Took part in the Nanchang Uprising, August 1. 1927, and in the Autumn Harvest uprisings, retreating with Mao's forces to Chingkangshan when the uprisings failed. He made the Long March, was a prominent political officer in the Eighth Route Army and the PLA in the war with Japan and in the civil war with Chiang. He was elected to the Central Committee in 1945 and to the Politburo in 1956. From 1950 on he worked in Peking, serving variously as a member of the National People's Congress Standing Committee, a vice-chairman of the National Defense Council, and the de facto head of the Political Department of the PLA.

Lominadze, Vissarion (1898-1934)— Joined the Bolshevik Party in March 1917. He was a leader of various Comintern-sponsored youth organizations, then served as Stalin's delegate to China, July to December 1927. He dominated the August 7, 1927, Emergency Conference of the CCP, a rump meeting of the Central Committee which deposed Ch'en Tu-hsiu (q.v.) as party general secretary. With Heinz Neumann, Lominadze directed the Canton insurrection of December 1927. After his return to the Soviet Union Lominadze opposed Stalin's policy of forced collectivization and was stripped of all his posts in 1930. He was expelled from the Communist Party in the fall of 1934 and committed suicide in December, at the beginning of the purge touched off by the assassination of Sergei Kirov.

Lu Ting-i (Lu Dingyi) (1901?-   )— Joined the Socialist Youth League in Shanghai in the early 1920s in Shanghai and in 1924 joined the CCP. Headed the Propaganda Department of the Communist Youth League from 1927 to 1934, from underground in Shanghai after Chiang Kai-shek's April 1927 coup and then from the Kiangsi Soviet area after 1931. He participated in the Long March. During the Sino-Japanese War he was deputy director of the Propaganda Department of the Eighth Route Army. He was elected to the Central Committee in 1945 at the Seventh Party Congress. That same year he was appointed head of the CCP's Propaganda Department, a post he held with the exception of a few years in the early 1950s until he was purged in the Cultural Revolution. He was elected to the Politburo in 1956, and in January 1965 he was made minister of culture. He was dismissed at the insistence of the Mao faction early in 1966 in the earliest wave of the purges of the Cultural Revolution. He was publicly beaten at a massive Red Guard rally in Peking in January 1967, then imprisoned until December 1978. He reemerged in the spring of 1979, when he began to write again for the Chinese press, in particular publishing reminiscenses highly critical of Mao's Great Leap Forward and defending P'eng Te-huai (q.v.).

Ma Chi (Ma Ji)—Pen name of Su Ta (Su Da). Su Ta joined the Trotskyist movement around 1945 while a student in Yunnan. He went into exile in Hong Kong after the CCP came to power. In the 1950s and 1960s he lived in Macao. In 1959 he wrote a pamphlet in Chinese entitled *The People's Communes* urging critical support to the organization of the rural People's Communes in China. He was a member of the Revolutionary Communist Party of China, the official Chinese section of the Fourth International, until 1978 when he broke with the RCP and joined another Trotskyist organization in Hong Kong, the Revolutionary Marxist League.

Mandel, Ernest (1923-   )—Joined the Belgian section of the Fourth International under the German occupation at the beginning of World War II. He was elected to the Central Committee in July 1941 and worked in the underground during the war. He was captured three times by the Nazis, escaped twice, and was deported to Germany shortly before the end of the war. He was elected to the International Secretariat of the Fourth International at the first postwar meeting of the International, a preconference held in Paris in March 1946. He sided with Michel Pablo (q.v.) in the 1953-63 split in the Fourth International. He helped to prepare the Reunification Congress, which took place in 1963. He has been a member of the United Secretariat, the day-to-day leading body of the International established at the time of reunification, since 1963. Mandel is widely known throughout the world for his writings on Marxist economic theory.

Mao Tse-tung (Mao Zedong) (1893-1976)—Attended the founding conference of the CCP in July 1921. He was elected to the CCP Central Committee in 1923, and became an alternate member of the KMT's Central Committee in 1924. He worked under Hu Han-min in the Shanghai KMT apparatus, then headed the KMT Propaganda Department, November 1925-May 1926. In March 1927 he was appointed head of the Wuhan KMT Central Land Commission. He was made an alternate member of the CCP Politburo at the August 7, 1927, rump Emergency Conference that deposed Ch'en Tu-hsiu as party general secretary. He was assigned to lead the section of the Autumn Harvest uprisings in Hunan. When this failed he was removed from the Politburo in November 1927. He founded the military base in the Chingkang mountains that led to the formation of the Kiangsi Soviet regime. He became party chairman during the Long March at the Tsun-i conference in 1935. He was the political head of the CCP in the Sino-Japanese War, in the civil war with Chiang Kai-shek, and headed the People's Republic of China from its establishment in 1949 until his death in September 1976. In his last decade he organized the Cultural Revolution as a purge of other groupings in the CCP and in the state bureaucracy. His faction, the so-called gang of four, collapsed after his death.

Mao Tun (Mao Dun) (1896-   )—Pen name of the left-wing novelist Shen Yenping (Shen Yanbing). Mao Tun was a founder of the influential Literary Research Society (Wen-hsueh yen-chiu hui) in Shanghai in 1920. He worked in the KMT Propaganda Department in Canton in 1925 along with Mao Tse-tung. After the break with the KMT in 1927, Mao Tun settled in Shanghai where he wrote a series of left-wing novels that established him as one of China's best-known twentieth-century literary figures. He was a founder with Lu Hsun of the League of Left-Wing Writers in 1930. Mao Tun generally sided with Lu Hsun in the clash in 1936 with the CCP's representative to the League, Chou Yang (q.v.). During the Sino-Japanese War he was active in propaganda work for the anti-Japanese resistance. He went into exile in Hong Kong during the civil war, then went to Peking in 1949, where he became a leading literary and cultural figure in the People's Republic. In 1949 he was made chairman of the All-China Association of Literary Workers (after 1953 renamed the Union of Chinese Writers), a post he held until the Cultural Revolution. He was also made minister of Culture in 1949, a post he held until January 1965. Mao Tun wrote little after 1949 and adapted himself to the CCP's attacks on other radical intellectuals. He came under mild attack in the Cultural Revolution but was one of the few CCP intellectuals who was not purged. In 1979 he was vice-chairman of the China Federation of Literary and Art Circles.

Marshall, George C. (1880-1959)—U.S. Army chief of staff, 1939-45. He was special ambassador to China in 1946-47, where he unsuccessfully urged Chiang Kai-shek to accept Mao Tse-tung's offer of a coalition government.

Marshall became Secretary of State early in 1947. He was the author of the European Recovery Program, known as the Marshall Plan, proposed in June 1947 to provide a massive inflow of capital into war-torn Europe to restabilize capitalism as a bulwark against socialist revolution. He later served as secretary of defense in the early stage of the Korean War, 1950-51.

Mensheviks—Literally, "minorityites." The minority faction in the Russian Social Democratic Labor Party formed at the Second Party Congress in 1903. They became a separate party after 1912. The Mensheviks supported the bourgeois Provisional Government created by the February 1917 Russian revolution and opposed the Bolshevik seizure of power in October. They remained part of the Second International.

Nagy, Imre (1895?-1958)—Hungarian CP leader. While premier of Hungary in 1953-55 he raised criticisms of the Soviet Union's domination of the country's politics and economy, leading to his removal and, early in 1956, his expulsion from the CP. He was reinstated in the party in the fall in response to student demonstrations, then was appointed premier on October 24, the first day of the 1956 Hungarian revolution. He took refuge in the Yugoslav embassy on November 4 during the Kremlin's invasion. He left the embassy on a safe-conduct pledge, but was arrested by Russian police, turned over to the new pro-Moscow government headed by Janos Kadar, and later executed.

Nieh Jung-chen (Nie Rongzhen) (1899-   )—Participated in the May Fourth Movement in 1919, then studied in Belgium. Joined the CCP in Europe in 1923. After his return to China late in 1925 he became a military instructor in Canton under Chou En-lai at the Whampoa Military Academy. He took part in the Nanchang Uprising, August 1, 1927, and in the Canton Commune of December 1927. He served as a political officer under Lin Piao in the early 1930s and on the Long March. He was commander of the 115th Division of the Eighth Route Army during the Sino-Japanese War. He was elected to the Central Committee in 1945. Nieh fought in the civil war, and after the CCP victory was commander of the Peking-Tientsin garrison until 1955. When ranks were instituted in the PLA in 1955 Nieh became one of the army's ten marshals, the top rank. In the late 1950s he shifted from military affairs to administration of science and technology. In particular he was put in charge of China's nuclear weapons program. He was denounced in the Cultural Revolution but not purged, remaining on the CC until the Eleventh Party Congress in 1977 when he was elected to the Politburo.

Pablo, Michel (1911-   )—Joined the Archio-Marxists, a Greek communist group close to the Trotskyist movement, in 1928. He represented one of two Greek Trotskyist groups at the Founding Congress of the Fourth International in 1938. (Pablo moved to France about that time.) He was elected to the European Secretariat of the Fourth International established by an underground conference in France in February 1944, and was elected secretary of the International Secretariat when it was reestablished after World War II at a preconference in March 1946. On the expectation of the imminent outbreak of a new world war, Pablo proposed at the beginning of 1952 that the European sections of the Fourth International join the mass Stalinist and Social Democratic parties in a "deep entry" tactic. This led to sharp disagreements in the Fourth International over the potential capacities of Stalinist parties to act in a revolutionary manner under the pressure of imperialist attack, as well as differences over Pablo's interpretation of democratic centralism. In 1953-54 the International split into two public factions: the International Secretariat faction, led by Pablo, and the International Committee faction, supported by P'eng, the majority of the British and French sections, and by the U.S. Socialist Workers Party. Pablo lost the leadership of the IS faction by 1961, when he came to head a minority tendency within it. He participated in the Reunification Congress in 1963, but was expelled from the Fourth International in 1965 for violations of discipline. He later led the Alliance Marxiste Révolutionnaire, which fused with the centrist Parti Socialiste Unifié in France in 1975. In 1977 he left the PSU and founded the Tendance Marxiste Révolutionnaire Internationale. He is also known under the name Michel Raptis.

Pai Ch'ung-hsi (Bai Chongxi) (1893-1966)—KMT general and associate of Li Tsung-jen (q.v.) in the so-called Kwangsi clique. Attended military schools from 1906, participating briefly in the revolution of 1911. Became an officer in the 1st Kwangsi Division in 1917. He joined the KMT in 1924, and served as deputy chief of staff of the National Revolutionary Army during the Northern Expedition. He was the central organizer for Chiang Kai-shek of the massacre of the CCP and workers' movement in Shanghai in April 1927. He led the troops that took Peking for the KMT in 1928, then was expelled from the party in 1929 along with Li Tsung-jen for plotting against Chiang. He participated with Li Tsung-jen in several unsuccessful coups against Chiang in 1929 and 1930-31, ending in a nominal reconciliation with the KMT government after the Japanese invasion of Manchuria in September 1931. Pai was deputy joint chief of staff of the KMT forces in the Sino-Japanese War. He remained in China to fight the CCP in the civil war after Chiang Kai-shek fled to Taiwan in January 1949. At the end of the year Pai also fled to Taiwan, where he was a member of the Central Executive Committee of the KMT until his death.

P'eng Chen (Peng Zhen) (1902?-

)—Joined the CCP in Shansi province in 1923. He worked as a labor leader in North China during and after the revolution of 1925-27 and spent a number of years in prison in the early 1930s. He was one of the CCP's main political functionaries in the North China Shansi-Chahar-Hopeh Border Region government during the Sino-Japanese War. He was elected to the Central Committee and Politburo at the Seventh Party Congress in 1945. He became secretary of the CCP's Peking Committee immediately after the city was captured in early 1949. He was appointed mayor of Peking in February 1951, a post he held until he was purged in 1966 in the Cultural Revolution. He ceased to appear in public in March 1966, then was publicly removed from his posts in the first week of June. On January 4, 1967, he and several other purged leaders, including Lo Jui-ch'ing (q.v.) were presented bound to a massive Red Guard rally in Peking where they were beaten on the stage. He first reappeared at a New Year's reception in Peking in January 1979, then became the principal public spokesperson for the meeting of the National People's Congress held in June 1979.

P'eng Te-huai (Peng Dehuai) (1898-1974)—Joined the army in his native Hunan in 1916. At the beginning of the Northern Expedition in 1926 he was a regimental commander under T'ang Sheng-chih (q.v.), who had recently joined the KMT. He joined the CCP in April 1928 and in July, with other CCP members in his unit, staged a military uprising at P'ing-chiang in northern Hunan, converting their forces into a section of the Red Army and meeting later in the year with Mao Tse-tung and Chu Te at Chingkangshan. He captured Changsha, the capital of Hunan, in July 1930 during the ill-fated attempt by the Li Li-san (q.v.) leadership to use the guerrilla armies to take major cities; P'eng held the city for only a week and then was forced to withdraw. He was one of the central leaders of the Red

Army during the Kiangsi Soviet period and on the Long March. He was elected to the CCP Central Committee in 1934 and to the Politburo in 1935. P'eng was deputy commander of the Eighth Route Army, under Chu Te, during the Sino-Japanese War. He commanded the First Field Army in the civil war with Chiang Kai-shek. P'eng led the Chinese troops in the Korean War, 1950-53. He was made minister of defense in 1954, a post that he held until September 1959, immediately following the Lushan plenum, when he was replaced by Lin Piao (q.v.) for disparaging Mao's Great Leap Forward. He was last seen in public in 1960. He was rehabilitated in an official state ceremony in December 1978. According to a January 1979 speech by his long-time subordinate Huang K'o-ch'eng (q.v.), who had been purged with P'eng and himself rehabilitated in 1978, P'eng was arrested in 1966 and died in prison.

Plekhanov, George (1856-1918)— Regarded as the founder of Russian Marxism, Plekhanov broke with the populists (Narodniks) in 1883 to found the Emancipation of Labor group, Russia's first Marxist organization. He became known as an outstanding theorist and an important contributor to the development of Marxist philosophy. Plekhanov was the main leader of the Russian Social Democratic Labor Party from its founding in 1898 until the split congress of 1903 where the Bolshevik and Menshevik factions were formed (qq.v.). He supported the Mensheviks in the split with Lenin, later becoming a social-patriot during World War I. He opposed the October 1917 Russian revolution.

Po I-po (Bo Yibo) (1907-   )—Joined the CCP about 1927 in Taiyuan, Shansi. Imprisoned in Peking for anti-Japanese activity, 1932-36. He was a regional CCP military commander, mainly in Shansi, during the Sino-Japanese War. Po was elected to the Central Committee in 1945. During the civil war with the KMT he was a government administrator in North China. After 1949 Po be-

came one of the CCP's top economic and financial specialists. He was minister of finance, 1949-53, and in 1956 became head of the State Economic Commission, the body that oversees the annual carrying out of the longer-range plans decided by the State Planning Commission. He was elected an alternate member of the Politburo in 1956. He was denounced as a supporter of Liu Shao-ch'i and Teng Hsiao-p'ing (qq.v.) in mid-1966 and disappeared. After more than a decade in prison, he reappeared at the June 1979 National People's Congress, where he was made a member of a three-man special economic commission to administer China's economy.

P'u-yi (Pu Yi) (1906-1967)—The last Manchu emperor of China. Nephew to the previous Kuang-hsü emperor, Pu-yi acceded to the throne as an infant in November 1908 under the nominal regency of his father, Prince Ch'un, but with the actual power of the government still in the hands of the Empress Dowager Tz'u-hsi, who had been the de facto ruler of China since 1861. In response to the republican revolution of October 1911, the Ch'ing court formally issued an abdication for P'u-yi in February 1912, ending the emperor system established by Ch'in Shih Huang (q.v.) in 221 B.C. P'u-yi retained his title and continued to live in the Forbidden City in Peking with an imperial entourage until 1924, after having renounced the Ch'ing dynasty's claim to administer the government. He later lived in a mansion in the Japanese concession in Tientsin. In 1932 he became the head of the Japanese puppet government in "Manchoukuo," the name given to Japanese occupied Manchuria. In March 1934 he assumed the title emperor. After the fall of Japan and the collapse of "Manchoukuo," P'u-yi was imprisoned for five years in the Soviet Union. In 1950 he was transferred to China, where he was imprisoned until the end of 1959. On his release he became a professed supporter of the CCP and of Maoism. He worked for a period in a mechanical repair shop, then, after 1963, in the National Political Library. He died of cancer.

Quatriéme Internationale—The French-language theoretical journal of the Fourth International. In the years 1953-63 it represented the views of the International Secretariat faction during the split in the International.

Radek, Karl Berngardovich (1885-1939)—Active in the German and Polish Social Democratic parties from 1910. A supporter of the Bolsheviks. Radek came to Russia on the "sealed train" with Lenin in April 1917. He was elected a member of the Presidium of the Communist International in its early years. He supported Trotsky's Left Opposition, but capitulated to Stalin in 1929. He worked as a Stalinist propagandist in the 1930s, but was arrested and became a defendant in the second Moscow frame-up trial, in 1937. He was sentenced to ten years and died in prison.

Rákosi, Mátyás (1892-1971)—Joined the Hungarian Social Democratic Party in 1910. A prisoner of war in Russia, 1915-18, he was a founding member of the Hungarian Communist Party in November 1918. He was a leader of the Hungarian Soviet Republic of 1919 and a close associate of Bela Kun. Later he was for several years a functionary of the Comintern. He was imprisoned in Hungary, 1925-40, afterward returning to the Soviet Union. In 1945 he returned to Hungary and was elected secretary-general of the Hungarian CP (after June 1953 the title became party first secretary). He became premier in 1952 but was removed as an extreme Stalinist in 1953. He regained the premiership in 1955 but was again forced out, in August 1956, shortly before the outbreak of the Hungarian revolution. He lived the rest of his life in the Soviet union. He was expelled from the Hungarian CP in 1962.

Roberts, Daniel (1918-1962)—Born in New York City, he joined the Social- ist Party in 1941 while a student at the University of California at Los Angeles. He left the SP a few years later and joined the Socialist Workers Party, rapidly becoming the Los Angeles branch organizer. In 1945 he transferred to Seattle. Roberts was elected an alternate member of the SWP National Committee in 1948 and a full member in 1954. He transferred to Newark, New Jersey in 1954, where he served as branch organizer and also began to write regularly for the *Militant*. From 1956 to 1961 he was managing editor and then editor of the *Militant*. He wrote on various political and theoretical questions, with China as one of his particular interests. He was forced to step back from his editorial responsibilities by the onset of Hodgkins disease, from which he died.

Roy, Manabendra N. (1887-1954)—Active in anti-British protests as a student in his native Bengal in 1915. Left India that year to travel through Asia, Europe, and the United States. He was recruited to the Communist movement in Mexico by Michael Borodin (q.v.) and was a founder of the Mexican Communist Party. He attended the Second Congress of the Comintern, where Lenin collaborated with him in writing the theses on the national and colonial questions. He headed the Comintern's Far Eastern Bureau and was elected to the Executive Committee of the Comintern at the Third Congress, in 1921. He went to China in May 1927, where he replaced Borodin at the head of the Comintern delegation. He was accused of a "rightist deviation" at the Sixth Comintern Congress in 1928 and expelled in 1929. He then returned to India, where he was imprisoned, 1931-36. On his release he joined the bourgeois Congress Party and in 1940 founded the Radical Democratic Party. He edited a publication called *The Radical Humanist* in the 1940s and 1950s.

Russian Social Democratic Labor Party (RSDLP)—Forerunner of the Communist Party. Its First Congress was held at Minsk in 1898, but was broken up by the police. The RSDLP split at its Second Congress (London, 1903) into Bolshevik and Menshevik wings. The two factions reunited at the Fourth Congress (Stockholm, 1906), only to split definitively in 1912. The Seventh Congress, held in Moscow in 1918, voted to change the name to the Russian Communist Party (Bolshevik).

Shachtman, Max (1903-1972)—An early member of the Young Communist League and a member of the American Communist Party's Central Executive Committee. He was expelled from the CP in October 1928 along with James P. Cannon and Martin Abern, the three becoming the founding leaders of the American Trotskyist movement. Shachtman was a member of the first National Committee elected at the founding conference of the Communist League of America (Opposition) in 1929. He participated in founding the Socialist Workers Party at the beginning of 1938. After the signing of the Soviet-German nonaggression pact in September 1939 and the Soviet invasion of Finland in November, Shachtman began to rapidly retreat from Trotsky's position of unconditional defense of the Soviet Union in a war with a capitalist power. In May 1940 he, Martin Abern, and James Burnham led a split from the SWP that set up the rival Workers Party. The WP evolved to the right for a number of years, finally dissolving into the Socialist Party in 1958. In the SP Shachtman became a leader of the party's right wing, supporting the U.S. government in its invasion of Vietnam in the 1960s and early 1970s.

Shen Yen-ping. *See* Mao Tun

Social Revolutionary Party (SRs)—Russian populist party founded in 1900. At its First Congress, held in Finland in 1905, it adopted a program projecting a struggle for a bourgeois-democratic republic through a mobilization of the peasantry. A majority of the SRs supported the bourgeois Kerensky government in 1917 and opposed the Bolshevik October revolution. One section of the party, the Left SRs, participated in a coalition government with the Bolsheviks, but then led an anti-Bolshevik insurrection in July 1918. The insurrection was suppressed and the Left SRs outlawed.

Soong Ch'ing-ling (Song Qingling) (1892-   )—A member of the wealthy, Americanized Soong family, she married Sun Yat-sen (q.v.) in 1914 and was his constant companion and political collaborator until his death in 1925. She was a member of the State Council of the KMT government at Wuhan in 1926-27. She opposed the suppression of the CCP in July 1927 and took refuge afterward in Moscow, where she remained for two years. During this period her sister Soong Mei-ling married Chiang Kai-shek. Soong Ch'ing-ling became the honorary chairwoman of Li Chi-shen's splinter bourgeois party, the Kuomintang Revolutionary Committee (qq.v.) when it was organized in 1947. She remained in China after the CCP victory and has held various honorary posts in the government of the People's Republic. She was not attacked in the Cultural Revolution, although she receded in prominence. She has been featured at "united front" meetings by the post-Mao government.

Sun Yat-sen (1866-1925)—Bourgeois nationalist leader of the Chinese revolution of 1911, and the founder of the Kuomintang. Sun joined the anti-Manchu underground in 1893. He organized the Hsing-chung hui (Revive China Society) in Honolulu in 1894. After an unsuccessful revolt in Canton in 1895 he went into exile in Japan. There he founded the T'ung-meng hui (Alliance Society) in 1905. The same year he formulated the ideology of the San Min Chu-I or Three People's Principles: nationalism, democracy, and the people's livelihood. He served briefly—in January 1912—as provisional president of China's first republic after the October 1911 revolution against the Ch'ing dynasty. He was forced to abdicate to General Yüan Shih-k'ai (q.v.). He formed the Kuomintang (KMT—Nationalist Party) (q.v.) in Peking in August 1912. He was again forced into exile in Japan, 1913-16, then succeeded in establishing a military government at Canton in 1917. He was expelled by local militarists in 1919 but regained power in 1920. In April 1921 he declared his Canton regime to be the sole legal government of China, although at that time its power did not extend beyond Kwangtung province. He was deposed by the Kwangtung warlord Ch'en Chiung-ming, a one-time ally, in 1922. After that he sought an alliance with the Soviet Union and the CCP. He returned to Canton in February 1923 and died in Peking in March 1925 during fruitless negotiations with the Northern warlords. It was only after his death, with the May Thirtieth Incident in 1925, that the revolutionary upheaval brought the KMT back to power in Canton (July 1925), paving the way for its unification of China later in the decade.

Swabeck, Arne (1890-   )—A founding member of the American Communist Party in 1919 (then called the Communist Labor Party). He became Chicago District Organizer and later a member of the party's Central Executive Committee. A supporter of the Cannon faction, Swabeck was one of the earliest CP leaders to declare his support to the Trotskyists when James P. Cannon (q.v.) was expelled from the party in the fall of 1928. He was elected to the first National Committee of the Communist League of America (Opposition) in 1929 and was a founder of the Socialist Workers Party in 1938. He visited Trotsky in Turkey in 1933, then served in the party center in New York, 1933-37. He was active afterward in Chicago from 1937 to the early 1950s, then in Los Angeles. He hailed the formation of the Chinese rural "People's Communes" in 1958 and in 1959 proposed critical support to the Mao regime. By the early 1960s he became an avowed Maoist and

was expelled from the SWP in 1967 for violations of discipline. He was later briefly associated with the then-Maoist Progressive Labor Party.

T'an Chen-lin (Tan Zhenlin) (1902-   )—Joined the CCP in eastern Hunan in 1926. T'an participated in the Autumn Harvest uprisings in September 1927 and was part of Mao Tse-tung's forces that retreated to Chingkangshan when the uprisings failed. He was a political officer in the Red Army in the Kiangsi Soviet period. He remained behind when the Long March took place in 1934-35, becoming a CCP leader in the Fukien area. His units were incorporated into the New Fourth Army in 1938 and participated in the Sino-Japanese War in South China. He was elected to the Central Committee at the Seventh Party Congress in 1945. He was a PLA commander active in the capture of Shantung province. He was made governor of Chekiang province in 1949. He was transferred to Peking in 1954, made a deputy CCP secretary-general under Teng Hsiao-p'ing in 1965, and elected to the Politburo in 1958. From 1957 he became the CCP's main agricultural spokesman. He strongly supported Mao's Great Leap Forward in 1958, but in the Cultural Revolution he sided with Liu Shao-ch'i, publicly defending Liu as late as February 1967, and organizing his own Red Guard groups to battle the Mao faction. He was denounced as a "counterrevolutionary traitor" by the Maoists in April 1967, and was arrested shortly after May Day of that year. He was among the earliest of those purged in the Cultural Revolution to be brought back into the leadership, regaining his seat on the Central Committee at the Tenth Party Congress in August 1973. He has not been reelected to the Politburo, however.

T'an P'ing-shan (Tan Pingshan) (1887-1956)—Joined Sun Yat-sen's T'ung-meng hui (Alliance Society) in 1906. T'an became a member of Li Ta-chao's (q.v.) communist study group in

Peking in 1920. He was elected to the Central Executive Committee of the KMT during the period of CCP entry, at the KMT's First National Congress, January 1924. He headed the KMT's Organization Department, 1924–May 1926. He was the Communist minister of agriculture in the Wuhan KMT government, March-June 1927, acting to suppress peasant land seizures. He took part in the Nanchang Uprising, August 1, 1927, and was the head of the short-lived CCP government set up there. He was made a scapegoat for the failure of the 1925-27 revolution at the August 7, 1927, Emergency Conference, and was expelled from the CCP in November. He then joined the so-called Third Party of Teng Yen-ta, but rejoined the KMT in 1937. He participated with Li Chi-shen (q.v.) in forming the Kuomintang Revolutionary Committee in 1947, which participated in the coalition government set up by the CCP after 1949. He was given nominal posts in the People's Republic after 1949.

T'ang Sheng-chih (Tang Shengzhi) (1890-   )—Hunanese militarist. T'ang joined the KMT in June 1926, participating in the Northern Expedition in command of six divisions in Hunan. He helped take Wuhan for the KMT in August–October 1926. T'ang became the military chief for the "left" KMT government at Wuhan after the split with Chiang Kai-shek in April 1927. He led the military suppression of the CCP in Wuhan in July 1927. Later he took part in several abortive revolts against Chiang Kai-shek. He remained in China after the CCP victory, becoming vice-chairman of the Hunan provincial government and, in 1958, a member of the Standing Committee of the National People's Congress.

T'ao Chu (Tao Zhu) (1906?-1969)—Became a student at the Whampoa Military Academy at Canton in 1926 and joined the CCP the same year. He took part in the Nanchang Uprising in August 1927, then headed the Fukien committee of the CCP, 1929-33. He was

imprisoned by the KMT, 1933-37. On his release he worked as a political officer of the New Fourth Army in Hupeh. He headed the party Propaganda Department in Yenan from 1940. During the civil war he was deputy director of the Political Department of the Northeast Field Army. After 1949 he was the head of the CCP's Central South Bureau and became the most important CCP functionary in South China, with his headquarters at Canton. He was elected to the Central Committee in 1956. T'ao was initially a central leader of the Cultural Revolution. He was brought to Peking in the summer of 1966 and added to the Politburo at the August 1966 plenum of the CC, which Mao packed with his followers. In January 1967 he was labeled "China's biggest bourgeois royalist" and arrested. He was officially rehabilitated in a state ceremony in December 1978, when it was revealed that he died in prison in November 1969 after a long period of torture.

Teng Hsiao-p'ing (Deng Ziaoping) (1904-   )—A native of Szechuan, Teng was in France on a work-study program, 1920-26. He joined the CCP in France in 1922. He was briefly in Moscow in 1926, then returned to China, where he became a political officer of the Kuominchün, the private army of Feng Yü-hsiang (q.v.), then allied to the KMT. When Feng sided with Chiang against the CCP in April 1927, Teng fled from Sian to Shanghai, where he worked underground until mid-1929, when he was sent to Kwangsi. In December 1929 he became political commissar of the Seventh Red Army; in October of the following year Teng brought his forces to the Kiangsi Soviet area where they merged with Mao's Red Army. He participated in the Long March, during which or shortly after he became deputy political commissar of Lin Piao's First Army Corps. After the outbreak of the Sino-Japanese War in 1937, Teng became political commissar of the 129th Division, one of the three main components of the Eighth Route Army. He was elected to the Central Committee at the Seventh Party Congress in 1945. He was an important military and political figure in the civil war, ending the war with the army that conquered Szechwan, Kweichow, Singiang, and Yunnan. Teng was transferred from the Southwest to Peking in 1952, where he was appointed a vice-premier of the Government Administration Council. In 1954 he was made secretary-general of the CCP Central Committee. In 1955 he led the purge of Jao Shu-shih and Kao Kang (qq. v.), and was immediately afterward made a member of the Politburo. He attended the Twentieth Congress of the CPSU in Moscow in February 1956, and was the reporter on this question at the CCP Eighth Congress in September of that year, where he endorsed Khrushchev's speech criticizing Stalin. (His title was changed to general secretary at this congress.) Teng became one of the main targets of Mao's Cultural Revolution in 1966, when he was denounced at an inner-party meeting in October and the report quickly leaked to the Red Guard press. He was stripped of all his posts and disappeared early in 1967, accused of plotting to restore capitalism. He was brought back into the government seven years later as Chou En-lai's deputy, and was restored to the Central Committee at the Tenth Party Congress in August 1973. He was dismissed again following the T'ien An Men demonstrations of April 1976. He was not officially rehabilitated until July 1977, nine months after the fall of the "gang of four," but by 1978 he had emerged as plainly the head of the Chinese government and party, although he is formally outranked by party Chairman Hua Kuo-feng and head of the National People's Congress Yeh Chien-ying (qq.v.).

Teng T'o (Deng Tou) (1911?-196?)—CCP journalist and propagandist. In 1938 he was editor of the *K'ang-ti pao* (Resistance News), the newspaper of the CCP's Shansi-Chahar-Hopeh Border Re-

gion government. Toward the end of the Sino-Japanese War he transferred to the KMT capital at Chungking, where he worked for the CCP press during the period of negotiations with Chiang Kai-shek. In 1952 Teng became editor in chief of the Peking *People's Daily,* the CCP's most important newspaper, a post he held until 1957. In 1959 he became a secretary of the Peking Municipal Party Committee under First Secretary P'eng Chen (q.v.). In March 1961, Teng T'o began to publish a series of articles in the *Peking Evening News* entitled "Evening Chats at Yenshan," and shortly after joined with Wu Han and Liao Mo-sha (qq.v.) in writing a series called "Notes from Three-Family Village" in the Peking Municipal Party Committee's journal *Frontline.* These were allegorical and satirical pieces lampooning the CCP's cultural dogmatism and censorship and criticizing the rising Mao cult. These articles were halted by party pressure in the fall of 1962. In April 1966 during the Cultural Revolution Teng, Liao, and Wu came under vitriolic attack by the Mao faction for their "Black Anti-Party and Anti-Socialist Line." Teng disappeared sometime in 1966 and was killed in prison. He was posthumously rehabilitated in the summer of 1979. *Notes from Three-Family Village* was republished in book form at that time.

Teng Tzu-hui (Deng Zihui) (1895-1972)—Joined the KMT in 1925 and the CCP in 1926. In 1927 he became a peasant organizer in his home province of Fukien, where he remained active until the beginning of the Sino-Japanese War in 1937, when he was assigned to the CCP's New Fourth Army. He became director of the army's Political Department after the attack on the CCP's troops by Chiang Kai-shek in January 1941 known as the New Fourth Army Incident. He was elected to the CCP Central Committee at the Seventh Party Congress in 1945. He was a liaison officer in East and Central China during the civil war, coordinating communication between the various CCP armies. In 1952 or 1953 he became head of the CCP's Rural Work Department, a position he held until the department was abolished in 1961. He was one of the CCP's central functionaries in the agricultural collectivization of the 1955-58 period. Teng is accused of having opposed Mao's adventurist Great Leap Forward, and from 1958 onward played little role in the Chinese government. He survived the Cultural Revolution and was reelected to the Central Committee at the Ninth Party Congress in April 1969.

T'ien Han (Tian Han) (1898-1968)— Became established as a playwright in Shanghai in 1922. He was a founder of the League of Left-Wing Dramatists in 1931, joining the CCP the same year. During the Sino-Japanese War he worked in the KMT capital at Chungking as a propagandist for the anti-Japanese resistance. After the establishment of the People's Republic, he became a member of the National Committee, and later a vice-chairman, of the All-China Federation of Literary and Art Circles. He was also chairman of the Union of Chinese Dramatists. One of this century's best-known Chinese playwrights, T'ian worked after 1949 to adapt many classical dramas to the modern stage and screen. He was a close associate of the CCP's chief literary bureaucrat, Chou Yang (q.v.), and in 1966 was denounced as one of the "Four Villains" (Chou Yang, T'ien Han, Yang Han-sheng, and Hsia Yen). He was part of a group of literary and political leaders brought bound and with humiliating signboards around their necks to a massive Red Guard rally in Peking, December 12, 1966. He was killed in prison. T'ien was posthumously rehabilitated in April 1979 and his plays were revived.

Ting Ling (Ding Ling) (1904-   )— The most famous woman writer in the Chinese Communist movement. Ting Ling was born in Hunan and studied in Shanghai and Peking, and had already published a number of short stories and several novels by the 1920s. She joined the CCP in Shanghai in 1930, also becoming a member of the League of Left-Wing Writers. In 1931, her husband, Hu Yeh-p'in, also a left-wing writer, was executed by the KMT. Ting Ling was imprisoned by the KMT, 1933-1935. In 1937 she went to the CCP's capital at Yenan, where she wrote on literary questions for the CCP press. In 1942 she published an essay, "Impressions of the March 8 Commemoration," using the occasion of International Women's Day to criticize the lack of equality for women in the CCP's stronghold. She was submitted to organized criticism sessions to force her to recant. In 1951 she won the Stalin Prize for Literature for her best-known novel, *The Sun Shines over Sangkan River*. She was made a vice-chairwoman of the All-China Association of Literary Workers in 1949 (after 1953 renamed the Union of Chinese Writers). In 1954 she was criticized by Chou Yang (q.v.), the CCP's principal cultural bureaucrat, for her support to the mildly independent *Literary Gazette* and its editor, Feng Hsueh-feng (q.v.). This criticism was renewed in 1955 in the campaign against Hu Feng (q.v.). Until 1957 the attacks on her were confined to the inner-circles of the writers' organizations, but in the "Antirightist" campaign in the fall of 1957, after the end of the "Hundred Flowers" movement, she became a central target of public attack in the CCP press. At that time she was removed from all her posts. Refusing to capitulate, she was exiled for twelve years to a remote village near the Soviet border in the Northeast. She was arrested during the Cultural Revolution, tortured by the Red Guards, and then held in solitary confinement for five years, 1971-75. On her release, in broken health, she was placed in a sanatorium, then exiled again to a poverty-stricken village in Shansi province. She was rehabilitated in June 1979, and made a deputy to the Chinese People's Political

Consultative Conference. She now lives in Peking.

Ts'ai Ho-sen (Cai Hesen) (1890-1931?)—A friend of Mao Tse-tung as a student activist in Changsha, Hunan, during World War I. Studied in France, 1919-21, where he joined the Socialist Youth League, a predecessor of the French branch of the CCP. Elected to the Central Committee of the CCP in July 1922, shortly after his return to China. He was the original editor of *Hsiang-tao chou-pao* (Guide Weekly), the CCP's most important journal. In 1925 he was a trade union organizer in Shanghai and was a leader of the May Thirtieth Movement. He spent all of 1926 in Moscow, returning to China in time for the Fifth CCP Congress, held in Hankow in April-May 1927, where he was elected to the Politburo. He sided with Ch'ü Ch'iu-pai against Ch'en Tu-hsiu (qq.v.) when the latter was ousted as party general secretary in August 1927. He developed differences with the Ch'ü leadership shortly afterward but remained in the CCP. He was arrested in Hong Kong in July 1931 and was later executed, either late in 1931 or early in 1932.

Tung Pi-wu (Dong Biwu) (1886-1975)—From a poor gentry family near Wuhan, Tung was trained as a classical scholar, then enlisted in the anti-Manchu army in the revolution of 1911. He worked with Sun Yat-sen in exile in Japan during most of 1913-17, was won over to Marxism in 1919, and was a founding member of the CCP. He was among the twelve persons who attended the official CCP First Congress in Shanghai in July 1921. He was active mainly in Hupeh during the revolution of 1925-27, heading the KMT Wuhan government's Peasants' and Workers' Bureau. After the break with the "left" KMT in July 1927 he escaped to Japan and then Moscow, returning to China only in 1932. He was mainly involved in educational work in the Kiangsi Soviet area. Tung was elected as an alternate member of the CCP Central Committee

in 1934, and became a full member at a plenum in 1938. He was in charge of health work on the Long March. In the period of the Sino-Japanese War he acted mainly as a liaison official in negotiations with the KMT government at Chungking.'He was put on the Politburo in 1945, and attended the founding conference of the United Nations in San Francisco. In the civil war with Chiang he headed the North China People's Government. After the founding of the People's Republic he held a series of government posts including that of vice-premier and chief justice of the Supreme People's Court. He survived the Cultural Revolution, remaining in the CCP's highest bodies until his death, although he was relatively inactive in his last years.

Ulanfu (Ulanhu) (1906-   )—Born in a village of the Tumet Banner, Inner Mongolia, Ulanfu is the highest ranking non-Chinese in the CCP leadership. He went to Peking to study at the Mongolian and Tibetan Institute in 1923. There he was recruited to the CCP by Li Ta-chao (q.v.). one of the party's central founders. In 1925 Ulanfu helped organize the Inner Mongolia People's Party. He spent five years in the USSR after 1925, returning to China in 1930 where he spent the next ten years in the then-Inner Mongolian province of Suiyuan. He spent 1941-44 at Yenan as head of the Nationalities Institute's Education Department. In 1945 he became an alternate member of the CCP Central Committee (he became a full member in 1956, when he also became an alternate member of the Politburo). In 1947 he was made head of the government of the Inner Mongolian Autonomous Region. From the fall of 1966 Ulanfu was besieged by Maoist Red Guards in his stronghold at Huhehot, Inner Mongolia. He retaliated with local troops, but in April 1967 Lin Piao sent in the People's Liberation Army, declared martial law, and stripped Ulanfu of his posts. He disappeared and was dropped from the

CC at the Ninth Party Congress in 1969. He was partially rehabilitated and reinstated on the Central Committee at the Tenth Congress in 1973, and restored to membership in the Politburo after the death of Mao, at the Eleventh Congress in 1977.

Wang Ching-wei (Wang Jingwei) (1883-1944)—Became an associate of Sun Yat-sen in 1905 while a student in Tokyo. He was imprisoned in 1910 for attempting to assassinate the Manchu prince regent, but was released by the 1911 revolution. He was elected the second-ranking member of the KMT executive at its First Congress, January 1924. He was elected chairman of the Nationalist government formed at Canton in July 1925. Wang became a leader of the left wing of the KMT, favoring the alliance with the CCP and the USSR. He was forced to resign after Chiang Kai-shek's March 20, 1926 anticommunist coup in Canton, and went into exile in Europe. After the KMT government moved to Wuhan at the beginning of 1927 he was invited to return to offset the growing power of Chiang Kai-shek. He arrived in China in April, taking charge of the Wuhan regime on the eve of Chiang's Shanghai bloodbath and declaration of a secessionist KMT regime at Nanking. Wang followed Chiang's example in purging the CCP and trade unions in Wuhan in July 1927. He led his forces in a reunification with Chiang in the fall of 1927. He clashed with Chiang on several occasions, including backing a military revolt against him in Peking in 1930. Wang was made head of the KMT's Executive Yüan, 1932-35, but his relations with Chiang steadily deteriorated. He went over to the Japanese imperialists and headed a collaborationist regime at Nanking, then under Japanese occupation, 1940-44. He died in Japan while undergoing medical treatment.

Wang Hung-wen (Wang Hongwen) (1936--   )—A member of the security police at Shanghai Seventeenth Cotton

Mill in 1966, he became a leader of the Maoist "Shanghai Workers' Revolutionary Rebel Headquarters" in November 1966. He was instrumental in breaking the independent workers' strikes that erupted in Shanghai in the fall of 1966, continuing into late 1967. In February 1967 he was appointed to the newly formed Shanghai Municipal Revolutionary Committee. He was elected to the Central Committee at the Ninth Congress in April 1969 at the close of the Cultural Revolution. At the Tenth Congress in August 1973 he was made a member of the Politburo and its Standing Committee, and elected the CCP's second vice-chairman, making him the third figure in the party hierarchy after Mao and Chou En-lai. He was arrested as one of the "gang of four" in October 1976 following Mao's death.

Wang Li (Wang Li)—A member of the CCP's Peking Municipal Party Committee and an editor of *Red Flag* in the 1960s, Wang supported the Mao faction in the purge of Peking Mayor P'eng Chen (q.v.) in the spring of 1966 and was afterward placed on the ruling Cultural Revolution Group, headed by Ch'en Po-ta and Chiang Ch'ing (qq.v.). After the arrest of T'ao Chu (q.v.) in January 1967, Wang became the head of the CCP's Propaganda Department. He won national fame in July 1967 when he and Hsieh Fu-chih (q.v.) were arrested by military rebels in Wuhan, where they had gone as Mao's emissaries. After their release, following a massive show of military force by Lin Piao's troops, Wang and Hsieh were given heroes' welcomes in Peking by the whole central party leadership. He was closely associated with the most fanatical wing of the Maoists such as Ch'i Pen-yu and General Hsiao Hua (qq.v.) and was reputedly a leader of the May 16 Group, denounced as "ultraleftist" in the fall of 1967, but later presented as a widespread conspiratorial network led by Lin Piao. Wang Li led an occupation of the Foreign Ministry in August 1967 and was accused of ordering the burning of the British mission in Peking on August 22. Wang was arrested sometime in the fall of 1967 and has not been heard of since.

Wang Ming. *See* Ch'en Shao-yü

Wang Shih-wei (Wang Shiwei) (d.1947)—Joined the CCP in 1926 and became known as a translator of Marxist works. He was sympathetic to the Chinese Trotskyists after their formation in 1929 and translated some of Trotsky's writings into Chinese (he continued to correspond with Ch'en Tu-hsiu until 1936). In the early 1930s he studied in the Soviet Union and was accepted by the CCP as an authority on Marxist theory. He went to Yenan in the late 1930s where he became a research fellow at the Central Research Institute. In March 1942 he published a two-part article entitled "The Wild Lily" that criticized the special privileges of the CCP hierarchy, which he said was evolving into a new ruling class. He also called for the independence of literature and art from party domination. Mao Tse-tung's May 1942 "Yenan Talks on Art and Literature" were largely an attack on Wang and on the novelist Ting Ling and poet Ai Ch'ing (qq.v.), disparaging their literary concepts as non-Marxist and insisting on strict party control over literary production. A fierce denunciation campaign began against Wang Shih-wei at the end of May and on June 2 he resigned from the CCP, but refused to concede that he was guilty of any crime. Under pressure of the CCP campaign, most of his cothinkers deserted him and he was arrested. He remained a prisoner until the spring of 1947, when the KMT's troops temporarily retook Yenan. He was shot by the CCP before they evacuated the city.

Wang Tung-hsing (Wang Dongxing) (1916-   )—Joined a CCP youth organization in 1927 and was chosen by Mao as his personal bodyguard sometime in the mid-1930s. In 1935 he was appointed to head a special security guard unit which was later renamed the Central Security Regiment, often called the 8341 Regiment. This unit since the 1930s has been assigned the job of protecting the central CCP leaders. In the 1960s the 8341 Regiment had 10,000 troops in it. After 1949, Wang concurrently held high posts in the Ministry of Public Security, the political police, and his 8341 Regiment was used for special investigations, reporting directly to Mao Tse-tung. In the late summer of 1966, during the Cultural Revolution, Wang was named head of the CCP's General Office, the party's organizational nervecenter. It was his 8341 Regiment that carried out the arrests of the high party officials denounced by Mao in the Cultural Revolution. Wang was first elected to the Central Committee at the Ninth Party Congress in April 1969, when he was also made an alternate member of the Politburo. He advanced to full Politburo membership at the Tenth Congress in 1973. After Mao's death he deserted the Mao faction, switching his allegiance to Hua Kuo-feng and using his troops to arrest the "gang of four" (Chiang Ch'ing, Chang Ch'un-ch'iao, Wang Hung-wen, and Yao Wen-yuan [qq.v.]). He became a party vicechairman at the Eleventh Congress in 1977 but came under attack at the end of 1978 for his long association with the "gang of four" and was removed from control over the 8341 Regiment and the General Office. He retains his seat on the Politburo.

Wu Han (Wu Han) (1909-196?)—Son of a landowning family in Chekiang, Wu studied in Shanghai and Peking in the late 1920s and early 1930s. He served as a teaching assistant at Tsinghua University, 1931-37, becoming known as a historian and an authority on the Ming period. During the Sino-Japanese War he was a professor of history at the Southwest Associated University at Kunming, 1937-46. In the postwar period he became a supporter of the Democratic League (q.v.) and contributed satirical articles to the CCP press in Yenan. He remained in China after 1949 and was made a delegate to the People's Political Consultative Conference. In 1952 he was made deputy mayor of Peking. He was concerned mainly with historical scholarship until about 1959, when he began to write extensively on the need to study the Chinese past in order to understand the present, and sought to develop a Marxist interpretation of Chinese history. His 1961 play, *Hai Jui Dismissed from Office,* revived a tactic he had used in the 1940s in using historical tales to indirectly criticize current officials. In this case his defense of the wrongly dismissed official Hai Jui against an intolerant emperor was taken as a barb at Mao Tse-tung for his dismissal of Defense Minister P'eng Te-huai (q.v.) in 1959. Wu also collaborated with Teng T'o and Liao Mo-sha (qq.v.) in writing the satirical column "Notes from Three-Family Village" in the Peking Municipal Party Committee's journal *Frontline.* The three, and their protector, Peking Mayor P'eng Chen (q.v.), were purged early in the Cultural Revolution. Wu's play about Hai Jui was attacked in the opening gun of the Cultural Revolution, Yao Wen-yuan's (q.v.) November 1965 article in the Shanghai *Wen Hui Pao.* Wu was arrested sometime in mid-1966 and committed suicide. He was posthumously rehabilitated at the end of 1978 and in 1979 *Notes from Three-Family Village* was reprinted in book form.

Wu Te (Wu De) (1910?-   )—A native of Hopeh, Wu studied at Peking National University, then, in the mid-1930s, became a labor organizer in Hopeh. He is believed to have joined the CCP shortly after the beginning of the Sino-Japanese War in 1937. He was a prominent CCP spokesman at the 1948 congress of the All-China Labor Federation at Harbin. He served in Tientsin, 1952-56 (he was mayor of the city, 1953-55). In 1956 he was transferred to the Manchurian province of Kirin, where he served as political commissar of the Kirin Military District (1958-66), and

held various posts in the educational and planning apparatuses. He was elected an alternate member of the CCP Central Committee in 1956. He was transferred to Peking in mid-1966 to replace the purged P'eng Chen (q.v.) as mayor of Peking. He became a full member of the CC in 1969 and was placed on the Politburo at the Tenth Party Congress in August 1973. With Peking garrison commander Ch'en Hsi-lien (q.v.), he was in charge of the suppression of the April 1976 T'ien An Men Square demonstrations. He was periodically under attack for this, beginning with demonstrations in Peking in January 1977, and was finally removed from his post in November 1978, although he still retained his seat on the Politburo.

Yang Ch'eng-wu (Yang Chengwu) (1912?-   )—Took part in a peasant revolt in west Fukien in 1929 and in 1930 was drafted into Chu Te's (q.v.) Fourth Red Army. Yang became a regimental political commissar in 1932. He played a prominent role in the battles with Chiang Kai-shek's forces during the Long March. He was a commander in the Eighth Route Army in Shansi and Hopeh during the Sino-Japanese War. His forces, operating under Lin Piao's general command, were in the forefront of the capture of Manchuria in the most decisive battles of the civil war with the KMT after 1946. Yang was commander of the Tientsin garrison, 1949-53. He became concurrently chief of staff of the North China Military Region in 1952. He was made an alternate member of the CCP Central Committee at the Eighth Party Congress in 1956. He was identified as a deputy chief of staff of the People's Liberation Army in 1959. He became acting chief of staff in 1966 after the purge of Lo Jui-ch'ing (q.v.). Yang was arrested in March 1968 and accused of plotting to overthrow Mao. He was rehabilitated after Mao's death and made a full member of the Central Committee at the

Eleventh Party Congress in August 1977.

Yang Han-sheng (Yang Hansheng)—Well-known playwright, short story writer, and film scenarist. Yang was closely associated with Chou Yang (q.v.) in Shanghai literary circles and was a leader of CCP work in left-wing cultural organizations from the early 1930s. He was prominent in the League of Left-Wing Writers and became the head of the Left-Wing Cultural Federation. He sided with Chou Yang against Lu Hsun, the founder and best-known member of the League of Left-Wing Writers, in the controversies of 1936 that led to the league's dissolution. Lu labelled the CCP representatives to the league (Chou Yang, Yang Hansheng, Hsia Yen, and T'ien Han [qq.v.]) the "Four Villains," a label that was revived by Chiang Ch'ing when she first began to attack this group in 1964. Yang and the others were purged in the summer of 1966. Yang was officially cleared of the charge of being a "counterrevolutionary" in February 1979, becoming active again in CCP literary functions in Peking.

Yao Wen-yuan (Yao Wenyuan) (1929?-   )—A minor critic for the Shanghai *Wen Hui Pao* in the 1960s, Yao was chosen by Chiang Ch'ing and Chang Ch'un-ch'iao (qq.v.) in early 1965 to draft an attack on Wu Han (q.v.) and the Peking intellectuals who had engaged in veiled criticisms of Mao in the early 1960s. The publication of this article in November 1965 was the opening gun of the Cultural Revolution. In May 1966 Yao authored a slanderous denunciation of Teng T'o (q.v.) for his "Evening Chats at Yenshan." About this time, following the purge of Peking Mayor P'eng Chen, Yao was elevated to membership in the ruling Cultural Revolution Group, headed by Ch'en Po-ta (q.v.) and Chiang Ch'ing. He became the principal journalistic interpreter of Mao's directives during the Cultural Revolution, was made the director of all the main communications media, and

used the press for a relentless promotion of the cult of Mao's authority and the persecution of dissent. He was elected simultaneously to the Central Committee and to the Politburo at the Ninth Party Congress in April 1969. In October 1976 he was arrested along with Chiang Ch'ing, Chang Ch'un-ch'iao, and Wang Hung-wen (q.v.), then labeled the "gang of four." He has been imprisoned without trial since his arrest.

Yeh Chien-ying (Ye Jianying) (1898-   )—Graduated from the Yunnan Military Academy in 1919. In the early 1920s he joined Sun Yat-sen's staff in Canton. He was an instructor at the Whampoa Military Academy. Yeh took part in the Northern Expedition as a divisional commander in the KMT's Fourth Army. He is believed to have joined the CCP in 1927. He helped plan the Nanchang Uprising of August 1, 1927, but was assigned to a unit elsewhere and did not take part. Yeh participated in the Canton Commune of December 1927, and after its defeat spent two years in the Soviet Union. He returned to Shanghai in 1931, then moved to the Kiangsi Soviet area the following year. He took part in the Long March. He spent the early years of the Sino-Japanese War as a liaison officer and military instructor in the KMT capital at Chungking. By the time of the New Fourth Army Incident in 1941 Yeh had returned to Yenan and been made chief of staff of the Eighth Route Army. He was elected to the CCP Central Committee at the Eighth Party Congress in 1945. He played a prominent role in the civil war in North China leading to the establishment of the People's Republic in 1949. As one of the few CCP leaders who spoke Hakka and Cantonese, he was made head of the South China Bureau, 1949-52. In 1954 he became secretary of the Central-South Bureau headquartered in Wuhan. He was made one of the PLA's ten marshals when ranks were instituted in 1955. He survived the Cultural Revolution, and was put on the Politburo at the

August 1966 Eleventh Plenum, packed by Mao's supporters. At the Tenth Party Congress in 1973 he was placed on the Politburo Standing Committee and made fourth vice-chairman of the CCP. He was acting defense minister from the fall of Lin Piao (q.v.) in 1971 until March 1978, when he retired from the armed forces and was given the honorific post of chairman of the National People's Congress.

Yeh T'ing (Ye Ting) (1897-1946)— Served in Ch'en Chiung-ming's Kwangtung Army in the early 1920s. Yeh joined the KMT in 1922. He studied military technique in Moscow, 1924-25, joining the CCP branch in Moscow in 1925. He commanded the 24th Division of Chang Fa-k'uei's 11th KMT Army in the Northern Expedition, bringing his troops over to the CCP at the time of the break with the Wuhan KMT. Yeh was, with Ho Lung and Chou En-lai (q.v.), one of the three central leaders of the Nanchang Uprising of August 1, 1927, from which the CCP's Red Army dates its founding. Following the defeat at Nanchang, Yeh and Ho retreated southward, taking Swatow briefly in September. Yeh was the commander of the CCP troops in the Canton Commune in December 1927. He was made a scapegoat for the failures of Stalin's putschist policy and withdrew from CCP activity for five years, living in Europe. He was appointed commander of the CCP-led New Fourth Army in South China in 1937. He was captured by Chiang's forces after the KMT attack of the New Fourth Army in January 1941 and imprisoned, 1941-46. He was killed in a plane crash while returning to Yenan after his release.

Yüan Shih-k'ai (Yuan Shikai) (1859-1916)—From 1885 to 1894 he was Chinese regent in Korea, then an imperial dependency. He supported the Dowager Empress Tz'u Hsi against the reform movement of 1898, and in return was made vice-regent of Chihli province (now Hopeh). He became the most powerful of the imperial generals in the last years of the Ch'ing court. He was assigned to the defense of the empire against the revolution of 1911, but instead he compelled the abdication of the last emperor, P'u Yi (q.v.), in February 1912. A few days later he also forced Sun Yat-sen to resign his brief presidency of the newly declared republic. Yüan ruled China as a military dictator from 1912 until his death. In 1914 he dissolved the nominal parliament, and in January 1916 he discarded the title of president of the republic and declared himself emperor. This immediately provoked a military rebellion in Yunnan, compelling Yüan to drop his imperial pretensions. He died shortly afterwards.

Zhdanov, Andrei (1896-1948)— Joined the Bolshevik Party in 1913. From 1924 to 1939 he was party secretary in Gorky Oblast in the Volga region east of Moscow. He became a candidate member of the CPSU Central Committee in 1925 and a full member in 1930. In 1935, following the assassination of Sergei Kirov, he was put in charge of the Leningrad party organization, where he was instrumental in carrying out Stalin's purges of the late 1930s. In 1939 he was promoted to the Politburo. He is best known for his role in the postwar period as Russia's cultural dictator, when he carried out Stalin's line of wholesale rejection of both foreign cultural influences and of traditional Russian literature and art. He also intervened in scientific discussions to determine the "correct" line in genetics, nuclear physics, and other areas according to preconceived schemas allegedly deduced from Marxist first principles.

Zinoviev, Gregory (1883-1936)— Joined the Russian Social Democratic Labor Party in 1901. Zinoviev was Lenin's closest associate during World War I. With Kamenev (q.v.) he opposed the decision for the October 1917 Bolshevik insurrection. After Lenin's death, in 1924 he formed a triumvirate with Stalin and Kamenev aimed at excluding

Trotsky from party leadership. He and Kamenev broke with Stalin in 1925 and during 1926-27 joined with Trotsky in the United Opposition. Expelled from the CPSU in November 1927 and exiled to Siberia, Zinoviev capitulated almost immediately and was readmitted to the party in 1928. Expelled again in 1932, he again recanted. Arrested in 1935 following the assassination of Sergei Kirov, he was sentenced to ten years on trumped-up charges. He was a principal defendant in the first Moscow show trial, 1936. He "confessed" and was executed.

Index

"After Reading Chiang Kai-shek's Speech of February 21" (P'eng), 23

Agrarian question, 68, 69, 153; in India, 66; in Indonesia, 67; in Russia, 51. *See also* Collectivization; Peasants

Agricultural cooperatives, 163. *See also* People's Communes

Agriculture:
—and irrigation, 182
—productivity of, 183-85, 220
—scale of, 173-74
—taxes on, 217
—and technology, 181

Ai Ch'ing, 418-19, 461g

Aidit, D. N., 275-76, 303, 461g

"Aid Korea" campaign, 118

All-China Federation of Literature and Art, 319, 400

All-Russian Congress of Soviets, 246, 247, 249

Alsop, Joseph, 331

American imperialism, 63-64, 67-68, 76-77, 79, 81, 82, 86, 123, 149, 390; and blockade, 118, 120, 393; and Chiang, 155-56

Anticommunist guerrillas, 116

Anti-Japanese campaign, 37

Anti-Japanese War. *See* Resistance War

Asia Oil Company, 120

Assimilation, 124-25

August 7 Conference (1927), 27

Autumn Harvest Uprising (1927), 27-28, 309, 382

Backyard blast furnaces, 214, 255, 270, 397

"Banning of the Confederation of Trade Unions in Shanghai and the Ensuing Responsibilities of the Workers in the City, The" (P'eng), 23

Basic Problems of the Chinese Revolution, The (P'eng), 26

Bloc of four classes, 23, 56, 57, 64, 154

Bolsheviks, 52-54, 461g

Borodin, Michael, 18-19, 461g

Boxer Movement (1900), 14, 435n

British imperialism, 76, 155, 156; in India, 66

Bukharin, Nikolai, 29, 297, 461-62g

Bureaucratic centralism, 228, 296

Bureaucratic privileges, 65, 238-43, 268

Canton–Hong Kong Strike Committee, 56, 103, 437n

Canton insurrection (1927), 28

Capitalism, 50, 355

Ceylon Trotskyists, 149

Chang Ch'un-ch'iao, 348, 357, 359, 462g; arrest of, 369; on class nature of USSR, 359

Chang Hsueh-liang, 89-90, 384-85, 462g

Chang Kuo-t'ao, 17, 19, 462g

Chang Tso-lin, 435n, 462g

Ch'en Hsi-lien, 349, 374, 462g

Ch'en I, 281, 284, 287, 462g

Ch'en Li-fu, 35-36, 462g

Ch'en P'ei-hsien, 375, 462-63g

Ch'en Pi-lan, 13-14n, 17, 34, 40, 41, 42; on Cultural Revolution, 417-33

Ch'en Po-ta, 281, 299, 307, 344, 463g; purge of, 337
Ch'en Shao-yü, 31-32, 33, 311, 463g; and Mao, 310
Ch'en Tu-hsiu, 15, 17, 26, 463g
—arrest of, 34-36
—on CCP-KMT collaboration, 20, 27
—on class nature of USSR, 38-39
—and Left Opposition, 30
—and Mao, 311
—and P'eng, 36, 37-38
Ch'en Yen-nien, 20, 463g
Ch'en Yun, 356, 463-64g
Cheng Ch'ao-lin, 31, 464g; arrest of, 149
Ch'eng Ch'ien, 76
Ch'i Pen-yu, 337, 346, 464g
Chiang Ch'ing, 281, 288, 299, 307, 346, 377, 464g; arrest of, 369; denunciation of, 364; and Mao, 377; and militia, 371
Chiang Kai-shek, 16, 56, 74, 75, 76, 85, 436n, 465g
—arrest of, 89
—and bankruptcy of regime, 79-80
—Canton coup of, 18, 25, 56
—and collapse of regime, 81, 155
—and Mao's arrest, 391
—and military dictatorship, 20
—and refusal to compromise, 156
—and "Resolution Adjusting Party Affairs," 19
—second coup of, 24
—Shanghai coup of, 57
Chiao, 96, 102, 105
Ch'ien feng (The Vanguard), 15
Chien Po-tsan, 277n
Ch'in Shih Huang, 350-51, 352, 465g
China: and capitalism, 354; class nature of, 34; compared with Russia, 21; as deformed workers' state, 169-70; feudal society in, 350
Chinese Communist Party, 14, 63, 71, 72, 115. *See also* Bureaucratic privileges; Collectivization of land; Eighth Party Congress;

Ninth Party Congress; Peasant army; Tenth Party Congress
—adventurism of, 250, 270
—and agrarian reform, 78, 86, 87, 118-19, 140, 146, 162, 163, 164, 252
—and agriculture, 187, 206, 222
—and bureaucracy, 125, 126, 201, 236-37
—and Canton coup, 18
—class nature of, 108-9, 142
—on class nature of USSR, 319
—and coalition government, 143, 157, 229
—and Comintern, 28, 79
—composition of, 130-31, 136
—early history of, 16
—economic policies of, 165-66
—and forced collectivization, 179, 191, 231, 254-55, 393
—foreign policy of, 167-68, 229, 275
—government of, 110-14, 161
—and guerrilla warfare, 141
—and imperialist property, 63-64
—and industrialization, 231
—and KMT, 14, 24, 55-56, 146, 386-87
—and Korean War, 115, 118-19, 120-21
—labor policies of, 117, 119, 166
—and Left-KMT, 18, 57
—and Left Opposition, 31
—and left turn, 87, 88
—mass base of, 94
—Municipal Party Committee of Peking of, 279
—nature of, 224-67
—opportunism of, 122, 124, 126, 135-36, 147, 154
—organization of, 280
—persecution of Trotskyists by, 104, 120, 145-46, 229, 245-46, 387-88
—and private property, 111, 113, 117, 120, 147, 159, 163, 165, 255, 392
—Red Army of, 78
—secret police of, 244-45
—size of, 282, 299

—statistical methods of, 219
—strategy of, 73, 86
—and U.S. imperialism, 121, 168
—and USSR, 89, 90-91, 121, 140-42, 144, 168, 227, 274, 391
—and workers, 112, 129, 131-32, 133-34, 148, 160

Chinese People's Republic, 64, 71

Chinese revolution, 14, 21, 22, 56; first (1911), 153-54; role of proletariat in, 14, 58, 73, 103; second (1925-27), 25, 49, 55, 64, 102, 154; third (1949), 97, 102, 104, 122, 153, 154, 158-59

"Chinese Revolution After the Sixth Congress, The" (Trotsky), 30

"Chinese Revolution and the Theses of Comrade Stalin, The" (Trotsky), 59

Chinese Revolutionary Communist Party, 41. *See also* Left Opposition; Communist League of China

Ch'ing dynasty, 465g

Ch'ing Ming festival, 363

Chou dynasty, 354

Chou En-lai, 19, 90n, 385, 465-66g
—in Cultural Revolution, 288
—death of, 361-62
—on First Five-Year Plan, 185
—Four Modernizations of, 363
—and Mao, 321, 344, 366-67
—on New Democracy, 392

Chou Kung, 352

Chou Yang, 279, 375, 422-24, 466g; on communes, 399

Chow Ching-wen, 238, 466g

Ch'ü Ch'iu-pai, 17, 26, 27, 33, 311, 382, 466g

Chu Te, 287, 356, 383, 466-67g

Chung-kuo fu-nü (Chinese Women), 17

Chung Yuan, 103

"Class Relations in the Chinese Revolution" (Trotsky), 58

Coalition government, 86, 91, 139, 143, 146, 151

Cold war, 90

Collectivization of land: by force, 177-78, 179; in Poland, 210-11; principles of, 43-44, 178; voluntary, 176, 177, 180, 216

Colonial revolution, 49

Comintern. *See* Communist International

Communes. *See* People's Communes

"Communes in China, The," 183, 192

"Communiqué of the State Statistical Bureau of China on the Revision of 1958 Agricultural Figures," 219

Communist International, 14, 55
—on CCP-KMT collaboration, 23
—and criticism of P'eng, 20
—and expulsion of Trotsky, 58
—Sixth Congress of, 29, 65
—Third Period theory of, 309, 439-40n

Communist League of China, 32, 40; national convention (1941) of, 39; provisional conference of, 37; third convention (1948) of, 40, 41. *See also* Left Opposition

Communist University of Toilers of the East, 13, 16

Communist Youth League, 41

Competition between state and private enterprises, 166

"Conciliators," 31, 32

Confucius, 351, 352-53, 467g

Constituent assembly, 69

Cooperative movement (1955), 179

Cuba, 67

Cultural Revolution, 268-93, 401-8
—as compared to May Fourth Movement, 329-34
—and education, 330, 375
—and factional struggle in CCP, 278-79, 281, 289-90
—and literature and art, 329-30
—and purges, 294, 375
—and security forces, 287-88
—and Shanghai workers' strike, 348, 403

Cultural Revolution Committee,

287
Cultural Revolution Group, 402

"Declaration of the Left Opposition," 31
Defeat of the Austrian Revolution, The (P'eng), 38
Deformed workers' state, 99-101, 169-70
Democratic centralism, 296
Democratic dictatorship of workers and peasants, 51, 53, 54
Democratic League, 76, 87, 249, 391, 392, 467g
De-Stalinization, 304, 313
"Draft Program of the Communist International—A Criticism of Fundamentals" (Trotsky), 62
"Draft Resolution on Chinese Communes" (Liang), 183
Dual power, 112, 137

Eastern European revolutions, 98-99, 125, 129, 161
Eighth Party Congress (1956), 64, 313, 394-95
8341 Regiment, 371
Engels, Frederick, 171, 173-74
"Evening Talks at Yenshan," 272, 274
Extraterritorial privileges, 167

Feng Hsüeh-feng, 16, 421, 467g
Feng Yü-hsiang, 435-36n, 467-68g
Five Anti Movement, 64, 166, 230, 252, 438n
Five principles of peaceful coexistence, 230, 257, 263, 394, 445n
Five-Year Plan, 64, 167, 185, 230, 252
Four Clean-ups Movement, 318
Four Modernizations, 363, 365, 376; criticized by Maoists, 367
Four News, 283
Four Olds, 283
Fourth International, 44, 106, 148, 171n; Transitional Program of, 68-69

Fourth National People's Congress, 355

Gang of four, 370, 371, 372; and Mao, 373
Germain, Ernest. *See* Mandel, Ernest
Gold yuan, 75, 439n
Gomulka, Wladyslaw, 177, 204, 468g
Great Leap Forward, 179, 184, 214, 221, 255, 257, 270, 397
Great Proletarian Cultural Revolution. *See* Cultural Revolution
Guatemala, 67

Hai Jui Dismissed from Office (Wu), 271, 273
"Hai Jui Scolds the Emperor" (Wu), 271
Han dynasty, 353
Han Hsien-ch'u, 349, 468g
Healy, Gerry, 44, 468g
History of the Russian Revolution (Trotsky), 38
Ho Lung, 287, 383, 468g
Ho Ming-fan, 380, 469g
Ho Meng-hsiung, 468-69g
Hsia Yen, 277n, 294, 469g
Hsiang-tao chou-pao (Guide Weekly), 13, 15
Hsiang Ying, 310, 384, 388, 469g
Hsiao Hua, 317, 469g
Hsieh Fu-chih, 287-88, 469-70g
Hsin ch'ing-nien (New Youth), 14
Hsu Shih-yu, 349, 371, 374, 470g
Hu Ch'iao-mu, 470g
Hu Feng, 420, 470-71g
Hu Shih, 327, 452n, 471g
Hua Kuo-feng, 370, 471g; appointed premier, 362; and Mao's authority, 373; and Mao's faction, 369
Huang K'o-ch'eng, 271, 471-72g
Huang Yung-sheng, 407, 472g
Hundred Flowers campaign, 243, 259-62, 268, 396, 447-48n
Hungarian revolution, 213; and CCP, 232, 260

I K'uan, 31, 41, 472g; arrest of, 149
Imperialism, 50, 59; and second Chinese revolution, 58. *See also* American imperialism; British imperialism; Japanese imperialism
"Imperialism and the Boxer Movement" (P'eng), 14
Impressionism, 266
India, 66, 83
Indonesia, 66-67, 303; Communist Party of, 275-76; coup d'etat in, 279, 401
Intellectuals, 78-79, 276-78. *See also* Cultural Revolution
Intensification of labor, 166, 167
International Executive Committee (Fourth International), 138
Internationalism, 253, 256
International Secretariat (Fourth International), 138
Iraq, 67
Isaacs, Harold, 440n
"Is Leninism Applicable to the National Peculiarities of China?" (P'eng), 21

Jacobins, 113
Jao Shu-shih, 359, 472-73g
Japanese imperialism, 74, 78, 154; and occupation of China, 33, 39

Kamenev, Lev B., 54, 473g
K'ang Sheng, 281, 307, 374, 473g
Kao Kang, 134, 359, 473g
Khrushchev, Nikita, 46, 232, 394; and de-Stalinization, 315
Khrushchevism, 292, 304
Korean War, 63-64, 230, 392-93; and Chinese revolution, 115, 118; and Sino-Soviet relations, 121
Kuan Feng, 346
Kuo Mo-jo, 278, 473-74g
Kuomintang, 14, 55, 474g; anti-Chiang factions of, 76; and CCP, 14, 24, 55-56, 146, 386-87; disintegration of, 155; military offensive (1946-47) of, 87; moderate group of, 22; national assembly (1946) of, 87
Kuomintang Revolutionary Committee, 76, 120, 392, 474g
Kwangsi clique, 76

Labor and Capital Consultative Conferences, 117
Land Reform Law, 117-18
Lao She, 330, 374-75g
Left Opposition, 30, 33, 34. *See also* Communist League of China
Left Opposition (Russian), 30; on industrialization and collectivization, 255-56
Left-wing Kuomintang, 25, 57
Legalists, 352-53
Lenin, V. I., 51-52, 54; on peasantry and collectivization, 171, 174-75, 176, 180
Lesson of the Defeat of the Spanish Revolution, The (P'eng), 38
Li Ching-ch'üan, 280, 284, 356, 375
Li Chi-shen, 76, 120, 475g
Li Fu-ch'un, 281, 475g
Li Hsien-nien, 284, 374, 475g
Li Hsueh-feng, 280, 284
Li Li-san, 33, 311, 475g
Li Ta, 380, 428-29, 476g
Li Ta-chao, 16, 476g
Li Tsung-jen, 76, 439n, 476g
Liang, John, 183, 192, 198-99, 212, 224, 264, 477g
Liao Mo-sha, 272, 477g
Lin Chieh, 346
Lin Hsi-ling, 260, 261, 269, 396, 477g
Lin Piao, 80n, 93n, 276-77, 477-78g
—and army, 280-81, 337, 402
—designated Mao's heir, 342, 370
—and differences with Mao, 337
—and Mao's cult, 341, 400
—and "Outline of Project 571," 343
—purge of, 335-60
—and Red Guards, 283-84
Lin Po-ch'ü, 321, 478g
Literacy campaign, 123
Liu Chia-liang, 38, 42, 478g

Liu Lan-t'ao, 280, 284, 375, 478g

Liu Pai-chien, 16

Liu Po-ch'eng, 286

Liu Shao-ch'i, 31, 280, 281, 291, 478-
79g
—on agriculture, 182, 312
—biography of, 295, 308-10
—on bureaucracy, 260, 396
—on communes, 315-16
—and Cultural Revolution, 306, 307
—and de-Stalinization, 313
—and differences with Mao, 307,
315, 320
—on education, 399
—on literature and culture, 317
—on permanent revolution, 258
—self-criticism of, 284-85

Lo I-nung, 16, 479g

Lo Jui-ch'ing, 244, 287, 320, 479g;
and arrest by Mao faction, 288;
on defense of China, 290

Lo Jung-huan, 317, 480g

Lominadze, Vissarion, 258, 480g

Long March, 309, 384

Lu Ting-i, 279, 285, 375, 480g

Ma Chi, 96, 102, 172, 178, 179-80,
184, 189, 216, 480g

Mandel, Ernest, 84, 94, 226, 480-
81g; on CCP regime, 110-11; on
class nature of CCP, 109

Mao Tse-tung, 15, 389, 481g
—on agriculture, 312
—and army, 276, 298, 306, 317, 342,
380
—on CCP-KMT collaboration, 386-
87
—and Chiang Kai-shek, 141, 381,
390
—and Chou En-lai, 344, 366-67
—on collectivization, 65
—on communes, 191, 206
—cult of, 274-75, 314, 315, 390
—death of, 369
—and education, 280
—fall of faction of, 371-73
—foreign policy of, 368
—and gang of four, 373, 377

—and Hungarian revolution, 276,
395
—and intellectuals, 276-78
—and Khrushchev, 395
—and Lin Piao, 337, 338
—and Liu Shao-ch'i, 307, 320
—military strategy of, 80
—and 1927 revolution, 380
—and opponents in CCP, 268, 355-
58
—and opportunism, 139, 154-55,
159-60, 387
—on peasants, 131, 133, 381-82
—and socialism in one country,
214, 218
—and Stalin, 229, 231-32, 320, 394
—and two stage theory, 63, 387
—and Wang Ming, 310-11
—and work in peasant movement,
308, 309

Mao Tse-tung Thought, 230, 274,
283, 295, 296, 315, 321, 330

Mao Tun. *See* Shen Yen-ping

Marcy, Sam, 445n

Marshall, George, 77, 146, 156, 481-
82g

Marx, Karl, 50

Mass pressure, 84

Material incentives, 371

May Fourth Movement (1919), 326-
29, 452-53n; and Cultural Revolution, 329-34; and culture, 329; and
Marxism, 331

May 16 Army Corps, 407

May Thirtieth Movement, 18, 23,
435n

Mensheviks, 51, 53, 482g

Militia, 207, 301, 349, 371

Million Brave Troops, 404-5

Moscow Trials, The (Trotsky), 38

Moving Force, The, 34

Moving Onward, 38

Nagy, Imre, 366, 368, 482g

National minorities, 302-3

"National Revolution and All
Classes, The" (Ch'en), 15

National Revolutionary Army, 22

National People's Congress, 246, 247, 248

New Democracy, 63-64, 92, 111, 122, 139, 159, 227, 252; economy of, 322, 387; end of, 393

New Fourth Army, 310, 388

"New Statutes of the CCP, The," 311

New Voice, 40

Ni Chih-fu, 372

Nieh Jung-chen, 356, 375, 482g

Nineteenth Route Army, 33, 436-37n

Ninth Party Congress (1969), 409-10

Nondefensism, 74

Northern Expedition, 20, 57, 436n

"Notes from Three-Family Village," 272, 274

"On New Democracy" (Mao), 131, 321, 322, 387

"On the Epoch-making Significance of the May Fourth Movement" (P'eng), 327

On the New Stage (Mao), 386

"On the Social Basis of Lin Piao's Anti-Party Clique" (Yao), 358

"On the Struggle Against Two Deviationist Lines" (P'eng), 38-39

Opium War (1840-42), 435n

"Outline of Project 571," 343

Pablo, Michel, 44, 91n, 215, 226, 257-58, 266, 482-83g

"Pabloism Reviewed" (P'eng), 44

Pai Ch'ung-hsi, 483g

Peaceful coexistence, 228, 235

"Peasant Question in France and Germany, The" (Engels), 174

Peasant army, 78, 97, 102, 122, 139, 154, 226; and CCP, 156

Peasants: and CCP, 198, 270; decline of, 173; living conditions of, 205, 217; rights of, 208

Peasant revolts, 78, 102

"Peking Coup d'Etat and the Merchants" (Mao), 15, 380

P'eng Chen, 238, 268, 274, 375, 483; and Mao, 279; purge of, 279, 280, 285

P'eng Shu-tse, 13, 29, 34, 37-38, 39, 41, 42, 43, 45
—arrest of, 34-36
—and Borodin, 19
—on Boxer movement, 14
—in CCP, 15-20
—and CCP-KMT collaboration, 20
—and Ch'en Tu-hsiu, 26-27, 36, 37-38
—on class nature of USSR, 38-39
—on class-collaboration, 15
—and Left Opposition, 30
—and Liu Shao-ch'i, 323
—on Mao's regime, 44
—and Mao Tse-tung, 322-23

P'eng Te-huai, 271, 286, 287, 483-84g; and communes, 398

People's Communes, 43, 172-223, 397
—administration of, 192-93, 199-200
—and community kitchens, 189, 190, 209, 222
—division of labor on, 203
—living conditions on, 205
—organization of, 196-97
—and peasants, 194-95, 198
—productivity of, 183-85
—scale of, 181, 193
—and status of women, 187-90
—taxes on, 205
—working day on, 185-86

People's Communes, The (Ma), 172

People's Congress, 246, 247-48; class content of, 249

People's Front, 65-66, 89

People's Liberation Army, 41, 286; and Cultural Revolution, 287, 337; and New Democracy, 322

People's Political Consultative Conference (1950), 117, 118, 147, 150, 160, 246, 392; and bourgeoisie, 160

Permanent revolution, 21, 26, 49, 52, 54, 64, 65, 72, 83, 127, 138, 249-51; and CCP, 258

Permanent Revolution, The (Trotsky), 62, 139, 250-51

Petöfi Club, 276, 319

PKI. *See* Indonesia

Plekhanov, George, 51, 484g

Po I-po, 284, 484g

Political revolution, 65, 225, 259; program for, 262-63

Post-war economic crisis, 75

Post-war growth of mass movement, 84-85

"Preliminary Draft Theses on the Agrarian Question" (Lenin), 175

"Present Revolutionary Crisis of the Rightward Tendency, The" (P'eng), 21

Problem of the Chinese Revolution, The (Ch'ü), 26

"Problem of the So-called 'Revolutionary Situation,' The" (Yuan), 103

Proletarian dictatorship, 94-95, 111, 124, 138; and permanent revolution, 139

Proletariat, The, 31

Provisional Government (Russian), 53

P'u-yi, 484-85g

Questions of the Chinese Revolution (Stalin), 58

Radek, Karl, 485g

Rákosi, Mátyás, 368, 485g

Reader's Magazine, 34

"Rearmament or Revisionism" (Ming), 106

Red Army, 63, 78; modernization of, 79, 80

Red Flag, 31, 33

Red Guards, 281, 282, 405-6

—and attacks on army commanders, 337

—and attacks on state officials, 284-85

—and Chiang and Ch'en, 299

—composition of, 283

—conflicts between groups of, 404

—dispersal of, 372

—local groups of, 403

—and seizure of power, 306

—and wall posters, 307

—and workers, 284, 306

Resistance War, 37-38, 74, 78, 131, 155

"Resolution Adjusting Party Affairs," 19, 56

"Resolution Concerning Party Work in the Army," 318

"Resolution on Some Questions in the History of Our Party," 311, 321

Results and Prospects (Trotsky), 52

Revolutionary Committee, 404, 406

Revolutionary Committee of the Kuomintang, 249

Revolution Betrayed, The (Trotsky), 38

Revolutions: role of peasantry in, 52; role of proletariat in, 50, 54; two stage theory of, 51, 54, 63, 68, 71, 92, 140, 159, 252

Roberts, Daniel, 212, 444n, 485g

Roy, Manabendra, 26, 485g

Russian revolution, 49-55, 159; role of proletariat in, 54

Russian Social Democratic Labor Party, 50, 485-86g

San-min chu-i (Three People's Principles), 19, 381, 385

Second Five-Year Plan, 65

Second World War, 63, 72, 83, 155

Sectarianism, 104, 106

Seeking the Truth, 40

Shachtman, Max, 266, 486g

Shang dynasty, 354

Shanghai General Labor Union, 103

Shanghai insurrection, 22, 23-24

Shen Yen-ping, 421-22, 481g

Sino-Japanese War. *See* Resistance War

Sino-Soviet Agreement of 1945, 141

Socialism in one country, 64-65

Socialist democracy, 201-2, 247

Socialist Workers Party (U.S.), 148-49, 171n, 225

Social Revolutionary Party (Russia), 486g

Soong Ch'ing-ling, 35, 486g

Soviets, 24, 53, 54, 57, 59, 60, 151, 201, 249, 299

Soviet Union, 77, 93n
—agriculture in, 171-72
—bureaucracy in, 235
—and CCP, 79, 82, 90-91, 142, 157, 169, 244
—and CCP bureaucracy, 234
—and China, 376-77
—class nature of, 304
—foreign policy of, 90
—occupation of Manchuria by, 79, 141, 157

Stalin, Joseph, 20, 25, 26, 28, 29, 54, 55-56, 60-61
—adventurism of, 28, 231
—and collectivization, 177, 178
—and CPSU, 154
—and frame-up trials, 151
—and Left-KMT, 25, 27
—and Old Bolsheviks, 150, 297
—opportunism of, 58, 59, 61
—and socialism in one country, 55, 65, 254
—and Trotsky, 26

Stalinism, 83, 92, 120, 124, 226-27, 230, 321; ideology of, 228, 389

Strategy for revolution, 50

Strikes, 75, 132, 348, 403

Struggle, The, 37

Students and Chinese revolution, 85, 86

Study Stalinist Ideology movement, 231-32

Sukarno, 67

"Summary and Perspectives of the Chinese Revolution" (Trotsky), 30

Sun Yat-sen, 153, 486-87g

Sung Jen-ch'iung, 280

Swabeck, Arne, 192, 213, 224, 264, 487g

Tai Huang, 260, 262

"Talks at the Yenan Forum on Literature and Art" (Mao), 418

T'an Chen-lin, 347, 356, 375, 487g

T'an P'ing-shan, 19, 487-88g

T'ang Sheng-chih, 382, 488g

T'ao Chu, 281, 286, 488g

"Tasks of the CCP in the Period of Resistance to Japan" (Mao), 387-88

Teng Hsiao-p'ing, 280, 281, 291, 488-89g
—attacks on, 314, 363, 366
—on the cult of the individual, 395
—and government, 361, 362
—and rectification campaign, 316, 398
—rehabilitation of, 347, 356, 375
—self-criticism of, 284-85

Teng T'o, 268, 269-70, 271, 272, 273, 279, 291, 489g

Teng Tzu-hui, 312, 489-90g

Tenth Party Congress (1973), 345-46, 348, 374

Ten Years of Storm (Chow), 238

Thermidor, 235, 446-47n

"Theses on the Ideological Rearmament" (Chiao), 105

"Third Chinese Revolution and Its Communes, The" (Swabeck), 192

"Third Chinese Revolution, the Communes and the Regime, The" (Liang and Swabeck), 224

Three People's Principles. *See* San-min chu-i

T'ien An Men demonstration, 361-65; public reaction to, 366

T'ien Han, 277n, 490g

Ting Ling, 418-19, 421, 490-91g

Trade Union Act, 117, 118

Tragedy of the Chinese Revolution, The (Isaacs), 41-42, 108

Transitional Program, The (Trotsky), 68-69

Transition from capitalism to socialism, 100
Trotsky, Leon, 25, 26, 30, 58-63, 71, 83, 108, 132-33
—on CCP-KMT collaboration, 25, 58, 382
—on class nature of CCP, 142
—on colonial revolution, 49
—on degeneration of USSR, 99
—on India, 66
—on industrialization, 255-56
—and Left Opposition, 30
—on permanent revolution, 138-39, 250-51, 254
—on Russian revolution, 52-54
Trotskyism, 26, 106; on class nature of China, 34
Trotskyist program, 388
Ts'ai Ho-sen, 17, 28, 491g
Tung Pi-wu, 238, 374, 491g
Twentieth Congress of the CPSU (1956), 46
Two Tactics of Social-Democracy in the Democratic Revolution (Lenin), 51

Ulanfu, 347, 356, 491-92g
Ultraoptimism, 104
"'Uninterrupted' Revolution in China" (Martin), 215
United front against U.S. imperialism, 305
U.S. *See* American imperialism
"Urgent Tasks Following the Establishment of Kuomintang-Communist Co-operation," 386
Usury, 164

Vietminh, 168
Vietnamese Trotskyists, 42

Wang Ching-wei, 25, 56, 57, 382,

492g; and purge of Communists, 27
Wang Fan-hsi, 38-39
Wang Hung-wen, 347-48, 372, 492g; arrest of, 369
Wang, Jen-chung, 286
Wang Li, 337, 346, 492-93g
Wang Ming. *See* Ch'en Shao-yu
Wang Shih-wei, 418-20, 493g
Wang Tung-hsing, 371, 493g
War Against the Japanese Imperialists, The (P'eng), 38
Warm Tide, 33
War of Resistance. *See* Resistance War
"Where is Healy Taking the Socialist Labour League?" (P'eng), 44
"Who is the Leader of the National Revolution?" (P'eng), 14
Women and communes, 187-90
Worker-peasant party, 110
Workers' and peasants' government, 23, 142
Workers' committees, 302
Wu Han, 271, 279, 291, 493-94g
Wu Te, 369, 494g

Yang Ch'eng-wu, 337, 494-95g
Yang Han-sheng, 424-25, 494g
Yao Wen-yuan, 401, 402, 495g; arrest of, 369
Yeh Chien-ying, 338, 370, 374, 495-96g
Yeh T'ing, 18, 310, 388, 496g
Yellow trade unions, 86, 439n
Young and Women, 40
Young Socialist League, 13n
Yüan Shih-k'ai, 453n, 496g
Yugoslavia, 84, 92n, 96, 124, 125, 129; Communist Party of, 91, 92, 93, 111, 144

Zhdanov, Andrei, 376, 419, 496g
Zinoviev, Gregory, 296, 496-97g